Analytical Political Economy

Analytical Political Economy

Edited by Roberto Veneziani and Luca Zamparelli

WILEY Blackwell

Registered Offices
John Wiley & Sons, Inc., 111 River Street, Hoboken, NJ 07030, USA
John Wiley & Sons Ltd, The Atrium, Southern Gate, Chichester, West Sussex, PO19 8SQ, United Kingdom

Editorial Office
9600 Garsington Road, Oxford, OX4 2DQ, UK

For details of our global editorial offices, for customer services, and for information about how to apply for permission to reuse the copyright material in this book please see our website at www.wiley.com/wiley-blackwell.

Library of Congress Cataloging-in-Publication Data

Names: Veneziani, Roberto, 1972– editor. | Zamparelli, Luca, editor.
Title: Analytical political economy / edited by Roberto Veneziani, Luca Zamparelli.
Description: Hoboken : Wiley-Blackwell, 2018. | Series: Surveys of recent research in economics | Includes index. |
Identifiers: LCCN 2018006239 (print) | LCCN 2018010004 (ebook) | ISBN 9781119483335 (pdf) |
    ISBN 9781119483311 (epub) | ISBN 9781119483366 (paperback)
Subjects: LCSH: Economics. | Economic policy. | Macroeconomics. | BISAC: BUSINESS & ECONOMICS /
    Economics / Macroeconomics.
Classification: LCC HB171.5 (ebook) | LCC HB171.5 .A483 2018 (print) | DDC 330–dc23
LC record available at https://lccn.loc.gov/2018006239

Cover Design: Wiley
Cover Image: © Evgenii_Bobrov/Gettyimages

Set in 10/12pt Times by Aptara Inc., New Delhi, India
Printed in Singapore by C.O.S. Printers Pte Ltd

10 9 8 7 6 5 4 3 2 1

For Vanda and Bruno. They know exactly why.
R.V.

To my mother, who made it possible.
L.Z.

CONTENTS

CONTENTS

1

ANALYTICAL POLITICAL ECONOMY

Roberto Veneziani

School of Economics and Finance
Queen Mary University of London

Luca Zamparelli

Department of Social and Economic Sciences
Sapienza University of Rome

This special issue collects 11 surveys on recent developments in Analytical Political Economy. Originally a branch of moral philosophy, political economy emerged as an autonomous discipline during the early stages of the industrial revolution, thanks to the analyses of French physiocrats and British classical political economists. It can be loosely defined as the social science that studies the production and distribution of wealth in a capitalist market economy. Abandoned in favour of the more neutral 'Economics', nowadays the term is still used to indicate approaches to economic analysis that lie beyond the boundaries of mainstream, neoclassical analysis rooted in the Walrasian general equilibrium tradition.

Contributions gathered in this volume survey a wide variety of topics and belong to different schools of thought. They are grouped together as they all review recent formal, rigorous economic research – both theoretical and empirical – that rejects at least some of the defining features of neoclassical economics; hence the name Analytical Political Economy.

Despite the heterogeneity, we can use some broad categories to describe the surveys comprised in this special issue. Papers by Reiner Franke and Frank Westerhoff, Corrado Di Guilmi, and Michalis Nikiforos and Gennaro Zezza deal with topics belonging to Keynesian macroeconomics. One of the fundamental claims of Keynes's analysis is that in a monetary economy there may be no tendency to full employment as investment and saving decisions are taken by different economic actors. In fact, the role of investors' beliefs, expectations and confidence about the future state of the economy is crucial in determining the equilibrium level of employment and economic activity (Keynes, 1936). Franke and Westerhoff review recent approaches to formalize and model 'animal spirits' in macrodynamic models that explicitly reject the rational expectation hypothesis. They do so by developing a canonical framework that is flexible enough to encompass two ways to model attitudes toward optimism and pessimism: the discrete choice and the transition probability approach, where individual agents face a binary decision and choose one of them with a certain probability. These assessments are adjusted – either upward or downward – in response to what agents observe, which leads to changes in aggregate sentiment and therefore in the relevant macroeconomic variables.

Di Guilmi surveys the growing literature sparked by the recent cross-fertilization of agent-based modelling and Post-Keynesian macroeconomics. He argues that agent-based modelling is fully consistent with the Post-Keynesian approach and that both areas of research can bene-fit from mutual engagement. The survey discusses how various models have solved the issues raised by the adoption of the bottom-up approach typical of agent-based models in a tradi-tionally aggregative structure and highlights the novel insights derived from this modelling strategy. The papers reviewed are grouped into four different categories: agent-based models that formalize Hyman Minsky's 'Financial Instability Hypothesis'; evolutionary models with Post-Keynesian features; neo-Kaleckian models with agent-based features; and Stock-Flow-Consistent agent-based models.

Stock-Flow-Consistent models are the focus of the analysis developed by Nikiforos and Zezza. They first illustrate the general features of the Stock-Flow-Consistent approach, force-fully showing that it is a framework capable of accounting for the real and the financial sides of the economy in an integrated way. They then discuss how the core Stock-Flow-Consistent model has been recently extended to address issues such as financialization and income dis-tribution, open economies and ecological macroeconomics.

The two papers by Amitava Dutt, and Daniele Tavani and Luca Zamparelli review the latest developments in models of growth and income distribution. The relation between growth and distribution has been central in political economy since the classical economists – Smith and Ricardo in particular – argued that the accumulation of capital must be financed by saving out of profits. The direction of causality has been later inverted by Post-Keynesian economists, who considered distribution as the adjusting variable, given the Keynesian assumption on the exogenous nature of investment (see Kurz and Salvadori, 1995 for an introduction to the discus-sion). Both papers develop unified frameworks, which, once coupled with different closures, can describe Classical-Marxian, Kaleckian, and Post-Keynesian heterodox growth models. Dutt extends the general framework to show how recent contributions have enriched the origi-nal theories with new topics such as money and inflation, finance and debt, multisector issues, open economy and environmental questions. Tavani and Zamparelli, instead, focus on endoge-nous technical change and use the unified structure to compare heterodox and neoclassical models of exogenous, semi-endogenous and endogenous growth.

The papers by Maria Nikolaidi and Engelbert Stockhammer, and Leila Davis focus on fi-nance and the financial sector. Minsky's 'Financial Instability Hypothesis' (Minsky, 1986) is arguably the most influential theory of financial markets in non-mainstream economics. It is a theory of endogenous cycles based on debt accumulation by the private sector. Times of eco-nomic stability and prosperity make borrowers and lenders progressively underestimate risk. Their optimism engenders an excessive expansion of credit, which, eventually, creates finan-cial bubbles and busts. Minsky's analysis was mostly qualitative but in the latest decades a number of scholars have formalized his intuitions in macroeconomic theoretical models.

Nikolaidi and Stockhammer review these efforts by distinguishing between models that focus on the dynamics of debt or interest, and models in which asset prices play a key role in the evolution of the economy. Within the first category of models they classify: Kalecki–Minsky models; Kaldor–Minsky models; Goodwin–Minsky models; credit-rationing Minsky models; endogenous target debt ratio Minsky models and Minsky–Veblen models. Within the second category of models, they distinguish between the equity price Minsky models and the real estate price Minsky models.

The work of Minsky is also central in the literature discussed by Davis. She surveys the empirical literature that has studied the effects of the post-1980 expansion of finance in advanced economies, or 'financialization', on capital accumulation. After introducing a range of empirical indicators to define what is indeed meant by 'financialization', she proposes to use three approaches to categorize the literature on financialization and investment. The first two approaches emphasize rising income flows between nonfinancial corporations and finance: first, growth in nonfinancial corporations' financial incomes and, second, growth in the payments of nonfinancial corporations to creditors and shareholders. The third approach emphasizes the most developed behavioural explanation linking financialization to reduced investment: shareholder value orientation.

The papers by Deepankar Basu, Simon Mohun and Roberto Veneziani, and Naoki Yoshihara survey a rather different strand of Analytical Political Economy, as they focus on recent advances in Marxian economics. Basu reviews empirical research in Marxist political economy, focusing in particular on: Marxist national accounts, probabilistic political economy, profitability analysis, and Classical-Marxian theories of growth and technical change. He also considers recent empirical studies focusing on the Classical-Marxian theory of relative prices and values, which is at the heart of the other two surveys. The labour theory of value states that the economic value of a commodity is determined by the amount of labour socially necessary to produce it (Marx, 1867). It lies traditionally at the core of Marxian economic analysis; and it is at the centre of innumerable disputes around the so-called "transformation problem," investigating the relationship between labour values and prices, and exploitation theory. Mohun and Veneziani adopt an axiomatic approach to interpret the 'transformation problem' as an impossibility result for a specific interpretation of value theory based on specific assumptions and definitions. They provide a comprehensive review of recent theoretical literature and show that, contrary to the received wisdom, there are various theoretically sound, empirically relevant and logically consistent alternative interpretations of the labour theory of value based on different assumptions and definitions. Yoshihara thoroughly analyses the development of exploitation theory in mathematical Marxian economics from the 1970s till today, with a special focus on the controversies surrounding the relation between profits and exploitation in capitalist economies, and its relevance for the definition of the concept of exploitation.

Finally, the paper by Omar Dahi and Firat Demir focuses on international trade and development economics, and in particular it analyses the cost-benefit literature on South–South versus South–North economic exchanges. After providing a discussion on the definition of the notions of 'North' and 'South' and offering a statistical overview of South–South economic relations, the paper provides a framework for situating the literature by reviewing the traditional targets of development as well as the benefits and drawbacks of integration into the global economy in both South–South and North–South directions.

References

Marx, K. (1867 [1977]) *Capital. A Critique of Political Economy*, Vol. I. London: Penguin.

Minsky, H.P. (1986) *Stabilizing an Unstable Economy*. New Haven: Yale University Press.

Keynes, J.M. (1936) *The General Theory of Employment, Interest, and Money*. London: Macmillan.

Kurz, H. and Salvadori, N. (1995) *Theory of Production: A Long-Period Analysis*. Cambridge: Cambridge University Press.

2

TAKING STOCK: A RIGOROUS MODELLING OF ANIMAL SPIRITS IN MACROECONOMICS

Reiner Franke

University of Kiel (GER)

Frank Westerhoff

University of Bamberg (GER)

1. Introduction

A key issue in which heterodox macroeconomic theory differs from the orthodoxy is the notion of expectations, where it determinedly abjures the rational expectations hypothesis. Instead, to emphasize its view of a constantly changing world with its fundamental uncertainty, heterodox economists frequently refer to the famous idea of the 'animal spirits'. This is a useful keyword that poses no particular problems in general conceptual discussions. However, given the enigma surrounding the expression, what can it mean when it comes to rigorous formal modelling? More often than not, authors garland their model with this word, even if there may be only loose connections to it. The present survey focusses on heterodox approaches that take the notion of the 'animal spirits' more seriously and, seeking to learn more about its economic significance, attempt to design dynamic models that are able to definitively capture some of its crucial aspects.[1]

The background of the term as it is commonly referred to is Chapter 12 of Keynes' *General Theory*, where he discusses another elementary 'characteristic of human nature', namely, 'that a large proportion of our positive activities depend on spontaneous optimism rather than on a mathematical expectation' (Keynes, 1936, p. 161). Although the chapter is titled 'The state of long-term expectation', Keynes makes it clear that he is concerned with 'the state of psychological expectation' (p. 147).[2]

It is important to note that this state does not arise out of the blue from whims and moods; it is not an imperfection or plain ignorance of human decision makers. Ultimately, it is due to the problem that decisions resulting in consequences that reach far into the future are not only

Analytical Political Economy, First Edition. Edited by Roberto Veneziani and Luca Zamparelli.

complex, but also fraught with irreducible uncertainty. 'About these matters', Keynes wrote elsewhere to clarify the basic issues of the *General Theory*, 'there is no scientific basis on which to form any calculable probability whatever' (Keynes, 1937, p. 114). Needless to say, this facet of Keynes' work is completely ignored by the 'New-Keynesian' mainstream.

To cope with uncertainty that cannot be reduced to a mathematical risk calculus, enabling us nevertheless 'to behave in a manner which saves our faces as rational economic men', Keynes (1937) refers to 'a variety of techniques', or 'principles', which are worth quoting in full.

(1) We assume that the present is a much more serviceable guide to the future than a candid examination of past experience would show it to have been hitherto. In other words, we largely ignore the prospect of future changes about the actual character of which we know nothing'.

(2) We assume that the *existing* state of opinion as expressed in prices and the character of existing output is based on a *correct* summing up of future prospects, so that we can accept it as such unless and until something new and relevant comes into the picture.

(3) Knowing that our own individual judgment is worthless, we endeavor to fall back on the judgment of the rest of the world which is perhaps better informed. That is, we endeavor to conform with the behavior of the majority or the average. The psychology of a society of individuals each of whom is endeavoring to copy the others leads to what we may strictly term a *conventional* judgment. (p. 114; his emphasis)[3]

The third point is reminiscent of what is currently referred to in science and the media as herding. As it runs throughout Chapter 12 of the *General Theory*, decision makers are not very concerned with what an investment might really be worth; rather, under the influence of mass psychology, they devote their intelligences 'to anticipating what average opinion expects the average opinion to be', a judgement of 'the third degree' (Keynes, 1936, p. 156). Note that it is rational in such an environment 'to fall back on what is, in truth, a *convention*' (Keynes, 1936, p. 152; Keynes' emphasis). Going with the market rather than trying to follow one's own better instincts is rational for 'persons who have no special knowledge of the circumstances' (p. 153) as well as for expert professionals.

If the general phenomenon of forecasting the psychology of the market is taken for granted, then it is easily conceivable how waves of optimistic or pessimistic sentiment are generated by means of a self-exciting, possibly accelerating mechanism. Hence, any modelling of animal spirits will have to attempt to incorporate a positive feedback effect of this kind.

The second point in the citation refers to more 'objective' factors such as prices or output (or, it may be added, composite variables derived from them). According to the first point, it is the current values that are most relevant for the decision maker. According to the second point, this is justified by his or her assumption that these values are the result of a correct anticipation of the future by the other, presumably smarter and, in their entirety, better informed market participants.

If one likes, it could be said that the average opinion also plays a role here, only in a more indirect way. In any case, insofar as agents believe in the objective factors mentioned above as fundamental information, they will have a bearing on the decision-making process. Regarding modelling, current output, prices and the like could therefore be treated in the traditional way as input in a behavioural function. In the present context, however, these ordinary mechanisms will have to be reconciled with the direct effects of the average opinion. It is then a straightforward idea that the 'fundamentals' may reinforce or keep a curb on the 'conventional' dynamics.

In the light of this discussion, formal modelling does not seem to be too big a problem: set up a positive feedback loop for a variable representing the 'average opinion' and combine it with ordinary behavioural functions. In principle, this can be, and has been, specified in various ways. The downside of this creativity is that it makes it hard to compare the merits and demerits of different models, even if one is under the impression that they invoke similar ideas and effects. Before progressing too far to concrete modelling, it is therefore useful to develop building blocks, or to have reference to existing blocks, which can serve as a canonical schema.

Indeed, modelling what may be interpreted as animal spirits is no longer virgin territory. Promising work has been performed over the last 10 years that can be subdivided into three categories (further details later). Before discussing them one by one, we set up a unifying frame of reference which makes it easier to site a model. As a result, it will also be evident that the models in the literature have more in common than it may seem at first sight. In particular, it is not by chance that they have similar dynamic properties.

The work we focus on is all the more appealing since it provides a micro-foundation of macroeconomic behaviour, albeit, of course, a rather stylized one. At the outset, the literature refers to a large population of agents who, for simplicity, face a binary decision. For example, they may choose between optimism and pessimism, or between extrapolative and static expectations about prices or demand. Individual agents do this with certain probabilities and then take a decision. The central point is that probabilities endogenously change in the course of time. They adjust upward or downward in reaction to agents' observations, which may include output, prices as well as the aforementioned 'average opinion'. As a consequence, agents switch between two attitudes or two strategies. Their decisions vary correspondingly, as does the macroeconomic outcome resulting from them.

By the law of large numbers, this can all be cast in terms of aggregate variables, where one such variable represents the current population mix. The relationships between them form an ordinary and well-defined macrodynamic system specified in discrete or continuous time, as the case may be. The animal spirits and their variations, or that of the average opinion, play a crucial role as the dynamic properties are basically determined by the switching mechanism.

Owing to the increasing and indiscriminate use of the emotive term 'animal spirits', causing it to become an empty phrase, we will in the course of our presentation distinguish between a weak and a strong form of animal spirits in macrodynamics. We will refer to a weak form if a model is able to generate waves of, say, an optimistic and pessimistic attitude, or waves of applying a forecast rule 1 as opposed to a forecast rule 2. A prominent argument for this behaviour is that the first rule has proven to be more successful in the recent past. A strong form of animal spirits is said to exist if agents also rush towards an attitude, strategy, or so on, simply because it is being applied at the time by the majority of agents. In other words, this will be the case if there is a component of herding in the dynamics because individual agents believe that the majority will probably be better informed and smarter than they themselves. To give a first overview, the weak form of animal spirits will typically be found in macro-models employing what is known as the discrete choice approach (DCA), whereas models in which we identify the strong form typically choose the so-called transition probability approach (TPA). However, this division has mainly historical rather than logical reasons.

The remainder of this survey is organized as follows. The next section introduces the two approaches just mentioned. It also points out that they are more closely related than it may appear at first sight and then sets up an abstract two-dimensional model that allows us to study the dynamic effects that they possibly produce. In this way, it can be demonstrated that it is the two approaches themselves and their inherent non-linearities that, with little additional effort, are conducive to the persistent cyclical behaviour emphasized by most of the literature.

Section 3 is concerned with a class of models that are concerned with heterogeneous rule-of-thumb expectations within the New-Keynesian three-equation model (but without its rational expectations). This work evaluates the fitness of the two expectation rules by means of the discrete choice probabilities. It is also noteworthy because orthodox economists have shown an interest in it and given it attention. Section 4 discusses models with an explicit role for herding, which, as stated, is a field for the TPA (and where we will also reason about the distinction between animal spirits in a weak and strong form).[4]

While the modelling outlined so far is conceptually attractive for capturing a sentiment dynamics, it would also be desirable to have some empirical support for it. Section 5 is devoted to this issue. Besides some references to laboratory experiments, it covers work that investigates whether the dynamics of certain business survey indices can be explained by a suitable application of (mainly) the TPA. On the other hand, it presents work that takes a model from Section 3 or 4 and seeks to estimate it in its entirety. Here, the sentiment variable is treated as unobservable and only its implications for the dynamics of the other, observable macro-variables are taken into account. Section 6 concludes.

2. The General Framework

The models we shall survey are concerned with a large population of agents who have to choose between two alternatives. In principle, their options can be almost anything: strategies, rules of thumb to form expectations, diffuse beliefs. In fact, this is a first feature in which the models may differ. For concreteness, let us refer in the following general introduction to two attitudes that agents may entertain and call them optimism and pessimism, identified by a plus and minus sign, respectively. Individual agents choose them, or alternatively switch from one to the other, on the basis of probabilities. They are the same for all agents in the population in the first case, and for all agents in each of the two groups in the second case.

It has been indicated that probabilities vary endogenously over time. This idea is captured by treating them as functions of something else in the model. This 'something else' can be one macroscopic variable or several such variables. In the latter case, the variables are combined in one auxiliary variable, most conveniently by way of weighted additive or subtractive operations. Again, the variables can be almost anything in principle; their choice is thus a second feature for categorizing the models.

Mathematically, we introduce an auxiliary variable, or index, which is, in turn, a function of one or several macroeconomic variables. Regarding the probabilities, we deal with two approaches: the DCA and the TPA. In the applications we consider, they typically differ in the interpretation of the auxiliary variable and the type of variables entering this function. However, both approaches could easily work with setting up the same auxiliary variable for their probabilities.

2.1 The Discrete Choice Approach

As a rule, the DCA is formulated in discrete time. At the beginning of period t, each individual agent is optimistic with probability π_t^+ and pessimistic with probability $\pi_t^- = 1 - \pi_t^+$. The probabilities are not constant, but change with two variables $U^+ = U_{t-1}^+$, $U^- = U_{t-1}^-$, which, in the applications, are often interpreted as the success or fitness of the two attitudes.[5] As the dating indicates, the latter are determined by the values of a set of variables from the previous or possibly also earlier periods. Due to the law of large numbers, the shares of optimists and pessimists in period t, n_t^+ and n_t^-, are identical to the probabilities, that is,

$$n_t^+ = \pi_t^+ = \pi^+ \left(U_{t-1}^+\right), \qquad n_t^- = \pi_t^- = \pi^- \left(U_{t-1}^-\right) = 1 - \pi^+ \left(U_{t-1}^+\right) \tag{1}$$

A priori there is a large variety of possibilities to conceive of functions $\pi^+(\cdot)$, $\pi^-(\cdot)$. In macroeconomics, there is currently one dominating specification that relates π^+, π^- to U^+, U^-. It derives from the multinomial logit (or 'Gibbs') probabilities. Going back to these roots, standard references for an extensive discussion are Manski and McFadden (1981) and Anderson *et al.* (1993). For the ordinary macroeconomist, it suffices to know the gist as it has become more broadly known with two influential papers by Brock and Hommes (1997, 1998). They applied the specification to the speculative price dynamics of a risky asset on a financial market, while it took around 10 more years for it to migrate to the field of macroeconomics. With respect to a positive coefficient $\beta > 0$, the formula reads:

$$\pi^+ \left(U_{t-1}^+\right) = \frac{\exp \left(\beta U_{t-1}^+\right)}{\exp \left(\beta U_{t-1}^+\right) + \exp \left(\beta U_{t-1}^-\right)} = \frac{1}{1 + \exp \left[\beta \left(U_{t-1}^- - U_{t-1}^+\right)\right]}$$

$$\pi^- \left(U_{t-1}^-\right) = \frac{\exp \left(\beta U_{t-1}^-\right)}{\exp \left(\beta U_{t-1}^+\right) + \exp \left(\beta U_{t-1}^-\right)} = \frac{1}{1 + \exp \left[\beta \left(U_{t-1}^+ - U_{t-1}^-\right)\right]} \tag{2}$$

($\exp(\cdot)$ being the exponential function).[6] Given the scale of the fitness expressions, the parameter β in (2) is commonly known as the *intensity of choice*. Occasionally, reference is made to $1/\beta$ as the propensity to err. For values of β close to zero, the two probabilities π^+, π^- would nearly be equal, whereas for $\beta \to \infty$, they tend to zero or one, so that almost all of the agents would either be optimistic or pessimistic.[7] The second equals sign follows from dividing the numerator and denominator by the numerator. It makes clear that what matters is the difference in the fitness.

Equations (1) and (2) are the basis of the animal spirits models employing the DCA. The next stage is, of course, to determine the fitnesses U^+, U^-, another salient feature for characterizing different models. Before going into detail about this further below, we should put the approach as such into perspective by highlighting two problems that are rarely mentioned. First, there is the issue of discrete time. It may be argued that (1) and (2) could also be part of a continuous-time model if the lag in (1) is eliminated, that is, if one stipulates $n_t^+ = \pi^+(U_t^+)$. This is true under the condition that the fitnesses do not depend on n_t^+ themselves. Otherwise (and quite likely), because of the non-linearity in (2), the population share would be given by a non-trivial implicit equation with n_t^+ on the left-hand and right-hand sides, which could only be solved numerically.

The second problem is of a conceptual nature. It becomes most obvious in a situation where the population shares of the optimists and pessimists are roughly equal and remain constant over time. Here, the individual agents would nevertheless switch in each and every period with a probability of one-half.[8] This requires the model builder to specify the length of the period. If the period is not too long then, for psychological and many other reasons, the agents in the model would change their mind (much) more often than most people in the real world (and also in academia). This would somewhat undermine the micro-foundation of this modelling, even though the invariance of the macroscopic outcomes n_t^+, n_t^- may make perfect sense.

Apart from being meaningful in itself, both problems can be satisfactorily solved by taking up an idea by Hommes *et al.* (2005). They suppose that in each period, not all agents but only a fraction of them think about a possible switch, a modification which they call discrete choice with asynchronous updating. Thus, let μ be the fixed probability *per unit of time* that an individual agent reconsiders his attitude, which then may or may not lead to a change. Correspondingly, $\Delta t \mu$ is his probability of operating a random mechanism for π_t^+ and π_t^- between t and Δt, while over this interval, he will unconditionally stick to the attitude he already had at time t with a probability of $(1 - \Delta t \mu)$. From this, the population shares at the macroscopic level at $t + \Delta t$ result like

$$n_{t+\Delta t}^+ = (1 - \Delta t \mu)\, n_t^+ + \Delta t \mu \pi^+ \left(U_t^+\right) = n_t^+ + \Delta t \mu \left[\pi^+ \left(U_t^+\right) - n_t^+\right]$$

$$n_{t+\Delta t}^- = (1 - \Delta t \mu)\, n_t^- + \Delta t \mu \pi^- \left(U_t^-\right) = n_t^- + \Delta t \mu \left[\pi^- \left(U_t^-\right) - n_t^-\right] \tag{3}$$

It goes without saying that these expressions reduce to (1) if the probability $\Delta t \mu$ is equal to one. Treating μ as a fixed parameter and going to the limit in (3), $\Delta t \to 0$, gives rise to a differential equation for the changes in n^+. It actually occurs in other fields of science, especially and closest to economics, in evolutionary game theory, where this form is usually called *logit dynamics*.[9] At least in situations where one or both reasons indicated above are relevant to the DCA, the continuous-time version of (3) with $\Delta t \to 0$ may be preferred over the formulation (1) and (2) in discrete time.

With a view to the TPA in the next subsection, it is useful to consider the special case of symmetrical fitness values, in the sense that the gains of one attitude are the losses of the other, $U^- = -U^+$. To this end, we introduce the notation $s = U^+$ and call s the switching index. Furthermore, instead of the population shares, we study the changes in their difference $x := n^+ - n^-$ (which can attain values between ± 1). Subtracting the population shares in (3) and making the adjustment period Δt infinitesimally small, a differential equation in x is obtained: $\dot{x} = \mu\{[\exp(\beta s) - \exp(-\beta s)]/[\exp(\beta s) + \exp(-\beta s)] - x\}$. The fraction of the two square brackets is identical to a well-established function of its own, the hyperbolic tangent (tanh), so that we can compactly write,

$$\dot{x} = \mu[\tanh(\beta s) - x] \tag{4}$$

The function $x \mapsto \tanh(x)$ is defined on the entire real line; it is strictly increasing everywhere with $\tanh(0) = 0$ and derivative $\tanh'(0) = 1$ at this point; and it asymptotically tends to ± 1 as $x \to \pm\infty$. This also immediately shows that x cannot leave the open interval $(-1, +1)$.

2.2 *The Transition Probability Approach*

The TPA goes back to a quite mathematical book on quantitative sociology by Weidlich and Haag (1983). It was introduced into economics by Lux (1995) in a seminal paper on a speculative asset price dynamics.[10] It took a while before, with Franke (2008a, 2012a), macroeconomic theory became aware of it.[11] The main reason for this delay was that Weidlich and Haag as well as Lux started out with concepts from statistical mechanics (see also footnote 16 below), an apparatus that ordinary economists are quite unfamiliar with. The following presentation makes use of the work of Franke, which can do without this probabilistic theory and sets up a regular macrodynamic adjustment equation.[12]

In contrast to the DCA, it is now relevant whether an agent is optimistic or pessimistic at present. The probability that an optimist will remain optimistic and that of a pessimist becoming an optimist will generally be different. Accordingly, the basic concept are the probabilities of switching from one attitude to the other, that is, transition probabilities. Thus, at time t, let p_t^{-+} be the probability *per unit of time* that a pessimistic agent will switch to optimism (which is the same for all pessimists), and let p_t^{+-} be the probability of an opposite change. More exactly, in a discrete-time framework, $\Delta t\, p_t^{-+}$ and $\Delta t\, p_t^{+-}$ are the probabilities that these switches will occur within the time interval $[t, t + \Delta t)$.[13]

In the present setting, we refer directly to the difference $x = n^+ - n^-$ of the two population shares. It is this variable that we shall call the aggregate *sentiment* of the population (average opinion, state of confidence or just animal spirits are some alternative expressions). In terms of this sentiment, the shares of optimists and pessimists are given by $n^+ = (1 + x)/2$, and $n^- = (1 - x)/2$.[14] With a large population, changes in the two groups are given by their size multiplied by the transition probabilities. Accordingly, the share of optimists decreases by $\Delta t\, p_t^{+-} (1 + x_t)/2$ due to the agents leaving this group, and it increases by $\Delta t\, p_t^{-+} (1 - x_t)/2$ due to the pessimists who have just joined it. With signs reversed, the same holds true for the population share of pessimistic agents. The net effect on x is described by a deterministic adjustment equation.[15] We express this for a specific length Δt of the adjustment period as well as for the limiting case when Δt shrinks to zero, which yields an ordinary difference and differential equation, respectively:[16]

$$x_{t+\Delta t} = x_t + \Delta t \left[(1 - x_t) p_t^{-+} - (1 + x_t) p_t^{+-} \right]$$
$$\dot{x} = (1 - x) p^{-+} - (1 + x) p^{+-} \tag{5}$$

Similar to the DCA, the transition probabilities are functions of an index variable. Here, however, as indicated in the derivation of equation (4), the same index enters p^{-+} and p^{+-}. That is, calling it a switching index and denoting it by the letter s, p^{-+} is supposed to be an increasing function and p^{+-} a decreasing function of s. We adopt this new notation because the type of arguments upon which this index depends typically differs to those of the functions U^+ and U^- in (1). In particular, s may positively depend on the sentiment variable x itself, thus introducing a mechanism that can represent a contagion effect, or 'herding'.

Regarding the specification in which the switching index influences the transition probabilities, Weidlich and Haag (1983) introduced the natural assumption that the *relative* changes of p^{-+} and p^{+-} in response to the changes in s are linear and symmetrical. As a consequence, the function of the transition probabilities is proportional to the exponential function $\exp(s)$. Analogously to the intensity of choice in (2), the switching index may furthermore be multiplied by a coefficient $\beta > 0$. In this way, we arrive at the following functional form:[17]

$$p_t^{-+} = p^{-+}(s_t) = v \, \exp(\beta s_t), \qquad p_t^{+-} = p^{+-}(s_t) = v \, \exp(-\beta s_t) \tag{6}$$

Technically speaking, v is a positive integration constant. In a modelling context, it can, however, be similarly interpreted to β as a parameter that measures how strongly agents react to variations in the switching index. Weidlich and Haag (1983, p. 41) therefore call v a *flexibility parameter*. Since the only difference between β and v is that one has a linear and the other has a non-linear effect on the probabilities, one of them may seem dispensable. In fact, we know of no example that works with $\beta \neq 1$ in (6). We maintain this coefficient for pedagogical reasons, because it will emphasize the correspondence with the DCA below.

Substituting (6) for the probabilities in (5) yields $\dot{x} = v[(1 - x) \exp(\beta s) - (1 + x) \exp(-\beta s)] = 2v\{[\exp(\beta s) - \exp(-\beta s)]/2 - x[\exp(\beta s) + \exp(-\beta s)]/2\}$. Making use of the definition of the hyperbolic sine and cosine (sinh and cosh), the curly brackets are equal to

$\{\sinh(\beta s) - x \cosh(\beta s)\}$. Since the hyperbolic tangent is defined as $\tanh = \sinh / \cosh$, equation (5) becomes

$$x_{t+\Delta t} = x_t + \Delta t\, 2\, v[\tanh(\beta s_t) - x_t]\cosh(\beta s_t)$$

$$\dot{x} = 2\, v[\tanh(\beta s) - x]\cosh(\beta s) \tag{7}$$

A comparison of equations (4) and (7) reveals a close connection between the TPA and the continuous-time modification of the DCA.[18] If we consider identical switching indices and $\mu = 2v$, then the two equations describe almost the same adjustments of the sentiment variable (because the hyperbolic cosine is a strictly positive function). More specifically, if these equations are integrated into a higher-dimensional dynamic system, (4) and (7) produce the same isoclines $\dot{x} = 0$, so that the phase diagrams with x as one of two variables will be qualitatively identical. When, moreover, these systems have an equilibrium with a balanced sentiment $x = 0$ from $s = 0$, it will be locally stable with respect to (7) if and only if it is locally stable with respect to (4).[19]

2.3 Basic Dynamic Tendencies

A central feature of the models we consider are persistent fluctuations. This is true irrespective of whether they employ the discrete choice or TPA. With the formulations in (4) and (7), we can argue that there is a deeper reason for this behaviour, namely, the non-linearity brought about by the hyperbolic tangent in these adjustments. Making this statement also for the discrete choice models, we follow the intuition that basic properties of a system using (4) can also be found in its discrete-time counterparts (2) and (3) (albeit possibly with somewhat different parameter values).

   To reveal the potential inherent in (4) and (7), we combine the sentiment equation with a simple dynamic law for a second variable y. Presently, a precise economic meaning of x and y is of no concern, simply let them be two abstract variables. Forgoing any further non-linearity, we posit a linear equation for the changes in y with a negative autofeedback and a positive cross-effect. Regarding x let us, for concreteness, work with the logit dynamics (4) and put $\mu = \beta = 1$. Thus, consider the following two-dimensional system in continuous time:

$$\dot{x} = \tanh[s(x, y)] - x$$

$$\dot{y} = \eta_x x - \eta_y y$$

$$s(x, y) = \phi_x x - \phi_y y \tag{8}$$

We fix $\phi_y = 1.80$, $\eta_x = \eta_y = 1.00$ and study the changes in the system's global behaviour under variations of the remaining coefficient ϕ_x. A deeper analysis of the resulting bifurcation phenomena when the dynamics changes from one regime to another is given in Franke (2014). Here, it suffices to view four selected values of ϕ_x and the corresponding phase diagrams in the (x, y)-plane.

   Since tanh has a positive derivative everywhere, positive values of ϕ_x represent a positive, that is, destabilizing feedback in the sentiment adjustments. By contrast, $\phi_y > 0$ together with $\eta_x > 0$ establishes a negative feedback loop for the sentiment variable: an increase in x raises y and the resulting decrease in the switching index lowers (the change in) x. The stabilizing effect will be dominant if ϕ_x is sufficiently small relative to ϕ_y. This is the case for $\phi_x = 0.90$, which is shown in the top-left diagram of Figure 1. The two thin solid (black) lines depict

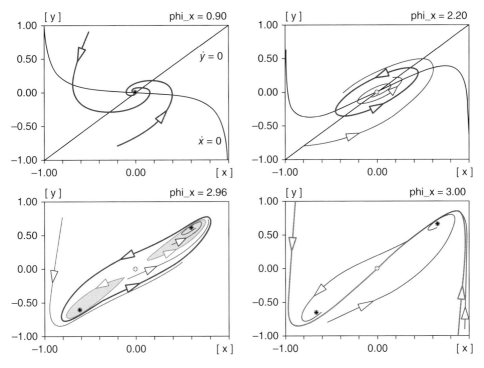

Figure 1. Phase Diagrams of (8) for Four Different Regimes.

the isoclines of the two variables; the straight line is the locus of $\dot{y} = 0$ and the curved line is $\dot{x} = 0$. Their point of intersection at $(x^o, y^o) = (0, 0)$ is the equilibrium point of system (8). Convergence towards it takes place in a cyclical manner.

The equilibrium (x^o, y^o) and the $\dot{y} = 0$ isocline are, of course, not affected by the changes in ϕ_x. On the other hand, increasing values of this parameter shift the isocline $\dot{x} = 0$ downward to the left of the equilibrium and upward to the right of it. The counterclockwise motions are maintained, but at our second value $\phi_x = 2.20$, they locally spiral outward, that is, the equilibrium has become unstable. Nevertheless, further away from the equilibrium, the centripetal forces prove dominant and generate spirals pointing inward. As a consequence, there must be one orbit in between that neither spirals inward nor outward. Such a closed orbit is indeed unique and constitutes a limit cycle that globally attracts all trajectories, wherever they start from (except the equilibrium point itself). This situation is shown in the top-right panel of Figure 1.

If ϕ_x increases sufficiently, the shifts of the $\dot{x} = 0$ isocline are so pronounced that it cuts the straight line at two (but only two) additional points (x^1, y^1) and (x^2, y^2). One lies in the lower-left corner and the other symmetrically in the upper-right corner of the phase diagram. First, over a small range of ϕ_x, these outer equilibria are unstable, after that, for all ϕ_x above a certain threshold, they are always locally stable. The latter case is illustrated in the bottom-left panel of Figure 1, where the parameter has increased to $\phi_x = 2.96$ (the isoclines are not shown here, so as not to overload the diagram).

The two shaded areas are the basins of attraction of (x^1, y^1) and (x^2, y^2), each surrounded by a repelling limit cycle. Remarkably, the stable limit cycle from $\phi_x = 2.20$ has survived these changes; it has become wider, encompasses the two outer equilibria together with their basins of attraction and attracts all motions that do not start there.

The extreme equilibria move towards the limits of the domain of the sentiment variable, $x = \pm 1$, as ϕ_x increases. They do this faster than the big limit cycle widens. Eventually, therefore, the outer boundaries of the basins of attraction touch the big cycle, so to speak. This is the moment when this orbit disappears, and with it all cyclical motions. The bottom-right panel of Figure 1 for $\phi_x = 3.00$ demonstrates that then the trajectories either converge to the saddle point (x^o, y^o) in the middle, if they happen to start on its stable arm, or they converge to one of the other two equilibria.

To sum up, whether the obvious, the 'natural' equilibrium (x^o, y^o) is stable or unstable, system (8) shows a broad scope for cyclical trajectories. Furthermore, whether there are additional outer equilibria or not, there is also broad scope for self-sustaining cyclical behaviour, that is, oscillations that do not explode and, even in the absence of exogenous shocks, do not die out, either.

3. Heterogeneity and Animal Spirits in the New-Keynesian Framework

3.1 De Grauwe's Modelling Approach

Given that the New-Keynesian theory is the ruling paradigm in macroeconomics, Paul De Grauwe had a simple but ingenious idea to challenge it: accept the three basic log-linearized equations for output, inflation and the interest rate of that approach, but discard its underlying representative agents and rational expectations. This means that, instead, he introduces different groups of agents with heterogeneous forms of bounded rationality, as it is called.[20] Expectations have to be formed for the output gap (the percentage deviations of output from its equilibrium trend level) and for the rate of inflation in the next period. For each variable, agents can choose between two rules of thumbs where, as specified by the DCA, switching between them occurs according to their forecasting performance. De Grauwe speaks of 'animal spirits' insofar as such a model is able to generate waves of optimistic and pessimistic forecasts, notions that are excluded from the New-Keynesian world by construction.[21]

The following three-equation model is taken from De Grauwe (2008a), which is the first in a series of similar versions that have subsequently been studied in De Grauwe (2010, 2011, 2012a,b). The term 'three-equation' refers to the three laws that determine the output gap y, the rate of inflation π and the nominal rate of interest i set by the central bank. The symbols $\pi^\star$ and $i^\star$ denote the central bank's target rates of inflation and interest, which are known and taken into account by the agents in the private sector.[22] All parameters are positive where, more specifically, a_y and b_π are weighting coefficients between 0 and 1. E_t^{agg} are the aggregated expectations of the heterogeneous agents using information up to the beginning of the present period t. They are substituted for the mathematical expectation operator E_t, the aforementioned rational expectations. Then, the three equations are:

$$y_t = a_y E_t^{agg} y_{t+1} + (1 - a_y) y_{t-1} + a_i \left[i_t - E_t^{agg} \pi_{t+1} - (i^\star - \pi^\star) \right] + \varepsilon_{y,t} \tag{9}$$

$$\pi_t = b_\pi E_t^{agg} \pi_{t+1} + (1 - b_\pi) \pi_{t-1} + b_y y_t + \varepsilon_{\pi,t} \tag{10}$$

$$i_t = c_i i_{t-1} + (1 - c_i) i^\star + c_\pi (\pi_t - \pi^\star) + c_y y_t + \varepsilon_{i,t} \tag{11}$$

Equation (9) for the output gap is usually referred to as a dynamic IS equation (in analogy to old theories contrasting investment with savings), here in hybrid form, which means that the expectation term is combined with a one-period lag of the same variable. The Phillips curve in (10), likewise in hybrid form, is viewed as representing the supply side of the economy. Equation (11) is a Taylor rule with interest rate smoothing, that is, it contains the lagged interest rate on the right-hand side.[23] The terms $\varepsilon_{y,t}$, $\varepsilon_{\pi,t}$ and $\varepsilon_{i,t}$ are white noise disturbances, interpreted as demand, supply and monetary policy shocks, respectively. Qualitatively little would change if some serial correlation were allowed for them.

The aggregate expectations in these equations are convex combinations of two (extremely) simple forecasting rules. With respect to the output gap, De Grauwe considers optimistic and pessimist forecasters, predicting a fixed positive and negative value of y, respectively. With respect to the inflation rate, he distinguishes between agents who believe in the central bank's target and so-called extrapolators, who predict that next period's inflation will be last period's inflation.[24] Accordingly, with $g > 0$ as a positive constant, n^{opt} as the share of optimistic agents regarding output, and n^{tar} as the share of central bank believers regarding inflation, expectations are given by

$$E_t^{opt} y_{t+1} = g, \quad E_t^{pess} y_{t+1} = -g$$

$$E_t^{tar} \pi_{t+1}, = \pi^\star \quad E_t^{ext} \pi_{t+1} = \pi_{t-1}$$

$$E_t^{agg} y_{t+1} = n_t^{opt} E_t^{opt} y_{t+1} + \left(1 - n_t^{opt}\right) E_t^{pess} y_{t+1}$$

$$E_t^{agg} \pi_{t+1} = n_t^{tar} E_t^{tar} \pi_{t+1} + \left(1 - n_t^{tar}\right) E_t^{ext} \pi_{t+1} \tag{12}$$

In other papers, De Grauwe alternatively stipulates so-called fundamental and extrapolative output forecasters, $E_t^{fun} y_{t+1} = 0$ and $E_t^{ext} y_{t+1} = y_{t-1}$. However, the dynamic properties of his model are not essentially affected by such a respecification.

The populations shares of the heterogeneous agents are determined by the suitably adjusted discrete choice equations (1) and (2). Denoting the measures of fitness that apply here by U^{opt}, U^{pess}, U^{tar} and U^{ext}, we have

$$n_t^{opt} = \frac{\exp\left(\beta U_{t-1}^{opt}\right)}{\exp\left(\beta U_{t-1}^{opt}\right) + \exp\left(\beta U_{t-1}^{pess}\right)}$$

$$n_t^{tar} = \frac{\exp\left(\beta U_{t-1}^{tar}\right)}{\exp\left(\beta U_{t-1}^{tar}\right) + \exp\left(\beta U_{t-1}^{ext}\right)} \tag{13}$$

Conforming to the principle that better forecasts attract a higher share of agents, fitness is defined by the negative (infinite) sum of the past squared prediction errors, where the past is discounted with geometrically declining weights. Hence, with a so-called memory coefficient $0 < \rho < 1$, superscripts $A = opt, pess, tar, ext$ and variables $z = y, \pi$ in obvious assignment,

$$U_t^A = -\sum_{k=1}^{\infty} \omega_k \left(z_{t-k} - E_{t-k-1}^A z_{t-k}\right)^2, \quad \omega_k = (1 - \rho)\rho^k$$

$$= -\rho \left\{ (1 - \rho)\left(z_{t-1} - E_{t-2}^A z_{t-1}\right)^2 + U_{t-1}^A \right\} \tag{14}$$

This specification of the weights ω_k makes sure that they add up to unity. The second expression in (14) is an elementary mathematical reformulation. It allows a recursive determination of the fitness, which is more convenient and more precisely computable than an approximation of an infinite series.

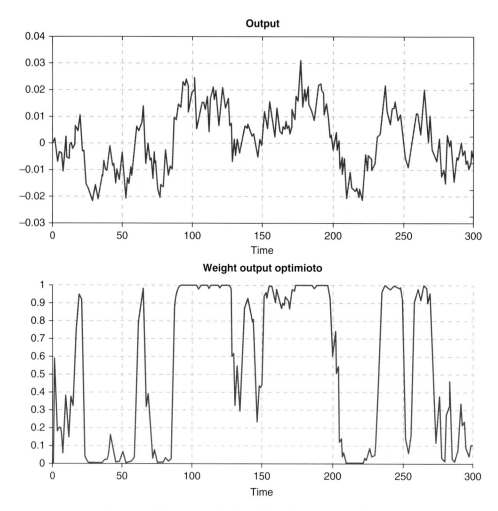

Figure 2. A Representative Simulation Run of Model (9)–(14).

Equation (14) completes the model. De Grauwe makes no explicit reference to an equilibrium of the economy (or possibly several of them?) and does not attempt to characterize its stability or instability. He proceeds directly to numerical simulations and then discusses what economic sense can be made of what we see. Depending on the specific focus in his papers, additional computer experiments with some modifications may follow.

A representative simulation run for the present model and similar models is shown in Figure 2. This example, reproduced from De Grauwe (2008a, p. 24), plots the time series of the output gap (upper panel) and the share of optimistic forecasters (lower panel). The underlying time unit is one month, that is, the diagram covers a period of 25 years. The strong raggedness of the output series is indicative of the stochastic shocks that De Grauwe assumes. In fact, the deterministic core of the model is stable and converges to a state with $y = 0$, $\pi = \pi^\star$ and $i = i^\star$. Without checking any stability conditions or eigenvalues, this can be inferred from various diagrams of impulse response functions (IRFs) in De Grauwe's work.

The fluctuations in Figure 2 are therefore not self-sustaining. De Grauwe nevertheless emphasizes that his model generates endogenous waves of optimism and pessimism. This characterization may be clarified by a longer quote from De Grauwe (2010):

> These endogenously generated cycles in output are made possible by a self-fulfilling mechanism that can be described as follows. A series of random shocks creates the possibility that one of the two forecasting rules, say the extrapolating one, delivers a higher payoff, that is, a lower mean squared forecast error (MSFE). This attracts agents that were using the fundamentalist rule. If the successful extrapolation happens to be a positive extrapolation, more agents will start extrapolating the positive output gap. The 'contagion-effect' leads to an increasing use of the optimistic extrapolation of the output-gap, which in turn stimulates aggregate demand. Optimism is therefore self-fulfilling. A boom is created. At some point, negative stochastic shocks and/or the reaction of the central bank through the Taylor rule make a dent in the MSFE of the optimistic forecasts. Fundamentalist forecasts may become attractive again, but it is equally possible that pessimistic extrapolation becomes attractive and therefore fashionable again. The economy turns around.
>
> These waves of optimism and pessimism can be understood to be searching (learning) mechanisms of agents who do not fully understand the underlying model but are continuously searching for the truth. An essential characteristic of this searching mechanism is that it leads to systematic correlation in beliefs (e.g. optimistic extrapolations or pessimistic extrapolations). This systematic correlation is at the core of the booms and busts created in the model. (p. 12)

Thus, in certain stages of a longer cycle, the optimistic expectations are superior, which increases the share of optimistic agents and enables output to rise, which, in turn, reinforces the optimistic attitude. This mechanism is evidenced by the co-movements of y_t and n_t^{opt} in Figure 2 and conforms to the positive feedback loop highlighted in a comment on the small and stylized system (8) above.[25] A stabilizing counter-effect is not as clearly recognizable. De Grauwe only alludes to the central bank's reactions in the Taylor rule, when positive output gaps and inflation rates above their target (which will more or less move together) lead to both higher nominal and real interest rates. This is a channel that puts a curb on y_t in the IS equation. In addition, a suitable sequence of random shocks may occasionally work in the same direction and initiate a turnaround.

The New-Keynesian theory is proud of its 'micro-foundations'. Within the framework of the representative agents and rational expectations, they derive the macroeconomic IS equation (9) and the Phillips curve (10) as log-linear approximations to the optimal decision rules of inter-temporal optimization problems. As these two assumptions have now been dropped, the question arises of the theoretical justification of (9) and (10). Two answers can be given.

First, Branch and McGough (2009) are able to derive these equations invoking two groups of individually boundedly rational agents, provided that their expectation formation satisfies a set of seven axioms.[26] The authors point out that the axioms are not only necessary for the aggregation result, but some of them could also be considered rather restrictive; see, especially, Branch and McGough (2009, p. 1043). Furthermore, it may not appear very convincing that the agents are fairly limited in their forecasts, and yet they endeavour to maximize their objective function over an infinite time horizon and are smart enough to compute the corresponding first-order Euler conditions.

Acknowledging these problems, the second answer is that the equations make good economic sense even without a firm theoretical basis. Thus, one is willing to pay a price for the convenient tractability obtained, arguing that more consistent attempts might be undertaken in the future. In fact, De Grauwe's approach also succeeded in gaining the attention of New-Keynesian theorists and a certain appreciation by the more open-minded proponents. This is indeed one of the rare occasions where orthodox and heterodox economists are able and willing to discuss issues by starting out from a common basis.

Branch and McGough (2010) consider a similar version to equations (9)–(11) where, besides naive expectations, they still admit rational expectations. However, the latter are more costly, meaning that they may be outperformed by boundedly rational agents in tranquil times, in spite of their systematic forecast errors. For greater clarity, the economy is studied in a deterministic setting (hence rational expectations amount to perfect foresight). The authors are interested in the stationary points of this dynamics: in general, there are multiple equilibria and the questions is which are stable/unstable, and what are the population shares prevailing in them.

Branch and McGough's analysis provides a serious challenge for the rational expectations hypothesis. Its recommendation to monetary policy is to guarantee determinacy in models of this type (this essentially amounts to the Taylor principle, according to which the interest rate has to rise more than one-for-one with inflation). Branch and McGough illustrate that, in their framework, the central bank may unwittingly destabilize the economy by generating complex ('chaotic') dynamics with inefficiently high inflation and output volatility, even if all agents are initially rational. The authors emphasize that these outcomes are not limited to unusual calibrations or *a priori* poor policy choices; the basic reason is rather the dual attracting and repelling nature of the steady-state values of output and inflation.

Anufriev *et al.* (2013) abstract from output and limit themselves to a version of (10) with only expected inflation on the right-hand side. Since there is no interest rate smoothing in their Taylor rule ($c_1 = 0$) and, of course, no output gap either, the inflation rate is the only dynamic variable. These simplifications allow the authors to consider greater variety in the formation of expectations and to study their effects almost in a vacuum. In this case, too, the main question is whether, in the absence of random shocks, the system will converge to the rational expectations equilibrium. This is possible but not guaranteed because, again, certain ecologies of forecasting rules can lead to multiple equilibria, where some are stable and give rise to intrinsic heterogeneity.

Maintaining the (stochastic) equations (9) and (10) (but without the lagged variables on the right-hand side) and considering different dating assumptions in the Taylor rule (likewise without interest rate smoothing), Branch and Evans (2011) obtain similar results, broadly speaking. They place particular interest in a possible regime-switching of the output and inflation variances (an important empirical issue for the US economy), and in the implications of heterogeneity for optimal monetary policy.

Dräger (2016) examines the interplay between fully rational (but costly) and boundedly rational (but costless) expectations in a subvariant of the New-Keynesian approach, which is characterized by a so-called rational inattentiveness of agents. As a result of this concept, entering the model equations for quarter t are not only contemporary but also past expectations about the variables in quarter $t + 1$. The author's main concern is with the model's ability to match certain summary statistics and, in particular, the empirically observed persistence in the data. Not least due to the flexible degree of inattention, which is brought about by the agents' switching between full and bounded rationality (in contrast to the case where all agents are fully rational, when the degree is fixed), the model turns out to be superior to the more orthodox model variants.[27]

3.2 Modifications and Extensions

The attractiveness of De Grauwe's modelling strategy is also shown by a number of papers that take his three-equation model as a point of departure and combine it with a financial sector. To be specific, this means that a financial variable is added to equation (9), (10) or (11), and that the real economy also feeds back on financial markets via the output gap or the inflation rate. It is here a typical conjecture, which then needs to be tested, that a financial sector tends to destabilize the original model in some sense; for example, output or inflation may become more volatile.

In an early extension of this kind is the integration of a stock market in De Grauwe (2008b). He assumes that an increase in stock prices has a positive influence on output in the IS equation and a negative influence on inflation in the Phillips curve (the latter because this reduces marginal costs). In addition, it is of special interest that the central bank can try to lean against the wind by including a positive effect of stock market booms in its interest rate reaction function. The stock prices are determined, in turn, by expected dividends discounted by the central bank's interest rate plus a constant markup. The actual dividends are a constant fraction of nominal GDP, that is, their forecasts are closely linked to the agents' forecasts of output and inflation.

In a later paper, De Grauwe and Macchiarelli (2015) include a banking sector in the baseline model. In this case, the negative spread between the loan rate and the central bank's short-term interest rate enters the IS equation in order to capture the cost of bank loans. Along the lines of the financial accelerator by Bernanke et al. (1999), banks are assumed to reduce this spread as firms' equity increases which, by hypothesis, moves in step with their loan demand. Besides y_t, π_t and i_t, the model contains private savings and the borrowing-lending spread as two additional dynamic variables. In the final sections of the paper, the model is extended by introducing variable share prices and determining them analogously to De Grauwe (2008b).

De Grauwe and Gerba (2015a) is a very comprehensive contribution that starts out from De Grauwe and Macchiarelli (2015), but specifies a richer structure of the financial sector, which also finds its way into the IS equation. One consequence of the extension is that capital now shows up as another dynamic variable, and that new types of shocks are considered.[28] Once again, the discrete choice version is contrasted to the world with rational expectations. In a follow-up paper, De Grauwe and Gerba (2015b) introduce a bank-based corporate financing friction and evaluate the relative contribution of that friction to the effectiveness of monetary policy. On the whole, it is impressive work, but, given the long list of numerical parameters to set, readers have to place their trust in it.

Lengnick and Wohltmann (2013) and, in a more elaborated version, Lengnick and Wohltmann (2016) choose a different approach to add a stock market to the baseline model.[29] There are two channels through which stock prices affect the real side of the economy. One is a negative influence in the Phillips curve, which is interpreted as an effect on marginal cost, the other is the difference between stock price and goods price inflation in the IS equation, which may increase output. The modelling of the stock market, on the other hand, is borrowed from the burgeoning literature on agent-based speculative demands for a risky asset. Such a market is populated by fundamentalist traders and trend chasers who switch between these strategies analogously to (13) and (14). The market is now additionally influenced by the real sector through the assumption that the fundamental value of the shares is proportional to the output gap. Furthermore, besides speculators, there is a stock demand by optimizing private households, which increases with output and decreases with the interest rate and higher real stock prices.

While in the simulations, the authors maintain the usual quarter as the length of the adjustment period in (9)–(11) for the real sector, they specify financial transactions on a daily basis and use time aggregates for their feedback on the quarterly equations. Even in isolation and without random shocks, the stock market dynamics is known for its potential to generate endogenous booms and busts. The spillover effects can now cause a higher volatility in the real sector. For example, it can modify the original effects of a given shock in the IRFs and make them hard to predict.[30] One particular concern of the two papers is a possible stabilization through monetary policy, another is a taxation of the financial transactions or profits. An important issue is whether a policy that is effective under rational expectations can also be expected to be so in an environment with heterogeneous and boundedly rational agents.

Scheffknecht and Geiger's (2011) modelling is in a similar spirit (including the different time scales for the real and financial sector), but limits itself to one channel from the stock market to the three-equation baseline specification. To this end, the authors add a risk premium ζ_t (i.e. the spread between a credit rate and i_t) to the short-term real interest rate in (9). The transmission is a positive impact of the change in stock prices on ζ_t, besides effects from y_t, i_t and the volatilities (i.e. variances) of y_t, π_t, i_t on this variable.

A new element is an explicit consideration of momentum traders' balance sheets (but only of theirs, for simplicity). They are made up of the value of the shares they hold and money, which features as cash if it is positive and debt if it is negative. This brings the leverage ratios of these traders into play, which may constrain them in their asset demands. Although the latter extension is not free of inconsistencies, these are ideas worth considering.[31]

4. Herding and Objective Determinants of Investment

The models discussed so far were concerned with expectations about an economic variable in the next period. Here, a phenomenon to which an expression like 'animal spirits' may apply occurs when the agents rush towards one of the two forecast rules. However, this behaviour is based on objective factors, normally publicly available statistics. Most prominently, they contrast expected with realized values and then evaluate the forecast performance of the rules.

In the present section, we emphasize that the success of decisions involving a longer time horizon, in particular, cannot be judged from such a good or bad prediction, or from corresponding profits in the next quarter. It takes several years to know whether an investment in fixed capital, for example, was worth undertaking. Furthermore, decisions of that kind must, realistically, take more than one dimension into account. As a consequence, expectations are multi-faceted and far more diffuse in nature. Being aware of this, people have less confidence in their own judgement and the relevance of the information available to them. In these situations, the third paragraph of the Keynes quotation in the introductory section becomes relevant, where he points out that 'we endeavor to conform with the behavior of the majority or the average', which 'leads to what we may strictly term a *conventional* judgment'. In other words, central elements are concepts such as a (business or consumer) sentiment or climate, or a general state of confidence. In the language of tough business men, it is not only their skills, but also their gut feelings that make them so successful.

Therefore, as an alternative to the usual focus on next-period expectations of a specific macroeconomic variable, we may formulate the following axiom: *long-term decisions of the agents are based on sentiment*, where, as indicated by Keynes, with agents' orientation towards the behaviour of the majority, this expression may also connote herding. In terms of 'animal spirits', we propose that in the models under consideration so far, we have animal spirits in a weak sense, whereas in the context outlined above we have animal spirits in a strong sense; animal spirits proper, so to speak.[32]

The discrete choice and TPAs can also be used to model animal spirits in the strong sense. Crucial for this is specifying arguments with which the probabilities are supposed to vary, that is, specifying what was called the fitness function or switching index, respectively. Such arguments may neglect an evaluation of short-term expectations, and they should provide a role for herding or contagion. The latter can be achieved conveniently by including a majority index, such that the more agents adhere to one of the attitudes, the higher *ceteris paribus* the probability that agents will choose it or switch to it.

In the following, we present a series of papers that follow this strategy. What they all have in common is that they pursue the TPA, and that their sentiment variable refers to the fixed investment decisions of firms. The models are thus concerned with a business sentiment. This variable is key to the dynamics because, acting *via* the Keynesian multiplier, investment and its variations are the driving forces of the economy; other components of aggregate demand play a passive role. Also, all of these models are growth models, a feature that makes them economically more satisfactory than most of the (otherwise meritorious) models described in the previous sections, which are stationary in the long run.

Let us therefore begin by specifying investment and the goods markets. Individual firms have two (net) investment options. These options are given by a lower growth rate of the capital stock g_{min}, at which firms invest if they are pessimistic, and a higher growth rate g_{max}, corresponding to an optimistic view of the world. Let g^o be the mean value of the two, $g^o = (g_{min} + g_{max})/2$, and x the sentiment of the firms as it was defined in Section 2.2, that is, the difference between optimistic and pessimistic firms scaled by their total number. Hence the aggregate capital growth rate is given by[33]

$$g = g(x) = g^o + \beta_{gx} x, \qquad \text{where} \qquad \beta_{gx} := (g_{max} - g_{min})/2 \qquad (15)$$

Being in a growth framework, economic activity is represented by the output-capital ratio u, which can also be referred to as (capital) utilization. Franke (2008a, 2012a) models the other components of demand such that, supposing continuous market clearing, IS utilization is a linear function of (only) the business sentiment,

$$u = u(x) = g(x)/\sigma + \beta_u \qquad (16)$$

where σ is the marginal aggregate propensity to save and β_u a certain positive, structurally well-defined constant. A consistency condition can (but need not) ensure that a balanced sentiment $x = 0$ prevails in a steady-state position.

For one part, the specification of the switching index includes the sentiment variable x, which can capture herding. The choice and influence of a second variable revolves around the rest of the economy. Franke (2008a) combines the sentiment dynamics with a Goodwinian struggle between capitalists and workers for the distribution of income. It is summarized in a real wage Phillips curve depending, in particular, on utilization $u = u(x)$ from (16). In this way, the wage share v becomes the second dynamic variable besides x. With a few simple manipulations, its changes can be described by

$$\dot{v} = \beta_v v (1 - v) x \qquad (17)$$

($\beta_v > 0$ another suitable constant). Regarding the sentiment, the idea is that *ceteris paribus* the firms tend to be more optimistic when the profit share increases (the wage share decreases).

With two coefficients $\phi_x, \phi_v > 0$ and the equilibrium wage share v^o, the switching index is thus of the form,[34]

$$s = s(x, v) = \phi_x \, x - \phi_v \, (v - v^o) \tag{18}$$

As derived in Section 2.2, equation (7), the sentiment adjustments read as follows (with $\beta = 2v = 1$),

$$\dot{x} = \{\tanh[s(x, v)] - x\} \, \cosh[s(x, v)] \tag{19}$$

To sum up, taking account of (18), the economy is reduced to two differential equations in the sentiment x and the wage share v. It could be characterized as a micro-founded Goodwinian model that, besides the innovation of the notion of business sentiment, includes a variable output-capital ratio and an investment function (the latter two features are absent in Goodwin's (1967) original model).

It may be observed that equations (17)–(19) have the same structure as system (8), apart from the slight distortions by $\cosh(\cdot)$ in (19) and the multiplication of x by $v(1 - v)$ in (17). Therefore, depending on ϕ_x, the isocline $\dot{x} = 0$ resembles the two upper panels of Figure 1, whereas the other isocline $\dot{v} = 0$ becomes a vertical line at $x = 0$. The latter rules out the multiple equilibria in the other two panels of Figure 1.

The dynamic properties are as described in the discussion of (8): the (unique) steady state is locally and globally stable if the herding coefficient ϕ_x is less than unity. Otherwise it is repelling, where the reflecting boundaries $x = \pm 1$ and the multiplicative factor $v(1 - v)$ in (17) ensure that the trajectories remain within a compact set. Hence (by the Poincaré–Bendixson theorem), all trajectories must converge to a closed orbit. Numerically, by all appearances, it is unique. Accordingly, if (and only if) herding is sufficiently strong, the economy enters a uniquely determined periodic motion in the long run. Regarding income distribution, it features the well-known Goodwinian topics, regarding the sentiment, phases of optimism give way periodically to phases of pessimism and vice versa.

Franke (2012a) specifies the same demand side (15) and (16). Its other elements are:

- A central bank adopting a Taylor rule to set the rate of interest; that is, the interest rate increases in response to larger deviations of utilization from normal and larger deviations of the inflation rate from the bank's target.
- A price Phillips curve with a so-called inflation climate π^c taking the role of its expectation term.
- An adjustment equation for the inflation climate, which is a weighted average of adaptive expectations and regressive expectations. The latter means that agents trust the central bank to bring inflation back to target (correspondingly, the weight of these expectations can be interpreted as the central bank's credibility).[35]

In spite of its structural richness, the economy can be reduced to two differential equations in the sentiment x and the inflation climate π^c. As a matter of fact, identifying π^c with y, the system has the same form as equation (8) in Section 2 (apart from the cosh term). Therefore, because of its business sentiment and, again, if herding is strong enough, the model can be viewed as an Old-Keynesian version of the interplay of output, inflation and monetary policy, or (in a somewhat risky formulation) of the macroeconomic consensus.[36]

For situations in which agents carry an asset forward in time, there is a problem with the transition probability and DCA alike, which should not be concealed. It arises from the fact that, with the switching between high and low growth rates in the investment decisions, the capital stocks of individual firms change from one period to another (in absolute and relative terms). On the other hand, the definition of the aggregate capital growth rate in (15) together with the macroscopic adjustment equation for the sentiment x implicitly presupposes that the groups of optimistic and pessimistic firms always have the same distribution of capital stocks. As a consequence, these equations are only an approximation. Apart from the size of the approximation errors, acknowledging this feature leads to the question of whether the errors may also accumulate in the course of time.

Yanovski (2014) goes back to the micro-level of the TPA to inquire into this problem. Considering a finite population, he models each firm and its probability calculus individually and also keeps track of the capital stocks resulting from these decisions (modelling that requires a few additional specifications to be made for the micro-level). In short, the author finds that the approximation problem does not appear to be very serious. Of course, every macro-model that uses the transition probability or DCA must be reviewed separately, but this first result is encouraging.

Interestingly, Yanovski discovers another problem, which concerns the size distribution of capital stocks: it tends to be increasingly dispersed over time. The result that some firms become bigger and bigger may or may not be attractive. Yanovski subsequently tries several specification details that may entail a bounded width of the size distribution in the long run. To them, it is crucial to relax the assumption of uniform transition probabilities, and that additional, firm-specific arguments are proposed to enter them. Within a parsimonious framework, these discussions can provide a better understanding of the relationships between micro and macro.[37]

Going back to macrodynamics, Lojak (2015) adds a financial side to the monetary policy and output-inflation nexus in Franke (2012a). Besides the different saving propensities for workers and rentiers households, which yield a more involved IS equation for goods market clearing, it makes the firms' financing of fixed investment explicit. This work distinguishes between internal sources, that is, the retained earnings of the firms, and external sources, that is, their borrowing from the rentiers (possibly with commercial banks as intermediates). In this way, a third dynamic variable is introduced into the model, the firms' debt-to-capital ratio. It feeds back on the real sector by a negative effect of higher indebtedness on the switching index for the business sentiment x (which again demonstrates the flexibility of this concept).

Motivated by the discussion of Minskian themes in other macro models, the author concentrates on cyclical scenarios and here, in particular, on the co-movements of the debt-asset ratio. While it is usually taken for granted that it lags capital utilization, the author shows that this is by no means obvious. This finding is an example of the need to carefully re-consider the dynamic features of a real-financial interaction.

In a follow-up paper, Lojak (2016) fixes the inflation rate for simplicity and drops the assumption of a constant markup on the central bank's short-term interest rate to determine the loan rate. Instead, the markup is now supposed to increase with the debt-asset ratio, d. This straightforward extension gives rise to additional strong non-linearities. Most amazingly, in the original cyclical scenario of the two-dimensional (x, d) dynamics, a second equilibrium with lower utilization and higher indebtedness comes into being (but not three as in Figure 1). It is also characterized by a locally stable limit cycle around it. The limit cycle around the 'normal' equilibrium is maintained, so that two co-existing cyclical regimes are obtained. Not all of the phenomena that one can here observe are as yet fully understood, which shows that it is work in progress and a fruitful field for further investigations. In particular, future research may consider the lending of commercial banks in finer detail, and animal spirits may then play a role in this sector as well.

5. Empirical Validation

Even if the discrete choice and transition probabilities are reckoned to be a conceptually attractive approach for capturing a sentiment dynamics, these specifications would gain in significance if it can be demonstrated that they are compatible with what is observed in reality, or inferred from it. A straightforward attempt to learn about people's decision-making are controlled experiments with human subjects in the laboratory. Regarding empirical testing in the usual sense, there are two different ways to try, a direct and a more indirect way. The first method treats a sentiment adjustment equation such as (3) or (5) as a single-equation estimation, where the variable x_t in (5) or the population shares n_t^+, n_t^- in (3) are proxied by an economic survey. In fact, several such surveys provide so-called sentiment or climate indices. The second method considers a model as a whole and seeks to estimate its parameters in one effort. Here, however, x or n^+, n^- remain unobserved variables, that is, only 'normal' macroeconomic variables such as output, inflation, etc., are included as empirical data. These three types of a reality check are considered in the following subsections.

5.1 Evidence from the Lab

Self-inspection is not necessarily the best method to find out how people arrive at their decisions. A more systematic way that approaches people directly in this matter are laboratory experiments. To begin with, they indeed provide ample evidence that the subjects use similarly simple heuristics to those considered in the models that we have presented; see Assenza *et al.* (2014a) for a comprehensive literature survey. A more specific point is whether the distribution of different rules within a population and its changes over time could be explained by the discrete choice or TPA. Several experiments at CeNDEF (University of Amsterdam) allow a positive answer with respect to the former. In the setting of a New-Keynesian three-equation model, Assenza *et al.* (2014b) find four qualitatively different macro-patterns emerging out of a self-organizing process where one of four forecasting rules tends to become dominant in the consecutive rounds of an experiment. The authors demonstrate that this is quite in accordance with the discrete choice principle.[38]

In another study by Anufriev *et al.* (2016), where the series to be forecasted are exogenously generated prior to the experiments and the subjects have to choose between a small numbers of alternatives given to them, a discrete choice model can in most cases be successfully fitted to the subjects' predictions. In particular, the experimenters can make inference about the intensity of choice, although different treatments yield different values. For all of these studies, however, it has to be taken into account that a full understanding of the results requires the reader to get involved in a lot of details.

5.2 Empirical Single-Equation Estimations

With respect to inference from empirical data, let us first consider surveys collecting information about the expectations or sentiment of a certain group in the economy. As far as we know, the first empirical test of this kind is Branch (2004). He is concerned with the Michigan survey where private households are asked on a monthly basis for their expectations about

future inflation. For his analysis, the author equips the respondents with three virtual predictor rules: naive (i.e. static) expectations, adaptive expectations and the relatively sophisticated expectations obtained from a vector autoregression (VAR) that besides inflation includes
unemployment, money growth and an interest rate. The fitness of these rules derives from
the squared forecast errors and a specific cost term (which has to be re-interpreted after the
estimations).

The model thus set up is estimated by maximum likelihood. The estimate of the intensity of
choice is significantly positive, such that all three rule are relevant (even the naive expectations)
and their fractions exhibit non-negligible fluctuations over time. It is also shown that this model
is markedly superior to two alternatives that assume the forecasts are normally distributed
around their constant or time-varying mean values across the respondents.

Branch (2007) is a follow-up paper using the same data. Here, the forecast rules entering the
discrete choice model are more elaborate than in his earlier paper. They are actually based on
explanations from a special branch of the New-Keynesian literature (which uses the concept
of limited information flows as it was developed in Mankiw and Reis, 2002). Thus, heterodox
economists will probably not be very convinced by this theory. Nevertheless, the heterogeneity
and switching mechanism introduced into the original New-Keynesian model with its homogeneous agents prove to be essential as this version provides a better fit of the data.

Several other business and consumer surveys lend themselves for testing theoretical approaches with binary decisions, because they already ask whether respondents are 'optimistic'
or 'pessimistic' concerning the changes of a variable or the entire economy. To accommodate
the possibility that a third, neutral assessment is also usually allowed for, it is assumed that
neutral subjects can be assigned half and half to the optimistic and pessimistic camp. Franke
(2008b) is concerned with two leading German surveys conducted by the Ifo Institute (Ifo
Business Climate Index) and the Center for European Research (ZEW Index for Economic
Sentiment), both of which are available at monthly intervals.

The respondents are business people and financial analysts, respectively. Because they are
asked about the future prospects of the economy, the aggregate outcome can be viewed as a
general sentiment prevailing in these groups. Given the theoretical literature discussed above,
this suggests testing the TPA with a herding component included. Franke formulates the corresponding sentiment changes in discrete time and extends equation (5) and its switching index
somewhat beyond what has been considered so far:

$$x_t = x_{t-1} + v[(1 - x_{t-1}) \exp(s_{t-1}) - (1 + x_{t-1}) \exp(-s_{t-1})] + \varepsilon_{x,t}$$

$$s_{t-1} = \phi_o + \phi_x x_{t-1} + \phi_{\Delta x} \Delta_{\tau_x} x_{t-1} + \phi_y y_{t-1} + \phi_{\Delta y} \Delta_{\tau_y} y_{t-1}$$

$$\Delta_{\tau_z} z_t = (z_t - z_{t-\tau_z})/\tau_z \qquad \text{for } z = x, y \tag{20}$$

where x_t is the Ifo or ZEW index, respectively, and y_t is the detrended log series of industrial
production (the output gap, in percent). Compared to previous discussions, three generalizations are allowed for in the switching index. (i) The coefficient ϕ_o measures a possible pre-
disposition to optimism (if it is positive) or pessimism (if it is negative). (ii) In addition to the
levels of x and y, first differences of the two variables can account for momentum effects. In
particular, herding has two aspects: joining the majority (represented by ϕ_x), and immediate
reactions to changes in the composition of the sentiment, which Franke (2008b, p. 314) calls
the moving-flock effect. (iii) There may be lags Δ_τ ($\tau = 1, 2, \ldots,$) in the first differences.

The intrinsic noise from the probabilistic decisions of a finite number of agents is neglected. Instead, the stochastic term $\varepsilon_{x,t}$ represents random forces from outside the theoretical

framework, that is, extrinsic noise. Thus, (20) can be estimated by non-linear least squares (NLS), with $\varepsilon_{x,t}$ as its residuals.

In the estimations of (20), a number of different cases were explored. Skipping the details and turning directly to the most efficient version where all of the remaining coefficients were well identified, a herding mechanism was indeed revealed for both indices. The majority effect, however, was of secondary importance and could be justifiably dismissed from the model (i.e. $\phi_x = 0$), so that herding was best represented by the moving-flock effect.

The arrival of new information on economic activity also plays a role. Relevant for both indices is again the momentum effect, while the level effect can be discarded for one index. Remarkably, the coefficient ϕ_y is negative when it is included (even in the version where $\phi_{\Delta y}$ is set equal to zero). A possible interpretation is that subjects in a boom already anticipate the subsequent downturn. Since it may not appear entirely convincing, the negative ϕ_y could perhaps be better viewed as a mitigation of the procyclical herding effect.

The finding of a strong role for the moving-flock effect is a challenge for theoretical modelling because incorporating it into our continuous-time framework would easily spoil a model's otherwise relatively simple mathematical structure. It would also affect its dynamic properties to some extent. The somewhat inconvenient features are discussed and demonstrated in Franke (2008a, pp. 249ff), but the issue has not been taken up in the following literature.

Subsequent to these results, Franke (2008b) considers two extensions of the estimation approach (20). First, he tests for cross-effects between the two indices, where he finds that the changes in the Ifo index (though not the levels) influence the respondents of the ZEW index, but not the other way around. This makes sense, given the specific composition of the two groups. The second extension tests for an omitted variable of unknown origin. This can be achieved by adding a stochastic variable z_t to the switching index in (20) and supposing, for simplicity, that its motions are governed by a first-order autoregressive process. Such a specification allows an estimation by maximum likelihood together with the Kalman filter, which serves to recover the changes in z_t. Again, an improvement is found for one index but not the other.

Lux (2009) uses the ZEW survey to estimate the TPA with an alternative and more elaborate method. To this end, he goes back to the micro-level and invokes the statistical mechanics apparatus, basically in the form of the Fokker–Planck equation in continuous time. In this way, he is able to derive the conditional transitional probability densities of the sentiment variable x_t between two months, and thus compute, and maximize, a likelihood function. The main conceptual difference in this treatment from the NLS estimation is that it makes no reference to extrinsic noise. Instead, it includes the intrinsic noise, so that it can also determine the finite number of 'autonomous' subjects in the sample.

The results are largely compatible with the references made about Franke (2008b). The likelihood estimation is potentially superior because it seeks to exploit more information, albeit at the cost of considerably higher computational effort. Ideally, NLS may be employed at a first stage to identify promising specifications, which then form the basis for more precise conclusions at a second stage.

In sum, it can be concluded from the two investigations by Franke and Lux that the TPA is a powerful explanation for the ups and downs in the expectation formation of the respondents in the two surveys, which does not need to rely on unobservable information shocks. For this good result, however, the specifications in the switching index are slightly more involved than in our theoretical discussions.

Ghonghadze (2016) recently conducted an NLS estimation in the spirit of equation (20) on a survey of senior loan officers regarding their bank lending practices. The respondents were asked whether they raised *versus* lowered the spreads between loan rates and banks' costs of funds, that is, a tightening *versus* an easing of lending terms. This work, too, finds evidence of social interactions within this group, albeit with a view to certain macroeconomic indicators.

Still being concerned with a single-equation estimation, Cornea-Madeira *et al.* (2017) is a contribution that tests the DCA by referring to empirical macroeconomic data. Their testing ground is the New-Keynesian Phillips curve, where regarding the expectations entering it, the agents can choose between naive forecasts and forecasts derived from an ambitious VAR that in addition to inflation takes account of the output gap and the rate of change of unit labour costs and of the labour share.[39] Again, the fitness of the two rules is determined by the past forecast errors. Since the population shares constituting the aggregate expectations can be ultimately expressed as functions of these macroeconomic variables, the Phillips curve can be estimated by NLS.

There are two structural parameters to be estimated, the slope coefficient for the marginal costs and the intensity of choice in the switching mechanism. Both of them have the correct positive sign at the usual significance levels. Overall, the predicted inflation path tracks the behaviour of actual inflation fairly well. The population share of the naive agents varies considerably over time, although it exhibits a high persistence. Interestingly, their fraction is relatively high or low during certain historical episodes. On average, the simplistic rule is adopted by no less than 67% of the agents.

The authors furthermore test this model against a number of alternatives, two of which are closely related to versions from the New-Keynesian estimation literature. All of them are rejected at a 95% confidence level. Also, robustness checks regarding alternative specifications of the VAR forecasting model and different empirical measures of marginal costs are undertaken. They show no need for any qualification of the previous conclusions. In sum, these results are a strong point in favour of the agents' heterogeneity plus a discrete choice switching mechanism.

The model investigated by Cornea-Madeira *et al.* (2017) may win another point because of its parsimony. On the other hand, a model with more parameters may be conceptually more satisfactory. Generally, modelling faces a trade-off between econometric efficiency and rich economic structure. For each single (non-trivial) case, this is a difficult problem of judgement, intuition and preferences.

5.3 *System Estimations*

A second estimation approach is concerned with an entire model into which a sentiment dynamics has been integrated. Accordingly, it seeks to estimate the parameters of the latter together with the parameters in the rest of the model, that is, it is about testing a joint hypothesis. While in the New-Keynesian mainstream literature, the dominant and widely applied system estimation method is Bayesian likelihood estimation, it is fraught with two difficulties: the model must have been linearized and it does not admit unobservable variables. Otherwise the mathematical and computational effort increases, and prohibitively so for non-specialists.

An alternative method can easily cope with these problems. It departs from the truism that no model can capture all aspects of the real world and that every model is built for a specific purpose. Therefore, a model is good if it fulfills its purpose; failures in other directions can and need to be tolerated. In the present context, a 'purpose' is given by a number of properties, often referred to as 'stylized facts', which can be filtered from reality and that researchers wish to be displayed in their models. Generally, these properties are quantified as summary statistics, which in econometric language are also called 'moments'.

A model will be unable to reproduce the desired empirical moments perfectly. Estimation means searching for parameter values such that the moments generated by the model come as close as possible to their empirical counterparts. Since a model usually has to be simulated to obtain these moments, one speaks of the *method of simulated moments*.

The crucial point is, of course, the choice of moments, which a number of econometric critics brand as arbitrary. It can, however, be argued that this feature is a virtue rather than a vice, because it requires researchers to be explicit about their priorities; readers can then decide whether they share or accept them. While in the present wording, a likelihood function can be said to take 'all moments' into account, this concept presupposes that the model is correctly specified. If, on the other hand, it is recognized that a model (by definition) is an abstract approximation to reality, then a discussion of the choice of the moments underlying an estimation appears to be more transparent.[40]

The moments can, moreover, provide a useful diagnosis for a model. By finding out that some moments are relatively well matched and that others are not, one learns more about the merits and demerits of a model than knowing that an objective function (be it a likelihood or something else) has been optimized, and perhaps having a technical econometric measure to summarize the goodness-of-fit.

Franke (2012b, 2016) applies the method of simulated moments to several discrete-time versions of Franke's (2012a) 'Old-Keynesian' model of the macroeconomic consensus with its three observable variables: quarterly output, inflation and the interest rate (all of them as percentage deviations from trend). The empirical moments employed are the variances and cross-covariances of these variables in the US economy with lags up to eight quarters, which gives a total of 78 statistics. Their informational value is, however, lower since the moments are not independent.

One of the model versions considered is a deterministic system; one has stochastic demand, cost push and monetary policy shocks added in the corresponding equations; a third version additionally allows two of them to take effect in the switching index and the adjustments of the inflation climate. Thus, nine parameters are to be estimated in the first and 14 parameters in the third version. Such a large number relative to the number of 'effective' moments requires great care in the minimization of the objective function that measures the distance between simulated and empirical moments, because it will typically have multiple local minima or extended valleys. The latter phenomenon will also deteriorate the precision of the parameter estimates (unless one chooses to fix some of them on the basis of other arguments or priorities). However, these problems would apply equally well to likelihood methods.

With respect to the so-called period of the Great Moderation (1982 – 2007), the thin (blue) solid line in Figure 3 illustrates that already the deterministic model achieves a respectable matching of the covariance profiles (recall that lags higher than eight quarters are not included in the estimation). The shaded areas indicate that the great majority of the model-generated moments lie inside the 95% confidence band of the empirical moments. The match is even better in the full stochastic version; see the bold (red) solid lines in the diagram.[41] However, a certain price must be paid for this improvement: the influence of the stochastic dynamics becomes so strong that the herding coefficient in the switching index (the analogue of ϕ_x in (18)) is relatively low and would imply stability of the steady state in the deterministic core of

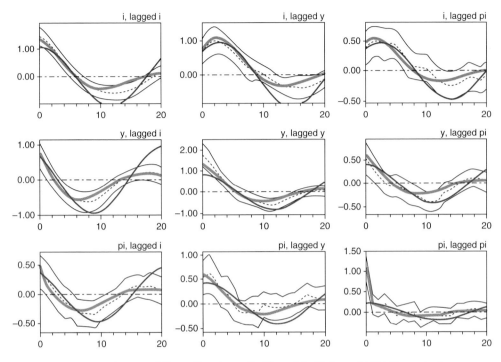

Figure 3. Auto- and Cross-Covariance Profiles of the Estimated 'Old-Keynesian' Model in Franke (2012b).

Note: y, pi and i designate the gaps of output, inflation and the interest rate, respectively. Shaded areas are the bootstrapped 95% confidence bands around the empirical moments (dotted lines). Other lines are explained in the text.

the model. In other words, it is the random shocks that keep the system in motion. Regarding the period of the Great Inflation (1960–1979), the coefficient is even close to zero.

In short, the model achieves a good or almost excellent matching of the chosen moments, which can also be quantitatively established in econometric terms. On the other hand, this result does not confirm the endogeneity of the cyclical behaviour of the economy. With the experience of the single-equation estimations above, one may now wonder about the possible presence of the so-called moving-flock effect, a question that has not yet been addressed in any master or PhD thesis.

An additional matter of concern in Franke's (2012b, 2016) contribution is the competitiveness of his model *versus* a corresponding (hybrid) New-Keynesian model (equations (9)–(11) with rational expectations in place of the boundedly rational expectations E^{agg}). Broadly speaking, both models are found to be equally successful at reproducing the auto-covariances of their three state variables. If one is more ambitious, however, it has to be noted that the auto-covariances and the raggedness of the inflation rate can hardly be reconciled in the New-Keynesian model: either it produces a good match of the former and a bad match of the latter, or vice versa. In the Old-Keynesian model, by contrast, the two types of moments are largely compatible, that is, a good match of one type may exist alongside at least an acceptable match of the other type. In this sense, the Old-Keynesian model may claim to do a better job.

Using Euro Area data and the same 78 second moments as Franke, the authors Jang and Sacht (2016a) estimate De Grauwe's model (with identically distributed shocks added) by the method of simulated moments. Regarding the coefficients in the discrete choice switching mechanism, they argue in favour of exogenously fixing a moderate intensity of choice $\beta = 1$ in (13) and a zero memory coefficient $\rho = 0$ in (14).[42] They furthermore provide detailed information about several other parameters. Especially the estimates of the monetary policy coefficients make good economic sense. At least to the naked eye, the matching itself is of a similar quality as in Figure 3, and slightly superior to the matching of the model's rational expectations version.[43]

Jang and Sacht (2016b) continue this line of research. In this paper, they consider four forecast rules (two of which with slightly more 'momentum' than before) and alternatively include two, three or all four in the model. Together with the rational expectations, they arrange a horse race for six model versions. With respect to US data and the Euro Area data, it is found in both cases that, when matching the same 78 moments as before, the interaction between the two new (and more dynamic) rules is almost as successful as all four rules together. In fact, insignificant values for the parameters characterizing the other two rules indicate that these are virtually ineffective. This finding supplies new knowledge in the search for efficient and parsimonious specifications within the De Grauwe framework. Besides, the rational expectations perform the worst, which is explained by the assumption of ruling out the lagged variables (i.e. the hybrid case) in equations (9) and (10).

Daring to provide a brief summary of these results, at least from a higher point of view and as a preliminary conclusion, it seems that the model approaches by Franke and De Grauwe receive similarly good and satisfactory empirical support from estimations by the method of simulated moments.

Another feature that bounded rationality models might possibly better capture than DSGE models are the kurtosis of the output growth rates, on which De Grauwe (2012a) puts great emphasis, or (better) a measure of fat tails in their distribution such as the shape parameter b of the exponential power distribution, which includes the normal distribution with $b = 2$ as a special case. There is some literature indicating that b is typically less than 2 (e.g. Fagiolo *et al.*, 2008), but Franke (2015) points out that once one separates the Great Moderation from the Great Inflation period, this 'stylized fact' is no longer so well founded. That is, it seems the shape parameter can only be measured with a limited empirical precision. It may nevertheless be worthwhile to explore whether this 'moment' could improve the existing estimation.

Finally, Brenneisen (2015) starts out from a recent paper by Liu and Minford (2014), who compare a purely forward-looking New-Keynesian model to a (very) simple version of De Grauwe's model. Estimating them by indirect inference, these authors conclude that the former model outperforms the latter. Brenneisen points out a number of unclear points in Liu and Minford's presentation, and then, instead, applies the method of simulated moments to the two models – whereby he arrives at the reverse conclusion. A more differentiated picture is obtained with respect to moderate extensions of the models.

Very informative in Brenneisen's contribution is a methodological issue regarding the precision of the parameter estimates. Distributions of the parameters can be computed by repeatedly re-estimating a model on the bootstrapped empirical moments, which is a sound but extremely time-consuming procedure. The author successfully tests a new econometric proposal for approximating these distributions by simulations of another random distribution, which can do without the re-estimations completely. This alternative device is relatively easy to implement and could prove useful in future applications of the method of simulated moments.

6. Conclusion

With respect to macroeconomics, this survey was concerned with recent attempts to translate aspects of the famous notion of the animal spirits into formal and rigorous modelling. To cope with the 'wilderness of bounded rationality', two approaches with a stylized micro-foundation were addressed: the DCA and the TPA. Before discussing their applications in the literature, it was revealed that they are more closely related than it might seem at first glance, and that they are well suited to endogenously generate persistent cyclical behaviour.

The literature presented here shows a considerable flexibility in building macrodynamic models from these tools, or incorporating them into existing models. As a first guideline for finding one's way around the many models, a distinction was offered between animal spirits in a weak sense and in a strong sense. The first expression merely points to a rush towards one of two attitudes, strategies or similar alternatives; the second involves an element of herding because, in a world of irreducible uncertainty, people think the majority knows better. The first variety is typically found in models that work with the DCA. The second can primarily be classified in models applying the TPA. However, this role allocation is based more on historical reasons rather than on a compelling inner logic.

Besides being theoretically attractive, the two approaches were also shown to have some empirical support. Overall, the material and ideas discussed can provide fruitful stimulations for future research that seeks to capture the formation of business or consumer sentiment, or of a general state of confidence, in a serious and structured way. Maybe this survey comes at a good time, before further modelling work in this direction abounds.

Acknowledgement

We wish to thank two anonymous referees for their constructive comments.

Notes

1. The term is so appealing that a number of orthodox economists also invoke it to adver-tise their models. In a branch of the dynamic stochastic general equilibrium literature, the term is used interchangeably with sunspot equilibria and self-fulfilling prophecies. It goes without saying that the discussion in the present paper has nothing to do with these (very elaborate) refinements of rational expectations, where observations of an exogenous stochastic process induce the agents to coordinate on recurrent switches between multiple equilibria; see, for example, Farmer and Guo (1994) and Galí (1994).
2. The actual term 'animal spirits' is mentioned in the same chapter on page 161.
3. A general review of Keynes' concepts can be found in Minsky (1975, Chapter 3). A more roughly sketched discussion focussing on their fruitfulness for macroeconomic modelling is given by Flaschel et al. (1997, Chapter 12.2). A good survey of the role of (psychologi-cal) expectations and confidence is provided by Boyd and Blatt (1988). In the wake of the financial crisis, Akerlof and Shiller's (2009) book on Animal Spirits brought the keyword to the attention of a wider audience.
4. For reasons of space, we skip a treatment of an early generation of relatively simple macro-models (some of which may still contain stimulating ideas). One branch (e.g. Westerhoff, 2006) already employed the DCA, while another branch (e.g. Westerhoff and Hohnisch, 2007) was inspired by Kirman's (1993) seminal ant model, which introduced a slightly

different specification from the TPA. This discussion is contained in an extended version of this paper (Franke and Westerhoff, 2017).

5. Although this is not done in the typical applications, U^+, U^- could also take account of direct social interactions, similar to the TPA in the next subsection. In the framework of an asset pricing model, Franke and Westerhoff (2012) compare several versions of a 'synthesis' of fitness and social interactions in U^+ and U^-. Brock and Durlauf (2001) is an often cited paper that discusses possible interaction effects at a level logically prior to the probabilities π_t^+ and π_t^-. Chang (2007) applies these ideas to a similar setting to Franke and Westerhoff.

6. An extension of (2) to more than two (but still a finite number of) options is obvious. A generalization to a continuous space of options, or 'beliefs', is also possible; see Brock *et al.* (2005), Diks and van der Weide (2005) and Pecora and Spelta (2017), who work with the concept of a so-called large type limit. For example, agents may have a prediction rule that is parameterized by a scalar or vector θ, which they are free to choose. Aggregate expected values, which are finite sums in a discrete choice model, are here integral expressions. They can be explicitly computed if the other parts of the model are sufficiently simple.

7. A remarkable alternative is the proposal by Chiarella and Di Guilmi (2015), who invoke the concept of maximum entropy inference in order to model the intensity of choice as an endogenous variable. It depends on the values of U_{t-1}^+ and U_{t-1}^- and can also become negative, which requires these fitnesses to be positive.

8. Hence, for example, the probability that an agent will maintain his attitude over only four consecutive periods is as low as $(1/2)^4 = 6.67\%$.

9. In this framework, a differential equation such as (in the present notation) $\dot{n}^+ = \mu\,[\pi^+ - n^+]$, which we obtain from (3) with $\Delta t \to 0$, can also be derived by making reference to a special case of the concept of a so-called revision protocol; see Lahkar and Sandholm (2008, p. 577) or, with a broader background, Ochea (2010, Chapter 2.2), who set $\mu = 1$.

10. Kirman (1993) is a slightly earlier and equally famous paper with a nice story about ants and two food sources between which they have to choose. It shares the same spirit as Lux (1995), but is specified differently and, as it emerged over time, somewhat less conveniently.

11. To be fair, there are some earlier (but now practically forgotten) examples.

12. The price for this simpler treatment is a loss of some information, but this would only become relevant if one wanted to take a higher, probabilistic point of view.

13. These probabilities are required to be less than one, but not necessarily p^{-+} and p^{+-} themselves.

14. Since $n^+ = n^+/2 + n^+/2 = (1 - n^-)/2 + n^+/2 = (1 + n^+ - n^-)/2 = (1 + x)/2$. The second relationship follows analogously.

15. Franke (2008a,b) gives a rigorous mathematical argument that includes a finite population size and the intrinsic noise which will thus be present. It is a more direct procedure than the treatment in statistical mechanics, which first sets up the Fokker–Planck equation and then derives the stochastic so-called Langevin equation from it, which, in turn, reduces to equation (5) below as the population becomes infinitely large. The intellectual copyright, however, is with Alfarano and Lux (2007, appendices A1 and A2).

16. At first sight, equation (5) seems to be identical to equation (2) in Lux (1995, p. 884). A subtle difference, however, is that here in (5), the variable x represents the *actual* value of the sentiment index of an infinitely large population, whereas in Lux's presentation, x is its *expected* value with respect to the stochastic system with a finite population. As indicated

by Lux (p. 895) himself, his equation (5) constitutes a quasi-deterministic dynamics. Its interpretation seems, however, somewhat problematic.

17. It corresponds to equation (3) in Lux (1995, p. 885), the right-hand side of which reads $v \exp(\pm\alpha x)$ and can be regarded as a special case of the present equation (4) with $\beta = \alpha$, $s = \alpha x$ and α representing the strength of infection or herd behaviour (a coefficient that we will employ as well below and designate ϕ_x).

18. This relationship with the suitable reformulation of the adjustment equations was established in Franke (2014).

19. This holds true since $\cosh(\beta s) = \cosh(0) = 1$ in such a case. It does not necessarily apply for other equilibria, because some entries in the Jacobian matrix derived from (7) will be 'distorted' by the factor $\cosh(\beta s) > 1$. Nevertheless, the phenomenon that an equilibrium is stable under the adjustments (4) and unstable under (7), or vice versa, will occur for only a narrow and special range of parameter values.

20. To be fair, Brazier et al. (2008) pursued a similar idea in an overlapping generations model with money growth and expectations about inflation, while Lines and Westerhoff (2010) employed a simple monetary model.

21. It has already been indicated in footnote 1 that the special branch of 'sunspot equilibria' within the DSGE literature makes reference to 'animal spirits', too, but that these concepts are fundamentally different from the mechanisms in the present models. As the term 'sunspots' suggests, the waves generated there have an exogenous source, while De Grauwe emphasizes their endogenous origin in his approach.

22. To be precise, $i^\star$ is the sum of the central bank's inflation target $\pi^\star$ and its estimate of the natural real rate of interest.

23. De Grauwe mostly simplifies his equations by putting $i^\star = \pi^\star = 0$.

24. It would be more appropriate to call the latter naive expectations; cf. De Grauwe and Macchiarelli (2015, p. 97).

25. De Grauwe (2010, p. 14) reports that the correlation between the fraction of optimists and the output gap is as high as 0.86. This requires the intensity of choice β to be sufficiently high and the memory coefficient ρ to be less than 1 (though only slightly so); see De Grauwe (2010, pp. 14f).

26. To be exact, the equations they obtain do not contain the lagged endogenous variable on the right-hand side. A model in a similar spirit but with more specific assumptions is studied by Massaro (2013).

27. The two precursory working papers Dräger (2010, 2011) may help generate a better understanding of the more elaborate parts of this analysis and of the conditions that may give rise to the superior results with the flexible-degree version.

28. There are lots of micro-foundation details in the first section. Unexperienced readers should not be deterred by this, but may proceed to Section 3.5, which provides a familiar, though more colourful picture.

29. In equations (9) and (10), they consider three types of expectations: targeting, naive and extrapolative expectations proper.

30. The reference for the authors' IRFs is not an equilibrium position, but an entire stochastic simulation run. Subsequently, the model is run a second time with the same random shocks, except for one shock in the initial period. The IRFs are then the difference in the variables from these two runs.

31. Two aspects are: (1) There is nobody in the model from which momentum traders could borrow, and whose balance sheet would be affected, too. (2) Neither the direct nor the indirect cost of borrowing shows up in the fitness function of momentum traders.

32. We consider the 'axiom' a useful first organizing principle for the macroeconomic literature that we cover. However, identifying long time horizons with strong animal spirits need not always be very helpful. As a referee has pointed out, in financial market models, fundamentalists have a longer time horizon than the technical traders, but nevertheless, the selection of the forecast rules may basically depend on their recent success (which would correspond to our weak form of animal spirits), or they may also involve a herding mechanism (which would be more in line with our classification as strong animal spirits); see Franke and Westerhoff (2012, p. 1198) to make this sketch more precise.

33. Recall from Section 2.2 that the shares of optimists and pessimists are $n^+ = (1 + x)/2$ and $n^- = (1 - x)/2$.

34. In addition, utilization may have a positive effect on the sentiment. By virtue of (16), however, this influence can be subsumed within the variable x.

35. Speaking of 'climate' might suggest that its changes are alternatively modelled by invoking transition probabilities a second time. As an interesting and somewhat puzzling aside, it can be noted that a higher credibility of the central bank tends to be destabilizing rather than stabilizing.

36. While heterodox theory should have an affinity to the model's 'Old-Keynesian' elements, a number of heterodox economists will not endorse it either, because the macroeconomic consensus is an emotive word to them (although the observation in the previous footnote may perhaps placate these sceptics somewhat).

37. The discussion can thus be more transparent than in the so-called bottom-up models with many heterogeneous agents (far more than two), which are creative but less 'canonical' than the approach under consideration here.

38. Two similar experimental studies for a financial market environment are Anufriev and Hommes (2012a,b).

39. The latter is included because the authors have marginal costs featuring in the Phillips curve. On the basis of econometric arguments, this treatment is finally reduced to a four-lag bivariate VAR in the output gap and the changes in the labour share.

40. It sometimes seems that the following fact is well known, but is subsequently merely put aside: 'maximum likelihood does the "right" efficient thing if the model is true. It does not necessarily do the "reasonable" thing for "approximate" models' (Cochrane, 2001, p. 293).

41. This estimation adds three further moments to the aforementioned 78 second moments. They characterize the raggedness in the time series of the output gap and the rates of inflation and interest.

42. Setting $\beta = 1$ is significantly superior to higher values such as 10 or 100, and insignificantly inferior to $\beta = 0.10$. The latter would, however, undermine the philosophy of the model as the decision between the two forecast rules is then close to tossing a coin.

43. Referring to the J-test, the authors conclude that they cannot reject the null hypothesis according to which the model-generated moments may also have been obtained from the real-world data generation process. Such an argument pre-supposes an optimal weighting matrix in setting up the objective moment distance function, whereas, as mentioned by the authors (p. 89), this assumption is not satisfied in their treatment. Nevertheless, this observation does not necessarily mean that their conclusion is wrong, only that other methods have to be tried to address this issue; for example, repeated re-estimations of the model as discussed in Franke (2012b) and Brenneisen (2015) (see also below).

References

Akerlof, G.A. and Shiller, R.J. (2009) *Animal Spirits*. Princeton and Oxford: Princeton University Press.

Alfarano, S. and Lux, T. (2007) A noise trader model as a generator of apparent power laws and long memory. *Macroeconomic Dynamics* 11(Supplement 1): 80–101.

Anderson, S., de Palma, A. and Thisse, J. (1993) *Discrete Choice Theory of Product Differentiation*. Cambridge, MA: MIT Press.

Anufriev, M., Assenza, T., Hommes, C. and Massaro, D. (2013) Interest rate rules and macroeconomic stability under heterogeneous expectations. *Macroeconomic Dynamics* 17: 1574–1604.

Anufriev, M., Bao, T. and Tuinstra, J. (2016) Microfoundations for switching behavior in heterogeneous agent models: An experiment. *Journal of Economic Behavior and Organization* 129: 74–99.

Anufriev, M. and Hommes, C. (2012a) Evolutionary selection of individual expectations and aggregate outcomes in asset pricing experiments. *American Economic Journal: Microeconomics* 4:4: 35–64.

Anufriev, M. and Hommes, C. (2012b) Evolution of market heuristics. *The Knowledge Engineering Review* 27: 255–271.

Assenza, T., Bao, T., Hommes, C. and Massaro, D. (2014a) Experiments on expectations in macroeconomics and finance. In J. Duffy (ed.), *Experiments in Macroeconomics (Research in Experimental Economics)*, Vol. 17 (pp. 11–70). Bingley, West Yorkshire: Emerald Group Publishing Limited.

Assenza, T., Heemeijer, P., Hommes, C. and Massaro, D. (2014b) Managing self-organization of expectations through monetary policy: A macro experiment. CeNDEF, University of Amsterdam, Working Paper 2014-07.

Bernanke, B.S., Gertler, M. and Gilchrist, S. (1999) The financial accelerator in a quantitative business cycle framework. In J.B. Taylor and M. Woodford(eds.), *Handbook of Macroeconomics*, Vol. 1 (pp. 1342–1393). Amsterdam: North-Holland.

Boyd, I. and Blatt, J.M. (1988) *Investment, Confidence and Business Cycles*. New York: Springer.

Branch, W. (2004) The theory of rationally heterogeneous expectations: Evidence from survey data on inflation expectations. *Economic Journal* 114: 592–621.

Branch, W. (2007) Sticky information and model uncertainty in survey data on inflation expectations. *Journal of Economic Dynamics and Control* 31: 245–276.

Branch, W.A. and Evans, G.W. (2011) Monetary policy and heterogeneous expectations. *Economic Theory* 47: 365–393.

Branch, W.A. and McGough, B. (2009) A New Keynesian model with heterogeneous expectations. *Journal of Economic Dynamics and Control* 33: 1036–1051.

Branch, W.A. and McGough, B. (2010) Dynamic predictor selection in a new Keynesian model with heterogeneous expectations. *Journal of Economic Dynamics and Control* 34: 1492–1508.

Brazier, A., Harrison, R., King, M. and Yates, T. (2008) The danger of inflating expectations of macroeconomic stability: Heuristic switching in an overlapping-generations monetary model. *International Journal of Central Banking* 4:2: 219–254.

Brenneisen, J.-N. (2015) Moment matching of heterogeneous expectations in a class of recent macroeconomic business cycle models. Unpublished master thesis, University of Kiel.

Brock, W.A. and Durlauf, S.N. (2001) Discrete choice with social interactions. *Review of Economic Studies* 68: 235–260.

Brock, W.A. and Hommes, C.H. (1997) A rational route to randomness. *Econometrica* 65: 1059–1095.

Brock, W.A. and Hommes, C.H. (1998) Heterogeneous beliefs and routes to chaos in a simple asset pricing model. *Journal of Economic Dynamics and Control* 22: 1235–1274.

Brock, W.A., Hommes, C.H. and Wagener, F.O.O. (2005) Evolutionary dynamics in markets with many trader types. *Journal of Mathematical Economics* 41: 7–42.

Chang, S.-K. (2007) A simple asset pricing model with social interactions and heterogeneous beliefs. *Journal of Economic Dynamics and Control* 31: 1300–1325.

Chiarella, C. and Di Guilmi, C. (2015) The limit distribution of evolving strategies in financial markets. *Studies in Nonlinear Dynamics and Econometrics* 19(2): 137–159.

Cochrane, J.H. (2001) *Asset Pricing*. Princeton: Princeton University Press.

Cornea-Madeira, A., Hommes, C. and Massaro, D. (2017) Behavioral heterogeneity in U.S. inflation dynamics. *Journal of Business Economics and Statistics*, forthcoming.

De Grauwe, P. (2008a) DSGE-modelling when agents are imperfectly informed. ECB, Working Paper Series No. 897.

De Grauwe, P. (2008b) Stock prices and monetary policy. Centre for European Policy Studies, Working Document No. 304.

De Grauwe, P. (2010) Top-down versus bottom-up macroeconomics. CESifo Working Paper No. 3020.

De Grauwe, P. (2011) Animal spirits and monetary policy. *Economic Theory* 47: 423–457.

De Grauwe, P. (2012a) Booms and busts in economic activity: A behavioral explanation. *Journal of Economic Behavior and Organization* 83: 484–501.

De Grauwe, P. (2012b) *Lectures on Behavioral Macroeconomics*. Princeton, NJ: Princeton University Press.

De Grauwe, P. and Gerba, E. (2015a) Stock market cycles and supply side dynamics: Two worlds, one vision? CESifo Working Paper No. 5573.

De Grauwe, P. and Gerba, E. (2015b) Monetary transmission under competing corporate finance regimes. London School of Economics, FinMaP-Working Paper, No. 52.

De Grauwe, P. and Macchiarelli, C. (2015) Animal spirits and credit cycles. *Journal of Economic Dynamics and Control* 59: 95–117.

Diks, C. and van der Weide, T. (2005) Herding, a-synchronous updating and heterogeneity in memory in a CBS. *Journal of Economic Dynamics and Control* 29: 741–762.

Dräger, L. (2010) Why don't people pay attention? Endogenous sticky information in a DSGE Model. University of Hamburg, DEP Discussion Papers Macroeconomics and Finance Series 2/2010.

Dräger, L. (2011) Endogenous persistence with recursive inattentiveness. University of Hamburg, DEP Discussion Papers Macroeconomics and Finance Series 3/2011.

Dräger, L. (2016) Recursive inattentiveness with heterogeneous expectations. *Macroeconomic Dynamics* 20: 1073–1100.

Fagiolo, G., Napoletano, M. and Roventini, A. (2008) Are output growth rate distributions fat-tailed: Evidence for OECD-countries. *Journal of Applied Econometrics* 23: 639–669.

Farmer, R. and Guo, J.T. (1994) Real business cycles and the animal spirit hypothesis. *Journal of Economic Theory* 63: 42–72.

Flaschel, P., Franke, R. and Semmler, W. (1997) *Dynamic Macroeconomics: Instability, Fluctuations, and Growth in Monetary Economies*. Cambridge, MA: MIT Press.

Franke, R. (2008a) Microfounded animal spirits and Goodwinian income distribution dynamics. In P. Flaschel and M. Landesmann (eds.), *Effective Demand, Income Distribution and Growth. Research in Memory of the Work of Richard M. Goodwin* (pp. 372–398). London: Routledge.

Franke, R. (2008b) Estimation of a microfounded herding model on German survey expectations. *Intervention: European Journal of Economics and Economic Policies* 5: 301–328.

Franke, R. (2012a) Microfounded animal spirits in the new macroeconomic consensus. *Studies in Nonlinear Dynamics and Econometrics* 16(4): 1–39.

Franke, R. (2012b) Competitive moment matching of a New-Keynesian and an Old-Keynesian model: Extended version. Working paper, University of Kiel. http://www.gwif.vwl.uni-kiel.de/en/working-papers (Last access July 2017).

Franke, R. (2014) Aggregate sentiment dynamics: A canonical modelling approach and its pleasant nonlinearities. *Structural Change and Economic Dynamics* 31: 64–72.

Franke, R. (2015) How fat-tailed is US output growth? *Metroeconomica* 66: 213–242.

Franke, R. (2016) Competitive moment matching of a New-Keynesian and an Old-Keynesian model. *Journal of Economic Interaction and Coordination*, forthcoming.

Franke, R. and Westerhoff, F. (2012) Structural stochastic volatility in asset pricing dynamics: Estimation and model contest. *Journal of Economic Dynamics and Control* 36: 1193–1211.

Franke, R. and Westerhoff, F. (2017) Taking stock: A rigorous modelling of animal spirits in macroeconomics (Extended version). Working paper, Universities of Kiel and Bamberg.

Galí, J. (1994) Monopolistic competition, business cycles, and the composition of aggregate demand. *Journal of Economic Theory* 63: 73–96.

Ghonghadze, J. (2016) Variation of lending terms and the financial instability hypothesis. Working paper, University of Kiel.

Goodwin, R.M. (1967) A growth cycle model. In C.H. Feinstein (ed.), *Socialism, Capitalism and Growth*. Cambridge: Cambridge University Press.

Hommes, C.H., Huang, H. and Wang, D. (2005) A robust rational route to randomness in a simple asset pricing model. *Journal of Economic Dynamics and Control* 29: 1043–1072.

Jang, T.-S. and Sacht, S. (2016a) Animal spirits and the business cycle: Empirical evidence from moment matching. *Metroeconomica* 67: 76–113.

Jang, T.-S. and Sacht, S. (2016b) Modelling consumer confidence and its role for expectation formation: A horse race. Working paper, Kyungpook National University and University of Kiel.

Keynes, J.M. (1936) *The General Theory of Employment, Interest and Money*. London: Macmillan.

Keynes, J.M (1937) The general theory of employment. *Quarterly Journal of Economics* 51: 109–123.

Kirman, A. (1993) Ants, rationality and recruitment. *Quarterly Journal of Economic* 108: 137–156.

Lahkar, R. and Sandholm, W.H. (2008) The projection dynamic and the geometry of population games. *Games and Economic Behavior* 64: 565–590.

Lengnick, M. and Wohltmann, H.-W. (2013) Agent-based financial markets and New Keynesian macroeconomics: A synthesis. *Journal of Economic Interaction and Coordination* 8: 1–32.

Lengnick, M. and Wohltmann, H.-W. (2016) Optimal monetary policy in a new Keynesian model with animal spirits and financial markets. *Journal of Economic Dynamics and Control* 64: 148–165.

Lines, M. and Westerhoff, F. (2010) Inflation expectations and macroeconomic dynamics: The case of rational versus extrapolative expectations. *Journal of Economic Dynamics and Control* 34: 246–257.

Liu, C. and Minford, P. (2014) Comparing behavioural and rational expectations for the US post-war economy. *Economic Modelling* 43: 407–415.

Lojak, B. (2015) Investor sentiment, corporate debt and inflation in a feedback-guided model of the business cycle. Unpublished master thesis, University of Kiel.

Lojak, B. (2016) Sentiment-driven investment, non-linear corporate debt dynamics and co-existing business cycle regimes. Metroeconomica (forthcoming).

Lux, T. (1995) Herd behaviour, bubbles and crashes. *Economic Journal* 105: 881–889.

Lux, T. (2009) Rational forecasts or social opinion dynamics: Identification of interaction effects in a business climate index. *Journal of Economic Behavior and Organization* 72: 638–655.

Mankiw, N.G. and Reis, R. (2002) Sticky information versus sticky prices: A proposal to replace the New Keynesian Phillips curve. *Quarterly Journal of Economics* 117: 1295–1328.

Manski, C. and McFadden, D. (1981) *Structural Analysis of Discrete Data with Econometric Applications*. Cambridge, MA: MIT Press.

Massaro, D. (2013) Heterogeneous expectations in monetary DSGE models. *Journal of Economic Dynamics and Control* 37: 680–692.

Minsky, H.P. (1975) *John Maynard Keynes*. New York: Columbia University Press.

Ochea, M. (2010) Essays on nonlinear evolutionary game dynamics. PhD thesis, University of Amsterdam: Book no. 468 of the Tinbergen Institute Research Series.

Pecora, N. and Spelta, A. (2017) Managing monetary policy in a New Keynesian model with many beliefs types. *Economics Letters* 150: 53–58.

Scheffknecht, L. and Geiger, F. (2011) A behavioral macroeconomic model with endogenous boom-bust cycles and leverage dynamics. FZID Discussion Paper 37-2011, University of Hohenheim.

Weidlich, W. and Haag, G. (1983) *Concepts and Models of a Quantitative Sociology. The Dynamics of Interacting Populations*. Berlin: Springer.

Westerhoff, F. (2006) Business cycles, heuristic expectation formation and contracyclical policies. *Journal of Public Economic Theory* 8: 821–838.

Westerhoff, F. and Hohnisch, M. (2007) A note on interactions-driven business cycles. *Journal of Economic Interaction and Coordination* 2: 85–91.

Yanovski, B. (2014) Introducing an elementary microstructure into macrodynamic models. Unpublished master thesis, University of Kiel.

3

THE AGENT-BASED APPROACH TO POST KEYNESIAN MACRO-MODELING

Corrado Di Guilmi

Economics Discipline Group, University of Technology Sydney
Centre for Applied Macroeconomic Analysis Australian
National University

1. Introduction

In recent years, a growing body of literature has stemmed from the cross-fertilization of agent-based (AB) modeling and Post Keynesian (PK) macroeconomics. A number of scholars (especially young researchers within the AB modeling community) have started embodying elements of PK theory in their models, in particular the consistency of stocks and flows and the endogeneity of money. At the same time, and perhaps as a consequence of this, junior researchers as well as established scholars in the heterodox field have started looking at AB modeling as a possible alternative to the standard aggregative PK modeling approach. The attention that the mainstream has been forced to give to some traditionally PK research topics have reinforced this trend. Obvious examples are the interaction between the financial sector and the real economy after the Great Recession and inequality after the publication of Piketty's book.

The review is preceded by some considerations about the reasons that have led to the cross-fertilization between the two fields. In particular, the paper highlights the complementarities and the common pillars from an epistemological perspective. In fact, although AB modeling is, in its essence, an agnostic modeling strategy developed outside the realm of social sciences, it is nevertheless peculiarly adept at integrating PK macro-modeling with formalized microeconomic foundations. Moreover, AB modeling can provide useful technical development of PK modeling and, by exposing young researchers and postgraduate students to the PK literature, can help establish and popularize PK economics as a sound alternative to neoclassical economics. AB modeling also benefits from this cross-fertilization: PK economics can represent a disciplining device for the modeler by narrowing down the degrees of freedom, supporting the construction of internally consistent models.

Within this stream of literature, models can be categorized into four different types: AB models that formalize Minsky's Financial Instability Hypothesis; evolutionary models with PK

Analytical Political Economy, First Edition. Edited by Roberto Veneziani and Luca Zamparelli.

features; structural neo-Kaleckian models with AB features; and stock-flow consistent (SFC) AB models. Particular attention is devoted to SFC-AB models, given their growing popularity. The papers have been selected not so much on the basis of their explicit reference to a PK tradition (as for example, papers that present neo-Kaleckian AB models), but with the aim of linking different contributions that have progressively narrowed the distance between the two camps and led to the formulations of original frameworks to combine the two approaches.

The defining characteristics of the different models are introduced to highlight their particular solutions to the main issues that the construction of a PK model in a bottom-up fashion presents. Three types of obstacles can be identified. The first issue concerns the reformulation of behavioral rules, originally intended for the whole economy or for sectors, at the single agent level. The second issue, related to the first, is the computation of aggregate quantities starting from individual variables (for example, the multiplier) or the allocation and matching in markets starting from aggregate quantities (for example, the allocation of aggregate demand among suppliers). The third set of issues concerns two main critical points in SFC-AB modeling: first, how to model agents' demography (for example, what happens to the assets of bankrupted firms and which is the source of new entrants' initial endowments) and, second, how to ensure that the decentralized interactions respect the accounting consistency at every stage of computer simulations.

The remainder of the paper is organized as follows. Section 2 investigates the reasons of the cross-fertilization of the two schools and the possible mutual benefits. Section 3 surveys the AB models that attempted to formalize Minsky's Financial Instability Hypothesis. Section 4 presents the main AB models that can be included within the structuralist neo-Kaleckian and evolutionary traditions while Section 5 is devoted to the SFC-AB models. Finally, Section 6 offers some concluding remarks.

2. Background

This section discusses some possible mutual benefits coming from the cross-fertilization of the two approaches and outlines the compatibility of PK theory and AB modeling in an epistemological and historical perspective.

2.1 *PK Economics and AB Modeling*

For the reader unfamiliar with PK economics or AB modeling (or both), let us introduce some preliminary definitions and concepts.

PK economics is a heterodox school rooted mostly in the work of John Maynard Keynes and Michal Kalecki. The term "Post Keynesian" was introduced by Eichner and Kregel (1975) to define an alternative paradigm to monetarism rooted in the Keynes–Kalecki tradition. The core PK economics is summarized by King (2015) in the six core propositions identified by Thirlwall (1993): unemployment is determined in the goods market and cannot be reduced to a microeconomic representation of the job market; involuntary unemployment exists and is due to deficiencies in effective demand; investment determines savings and not *vice versa*; money is not neutral; the classical quantity theory of money is misleading; and given fundamental uncertainty, investment is determined by "animal spirits" and not by the solution to an optimization problem. Lavoie (2014) identifies five conceptual pillars of PK economics, which are discussed in Subsection 2.3 in order to compare them with the main features of AB modeling.

Operationally, PK theory is applied by a variety of different models, which are typically aggregative. Lavoie (2014, p. 43) identifies five different strands of PK authors: fundamentalist Keynesians, Kaleckians, Sraffians, Institutionalists, and Kaldorians. However, he recognizes that this classification is somewhat arbitrary since PK theory represents an internally consistent body of knowledge, and many PK models are a crossover among different strands. Accordingly, despite this eclecticism, we can coherently use the generic expression PK modeling.

AB modeling has been originally developed for the study of complex systems. The view of an economic system as complex is therefore central to AB modeling. A complex system can be defined as *a system composed of different parts or subparts whose interaction among themselves and with the environment gives rise to emergent behaviors.* Some elements of this characterization are worth stressing here. First, the central role that interaction and feedback effects play in the evolution of a complex system implies that agents can be heterogeneous and connected among themselves in multiple ways. Second, the presence of feedback effects can potentially generate nonlinear or chaotic dynamics. Third, as a consequence, the actions of single agents do not influence the system evolution in a predictable manner.

Leigh Tesfatsion defines AB modeling as *the computational modeling of economic processes as open-ended dynamic systems of interacting agents.*[1] AB models are computationally solved by means of computer simulations and are used to represent systems with no predefined state of spaces, in which nonlinear, chaotic, or out-of-equilibrium behaviors are possible.

2.2 *Microfoundations and Cross-Fertilization*

Prior to discussing the theoretical overlap between the two modeling approaches, an inescapable underlying methodological question must be addressed: *is microfoundation compatible with PK macro-modeling?* In order to address the question, we need to eliminate a terminological ambiguity. As King (2015) and Skott (2012) imply, the term *microfoundation* has traditionally identified the neoclassical treatment of the micro-level analysis in macroeconomics. It usually implies an intertemporal optimization over an infinite time horizon by a representative agent endowed with perfect knowledge and perfect rationality. Abstracting from the fact that such microfoundation of macro-models is grossly flawed (see Kirman, 1992; Colander *et al.*, 2008; Stiglitz and Gallegati, 2011, among many others), King (2015) and Skott (2012), from different perspectives, convincingly argue that this microfoundation is evidently incompatible with PK economics. While the term bottom-up might be preferable as more generic, in this paper we will use microfoundation to generically indicate the set of explicit assumptions adopted in a macroeconomic model to characterize the economic agents and underpin the underlying microeconomic behavior.

Di Guilmi *et al.* (2017) illustrate how the aggregation method proposed by AB modeling can overcome the simplification induced by the adoption of the representative agent. As they show, the exact aggregation of AB modeling is effective although it does not solve the issue of establishing an explicit relationship between micro- and macro-variables, in contrast with a microfoundation approach based on statistical mechanics (on this point see also Foley, 2017). Aggregative PK models circumvent the aggregation problem by using microeconomic behavioral rules to infer macroeconomic relationships (for example, production for investment functions). Such an approach is formally incorrect (Di Guilmi *et al.*, 2017), and basically amounts to averaging out possible differences among agents, similarly to the aggregation method based on the representative agent.

According to Schoder (2017), the traditional treatment of microeconomic behavior in PK macro-models suffers from three types of inconsistencies. The first is methodological: while the macroeconomic level is presented formally, the microeconomic behavior is verbally described. This type of inconsistency may give rise to a second one: internal inconsistency, which occurs when different behavioral rules are mutually inconsistent. The third type of inconsistency is ontological: while the postulated rules are invariant to endogenous changes in the microenvironment, the model implicitly assumes them to endogenously adjust.

Further considerations could be added about the possible advantages of a more formal microfoundation for PK models (from the possibility of a wider engagement with the rest of the profession to a wider diffusion of PK ideas and tenets), but to remain within the scope of the present paper, the following discussion focuses on the compatible features of PK theory and AB modeling.

A deeper integration with PK economics can also benefit AB modeling. The fact that AB models are open-ended dynamical systems allows for a wider range of results compared to a standard general equilibrium approach, but it may also represent an issue for the identification of AB models and their application in policy analysis. More specifically Foley (2017), who has always advocated a wide adoption of AB modeling in economics, identifies a deep methodological issue with AB modeling related to their closure: the almost unlimited number of possible representations of agents' interactions, even in small systems. Given the sensitivity of results and policy indications to the model's specification, the presence of such a wide range of possible modeling choices can undermine the credibility of the model and consequently limit the usefulness of an AB representation of the economy. In his opinion, the rejection of the Walrasian type of equilibrium by AB scholars should not imply a rejection of the notion of equilibrium altogether but its replacement with sounder alternatives, such as the statistical equilibrium of complex systems in which the entropy is maximized.

In this respect, PK theory can provide a disciplining device for AB modeling from two different perspectives. First, by referring to a tradition with consolidated behavioral and structural assumptions, it can help limit the degrees of freedom for the modeler. Given its agnostic nature, an AB model can house any set of assumptions and elements, even from different traditions or modeling approaches. A too eclectic mix can undermine the internal consistency of a model and generate a range of possibly self-contradictory results. PK economics can represent a theoretical reference for constructing an internally consistent economic framework. Second, PK economics can lessen the identification problem of AB models by restricting the range of possible results and by providing a reference for an economic interpretation of the results well embedded in a consolidated literature.

While in theory every school of thought in macroeconomics could provide a reference for an internally consistent model and the interpretation of the results, the next subsection argues that PK theory significantly overlaps with the AB modeling approach.

2.3 *PK Pillars and AB Modeling*

Lavoie (2014) identifies five conceptual pillars of PK theory that he uses to stress the differences with the mainstream neoclassical approach. However, this theoretical synthesis can be used to show the compatibility of PK with the AB modeling approach, as shown by table 1. The first pillar identified by Lavoie is the epistemological realism of PK economics: "*The objective of economics is to be able to tell a relevant story and to explain the way the economy actually works in the real world.*" AB modeling, not being constrained by the analytical solvibility

Table 1. Presuppositions of PK Theory and AB Model

Presuppositions	PK	AB modeling
Epistemology/Ontology Rationality	Realism Environment-consistent rationality, satisficing agent	Realism Limited rationality, heuristics
Method Economic core	Holism, organicism Production, growth, abundance	Complexity Open-ended evolving systems
Political core	Regulated markets	Agnostic

Note: Adapted from table 1.3 in Lavoie (2014).

or by the necessity to find a stable equilibrium point, but rather aiming to reproduce realistic emergent properties at the aggregate level, is able to incorporate real-world behavioral features of economic agents. This is in stark contrast with the instrumentalism of the neoclassical approach, for which a theory must provide accurate predictions and identify the equilibrium point of the economy.

The second pillar concerns ontology. From this perspective, as Lavoie (2014, p. 17) recognizes, holism is a unifying character for PK economics and AB modeling for two reasons. First, in AB modeling, interactions among agents obey behavioral rules which constitute a complex social structure, providing a counterpart to the PK concept of institutional structure. Second, in AB modeling the emergent properties of the system are not implied by the behaviors of single agents but rather generated by their interaction: "*emergent properties can be considered as macroeconomic paradoxes, or fallacies of composition*" (Lavoie, 2014, p. 17).

The third pillar considers the type of rationality of economic agents. Both PK theory and AB modeling reject the hyperrationality assumption of the Neoclassical approach, preferring a procedural rationality or heuristics (see Dosi *et al.*, 2005, for the AB model camp). From this perspective, Roos (2015) strongly argues that AB models are able to incorporate the radical uncertainty that permeates real-world decision making, as stressed by PKs, in contrast with the full knowledge and perfect rationality of Neoclassical theory, which rules out by construction radical uncertainty.

The fourth pillar concerns the focus of the analysis and the fact that in PK theory the economy is assumed to work within the production frontier and therefore exchange is less relevant than production and growth. From this perspective, it is worth stressing that AB models are open-ended systems and consequently they are not constrained by the necessity to identify internal and optimal equilibrium solutions and by the necessary assumption of decreasing returns.

The last conceptual pillar of PK economics is related to the political core of the theory, which is the impossibility of having free markets: the market is an institution and therefore created (and regulated) by a system of norms. Being a methodology, it is not possible to attach labels to AB modeling. However, while not being an embedded characteristic of AB modeling, this political presupposition can nevertheless be modeled and tested by AB models.

Cogliano and Jiang (2016) argue for AB modeling as a suitable alternative for PK and in general heterodox models building on Lavoie's arguments. According to them, AB modeling represents a promising possibility for all the heterodox branches in economics. All heterodox schools tend to "*share one theoretical commonality, that is, economic outcomes are, to a large extent, determined by the relation(s) between socioeconomic structure and the agents who reside in it*" (Cogliano and Jiang, 2016). In PK economics, this is represented by the fact that macroeconomic phenomena, such as inflation and unemployment, are the unintended consequences of the influence exerted by the capitalist structures and institutions on the individual behaviors. They argue that AB modeling is well-equipped for representing this theoretical structure for two main reasons. First, for its flexibility and the heterogeneity of agents. Second, for its evolutionary nature, which allows for continuous and bidirectional feedback between institutions and agents, both endowed with proper behavioral rules. The potential of AB modeling as a replacement of mainstream Neoclassical economics is also stressed by Harcourt and Kriesler (2013, p. 50).

Besides the general limits of AB modeling highlighted by Foley (2017), the possible drawbacks of the reformulation of PK macro-models as AB models are related to the three modeling issues identified in the introduction: the adaptation of macro-behavioral rules at the single-agent level; the need of a different closure for the model; and how to ensure the consistency of all stocks and flows. The solution to these issues and the need of using explicit functional forms for all the model's behavioral assumptions can on the one hand force the introduction of simplifications that might jeopardize the qualitative insights that are attainable in traditional aggregative models,[2] and on the other hand, imply the introduction of additional assumptions whose consistency with the PK approach must be verified.

3. The Financial Instability Hypothesis in AB Models

This section surveys non-SFC-AB models that have attempted to formalize Minksy's Financial Instability Hypothesis. A Minskyan pattern for the credit cycle is a common feature of many of the models reviewed in this paper, but this section exclusively concerns itself with those models that have explicitly attempted to model the Financial Instability Hypothesis. Minskyan SFC-AB model are included in Section 5 in order to provide a comprehensive overview of that particular modeling method.

As Bucciarelli and Silvestri (2013) remark, the development of AB modeling and, in general, of computational economics has opened new perspectives for the modeling of Minsky's Financial Instability Hypothesis.

AB modeling is a suitable modeling approach for formalizing the Financial Instability Hypothesis for two main reasons. The first reason is stressed by Bucciarelli and Silvestri (2013) and is related to Minsky's skepticism about the oversimplification required by formalized modeling and his more sympathetic view of computer simulation. Despite a robust analytical background, Minsky favored a more qualitative, rather than quantitative, presentation. According to Foley (2001), the main reason "*was his recognition that the formal, statistical methods adopted by contemporary economists are inherently hostile to critical and qualitative insights into the performance of markets as human and social institutions.*" On the contrary, he entertained the idea that "*it might be that the most meaningful way to test propositions as to the cause and effect of financial instability will be through simulation studies, where the simulation models are redesigned to reflect alternative ways that financial instability can be induced*" (Minsky, 1972). He indeed applied simulation techniques in nonlinear models inspired by the Financial Instability Hypothesis (see Delli Gatti *et al.*, 1999, as a matter of example).

The second reason is related to the fact that AB modeling, besides involving computer simulations, are based on a bottom–up approach which appears to be particularly suitable for the formal Minskyan analysis. Indeed, the focus of the Financial Instability Hypothesis is the heterogeneity of agents' financial conditions and their evolution along the cycle. At different points of his 1975 book, Minsky stresses the need for a consistent microeconomic analysis and the consideration of agents' interaction: "*an ultimate reality in a capitalist economy is the set of interrelated balance sheets among the various units*" (Minsky, 1975, p. 116).

As in traditional PK modeling, most Minskyan models are aggregative (see the surveys in Nasica, 2000; Lavoie, 2009). This modeling strategy runs the risk of missing the essential part of the story: "*the composition of Ponzi, hedge, and speculative finance in any given sector can fluctuate without any changes in the aggregate balance sheet, provided that the increase in Ponzi finance is counterbalanced by improvements in the balance sheets of the remaining hedge and speculative units*" (Dos Santos, 2005). As Taylor and O'Connell (1985) explicitly recognize, "*shifts of firms among classes as the economy evolves in historical time underlie much of its cyclical behavior. This detail is rich and illuminating but beyond the reach of mere algebra.*"

3.1 Financial Fragility Models

The models presented here draw from the New-Keynesian literature about financial fragility which has been largely inspired by Hyman Minsky (see Bernanke and Gertler, 1989; Greenwald and Stiglitz, 1993), though without explicit recognition. For this reason, Nasica (2000) includes this stream of New-Keynesian literature in his review of Minskyan models. This literature has paved the way for the AB modeling approach to PK macro-modeling by showing the potential of AB modeling for a deeper integration of the financial sector into macroeconomic modeling, highlighting some of the complementarities discussed in Section 2, and in general by proposing AB model as a well distinguished alternative to the mainstream.

One of the most popular papers in this literature is Delli Gatti *et al.* (2005), which has been further developed and extended by the following Delli Gatti *et al.* (2007, 2010); Gallegati *et al.* (2007); Russo *et al.* (2007) among others. These models combine the core idea of Minsky's Financial Instability Hypothesis, according to which business fluctuations have a financial origin, with the New-Keynesian informational asymmetries in the credit market.

Delli Gatti *et al.* (2005) present an AB model version of Greenwald and Stiglitz (1993) with heterogeneous firms that interact through the credit sector. The model is substantially supply-driven with uncertainty on the demand side exogenously modeled through an idiosyncratic shock on the final goods' price. The economy is composed by a goods market and a credit market with a large number of heterogeneous firms, and one banking sector. As in Greenwald and Stiglitz (1993), firms are equity-constrained and can raise funds only on the credit market. They default when their internal finance A becomes null. Accordingly, firms set their investment expenditure, and consequently their demand for credit, as dependent on the banks' interest rates. The total credit supply, in turn, is a multiple of the banks' equity base, which is negatively affected as borrowing firms become insolvent. The total supply of credit L^s is allotted to each firm proportionally to its size and to the available cash according to the rule:

$$L_{it}^s = \lambda L_t^s \frac{K_{it-1}}{K_{t-1}} + (1 - \lambda)L_t^s \frac{A_{it-1}}{A_{t-1}} \tag{1}$$

where $\lambda > 0$, $K_{t-1} = \sum_i K_{it-1}$ is aggregate capital, and $A_{t-1} = \sum_i A_{it-1}$ is the total amount of internal finance. The interest rate equates the demand and supply of credit for each firm. As a consequence, each firm will face a different cost of borrowing, which will be higher (lower) the worse (better) are the financial conditions of both the single firm and the other firms in the economy. Hence, Delli Gatti *et al.* (2005) devise a system of indirect interaction with a clear Minskyan flavor: as the economy grows, firms are able to fulfill their credit obligations, pushing down the interest rate and, as a consequence, raising the level of investment for all the other firms in the economy in a virtuous cycle. When the amount of debt in the economy grows, more and more firms will default, forcing the banking sector to raise interest rates causing more bankruptcies and a reduction of economic activity.

The paper provides a good example of the additional insights that an AB model can provide not only with respect to the original representative agent model by Greenwald and Stiglitz (1993), but also with respect to aggregative models. The model is stylized but nevertheless able to replicate several pieces of empirical evidence, in particular with reference to the distribution of firm-level variables. The paper also presents a discussion about how idiosyncratic multiplicative shocks and (indirect) interaction can lead to the emergence of right-skewed distributions, especially for size and growth rates, starting with uniform initial conditions.

With its simple structure, the model shows how the interaction among agents following heuristic rules can generate nonlinearities and lead to realistic aggregate results which are not directly implied by agents' behaviors. Such an outcome stresses the necessity of a holistic modeling approach which embodies fundamental uncertainty. This paper represents a good example of how AB models are well equipped to effectively incorporate these elements in their representation of the macroeconomy.

Among the subsequent developments, it is worth mentioning Delli Gatti *et al.* (2010), which extend this approach by allowing for heterogeneity in the banking sector and introducing capital goods producing firms, thus enabling agents to directly interact. The economy is modeled as a multilayered network in which firms have connections with credit suppliers and with input suppliers. The formation of links in this network is random: each goods producing firm can see only a subset of potential suppliers of inputs and credit and will try to obtain inputs or credit from those among them who offer the best conditions. The endogenous network formation provides additional detail with respect to Delli Gatti *et al.* (2005) for the study of financial contagion and its effects on the phase transitions in the business cycle.

The model is able to replicate empirical evidence about firms' distributions. As for the network, the random matching mechanism affects the degree distribution making big crises more likely when the credit market is more concentrated.

The network representation of a financial fragility model makes more evident the role of institutional structures and provides a more detailed representation of the complex chain of feedback effects that determine the aggregate outcomes. The fundamental uncertainty in which single units operate is represented by the matching mechanism: agents can see only a random subset of possible matches. As shown in the reminder of the paper, this type of matching mechanism is a common feature in AB models with networks.

3.2 *Minskyan Models with Different Classes of Agents*

This second group of papers within the Minskyan tradition uses AB modeling to link the business cycle to the density of agents in the different groups identified by Minsky (hedge, speculative, and Ponzi units).

One of the first contributions in this area is the AB model by de Freitas and Lima (2007). They propose a model with a fixed number of firms, which form expectations about future demand according to a predetermined set of possible rules and consequently determine their need of funding to finance production with labor as the only input. Aggregate demand follows an exogenous autoregressive process. It is assumed to be the sum of a number of demands (all of equal amount) of consumers who randomly match with firms on the goods market. Consequently, firms may accumulate unwanted inventories. Each firm has a specific markup and the firms with the highest leverage can imitate the pricing behavior of f randomly surveyed competitors.

As Foley (2001) remarks, one of the central issues in modeling Minsky's theory of business cycles is the formalization of the mechanism that leads the financial sector to expand the supply of finance during upturns and to restrict it in the subsequent downturns. In de Freitas and Lima (2007), money is fully endogenous and the banking sector applies a variable mark-up to the policy rate. In particular, banks calculate a risk-adjusted mark-up which depends on the previous period's default rate, implementing an indirect interaction mechanism similar to the one in Delli Gatti *et al.* (2005). Formally, the mark-up h at time t is given by

$$h_t = \frac{1 + h_{t-1}}{1 - d_{t-1}} \tag{2}$$

where d is the percentage of defaulted debt.

Firms are classified as: hedge if their cash flow (generated by interest accrued on deposits and sales revenue) is enough to repay both the interest and the principal of debt, speculative if the cash flow is big enough to repay at least the interest, and Ponzi if they need to rollover both the interest and the principal component of debt.

Through computer simulations, de Freitas and Lima (2007) test the dependence of systemic financial fragility (measured by the proportion of the three types of agents) on the parameters of the model, for example, on the effectiveness of the matching process in the goods market and the sensitivity of firms' price mark-up on macroeconomic conditions. Simulations show how the distribution of firms across the three financing regimes is sensitive to the flexibility of price mark-ups (proxied by the parameter f) and the size of the sample of firms surveyed by consumers. The output and credit cycles appear to be strictly correlated but the distribution of firms for financing regimes does not display any pattern.

Despite the fact that sensitivity study involves factors that are not central in Minsky's narrative (such as informational asymmetries and local imitation), and the investigation of financial fragility does not clarify its genesis and diffusion process, this paper is an interesting pioneering attempt to explore the potential of AB modeling in a Minskyan model.

As in Delli Gatti *et al.* (2010), a random matching mechanism and local interaction are used to represent the fact that agents face an uncertain and evolving environment and adopt heuristic rules.

Chiarella and Di Guilmi have developed the above line of research in three different papers (Chiarella and Di Guilmi, 2011, 2012b, 2017). Chiarella and Di Guilmi (2011) adapt in an AB framework the aggregative Minskyan model by Taylor and O'Connell (1985). Firms are heterogeneous in size and financial condition, and are subjected to idiosyncratic shocks.

Two contributions of this paper are worth emphasizing. First, the model is solved both numerically and analytically, following the aggregation method proposed by Aoki and Yoshikawa (2006) and Di Guilmi (2008). This method is particularly suitable for representing the Minskyan dynamics of the business cycle as it groups agents in clusters according to measurable characteristics. In order to keep the derivation as simple as possible, Chiarella and

Di Guilmi (2011) reduce the number of categories to two, grouping together speculative and Ponzi in the classification of de Freitas and Lima (2007).

The second contribution is the procyclicality in the financial sector's propensity to lend through a Tobinian system which determines the total amount of wealth in an endogenous money setting.[3] The prices of the two types of equities (stocks issued by hedge and by speculative firms) are quantified as clearing market prices. Capital gains (losses) determine the availability of credit and, consequently, the lending interest rate.

As shown by both simulations and analytical solution, asset price booms generate cheaper credit and more investment in a virtuous cycle, which is also the cause of growth in the proportion of speculative firms. The share of investors' portfolio allocated to hedge or speculative firms' equities depends on a stochastic mechanism: when a series of shocks reduces the proportion of wealth invested in speculative firms' shares, their financial condition worsens. The most financially distressed firms will default, reducing investors wealth and setting the stage for a further worsening in credit conditions. The higher cost of credit will squeeze firms' investment and the previous virtuous cycle is reversed.

The paper provides a microeconomic explanation of macroeconomic phenomena in line with Minsky's theory, rooted in a complexity perspective. During booms, the capital and the debt of speculative firms grow faster until the system hits a critical leverage threshold, while hedge firms have a steady rate of growth over time. Hence, the variation in the balance sheet structure of speculative units is at the root of short-term fluctuations and changes in firm size distribution over the cycle.

Chiarella and Di Guilmi (2012b, 2017) extend this framework using Minsky's original classification of firms into three categories and solving the model only numerically. In particular, Chiarella and Di Guilmi (2012b) add a government sector that runs anticyclical fiscal policy, and Chiarella and Di Guilmi (2017) also include a central bank that sets the reference interest rate with different types of Taylor rules. Consistently with PK theory,[4] they show that an active fiscal policy can curb the amplitude of the boom-bust cycles whereas an active monetary policy can possibly generate undesired effects due to the complex chain of effects on firms' behavior generated by a change in the policy rate. Chiarella and Di Guilmi (2017) also find that endogenous credit can contribute to keep goods price inflation low during stock market booms. In both papers, the simulations reveal a strict correlation between the cycle and the evolution of the densities of agents in the three groups, and the consideration of the three financial regimes adds further detail to the analysis of the joint dynamics of firms' financial fragility and the macroeconomy.

4. AB Model Applications in Structuralist-Neo-Kaleckian and Evolutionary Models

As argued by Setterfield and Gouri Suresh (2016), AB models are suitably equipped to deal with path-dependency in a Keynesian and Schumpeterian sense. Their argument relies on three observations. First, AB models represent the economy as a complex system with nonlinearities and high sensitivity to initial conditions. Second, two of the defining features of AB models are agent heterogeneity and interaction, which are also found in different definitions of path-dependence (such as hysteresis and lock-in). Third, AB models are open-ended and their final outcome can only be identified through computational techniques (Arthur, 2013).

Following Setterfield and Gouri Suresh's suggestion, this section groups together AB models developed by Giovanni Dosi and his research group at Sant'Anna in Pisa, Italy, which combine a Schumpeterian evolutionary approach with some PK characteristics (presented in

Subsection 4.1), and structuralist and Neo-Kaleckian models with AB features developed by Mark Setterfield and coauthors (presented in Subsection 4.2).

4.1 Evolutionary Models with PK Features

Dawid (2006) provides a review of AB models with technological change and innovation. Given its nature and scope, AB modeling has been widely used by evolutionary economists. For the purposes of this review, the series of models defined as "Keynes-Schumpeter" is of particular interest (Dosi *et al.*, 2008, 2010, 2013, 2015). This type of models has proved to be able to replicate a large number of stylized facts and to be flexible enough to be adapted in different contexts (see, for example, Dosi *et al.*, 2016, for an assessment of job market reforms). These models originally combine an evolutionary approach with technological change and some elements of PK macroeconomics. In particular, they merge an evolutionary approach (Nelson and Winter, 1982) with Keynesian effective demand to answer the question "*How does aggregate demand modulate the diffusion and the macro-impact of technological innovations?*" (Dosi *et al.*, 2010).

Whereas some elements of this framework are not PK, for example, the supply-side determination of innovation,[5] the most recent versions (such as Dosi *et al.*, 2013) embody some essential PK elements and, interestingly, achieve PK conclusions in terms of policy. The elements that are related to the traditional PK literature are the Minskyan credit cycle and its effects on the macroeconomy (which is modeled in line with Delli Gatti *et al.*, 2005) and a Kaleckian modeling of the functional distribution of income, which depends on the firms' price mark-up.

The latest versions of this model present two industrial sectors (capital goods and consumption goods), a banking sector with heterogeneous banks that set their lending rates depending on the risk class of their borrowers, a government that collects taxes and decides the level of expenditure and the unemployment benefits, and a central bank that sets the policy rate to steer the economy toward its inflation and unemployment targets.

The result is a fairly large and complex model. However, the results of the simulations are neat and the authors provide an in-depth sensitivity analysis of the relevant parameters. Dosi *et al.* (2016) enrich the previous papers by studying the effects of joint variations in the core parameters thanks to recent techniques of global sensitivity analysis for numerical systems.

The results of the simulations in Dosi *et al.* (2013) identify fiscal policy as the best tool to smooth the cycle and reduce inequality. The microeconomic detail enriches the evaluation of policy, showing that fiscal policy has a greater impact the larger is the degree of inequality in income distribution. In particular, an increase in the tax rate and in the size of the unemployment benefit as a percentage of the average market wage reduce the standard deviation of GDP growth rates, make full-employment more likely, and reduce the probability of a crisis. These effects are stronger when the functional distribution of income is more skewed toward wages. A well-designed fiscal policy can also foster innovation and prevent the economy from falling into long-term stagnation. Overall, the numerical results prove that austerity measures are self-defeating and that monetary policy should abandon interest rate targeting in order to complement and support the stabilizing effort of the government.

4.2 Kaleckian Models with AB Features

Different from the other models surveyed in this paper, which are constructed in a bottom–up fashion, Suresh and Setterfield (2015) (but see also Gibson and Setterfield, 2015a, b) build a standard aggregative structural model and then reformulate only the relevant equations to account for heterogeneity in the firm sector. Building on Setterfield and Budd (2011), the path-dependency of the economic system is investigated by Suresh and Setterfield (2015) focusing on the "state of long-run expectations" as the reaction of agents to fundamental uncertainty in the Keynesian sense. In particular, firms heuristically revise upward (downward) their investment strategy looking at their capacity utilization in the previous unit of time according to a composite criterion whose main determinant is

$$\kappa \Delta u_{jt-1} + (1 - \kappa)\Delta u_{t-1} \geq (\leq)c$$

where u_{jt-1} and u_{t-1} are the capacity utilization for, respectively, the single firm and the whole economy, and κ, c are constant.[6] The parameter $0 \leq \kappa \leq 1$ quantifies the "degree of isolation" of a firm. Firm j uses adaptive expectations about its future capacity utilization: $u^e_{jt} = u_{jt-1}$.

In the simulations, an idiosyncratic shock is exogenously introduced in the capacity utilization in the second period in order to measure the magnitude of the standard deviation of the distribution of capacity utilization as a function of the parameter κ. The numerical results suggest a nonlinear relationship which displays a reverse-U shape, with critical points located at $\kappa = \{0.4, 0.85\}$.

The network effects of financial constraints are investigated by Gibson and Setterfield (2015a). They focus on the short run and, in particular, the role of financial constraints for firms when lending agents have heterogeneous expectations (namely, bull or bear). The aim of the paper is to show the possible additional insights on the real-financial interaction coming from integrating AB modeling into a structuralist perspective.

Gibson and Setterfield (2015a) build a static network to connect financial agents among themselves and with firms. Firms make decisions about investment on the basis of their capacity utilization and profit rate. They consequently determine the level of aggregate demand, which is allocated to each firm with an algorithm that ensures that for each firm capacity utilization is strictly lower than 1. When the value of investment is higher than retained profits firms demand credit from the lender (financial agent) to which they are connected. The lender uses a Bayesian procedure to update her forecast. Looking at the forecast and the availability of capital (directly or through lending from other financial agents), the lender decides whether to approve the loan requested by the firm. In case of a negative decision, the firm's investment is not realized. Financial networks are either random or subject to preferential attachment, and either weighted or unweighted by shares of capital stock.

In contrast to other models of real-financial networks (as the cited Delli Gatti *et al.*, 2010, among others), in this paper a more interconnected system appears to be more resilient to financial shocks and less prone to crashes. This result is probably affected by the mechanisms of link formation and the consequent transmission of financial distress. In both weighted and preferentially attached networks, the number of loans denied is larger. However, the mechanism of link formation does not affect GDP growth, only the distribution of growth rates: large firms grow faster due to their easier access to credit. Financial crashes are more likely to occur in a network with preferential attachment.

This set of models represents a hybrid between purely structural aggregative models and AB models, built through a sort of *disaggregation* process. Different from typical AB models, in the simulations some results are subject to further *ex post* analytical manipulations before being fed back to the model and as a consequence it is not clear whether the final macroeconomic results can genuinely be considered emergent properties.

5. SFC-AB Models: Toward a New Benchmark?

In recent years, stock-flow consistency has become more and more popular in macroeconomic AB models with PK features.[7] At the same time, PK scholars have started microfounding their SFC models using an AB approach.

5.1 SFC-AB Models with PK Features

Seppecher (2010) and the following Seppecher and Salle (2015) present a SFC-AB model, called Jamel (Java Agent-based Macro-Economic Laboratory), in which the phase transitions during business cycles are determined by the *opinion dynamics*, as modeled in De Grauwe (2008). In particular, consumers and firms can be optimistic or pessimistic about, respectively, their consumption decisions and the targeted level of leverage. The model combines non-PK elements (for example, a Calvo pricing mechanism for price adjustment) together with PK tenets. Credit supply is perfectly elastic at a fixed interest rate, which is increased to a constant higher rate when a borrowing firm is forced to rollover its debt.

Each agent (household or firm) decides about her attitude looking either at her own past situation with a predefined probability $1 - p$ or to a given subset of neighboring agents with a probability p. The simulations in Seppecher and Salle (2015) produce realistic dynamics of a business cycle, which is driven by endogenous waves of optimism and pessimism among agents: market sentiment pushes up consumer spending and distributed profits, leading to a boost in aggregate demand that increases the level of employment and profits. However some agents remain pessimistic and can spread their pessimism to other agents, depending on the size of the parameter p. If this contagion reaches a critical threshold, the virtuous cycle is reversed and the economy enters into a recession, with reduced consumption and deleveraging.

The paper enriches the analysis of financial fragility with original insights about the role of opinion dynamics in the propagation of shocks through random networks. Network effects can be clearly assessed through the sensitivity study of the parameter p, which reveals that for stronger imitation effects the volatility of the output gap generally increases because of the faster transmission of changing sentiment among consumers.

Bruun provides a few early attempts of SFC-AB models that are generically qualified as Keynesian. Among these, Bruun (2010) is more directly related to traditional SFC models, and proposes a representation of a three-sector economy with producers of investment goods, producers of consumption goods, and consumers. One of the most original features of the model is that the distributional effects are investigated using thresholds for negative wealth (below which households reduce consumption) and positive wealth (above which households increase consumption). In this setting, the sensitivity study reveals that the exogenous creation of inequality (low threshold for poor household and high threshold for rich household) generates faster growth but also sets a limit for it due to the transfer of wealth to the upper tail of the distribution. Unfortunately, these results are not further investigated and related with the other similar contemporary studies on this topic.

Riccetti *et al.* (2015) introduce stock-flow consistency in a model that borrows from Riccetti *et al.* (2013) and from Delli Gatti *et al.* (2005, 2010). Although the model is, strictly speaking, not PK (for example, money is not endogenous), it is worth mentioning here because in this model business fluctuations are due both to Minskyan financial dynamics of the type seen in Delli Gatti *et al.* (2005, 2010) and to original Goodwin-type effects originating in the labor market. The economy is composed of a set of heterogeneous firms, households and banks, together with a central bank and a government. Agents randomly match in the goods, credit and labor markets and heuristically revise their behavior accordingly to their situation in the previous unit of time. In particular at time t, a worker revises up (down) her satisficing wage if she was employed (unemployed) at time $t-1$. This simple behavioral rule creates Goodwin dynamics that interact with the credit market conditions. Banks linked to defaulted firms lose a fraction of their loans while defaulted firms are replaced by new ones with a fresh endowment of net worth and a targeted leverage ratio of 1.

The realization of Goodwin cycles as an emergent property based on a heuristic behavior at the agent-level adds an interesting perspective for the study of this type of dynamics. The bargaining power of the workers is differentiated across individuals and becomes endogenous. This allows for the identification of more specific policy prescriptions, such as the government's acyclical hiring of workers. From the simulations, the authors conclude that this type of fiscal policy is effective at stabilizing the economy. The simulations also highlight the correlation between debt cycles and business cycles, and in particular the amplifying effect of financial factors on the business cycle.

Russo *et al.* (2016) further develop this framework by introducing a consumption function with habit formation. This extension allows the authors to shed light on the empirical finding by Cynamon and Fazzari (2013) and Perugini *et al.* (2016), among others, that the redistribution of income toward the top earners observed since the 1980s has not resulted in stagnation due to the increase in the availability of consumer credit and the consequent use of leverage to finance consumption by the poorest households. Using two sets of simulations (with and without consumer credit), the model reproduces one of the main empirical findings of the cited papers: the availability of credit and the resulting increase in leverage make financial crises more likely. As a consequence, policy makers face a trade-off between stability and fast growth. Higher leverage is at the root of wealth inequality, because of the growing interest burden faced by borrowing households, and interestingly, Monte Carlo replications show that the presence of consumer credit has a negative effect on average output employment in each run.

The Eurace model (Raberto *et al.*, 2012) is a very articulated and large AB model which aims to replicate in detail the features of a real economy. The version presented in Raberto *et al.* (2012) consists of a goods production sector, a capital producing firm, a household sector, a banking sector, a government, and a central bank. The model presents some essential PK features, a demand-driven goods market, a standard mark-up pricing rule, and endogenous money,[8] together with some significant departures from the typical PK model architecture, such as a Cobb–Douglas production function for firms in the consumption goods sector and the determination of investment on the basis of a cost-minimizing approach. Another difference with a standard PK model is the consumption decision, modeled as buffer-stock saving behavior (Carroll, 2001).

Firms' expectations about future demand are quantified using a weighted average over the past periods, considering the amount of inventories. The matching in the goods, labor, and credit markets occurs after a local search over a random subset of counterparts. Once consumption for household h is determined, the allocation among the different firms f obeys the following logit model:

$$Prob_{h,f} = \frac{exp(-\Lambda log\ p^f)}{\sum_f exp(-\Lambda log\ p^f)} \tag{3}$$

where Λ is a parameter and p^f is the price of output for firm f (given that firms have different technology, they will also have different costs and prices).

Firms face two types of bankruptcies: insolvency bankruptcy and illiquidity bankruptcy. In the former, equity goes to zero and debt is restructured, forcing the defaulted firm to adopt a lower leverage target. In the latter, firms still have some residual equity. In both cases, firms do not disappear but simply cease production and try to raise new capital in the financial market in order to restart their activity, ensuring the accounting consistency for stocks and flows. The central bank follows an inflation targeting rule.

The simulations reveal a Minskyan pattern in which the debt cycle is at the root of the business cycle. In particular, the regulatory rule for banks causes a credit squeeze at the peak of the cycle when the more leveraged firms default, causing a reduction in capital to the lending banks. Computational experiments with different regulatory constraints confirm the dependence of the real economy on the credit market.

As argued by Lengnick (2013), the degree of complexity of very large AB models, while allowing a comprehensive representation of an economic system, makes it problematic to identify the causal relationships and thus to unambiguously interpret the results, justifying the concerns expressed by Foley (2017) for AB modeling. However, Raberto et al. (2012) can provide an example of how an SFC representation can to some extent discipline the construction of such a large model by limiting the number of modeling options.

This framework has been subsequently used by Erlingsson et al. (2014) to study the real effects of a housing market bubble. Dawid (2015) and Dawid et al. (2016) propose a policy-oriented variant of this model, aimed at a specific application to the European Union economies.

5.2 PK SFC-AB Models

Kinsella et al. (2011) is probably the first paper with a typical SFC model in an AB setting. The model consists of four sectors: firms and households, which are modeled at agent-level, banks, which are treated as an aggregate sector, and the government.

Households have a limited life-span (75 years) and can accumulate wealth, through savings, and increase their job skills, through debt-financed education and learning-by-doing. After 75 periods, each household is replaced by a newborn one, which inherits its parent's wealth but not the working skills. Firms spend their profit in either expanding their productive capacity or, alternatively, engaging in risky innovation according to a fixed probability. The matching on the labor market occurs randomly. The offered wage depends on the financial resources of the employer and on the level of education of the potential employee; the demanded wage depends on the household's wealth, skills, and education plus a random component quantifying the relative bargaining power. Money is endogenous as the banking sector elastically supplies credit to households and firms (even though at a variable rate that depends on the loans' profitability). However, the accumulation of debt is limited as agents are bankrupted when their negative money reaches a given threshold.

To ensure stock-flow consistency, defaulted firms and households create bad debt for banks. Bankrupted firms are immediately replaced and their initial endowment is supplied by the government at no cost. Aggregate demand is allocated to each firm according to an index based on the productivity of its workers and its productive capacity.

Simulations of the model show fairly realistic dynamics of the macroeconomic variables and a Pareto distribution of income for the top 5% with a Pareto parameter close to the one empirically detected. The bottom 95% are distributed according to a gamma or exponential distribution.

Finally, it should be noted that the conclusions of Kinsella *et al.* (2011), stressing the negative macroeconomic consequences of unfettered market in terms of "winners" and "losers," are close to the political core of PK economics (Lavoie, 2014) discussed in Section 2.3.

The authors show that the AB modeling approach allows for a more realistic and complex representation of an evolving economy with inter-generational dynamics than the one possible in aggregative (or in representative agent) models. The simulations generate a realistic distribution of household income, and the authors provide an explanation for this piece of evidence based on statistical physics (Foley, 1994). The authors do not further explore this avenue to study, for example, the dynamics of the distribution over the cycle or possible policy implications.

The latest generation of this class of models is explicitly identified as SFC-AB models in order to stress the continuity with the two original literature. They are often the result of collaborations between scholars from both camps (Godin, 2015).

Carvalho and Di Guilmi (2014) and Di Guilmi and Carvalho (2017) develop microfounded neo-Kaleckian models to study the joint dynamics of leverage, inequality, and the business cycle. The originality of these contributions is their use of the standard SFC structure, conventions, and analysis, but built in a bottom–up fashion, starting with the microeconomic behavioral equations.

Both papers present SFC-AB models that are analytically solved by the master equation techniques introduced by Aoki and Yoshikawa (2006) and Di Guilmi (2008) in order to derive the aggregate equations of the SFC model from the agents' behavioral rules. The result is a dynamical system that includes micro-level variables; the analysis of steady state and stability is used to integrate and interpret the numerical outcomes of the Monte Carlo simulations. Consequently, the social accounting matrix and the SFC dynamical system feature micro-level variables. Both models are closed in a Keynesian fashion by the functional identification of a multiplier that allows for the contemporaneous determination of aggregate demand and demand for labor.

Carvalho and Di Guilmi (2014) study the interaction of wealth and income inequality, functional distribution of income (which is exogenous and constant) and the business cycle proposing an SFC-AB model on the household side while the firm side is modeled as an aggregate as in the traditional PK-SFC literature. The sensitivity study of both the numerical results and the analytical solution highlights the effect of the functional distribution of income on the cycle. In particular, a higher share of profits on total output makes the system more volatile and the personal distribution of income more skewed.

Di Guilmi and Carvalho (2017) complement their previous paper by modeling the production side as an AB model while keeping the other sectors of the economy as aggregates. For analytical tractability, they use a stylized version of Minsky's classification criteria dividing firms in hedge and speculative and not allowing for Ponzi behavior. Aggregate demand is allocated according to firms' size with a stochastic preferential attachment shock that partially redistributes demand across firms. Firms with a leverage ratio higher than a fixed threshold are bankrupted and their capital is reallocated at zero cost to continuing and newborn firms.

Both numerical and analytical results investigate the effect of firms' behavioral parameters on the stability of the system, in particular a more conservative attitude of hedge firms has the undesired effect of making the expansionary phase more reliant on speculative firms and, therefore, more unstable. A functional distribution of income more geared toward profits has a destabilizing effect on the economy.

By integrating statistical mechanic and AB modeling approaches, these papers indicate a possible avenue for overcoming the identification issue stressed by Foley (2017). Thanks to the analytical solution, the steady state of the model can be determined and the conditions for its existence identified. Moreover, since the macroeconomic variables can be expressed as a function of microeconomic quantities, the causal links can be clearly analyzed. Given its analytical complexity, applications of this method may face a trade-off between tractability and degree of sophistication.

Michell (2014) presents an SFC-AB model to investigate the Steindlian idea of the natural emergence of oligopoly in competitive markets, and the consequent fall in the rate of investment and modifications in the functional distribution of income, which is therefore endogenous in this model. The paper proposes a Kaleckian growth model in which firms set their targets for output, fixed capital investment, and loans. As in Di Guilmi and Carvalho (2017), the firm sector is microfounded while the household and banking sectors are modeled as aggregates. Due to the numerical solution used by Michell (2014), the model presents a different closure from Di Guilmi and Carvalho (2017): the macroeconomic variables are either obtained as a sum of the microeconomic quantities in the productive sector, or quantified by means of a system of equations in a typical SFC fashion. As such, output and aggregate expenditure (households' consumption plus investment) may differ. Aggregate demand is allocated to each firm using a mechanism similar to Di Guilmi and Carvalho (2017), with an additional parameter to govern the proportions of demand allocated according to size and stochastic shock, respectively. Michell (2014) shows that, when the size of the shock is relatively small, the model confirms Steindl's intuition: starting from a uniformly distributed capital endowment, market concentration rapidly increases, the functional distribution shifts toward profits, and the rate of investment falls. However, the size of the shock is probably too big for a fair assessment: when the stochastic element accounts for 30% of the criterion for demand allocation, the dispersion of firm-level variables is unrealistically large.

The author demonstrates the potential of AB microfoundations for SFC analysis from two different perspectives. First, it highlights the micreconomic behavioral and structural details of the joint evolution of market concentration, leverage, and investment that cannot be captured when intrasectoral flows are not modeled (as in standard aggregate SFC models). Second, the AB microfoundations enable the model to reconcile the procyclicality of debt implied by Minsky's Financial Instability Hypothesis with the Kaleckian theory of procyclicality of profits, showing that while the proportion of firms in financial distress is rising, the net financial position of the productive sector improves thanks to the accumulation of cash by the largest units.[9]

Caiani et al. (2016) propose an SFC-AB model that aims to be general enough to define a benchmark for this class of models. The model is composed of a large number of heterogeneous households, firms (divided in capital goods and consumption goods producing firms), banks, a government sector, and a central bank. The agents interact in different markets (consumption goods, capital goods, labor, credit, and deposit) through a random matching mechanism borrowed from Riccetti et al. (2015). The duration of bank loans is set at 20 periods, and in each period the borrowers pay the one-period interest plus a share of the principal. Since a firm resorts to borrowing finance (randomly matching with a bank) whenever the operating cash flow is not enough to face its expected financial commitments, at a given point in time each firm can have multiple active loan contracts.

Firms and banks can default when their equity is wiped out but, in order to maintain their number constant, they are bailed in by the households who own their capital, and by depositors. Money is endogenous but, as in Riccetti et al. (2015) and Dosi et al. (2013), credit rationing may occur as a consequence of a prudent behavior of banks. In particular, the supply of credit depends on the capital ratio of the lending bank and the riskiness of the borrower, measured by the probability of default during the life of the loan and its operating cash flow and value of collateral.

The main contribution of Caiani *et al.* (2016) is methodological as they identify the crucial issues for the development of consistent and usable SFC-AB models and propose original solutions to them. The most important contribution concerns the calibration and accounting validation of the model. As Caiani *et al.* (2016) correctly remark, many of the existing SFC-AB models have a consistent structure of stock and flows as defined by their behavioral and accounting equation but, when it comes to the implementation of the numerical simulations, the initial calibration may not respect this accounting consistency. Their solution consists in: first, deriving an aggregate version of the model; second, identifying a steady state in which real variables are constant and nominal variables grow at a constant rate; third, numerically solving the model for the initial conditions and some of the parameters by considering as exogenous parameters those for which empirical estimates are available and those that the authors want to control. Furthermore, the initial duration of loans[10] and the matching in the various market is set in order to ensure the accounting consistency.

This innovative calibration procedure allows the authors to analyze the time series produced by the simulations from the beginning and not after a *burn-in* phase, as is standard practice in AB models. Caiani *et al.* (2016) argue against this practice because of its arbitrariness and the strong path-dependency of AB models.

The numerical simulations of this model are run by means of a platform appositely developed for AB model-SFC, named *Java Macro Agent Based* (JMAB) tool suite. The results of the model are in line with a number of stylized facts as detected by the empirical literature. The time series of macro-variables match their empirical counterparts for volatility, auto- and cross-correlation as do the distributions of firm-level variables (size, growth rates, bad debt, and bankruptcies). As for the network structure, the degree distribution for banks is right-skewed, and the number of degrees per bank is higher than the number of degrees for firms. The analysis of the results is completed by a robustness check, which demonstrates that these outcomes are not determined by the choice of the parameter set.

6. Concluding Remarks

This paper provides an overview of the literature about PK-AB modeling and AB models with PK features. Within this literature, four different streams can be isolated: Minskyan AB models; evolutionary AB models with PK features; AB models belonging to the neo-Kaleckian and structuralist traditions; and SFC-AB models. In surveying the various papers, it is argued that this cross-fertilization can benefit and enrich both AB and PK modeling approaches.

The construction of a microfounded PK macro-model faces three main challenges. The first is the elaboration of microbehavioral rules consistent with the traditionally aggregative structure of PK macro-models. As mentioned in the introduction, aggregative PK models often use microeconomic behavioral rules to infer macroeconomic relationships. Consequently, most of the models surveyed here manage to adapt the PK aggregate equations at the agent level, introducing in some cases specific micro-variables. In some instances, when the microeconomic detail was not essential to the analysis, sectors have been kept as aggregate.

The second issue is twofold and concerns, on the one hand, the computation of the relevant aggregate quantities and, on the other hand, the allocation and matching in markets where only aggregate quantities are known. The former is usually solved by devising a time-structure that allows for the determination of the variables in a logically consistent manner. Only in one instance the usual Keynesian closure with the multiplier is adopted. For the latter issue, a range of possible criteria (from size to price to uniform distribution) have been proposed.

Finally, SFC-AB modeling faces two main specific types of issues. The first consists in modeling agents' demography: what happens to the assets of bankrupted agents and where does the endowment of newborn agents come from? In most cases, the issue is avoided by keeping the number of agents constant with different mechanisms: immediately replacing defaulted firms, keeping them temporarily inactive or bailing them in. Only in one instance the replacement is not one-to-one and stock-flow consistency is ensured by the redistribution of firms' assets to continuing firms and new entrants. The second type of issues specific for SFC-AB modeling is how to ensure the consistency of stocks at any stage of computer simulations. While all the surveyed models present a structure of behavioral equations that ensures the consistency of stocks and flows (verified for the models in Subsection 5.2 by a social accounting matrix), Caiani *et al.* (2016) is so far the only paper in which this problem is explicitly discussed, providing an original initialization algorithm that ensures the accounting consistency from period zero of the simulations.

The microfoundation through an AB approach provides a number of potential insights. The review shows that it is possible to associate the evolutionary dynamics of agents to the different phases of the business cycle and to identify which microeconomic conditions (agents behaviors, endowments, or financial situations) guarantee faster or sustainable growth. Policy analysis is enriched in two main ways. First, a policy measure can be differentiated by classes of agents (for example, unemployed workers) and its impact can be assessed not only with reference to the macroeconomy but also to single social classes, groups, or individuals. Moreover, the distributional effects of a policy can be evaluated in full detail. Second, in assessing a particular policy, AB modeling can shed light on the unintended or undesired consequences that can be generated by the complex interaction of agents. As for the social structure, AB models with networks are able to investigate the aggregate outcomes generated by different types of social norms and institutions (represented, for example, by different types of connectivity, information flows, and mechanisms of link creation).

AB modeling can benefit from the cross-fertilization because PK economics can represent a benchmark for limiting the degrees of freedom in building the model and a reference for the interpretation of the results addressing the concerns expressed by Foley (2017). These concerns appear to be legitimate in particular for large-scale models. A possible solution is a deeper integration between AB models and statistical mechanics, which can also open new directions of research for PK economics.

Ackowledgments

The author wishes to thank Timo Henckel, Alberto Russo, and two anonymous referees for helpful comments. The usual caveats apply.

Notes

1. See Leigh Tesfatsion's website at http://www2.econ.iastate.edu/tesfatsi/ace.htm.
2. For a more general discussion on formalization in heterodox economics, see Lavoie (2014, pp. 44–47).
3. See Chiarella and Di Guilmi (2012a) for more specific treatment of this point.

4. The effectiveness in demand management of fiscal policy in comparison to the dubious effects of monetary policy has always been a tenet of Keynesian and PK economics (see, for example, King, 2015, pp. 82–85).
5. The variation in productivity over time follows a stochastic process in which the aggregate demand has little role, although the investment in R&D depends on the firm's market share. PK growth models (such as Dutt, 1990) generally assume demand-driven innovation according to Verdoon's law (McCombie and Thirlwall, 1994).
6. In Setterfield and Budd (2011), the parameter κ is differentiated across firms.
7. Although this is not true for AB modeling in general (see, for example, the review in Chen and Gostoli, 2014).
8. It should be noted that the supply of credit is infinitely elastic at the policy rate plus a risk premium only if the lending institution satisfies a Basel II-style regulatory requirement.
9. Michell (2014) notes that this result may also cast doubts on the realism of a pure horizontalist modeling of the banking sector which neglects the different degrees of creditworthiness of borrowers.
10. Loans are initialized with different residual life to ensure that they do not all expire at the same time, possibly distorting the evolution of the macroeconomy.

References

Aoki, M. and Yoshikawa, H. (2006) *Reconstructing Macroeconomics*. Cambridge: Cambridge University Press.

Arthur, B. (2013) Complexity economics: a different framework for economic thought. Working Papers, SFI.

Bernanke, B. and Gertler, M. (1989) Agency costs, net worth, and business fluctuations. *American Economic Review* 79: 14–31.

Bruun, C. (2010) The economics of Keynes in an almost stock-flow consistent agent-based setting. In S. Zambelli (ed.), *Computable, Constructive and Behavioural Economic Dynamics* (pp. 442–461). Routledge.

Bucciarelli, E. and Silvestri, M. (2013) Hyman p. Minsky's unorthodox approach: recent advances in simulation techniques to develop his theoretical assumptions. *Journal of Post Keynesian Economics* 36: 299–324.

Caiani, A., Godin, A., Caverzasi, E., Gallegati, M., Kinsella, S. and Stiglitz, J.E. (2016) Agent based-stock flow consistent macroeconomics: towards a benchmark model. *Journal of Economic Dynamics and Control* 69: 375–408.

Carroll, C.D. (2001) A theory of the consumption function, with and without liquidity constraints. *Journal of Economic Perspectives* 15: 23–45.

Carvalho, L. and Di Guilmi, C. (2014) Income inequality and macroeconomic instability: a stock-flow consistent approach with heterogeneous agents. CAMA Working Papers 2014-60, Centre for Applied Macroeconomic Analysis, Crawford School of Public Policy, The Australian National University. https://ideas.repec.org/p/een/camaaa/2014-60.html.

Chen, S.-H. and Gostoli, U. (2014) Behavioral macroeconomics and agent-based macroeconomics. In S. Omatu, H. Bersini, J.M. Corchado, S. Rodríguez, P. Pawlewski, and E. Bucciarelli, eds., *11th International Conference on Distributed Computing and Artificial Intelligence* (pp. 47–54). Cham: Springer International Publishing.

Chiarella, C. and Di Guilmi, C. (2011) The financial instability hypothesis: a stochastic microfoundation framework. *Journal of Economic Dynamics and Control* 35: 1151–1171.

Chiarella, C. and Di Guilmi, C. (2012a) A reconsideration of the formal Minskyan analysis: microfoundations, endogenous money and the public sector. In G.I. Bischi, C. Chiarella and I. Sushko (eds.),

Global Analysis of Dynamic Models in Economics and Finance (pp. 63–81). Springer-Verlag: Berlin Heidelberg.

Chiarella, C. and Di Guilmi, C. (2012b) The fiscal cost of financial instability. *Studies in Nonlinear Dynamics and Econometrics* 16: 1–29.

Chiarella, C. and Di Guilmi, C. (2017) Monetary policy and debt deflation: some computational experiments. *Macroeconomic Dynamics*, 21: 214–242.

Cogliano, J.F. and Jiang, X. (2016) Agent-based computational economics: simulation tools for heterodox research. In F.S. Lee and B. Cronin (eds.), *Handbook of Research Methods and Applications in Heterodox Economics* (pp. 253–271). Edward Elgar.

Colander, D., Howitt, P., Kirman, A., Leijonhufvud, A. and Mehrling, P. (2008) Beyond DSGE models: toward an empirically based macroeconomics. *American Economic Review* 98: 236–240.

Cynamon, B. and Fazzari, S. (2013) Inequality and household finance during the consumer age. Working Paper 752, Levy Economics Institute.

Dawid, H. (2006) Agent-based models of innovation and technological change. In L. Tesfatsion and K.L. Judd (eds.), *Handbook of Computational Economics, Handbook of Computational Economics* (Vol. 2, Chap. 25,pp. 1235–1272). Elsevier.

Dawid, H. (2015) *Modeling the Economy as a Complex System*. IPEA, pp. 191–216.

Dawid, H., Harting, P., van der Hoog, S. and Neugart, M. (2016) A heterogeneous agent macroeconomic model for policy evaluation: improving transparency and reproducibility.

de Freitas, G.G. and Lima, G.T. (2007) debt financing and emergent dynamics of a financial fitness landscape, Anais do XXXV Encontro Nacional de Economia [Proceedings of the 35th Brazilian Economics Meeting] 064, ANPEC - Associação Nacional dos Centros de Pósgraduação em Economia [Brazilian Association of Graduate Programs in Economics]. https://ideas.repec.org/p/anp/en2007/064.html.

De Grauwe, P. (2008) Animal spirits and monetary policy. CESifo Working Paper Series 2418, CESifo Group Munich.

Delli Gatti, D., Gallegati, M. and Minsky, H.P. (1999) Financial institutions, economic policy, and the dynamic behavior of the economy. Macroeconomics 9903009, EconWPA. http://ideas.repec.org/p/wpa/wuwpma/9903009.html.

Delli Gatti, D., Di Guilmi, C., Gaffeo, E., Giulioni, G., Gallegati, M. and Palestrini, A. (2005) A new approach to business fluctuations: heterogeneous interacting agents, scaling laws and financial fragility. *Journal of Economic Behavior and Organization* 56: 489–512.

Delli Gatti, D., Di Guilmi, C., Gallegati, M. and Giulioni, G. (2007) Financial fragility, industrial dynamics, and business fluctuations in an agent-based model. *Macroeconomic Dynamics* 11: 62–79.

Delli Gatti, D., Gallegati, M., Greenwald, B., Russo, A. and Stiglitz, J.E. (2010) The financial accelerator in an evolving credit network. *Journal of Economic Dynamics and Control* 34:1627–1650.

Di Guilmi, C. (2008) *The Generation of Business Fluctuations: Financial Fragility and Mean-Field Interaction*. Peter Lang Publishing Group: Frankfurt/M.

Di Guilmi, C. and Carvalho, L. (2017) The dynamics of leverage in a Minskyan model with heterogeneous firms. *Journal of Economic Behavior and Organization*, forthcoming.

Di Guilmi, C., Gallegati, M. and Landini, S. (2017) *Interactive Macroeconomics*. Cambridge: Cambridge University Press.

Dos Santos, C.H. (2005) A stock-flow consistent general framework for formal Minskyan analyses of closed economies. *Journal of Post Keynesian Economics* 27: 712–735.

Dosi, G., Marengo, L. and Fagiolo, G. (2005) Evolutionary principles of economics, Cambridge. In K. Dopfer (ed.), *Learning in Evolutionary Environment*. Cambridge: Cambridge University Press.

Dosi, G., Fagiolo, G. and Roventini, A. (2008) The microfoundations of business cycles: an evolutionary, multi-agent model. *Journal of Evolutionary Economics* 18: 413–432.

Dosi, G., Fagiolo, G. and Roventini, A. (2010) Schumpeter meeting Keynes: a policy-friendly model of endogenous growth and business cycles. *Journal of Economic Dynamics and Control* 34: 1748–1767.

Dosi, G., Fagiolo, G., Napoletano, M. and Roventini, A. (2013) Income distribution, credit and fiscal policies in an agent-based Keynesian model. *Journal of Economic Dynamics and Control* 37: 1598–1625.

Dosi, G., Fagiolo, G., Napoletano, M., Roventini, A. and Treibich, T. (2015) Fiscal and monetary policies in complex evolving economies. *Journal of Economic Dynamics and Control* 52: 166–189.

Dosi, G., Pereira, M.C., Roventini, A. and Virgillito, M.E. (2016) When more flexibility yields more fragility: the microfoundations of Keynesian aggregate unemployment. LEM Papers Series 2016/06, Laboratory of Economics and Management (LEM), Sant'Anna School of Advanced Studies, Pisa, Italy.

Dutt, A.K. (1990) *Growth, Distribution and Uneven Development*. Cambridge: Cambridge University Press.

Eichner, A.S. and Kregel, J.A. (1975) An essay on post-Keynesian theory: a new paradigm in economics. *Journal of Economic Literature*, 13: 1293–1314.

Erlingsson, E.J., Teglio, A., Cincotti, S., Stefansson, H., Sturluson, J.T. and Raberto, M. (2014) Housing market bubbles and business cycles in an agent-based credit economy. *Economics: The Open-Access, Open-Assessment E-Journal* 8. https://doi.org/10.5018/economics-ejournal.ja.2014-8.

Foley, D.K. (1994) A statistical equilibrium theory of markets. *Journal of Economic Theory* 62: 321–345.

Foley, D.K. (2001) Hyman Minsky and the dilemmas of contemporary economic method. In R. Bellofiore and P. Ferri (eds.), *Financial Fragility and Investment in the Capitalist Economy: The Economic Legacy of Hyman Minsky* (Vol. I). Edwar Elgar.

Foley, D.K. (2017) Crisis and theoretical methods: equilibrium and disequilibrium once again. Working Papers 1703, New School for Social Research, Department of Economics. http://EconPapers.repec.org/RePEc:new:wpaper:1703.

Gallegati, M., Delli Gatti, D., Gaffeo, E., Giulioni, G. and Palestrini, A. (2007) *Emergent Macroeconomics*. Springer.

Gibson, B. and Setterfield, M. (2015a) Intermediation, money creation, and Keynesian macrodynamics in multi-agent systems. Working Papers 1511, New School for Social Research, Department of Economics.

Gibson, B. and Setterfield, M. (2015b) Real and financial crises in the Keynes-Kalecki structuralist model: an agent-based approach. Working Papers 1517, New School for Social Research, Department of Economics.

Godin, A. (2015) Special issue: post-Keynesian stock-flow consistent modelling editorial to the special issue. *European Journal of Economics and Economic Policies* 12: 29–31.

Greenwald, B. and Stiglitz, J.E. (1993) Financial markets imperfections and business cycles. *Quarterly Journal of Economics*.

Harcourt, G.C. and Kriesler, P. (eds). (2013) *The Oxford Handbook of Post-Keynesian Economics, Volume 2: Critiques and Methodology*. Oxford University Press.

King, J.E. (2015) *Advanced Introduction to Post Keynesian Economics*. London: Edward Elgar.

Kinsella, S., Greiff, M. and Nell, E.J. (2011) Income distribution in a stock-flow consistent model with education and technological change. *Eastern Economic Journal* 37: 134–149.

Kirman, A.P. (1992) Whom or what does the representative individual represent? *Journal of Economic Perspectives* 6: 117–136.

Lavoie, M. (2009) Towards a post-Keynesian consensus in macroeconomics: reconciling the Cambridge and Wall Street views. In E. Hein, T. Niechoj, and S. Engelbert (eds.), *Macroenomic Policies on Shaky Foundations - Wither Mainstream Economics?* (pp. 75–99). Marburg: Metropolis Verlag.

Lavoie, M. (2014) *Post-Keynesian Economics: New Foundations*. Edward Elgar.

Lengnick, M. (2013) Agent-based macroeconomics: a baseline model. *Journal of Economic Behavior and Organization* 86: 102–120.

McCombie, J. and Thirlwall, A.P. (1994) *Economic Growth and the Balance of Payments Constraint*. New York: St Martin's Press.

Michell, J. (2014) A Steindlian account of the distribution of corporate profits and leverage: a stock-flow consistent macroeconomic model with agent-based microfoundations. Working Papers PKWP1412, Post Keynesian Economics Study Group (PKSG).

Minsky, H.P. (1972) Financial stability revisited: the economics of disaster. Technical report, Board of Governors of the Federal Reserve System, Reappraisal of the Federal Reserve Discount Mechanism, Vol. 3, Washington, DC, pp. 95–136.

Minsky, H.P. (2008) *John Maynard Keynes* (1st edn). McGraw-Hill, 1975.

Nasica, E. (2000) *Finance, Investment, and Economic Fluctuations: An Analysis in the Tradition of Hyman P. Minsky.* Edward Elgar.

Nelson, R.R. and Winter, S.G. (1982) *An Evolutionary Theory of Economic Change.* Harvard University Press.

Perugini, C., Hölscher, J. and Collie, S. (2016) Inequality, credit and financial crises. *Cambridge Journal of Economics* 40: 227. + https://doi.org/10.1093/cje/beu075.

Piketty, T. (2014) *Capital in the Twenty-First Century.* Cambridge: Harvard University Press.

Raberto, M., Teglio, A. and Cincotti, S. (2012) Debt, deleveraging and business cycles: an agent-based perspective. *Economics - The Open-Access, Open-Assessment E-Journal* 6: 1–49.

Riccetti, L., Russo, A. and Gallegati, M. (2013) Leveraged network-based financial accelerator. *Journal of Economic Dynamics and Control* 37: 1626–1640.

Riccetti, L., Russo, A. and Gallegati, M. (2015) An agent based decentralized matching macroeconomic model. *Journal of Economic Interaction and Coordination* 10: 305–332.

Roos, M.W.M. (2015) The macroeconomics of radical uncertainty. Ruhr Economic Papers 592, RWI - Leibniz-Institut für Wirtschaftsforschung, Ruhr-University Bochum, TU Dortmund University, University of Duisburg-Essen.

Russo, A., Catalano, M., Gaffeo, E., Gallegati, M. and Napoletano, M. (2007) Industrial dynamics, fiscal policy and R&D: evidence from a computational experiment. *Journal of Economic Behavior & Organization* 64: 426–447.

Russo, A., Riccetti, L. and Gallegati, M. (2016) Increasing inequality, consumer credit and financial fragility in an agent based macroeconomic model. *Journal of Evolutionary Economics* 26: 25–47.

Schoder, C. (2017) A critical review of the rationale approach to the microfoundation of post-Keynesian theory. *Review of Political Economy* 29: 171–189.

Seppecher, P. (2010) Flexibility of wages and macroeconomic instability in an agent-based computational model with endogenous money. Copyright - Copyright FEDERAL RESERVE BANK OF ST LOUIS 2010; Last updated - 2015-10-03.

Seppecher, P. and Salle, I. (2015) Deleveraging crises and deep recessions: a behavioural approach. *Applied Economics* 47, 3771–3790.

Setterfield, M. and Budd, A. (2011) A Keynes-Kalecki model of cyclical growth with agent-based features. In P. Arestis (ed.), *Microeconomics, Macroeconomics and Economic Policy: Essays in Honour of Malcolm Sawyer* (pp. 228–250). London: Palgrave Macmillan UK. https://doi.org/10.1057/9780230313750_13.

Setterfield, M. and Gouri Suresh, S. (2016) Multi-agent systems as a tool for analyzing path-dependent macrodynamics. *Structural Change and Economic Dynamics* 38: 25–37.

Skott, P. (2012) Pluralism, the Lucas critique, and the integration of macro and micro. UMASS Amherst Economics Working Papers 2012-04, University of Massachusetts Amherst, Department of Economics.

Stiglitz, J.E. and Gallegati, M. (2011) Heterogeneous Interacting Agent Models for Understanding Monetary Economies. *Eastern Economic Journal* 37: 6–12.

Suresh, S.G. and Setterfield, M. (2015) Firm performance, macroeconomic conditions, and "animal spirits" in a post Keynesian model of aggregate fluctuations. *Journal of Post Keynesian Economics* 38: 38–63.

Taylor, L. and O'Connell, S.A. (1985) A Minsky crisis. *Quarterly Journal of Economics* 100: 871–885.

Thirlwall, A.P. (1993) The renaissance of Keynesian economics. *Quarterly review Banca Nazionale del Lavoro, Roma* 46: 327–337.

4

STOCK-FLOW CONSISTENT MACROECONOMIC MODELS: A SURVEY

Michalis Nikiforos

Levy Economics Institute of Bard College

Gennaro Zezza

Universita' di Cassino e del Lazio Meridionale, and Levy Economics Institute of Bard College

1. Introduction

The stock-flow consistent (henceforth SFC) approach to macroeconomic modelling has become increasingly popular among economists of different persuasions. Despite its roots going back at least five decades, its popularity increased exponentially after the recent crisis of 2007–2009. Two factors played a significant role in that: first, the 2007 publication of *Monetary Economics*, by Wynne Godley and Marc Lavoie (2007a), a book that summarizes and synthesizes the basic principles and modelling methods; and second, the recognition that models and policy analyses based on the SFC framework (e.g. Godley, 1999a) were able to predict the crisis, which caught the majority of the profession by surprise. For these two reasons, the years of the Great Recession are a demarcation point in time that separates the early period of the development of the SFC approach from the more recent period.

The main characteristic and advantage of the SFC approach is that it provides a framework for treating the real and the financial sides of the economy in an *integrated* way. In a modern capitalist economy, the behaviour of the real side of the economy cannot be understood without reference to the financial side (money, debt and assets markets). Although this is a general statement, it became particularly evident during the recent crisis and the slow recovery that followed (hence the aforementioned surge in the popularity of SFC models). For that reason, the SFC approach is an essential tool if one wants to examine the political economy of modern capitalism in a rigorous and analytical way.

The roots of the SFC approach go back to the late 1960s and 1970s, a 'hard time' for Keynesian economists, who saw their influence decline in favour of monetarism and then later New Classical economics (Dos Santos, 2006). The two main figures in these nascent years were

Analytical Political Economy, First Edition. Edited by Roberto Veneziani and Luca Zamparelli.

Wynne Godley at the University of Cambridge and James Tobin at Yale University. Godley, after working for 14 years at the Treasury, joined the University of Cambridge as the director of the Department of Applied Economics, within which he also formed the Cambridge Economic Policy Group. His writings at the time – most done together with Francis Cripps – contain the basic elements of the principles of SFC modelling that we will discuss below (Godley and Cripps, 1974, 1983; Cripps and Godley, 1976, 1978). Since these early days, the two basic characteristics of Godley's approach are an effort to combine economic theory and policy (not surprising for someone who had spent 14 years at the Treasury) and successive attempts to build rigorous models that combine the real and the financial sides of the economy.[1]

The work of Godley was highly influenced by Nicholas Kaldor. The two met while Godley was at the Treasury and it was Kaldor who brought him to Cambridge. Among other things, it was discussions with Kaldor that led Godley to identify and recognize the importance of the 'three balances', which we will discuss in some detail in Section 4. Kaldor had already mentioned these balances three decades earlier (Kaldor and Barna, 1944), though without then recognizing their importance.

At the same time, on the other side of the Atlantic, James Tobin developed a similar approach, which came to be known as the 'pitfalls' approach. The approach was developed in a series of papers, many of which were co-authored with William Brainard (Brainard and Tobin, 1968; Tobin, 1969; Backus et al., 1980), and was summarized in Tobin's Nobel Prize lecture (Tobin, 1982). According to Tobin, the main pitfall in financial model building is the failure to explicitly model that 'the prices and interest rates determined in these [financial] markets and the quantities to which they refer *both influence and are influenced by the "real economy"* [...]. These *interdependencies* are easy to acknowledge in principle but difficult to honour in practice, either in theoretical analysis or in empirical investigation' (Brainard and Tobin, 1968, p. 99; emphasis added). The aim of Tobin's research project was thus to provide an analysis that properly takes care of these interdependencies. As we will discuss in more detail in Section 2.2, among other things, Tobin set out the principles that determine portfolio choice within these models.

The latest part of this long first phase of the formation of the SFC approach started in 1994 when Godley arrived at the Levy Economics Institute of Bard College and ends with the publication of *Monetary Economics* (the book was the result of a long research project, undertaken together with Marc Lavoie from the University of Ottawa). At the same time, and in accordance with his preference for a combination of theory and policy, Godley created the Levy Macroeconomic Model, a policy model based on SFC principles that proved successful in predicting the downturn of 2001 and the Great Recession.

As we mentioned above, since the publication of *Monetary Economics* there have been extensive contributions to the literature adopting the SFC method to examine a variety of issues. The purpose of this paper is to provide a detailed survey of this literature, as well to show how this approach provides innovative contributions to policy debates related to austerity policies, balance of payment imbalances, long-term sustainable growth, etc. Towards that goal, in the next section we provide an overview of the basic principles of SFC modelling, which will also act as an entry and a reference point for the discussion that will follow. These principles can be divided into two broad categories. First, the building of the models starts with a lot of attention to accounting consistency. In the words of Taylor (2004b, p. 206), making sure that the accounting is right is often 'the best way to attack a problem in economics'. Careful accounting can lead to interesting conclusions in its own right because it imposes certain constraints and reduces the degrees of freedom of the model. The second category consists of the closure and the behavioural specifications of the model. SFC models have a post-Keynesian closure, in the sense that demand matters and full employment is not considered to be the general state of the economy. Moreover, and based on the early insights of Godley and Tobin, there is a thorough modelling of the real and the financial sides of the economy and of their *interdependencies*. The accounting structure of the model provides the basis for these modelling exercises.

The emphasis on careful accounting reveals the intellectual kinship of the SFC approach to national accounts-based macroeconomic models, first introduced by Richard Stone (e.g. Stone and Brown, 1962) as part of his wider pioneering work on national accounts. Stone preceded Godley as the first director of the Department of Applied Economics at the University of Cambridge. Stone's methodology was further developed as a base for fixed-price, multiplier-type analysis based on large social accounting matrices (Pyatt and Round, 1977, 1979; Pyatt, 1988; Round, 2003a, 2003b) and also then used as the accounting framework for computable general equilibrium (CGE) models (Johansen, 1960; Taylor and Black, 1974; Adelman and Robinson, 1978; Taylor *et al.*, 1980; Dervis *et al.*, 1982; Taylor, 1990; Dixon and Jorgenson, 2013).

Moreover, the integrated treatment of the financial and the real sectors provides a natural way to examine issues related to financial fragility and its links to the real economy. It is thus no coincidence that the work of Hyman Minsky (1975, 1986) has been very influential on the SFC literature. A lot of Godley's models and analyses formalize Minskyan ideas, while there is a considerable number of more recent papers that treat Minskyan themes in an SFC framework (Minsky also played an instrumental role in Godley's coming to the Levy Economics Institute).

Finally, it is worth mentioning that the principles of SFC analysis in one form or another were advocated and used by various scholars in parallel and sometimes crossing paths with the abovementioned protagonists. Paul Davidson (1968a) was one of the first to emphasize that money balances need to be taken into account in models of capital accumulation; he also provided an early exploration of the implications of portfolio choice for economic growth (Davidson, 1968b). Stock-flow consistency is a central element in the work of Alfred Eichner (e.g. 1987), who also emphasized the interdependences of the real and financial sectors and the need for a combined treatment. Lance Taylor arrived at the SFC approach through his extensive work on CGE models (cited above) and the structuralist theory of growth, distribution and finance [see Taylor, 1983, 1991; Taylor and O'Connell, 1985; Taylor (2008) provides a review of *Monetary Economics*]. Another author within the post-Keynesian tradition who has consistently been using rigorous analytical SFC models is Peter Skott (e.g. 1989). Finally, in addition to these Keynesian scholars, Duncan Foley (1982, 1986) used an (essentially) SFC model to formalize the circuit of capital originally proposed by Marx (1978) in volume II of *Capital*.

The rest of the paper proceeds as follows. The basic principles of SFC modelling are laid out in Section 2. In the first Subsection (2.1), we discuss the accounting principles and in the second Subsection (2.2) the closure and treatment of the real and financial sides of the economy in a generic SFC model. Section 3 presents how various contributions have extended and/or modified this generic treatment to examine issues related to the monetary circuit, financialization and changes in income distribution. In Section 4, we discuss how the basic model can be extended to deal with the implications of open-economy macroeconomics. The open-economy model allows us to introduce the 'three balances approach', which is one of the main building blocks of SFC analysis. The theoretical open-economy models allow us to discuss SFC models for whole countries as concrete economic policy tools in Section 5. Then, in Section 6, we present recent contributions of SFC applications to environmental issues. In recent years there has been an effort to use the SFC approach together with agent-based modelling, which we discuss in Section 7.

In Section 8, we conclude with a discussion of the name 'SFC'. We argue that the name is sometimes misleading and confusing; as we already mentioned, accounting consistency is just one side of the SFC approach, with a demand-led economy and an explicit treatment of the financial side being the other.

Finally, we need to say that there were two excellent survey papers of the SFC literature before this one: the first is Dos Santos (2006), written in the early era of SFC modelling, which tries to locate the SFC approach within different strands of Keynesian macroeconomic thought; and the second is Caverzasi and Godin (2015). The purpose of our paper is of course to update these surveys with the burgeoning recent literature, but also approach some issues from a different angle. In particular, we aim to provide a survey that is pedagogical and rigorous but also accessible to the non-specialist reader. Moreover, along the discussion we try to make clear the links between the theoretical elements underpinning the SFC methodology and broader macroeconomic debates, for example, the 'twin-deficits' hypothesis or the impact of austerity. Finally, our paper discusses some questions that cannot be found in these other papers, such as the meaning of the name SFC.

2. Basic Principles

2.1 Accounting Consistency

We can identify four main accounting principles of SFC macroeconomic modelling:

1. *Flow consistency*: Every monetary flow comes from somewhere and goes somewhere. As a result, there are no 'black holes' in the system. For example, the income of a household is a payment for a firm, and the exports of one country are the imports of another. In the jargon of the System of National Accounts (SNA) (European Commission *et al.*, 2009), this type of flow consistency between units (household-firm; country A–country B) is called 'horizontal' consistency. Another type of flow consistency is 'vertical' consistency, meaning that every transaction involves at least two entries within each unit, usually referred to as 'credit' and 'debit'. For example, when a household receives income, its deposits are credited by the same amount.
2. *Stock consistency*: The financial liabilities of an agent or sector are the financial assets of some other agent or sector. For example, a loan is a liability for a household and an asset for a bank; a Treasury bond is a liability for the government and an asset for its holder. As a result, the net financial wealth of the system as a whole is zero.
3. *Stock-flow consistency*: Every flow implies the change in one or more stocks. As a result, the end-of-period stocks are obtained by cumulating the relevant flows, and taking into account possible capital gains. More formally, $\Omega_t = \Omega_{t-1} + F_t + CG_t$, where Ω_t is the monetary value of the stock at the end of period t, F_t is the relevant flow and CG_t are net capital gains. Thus, stock-flow consistency implies that positive net saving leads, *ceteris paribus*, to an increase in net wealth and vice versa. For example, when the net saving of a household is positive, one or more of its assets increase (or one or more liabilities decrease) and its net wealth – save for capital gains – also increases.

Obviously, this equation can be rewritten as $\Delta\Omega_t = F_t + CG_t$, where Δ is the difference operator. From this perspective, the *change* in the stock, which is a flow in itself, is equal to the related flow and the capital gains. Stock-flow consistency is thus a logical corollary of the 'vertical' flow consistency. The flow-of-funds (FoF) accounts usually have separate tables for the flows ($\Delta\Omega_t$) and the level of stocks (Ω_t) of financial assets.[2]

4. *Quadruple entry*: These three principles, then, imply a fourth one: that every transaction involves a *quadruple entry* in accounting. For example, when a household purchases a product from a firm, the accounting registers an increase in the revenues of the firm and the expenditure of the household, and at the same time a decrease in at least one asset (or increase in a liability) of the household and correspondingly an increase in at a least one asset of the firm. Quadruple-entry bookkeeping was introduced by Morris Copeland (1947, 1949) and is now the fundamental accounting system underlying the SNA because it ties together the various types of accounting consistency and therefore guarantees the accounting consistency of the system as a whole (European Commission *et al.*, 2009, p. 50).

Among others things, these principles mean that the accounting structure of the SFC models follows that of the SNA – albeit with a varying level of detail determined by the research question that the model wants to address. The accounting structure of the SFC models is summarized within two matrices: the balance-sheet matrix and the transactions-flow matrix.

We can make the above clearer by introducing the accounting structure of a baseline model. Table 1 presents the balance-sheet matrix of a closed economy divided into five sectors: households, firms, government, the central bank and banks. We assume the existence of six financial assets: high-powered money (HPM), deposits, loans, bills, bonds and equities. These assets have one important difference related to their rate of return: the nominal rate of return of HPM is zero, while deposits, loans and bills have a nominal rate of return equal to their respective interest rate. On the other hand, the overall rate of return on bonds and equity consists of their income return (interest and dividends, respectively) but also of the possible capital gains.

The positive sign in the matrix denotes an asset and the negative a liability; the subscript denotes the holder of the related instrument. For example, bills (B) are a liability for the government but an asset for households, banks and the central bank. The principle of stock consistency is captured in the matrix by the sum of each row of financial assets being equal to zero. To continue with the bills, the amount of government liabilities under this form of bills is exactly equal to the holdings of bills on behalf of the other sectors, so that $B_g = B_h + B_b + B_{cb}$.

Table 1. Balance-Sheet Matrix.

	(1) Households	(2) Production Firms	(3) Government	(4) Central Bank	(5) Banks	(6) Total
(A) Fixed capital		$+PK$				$+PK$
(B) HPM	$+H_h$			$-H_{cb}$		0
(C) Deposits	$+D_h$				$-D_b$	0
(D) Loans	$-L_h$	$-L_c$			$+L_b$	0
(E) Bills	$+B_h$		$-B_g$	$+B_{cb}$	$+B_b$	0
(F) Bonds	$+p_{bl}BL_h$		$-p_{bl}BL_g$	$+p_{bl}BL_{cb}$	$+p_{bl}BL_b$	0
(G) Equities	$+p_eE_h$	$-p_eE_c$			$+p_eE_b$	0
(H) Balance (net worth)	$-V_h$	$-V_c$	$-V_g$	$-V_{cb}$	$-V_b$	$-PK$
(I) Sum	0	0	0	0	0	0

An important conclusion of this accounting exercise is that the common conception that government debt is a liability for future generations is misguided. Assuming that the government debt is not held by foreigners, Table 1 is telling us that it is a liability for the government and thus the taxpayers of the economy, but *at the same time* it is an asset of households and other domestic sectors. The 'future generations' that will have to pay for this debt – if they will have to – will also earn the proceeds of these payments.

The only tangible asset in Table 1 is fixed capital, which is an asset of the firms. Because of the stock consistency, all financial assets and liabilities cancel out. As a result, the overall net worth of the economy is equal to the value of the tangible assets – in this case, the fixed capital.

An important decision one needs to make when building an SFC model is how many assets to include. The more assets one includes, the more realistic the model becomes and the more real features of an actual economy it can potentially capture; however, this comes at the cost of the model becoming exponentially more complicated and less intuitive. For instance, in Table 1, residential capital has been omitted from the matrix. A second, related decision has to do with the holders of each asset. In reality, every sector holds (almost) every asset, but in a model one may choose to focus on only certain holders of each asset to keep the model as simple as possible.[3] These questions have to be addressed in relation to the research question at hand.

The accounting skeleton of the model is completed with the transactions-flows matrix, presented in Table 2. The matrix may seem intimidating to an inexperienced eye but it is not that complicated. Starting from column (2) in the upper part of the table we can see that – following the national accounts – total output is decomposed on the expenditure side into total consumption (*PC*), investment (*PI*) and government expenditure (*PG*), and on the income side into wages (*W*) and profits (Π).

A convention of the matrix is that sources of funds are denoted with a plus sign and uses of funds with a minus sign. Horizontal flow consistency requires that for each category of transactions the flow and uses of funds sum to zero. For example, in row (D) we see that the wages are a use of funds for the firms but a source of funds for the households. The other income sources of funds for the households are the distributed profits ($\Pi_{c,d}$) and the interest income on the various assets they are holding. On the other hand, a household's major uses of funds are the purchase of consumption goods, paying taxes (T_h) and the interest on their loans. The latter is equal to the interest rate on loans times the stock of their loans in the previous period ($r_{l-1}L_{h-1}$).

The difference between the overall sources and uses of funds is equal to the net lending of the sector. In the case of the household sector that is:

$$NL_h = [W + \Pi_{c,\,d} + r_{d-1}D_{h-1} + r_{b-1}B_{h-1} + r_{bl-1}BL_{h-1}] - [PC + T_h + r_{l-1}L_{h-1}] \quad (1)$$

Vertical accounting consistency requires specifying where this net lending goes. As we can see at the bottom part of column (1), positive net lending means an increase in the various financial assets held by the households (denoted with a minus sign since this is a use of funds) or a decrease in their loans. An important decision, which we will discuss in more detail in the following section, is how the households and the other sectors allocate not only their net lending, but also their already accumulated wealth among these assets. Overall, vertical consistency requires that the sum of each column of the table is also equal to zero.

The rest of the matrix can be read in a similar way, so we do not need to go through every entry. Four more comments are in order here. First, whenever a payment implies a change

Table 2. Transactions-Flows Matrix.

	(1)	(2)	(3)	(4)	(5)	(6)	(7)
		NFC					
	Households	Current	Capital	Government	Central Bank	Banks	Total
Transactions							
(A) Consumption	$-PC$	$+PC$					0
(B) Investment		$+PI$	$-PI$				0
(C) Gov. Expenditure		$+PG$		$-PG$			0
(D) [memo: Output]		$[PY]$					
(E) Wages	$+W$	$-W$					0
(F) NFC Profits	$+\Pi_{c,d}$	$-\Pi_c$	$+\Pi_{c,r}$				0
(G) Taxes	$-T_h$		$-T_c$	$+T$		$-T_b$	0
(H) C.B. Profits				$+\Pi_{cb}$	$-\Pi_{cb}$		0
(I) Interest on Deposits	$+r_{d-1}D_{h-1}$					$-r_{d-1}D_{h-1}$	0
(J) Interest on Loans	$-r_{l-1}L_{h-1}$		$-r_{l-1}L_{c-1}$			$+r_{l-1}L_{b-1}$	0
(K) Interest on Bills	$+r_{b-1}B_{h-1}$			$-r_{b-1}B_g$	$+r_{b-1}B_{cb-1}$	$+r_{b-1}B_{b-1}$	0
(L) Interest on Bonds	$+r_{bl-1}BL_{h-1}$			$-r_{bl-1}BL_g$	$+r_{bl-1}BL_{cb-1}$	$+r_{bl-1}BL_{b-1}$	0
Flow of Funds							
(M) [memo: Net Lending]	$[NL_h]$		$[NL_c]$	$[NL_g]$	$[NL_{cb}]$	$[NL_b]$	0
(N) Δ in HPM	$-\Delta H_h$				$+\Delta H$		0
(O) Δ in Deposits	$-\Delta D_h$					$+\Delta D_b$	0
(P) Δ in Loans	$+\Delta L_h$		$+\Delta L_c$			$-\Delta L_b$	0
(Q) Δ in Bills	$-\Delta B_h$			$+\Delta B_g$	$-\Delta B_{cb}$	$-\Delta B_b$	0
(R) Δ in Bonds	$-p_{bl}\Delta BL_h$			$+p_{bl}\Delta BL_g$	$-p_{bl}\Delta BL_{cb}$	$-p_{bl}\Delta BL_b$	0
(S) Δ in Equities	$-p_e\Delta E_h$		$+p_e\Delta E_c$			$-p_e\Delta E_b$	0
(T) Sum	0	0		0	0	0	0

in the stock of real or financial wealth it is a good idea to record it separately in the capital account. Therefore, in principle, all entries in the FoF part of the table should appear in a 'financial/capital account' column of each sector, with net lending transferred from the current account to the capital/financial account. In that sense the households would transfer their net lending to their capital account and this account would then record the changes in their assets and liabilities. For reasons of simplicity and economy of space, we opted for a simpler layout with one account for each sector.

The only sector where we cannot apply this simplifying treatment is the corporate sector. Investment (PI) is a transaction that takes place within the corporate sector: some firms buy investment goods from other firms that produce them. Similarly, the retained profits ($\Pi_{c,r}$) are also an income 'transfer' that takes place within the sector. To capture these intrasectoral transactions in a consistent way, we need to have the capital account of the firms in column (3). The difference between retained profits (net of taxes and interest payments) and investment is equal to the net lending of firms. At the lower part of the table we see that a negative lending (a net borrowing) is covered either by the issuance of new equity or by taking on more loans.

$$NL_c = \Pi_{c,r} - T_c - r_{l-1}L_{c-1} - PI = \Delta L_c + p_e\Delta E \qquad (2)$$

Second, the horizontal consistency also applies to the FoF part of the matrix, so that the overall change in every asset is equal to the change in the corresponding liability. For example, the increase in the loans offered by banks is equal to the increase in the loans assumed by households and firms; therefore, the stock consistency of the system is maintained. Algebraically, that means that the sum of each row in the lower part of the matrix is also zero.

The end-of-period values of the assets in the balance-sheet matrix (Table 1) are equal to their value at the beginning of the period plus the change during the period (as captured in the lower part of Table 2) and possible capital gains. In that sense, the FoF subtable provides the link between the balance-sheet matrices of successive periods. For example, in the case of the stock of loans – which do not have a price and therefore no capital gains are involved – their end-of-period value is:

$$L_h = L_{h-1} + \Delta L_h \tag{3}$$

with the latter term of the equation coming from the FoF subtable. In the case of assets with an explicit price, the end-of-period stock needs to take capital gains into account. So, the end-of-period stock of equities is:

$$p_e E = p_{e-1} \cdot E_{-1} + p_e \cdot \Delta E + \Delta p_e \cdot E_{-1} \tag{4}$$

where the last term ($\Delta p_e \cdot E_{-1}$) captures the capital gains, which are equal to the change in the value of the stock of equities at the end of the previous period (E_{-1}) due to changes in their prices (Δp_e). The institutions that produce FoF data usually provide a separate matrix, the so-called 'revaluation matrix', with information on the revaluation of the assets.

Finally, another important corollary of doing the accounting right is that the sum of the net lending of the sectors of our system is equal to zero:

$$NL_h + NL_c + NL_g + NL_{cb} = 0 \tag{5}$$

This is an important insight that was first pursued consistently by Godley in the late 1970s (Godley and Cripps, 1983). Although it is a simple accounting identity, it has far-reaching consequences for macroeconomic analysis and it is a good example of why a careful specification of the accounting structure of a model is essential.

One of the most important of these consequences is that negative net lending on behalf of a sector will tend to increase its debt-to-income ratio. For example, if we assume that the net lending of the banking sector in equation (5) is zero and the government is running large surpluses, then the private sector (households and firms) *must* be running large deficits, which in turn leads, *ceteris paribus*, to an increase in the indebtedness of that sector. A prolonged period with such a configuration can lead the private sector – to use the Minskyan terminology – from a hedge, to a speculative, and then a 'Ponzi' position (Minsky, 1975, 1986). This is an important point of contact between the SFC approach and the Minskyan analysis of financial markets and it also emphasizes the inter-linkages between the balance sheets of each sector and the net lending position of the *other* sectors.

Another way to portray the accounting skeleton of an economy is the so-called social accounting matrix (SAM). The SAM methodology was first introduced by Richard Stone and was then further developed as a base for multiplier fixed-price as well as for CGE models (see the references in the introduction). For reasons of economy of space we discuss the SAM exposition in an accompanying online appendix. For here it suffices to say that in a macro model, the choice between a transactions-flow matrix and a SAM is a matter of taste. If properly constructed, both matrices can convey the same information and guarantee the accounting consistency of the model.

2.2 Closure, Behavioural Specification and Equilibrium

Accounting consistency is a very important part of SFC methodology. Doing the accounting correctly reduces the degrees of freedom of a model and provides some important insights by itself. However, as Taylor and Lysy (1979) demonstrated in the context of CGE models, the conclusions of a model crucially depend on its 'closure' (the direction of causality among the macroeconomic variables). In that respect, the SFC literature has developed mostly inside the Keynesian school: it is the aggregate demand that sets the tone for the economy not only in the short run but also in the long run. Neoclassical macroeconomic models are – or should be – SFC, and thus satisfy the principles of the previous subsection.[4] However, in such models economic activity is determined from the supply side and finance plays a minor role.

Another important part of the model is its behavioural specification. From a technical point of view, if a model needs to determine n endogenous variables, and its accounting skeleton provides us with k independent accounting identities, we need $n-k$ more equations to solve the model.[5] These equations are provided by the specification of the behaviour of the various agents and sectors of the model.

There are five broad categories of behavioural assumptions that one needs to make. First, we need to specify how the agents determine their expenditure. In the model of Table 2, we need to specify a consumption function, an investment function and a government expenditure function. The latter is usually treated as a discretionary policy instrument, or modelled as a reaction function. The most common specification of the consumptions function is:

$$C_h = \alpha_1 \, Y_{h,d} + \alpha_2 \left(\frac{V_{h-1}}{P_{-1}} \right) \tag{6}$$

where $PY_{h,d} = PY_h - T_h$ is the nominal disposable income of the households and α_1, α_2 are positive constants. In other words, real consumption is assumed to be a function of real disposable income and the lagged real wealth. On the other hand, the investment function is usually a variant of the following specification:

$$g = \frac{I}{K} = \beta_0 + \beta_1 \frac{\Pi_{c,r-1}}{(PK)_{-1}} - \beta_2 \frac{L_{c-1}}{(PK)_{-1}} + \beta_3 \frac{L_{c-1} + p_{e-1}E_{c-1}}{(PK)_{-1}} + \beta_4 \frac{Y_{-1}}{K_{-1}} \tag{7}$$

Investment (normalized for capital stock) is a positive function of retained profits ($\Pi_{c,r-1}/(PK)_{-1}$), the degree of indebtedness ($L_{c-1}/(PK)_{-1}$), the valuation ratio ($q = [L_{c-1} + p_{e-1}E_{c-1}]/(PK)_{-1}$) and capacity utilization (Y_{-1}/K_{-1}).[6]

An important feature of both consumption and investment as specified above is that they depend on past values of stocks of assets and liabilities (the stock of wealth, of loans, of capital, etc.). In other words, the stocks, as determined at the end of each period, feed back into the flows of the next period, which in turn determine the stocks of that period and so on. This makes the model dynamic, and the position of the system at every time period is determined by its historical path.

The second category of behavioural assumptions is related to how the agents finance their expenditure and possible net borrowing position. In our example, one needs to specify: how the government decides the portion of its deficit that is covered through short-term bills and long-term bonds; how the firms will cover a possible discrepancy between investment and retained profits; and finally how households decide how much of their expenditure will be financed with new loans. It is common to specify this set of decisions as simple linear functions, for example, the demand for loans on behalf of households is a constant proportion of their income (Godley and Lavoie, 2007a, ch. 11) or that firms finance a fixed proportion of their investment with new equities (Lavoie and Godley, 2001; Taylor, 2004a, ch. 8; Godley and Lavoie, 2007a, ch. 11). It goes without saying that a more sophisticated specification is possible, albeit at the cost of increasing the complexity of the model.

The third category of behavioural assumptions is how agents, especially households, allocate their wealth. With reference to Tables 1 and 2, we can see that a household's decision on how much to consume and borrow also implies how much they will save, which in turn – together with the stock of wealth from the previous period and possible capital gains – determines the value of their stock of wealth at the end of the period. The question then is how households allocate this wealth between various possible assets. If there are m possible assets, one needs to specify the demand for $m - 1$ of them, with the demand for the last one following residually.

Assets are usually allocated according to 'Tobinesque' principles (Tobin, 1969, 1982; Godley, 1999b; Godley and Lavoie, 2007a, ch. 5). More formally, the demand for the various assets is specified as:

$$a = \lambda_0 + \Lambda R + \lambda_m (Y_{d,h}/V_h) \tag{8}$$

where a is a vector of the demand for m assets as a share of total wealth, λ_0 is a vector of constants, R is a vector of the (expected) real rates of returns of the various assets and Λ is a square matrix of the effects of the returns of the assets on their demand and the demand for the other assets (with the main diagonal of the matrix capturing the effect of the rate of return of each asset on its own demand). Finally, λ_m is a vector that captures the effect of disposable income on the demand for the assets. The size of the vectors and the order of Λ is m. The real rate of returns for each asset is comprised by its income yield (interest or dividend) and capital gains corrected for inflation.

The logical constraints on these vectors are: (i) that the sum of the elements of λ_0 is equal to unity, meaning that the sum of the shares of each asset are equal to unity; and (ii) that the sum of each of the columns of Λ and the elements of λ_m are equal to zero, meaning that an increase in the demand for an asset – due to a change in the return on an asset or disposable income – needs to be matched with an equiproportional decrease in demand for one or more other assets. To close the specification of the parameters of equation (8), Godley (1996) proposed an additional constraint: the sum of each row of Λ needs to be equal to zero, meaning that the effect of a change in the return on an asset, all other returns remaining equal, should, in principle, be the same as the effect of an equiproportional change of the other returns, with the specific return remaining constant. A common alternative to this horizontal constraint follows Friedman (1978) and Karacaoglu (1984) and assumes that the Λ is symmetric. The symmetry constraint implies the horizontal adding-up constraint, but not the other way around.

It is worth pointing out a substantial difference between Tobin and Godley on the issue of portfolio behavior. Tobin's main contribution was to explain what happens when portfolios are not at their equilibrium value, for a given level of output, describing the transition towards the equilibrium portfolio (e.g. Tobin 1969, 1982). On the other hand, Godley assumes that agents succeed in achieving their desired portfolios in each period, and examines the consequences of various shocks on real and financial variables, thus examining the interaction between stocks of assets and real variables (including output) during the transition (e.g. Godley 1999b; Godley and Lavoie 2007a: ch. 5).

A fourth set of behavioural assumptions is related to the specification of productivity growth, wages and inflation. The SFC literature so far has not focused on productivity issues. As a result, productivity is usually assumed to be constant or in some cases to grow at an exogenously given rate. Inflation is the result of the conflict between wage earners and their employers. The former are posited to have certain real wage aspirations that depend on labour productivity and the state of the labour market, and the nominal wage reacts – through a certain parameter – to the gap between the targeted and actual wage. The price level is then determined with a markup on the unit cost of production.

To close the system, one then needs to specify a final (fifth) set of assumptions about the behaviour of the financial system. More specifically, we need to specify the behaviour of the banks and how monetary policy is conducted. For example, with regard to the latter, a common assumption is that the central bank buys any quantity of government liabilities that are not demanded by the private sector and supplies an amount of HPM equal to its demand. In that way, it is able to exogenously set the interest rate and the quantity of money becomes endogenous; this is in opposition to the common neoclassical quantity theory of money, where it is the central bank that exogenously determines the quantity of money. When it comes to the banks, we again need to specify what assets are issued by other entities, what quantities of these assets they choose to hold and, very importantly, how they supply credit. Common specifications include a purely Wicksellian type of banking sector, where banks supply whatever loans are demanded (for example, this is the running assumption in most chapters of Godley and Lavoie (2007a)) or some kind of credit rationing (e.g. Le Heron and Mouakil, 2008; Caiani *et al.*, 2016).

The accounting skeleton, as sketched in the previous section, *together with* the demand-led closure, *and* the behavioural assumptions for the components of aggregate demand, *and* the explicit treatment of financial assets allows for an *integrated* analysis of the real and the financial sides of the economy. These kinds of models are diametrically opposed to models that have dominated macroeconomic discourse over the last three decades, where the real variables are independent from the monetary variables. In SFC models, decisions made by the agents of the economy on debt, credit and assets and liabilities allocation have an impact on the determination of the real variables and vice versa. As the recent crisis made very clear, this is a better way to understand a modern capitalist economy.

In the short run, 'equilibrium' is reached through price adjustments in financial markets, while output adjustments guarantee that overall saving is equal to investment. However, such 'equilibrium' is not a state of rest, since the expectations that drive expenditure and portfolio decisions may not be fulfilled, and/or the end-of-period level for at least one stock in the economy is not at its target level, so that such discrepancies influence decisions in the next period.

In theoretical SFC models, the long-run equilibrium is defined as the state where the stock–flow ratios are stable. In other words, the stocks and the flows grow at the same rate. The system converges towards that equilibrium with a sequence of short-run equilibria, and thus follows the Kaleckian dictum that 'the long-run trend is but a slowly changing component of a chain of short-run situations; it has no independent entity' (Kalecki, 1971, p. 165). The adjustment takes place because stocks and stock–flow ratios are relevant for the decisions of the agents of the economy. If stocks did not feed back into flows, the model may generate ever-increasing (or decreasing) stock–flow ratios: a result that might be SFC, but at the same time unendurable. The convergence towards the long-run equilibrium also depends on more conventional hypotheses regarding the parameters of the model.

The relevance of stocks also implies that agents have some desired stock–flow 'norm' that they are trying to achieve. For example, using the identity $\Delta V = PY_{h,d} - PC_h$ we can rewrite the consumption function of equation (6) as:

$$\frac{\Delta V_h}{P} = \alpha_2 \left[\alpha_3 Y_{h,d} - \left(\frac{V_{h-1}}{P_{-1}} \right) \right] \tag{9}$$

where $\alpha_3 = (1 - \alpha_1)/\alpha_2$ is the ratio of wealth to income (a stock–flow norm) that households target. The change in wealth, and thus also consumption, is a reaction to the discrepancy of this norm from the actual ratio. When the ratio of (lagged) wealth to income is lower than the norm (when the term in square brackets is positive), households will adjust their behaviour accordingly to move closer to their target. In the long-run equilibrium the stock–flow norm is achieved.

Besides its theoretical interest, at a practical level and in more policy-oriented analyses, a so-defined long-run equilibrium can act as a benchmark because a situation that is characterized by a constant increase (or decrease) of a stock–flow ratio is likely to be unsustainable. For example, Godley (1999a) characterized the configuration of the U.S. economy as unsustainable because of the high net borrowing of the private sector, which led to a continuous increase in its debt-to-income ratio.

3. Extensions: Finance, the Monetary Circuit and Income Distribution

As mentioned above, the main purpose of the SFC approach is to provide an integrated framework for treating the linkages between the real and financial sectors. For that reason, the baseline model of the previous section can be, and has been, extended to examine issues of this kind, the treatment of which does not allow abstraction from either the real or the financial side of the economy.

Some important extensions of the model are related to financialization, that is, 'the increasing role of financial motives, financial markets, financial actors, and financial institutions in the operation of the domestic and international economies' (Epstein, 2005, p. 3). Two integral parts of the process of financialization – which have also been treated in the literature – are the new perspective on corporate governance that prioritizes shareholder value as the ultimate goal of a firm (Lazonick and O'Sullivan, 2000) and the increase in income inequality that has accompanied these trends over the last three-and-a-half decades.

Moreover, in highlighting real financial interactions the SFC approach has many similarities to the theory of the monetary circuit (TMC), usually associated with Augusto Graziani (2003). Such similarities were noted early (Godley 2004; Lavoie, 2004) and paved the way for a number of circuitist analyses of the developments in the financial sector (Bellofiore and Passarella, 2010; Passarella, 2012, 2014; Botta et al., 2015; Sawyer and Passarella, 2017), as well as comparisons between the TMC and SFC approaches (Zezza, 2012).

In a fairly complex model, Botta et al. (2015) disaggregate the household sector into 'workers' and 'rentiers', and introduce special purpose vehicles, money market mutual funds, investment funds and 'broker and dealers' as parts of the financial sector, with a high level of detail in the balance sheet for each sector, where they consider two real assets (productive capital and housing) and nine financial assets (loans, mortgages, deposits, obligations of financial and nonfinancial firms, money shares, longer shares, asset-backed securities and repos). They provide a very rich and enlightening view of a complex, modern financialized economy, but do not attempt to provide formal behavioural rules for portfolio management, nor a closure for their model, which therefore is limited to a (very interesting) accounting framework.

Sawyer and Passarella (2017) adopt a simpler accounting structure, distinguishing only banks from other financial intermediaries, and only consider loans, deposits, securities and derivatives; however, they provide a full-blown 'behavioural' model, which they use for simulating the impact of different shocks to the economy. They show how the TMC distinction between 'initial finance' (the creation of liquidity to finance the start of the production process) and 'final finance' (the sources of funds for investment) is very relevant for understanding financialization. They also distinguish between workers and rentiers in order to examine the role of changes in the personal distribution of income due to financialization, showing that the transformation of household loans into financial products, along with the effect of the class divide on access to bank credit, are the main drivers of a worsening in income distribution and an increase in household debt.

An early SFC treatment of financialization (not explicitly linked to TMC) is Skott and Ryoo (2008). They demonstrate that the effects of financialization critically depend on whether we assume a labour-constrained 'mature' economy or a 'dual' economy. Further work that addresses financialization and income distribution is van Treeck (2009), who pays particular attention to the shareholder value orientation. The simulations of his model reproduce some central stylized facts of financialization, like the decoupling of profitability from investment and the increase in income inequality. Related to that, Dallery and van Treeck (2011) develop a model to study the conflicting claims among workers, shareholders and managers, using model simulations to generate patterns resembling the stylized facts of a 'Fordist regime', where capital accumulation is the primary objective of managers, and a 'financialization regime', where the maximization of shareholder value is the primary goal.

A large number of contributions adopt the SFC methodology to formalize Minskyan concepts, especially after the 2007–2009 recession, which brought Minsky back into fashion (Dos Santos, 2005; Dos Santos and Macedo e Silva, 2009; Bellofiore and Passarella, 2010; Morris and Juniper, 2012; Dafermos, 2015). Well before the recession, Dos Santos (2005) noted that the attempts at formalizing Minsky's 'financial instability hypothesis' were lacking a common ground, while the SFC approach could provide a framework where many of Minsky's insights, such as the interrelation among balance sheets, could be better dealt with. Later contributions, such as Dos Santos and Macedo e Silva (2009), tried to show how SFC models could provide a starting point for a dynamic analysis of a business cycle with Minskyan features, a result that is achieved with a model of greater complexity by Dafermos (2015), who combines Godley's New Cambridge approach with some Minskyan assumptions. In his model, private expenditure is driven by a target net-assets-to-income ratio, but such a target ratio – following Minsky – changes over the cycle as a result of changes in expectations and the conventions of borrowers and lenders. In this way, the model is useful for understanding how instability can emerge and which policies are appropriate to counter such instability. Similarly, Le Heron (2011) uses a Minskyan SFC model that explicitly incorporates the role of expectations and confidence of the private sectors (households, firms, banks). He shows that the erosion of confidence is a central transmission channel of a financial crisis with strong self-fulfilling characteristics.

The SFC approach to a closed economy has also been used for a more detailed treatment of the household sector, which allows one to deal with issues related to the distribution of income. Dafermos and Papatheodorou (2015) develop a model with rich detail in household groups, which are split among low and high skilled, employed and unemployed and entrepreneurs.

This framework allows the authors to consistently address the link between the functional and the personal distribution of income.

In a more recent paper, Nikiforos (2016) presents a model that shows how, in the face of an increase in income inequality, the decrease in the saving rate (and thus the increase in the indebtedness) of the households at the bottom 90% of the distribution was a prerequisite for the maintenance of full employment in the three decades before the crisis. In turn, the asset bubbles of the period were necessary for sustaining this process. Nikiforos, following Godley (1999a), Zezza (2011) and Papadimitriou *et al.* (2014d), calls the increase in income inequality the 'eighth unsustainable process' of the U.S. economy and argues that a decrease in inequality is necessary for sustainable growth in the future.

The core model has also been extended to include more than one real asset. The role of the housing market bubble in the Great Recession of 2007–2009 led to SFC models that treated residential capital separately and examined the relation between real estate prices and income distribution. Zezza (2007, 2008) built models to explore the distributional implications of the housing market boom. Similar arguments have been put forward by Lavoie (2009) and Nikolaidi (2015). Finally, in a recent paper, Herbillon-Leprince (2016) extends the model to include – in addition to residential capital – land owned by a capitalist-landowner sector and whose supply is constant.

4. Modelling the Open Economy

The discussion so far has been limited to closed-economy models. However, open-economy models are able to provide significant insights at both a theoretical and a practical level. This is a statement that applies to all macroeconomic models, but is especially true for SFC models.

Introducing the open economy in a consistent way means that one needs to specify the structure of the domestic *and* the foreign economy, as well as the interactions between them. As in the case of the closed economy, we can start from the balance sheets. Table 3 presents the balance sheets of various sectors for a two-economy model. The sectoral decomposition of the two economies is the same as in the closed-economy model of Section 2, as are the available assets. The difference is that there are financial assets issued domestically and in the foreign country. Agents hold assets and assume liabilities issued both in their country and abroad. The symbol * denotes abroad. When it comes to assets, the superscript * denotes assets issued abroad, while the subscript * refers to assets held abroad. So, for example H_h^* is foreign HPM held by domestic households, while H_{h*}^* is foreign HPM held by households abroad. The balance sheets of each economy are denominated in local currency. Therefore, the assets issued abroad are converted into domestic currency with the use of the exchange rate (ε), that is, the number of domestic currency units per foreign currency unit. As a result, all the assets issued in the foreign economy are included on the domestic balance sheets, multiplied by ε and vice versa.

In Table 3, we have assumed that the agents of each economy hold the same types of domestic and foreign assets. For example, households in both countries hold all types of assets and assume loans issued both from the banks of their countries and banks abroad. The only exception is the central banks of the two countries. Implicitly, an underlying assumption for Table 3 is that foreign currency has the special status of a reserve currency, so the domestic central bank holds foreign assets as reserves while the foreign central bank (presumably that of the U.S.) holds no foreign asset.

Accounting consistency dictates that the financial assets of someone are the liabilities of others; therefore, each row of the table (adjusted by the exchange rate) sums to zero and the

Table 3. Balance-Sheet Matrix for Two Economies.

		(1) Households	(2) Production Firms	(3) Government	(4) Central Bank	(5) Banks	(6) [XR]	(7) Households	(8) Production Firms	(9) Government	(10) Central Bank	(11) Banks	(12) Total
					Domestic Economy						*Foreign Economy*		
Domestically issued assets	(A) Fixed capital		$+PK$						$+P^*K^*$				$+PK + \varepsilon P^* K^*$
	(B) HPM	$+H_h$			$-H_{cb}$		[ε]	$+(1/\varepsilon)H_{h*}$					0
	(C) Deposits	$+D_h$				$-D_b$	[ε]	$+(1/\varepsilon)D_{h*}$					0
	(D) Loans	$-L_h$	$-L_c$			$+L_b$	[ε]	$-(1/\varepsilon)L_{h*}$	$-(1/\varepsilon L_{c*})$				0
	(E) Bills	$+B_h$		$-B_g$	$+B_{cb}$	$+B_b$	[ε]	$+(1/\varepsilon)B_{h*}$				$+(1/\varepsilon)B_{b*}$	0
	(F) Bonds	$+p_{BL}BL_h$		$-p_{bl}BL_g$	$+p_{bl}BL_{cb}$	$+p_{BL}BL_b$	[ε]	$+(1/\varepsilon)p_{BL}BL_{h*}$				$+(1/\varepsilon)p_{BL}BL_{b*}$	0
	(G) Equities	$+p_e E_h$	$-p_e E_c$			$+p_e E_b$	[ε]	$+(1/\varepsilon)p_e E_{h*}$				$+(1/\varepsilon)p_e E_{b*}$	0
Foreign issued assets	(H) HPM	$+\varepsilon H_h^*$			$-\varepsilon H_{cb}^*$		[ε]	$+H_*^*$			$-H_{cb*}^*$		
	(I) Deposits	$+\varepsilon D_h^*$					[ε]	$+D_*^*$				$-D_{b*}^*$	0
	(J) Loans	$-\varepsilon L_h^*$	$-\varepsilon L_c^*$				[ε]	$-L_{h*}^*$	$-L_{c*}^*$			$+L_{b*}^*$	0
	(K) Bills	$+\varepsilon B_h^*$			$+\varepsilon B_{cb}^*$	$+\varepsilon B_b^*$	[ε]	$+B_{h*}^*$		$-B_{g*}^*$	$+B_{cb*}^*$	$+B_{b*}^*$	0
	(L) Bonds	$+\varepsilon p_{bl}^* BL_h^*$			$+\varepsilon p_{bl}^* BL_{cb}^*$	$+\varepsilon p_{bl}^* BL_b^*$	[ε]	$+p_{BL}^* BL_{h*}^*$		$-p_{bl}^* BL_{g*}^*$	$+p_{bl}^* BL_{cb*}^*$	$+p_{bl}^* BL_{b*}^*$	0
	(M) Equities	$+\varepsilon p_e^* E_h^*$				$+\varepsilon p_e^* E_b^*$	[ε]	$+p_e^* E_{h*}^*$	$-p_e^* E_{c*}^*$			$+p_e^* E_{b*}^*$	0
	(N) Net worth	$-V_h$	$-V_c$	$-V_g$	$-V_{cb}$	$-V_b$		$-V_{h*}^*$	$-V_{c*}^*$	$-V_{g*}^*$	$-V_{cb*}^*$	$-V_{b*}^*$	$-PK - \varepsilon P^* K^*$
	(O) Sum	0	0	0	0	0		0	0	0	0	0	0

overall net financial asset position (NFA) of the whole system is zero as well. The overall net worth of the two economies combined is equal to their tangible assets, whose value in domestic currency units is $PK + \varepsilon P^* K^*$. Since, the overall NFA of the system is zero, if one country has a positive NFA, then the other's is negative: $NFA = -NFA_*$.

The transactions-flow matrix (Table 4) is also easily understood based on the principles laid out in Section 2. A few comments are important. First, as we can see in rows (E) and (F), accounting consistency dictates that the exports of one country are the imports of the other country. This is a trivial but often neglected point. The policy recommendations advising that all countries should try to increase their competitiveness and pursue export-led growth violate this principle, as one country cannot pursue export-led growth if at least one other country does not absorb these exports.

Another difference of the open-economy transactions-flow matrix is that the sectors receive and pay income abroad based on the respective foreign-denominated assets and liabilities they hold. For example, because they hold equities of foreign firms, domestic households now receive dividends from abroad ($\varepsilon \Pi^*_{c,d}$), as well as interest income on deposits at foreign banks, and bills and bonds issued abroad. In turn, they pay interest for loans they have taken from foreign banks. The net income transfers together with the trade balance sum up to the current account balance, or the net lending of the foreign sector (NL_f). A positive trade balance and a positive net interest income contribute to a positive current account balance (or to a negative NL_f; i.e. the foreign sector is a 'net borrower').

As in the case of the closed economy, positive net lending for a sector leads to an increase in the sector's NFA. For reasons of economy of space, the FoF part of Table 4 does not present the changes in every asset and liability in detail; it summarizes the change in the net financial position in domestic and foreign assets.

Moreover, as before, the sum of the net lending of the various sectors of the economy is equal to zero. The important thing here is that now the net lending of the foreign sector is included in this identity. If we group the domestic sectors into a private and a government sector, this implies that:

$$NL_p + NL_g + NL_f = 0 \tag{10}$$

where NL_p is the net lending position of the private sector. In the related literature, equation (10) is often referred to as the 'three balances' or the 'fundamental identity' (Lavoie, 2014, p. 258). The examination of the three balances in conjunction with total income can help us identify which component of aggregate demand contributes to growth. The net lending position of each sector also gives us information about the trajectory of its debt and net worth.

This kind of analysis based on the three balances was the central axis of Wynne Godley's *Seven Unsustainable Processes* (1999a), the most famous piece on economic policy based on SFC methodology. The main idea of Godley's argument is that during the 1990s, the United States experienced a large exogenous increase in their current account deficit (due to the 'successful invasion' of their markets by foreign competitors) and the government consolidated its budget (2000 was the only year in the post-war period that the government sector achieved a surplus). As a result, and based on equation (10), the only way for the economy to sustain the robust growth of the period was through a large increase in net borrowing and thus the indebtedness of the private sector. In fact, the rate of the accumulation of debt was so fast that despite the high growth rate of the economy, it led to a continuous increase in the debt-to-income ratio of the private sector – a Minskyan process where the private sector moves from a hedge, to a speculative and then a Ponzi position. As we explained above, a process that entails a

Table 4. Transactions-Flow Matrix for Two Economies.

Columns (1)–(7): Domestic Economy. Columns (8)–(14): Foreign Economy. NFC comprises Current/Capital: columns (2)–(3) (domestic) and (9)–(10) (foreign).

	(1) Households	(2) Current	(3) Capital	(4) Government	(5) Central Bank	(6) Banks	(7) [XR]	(8) Households	(9) Current	(10) Capital	(11) Government	(12) Central Bank	(13) Banks	(14) Total
(A) Transactions														
(B) Consumption	$-PC$	$+PC$						$-P^*C^*$	$+P^*C^*$					0
(C) Investment		$+PI$	$-PI$						$+P^*I^*$	$-P^*I^*$				0
(D) Gov. Expenditure		$+PG$		$-PG$					$+P^*G^*$		$-P^*G^*$			0
(E) Domestic Exports		$+PX$					$[\varepsilon]$		$-P^*M^*$					0
(F) Domestic Imports		$-PM$					$[\varepsilon]$		$+P^*X^*$					0
(G) *[memo: Output]*		$[PY]$							$[P^*Y^*]$					
(H) Wages	$+W$	$-W$						$+W^*$	$-W^*$					0
(I) Dom. Profits	$+\Pi_{c,d}$	$-\Pi_c$	$+\Pi_{c,r}$				$[\varepsilon]$	$+(1/\varepsilon)\Pi_{c,d*}$						0
(J) For. Profits	$+\varepsilon\Pi^*_{c,d}$						$[\varepsilon]$	$+\Pi^*_{c,d*}$	$-\Pi^*_c$	$+\Pi^*_{c,c}$				0
(K) Taxes	$-T_h$		$-T_c$	$+T$		$-T_b$		$-T^*_h$		$-T^*_c$	$+T^*$		$-T^*_b$	0
(L) C.B. Profits				$+\Pi_{cb}$	$-\Pi_{cb}$						$+\Pi^*_{cb}$	$-\Pi^*_{cb}$		0
Interest on														
(M) Dom. Deposits	$+r_{d-1}D_{h-1}$					$-r_{d-1}D_{b-1}$	$[\varepsilon]$	$+(1/\varepsilon)r_{d-1}D_{h*-1}$						0
(N) Dom. Loans	$-r_{-1}L_{h-1}$		$-r_{-1}L_{c-1}$			$+r_{-1}L_{b-1}$	$[\varepsilon]$	$-(1/\varepsilon)r_{-1}L_{h*-1}$		$-(1/\varepsilon)r_{-1}L_{c*-1}$				0
(O) Dom. Bills	$+r_{b-1}B_{h-1}$			$-r_{b-1}B$	$+r_{b-1}B_{cb-1}$	$+r_{b-1}B_{b-1}$	$[\varepsilon]$	$+(1/\varepsilon)r_{b-1}B_{h*-1}$					$+(1/\varepsilon)r_{b-1}B_{b*-1}$	0
(P) Dom. Bonds	$+r_{bl-1}BL_{h-1}$			$-r_{bl-1}BL$	$+r_{bl-1}BL_{cb-1}$	$+r_{bl-1}BL_{b-1}$	$[\varepsilon]$	$+(1/\varepsilon)r_{bl-1}BL_{h*-1}$					$+(1/\varepsilon)r_{bl-1}BL_{b*-1}$	0
(Q) For. Deposits	$+\varepsilon r^*_{d-1}D^*_{h-1}$						$[\varepsilon]$	$+r^*_{d-1}D^*_{h*-1}$					$-r^*_{d-1}D^*_{b*-1}$	0
(R) For. Loans	$-\varepsilon r^*_{-1}L^*_{h-1}$		$-\varepsilon r^*_{-1}L^*_{c-1}$				$[\varepsilon]$	$-r^*_{-1}L^*_{h*-1}$		$-r^*_{-1}L^*_{c*-1}$			$+r^*_{-1}L^*_{b*-1}$	0
(S) For. Bills	$+\varepsilon r^*_{b-1}B^*_{h-1}$				$+\varepsilon r^*_{b-1}B^*_{cb-1}$	$+\varepsilon r^*_{b-1}B^*_{b-1}$	$[\varepsilon]$	$+r^*_{b-1}B^*_{h*-1}$			$-r^*_{b-1}B^*$	$+r^*_{b-1}B^*_{cb*-1}$	$+r^*_{b-1}B^*_{b*-1}$	0
(T) For. Bonds	$+\varepsilon r^*_{bl-1}BL^*_{h-1}$				$+\varepsilon r^*_{bl-1}BL^*_{cb-1}$	$+\varepsilon r^*_{bl-1}BL^*_{b-1}$	$[\varepsilon]$	$+r^*_{bl-1}BL^*_{h*-1}$			$-r^*_{bl-1}BL^*$	$+r^*_{bl-1}BL^*_{cb*-1}$	$+r^*_{bl-1}BL^*_{b*-1}$	0
Flow of Funds														
(U) *[memo: Net Lending]*	$[NL_h]$		$[NL_c]$	$[NL_g]$	$[NL_{cb}]$	$[NL_b]$	$[\varepsilon]$	$[NL^*_h]$		$[NL^*_c]$	$[NL^*_g]$	$[NL^*_{cb}]$	$[NL^*_b]$	0
(V) Δ in NFA	$-\Delta NFA_h$		$-\Delta NFA_c$	$-\Delta NFA_g$	$-\Delta NFA_{cb}$	$-\Delta NFA_b$	$[\varepsilon]$	$-\Delta NFA_{h*}$		$-\Delta NFA_{c*}$	$-\Delta NFA_{g*}$	$-\Delta NFA_{cb*}$	$-\Delta NFA_{b*}$	0
(W) Δ in NFA*	$-\Delta NFA^*_h$		$-\Delta NFA^*_c$	$-\Delta NFA^*_g$	$-\Delta NFA^*_{cb}$	$-\Delta NFA^*_b$	$[\varepsilon]$	$-\Delta NFA^*_{h*}$		$-\Delta NFA^*_{c*}$	$-\Delta NFA^*_{g*}$	$-\Delta NFA^*_{cb*}$	$-\Delta NFA^*_{b*}$	0
(X) Sum	0	0	0	0	0	0		0	0	0	0	0	0	0

continuous increase of a stock–flow ratio is unsustainable. A more formal discussion of Godley's argument can be found in Nikiforos (2016).

Therefore, the three balances approach ties together the performance of the foreign sector and the fiscal stance of the government with the trajectory of the balance sheets of the private sector and the performance of the economy. This approach remains a central aspect of the Levy Institute's policy analyses for the USA economy, which are produced with updated versions of the model that Godley created in the 1990s and used for his 'Seven Unsustainable Processes'; the same is true for the SFC macroeconometric model that we recently developed for the Greek economy (Papadimitriou et al., 2013a). One of the main underlying assumptions of the austerity policies in Greece and elsewhere in Europe is that austerity (a steep increase in NL_g) will improve the competitiveness of the country and thus decrease NL_f without a negative effect on the growth rate. In reality, although austerity has led to an increase in NL_g and a decrease in NL_f, the adjustment took place through the output: the operation succeeded, but the patient died. An analysis of eurozone imbalances through the prism of the three balances is also provided in Semieniuk et al. (2011).

Notice that the analysis of the three balances requires the specification of the closure of the model. More precisely, one needs to define: (i) if the economy is demand-led or supply-led; and (ii) how the causality runs between the net lending of the three sectors. For example, in 'Seven Unsustainable Processes', Godley (1999a) assumes a demand-led economy where the increase in the trade deficit is exogenous – due to the successful invasion of the USA markets – and thus the causality runs from NL_f to the domestic sector. In the case of the USA, the possibility that the causality is running this way has also been highlighted by Darrat (1988) and Stiglitz (2010, ch. 8). In the case of the eurozone, many authors have argued that the high private and public deficits of the peripheral countries are simply the mirror image of the exogenous decrease of the current account balance due to the real exchange rate appreciation, the decrease in the transfers to these countries and the structural deficiencies of the eurozone (Arghyrou and Chortareas, 2008; Eichengreen, 2010; Chen et al., 2013; Flassbeck and Lapavitsas, 2013; Nikiforos et al., 2015; Kang and Shambaugh, 2016).

On the other end, neoclassical economists usually maintain a different causal story, where the causality runs from the domestic sector – especially the government – to the foreign sector. This is the so-called 'twin-deficits hypothesis' (Volcker, 1984; Abell, 1990). According to this hypothesis, a decrease in NL_g (or NL_p) creates inflation and thus has a negative impact on competitiveness, with the result being that NL_f increases. Thus, austerity can help increase competitiveness without a negative impact on the growth rate. Several studies that supported this interpretation provided the theoretical underpinnings of the austerity policies in the eurozone periphery (Blanchard and Giavazzi, 2002; Decressin and Stavrev, 2009; Jaumotte and Sodsriwiboon, 2010; Schmitz and von Hagen, 2011). A different neoclassical closure is the so-called 'Ricardian equivalence', where a change in NL_g leads to an equivalent change in NL_p in the opposite direction, leaving NL_f unchanged (Barro, 1974).

The three balances approach can be extended within a two-country framework, like that in Table 4. In this case, the accounting identity of equation (10) needs to hold for each country individually, with the additional constraint that the net lending of one country is equal to the net borrowing of the other:

$$NL_p + NL_g + NL_f = 0$$
$$NL_p^* + NL_g^* + NL_f^* = 0 \qquad\qquad (11)$$
$$NL_f = -NL_f^*$$

Combing these three equations we get:

$$NL_p + NL_g = -NL_f = NL_f^* = -\left(NL_p^* + NL_g^*\right) \tag{12}$$

Equation (12) shows how the balance of the sectors of the two countries – and therefore also their balance sheets – are connected. From this equation it becomes clear that by accounting principle it is impossible for both countries to simultaneously increase their current account balance: the surpluses of one country need to be absorbed by another. Another implication of this equation is that it is impossible to have foreign surpluses in one country and at the same time domestic surpluses – private or public – in the other. This simple accounting rule is often forgotten in the eurozone, where officials defend the trade surpluses of the north and demand the south decreases its public and private domestic borrowing.

Another complication that arises in an open-economy framework is that one needs to define the mechanisms that determine the exchange rate. The economic performance of the economy, the portfolio choice of the agents and the decisions of the policymakers are the main determinants of the exchange rate. In turn, the exchange rate will affect the performance of exports and imports, but also the portfolio choice of the agents (since it will affect the price of foreign assets in domestic currencies). This is yet another channel where the real and financial sides of the economy are integrated within the SFC framework. For example, a change in the portfolio preferences of the agents will tend to change the exchange rate and this will feed back into the real economy.

The centre of gravity of the open-economy SFC literature is – as with other themes – the treatment in Godley and Lavoie (2007a). In chapter 6, they first introduce an economy with two regions but a common government and then sketch a 'gold-standard'-like two-country model, with the exchange rate being treated as a constant, where the central bank of each country holds gold reserves in addition to the domestic government bills. The foreign deficit of a country is matched by gold outflows and vice versa.

There are two important results of this simple model that carry over to the more complicated models they introduce later. First, after a negative shock to net exports, the private sector does not receive any signal that something is wrong and its demand for assets and money are not affected. Second, the reduction in the gold reserves of the central bank is automatically compensated for by an increase in its holding of government securities (since the foreign deficit that precedes the former leads to government deficits and, thus, to the latter), and therefore the supply of money adjusts – endogenously – to meet its demand. These results stand in stark contrast with conventional wisdom, which posits that there is some automatic adjustment of the foreign balance.[7] In the absence of an automatic correction the government needs to intervene and correct the imbalances.

Chapter 12 introduces a two country model where the exchange rate is determined endogenously to clear the international transactions for goods and financial assets. To close the model, they assume that private sector demand for foreign financial assets is always satisfied and therefore the exchange rate is pinned down by the demand for and supply of the reserves of the central bank (of the country that does not issue the reserve currency). This is a common closure for the exchange rate in the literature, although there are several other possibilities. Godley and Lavoie distinguish between a regime where the central bank chooses to keep its reserves constant and allows the exchange rate to fluctuate, and three regimes with fixed exchange rates along the lines of their model in chapter 6. Their model shows again that there is no intrinsic mechanism that will correct possible foreign imbalances and that there has to be active government intervention. Exchange rate adjustment can be effective in correcting foreign imbalances, as purely speculative behaviour is left outside of the model. Finally, a change in the liquidity preference of households can affect the exchange rate and then the real economy through the asset markets.

The analysis of these two chapters in Godley and Lavoie (2007a) builds on the work of the two authors in the years before the publication of the book. The first attempt towards a full SFC model for an open economy is Godley (1999c). Lavoie (2003) builds a fixed exchange rate model for the eurozone, which forms the basis for chapter 6, and in Godley and Lavoie (2003, 2005) one can find the first insights for chapter 12. Finally, Godley and Lavoie (2007b) present a three-country model that discusses the eurozone economy. In a somewhat prophetic manner, they stress that the situation in the eurozone in the presence of imbalances would be sustainable as long as the European Central Bank (ECB) was willing to accumulate an ever-rising quantity of bills from the 'weak' country (the country with external deficits). If not, interest rates in the weak country would keep on rising. The only alternative would be for the government of the weak country to endogenize fiscal policy: essentially to create a recession that would decrease imports and rebalance the current account. An interesting feature of the model is that it demonstrates the interconnectedness of countries, since the fiscal and external deficits of the weak country could arise through no fault on its own, as they could be caused by an improvement in the export performance of other members vis-à-vis the rest of the world. These are important insights if one wants to understand the current situation in the eurozone and the policies that have been adopted in the last 7 years. Another paper of this first generation of open-economy SFC models is by Izurieta (2003), who was working with Godley at the Levy Institute at the time. The paper presents a two-country model and examines the implications of the dollarization of an economy. The conclusions of the paper echo the results of the fixed exchange rate models of Godley and Lavoie.

Another fully articulated open-economy SFC model from the same period was built by Lance Taylor (2004a, ch. 10, 2004b), who employs a different closure for the model. Internally, in each economy the interest rate is determined endogenously based on an IS-LM mechanism and the exchange rate is determined based on the uncovered interest parity condition through arbitrage. Taylor reaches the same conclusion with regards to the (in)ability of an economy to self-correct external imbalances.

These insights and the techniques of this first generation of open-economy SFC models have been used in more recent contributions on various topics. Lavoie and Zhao (2010) build a three-country model (USA, eurozone and China) where the exchange rate between China and the USA is fixed, and examine the results of the diversification of Chinese foreign reserves. They show that both the Chinese and USA economy benefit, because the increase in the demand for European assets leads to the appreciation of the euro. Their model also generates path dependence. Lavoie and Daigle (2011) examine the role of exchange rate expectations. Based on chapter 12 of Godley and Lavoie (2007a), they build a model of exchange rate expectations with two types of agents: the so-called 'fundamentalists' and 'chartists'. The former expect that the exchange rate will revert to a level that they perceive as fundamental, while the latter follow the market trend. The model shows that expectations play a role, and if the 'chartists' are overrepresented, expectations can be destabilizing. Flexible exchange rates in that case will not remove global imbalances.

Mazier and Tiou-Tagba Aliti (2012) build a three-country model along the lines of Lavoie and Zhao (2010) and examine scenarios with pegged and flexible dollar-Yuan parity. They conclude that the flexible parity could be an important way to address the global imbalances. Addressing the global imbalances is also the subject of Valdecantos and Zezza (2015). Within a four-country model, they examine the effects of introducing an international clearing union and a Bancor model, as proposed by Keynes's at Bretton Woods, and show that the implementation of these proposals leads to an elimination of global imbalances.

Finally, Greenwood-Nimmo (2014) discusses the role and effects of stabilization policies and extends the two-country model of Godley and Lavoie (2007a, ch. 12) with the introduction of persistent inflationary pressures (because of conflicting claims) and cyclicality of aggregate demand (achieved through the endogenization of the propensities to consume to changes in the interest rate). The simulations of the model show that a combination of fiscal and monetary policies outperforms each of these policies when operated in isolation. Moreover, the autonomous pursuit of inflation targeting policies by both central banks leads to excessive exchange rate volatility compared to a situation in which one central bank plays is the leader in setting the interest rate.

The discussion above shows that the SFC framework is particularly appropriate for examining issues related to a monetary union like the eurozone. As we explained, Lavoie (2003) and Godley and Lavoie (2007b) present models specifically for the eurozone, while much of the discussion in their book implicitly or explicitly refers to it. The publication of the book, together with the increasing popularity of the SFC approach and the fact that many scholars who have adopted it are based in Europe, has led to a series of contributions that examine eurozone-related issues.

In a properly calibrated model, Duwicquet and Mazier (2010) examine the usual argument that financial integration can help make a currency union an optimum currency area. In particular, they examine the stabilization effects of holding foreign assets and intra-zone credits. They conclude that the former indeed has stabilizing effects, albeit small, while the latter does not have specific stabilization effects. An extension of this analysis is provided in Duwicquet and Mazier (2012), where it is argued that intra-zone credit has a stabilization effect if the non-resident banks do not ration their purchases of T-bills from deficit countries. The adjustment mechanisms of the eurozone is the topic of another paper (Duwicquet et al., 2012), which argues that the creation of a federal budget and issuing of eurobonds could have a stabilizing role. In a similar vein, Mazier and Valdecantos (2015) use a four-country model and suggest that the introduction of a 'multi-speed' Europe, with separate currencies for the north and the south, could have a stabilizing role. The same model is used by Mazier and Valdecantos (2014), who propose the introduction of a clearing union and a Bancor system for the eurozone, arguing that the TARGET2 system provides the necessary infrastructure for the implementation of such a proposal. Finally, Kinsella and Khalil (2011) build a two-country model and discuss the process of debt deflation in a small, open economy (an appropriate issue for Ireland, where Kinsella is based). They conclude that within a monetary union, the duration of the debt deflation spiral is prolonged.

5. Empirical Models for Whole Countries

One of the main reasons for the recent surge in the popularity of SFC modelling is certainly related to the recognition that Wynne Godley and models based on the SFC approach were able to predict the 2001 USA recession (e.g. Godley 1999a), and later the Great Recession of 2007–2009 (Godley and Zezza, 2006; Godley et al., 2007).[8] This recognition came from academic economists (e.g. Bezemer 2010), but was also widely shared in the press (Chancellor, 2010; Wolf, 2012; Schlefer, 2013).

Although the SFC theoretical methodology was fully formalized later, as discussed in the previous sections, the central features of SFC empirical models were already present in

Godley's work at the time of the Cambridge Economic Policy Group in the 1970s (Godley and Cripps, 1974, 1983; Cripps and Godley, 1976, 1978). This early SFC empirical approach was aimed at determining the drivers of sectoral financial balances (see equation (10), above) by building a set of accounting identities for monetary transactions and determining the components of trade, aggregate private demand and prices through econometric estimates. From that point of view, the modelling methodology was in the 'Cowles Commission' tradition of other Keynesian empirical models of the time (Fair, 2012). An important difference was the choice of treating private domestic demand as an *aggregate* – that is, the combination of household consumption and business investment. This approach aimed at introducing what came to be labelled the 'New Cambridge hypothesis' about the private sector financial balance, as a contribution to the Keynesian debate of the time on the UK economy. As Dos Santos and Macedo e Silva (2010, pp. 22–23) explain the 'private financial balance of the British economy had been relatively small and stable for many years—so that any (conventional Keynesian) attempts to increase effective demand by means of a relaxation of fiscal policy would only worsen the British current account balance'.

This same approach guided the development of models for Denmark (Godley and Zezza, 1992), the USA (Godley, 1999a; Zezza, 2009) and, more recently, Greece (Papadimitriou et al., 2013a). The models for the USA and Greece have routinely been used by the Levy Institute to examine the medium-run prospects of the USA economy and simulate the effects of alternative policy options or other macroeconomic scenarios.[9] Their ability to better project the trajectories of these economies relative to other neoclassical-oriented Dynamic Stochastic General Equilibrium (DSGE)-type models has contributed to spreading the interest in the SFC approach.

The main features of what could be labelled as the 'Godley–Levy' empirical SFC models are thus the attention to modelling real aggregate private sector demand as a function of real disposable wealth and the real opening stock of net financial wealth, determining an implicitly stable stock–flow ratio ('norm') towards which the economy would converge in the absence of external shocks. The introduction of additional variables – mainly related to credit and net capital gains – determines deviations from the stock–flow ratio, where such deviations may take a very long time to die out (Zezza, 2009). On the other hand, the Tobinesque approach to portfolio management is kept to a minimum – or it is absent. The Godley–Levy models capture the main channel of transmission from the financial side of the economy to the real side, namely:

1. every stock of financial assets implies a flow of income from capital from the debtor to the creditor (this usually implies a considerable amount of work reconstructing who-to-whom payments from national accounts, whenever they are not available);
2. flows of new credit have an impact on expenditure decisions; and
3. the end-of-period stock of net financial wealth (or debt) has an impact on expenditure and saving decisions.

What are neglected, given the absence of portfolio management, are the macroeconomic consequences of shifts in financial portfolios, which are likely to be small in many practical cases.

Since the purpose of the Godley–Levy SFC models is to perform policy simulations in order to minimize concerns over the Lucas critique (Lucas, 1976), model parameters are estimated with econometric techniques that ensure – as far as possible – that their values would not change over a shocked simulation period.[10]

A somewhat different methodology has been applied to developing empirical SFC models for Ireland (Kinsella and Tiou-Tagba Aliti, 2012a). In this case, the focus is on reconstructing the balance sheets of the main sectors of the economy for a country where statistical information for flows and stocks is not complete. This leads Kinsella and Tiou-Tagba Aliti (2012b) to propose the adoption of calibration methods for determining parameter values, where parameters may change over time. In some cases, the calibration method can also produce time series for missing statistical information (Godin et al., 2012). This approach is certainly useful in adapting a theoretical model to empirical time series in order to get 'informed intuition' (Godley and Lavoie, 2007a, p. 9) on how the economy actually works, but may pose severe limitations in using the model for forecasting purposes (whenever the future value of parameters may not be assumed to remain stable).

A similar approach in terms of parameter calibration has been adopted in Miess and Schmelzer (2016a, 2016b). They develop a model for Austria with rich institutional detail, and a detailed disaggregation of the financial sector with seven classes of financial assets. Parameters are calibrated over the observed sample, and their trend is used to project their value over the out-of-sample period. In practice, most parameters are projected to remain fixed at their last value in out-of-sample simulations. The authors use the model to produce a baseline scenario up to 2025, which is used as a benchmark to evaluate alternative scenarios for different fiscal policies.

A recent model for the UK (Burgess et al., 2016) is probably the most complex SFC model so far estimated from national accounting statistics for a real economy. Similar to the Godley–Levy models, its purpose is to perform scenario analysis over the medium term. On the other hand, compared to the Godley–Levy models, there is greater institutional detail, with the economy disaggregated into six sectors (households, non-financial corporations, government, banks, insurance companies and pension funds and the foreign sector). The approach used for identifying parameter values is a mixture of econometric estimation, calibration and (arbitrary) coefficient restrictions, which allows for a rich and complex model for portfolio management that would not have been feasible by adopting only econometric techniques.

In all the aforementioned applied SFC post-Keynesian models, output is driven by demand, with little attention to supply-side constraints. An exception is a Structuralist-SFC model for Argentina by Valdecantos (2012) that distinguishes among three goods – agricultural, non-agricultural and intermediate – and shows that, especially in the context of less-developed economies, several complications may arise when supply constraints are binding, for example, when the price of agricultural goods are determined in the international markets or if the growth rate is constrained by the balance of payments (Thirlwall, 1979). Finally, Escobar-Espinoza (2016) builds an applied SFC model for Colombia following the Godley–Levy approach, and shows that even in the case of a developing country it can perform satisfactorily and provide some useful insights.

We are not aware of other complete SFC models for whole countries. Several authors employ econometric techniques to estimate parameters of their theoretical models, thus partially calibrating them to a specific country (e.g. Clevenot et al., 2010).

6. SFC and Agent-Based Modelling

The use of agent-based models (henceforth ABM) is an approach that has been gaining favour very quickly over the last few years. Epstein and Axtell (1996), Tesfatsion and Judd (2006) and LeBaron and Tesfatsion (2008) provide an extensive treatment of the use of ABM in economics and the social sciences; most of the papers cited in this section explain the advantages of ABM, as well. The basic idea of ABM is that a modern capitalist economy is a *complex* system of *interacting* agents and we can gain a lot in our effort to understand such a system by precisely studying its complexity (Farmer and Foley, 2009). Such an approach is obviously diametrically opposed to the neoclassical idea that one can understand the basic features of a capitalist economy by studying the behaviour of a Robinson Crusoe economy.

Thus, economic processes are studied through the interaction of numerous heterogeneous agents, classified in various sectors. As in any model, the classification follows the related theory and the issue under examination. The properties of the model emerge from the (microeconomic) behaviour of the agents from the 'bottom-up'. In that sense, ABM can shed light on how the macroeconomic variables and phenomena (e.g. GDP, leverage, economic fluctuations) are determined endogenously through the interaction of multiple heterogeneous agents. In that sense, ABMs are able to provide the sought-after micro-foundations. More interestingly, in ABM there is an endogenous emergence of various distributions and networks within the economy (e.g. the distribution of the size of the firms, the income and wealth of households or the network structure of the banking sector).

ABM is a *methodological* approach and therefore the conclusions one reaches with the use of a related model crucially depend on the theory behind the model and the specification of the behaviour of the agents. Therefore, although the overall vision of most of the scholars who develop ABM for economic applications is not neoclassical, one could reach neoclassical results by assuming an 'appropriate' behaviour for the agents of the model.

The advantages of agent-based and SFC models have led many researchers to call for a combination of the two approaches. The basic idea is that in an agent-based SFC model each sector of the transactions-flow matrix is populated with several agents (e.g. n households, m firms and k banks). The government and the central bank are usually treated as one agent each. Moreover, instead of specifying behavioural rules for each sector as a whole, the modeller specifies rules for the behaviour of the individual agents and on the matching between the agents (e.g. how do the household choose where to buy their consumption goods among the different firms or how do the firms and households choose where to deposit their money and where to take their loans from among the banks).

The first systematic effort to build an agent-based SFC model is the EURACE model, the outcome of a collaborative effort of researchers at various European universities. In the words of Deissenberg *et al.* (2008), EURACE is a 'massive' model: at a spatial level it is subdivided at the European regional level, while its temporal resolution is the business day. There are three types of agents (households, firms and the banks), each located in a specific region, with five types of markets (consumption goods, investment goods, labour, credit and financial assets). Cincotti *et al.* (2010) use the EURACE model to study the business cycle and show that when firms pay a higher fraction of their earnings as dividends, the amplitude of the business cycle increases because they compensate for the lower retained earnings with more borrowing and leverage. In a related study, Raberto *et al.* (2012) examine the relation between debt and the macroeconomic performance of an economy. They show that the effect of debt on growth is not certain *a priori*: more debt can foster or inhibit growth, a result that echoes the debt-led and debt-burdened classifications of Taylor (2004a, ch. 8).

The EURACE model has been further developed more recently by researchers at the University of Bielefeld, and renamed 'Eurace@Unibi' (Dawid *et al.*, 2011, 2012, 2016b). This latest incarnation of the model has been used for various applications.[11] For example, Dawid *et al.* (2014) use the model to study economic convergence across European regions. With fully integrated labour markets, they show that investment in human capital in weaker regions has a positive effect on the performance of the stronger regions, but a negative effect for the weaker ones. On the contrary, subsidies for high-technology industries in the weaker regions lead to convergence. In a related paper, Dawid *et al.* (2016a) examine economic convergence in relation to fiscal policy. They show that debt-burden sharing does not have a significant effect on convergence. Convergence of per capita consumption can emerge as a result of fiscal transfers, although the authors show that technology-oriented subsidies are the most sustainable way for regional convergence. Finally, Hoog and Dawid (2015) examine business fluctuations in relation to banking regulation. They find that liquidity regulations, as opposed to capital requirements, dampen the business cycle more effectively.

An early explicitly agent-based SFC model was built by Kinsella *et al.* (2011). They show how in such a model, power-law dynamics emerge for several variables, such as the size of the firm and income distribution. In the same year, another early call to combine ABM with the SFC approach is found in Bezemer (2011). He shows that a careful modelling of an economy's financial structure can give rise to non-linear behaviours and endogenous crises, unlike the DSGE models. However, the model utilized towards that purpose is an aggregate macro-model and not agent based.

The combination of ABM and the SFC approach also lies at the heart of 'Jamel', an acronym for 'Java agent-based macroeconomic laboratory', which is a platform for modelling and simulating complex monetary economies (Seppecher, 2012a). Jamel has been used for various interesting modelling exercises. Seppecher (2014) presents a model of a monetary theory of production, which explicitly takes into account the relations between production, money and time and how these determine interest and profits. Seppecher (2012b) presents a model where the introduction of more flexibility in wages and the labour market creates instability and leads to the formation of deflationary spirals: a result that echoes the famous chapter 19 of *The General Theory* (Keynes, 2013 [1936]). Seppecher and Salle (2015) augment the Jamel platform with endogenous waves of optimism, which affect the leverage decisions of firms and households. This mechanism exacerbates the usual credit cycle. Finally, and related to that, Seppecher *et al.* (2016) propose a model where firms adapt and explore new strategies of leverage. This kind of behaviour of the firms leads to oscillations in the macroeconomic performance of the economy. In the upswing, firms tend to adopt more and more high-leverage strategies. At that phase, firms that resist this kind of strategy face the danger of low profitability and extinction. However, when the leverage of the overall system increases too much, the downswing begins. At this phase, individual firms are unable to adapt fast enough and there is a 'brutal' cleaning of the high-leverage firms and the firms with low leverage have better chances of survival.

Credit cycles as the result of firm leverage are also modelled in Riccetti *et al.* (2015), where the firms are assumed to have an endogenous leverage target level. In a similar vein, Carvalho and Di Guilmi (2014) model credit cycles, which originate from the household and not from the firm sector. A distinctive characteristic of their approach as opposed to the majority of the literature is that they are able to solve their model analytically and not numerically.

Finally, Caiani *et al.* (2016) propose an agent-based SFC model as a benchmark for future-related research. They pay special attention to how the model can be validated based on real data and they propose rules for the calibration and display of such a model. Based on this model, Schasfoort *et al.* (2016) examine the transmission mechanisms of monetary policy and conclude that the transmission of monetary policy depends on the composition of the balance sheets of the sectors of the economy.

The above show that there is a nascent but very active and growing literature that aims at combining the SFC approach with agent-based micro-foundations. These kinds of models can be complementary to the more standard macroeconomic models mentioned above and shed light into corners where an aggregate model does not have much to say.

7. SFC Ecological Models

Many environmental processes that interact with the economy, such as pollution or the availability of natural resources, exhibit characteristics that can be formalized through the stock–flow relationship. For instance, the flow of CO_2 emissions will depend on industrial processes in a given region, and cumulates in a stock of CO_2 pollution, which in turn has adverse consequences on quality of life and the economy. These aspects, together with the formal rigor of the SFC literature, are stimulating a number of studies that adopt the SFC approach to address environmental problems.[12]

An important link between economic modelling and environmental sustainability is the determination of sustainable economic growth rates. Jackson and Victor (2015) develop an SFC model to show that when interest rates are positive the system can replicate itself in a stationary state and therefore diminish threats to environmental sustainability. In Jackson and Victor (2016) they show that under specific assumptions slower growth would not imply an increase in inequality, and would therefore be socially sustainable. In Jackson et al. (2014) they discuss how the links between the impact on the environment and the economy can be detailed using I-O matrices, although these issues have not been developed in later works.

Berg et al. (2015) develop a formal integration of the SFC and the I-O approach, taking energy into account.[13] They use their model to study energy-related problems, with attention to the conditions for system stability.

A complex multi-sectoral SFC model with an explicit treatment of the energy sector that has been calibrated for the European Union is presented in Naqvi (2015). The model is simulated to examine policies that can address growth, distribution and environmental sustainability. The same model structure, albeit without the energy sector, is deployed in a two-region north–south model in Dunz and Naqvi (2016), where the purpose is to study the impact of interregional transfers to foster 'clean investment'.

Finally, an ambitious model in Dafermos et al. (2017) provides additional insights. In this model, the monetary and the physical stocks are determined based on SFC accounting principles and the laws of thermodynamics. The authors adopt the distinction, proposed by Georgescu-Roegen (1971), between stock–flow and fund–service resources. Output is demand determined; however, supply constraints might arise as a result of environmental changes or the exhaustion of natural resources. Climate change and finance have direct and indirect effects on aggregate demand and investment plans. This is important because 'green' investment is treated separately from 'conventional' investment in the economic part of the model, and therefore investment shifts affect ecological efficiency.

Dafermos et al. (2017) calibrate the model using global data to produce simulations over a 100-year time horizon under different assumptions of the impact of financial fragility on macroeconomic activity, as well as on the financing of green investment. In their simulations, the negative impact of environmental change is reinforced as the contractionary effects of a high leverage increase. Finally, they show that better terms of credit for green investment have positive effects both for environmental sustainability and financial stability.

Summing up, SFC models that treat the economy as part of a more global system (i.e. where the environment plays a relevant role) are one of the most promising areas of research for SFC modellers.[14] However, greater attention needs to be paid to a number of other systemic variables – such as population growth and migration, constraints to growth given by scarcity of natural resources, etc. – in order to provide a valid alternative to mainstream models, which are usually more detailed in their treatment of the environment, but lack any attention to the role of the financial sector, and are empirically weak because of their assumption of full employment.

8. Instead of Conclusion: Onomastics

The present paper discussed the SFC approach to macroeconomic modelling. We started with a short outline of the intellectual roots of the approach, pioneered by the work of Wynne Godley at Cambridge and James Tobin at Yale. In Section 2, we explained the basic principles of the model: the accounting consistency, the demand-led closure and the various alternative behavioural specifications, as well as the treatment of the financial side of the economy. Section 3 presented how the basic model has been used and modified to address various issues related to the monetary circuit, financialization and income distribution. In Section 4, we surveyed the literature on open-economy SFC models and in Section 5 the empirical models for whole countries. Section 6 discussed how the SFC approach has been used in conjunction with the ABM approach, and Section 7 explained the usefulness of SFC modelling for treating environmental issues. Instead of a conclusion, we can discuss here one last issue: the name 'SFC'. The related analysis that follows – besides being interesting in its own right – can act as a summary and further clarify the issues we discussed in the previous sections.

The name 'SFC' has existed in the literature for a long time as a reference to models with the characteristics described in Section 2 (e.g. Davis, 1987a, 1987b). However, it was only established as a 'brand name' after Claudio Dos Santos's PhD dissertation at The New School for Social Research entitled 'Three Essays on Stock-Flow Consistent Macroeconomic Modeling' (Dos Santos, 2003).[15]

The name has been a source of confusion among friends and foes of the SFC approach for two reasons. First, it has misled people to believe that it describes what Krugman (2013) called 'hydraulic' macroeconomic models, devoid of behavioural underpinnings, which is essentially 'accounting, not economics' (Wren-Lewis, 2016).[16] Second, people who are not familiar with the SFC approach contend – rightly – that stock–flow consistency is a characteristic of various classes of models. For example, the Solow (1956)–Swan (1956) model or Ramsey-type (1928) models are indeed SFC. From that point of view, it is wrong to use stock–flow consistency as the demarcating characteristic of the type of models described here. We discuss these issues in the following paragraphs.

To begin with, as we explained in the previous sections (especially in Section 2.1), proper accounting reduces the degrees of freedom of a model (or an analysis) and protects the modeller from certain common fallacies. In the course of the discussion in the previous sections we gave many related examples. For instance, in our discussion of the three balances we explained that by accounting principle the sum of the net lending of the foreign sectors of all the economies taken together is also equal to zero. Since the deficit of an economy cannot decrease if the surplus of another economy does not decrease as well, this simple accounting principle invalidates the growth paradigm proposed by many economists and international organizations who advocate that every country should pursue export-led growth by trying to increase its competitiveness (through 'structural reforms', etc.). The problem here is that although the models of these economists and organizations are indeed SFC at the individual economy/country level, they violate 'accounting consistency' at the international level. Certain cases of fallacy of composition like this are due to the violation of simple accounting rules.

Besides that, accounting consistency is the method that brings together the real and financial sides of the economy and allows the modeller to track down how the agents' decisions about their real variables affect the nominal assets of their balance sheets and how these changes feedback on their 'real' decisions. The balance-sheet matrix (Table 1) and the transactions-flow matrix (Table 2) are thus indispensable tools for the analysis of a *monetary* economy. For all these reasons, the best way to start solving an economic problem is by ensuring that the accounting is right.

However, the SFC approach goes beyond simple accounting. As we explained in Section 2.2, another very important characteristic is that the basic closure is Keynesian. SFC models do not assume Say's law and full employment in the short run or that the economy will converge towards such a state in the medium/long run. Arguably, this is Keynes's most important contribution to macroeconomic theory. He demonstrated that the *general* state (hence *The General Theory*) of the capitalist economy is not one of full employment and there is no natural tendency of the economy to gravitate towards full employment. The full employment equilibrium envisaged by neoclassical economics is just a *special* case. This choice of closure allows then for an *integrated* treatment of the real and financial sectors of the economy, where the latter – debt, leverage, the stock market, etc. – matters for the behaviour of the agents and therefore the performance of the former. SFC models are driven by this kind of closure and a sophisticated treatment of the financial sector, and are thus far from 'hydraulic' or without any behavioural content.

The world of neoclassical models – like the stochastic Ramsey-type DSGE models that are widely used in academia and policymaking – is on the exact opposite side. These models are indeed SFC, in the sense that the flows of the models accumulate into stocks. However, they are supply-side full-employment models at heart: the *general* state is supply determined, and characterized by full employment (or a 'natural' rate of unemployment). The introduction of (*ad hoc*) rigidities allows them to derive some Keynesian results in the short run as a special case. However, in the medium run, the economy always returns to full employment or to its natural rate of unemployment. This is not just an esoteric theoretical issue. In the CBO's projections for the USA economy (or the official projections in the European periphery countries), which are derived from DSGE models, demand effects vanish after a couple of years and the economy reverts to a fully supply-side-determined equilibrium. In these types of models, fluctuations are mainly due to 'shocks' to productivity or other variables on the real side of the economy.

Moreover, this kind of closure ties the model in such a way that it allows a very minor role (if any) for finance. There is the so-called dichotomy between the real and the financial sides of the economy, where financial complications do not really matter for the real outcome of the economy. Finance is, to use another classical metaphor, just a 'veil' that can affect nominal variables but not the real ones. Various related properties that are widespread in neoclassical economics, like the 'neutrality of money' or the Modigliani and Miller (1958) theorem, emanate from this supply-side, full-employment choice of closure.

The only way to break this dichotomy is to introduce some kind of friction. Following Bernanke and Gertler (1989), Kiyotaki and Moore (1997) and Bernanke *et al.* (1999), in the related 'financial' DSGE literature these frictions usually take the form of informational asymmetries and/or incomplete markets. In these models, the financial frictions amplify the effects of shocks to productivity. However, these processes are only transitory and, as is usual with every kind of 'friction' DSGE model the economy tends to return to its supply-determined, full-employment equilibrium in the medium run, where finance does not play any role. It is telling that Bernanke, one of the architects of the 'financial frictions' DSGE models, was the same person who coined the term 'Great Moderation' 3 years before the Great Recession (Bernanke, 2004).

In that sense, it was no accident that the DSGE models ignored the situation in the financial markets or the build-up of private debt in the 1990s or the 2000s. It was exactly the opposite; these models – albeit SFC in the literal sense – *by assumption* keep the real and the financial sides separate. As we explained in the course of this paper, the purpose of the Keynesian-type SFC models is antipodal: to provide an *integrated* approach to credit, money, income, production and wealth (as the subtitle of Godley and Lavoie (2007a) reads), where the real and the financial sides matter for each other both in the short and long run.

In conclusion, it is true that the name 'SFC' is misleading and sometimes confusing for what the post-Keynesian SFC approach wants to convey. Accounting consistency is just one of the pillars of the analysis, which is combined with a demand-led closure and a sophisticated and realistic treatment of the financial side of the economy. It is probably too late to change the name, but what we mean by it should be clear by now.

Onomastics aside, for the reasons explained in this paper, the SFC approach to macroeconomic analysis combines many advantages for a rigorous analysis and understanding of the political economy of capitalism.

Acknowledgements

We would like to thank three anonymous referees as well as Roberto Veneziani and Luca Zamparelli for very detailed and useful comments and suggestions. The usual disclaimer applies.

Notes

1. Cripps and Lavoie (2017) provide a biographical discussion of Godley's works and methods.
2. In the United States, the FoF accounts are released by the Federal Reserve System, and are also published as 'integrated macroeconomic accounts' by the Bureau of Economic Analysis. In the eurozone, these accounts are usually called 'financial accounts' and are published by the national central banks and Eurostat, but they have a broadly similar format.
3. For example, in the present case we have implicitly assumed that only firms issue equities, which are held by households, the banks and the central bank.
4. One important counterexample is the famous textbook IS-LM model, which is not SFC. For the implications of stock-flow inconsistency in the IS-LM model, see Godley and Shaikh (2002).
5. Note that the identities resulting from the transaction matrix are such that one can be obtained as a linear combination of the others, and must therefore be dropped from the simulation to avoid over-determination. This is the so-called 'redundant equality' (Godley and Lavoie, 2007a, p. 14). The same applies to the identities embedded in the balance sheet.

6. The specification of investment is famously difficult and controversial, but at the same time necessary within a Keynesian framework. Equation (7) builds on the recent post-Keynesian and Kaleckian literature (Steindl, 1952; Rowthorn, 1981; Taylor, 1983; Dutt 1984; Minsky, 1986; Bhaduri and Marglin, 1990) and the so-called 'q-theory of investment', as proposed by James Tobin (Brainard and Tobin, 1968; Tobin 1969). Variants of this specific functional form within an SFC model can be found in Lavoie and Godley (2001) and have been subsequently used in other forms by Taylor (2004a, ch. 8) and Godley and Lavoie (2007a, ch. 11). Fazzari and Mott (1986) and Ndikumana (1999) have found empirical evidence that supports it.

7. The automatic stabilization of the foreign balance goes back to the price-specie flow mechanism of David Hume (2008) and is present in the IS-LM-BP type of models (Fleming, 1962; Mundell, 1963). The mechanism of the automatic correction is based on the assumption that the quantity of money is supply determined.

8. It is worth mentioning that Godley (1999a, p. 5) argues that if the process continues for eight more years, there will be a 'sensational day of reckoning'. Eight years after 1999 was 2007!

9. Recent publications using the model for the United States include Papadimitriou *et al.* (2013c, 2014d, 2015a, 2016b) and Nikiforos and Zezza (2017). Publications on Greece include Papadimitriou *et al.* (2013b, 2014a, 2014b, 2014c, 2015b, 2016a).

10. This is usually achieved adopting co-integration techniques, therefore verifying that explanatory variables are weakly exogenous.

11. The full list of the publications based on Eurace@Unibi model can be found at: http://www.wiwi.uni-bielefeld.de/lehrbereiche/vwl/etace/Eurace_Unibi/

12. A useful reference for a post-Keynesian approach to 'ecological macroeconomics', which rests on the monetary circuit theory rather than the SFC approach, is in Fontana and Sawyer (2016).

13. The integration of the SFC methodology into I-O based models is recognized as a potentially fruitful new research area (Kratena and Temursho, 2017).

14. See also Cahen-Fourot and Lavoie (2016) for a SFC-based critique of macroeconomic closures in ecological economics.

15. As Cripps and Lavoie (2017, p. 944) point out, several other names have been proposed along the way: *real stock–flow monetary model*, the *financial stock–flow coherent approach* or the *sectorial stock–flow coherent approach*.

16. It is worth saying that the term 'hydraulic Keynesianism' refers to the neoclassical synthesis, IS-LM type of Keynesianism and not to the kind of Keynesian economics Godley and the Cambridge (UK) economists practiced (Coddington, 1976). Ironically, Krugman has been the most vocal contemporary defender of the IS-LM model (e.g. Krugman, 2000).

References

Abell, J.D. (1990) Twin deficits during the 1980s: an empirical investigation. *Journal of Macroeconomics* 12(1): 81–96.

Adelman, I. and Robinson, S. (1978) *Income Distribution Policy in Developing Countries: A Case Study of Korea*. Stanford, CA: Stanford University Press.

Arghyrou, M.G. and Chortareas, G. (2008) Current account imbalances and real exchange rates in the euro area. *Review of International Economics* 16(4): 747–764.

Backus, D., Brainard, W.C., Smith, G. and Tobin, J. (1980) A model of U.S. financial and nonfinancial economic behavior. *Journal of Money, Credit and Banking* 12(2): 259–293.

Barro, R.J. (1974) Are government bonds net wealth? *The Journal of Political Economy* 82(6): 1095–1117.

Bellofiore, R. and Passarella, M.V. (2010) Minsky, the monetary circuit and the current crisis: a SFC monetary accounting framework. Paper presented at the conference "Can it happen again? Sustainable policies to mitigate and prevent financial crises," Macerata, October 1–2.

Berg, M., Hartley, B. and Richters, O. (2015) A stock-flow consistent input-output model with applications to energy price shocks, interest rates, and heat emissions. *New Journal of Physics* 17(1): 015011.

Bernanke, B. (2004) The great moderation: remarks by governor Ben S. Bernanke. Meetings of the Eastern Economic Association, Washington, DC, February 20.

Bernanke, B. and Gertler, M. (1989) Agency costs, net worth, and business fluctuations. *The American Economic Review* 79(1): 14–31.

Bernanke, B., Gertler, M., and Gilchrist, S. (1999) The financial accelerator in a quantitative business cycle framework. In J.B. Taylor and M. Woodford (eds.), *Handbook of Macroeconomics*, Vol. 1, Part C. Philadelphia: Elsevier Science B.V.

Bezemer, D.J. (2010) Understanding financial crisis through accounting models. *Accounting, Organizations and Society* 35(7): 676–688.

Bezemer, D.J. (2011) *Causes of financial instability: don't forget finance*. Levy Institute Working Paper 655. Annandale-on-Hudson, NY: Levy Economics Institute of Bard College.

Bhaduri, A. and Marglin, S. (1990) Unemployment and the real wage: the economic basis for contesting political ideologies. *Cambridge Journal of Economics* 14(4): 375–393.

Blanchard, O. and Giavazzi, F. (2002) Current account deficits in the euro area: the end of the Feldstein Horioka puzzle? *Brookings Papers on Economic Activity* 33(2): 147–210.

Botta, A., Caverzasi, E. and Tori, D. (2015) Financial-real side interactions in the monetary circuit: loving or dangerous hugs? *International Journal of Political Economy* 44(3): 196–227.

Brainard, W.C. and Tobin, J. (1968) Pitfalls in financial model building. *The American Economic Review* 58(2): 99–122.

Burgess, S., Burrows, O., Godin, A., Kinsella, S. and Millard, S. (2016) *A dynamic model of financial balances for the United Kingdom*. Bank of England Staff Working Paper No. 614, September. London: Bank of England.

Cahen-Fourot, L. and Lavoie, M. (2016) Ecological monetary economics: a post-Keynesian critique. *Ecological Economics* 126: 163–168.

Caiani, A., Godin, A., Caverzasi, E., Gallegati, M., Kinsella, S. and Stiglitz, J.E. (2016) Agent based-stock flow consistent macroeconomics: towards a benchmark model. *Journal of Economic Dynamics and Control* 69: 375–408.

Carvalho, L. and Di Guilmi, C. (2014) Income inequality and macroeconomic instability: a stock-flow consistent approach with heterogeneous agents. CAMA Working Paper No. 60/2014. Canberra: Centre for Applied Macroeconomic Analysis, Australian National University.

Caverzasi, E. and Godin, A. (2015) Post-Keynesian stock-flow-consistent modelling: a survey. *Cambridge Journal of Economics* 39(1):157–187.

Chancellor, E. (2010) The dreadful potential of frugality. *Financial Times*, June 6. https://www.ft.com/content/a7df74f6-7002-11df-8698-00144feabdc0 (accessed 10 October, 2017).

Chen, R., Milesi-Ferretti, G.M. and Tressel, T. (2013) External imbalances in the eurozone. *Economic Policy* 28(73): 101–142.

Cincotti, S., Raberto, M. and Teglio, A. (2010) Credit money and macroeconomic instability in the agent-based model and simulator eurace. *Economics: The Open-Access, Open-Assessment E-Journal* 4: 1–32.

Clevenot, M., Guy, Y. and Mazier, J. (2010) Investment and the rate of profit in a financial context: the French case. *International Review of Applied Economics* 24(6): 693–714.

Coddington, A. (1976) Keynesian economics: the search for first principles. *Journal of Economic Literature* 14(4): 1258–1273.

Copeland, M.A. (1947) Tracing money flows through the United States economy. *American Economic Review* 37(2): 31–49.

Copeland, M.A. (1949) Social accounting for moneyflows. *The Accounting Review* 24(3): 254–264.

Cripps, F.T. and Godley, W. (1976) A formal analysis of the Cambridge Economic Policy Group Model. *Economica* 43(172): 335–348.

Cripps, F.T. and Godley, W. (1978) Control of imports as a means to full employment and the expansion of world trade: the UK's case. *Cambridge Journal of Economics* 2(3): 327–334.

Cripps, F.T. and Lavoie, M. (2017) Wynne Godley (1926–2010). In R. Cord (ed.), *The Palgrave Companion to Cambridge Economics*. Basingstoke, UK: Palgrave Macmillan.

Dafermos, Y. (2015) *Debt cycles, instability and fiscal rules: a Godley-Minsky model*. University of the West of England, Economics Working Paper Series 1509. Bristol: University of the West of England.

Dafermos, Y. and Papatheodorou, C. (2015) Linking functional with personal income distribution: a stock-flow consistent approach. *International Review of Applied Economics* 29(6): 787–815.

Dafermos, Y., Nikolaidi, M. and Galanis, G. (2017) A stock-flow-fund ecological macroeconomic model. *Ecological Economics* 131: 191–207.

Dallery, T. and van Treeck, T. (2011) Conflicting claims and equilibrium adjustment processes in a stock-flow consistent macroeconomic model. *Review of Political Economy* 23(2): 189–211.

Darrat, A.F. (1988) Have large budget deficits caused rising trade deficits? *Southern Economic Journal* 54(4): 879–887.

Davidson, P. (1968a) Money, portfolio balance, capital accumulation, and economic growth. *Econometrica* 36(2): 291–321.

Davidson, P. (1968b) The demand and supply of securities and economic growth and its implications for the Kaldor-Pasinetti versus Samuelson-Modigliani controversy. *The American Economic Review* 58(2): 252–269.

Davis, E.P. (1987a) A stock-flow consistent macro-econometric model of the UK Economy—part II. *Journal of Applied Econometrics* 2(4): 259–307.

Davis, E.P. (1987b) A stock-flow consistent macro-econometric model of the UK economy—part I. *Journal of Applied Econometrics* 2(2): 111–132.

Dawid, H., Gemkow, S., Harting, P. and Van derHoog, S. (2011) Eurace@Unibi Model v1.0 User Manual. Available at: https://pub.uni-bielefeld.de/publication/2622083.

Dawid, H., Gemkow, S., Harting, P., Van derHoog, S. and Neugart, M. (2012) *The Eurace@Unibi Model: an agent-based macroeconomic model for economic policy analysis*. Bielefeld Working Papers in Economics and Management No. 05–2012. Bielefeld, Germany: Bielefeld Graduate School of Economics and Management.

Dawid, H., Harting, P. and Neugart, M. (2014) Economic convergence: policy implications from a heterogeneous agent model. *Journal of Economic Dynamics and Control* 44(July): 54–80.

Dawid, H., Harting, P. and Neugart, M. (2016a) Fiscal transfers and regional economic growth. Bielefeld Working Papers in Economics and Management, No. 09–2016. Bielefeld, Germany: Bielefeld Graduate School of Economics and Management.

Dawid, H., Harting, P., van derHoog, S. and Neugart, M. (2016b) *A heterogeneous agent macroeconomic model for policy evaluation: improving transparency and reproducibility*. Bielefeld Working Papers in Economics and Management, No. 06–2016. Bielefeld, Germany: Bielefeld Graduate School of Economics and Management.

Decressin, J. and Stavrev, E. (2009) *Current accounts in a currency union*. IMF Working Paper 09/127. Washington, DC: International Monetary Fund.

Deissenberg, C., van derHoog, S. and Dawid, H. (2008) EURACE: a massively parallel agent-based model of the European economy. *Applied Mathematics and Computation* 204(2): 541–552.

Dervis, K., de Melo, J. and Robinson, S. (1982) *General Equilibrium Models for Development Policy*. Cambridge, UK: Cambridge University Press.

Dixon, P.B. and Jorgenson, D. (2013) *Handbook of Computable General Equilibrium Modeling*. Amsterdam: North Holland.

Dos Santos, C.H. (2003) *Three essays on stock-flow consistent macroeconomic modeling*. Ph.D. Thesis. New York: The New School for Social Research.

Dos Santos, C.H. (2005) A stock-flow consistent general framework for formal Minskyan analyses of closed economies. *Journal of Post Keynesian Economics* 27(4): 711–736.

Dos Santos, C.H. (2006) Keynesian theorising during hard times: stock-flow consistent models as an unexplored 'frontier' of Keynesian macroeconomics. *Cambridge Journal of Economics* 30(4): 541–565.

Dos Santos, C.H. and Macedo e Silva, A.C. (2009) *Revisiting (and Connecting) Marglin–Bhaduri and Minsky: an SFC look at financialization and profit-led growth*. Levy Institute Working Paper 567. Annandale-on-Hudson, NY: Levy Economics Institute of Bard College.

Dos Santos, C.H. and Macedo e Silva, A.C. (2010) *Revisiting 'New Cambridge': the three financial balances in a general stock–flow consistent applied modeling strategy*. Levy Institute Working Paper 594. Annandale-on-Hudson, NY: Levy Economics Institute of Bard College.

Dunz, N. and Naqvi, A. (2016) Environmental and labor policies in a north-south SFC model. Unpublished manuscript. Available at: http://www.boeckler.de/pdf/v_2016_10_21_dunz.pdf.

Dutt, A.K. (1984) Stagnation, income distribution and monopoly power. *Cambridge Journal of Economics* 8(1): 25–40.

Duwicquet, V. and Mazier, J. (2010) Financial integration and macroeconomic adjustments in a monetary union. *Journal of Post Keynesian Economics* 33(2): 331–368.

Duwicquet, V. and Mazier, J. (2012) Financial integration and stabilization in a monetary union without or with bank rationing. In D.B. Papadimitriou and G. Zezza (eds.), *Contributions in Stock-Flow Modeling*. Basingstoke: Palgrave Macmillan.

Duwicquet, V., Mazier, J. and Saadaoui, J. (2012) Exchange rate misalignments, fiscal federalism and redistribution: how to adjust in a monetary union. MPRA Paper No. 48697, University Library of Munich, Germany.

Eichengreen, B. (2010) Imbalances in the Euro Area. Unpublished manuscript. Available at: http://eml.berkeley.edu/~eichengr/Imbalances_Euro_Area_5-23-11.pdf.

Eichner, A.S. (1987) *The Macrodynamics of Advanced Market Economies*. New York: M.E. Sharpe.

Epstein, G.A. (2005) *Financialization and the World Economy*. Northampton, MA: Edward Elgar Publishing.

Epstein, J. and Axtell, R. (1996) *Growing Artificial Societies: Social Science from the Bottom-Up*. Washington, DC: MIT Press and Brooking Press.

Escobar-Espinoza, A. (2016) Stock-Flow Consistent Models for Developing Countries: The Case of Colombia. Unpublished manuscript. Available at: https://www.gtap.agecon.purdue.edu/resources/download/8168.pdf.

European Commission, International Monetary Fund, Organisation for Economic Co-operation and Development, United Nations, and World Bank. (2009) *System of National Accounts 2008*. New York: United Nations.

Fair, R.C. (2012) Has macro progressed? *Journal of Macroeconomics* 34(1): 2–10.

Farmer, J. and Foley, D. (2009) The economy needs agent-based modelling. *Nature* 460(7256): 685–686.

Fazzari, S.M. and Mott, T.L. (1986) The investment theories of Kalecki and Keynes: an empirical study of firm data, 1970–1982. *Journal of Post Keynesian Economics* 9(2): 171–187.

Flassbeck, H. and Lapavitsas, C. (2013) The systemic crisis of the euro—true causes and effective therapies. In *STUDIEN*. Berlin: Rosa-Luxemburg-Stiftung. Available at:http://www.erensep.org/images/pdf/2013-05-01_lapavitsas_flassbeck.pdf

Fleming, J. (1962) Domestic financial policies under fixed and under floating exchange rates. *IMF Staff Papers* 9(3): 369–380.

Foley, D.K. (1982) Realization and accumulation in a Marxian model of the circuit of capital. *Journal of Economic Theory* 28(2): 300–319.

Foley, D.K. (1986) *Money, Accumulation, and Crisis*. London: Hardwood Academic Publishers.

Fontana, G. and Sawyer, M. (2016) Towards post-Keynesian ecological macroeconomics. *Ecological Economics* 121(January): 186–195.

Friedman, B.M. (1978) Crowding out or crowding in? Economic consequences of financing government deficits. *Brookings Papers on Economic Activity* 9(3): 593–641.

Georgescu-Roegen, N. (1971) *The Entropy Law and the Economic Process*. Cambridge, MA: Harvard University Press.

Godin, A., Tiou-Tagba Aliti, G. and Kinsella, S. (2012) Method to Simultaneously Determine Stock, Flow, and Parameter Values in Large Stock Flow Consistent Models. Unpublished manuscript. Available at: https://papers.ssrn.com/sol3/papers.cfm?abstract_id=2094996

Godley, W. (1996) Money, finance and national income determination: an integrated approach. Levy Institute Working Paper 167. Annandale-on-Hudson, NY: Levy Economics Institute of Bard College.

Godley, W. (1999a) *Seven Unsustainable Processes: Medium-Term Prospects and Policies for the United States and the World. Strategic Analysis*. Annandale-on-Hudson, NY: Levy Economics Institute of Bard College.

Godley, W. (1999b) Money and credit in a Keynesian model of income determination. *Cambridge Journal of Economics* 23(4): 393–411.

Godley, W. (1999c) *Open economy macroeconomics using models of closed systems*. Levy Institute Working Paper 281. Annandale-on-Hudson, NY: Levy Economics Institute of Bard College.

Godley, W. (2004) Weaving cloth from Graziani's thread. Endogenous money in a simple (but complete) Keynesian model. In R. Arena and N. Salvadori (eds.), *Money, Credit and the Role of the State: Essays in Honour of Augusto Graziani*. Aldershot: Ashgate.

Godley, W. and Cripps, F.T. (1974) Demand, inflation and economic policy. *London and Cambridge Economic Bulletin* 84(1): 22–23.

Godley, W. and Cripps, F.T. (1983) *Macroeconomics*. New York: Oxford University Press.

Godley, W. and Lavoie, M. (2003) *Two-country stock-flow-consistent macroeconomics using a closed model within a dollar exchange regime*. Cambridge Endowment for Research in Finance, Working Paper No. 10. Cambridge, UK: Cambridge Endowment for Research in Finance. Available at: http://www.dspace.cam.ac.uk/bitstream/1810/225206/1/wp10.pdf.

Godley, W. and Lavoie, M. (2005) Comprehensive accounting in simple open economy macroeconomics with endogenous sterilisation or flexible exchange rates. *Journal of Post Keynesian Economics* 28(2): 277–312.

Godley, W. and Lavoie, M. (2007a) *Monetary Economics: An Integrated Approach to Credit, Money, Income, Production and Wealth*. London: Palgrave MacMillan.

Godley, W. and Lavoie, M. (2007b) A simple model of three economies with two currencies: the Eurozone and the USA. *Cambridge Journal of Economics* 31(1): 1–23.

Godley, W. and Shaikh, A.M. (2002) An important inconsistency at the heart of the standard macroeconomic model. *Journal of Post Keynesian Economics* 24(3): 423–443.

Godley, W. and Zezza, G. (1992) A simple stock flow model of the Danish economy. In H. Brink (ed.), *Themes in Modern Macroeconomics*. London: Palgrave Macmillan.

Godley, W. and Zezza, G. (2006) *Debt and Lending: A Cri de Coeur*. Policy Note, no. 4. Annandale-on-Hudson, NY: Levy Economics Institute of Bard College.

Godley, W., Papadimitriou, D.B., Hannsgen, G. and Zezza, G. (2007) *The U.S. Economy: Is There a Way Out of the Woods?* Strategic Analysis, November, 11. Annandale-on-Hudson, NY: Levy Economics Institute of Bard College.

Graziani, A. (2003) *The Monetary Theory of Production*. Cambridge, UK: Cambridge University Press.

Greenwood-Nimmo, M. (2014) Inflation targeting monetary and fiscal policies in a two-country stock-flow-consistent model. *Cambridge Journal of Economics* 38(4): 839–867.

Herbillon-Leprince, S. (2016) A Stock-Flow Consistent Model with Real Estate and Land. Unpublished manuscript. Available at: https://www.boeckler.de/pdf/v_2016_10_21_herbillon-leprince.pdf

Hoog, S. and Dawid, H. (2015) *Bubbles, crashes and the financial cycle: insights from a stock-flow consistent agent-based macroeconomic model*. Bielefeld Working Papers in Economics and

Management, No. 01–2015. Bielefeld, Germany: Bielefeld Graduate School of Economics and Management.

Hume, D. (2008) *Selected Essays*. Oxford: Oxford University Press.

Izurieta, A. (2003) Dollarization as a tight rein on the fiscal stance. In L.-P. Rochon and M. Seccareccia (eds.), *Dollarization: Lessons from Europe and the Americas*. London: Routledge.

Jackson, T. and Victor, P.A. (2015) Does credit create a 'growth Imperative'? A quasi-stationary economy with interest-bearing debt. *Ecological Economics* 120: 32–48.

Jackson, T. and Victor, P.A. (2016) Does slow growth lead to rising inequality? Some theoretical reflections and numerical simulations. *Ecological Economics* 121: 206–219.

Jackson, T., Drake, B., Victor, P.A., Kratena, K. and Sommer, M. (2014) Foundations for an ecological macroeconomics: literature review and model development. WWWforEurope Working Paper No.65. Vienna: WWWforEurope. Available at: http://www.foreurope.eu/fileadmin/documents/pdf/Workingpapers/WWWforEurope_WPS_no065_MS38.pdf

Jaumotte, F. and Sodsriwiboon, P. (2010) *Current account imbalances in the southern Euro area*. IMF Working Paper No. 10/139. Washington, DC: International Monetary Fund. Available at: http://www.imf.org/external/pubs/cat/longres.aspx?sk=23940

Johansen, L. (1960) *A Multi-Sectoral Study of Economic Growth*. Amsterdam: North-Holland.

Kaldor, N. and Barna, T. (1944) The quantitative aspects of the full employment problem in Britain. Appendix C in W.H. Beveridge (ed.), *Full Employment in a Free Society*, London: Allen & Unwin.

Kalecki, M. (1971) *Selected Essays on the Dynamics of the Capitalist Economy*. Cambridge, UK: Cambridge University Press.

Kang, J.S. and Shambaugh, J.C. (2016) The rise and fall of European current account deficits. *Economic Policy* 31(85): 153–199.

Karacaoglu, G. (1984) Absence of gross substitution in portfolios and demand for finance: some macroeconomic implications. *Journal of Post Keynesian Economics* 6(4): 576–589.

Keynes, J.M. (2013) [1936]. The general theory of employment, interest and money. In E. Johnson and D. Moggridge (eds.), *The Collected Writings of John Maynard Keynes, Volume VII*. Cambridge, UK: Cambridge University Press.

Kinsella, S. and Khalil, S. (2011) Debt-deflation in a stock flow consistent macromodel. In D.B. Papadimitriou and G. Zezza (eds.), *Contributions in Stock-Flow Consistent Modeling: Essays in Honor of Wynne Godley*. Basingstoke, UK: Palgrave MacMillan.

Kinsella, S. and Tiou-Tagba Aliti, G. (2012a) Towards a Stock Flow Consistent Model for Ireland. Unpublished manuscript.

Kinsella, S. and Tiou-Tagba Aliti, G. (2012b) Simulating the Impact of Austerity on the Irish Economy Using a Stock-Flow Consistent Model. Unpublished manuscript. Available at: https://papers.ssrn.com/sol3/papers.cfm?abstract_id=2157420.

Kinsella, S., Greiff, M. and Nell, E.J. (2011) Income distribution in a stock-flow consistent model with education and technological change. *Eastern Economic Journal* 37(1): 134–149.

Kiyotaki, N. and Moore, J. (1997) Credit chains. *Journal of Political Economy* 105(21): 211–248.

Kratena, K. and Temursho, U. (2017) Dynamic econometric input-output modeling: new perspectives. In R. Jackson and P. Schaeffer (eds.), *Regional Research Frontiers, Vol. 2*. Basel: Springer International Publishing.

Krugman, P. (2000) How complicated does the model have to be? *Oxford Review of Economic Policy* 16(4): 33–42.

Krugman, P. (2013) Wynne Godley and the Hydraulics. *The New York Times*, September 13. https://krugman.blogs.nytimes.com/2013/09/13/wynne-godley-and-the-hydraulics/

Lavoie, M. (2003) A fully coherent post-Keynesian model of the Euro zone. In P. Arestis, M. Baddeley and J.S.L. McCombie (eds.), *Globalization, Regionalism and Economic Activity*. Cheltenham, UK: Edward Elgar.

Lavoie, M. (2004) Circuit and coherent stock-flow accounting. In R. Arena and N. Salvadori (eds.), *Money, Credit, and the Role of the State: Essays in Honour of Augusto Graziani*. Aldershot: Ashgate.

Lavoie, M. (2009) *Towards a post-Keynesian consensus in macroeconomics: reconciling the Cambridge and Wall Street views*. Research on Banking International and National Systems Or Networks, Working Paper 08-05. Ottawa: University of Ottawa.

Lavoie, M. (2014) *Post-Keynesian Economics: New Foundations*, Cheltenham, UK: Edward Elgar

Lavoie, M. and Daigle, G. (2011) A behavioural finance model of exchange rate expectations within a stock-flow consistent framework. *Metroeconomica* 62(3): 434–458.

Lavoie, M. and Godley, W. (2001) Kaleckian models of growth in a coherent stock-flow monetary framework: a Kaldorian view. *Journal of Post Keynesian Economics* 24(2): 277–312.

Lavoie, M., and Zhao, J. (2010) A study of the diversification of China's foreign reserves in a three-country stock-flow consistent model. *Metroeconomica* 61(3): 558–592.

Lazonick, W. and O'Sullivan, M. (2000) Maximizing shareholder value: a new ideology for corporate governance. *Economy and Society* 29(1): 13–35.

LeBaron, B. and Tesfatsion, L. (2008) Modeling macroeconomies as open-ended dynamic systems of interacting agents. *The American Economic Review* 98(2): 246–250.

Le Heron, E. (2011) Confidence and Financial crisis in a Post-Keynesian Stock-Flow Consistent Model, *Intervention–European Journal of Economics and Economic Policies*, 8(2): 361–388.

Le Heron, E. and Mouakil, T. (2008) A post-Keynesian stock flow consistent model for dynamic analysis of monetary policy shock on banking behavior. *Metroeconomica* 59(3): 405–440.

Lucas, R.E. (1976) Econometric policy evaluation: a critique. *Carnegie-Rochester Conference Series on Public Policy* 1: 19–46.

Marx, K. (1978) *Capital: A Critique of Political Economy*, Vol. II. London: Penguin Books.

Mazier, J. and Tiou-Tagba Aliti, G. (2012) World imbalances and macroeconomic adjustments: a three-country stock-flow consistent model with fixed or flexible prices. *Metroeconomica* 63(2): 358–388.

Mazier, J. and Valdecantos, S. (2014) Gathering the Pieces of Three Decades of Monetary Coordination to Build a Way out of the European Crisis. Unpublished manuscript. Available at: https://www.boeckler.de/pdf/v_2014_10_30_valdecantos_mazier.pdf

Mazier, J. and Valdecantos, S. (2015) A multi-speed Europe: is it viable? A stock-flow consistent approach. *European Journal of Economics and Economic Policies: Intervention* 12(1): 93–112.

Miess, M. and Schmelzer, S. (2016a) Stock-flow consistent modelling of real-financial cycles and balance sheet dynamics. Preliminary Work-in-Progress Version for 13th EUROFRAME Conference, Utrecht, June 10. Available at: http://www.euroframe.org/files/user_upload/euroframe/docs/2016/conference/Session%206/EUROF16_Miess_etal.pdf

Miess, M. and Schmelzer, S. (2016b) Extension of the empirical stock-flow consistent (SFC) model for Austria: implementation of several asset classes, a detailed tax system and exploratory scenarios. Research Report. Available at: http://irihs.ihs.ac.at/4135/.

Minsky, H. (1975) *John Maynard Keynes*. New York: Columbia University Press.

Minsky, H. (1986) *Stabilizing an Unstable Economy*. New Haven, CT: Yale University Press.

Modigliani, F. and Miller, M.H. (1958) The cost of capital, corporation finance and the theory of investment. *The American Economic Review* 48(3): 261–297.

Morris, N. and Juniper, J. (2012) Modern Money Theory (MM) and Minsky: towards a stock-flow-consistent (SFC) synthesis. In *AHE Panel on Modern Monetary Theory* at "Political economy and the outlook for capitalism," a Joint conference of the AHE, IIPPE, and FAPE, July 5–7, Paris.

Mundell, R.A. (1963) Capital mobility and stabilization policy under fixed and flexible exchange rates. *The Canadian Journal of Economics and Political Science / Revue Canadienne d'Economique et de Science Politique* 29(4): 475–485.

Naqvi, A. (2015) *Modeling growth, distribution, and the environment in a stock-flow consistent framework*. Institute for Ecological Economics Working Paper 2/2015. Vienna: Vienna University of Economics and Business.

Ndikumana, L. (1999) Debt service, financing constraints, and fixed investment: evidence from panel data. *Journal of Post Keynesian Economics* 21(3): 455–478.

Nikiforos, M. (2016) A nonbehavioral theory of saving. *Journal of Post Keynesian Economics* 39(4): 562–592.

Nikiforos, M. and Zezza, G. (2017) *The Trump Effect: Is This Time Different?* Levy Institute Strategic Analysis, April. Annandale-on-Hudson, NY: Levy Economics Institute of Bard College.

Nikiforos, M., Carvalho, L. and Schoder, C. (2015) 'Twin Deficits' in Greece: in search of causality. *Journal of Post Keynesian Economics* 38(2): 302–330.

Nikolaidi, M. (2015) *Securitisation, Wage Stagnation and Financial Fragility: A Stock-Flow Consistent Perspective*. Greenwich Papers in Political Economy no. GPERC27. London: University of Greenwich.

Papadimitriou, D.B., Nikiforos, M. and Zezza, G. (2013a) A Levy Institute Model for Greece. Levy Institute Technical Report. Annandale-on-Hudson, NY: Levy Economics Institute of Bard College.

Papadimitriou, D.B., Nikiforos, M. and Zezza, G. (2013b) The Greek Economic Crisis and the Experience of Austerity. Levy Institute Strategic Analysis, July. Annandale-on-Hudson, NY: Levy Economics Institute of Bard College.

Papadimitriou, D.B., Hannsgen, G. and Nikiforos, M. (2013c) *Is the Link between Output and Jobs Broken?* Levy Institute Strategic Analysis, March. Annandale-on-Hudson, NY: Levy Economics Institute of Bard College.

Papadimitriou, D.B., Nikiforos, M. and Zezza, G. (2014a) *Is Greece Heading For a Recovery?* Levy Institute Strategic Analysis, December. Annandale-on-Hudson, NY: Levy Economics Institute of Bard College.

Papadimitriou, D.B., Nikiforos, M. and Zezza, G. (2014b) *Prospects and Policies for the Greek Economy*. Levy Institute Strategic Analysis, February. Annandale-on-Hudson, NY: Levy Economics Institute of Bard College.

Papadimitriou, D.B., Nikiforos, M. and Zezza, G. (2014c) Will Tourism Save Greece? Levy Institute Strategic Analysis, August. Annandale-on-Hudson, NY: Levy Economics Institute of Bard College.

Papadimitriou, D.B., Nikiforos, M., Zezza, G. and Hannsgen, G. (2014d) *Is Rising Inequality a Hindrance to the US Economic Recovery?* Levy Institute Strategic Analysis, April. Annandale-on-Hudson, NY: Levy Economics Institute of Bard College.

Papadimitriou, D.B., Hannsgen, G., Nikiforos, M. and Zezza, G. (2015a) Fiscal Austerity, Dollar Appreciation, and Maldistribution Will Derail the US Economy. Levy Institute Strategic Analysis, May. Annandale-on-Hudson, NY: Levy Economics Institute of Bard College.

Papadimitriou, D.B., Nikiforos, M. and Zezza, G. (2015b) *Greece: Conditions and Strategies for Economic Recovery*. Levy Institute Strategic Analysis, May. Annandale-on-Hudson, NY: Levy Economics Institute of Bard College.

Papadimitriou, D.B., Nikiforos, M. and Zezza, G. (2016a) *Greece: Getting Out of the Recession*. Levy Institute Strategic Analysis, October. Annandale-on-Hudson, NY: Levy Economics Institute of Bard College.

Papadimitriou, D.B., Nikiforos, M. and Zezza, G. (2016b) *Destabilizing an Unstable Economy*. Levy Institute Strategic Analysis, March. Annandale-on-Hudson, NY: Levy Economics Institute of Bard College.

Passarella, M. (2012) A simplified stock-flow consistent dynamic model of the systemic financial fragility in the 'new capitalism'. *Journal of Economic Behavior & Organization* 83(3): 570–582.

Passarella, M. (2014) Financialization and the Monetary Circuit: A Macro-Accounting Approach. *Review of Political Economy* 26(1): 107–127.

Pyatt, G. (1988) A SAM approach to modelling. *Journal of Policy Modeling* 10(3): 327–352.

Pyatt, G. and Round, J.I. (1977) Social accounting matrices for development planning. *Review of Income and Wealth* 23(4): 339–364.

Pyatt, G. and Round, J.I. (1979) Accounting and fixed price multipliers in a social accounting matrix framework. *The Economic Journal* 89(356): 850–873.

Raberto, M., Teglio, A. and Cincotti, S. (2012) Debt, deleveraging and business cycles: an agent-based perspective. *Economics—The Open-Access, Open-Assessment E-Journal* 6: 1–49.

Ramsey, F.P. (1928) A mathematical theory of saving. *The Economic Journal* 38(152): 543–559.

Riccetti, L., Russo, A. and Gallegati, M. (2015) An agent based decentralized matching macroeconomic model. *Journal of Economic Interaction and Coordination* 10(2): 305–332.

Round, J.I. (2003a) Constructing SAMs for development policy analysis: lessons learned and challenges ahead. *Economic Systems Research* 15(2): 161–183.

Round, J.I. (2003b) Social accounting matrices and SAM-based multiplier analysis. In F. Bourguignon and L.A. Pereira da Silva (eds.), *The Impact of Economic Policies on Poverty and Income Distribution: Evaluation Techniques and Tools*. Washington, DC and New York: World Bank and Oxford University Press.

Rowthorn, R. (1981) *Demand real wages and economic growth*. Thames Papers in Political Economy No 81/3. London: Thames Polytechnic and Northeast London Polytechnic.

Sawyer, M. and Passarella, M.V. (2017) The monetary circuit in the age of financialisation: a stock-flow consistent model with a twofold banking sector. *Metroeconomica* 68(2): 321–353.

Schasfoort, J., Godin, A., Bezemer, D., Caiani, A. and Kinsella, S. (2016) Monetary policy transmission mechanisms in an agent-based macroeconomic model. Paper presented at "Social Simulation, the Universe and Everything," Rome, September 19–23. Available at: http://ae2016.it/public/ae2016/files/AE_2016_paper_5.pdf.

Schlefer, J. (2013) Embracing Wynne Godley, an economist who modeled the crisis. *The New York Times*, September 10. Available at: http://www.nytimes.com/2013/09/11/business/economy/economists-embracing-ideas-of-wynne-godley-late-colleague-who-predicted-recession.html.

Schmitz, B. and von Hagen, J. (2011) Current account imbalances and financial integration in the Euro area. *Journal of International Money and Finance* 30(8): 1676–1695.

Semieniuk, G., van Treeck, T. and Truger, A. (2011) *Reducing economic imbalances in the Euro area: some remarks on the current stability programs, 2011–14*. Levy Economics Institute Working Paper 694. Annandale-on-Hudson, NY: Levy Economics Institute of Bard College.

Seppecher P. (2012a) *Jamel, a Java Agent-Based MacroEconomic Laboratory*. HAL Archives Working Paper halshs-00697225. Lyon: Centre pour la Communication Scientifique Directe. Available at: http://econpapers.repec.org/paper/halwpaper/halshs-00697225.htm.

Seppecher P. (2012b) Flexibility of wages and macroeconomic instability in an agent-based computational model with endogenous money. *Macroeconomic Dynamics* 16(S2): 284–297.

Seppecher, P. (2014) *Monnaie Endogène et Agents Hétérogènes Dans Un Modèle Stock-Flux Cohérent*. HAL Archives Working Paper hal-01071391. Lyon: Centre pour la Communication Scientifique Directe.

Seppecher, P. and Salle, I. (2015) Deleveraging crises and deep recessions: a behavioural approach. *Applied Economics* 47(34–35): 3771–3790.

Seppecher, P., Salle, I. and Lang, D. (2016) Is the market really a good teacher?: market selection, collective adaptation and financial instability. 20th Conference of the Research Network Macroeconomics and Macroeconomic Policies, "Towards Pluralism in Macroeconomics?" October 20–22, Berlin.

Skott, P. (1989) *Conflict and Effective Demand in Economic Growth*. Cambridge, UK: Cambridge University Press.

Skott, P. and Ryoo, S. (2008) Macroeconomic implications of financialisation. *Cambridge Journal of Economics* 32(6): 827–862.

Solow, R.M. (1956) A contribution to the theory of economic growth. *The Quarterly Journal of Economics* 70(1): 65–94.

Steindl, J. (1952) *Maturity and Stagnation in American Capitalism*. Oxford: Basil Blackwell.

Stiglitz, J.E. (2010) *Freefall: America, Free Markets, and the Sinking of the World Economy*. New York: W. W. Norton.

Stone, R. and Brown, A. (1962) *A Computable Model of Economic Growth*. London, UK: Chapman & Hall.

Swan, T.W. (1956) Economic growth and capital accumulation. *Economic Record* 32(2): 334–361.

Taylor, L. (1983) *Structuralist Macroeconomics*. New York: Basil Books.

Taylor, L. (1990) Structuralist CGE Models. In L. Taylor (ed.), *Socially Relevant Policy Analysis: Structuralist Computable General Equilibrium Models for the Developing World*. Cambridge, MA: MIT Press.

Taylor, L. (1991) *Income Distribution, Inflation, and Growth: Lectures on Structuralist Macroeconomic Theory*. Cambridge, MA: MIT Press.

Taylor, L. (2004a) *Reconstructing Macroeconomics: Structuralist Proposals and Critiques of the Mainstream*. Cambridge, MA: Harvard University Press.

Taylor, L. (2004b) Exchange rate indeterminacy in portfolio balance, Mundell–Fleming and uncovered interest rate parity models. *Cambridge Journal of Economics* 28(2): 205–227.

Taylor, L. (2008) A Foxy Hedgehog: Wynne Godley and macroeconomic modelling. *Cambridge Journal of Economics* 32(4): 639–663.

Taylor, L. and Black, S.L. (1974) Practical general equilibrium estimation of resource pulls under trade liberalization. *Journal of International Economics* 4(1): 37–58.

Taylor, L. and Lysy, F.J. (1979) Vanishing income redistributions: Keynesian clues about model surprises in the short run. *Journal of Development Economics* 6(1): 11–29.

Taylor, L. and O'Connell, S.A. (1985) A Minsky crisis. *The Quarterly Journal of Economics* 100(Supplement): 871–885.

Taylor, L., Bacha, E.L., Cardoso, E.A. and Lysy, F.J. (1980) *Models of Growth and Distribution for Brazil*. New York: Oxford University Press.

Tesfatsion, L. and Judd, K.L. (2006) *Handbook of Computational Economics: Agent-Based Computational Economics*. Amsterdam: North Holland.

Thirlwall, A. (1979) The balance of payments constraint as an explanation of international growth rate differences. *BNL Quarterly Review, Banca Nazionale del Lavoro* 32(128): 45–53.

Tobin, J. (1969) A general equilibrium approach to monetary theory. *Journal of Money, Credit and Banking* 1(1): 15–29.

Tobin, J. (1982) Money and finance in the macroeconomic process. *Journal of Money, Credit and Banking* 14(2): 171–204.

Valdecantos, S. (2012) Macroeconomic Dynamics in Argentina in the Light of a Structuralist-Post Keynesian Stock-Flow Consistent Model. Unpublished manuscript. Available at: https://archive.org/stream/Jecs20xx/Eje1/Eje1.3/01.03.Valdecantos_djvu.txt.

Valdecantos, S. and Zezza, G. (2015) Reforming the international monetary system: a stock-flow-consistent approach. *Journal of Post Keynesian Economics* 38(2): 167–191.

van Treeck, T. (2009) A synthetic, stock-flow consistent macroeconomic model of financialisation. *Cambridge Journal of Economics* 33(3): 467–493.

Volcker, P.A. (1984) Facing up to the Twin Deficits. *Challenge* 27(1): 4–9.

Wolf, M. (2012) The balance sheet recession in the US. *Financial Times*, July 19.

Wren-Lewis, S. (2016) Heterodox economics, mainstream macro and the financial crisis. *Mainly Macro* blog, August 29. https://mainlymacro.blogspot.com/2016/08/heterodox-economics-mainstream-macro.html.

Zezza, G. (2007) The U.S. housing market: a stock-flow consistent approach. *Ekonomia* 10(2): 89–111.

Zezza, G. (2008) U.S. growth, the housing market and the distribution of income. *Journal of Post Keynesian Economics* 30(3): 379–405.

Zezza, G. (2009) Fiscal policy and the economics of financial balances. *Intervention. European Journal of Economics and Economic Policies* 6(2): 289–310.

Zezza, G. (2011) Income distribution and borrowing: growth and financial balances in the US economy. In P. Arestis, R. Sobreira and J.L. Oreiro (eds.), *The Financial Crisis: Origins and Implications*. Basingstoke and New York: Palgrave Macmillan.

Zezza, G. (2012) Godley and Graziani: stock-flow consistent monetary circuits. In D.B. Papadimitriou and G. Zezza (eds.), *Contributions in Stock-Flow Consistent Modeling: Essays in Honor of Wynne Godley*. Basingstoke: Palgrave MacMillan.

Supporting Information

Additional Supporting information may be found in the online version of this article at the publisher's website:

Table A1. A Social Accounting Matrix for the Real Sector.
Table A2. A Social Accounting Matrix with FoF information.

5

HETERODOX THEORIES OF ECONOMIC GROWTH AND INCOME DISTRIBUTION: A PARTIAL SURVEY

Amitava Krishna Dutt

University of Notre Dame
and FLACSO-Ecuador

1. Introduction

Theories of economic growth are often seen to originate in Harrod (1939) and Domar (1946), but they emerged much earlier, at least as far back as the classical economists, Smith, Malthus, and Ricardo, followed by Marx. The focus of analysis then shifted from economic expansion as a whole to resource allocation and the study of individuals and their interactions in markets. The earlier tradition was revived by Harrod and Domar after the development of Keynes's theory of effective demand. While several early theories of economic growth after the 1940s, most notably those of Kahn (1959) and Robinson (1956, 1962), continued in the Keynesian tradition, and economists such as Kaldor (1955–56, 1957) and Pasinetti (1962), drew on classical-Marxian as well as Keynesian approaches, growth theory from the mid-1950s became increasingly dominated by neoclassical (NC) theories that combined the theory of resource allocation with the theory of the growing economy as a whole.[1] Initially, pioneered by Solow (1956) and Swan (1956), and further developed – drawing on earlier work of Ramsey (1928) – especially by taking into account optimization, NC growth theory became mainstream growth theory. After a lull in interest in growth, "new" or "endogenous" growth theory emerged in the late 1980s, especially with the contributions of Romer (1986) and Lucas (1988),[2] and this approach, together with the old NC one, is now mainstream or "orthodox" growth theory.[3]

Despite the dominance of these theories, a sizeable number of economists have continued developing growth theories in the classical-Marxian, Keynesian, Cambridge, and related traditions, which can be described as being "heterodox." The purpose of this paper is to provide a brief survey of some of these heterodox theories. Because, as we shall see, growth and distribution are usually examined together on account of their interaction, we will refer to them as theories of economic growth and income distribution.[4]

Analytical Political Economy, First Edition. Edited by Roberto Veneziani and Luca Zamparelli.
Chapters © 2018 The Authors. Book compilation © 2018 John Wiley & Sons Ltd. Published 2018 by John Wiley & Sons Ltd.

Since economic growth is generally measured by the rates of growth of total or per capital output and income, its study examines the determinants of these growth rates. Although this can employ different methods, we will examine growth *theories*, by which we mean growth models that more or less explicitly make assumptions about the economy and derive their implications. We will not examine broader and less formal theoretical approaches or empirical contributions on the determinants of growth and distribution or the "testing" different theories and their implications. Growth theories can be *conceptualized* in different ways. One is by distinguishing between static and dynamic theories, the former concerning the economy at a point in time, and the latter on how it moves over time and hence with growth. Another is by distinguishing between what happens now and in the very near future, what can be called the short run, and what occurs in the more distant future, what can be called the medium or long runs, or with growth. Yet, another focuses on what are considered the major forces behind the growth process, for instance, capital accumulation, labor force growth, technical change, and institutional and structural change. Although the first two ways will be discussed, we will see that these distinctions are somewhat murky; we therefore focus mainly on the third way, focusing on the major factors that drive economic growth and the forces that, in turn, determine these factors.

To explain the term "heterodox," especially given the dominance of "orthodox" theories, we may distinguish between them along different dimensions. The *epistemological* one refers to principles used in organizing analysis without specifying, and therefore consistent with, any aspect of the real world. This is often seen as the defining dimension the NC (now the orthodox) approach, and involves explaining phenomena in terms of the optimizing behavior of individuals that have objectives, preferences, constraints, and beliefs. Since nothing is specified about the real world, for instance, what the constraints and preferences are, in principle, any real-world outcomes can be explained with it. Other approaches to economics do not have such a clearly enunciated organizing principle, but Marxian approaches can interpreted as taking class struggle (without specifying specific classes and their relations) as the foundation, and post-Keynesian approaches can be taken to focus on the implications of uncertainty about the future and the role of aggregate demand (without necessarily taking the view that aggregate demand is the main driver of growth or which aspects of aggregate demand are important).[5]

The *ontological* dimension refers to ideas about the real world, in terms of assumptions or conclusions,[6] which are added to the organizing principle to develop the theory. Orthodox growth theory depicts the economy as always fully utilizing its resources such as labor (as a conclusion). Old NC growth theory assumes that: factor prices are flexible; production technology reflects smooth substitutability between different inputs (like labor and capital) and constant returns to scale, that all saving is automatically invested, so that income not consumed creates a demand for investment goods so that the supply of and demand for goods are always equal; perfect competition prevails; there are no distortions such as externalities; and there is perfect information, or at least objectively known probabilities about the future. The economy grows in the long run at its natural rate given exogenously by labor supply growth and rate of technical change. New growth theory also examines full employment growth, but allows for endogenous growth because technical change responds to economic factors (such as saving behavior) even in the long run. Some NC growth theorists, especially in new growth theory, introduce distortions or market imperfections (such as externalities and imperfect competition). Heterodox approaches do not view the economy as fully utilizing all its resources, and stress the role of power relations between classes and groups (that may be interpreted as "rigidities" in the orthodox sense), and examine ways in which people and organizations respond to uncertainty (where there are no objective probability distributions concerning future outcomes) rather than risk (where such distributions exist). In them, growth, except in special situations, does not imply full employment, and the economy can be subject to cycles, instability, and crises.

The *normative* dimension refers to what is considered good for society or, at least, an improvement. The NC approach usually evaluates this in terms of individual utility functions, and takes social improvements to reflect only what is considered by individuals to be improvements. Thus, efficiency, in the sense of Pareto optimality, is considered good. Although in some cases, the approach does take into account distribution, a tendency that is growing, the focus remains on efficiency, and distributional issues between the rich and poor are often ignored using representative agents. In contrast, heterodox economists emphasize distribution. A high rate of economic growth is not necessarily a good thing, since even subjective well-being may not necessarily rise with economic growth (see Easterlin, 2001). Neither is the normative focus on individual preferences, which can be endogenous and be manipulated by the powerful, justified. However, heterodox economists do not reject the importance of growth if it increases employment, reduces unemployment, is fairly distributed, provides more resources for improving well-being in general, and makes it politically more feasible to improve the lot of the disadvantaged using government policies (see Friedman, 2005). This normative importance of distribution is related to the ontological view that growth and distribution are related and to the epistemological approach of focusing on class and power rather than on individuals.

The literature on heterodox growth theories is large and growing, and covers a variety of approaches and issues, which makes it impossible to provide anything like a comprehensive survey within the confines of a survey article. This paper attempts to review some major heterodox models that have attracted the most attention, and some of the major issues that these models cover, with the objective of providing a flavor of the literature and a view of its main contours. It proceeds in three steps. In Section 2, it examines a general framework that is used for presenting some equilibrium versions of the more popular and other related models. Section 3 explicitly examines dynamics. Section 4 modifies the general framework to examine models involving productivity growth and technical change, money and inflation, finance and debt, additional distributional issues, sectoral consideration, the open economy, and the environment. After this, Section 5 provides some concluding remarks. It should be noted that this survey is "partial" not only because space constraints prevent a more comprehensive coverage, but also because its method of starting from a general framework, even when it is modified, has arguably led to some partiality in favor of models of the classical-Marxian, post-Keynesian–Kaleckian, and closely related traditions,[7] and the relative or even complete neglect of other heterodox traditions.[8]

2. A General Framework and Alternative Models

A simple way of presenting the main elements of a variety of heterodox theories of growth and distribution is to start with a general framework and show how different theories can be developed to complete it. The framework makes some assumptions, mostly simplifying ones that can be modified to address additional issues.

2.1 *The General Framework*

The framework assumes that one good is produced in a closed economy without government fiscal activity, with two homogeneous inputs, capital (which is the same as the output and is nondepreciating), and labor. The economy is a capitalist one with only two classes, in which capital is owned by capitalists who receive profits from organizing production employing workers who can be hired and fired instantaneously, and receive wages. Explicit discussion of financial issues is eschewed. Given these assumptions, we can write two accounting identities. The first, for production, showing that the money value of production is equal to the value of consumption plus the value of actual investment, is

$$PY = PC + P\dot{K} \tag{1}$$

where P is the price level, Y, real output, C, real consumption, K, capital stock, and the over-dot denotes the time rate of change, so that $\dot{K} = dK/dt$ is the real level of actual investment. The second, for income, showing that total income is the sum of wages and profits, is

$$PY = WL + rPK \tag{2}$$

where W is the money wage, L is the level of employment, and r the rate of profit (nominal value of profits divided by the value of capital, PK).

The labor–output ratio is fixed at $a_0 = L/Y$ and the minimum capital requirement per unit of output is a_1 is also fixed,[9] so that

$$a_1 \leq K/Y \tag{3}$$

where the asymmetry for labor and capital occurs because firms hire only as much labor as they need, but hold on to their installed capital even if they do not fully utilize it. Dividing equations (1) and (2) by PY, we obtain

$$1 = ca_0 + \frac{g}{u} \tag{4}$$

$$1 = wa_0 + \frac{r}{u} \tag{5}$$

where $c = C/L$ is the consumption–labor ratio (including capitalist consumption), $g = \hat{K}$, the rate of growth of capital where the over-hat represents the growth rate of the variable, $u = Y/K$, a measure of capacity utilization, and $w = W/P$, the real wage. Equations (4) and (5) comprise a system of two equations in five variables (c, g, u, w, and r).[10] They provide a useful and fairly general framework for examining the determinants of growth, measured by g, and income distribution (in functional terms distinguishing between capital and labor, and in personal terms, distinguishing between rich capitalists and relatively poor workers) measured by r and w, but they cannot determine the values of the five variables. Three more independent equations are needed to have a shot at "closing" the system.[11]

We now examine different models that use additional equations, four of which are especially well known. Although they, and the theories underlying them, were not developed – with some having a long pedigree – to provide alternative closures of this framework, and sometimes take other forms, this approach provides a convenient way of comparing and contrasting their main features.

2.2 The Classical-Marxian Model

One model, usually called the classical-Marxian or neo-Marxian model (henceforth the CM model), adds the three equations

$$g = s_c \, r \tag{6}$$

$$u = 1/a_1 \tag{7}$$

and

$$w = \bar{w} \tag{8}$$

where $s_c < 1$. Equation (6) follows from the assumption made in all the models considered in this section that only capitalists save from their profit income (their only form of income), and workers consume all their income (from wages), and the assumption made in most of the models that capitalists save a fixed fraction, s_c, of their income.[12] These considerations imply that

$$g^S = s_c\, r \tag{9}$$

where $g^S = \frac{S}{K}$, where S is the real saving. The equation also assumes that firms plan to automatically invested all saving, so that saving results in capital accumulation, or

$$g^S \equiv g^I = g \tag{10}$$

where $g^I = I/K$, where I is planned real investment. Equation (7) follows from the assumption of full capacity utilization, so that (3) holds as an equality. In some versions, capacity utilization is assumed not to be at "full" capacity, but at some normal, desired, or targeted capacity utilization rate, which is less than the maximum level, so that

$$u = \bar{u} < 1/a_1 \tag{11}$$

which implies that in equilibrium, firms may hold some excess capacity, with capacity utilization given at some exogenously fixed level $\bar{u}$. In the classical-Marxian approach, this assumption is usually justified by the process of competition, one version of which portrays firms as trying to obtain as large a share of the market as possible, which deters them from leaving undesired excess capacity. Equation (8) assumes that the real wage is given exogenously at the level $\bar{w}$. Different versions of the approach explain this fixed level in different ways, some in terms of subsistence, which can be taken to be biological, or also including ethical and historical elements, some in terms of income opportunities in subsistence sectors outside the capitalist system, and some in terms of the relative power of workers and capitalist firms, or the "state of class struggle." In the last interpretation, the equation is sometimes rewritten in the form

$$\omega = a_0 w = \bar{\omega} \tag{12}$$

where ω is the labor share in income and $\bar{\omega}$ denotes its exogenously fixed level, with a higher level of $\bar{\omega}$ reflecting greater power of workers vis-à-vis firms; with a_0 taken to be given, equations (8) and (12) both imply a fixed real wage. The assumption can be explained, as in the approaches of Malthus and Ricardo, by population dynamics, according to which a temporary increase (decrease) in the actual wage above (below) its subsistence level increases (reduces) the population, and thereby reduces (increases) the wage, returning it to its subsistence level. It can also be explained, as in Marx's writings, by the existence of a reserve army of the unemployed, replenished by the loss of employment in the subsistence sector due to competition from the capitalist sector and the privatization of agricultural land by legal changes, and (if technical change is allowed) by labor saving technical change, occasionally by the slowing down of capitalist accumulation and employment growth, by social changes that make additional people (for instance, women) enter the labor market, and (if open economy considerations are allow) by immigration and capital outflows, among other mechanisms.

$$1 = wa_0 + ra_1.$$

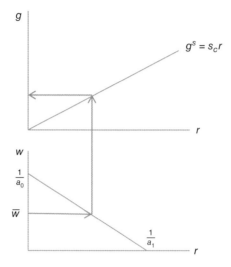

Figure 1. The Classical-Marxian Model.

Equations (4)–(8) comprise a system of five equations and five variables. Substituting equation (7) into equations (4) and (5) yields what are referred to as the consumption-growth and wage-profit frontiers (showing the maximum possible level of one variable in the equation given the value of the other),

$$1 = ca_0 + ga_1 \tag{13}$$

$$1 = wa_0 + ra_1 \tag{14}$$

Substituting equation (8) or (12) into equation (14) determines r, where profit can be seen as the surplus after the payment of wages (assuming that $wa_0 < 1$), which explains the name surplus approach sometimes given to the approach. Substituting this value of r into equation (6) determines the growth rate of capital, g, from which equation (13) determines c. Graphically, the model is shown in Figure 1, where the lower part of the figure shows the wage-profit frontier from equation (14), and the upper part shows the relation between growth and the rate of profit from equation (8); given $\bar{w}$, r is determined in the lower part, which then determines g in the upper part, as shown by the arrows. Since the output–capital ratio is fixed, total production grows at rate g and, if there is a given rate of population growth, this determines the rate of growth of per capita income and production. Growth in this model is not constrained by labor supply, but determined by saving and capital accumulation; a rise in the real wage or wage share reduces saving, capital accumulation and growth by reducing profits.

Despite capturing some central features of the classical-Marxian approach, this model is an oversimplified version of the different growth theories of the classical economists and Marx. Smith emphasized increases in labor productivity due to the division of labor made possible by market expansion. Ricardo examined the interaction of a manufacturing sector and an agricultural sector, in which there is diminishing returns to labor that is employed on increasingly less fertile land, and introduces landlords who receive rent from it; growth eventually comes to a halt with the economy reaching a stationary state as rent increases and squeezes profit. For Malthus, a high rate of saving is not always good for growth because it leads to a general glut of commodities, thereby reducing profit. The model is actually closer to a simplified version of Marx's theory, although he introduces complications involving technical change and the possibly falling rate of profit, the endogenous dynamics of capital-labor conflict, credit and finance, and the possibility of crisis due to the hoarding of money, among other things. We will examine these complications later.

2.3 *Post-Keynesian and Kaleckian Models*

Following the rise of Keynesian economics and the emphasis on the role of aggregate demand, growth models began to acknowledge that all saving is not automatically invested, and planned investment is a determinant of growth. In these models, like the CM model, output is not determined by labor supply, and unemployed labor is always assumed to exist. Models with these characteristics have sometimes been called post-Keynesians models, although they are closely related to Kalecki's models; we may therefore call them, collectively, post-Keynesian–Kaleckian (PKK) models.[13]

An early PKK model that fits into our general framework was developed by Robinson (1956, 1962).[14] This model, which has been called the neo-Keynesian (NK) model (Marglin, 1984; Dutt, 1990a), adds equations (6), (7) (or equation (11)), and

$$g = g(r) \tag{15}$$

where the function g satisfies $g' > 0$. Equation (7) can be justified using the concept of classical competition discussed earlier or in terms of pure competition with price-taking firms that produce all that they can. Equation (15) incorporates an investment function according to which planned investment increases with the rate of profit,

$$g^I = g(r) \tag{16}$$

and the market-clearing condition in the goods market, which implies that saving is equal to planned investment, so that

$$g^I = g^S = g \tag{17}$$

This equation, an equilibrium condition, is different from (10) where planned investment is identically equal to saving. Equation (6) follows from saving equation (9) and the right-hand equality of equation (17). Equation (16), according to Robinson (1962), makes investment plans a positive function of expected profits in the future, and takes the current profit rate to be a guide to expected profit rate. Subsequent contributions have also invoked financial considerations: a higher r allows firms to have more internal financing, and also allows them to obtain more external financing because they have more internal funds. The position of the function depends on expectations, or what Keynes (1936) refers to as animal spirits, that is, the spontaneous urge to action.

Equations (6) and (15) determine g and r, as shown by the upper part of Figure 2, which, with (for instance) full capacity utilization, determines w in the lower part of the figure as shown by equation (14); equation (13) solves for c. Equilibrium in the goods market is achieved by the fact that excess demand (supply) increases (reduces) P that, given W (for simplicity), reduces (increases) w that, according to equation (14), increases (reduces) r. A stable adjustment to equilibrium requires that the g^I curve in Figure 2 is flatter than the g^S line, or $s_C > g'$.[15] Starting

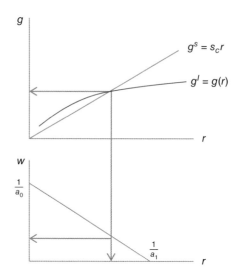

Figure 2. The New-Keynesian Model.

from an equilibrium, an increase in animal spirits shifts the investment curve upward, increasing the equilibrium levels of g and r, and reduces w, illustrating how an exogenous increase in investment brings about an increase in saving by reducing the real wage through forced saving by redistributing income from workers who do not save; like the CM model, a higher growth rate is associated with a lower real wage (and hence more inequality), although for this model, the increase in growth causes the increase in inequality, while in the CM model, the increase in inequality causes an increase in growth. An increase in s_c rotates the saving line upward and reduces the equilibrium levels of g and r and increases w, illustrating the paradox of thrift result according to which an increase in saving reduces aggregate demand, the profit rate, and reduces equilibrium investment and saving; this inverse relation between the capitalist saving rate and the growth rate is the opposite of the result found for the CM model.

While the NK model takes the price level to be the equilibrating variable in the goods market, an alternative approach, following the work of Kalecki (1971) and Steindl (1952), and arguably more faithful to Keynes, takes output to be the equilibrating variable. A model drawing on Kalecki and Steindl, independently developed by Dutt (1984) and Rowthorn (1982),[16] assumes that firms hold excess capacity and adjust output in response to demand, setting the price as a markup on labor costs, so that

$$P = (1 + z) \, W a_0 \tag{18}$$

where z, the markup rate, taken to be given, is dependent on factors such as the degree of industrial concentration and the state of class struggle. This implies that the real wage is given by

$$w = \frac{1}{(1 + z) \, a_0} \tag{19}$$

Since firms hold excess capacity, equations (7) or (11) do not hold, and u becomes a variable. It is then appropriate to assume, following Steindl (1952), that planned investment depends on

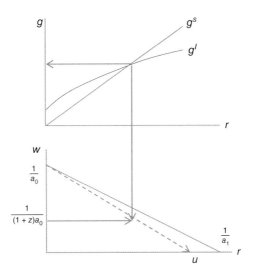

Figure 3. The Kalecki–Steindl Model.

both the rate of profit and on the rate of capacity utilization. Thus, investment (with investment being equal to actual accumulation through output adjustment) is given by

$$g = g\,(r, u) \tag{20}$$

with the partials satisfying $g_r > 0$ and $g_u > 0$ because a higher level of capacity utilization increases planned investment and more excess capacity deters it.

Equations (18) or (19) and (20), as well as the equation (6) showing saving – which is the same as in the CM and NK models – are added to equations (4) and (5) to complete this model, which can be called the Kalecki–Steindl (KS) model.[17] To show how equilibrium is determined, equations (5) and (18) yield

$$r = \frac{z}{1+z}u \tag{21}$$

which shows that as u increases, firms obtain a higher return on their capital. Substituting for u from this into equation (20), we get a positively sloped curve showing that an increase in r, both directly and because of the implied increase in capacity utilization, increases the level of planned investment, as shown by the g^I curve in the upper part of Figure 3. Equations (20) and (21) with equation (6) determine the equilibrium values of r and g, as shown by the intersection of the g^I and g^S curves in Figure 3. Equation (19) determines w, and the equilibrium configuration of w and r is shown in the lower part of Figure 3, and must occur on or inside the wage-profit frontier to satisfy (3). The economy is on the wage-profit line shown by the dashed line in the lower part of the figure, where the horizontal intercept of that line shows the level of capacity utilization. The adjustment to equilibrium takes place through variations in capacity utilization that, according to equation (21), also implies changes in r. If there is excess demand (supply) in the goods market, u increases (decreases), changing r according to equation (21); the stability of equilibrium requires, as in Figure 3, that the g^I line is flatter than the g^S line which, for this model, or that $g_r + \frac{1+z}{z}g_u < s_C$. The rate of growth of capital, and given the equilibrium capacity utilization rate, of output, determined by the positions of the saving and investment lines, is therefore determined by s_c and the investment parameters and the markup rate, z, which is held constant in drawing the investment line. An increase in autonomous investment (or animal spirits) increases the equilibrium g and r, while an increase in s_c reduces them, as in the NK model; these changes, however, reflect changes in u in this model, while they reflect changes in w in the NK model. An increase in the wage share, which for this model is given by $\omega = 1/(1 + z)$, due to a fall in the markup, z, implies that the investment line in Figure 3 moves up, increasing equilibrium g and r; it also increases the real wage, w, as shown by equation (19), implying that the economy moves to the northeast in the lower part of the diagram, to a higher wage-profit line, implying that equilibrium u also increases. These results, which are in sharp contrast to those of both the CM and NK models, distinguish this model from them on account of the fact that it reflects wage-led expansion in capacity utilization (an increase in ω implies an increase in u), wage-led growth (an increase in ω implies an increase in g and the growth rate of output), and what has been called the paradox of cost (an increase in the wage cost increases r).

Although these results go against earlier dominant ideas such as the CM notion that an increase in inequality is required for a higher rate of growth since it increases saving, or the NK idea that higher growth is possible due to an increase in inequality caused by forced saving, they are not really new ideas. There is a long tradition that takes the view that a high level of inequality and low wages depresses growth by reducing aggregate demand, found in the writings of Sismondi, Marx, Hobson, Kalecki (1971), Baran, and Sweezy, among others (see Bleaney, 1976), ideas that are resurfacing even in mainstream discussions of the 2007–2008 recession. The model shows that when the markup falls, real wage and the wage share increase, increasing the share of income to the group that consumes more of their income, it increases consumption demand, aggregate demand, and output, which, in turn, increases capacity utilization, the rate of profit, and investment, which increases growth.

Several variants of this model have been developed by modifying the investment function given by equation (20).[18] A simplified version assumes

$$g = g(u) \tag{22}$$

with $g' > 0$, for which a specific linear version (Amadeo, 1986) is

$$g = \alpha_0 + \alpha_u(u - \bar{u}) \tag{23}$$

where $\alpha_i > 0$ are parameters of the investment function, which states that if u is at its normal or targeted level $\bar{u}$, capital stock will grow at the rate α_0, but will grow faster (slower) when u is greater (less) than $\bar{u}$. These variants, like the basic KS model, imply wage-led growth.

In a particularly influential version developed by Bhaduri and Marglin (1990), which will be referrred to as the BM model, the investment function is written in the form

$$g = g(\pi, u) \tag{24}$$

with $g_\pi > 0$ as well as $g_u > 0$ (see also Kurz, 1990), where π is the profit share (where $\pi = 1 - \omega$), and the unambiguous effects of a change in the wage share do not follow. Bhaduri and Marglin analyze what they see as the short-run effects on capacity utilization (and not growth); however, this function also implies that when the profit share increases, u, r, and g may rise or fall. In this model, the increase in π (due to a rise in the markup) distributes income from workers to capitalists and tends to reduce consumption demand as in the KS model, the increase, for a given u, has a positive effect on investment, which means that the effect on aggregate demand is ambigous. The effects depend on the relative sizes of g_u and g_π (as well as s_C). If g_u is large and g_π small, when π rises r, u and g fall, but if the opposite is true, all of these can rise. In the intermediate case, it is possible for u to fall and g to rise, but it is not possible for u to rise and g to fall, since the increase in the profit share and the resultant increase in capacity utilization both increase accumulation. Bhaduri and Marglin justify their investment function by arguing that investment depends on the expected future rate of profit, and that firms form their expectation based on the current profit share and capacity utilization, because of the relation shown by equation (21), noting that $\pi = z/(1 + z)$. They criticize the KS model with its investment function given by equation (20) for not taking into account the dependence of the rate of profit on the rate of capacity utilization given by equation (21). Thus, they argue that even if in their own formulation, the assumption that the partial derivative of g with respect to u (for a given π) is positive, the stronger assumption that the partial derivative of g with respect to u for the KS model may not be (since by taking r to be given, it ignores the effect of a change in u through r), that is, the latter model makes the positive effect of u on g unwarrantedly strong. However, whether or not this stronger assumption is satisfied is an empirical matter concerning how investment responds to u given r. Be that as it may, by allowing investment to depend on the profit *share* rather than the profit *rate*, they have drawn attention to the possibility that a rise in the profit share can reduce growth or increase it, so that, as the subsequent literature has termed it, growth may be wage led (when a rise in ω or fall in π increases g) or profit led (when the rise in π increases g).[19] Of course, for the CM model with full capacity utilization, growth is necessarily profit led, but the novelty of this contribution is in showing the positive and negative effects of an exogenous change in the profit share on growth even when growth is determined by aggregate demand.

A key characteristic of the KS (and BM) model is that the equilibrium rate of capacity utilization is endogenously determined. It is argued by its critics that, although firms may wish to hold excess capacity (for instance, to meet unanticipated changes in demand or to take advantage of scale economies in investment), it is implausible that in equilibrium, firms will hold *any* amount of excess capacity as determined by the model rather than some exogenously given planned or desired level of capacity utilization, $\bar{u}$ (see, for instance, Committeri, 1986; Auerbach and Skott, 1988). It is argued that the economy cannot be in equilibrium if u does not satisfy equation (11) because firms are likely to reduce (increase) investment it if their capacty utilization is less (more) than what they desire or make some other adjustment. In the KS model in which investment is given by equation (23) for simplicity, the equilibrium level of capacity utilization is given by $u = (\alpha_0 - \alpha_u \bar{u})/(s_c \pi - \alpha_u)$ which, except by accident, will not satisfy equation (11). If we insist that it is, then we must have $g = \alpha_0 = s_c \pi \bar{u}$. But what will make the second equality hold? One possibility is to allow π to change over time, which can be explained by assuming that fims reduce their markup whenever $u < \bar{u}$ (and vice versa), the equilibrium is very similar to that in the NK model with the differrence that a_1 is replaced by $1/\bar{u}$ and that we replace equation (15) by (23). But since in this model, after ajustments in the profit share are completed and the model is in equilibrium, income distribution is no longer exogenous, it cannot examine of the effect of an exogenous change in income distribution on growth. Another possibility is to allow α_0 to adjust due to deviations of g from α_0, which produces a diffeent model, the implications of which will be analyzed in the next section, where it will be shown that equilibrium is unstable. Thus, the critics argue that with plausible investment behavior, there is no stable equilibrium with endogeneous capacity. As we shall see below, the model can be stabilized (that is, made to converge to an equilibrium or cycle around it) by introducing other features into it. In such a model, with capacity utization at (or hovering around) its normal level, $g = \alpha_0$ (from equations (11) and (23)). A change in the wage share will not affect the equilibrium growth rate and wage-led growth is no longer possible.

These arguments do not necessarily imply that the model with endogenous capacity utilization is logically incoherent, as argued by some critics.[20] First, the equilibria need not be interpreted as depicting an actual economy in which all relevant variables (such as growth rates and the capacity utilization rate) are constant, but as notional equilibria in which some parametes are artificially frozen to abstract from the effects of their changes (such as those of α_0), so that at equilibrium, not all things are "fully" adjusted to some planned values; the equilibria, in other words, represent some rough averages of variables that are changing due to the effects of shocks, rather than a self-repeating state. Second, in an uncertain environment firms need not have any specific desired level of capacity utilization, but be satisfied with remaining within an acceptable range of values, within which an equilibium with endogenous capacity utilization is possible. Third, even if firms have a particular desired level of capacity utilization, this level may be endogenous; under plausible assumptions to be mentioned later, this implies wage-led growth. Fourth, firms may have multiple possibily mutually inconsistent goals concerning $\bar{u}$, such as obtaining a desired makup or a desired internal finance ratio and may be satisfied with different degrees of the achievement of these goals without having a clear optimal weighted average of them as the overriding one, which make it endogenous.

2.4 Other Models

Although the CM and PKK models are best known in the heterodox growth literature, there are others that can also be examined in terms of the general framework.

A widely discussed model assumes that the same saving function used in the previous models, so that equation (6) holds, that capacity utilization is fully utilized or at its normal level due to perfect or classical competition, so that equations (7) or (11) hold, and that

$$g = n \tag{25}$$

where n is the exogenously given rate of growth of labor supply. The last equation assumes that growth occurs with full employment or a constant unemployment rate, since in this model (with given labor–output and capital–output ratios) capital, output and employment grow at the same rate. Here, g is determined from equation (25), after which equation (6) determines r, from which equations (13) and (14) determine c and w (in the case with full capacity, the case with normal capacity replaces (7) by (11)). This model can be interpreted as an NC one (see Dutt, 1990a) in which real wage variations adjust the rate of growth of employment to the rate of growth of labor supply, n, although it does not share the standard NC characteristics of factor substitution and ignoring class distinctions. Or it can be interpreted in terms of investment, and hence, capital accumulation, adjusting to labor supply growth, as in the Cambridge models of Kaldor (1955–56) and Pasinetti (1962). For this model, an increase in the saving rate of capitalists has no effect on the growth rate, which is determined by labor supply growth, but reduces the rate of profit and increases the real wage: this can be explained by the fact that the change increases saving, investment, and capital accumulation (without an independent investment function), which increases the rate of growth of labor demand, which increases the real wage and reduces the rate of profit.

Some other models modify the saving assumption in equation (6), replacing it with

$$g = -c_c + s_c r \tag{26}$$

adding $c_c = C_c/K$, "autonomous" capitalist consumption (that does not depend on the rate of profit) C_c as a ratio of capital stock, as a new variable, where it is assumed that C_c grows at a constant rate, $\bar{g}^c$.[21] This exogenous growth of the autonomous part of capitalist consumption may be explained by changes in social norms that keep increasing capitalist consumption as capitalists seek to keep up with each other's consumption and are induced to do so through sales promotion activities of sellers. Since in this model, c_c is a variable with a value that is determined by the model in equilibrium C_c and K must grow at the same rate, we have

$$\bar{g}^c = g \tag{27}$$

Serrano (1995) and Freitas and Serrano (2015) have developed a model with this assumption, adding to it an exogenously given distribution along CM or KS lines, shown by equation (8) or (19) that fix the profit share, π, and an autonomous investment function, say equation (23).[22] This model has an independent investment function as in the PKK models, and does not have growth determined by labor supply as in the NC model and does not insist on capacity utilization being at full or normal capacity as in CM models and can therefore be said to be in the PKK tradition. Two variants of this model may be examined (following Lavoie, 2016). One takes α_0 to be a constant as before, determines g from equation (27), u for this value of g from equation (21), and r from equation (21) that implies $r = \pi u$. For this model, growth is determined by autonomous consumption demand growth. An increase in this growth rate increases g and output and u by increasing aggregate demand, which increases the rate of profit; an increase in π leaves g and u unchanged and increases r; and an increase in α_0 increases u and r but leaves g unchanged. The other variant makes α_0 a variable and adds the equation

$$\alpha_0 = \bar{g}^c \tag{28}$$

that is, the "autonomous" rate of growth of capital, or the part of investment that is independent of $u - \bar{u}$, is determined by the exogenously given rate of growth of capitalist consumption. Equations (23), (27)), and (28) imply that equation (11) is satisfied, so that the level of capacity utilization is determined at its normal level without *assuming* it to be so but as a *result* of other equations of the model. This model thus behaves like a CM model with capacity utilization at its normal level and with distribution exogenously given, but growth is determined by autonomous consumption demand growth; c_c in equation (13) adjusts to bring saving and investment to equality, with its equilibrium level being $c_c = s_c \pi \bar{u} - \bar{g}^c$. An increase in the profit share for this model leaves g and u unchanged, but increases r and c_c.

2.5 Concluding Comments

The method of starting with a general framework with accounting relations such as equations (4) and (5), and introducing alternative sets of additional equations to obtain complete models can be viewed as an epistemological approach for analyzing growth and distribution, or for that matter, any aspects of social reality. It is an alternative to the NC organizing principle of explaining phenomena in terms of the optimizing agent. It does not focus on individual behavior, but looks at the overall structure of the system, and can therefore be related to what is called the "structuralist" approach that views the system as a whole in terms of accounting identities and then fills in behavioral, institutional, and other structural characteristics of the system to analyze the system.[23] Although here we have focused on flow accounting identities such as income and production accounts, this approach can incorporate relations between stocks and between stocks and flows, as made explicit in stock-flow consistent models (see below). Moreover, they can be used to analyze not only relations between variables at a point in time (what have been called synchronic relations) but also the evolution of the system over time, when laws of motion are introduced (to study diachronic relations involving what are called structural change, see below).

Using a common framework provides a simple way of comparing and contrasting different models representing different visions of the growth process and distribution, some of which may be relevant for some contexts, some periods, and some places (so there is no need to attempt to choose between them in general on empirical grounds). These models thus add ontological content to the epistemological approach. They imply, for instance, that growth may be determined by saving and distribution (the CM model), by labor supply growth (the NC model), and by aggregate demand (such as PKK models). They also show how distribution can affect growth and be affected by it in different ways, for instance, growth can be wage led or profit led, or be independent of distribution, and sometimes distribution is mainly determined by growth.

However, the approach discussed so far excludes many aspects of growth and distribution. First, although the framework and models can be seen as dynamic ones because they determine a number of variables in growth rate forms, they are also static ones in the sense that all variables are determined in equilibrium, with only some informal discussion of adjustment processes. They, however, can be used as the basis for explicitly analyzing dynamic process, by distinguishing between different "runs" such as the short and long runs, as shown in Section 3. Second, the framework is quite simple, for instance, assuming given techniques, a closed economy, and one sector, thereby ignoring the possible role of technical change, open economy considerations, and structural change involving sectors. But it can be used to analyze the role of these and other factors by modifying it, as shown in Section 4. Third, the approach and its extensions analyze time in a specific way, that is, in terms of flows and stocks and relations between them that may change over successive periods and does not include processes that involve different durations of time. An example of a CM model that does the latter using what is called a circuit of capital framework is developed by Foley (1982) and has been applied to other approaches (see Dos Santos, 2015; Vasudevan, 2016). This is a potentially interesting method for modeling dynamics, but seems to be tractably analyzed only in terms of a limiting steady-state framework, and so far has not yielded insights that cannot be obtained from the standard approach.

3. Dynamics

As noted earlier, the models discussed in the previous section analyze the determination of growth and distribution in equilibria or steady state, and do not analyze the dynamics over time explicitly. In this section, we modify some of the models discussed earlier by examining the dynamics of some parameters held constant in them, without otherwise changing the basic framework. The method distinguishes between a short run that takes some things as given, and a long run that examines how these givens change over time to examine whether the system arrives at a stable long-run equilibrium or result in cycles, and the possibility of instability. The analysis also implies the growth process can reflect different "closures" in different runs, so that models can be, say, CM in one run and the NC one in another, or the KS one in one run and the CM one in another.

3.1 The Dynamics of Investment and Consumption

The dynamics of investment can be examined in models having investment functions, that is, PKK and related models. A simple model with the explicit dynamics of investment assumes that the investment–capital ratio is given in the short run at the level g (as in the KS model mentioned in footnote 18), and in the long run changes according to

$$\dot{g} = \Theta \left[g^d - g \right] \tag{29}$$

where $\Theta > 0$ is a speed-adjustment constant which will be used in different models to save notation, and where desired investment, g^d is given by one of the investment functions of Section 2.3, such as equation (20) written as

$$g^d = g\,(r, u) \tag{30}$$

Equation (29) provides a simple way of taking into account lags in investment, emphasized by Kalecki (1971), by making current investment depend on the past, and making it change in response to its deviation from desired investment. Using all of the other equations of the KS model, this equation implies that in short-run equilibrium, when the goods market clears, we have

$$u - \frac{g}{s_c \pi} \tag{31}$$

which is stable and long-run adjustment, in which equation (31) always holds, takes place according to variations in g seen by substituting equations (21), (30), and (31) in equation (29). If $s_c \pi > g_r \pi + g_u$, the adjustment is stable, and the long-run equilibrium is exactly as in the KS model of Section 2.3. If, however, this inequality is not satisfied, long run equilibrium is unstable. This instability can be shown more starkly from the KS model with the investment function of equation (23) with α_0, autonomous investment, given in the short run, but changing in the long run according to the equation

$$\dot{\alpha}_0 = \Theta \left[g - \alpha_0 \right] \tag{32}$$

Following Lavoie (1995a), among others, α_0 can be interpreted as the expected rate of growth so that the investment function of equation (23) implies that firms plan to increase their capital stock at the expected rate of growth if actual and normal capacity utilization are equal, but to invest more (or less) than that if actual capacity utilization exceeds (or is less than) the desired level, and equation (26) assumes that firms adjust their expectations about the future growth rate adaptively in response to the deviation of expected growth from actual growth.[24] For this model, short-run equilibrium implies that $u = (\alpha_0 - \alpha_u \bar{u})/(s_c \pi - \alpha_u)$. In the long run, equations (23) and (32) imply that $\dot{\alpha}_0 = \Theta \alpha_u [u - \bar{u}]$ which shows, using the short-run equilibrium value of u, that $\dot{\alpha}_0$ increases with α_0, implying that long-run equilibrium, which occurs at the value $\alpha_0 = g = s_c \pi \bar{u}$, is necessarily unstable. This property is referred to as Harrodian knife-edge instability, for which, an increase (decrease) in planned investment leads to an increase (decrease) in capacity utilization by increasing (decreasing) effective demand, which leads to an increase (decrease) in growth expectations and therefore investment. Although this model is not exactly the same as Harrod's (1939) model, which is in discete time and is not explicit about adjustments in capacity utilization, it has been taken by Flaschel et al. (1999), Hein (2014), and others to formalize the model and demonstrate this Harodian knife-edge instability property.[25] This model can be extended to allow $\bar{u}$ to change depending negatively on the gap between α_0 and g (for instance, because if growth is expected to be higher than what it is now, firms will want to increase their desired excess capacity as a competitive weapon against possible entrants). This model implies that in long-run equilibrium $\alpha_0 = g$ and equation (11) is satisfied, but there is wage-led growth because $\bar{u}$ is endogenous (see Hein *et al.*, 2012).

The dynamics of consumption can be examined, for instance, in the model with autonomous growth in capitalist consumption of Section 2.4, by assuming that c_C is given in the short run in which u adjusts to clear the goods market, but in the long run, it adjusts according to $\hat{c}_C = \bar{g}^c - g$, which follows from the definition of c_C. Using the investment function given by equation (23) with autonomous investment given by equation (28), it follows that the model behaves like a KS model in the short run, with $u = (\bar{g}^c + c_C - \alpha_u \bar{u})/(s_c \pi - \alpha_u)$, but with (under some conditions) growth of capital and output converging in the long run to the growth rate of autonomous capitalist consumption, $\bar{g}^c$ with $u = \bar{u}$, as in the model of Section 2.4. A reduction in π in this model implies that u and g increase in the short run, but in the long run, they return to their initial levels; thus, the reduction in π reduces the average rate growth (so that growth is wage led in the average sense) over the adjustment period, despite the fact that long-run equilibrium rate of growth is unchanged (see Lavoie, 2016, for an analysis that also involves the investment adjustment shown in equation (32) and requires additional stability conditions).

3.2 *The Dynamics of Distribution*

The dynamics of distribution involving changes in w (or the wage or profit share) can be analyzed extending any model in which distribution taken to be a parameter, such as the CM and KS models. One simple model takes the CM model with w given in the short run, but allows the real wage to adjust according to the equation $\hat{w} = \Theta[g - n]$, where n is the given rate of labor supply growth, which states that growth rate of the real wage depends on how fast employment grows compared to labor supply. In the short run, the model is CM but in the long run, with w adjusting, the economy converges to an equilibrium in which equation (25) is satisfied, so that in long-run equilibrium is an NC or Cambridge model of Section 3.4. Another model, with given markup and hence profit share is KS in the short-run, but allows long-run adjustment in the markup (and hence the profit share) according to the gap between actual and normal capacity utilization (with firms increasing markups at a higher rate when capacity utilization is higher) according to $\hat{\pi} = \Theta[u - \bar{u}]$ (see Taylor, 1983); it thus becomes NK in long-run equilibrium, formalizing the discussion of Section 2.3.

In the pioneering model that endogenizes distribution, Goodwin (1967) uses the CM model, but amends it to take into account labor productivity growth at a given rate (which is not central to the model), allows labor supply grows at the given rate n, and most importantly, assumes that the rate of growth of the real wage (it is constant in the short run) is a linear function of the employment rate, a measure of labor market tightness. Goodwin shows that the model can expressed the in the Lotka–Volterra form involving two state variables, the wage share, ω, and the employment rate, $e = L/N$, where N is labor supply, which implies that the economy exhibits (concentric) cycles, whatever the initial values of the state variables (with the rate of growth of one variable depending on the level of only the other variable). High levels of capital accumulation and hence employment growth increase the employment rate that then increases the real wage, thereby squeezing profits, saving, and the rate of capital accumulation. The growth rate of the economy cycles around its NC level with cyclical changes in the wage due to the tightening and loosening of the labor market. This model has been modified it in various ways, for instance, by introducing nominal wage and price changes and by using nonlinear wage change functions (Desai, 1973; Veneziani and Mohun, 2006).

3.3 *Dynamics of Distribution and Aggregate Demand*

While Goodwin's model is CM and ignores aggregate demand considerations, several contributions introduce aggregate demand dynamics within its framework. Skott (1989) combines features related to the PKK tradition assuming that the saving–income ratio increases with the profit share and the investment–output ratio depends positively on the profit share and capacity utilization, with labor market dynamics using an employment growth function. In the short-run employment and output, capital stock and labor supply are given, and the goods market clears through variations in the price level and hence the profit share, as in the NK model. In the long-run employment and output change, depending positively on the profit share because greater profitability induces firms to increase employment and output and negatively on the employment rate, since tighter labor markets reduce the opportunity of firms for increasing employment, the stock of capital changes according to the investment function and labor supply grows at an exogenously fixed rate. An important feature of the model is Harrodian instability along the lines examined by Kaldor (1940), according to which investment responds strongly to the capacity utilization rate (more so than does saving) at intermediate levels of capacity utilization and weakly at low and high levels. The dynamics are examined in terms of the state variables capacity utilization, u, and the employment rate, e. At long-run equilibrium, with $\hat{u} = \hat{e} = 0$, we get $\hat{Y} = \hat{K} = n$, so that growth is determined by labor supply growth as in the NC closure (although capital is not fully utilized), but this long-run equilibrium is very likely to be locally unstable because of the unstable adjustment of output around long-run equilibrium due to Harrodian instability, and under fairly general conditions, the economy will fluctuate around the long-run equilibrium on a stable limit cycle.

Dutt (1992b) combines the KS and NK models to examine the cases of both excess and full capacity utilization using nominal wage and price dynamics involving conflict inflation that will be discussed in a later section, in which the real wage targeted by workers depends on the employment rate (with labor supply growing at an exogenous rate) and the markup target of firms depends on the capacity utilization rate. The model implies cycles in which the economy can alternate between excess capacity and full capacity utilization; there is a stable long-run equilibrium in which the economy converges to growth at rate n with full capacity, and growth is profit led as in the Goodwin model; however, this is so only in a zone of stability, outside which the economy will eventually experience a crisis of demand with a falling real wage and falling rates of capacity utilization and growth, since with excess capacity, the model experiences wage-led growth.

A simpler model examining the dynamics of only the state variables profit or wage share and the rate of capacity utilization has been developed by Barbosa-Filho and Taylor (2006) by assuming reduced-form wage share change and capacity utilization change equations to produce cycles with aggregate demand fluctuations by proxying the employment rate by the capacity utilization rate; the model is used mainly to examine U.S. business cycles. A similar model that focuses on the dynamics of the growth of capital stock (due to lags in investment), rather than slow output adjustment, and the profit share has been developed by Assous and Dutt (2013) to incorporate wage-led and profit-led growth effects of the profit share using a BM investment function, which also takes into account labor and goods market effects. In the short run, distribution and the growth rate of capital are fixed and adjustments in u clear the goods market, but in the long run, the change in the profit share depends on the profit share and the rate of capacity utilization, and the growth rate changes according to equation (29). Although the change in the profit share normally depends negatively on the profit share, for intermediate levels of π, it may respond positively due labor market effects (with a rise in the profit share reducing aggregate demand in a wage-led regime and hence increasing unemployment). With this nonlinearity, a variety of outcomes are possible, including instability, limit cycles, and hysteresis in which an exogenous downward aggregate demand shock followed by policy induced expansion may not restore growth.

4. Modifying the General Framework

The issues that can be addressed using models based on the general framework are limited by its simplifying assumptions. The models surveyed so far have abstracted from a host of considerations that have played a prominent part in heterodox theories of growth and distribution, such as technical change, money and inflation, finance and debt, distributional issues going beyond the stark worker/capitalist distinction, sectoral interactions, open economy considerations, and the environment. This section examines heterodox contributions on growth and distribution that incorporate these issues. Since the literature on them is large, each requiring its own survey paper, we must be content with brief reviews providing just a flavor of models related to those discussed in earlier sections.

4.1 Productivity Growth and Technical Change

Although our general framework has abstracted from productivity growth and technical change, these factors have played an important role in the writings of those who have inspired heterodox growth theories, including Smith, Marx, Schumpeter (1934), and, more recently, Kaldor (1957, 1961). The framework can be modified to analyze productivity growth and technical change by examining changes in a_0 and a_1,[26] and heterodox theories have done so mainly by making the rate of labor productivity growth, $\tau = -\hat{a}_0$, a variable while keeping a_1 a constant, in order to analyze steady-state growth paths (as in NC growth theories), but implications of changes in the latter have also been considered. With a_1 and the actual rate of capacity utilization being determined in equilibrium or constant, we get $\hat{L} = g - \tau$. Heterodox growth theories, however, do not always equate productivity growth and technical change, since the former is also seen as being caused by changes in social relations and norms rather than new methods of production, and the latter need not involve changes in productivity as shown by input–output relations in a macro framework, but changes in other parameters, such as consumption and investment parameters due to product innovation.

Although some heterodox models examine the consequences of exogenous changes in the levels or rates of growth of productivity, many endogenize τ. One popular approach makes τ depend on capital deepening, as in Kaldor's (1957) technical progress function, so that it depends positively on the rate of growth of the capital–labor ratio, or on scale economies as in Smith (for whom the division of labor is limited by the size of the market) and learning by doing in production and investment (following Arrow, 1962), so that it depends positively on the rate of growth of capital. Another popular approach, based on profitability, makes τ depend positively on the wage share because an increase in ω makes firms want to adopt labor-saving innovations at a faster rate as the profitability of existing techniques erodes (Taylor, 1991;

Duménil and Lévy, 2003; Foley, 2003). Other formulations include making τ depend positively on the rate of growth of the real wage on dynamic efficiency wage grounds (You, 1994), on the degree of monopoly along Schumpeterian lines (Lima, 2000), on labor market tightness (Bhaduri, 2006; Dutt, 2006b) so that the rate of change in τ depends positively on the difference between the rates of growth of employment and labor supply, and human capital accumulation due to education expansion (Dutt and Veneziani, 2011–12). Some models focus on changes in a_1, with capital productivity rising due to government investment in infrastructure (Tavani and Zamparelli, 2016) or falling with increases in τ to reflect that more capital per unit of output is required for achieving more rapid increases in labor productivity growth (Dutt, 2013).

In general, in heterodox growth models with unemployed labor, an increase in labor productivity or its rate of growth does not increase growth as it does in NC models with full employment, since the result may be to increase unemployment with output being determined by capital stock or aggregate demand. However, the precise effects depend on the specific model used and the parameters changed by technical change. Only a few examples using some CM and PKK models are given here. CM models with technical change typically assume that the wage share rather than the wage rate is exogenously given, so in the basic model, an increase in τ only has the effect of increasing the rate of growth of real wage without affecting output growth. However, if a change in τ is allowed to affect the wage share, for instance, because the rate of growth of the wage depends on the gap between employment growth and labor supply growth and productivity growth without fully adjusting to it, an increase in the parameter in a Smith–Arrow labor productivity growth function has the effect of reducing the wage share ω, and increasing r and g, and having an unclear effect on employment growth (see Dutt, 2013). This result, that rather than affecting growth directly, the effect of technical change depends on how it affects distribution, and how the change in distribution affects total saving is a rather general one in CM models (see, for instance, Dutt and Veneziani, 2011–12, in a model with high-skilled labor with human capital and low-skilled labor without it). Regarding capital productivity, continuing changes in it are incompatible with equilibrium outcomes (Foley & Michl, 1999; Duménil and Lévy, 2003). However, when there is a level change in capital productivity – for instance, when a higher labor productivity growth rate due to profitability reasons results in lower capital productivity – technical change may lead to a falling rate of profit as in Marx's theory, although not necessarily so, because of a possible decline in the wage share (Dutt, 2013). In PKK models, in which growth is determined by aggregate demand an increase in τ does not increase growth, but only reduces employment growth, unless some component of aggregate demand is positively affected by it. Rowthorn (1982), following Kalecki (1971), assumes that investment depends positively on the rate of technical change, and this, with a Smith–Arrow technical change function results in dual-sided relationship in which both capital accumulation and technical change affect each other positively. It is possible that some types of technical change can result in increases in consumption and investment parameters due to what have been called epochal changes in processes and products, and such changes can increase growth, while others may not. Technical change can also affect industrial concentration and the markup in a KS model with a BM investment function; the growth and distributional outcome depends on the precise relation between industrial concentration and technical change (see Lima, 2000). The assumption that labor productivity growth depends on the tightness of the labor market has been shown to imply that exogenous changes in aggregate demand can have a permanent effect on growth by inducing changes in labor productivity growth and the so-called natural rate of growth, with a stationary level of the unemployment rate (see Dutt, 2006b) by examining the interaction of aggregate demand and aggregate supply growth, implying that the model can have both NC and PKK features but have results like the latter.

4.2 *Money and Inflation*

Although money has an important role in the writings of Marx (for instance, in his analysis of the circuit of capital and hoarding rather than investing), and Keynes (for instance, in the discussion of uncertainty and liquidity preference), the explicit introduction of money in heterodox growth models is relatively recent. Most heterodox growth models that explicitly do so assume that money supply is determined endogenously by the demand for it at a given interest rate, because the demand for loans creates deposits and because central banks are lenders of last resort (see Lavoie, 2014). This is in sharp contradiction with many early NC growth models, which assume that the growth rate of money supply is given exogenously, given central bank policy and a fixed money multiplier. NC models typically view inflation to be the result of excessive money supply growth with the economy growing with an exogenously given growth rate given by labor supply growth and labor productivity growth, according to the quantity theory of money.[27] Heterodox growth theories, partly because money supply is endogenous, cannot explain inflation in this way and instead emphasize the importance of social conflict in terms of what has been called conflict inflation (see Rowthorn, 1977).

This analysis of inflation usually proceeds using a wage change equation and a price change equation. The former assumes that rate of change in the money wage, $\hat{W}$, depends positively on the gap between the actual real wage and the target real wage of workers .The price change equation assumes that the rate of inflation, $\hat{P}$, depends, in the case in which output is a full (or normal) capacity utilization, on the excess demand for goods, that is, the amount by which planned investment exceeds saving (Marglin, 1984), and in the case in which there is excess capacity, on the amount by which the actual real wage exceeds the target real wage firms based on their targeted markup, so that firms try to increase the actual markup (Dutt, 1990a). These two equations are combined to derive the rate of growth of the real wage, $\hat{w}$, which helps to determine the equilibrium real wage when $\hat{w} = 0$. This real wage determines the other variables of particular model chosen. For instance, in the NK model with full capacity utilization, there is persistent excess demand and the actual saving and investment at the rate of profit determined by this real wage is not equal to planned investment, and the wage target of workers is also not met, as in Robinson's (1956, p. 48) inflation barrier approach; an exogenous increase the real wage target of workers increases inflation and w, and reduces r and g, implying stagflation (Marglin, 1984).

The models can be extended in various ways, for instance, making wage and price changes depend on expected price and wage changes, the targeted real wages of firms depend on the interest rate (with a higher interest rate implying a lower targeted real wage to enable firms to increase their markup in an attempt to cover higher interest costs) and capacity utilization, and the targeted real wage of firms depend on the employment rate. The endogenization of the two targets is shown in Dutt (1992b) to result in cycles and the possibility of crises, as noted in Section 3.3. If the exogenously given interest rate is increased by central bank policy to reduce inflation, some of the models imply stagflation with a worsening of the distribution of income; for instance, in a KS model, the increase in the interest rate reduces the real wage by reducing the real wage targeted by firms and reduces consumption demand and investment demand, and the rise in the interest also reduces investment by increasing the cost of capital, which reduces growth; inflation may fall in the long run by reducing the real wage target of workers, but this may take a long time during which distribution worsens and the growth of output and employment fall. The results are not very different but somewhat more complicated if, contrary to the models discussed so far, money supply is given in the short run by the stock of high powered money and a given money multiplier, but adjusts in the long run according to the change in the government budget deficit as determined by an exogenous government deficit–capital ratio (see Taylor, 1991); thus, endogenous money in the sense that money supply adjusts endogenously due to bank and central bank behavior to the demand for money is not essential for showing how conflict and aggregate demand have a major role in determining growth, inflation, and distribution.

4.3 *Finance and Debt*

While introducing money and the interest rate, the discussion of Section 4.2 did not explicitly introduce borrowing and debt, or allow for changes in the price of assets, which have had important roles in heterodox analysis, especially in the writings of Keynes (1936) and Minsky (1986). Such financial issues have been introduced mostly into different PKK models (see, for instance, Taylor, 2004; Hein, 2008, 2014; Shaikh, 2016), with the analysis differing according to which specific models are used, whose borrowing is emphasized, which assets are considered, how asset markets arc modeled, and on how financial factors affect the real economy (through investment and saving functions and by directly affecting distribution).

Most models focus on the financing decision of firms, which can finance their investment in fixed capital (a few models – see Taylor, 1983 – also introduce working capital) from internal savings, borrowing from banks or the public, and issuing stocks or bonds, taking into account the alternative of "investing" in financial assets. High returns to financial assets – for instance, due to an increase in the interest rate influenced by monetary policy,[28] or by an increase in liquidity preference due to heightened uncertainty – in general reduces investment, as discussed earlier. In addition to including variables such as the profit rate or share, the rate of capacity utilization and the interest rate in the investment functions, they also introduce the internal saving by firms, the debt level of firms usually expressed as a ratio of capital stock, a quantitative measure of liquidity in the system that is affected by the monetary authorities, and the stock market valuation of firms. Steindl (1952) shows that an increase in the internal saving rate of firms has an ambiguous effect on growth: since dividend recipients consume a portion of their income, it reduces consumption, but in the long run, this can be countered by the fact that the capital stock of firms increases and firm debt decreases, so that investment increases. Shaikh (2009, 2016) endogenizes the saving rate of firms to show how this mechanism can address the Harrodian knife-edge instability problem. The incorporation of debt into the Steindl model also results in possible instability in the model even without a change in the interest rate as increasing indebtedness reduces investment and growth over time, and if the model is stable, wage-led growth may not prevail (see Dutt, 1995). With a Harrodian adjustment mechanism in the goods market, Taylor (2012) shows that debt dynamics and consequent Minsky-like effects on the interest rate can serve as a stabilizer because an increase in capacity utilization leads to increases in investment, debt, and the interest rate, which, in turn, reduces investment spending and brings about a downturn. Taylor (2012) examines the effects of changes in stock prices that not only affect investment but also consumption spending of financial wealth holders in different PKK models. Duménil and Lévy (1999) introduce a measure of credit availability in quantity terms into the investment function, and assume that the central bank adjusts credit availability to make u adjust to a given target level $\bar{u}$ (to influence inflation). They obtain a KS model with excess capacity with given distribution in the short run and a CM model, also with given distribution, but with $u = \bar{u}$ in the long run.

The effects of government borrowing and debt have been examined both for CM and PKK models. For CM models, Michl (2009) introduces government spending, taxes, and borrowing within an intertemporal optimizing framework in which only capitalists leave bequests to show that public debt can make income distribution less equal because capitalists own on the bulk of the debt, while workers also have to service it, and reduce growth by reducing saving and investment because of tax payments. However, You and Dutt (1996) show in a KS model that debt-financed government spending can be expansionary (because of government expenditure and the payment of interest on debt) and it is also possible that because of the increase in growth and employment, and an increase in the wage share of income, income equality can improve despite the fact that capitalists hold all the debt. The implications for growth, of course, get complicated if debt expansion increases the interest rate and crowds out private investment as they do in NC models, and if government spending on infrastructure crowds in private investment (see Taylor, 1991), the two having opposite effects.

Consumer borrowing has received some recent attention in PKK models. Dutt (2006a) examines a KS growth model in which workers borrow, assuming a given debt to income (net of interest payments) ratio that can be set by themselves or by banks and in which capitalists receive interest income at a fixed rate, in addition to profits from production. The dynamics of debt accumulation and investment using equation (29) shows the possibility of cyclical growth and implies that while borrowing is expansionary in the short run, it may reduce growth by worsening distribution due to an increase in the debt–capital ratio that redistributes income from debtor workers to creditor capitalists who have a higher propensity to save. While in this model, instability can arise if debt accumulation increases the interest rate, Hein (2014) shows that it can also arise if borrowing is driven by supply of credit, that is, when an increase in borrowing leads to an increase in debt, which increases the income of lenders who then lend more. Ryoo (2010) develops a model with both firm and household financing, building on the Harrod–Kaldor approach of Skott (1989) discussed in Section 3.3, to produce both short cycles due to the interaction of distributional dynamics and aggregate demand and long waves due to financial factors, following Minsky's (1986) suggestion.

Two further issues regarding models of finance, growth, and distribution should be mentioned. First, in terms of actual phenomena, financialization has been a popular theme in post-Keynesian models (see, for instance, Stockhammer, 2004; Palley, 2008; Skott and Soon, 2008; van Treeck, 2009; Hein and van Treeck, 2010). Financialization is interpreted as the imposition by shareholders of higher dividend payout ratios that reduce firm saving, and an expansion of consumer borrowing, the effects of which have been discussed above. It is also seen as shifting the distribution of income between workers, managers, and stockholders through a variety of channels. Since these groups have different propensities to consume, this can further affect aggregate demand and growth: for instance, an increase in the rate of interest can increase the markup, which reduces real wages and aggregate demand, as discussed earlier, and the effect of a redistribution to financiers or rentiers depends on whether profit recipients or interest recipients have a higher propensity to save. The implications of these changes, obviously, depend on whether the model is CM or PKK (see Dutt, 1989, for a CM model; Lavoie, 1995b for a PK model; and Dutt, 2016, for both). Second, concerning method, in modeling asset markets, growth models often track the balance sheets of asset holders and financial institutions focusing on how stocks are affected by flows such as income, saving, and borrowing (see Taylor, 1983, 2012; Skott, 1988), but not all of them do so explicitly, which can result in possible inconsistencies. Lavoie and Godley (2001–12) and Godley and Lavoie (2007) have introduced what has come to be called stock-flow consistent models that explicitly trace how all flows of different financial and real variables add to stocks in a consistent manner, but except in simpler models, this method requires the use of numerical simulation techniques (for a survey of PKK stock-flow consistent models, see Caverzasi and Godin, 2015).

4.4 Distribution beyond Two Distinct Classes

Our framework has analyzed inequality in terms of the distribution of income between two classes, capitalists who only receive profit income and workers who only receive wage income. This strict dichotomy cannot capture the complexity of class and distributional issues in the real world, and a number of models have modified the framework to allow workers and capitalists to receive different kinds of incomes, added additional classes, and examined nonclass distributional groups.

Kaldor (1955–56) allowed for saving both from profit income and wage income, assuming that the constant saving rate out of profit is greater than that out of wages. Pasinetti (1962) criticized Kaldor for not taking into account the capital stock of wage recipients despite the fact that they save. While this criticism can be deflected by interpreting Kaldor as distinguishing profit and wage income involving firms and households, and not between classes, Pasinetti's solution – examining two classes, and allowing workers to receive both wage income and profit income from their capital – has proved to be fruitful. Assuming that the two classes receive the same return, r, from the capital they own, K_i, where $K_C + K_W = K$ and where the subscripts denote capitalists and workers, each class saves a constant fraction of their income, so that $S_C = s_C r K_C$ and $S_W = s_W (r K_W + wL)$, with $s_c > s_w$ (with capitalists having a higher propensity to save), full capacity utilization prevails and investment maintains full employment, so that equations (7) and (25) hold. At long-run equilibrium, when the capitalist share of capital, $k_c = K_c/K$, is constant, which implies that $\hat{K}_C = g$, or $s_c r = n$. Thus, the long-run equilibrium r, which measures distribution, is independent of s_w, that is, worker behavior, a result that has come to be known as the Pasinetti paradox. The model has also been used to examine the dynamics of k_c over time, analyzing how the distribution of income and wealth change over time, and whether over time capitalists tend toward owning all the capital or none of it.

While this model considers the Cambridge closure of Section 2.3, it has been extended in numerous directions (including some by Pasinetti, 1983a), introducing more general saving functions, fiscal and monetary policy, differential rates of return on capital owned by different classes, saving by firms, factor substitution, and open economy considerations. The Pasinetti paradox has been found to hold even under many of these modifications of the model, though not in all. Conditions under which, in the limit, workers own all the capital have been explored, but they have been found to be unlikely to be satisfied. The model has also been extended to the case in which full employment growth does not prevail, in Darity (1981) by introducing an independent investment function that makes investment depend on the rate of profit and allowing for substitution in production, and in Dutt (1990c) in a version of the KS model. The latter implies that even if a Pasinetti paradox-type result holds, so that, $s_c r = g$, since g depends on the profit share, workers as a group can affect distribution. Moreover, wage-led growth becomes more likely since not only is current income redistributed toward workers, but in the long run, and as a consequence, wealth is also redistributed towards them.

Since in recent years, in many countries, top incomes also include not just capital income but what also is counted as wage income, some models allow capitalists to do managerial work and receive wage income in addition to profit income. Palley (2013) introduces managerial pay into a Kaleckian model with a BM investment function in which monopoly power, through the markup, determines the distribution of income between profit and wages, and labor market bargaining along Marx–Goodwin lines determines the wage bill between workers and managers. Also, introducing changes in hours of work and technical change due to learning by doing, the model shows how changes in the distribution between profits and wages and between workers and managers together determine the overall distribution of income. Dutt (2016) develops a general framework with two groups – the top, consisting of financiers and top managers who receive financial returns, managerial pay and profits, and the rest, consisting of workers who receive a wage also save and obtain interest income and explores a CM and a KS model with investment lags, to examine the effects of increasing managerial pay and financialization for growth and income distribution. With managers able to raise productivity and reduce the share of wage income going to the rest, the models imply different effects of distribution on growth depending on whether the economy has CM or KS characteristics and whether the top share increases due to financialization or an increase in top management income.

Some models go beyond two classes. Pasinetti's (1960) formulation of Ricardo's growth analysis introduces land and landlords who receive rent and shows in a CM model that accumulation leads to diminishing returns to labor as agricultural production extends to less fertile lands, which increases rents and leads to a stationary state since landlords, unlike capitalists, do not save. Dutt (1989) introduces a financier or rentier class that receives interest income as opposed to industrial capitalists who receive profits to show how the former class can slow down growth, Tavani and Vasudevan (2014) adds a separate managerial class in a KS model, endogenizing the relative wage of workers and managers, and Palley (2015) adds a middle class consisting of middle and top management into a KS model with a general production function with managerial inputs in addition to capital and labor and with endogenous technical change. In general, these models imply a more complex relation between income inequality and growth than models with capitalists and workers. Additional classes have also been introduced by subdividing workers into different groups, such as low- and high-skilled workers in a CM model in Dutt and Veneziani (2011–12) to examine the effects of an expansion of education, and short and long term labor in Dutt *et al.* (2015) in a KS model to examine the possible negative demand effects of greater labor market flexibility.

There are a few models that go beyond classes to examine gender and ethnic distribution. Braunstein *et al.* (2001) examine gender issues in a macroeconomic framework by analyzing the implications of care work at home – provided mainly by women – as an input into current and future labor that enters into the market production process using a BM model in which investment takes the form of capital accumulation as well as adding to human capabilities. Dutt (2017) examines the interaction of class and ethnic inequality under different assumptions on how, for instance, ethnic inequality can affect the market and political power of workers by increasing working class disunity. However, only a beginning has been made here and the area remains wide open.

4.5 *Multisector Issues*

Heterodox theories of growth and development have long emphasized taking into account multiple sectors, including those of Ricardo on agriculture and manufacturing, Marx on consumption and capital goods, Kalecki on sectors with fixed and flexible pricing, and structuralist economists who emphasize the role of structural change involving sectors in the development process.

Some heterodox multisector models analyze issues that cannot be addressed in one-sector models. Sraffa's (1960) critique of NC economic theory involved taking into account the different commodities used in the production of other commodities, which exposed the problems with the assumption of homogeneous capital with well-defined marginal product for explaining income distribution (see Harcourt, 1972). This approach has been used to examine the implications of different types of models, for instance, along CM and KS lines, and to examine the implications of the intersectoral mobility of capital in terms of the classical notion of competition and whether classical competition is consistent with monopoly power (see Dutt, 1990a; Shaikh 2016).

While systematic differences between sectors are not crucial for these models, other models focus on them, only a few of which are mentioned here (but see Dutt, 1990b). First, some models introduce different production conditions and social relations of production between different sectors, an important example being those featuring agriculture–industry interaction in which agriculture requires land for production but industry does not. Kaldor's (1979) theory along CM lines has surplus labor in peasant agriculture, which fixes the industrial wage in terms of the agricultural good, and the productivity of agricultural land depends positively on agricultural capital, which is augmented by peasants investing their savings; Thirlwall's (1986) formalization stresses the role of the agriculture–industry terms of trade in affecting industrial profitability and growth. Other models of agriculture–industry interaction include those of Taylor (1983), in which the industrial sector has markup pricing and excess capacity along KS lines, the agricultural sector is flex price along NK lines and capital moves between sectors, to show how agricultural expansion can increase the market for industrial goods, and those involving increasing returns and technical change in industry (Ros, 2001; Rada 2007). Second, there are models in which different classes consume different goods, for example, the rich consume luxury goods and the poor consume necessities. Taylor and Bacha (1976) show the possibility of an inequalizing spiral in which an increase in the relative wages of richer high skilled workers increases the size of the luxury goods sector, which excites animal spirits and growth, exacerbating inequality. However, if, investment is not stimulated by the growth of the luxury sector and excess capacity emerges in it as in KS models, inequalizing stagnation results (see Taylor, 1983). Third, different sectors can experience different rates of technical change and learning by doing, a theme also addressed by Kaldor (1966) and this, coupled with different demand patterns for different sectors, can lead to growth problems. When applied to manufacturing and services, if the latter experiences no labor productivity growth, but its demand is maintained due to low-price and high-income elasticities of demand, Baumol (1967) shows in an NC full employment setting that the service sector share of employment increases over time and overall productivity growth declines. Wolff (1987) uses Marx's notion of productive labor as that engaged in actual production and unproductive labor as that engaged in circulation activity, to show the same result, although in a model with full employment. However, this result does not necessarily survive in models that do not assume full employment: for instance, in a KS model, a long-run relative expansion of the unproductive sector can increase the rate of growth of the productive sector by increasing aggregate demand (Dutt, 1992a). Pasinetti (1983b) provides a more general discussion of intersectoral differences in rates of technical change and demand patterns in a multisector sector, and technical change is also analyzed in multisector evolutionary growth models related to the work of Schumpeter (see Metcalf and Foster, 2010).

4.6 *The Open Economy*

Heterodox economists have examined economic interactions between countries for a long time, for instance, in Marxist and related theories of imperialism and dependency (see Brewer, 2002), Keynes's recognition of trade surpluses for increasing aggregate demand and employment and structuralist ideas on the problems of the international pattern of specialization for the international terms of trade, technical change, and foreign exchange constraints, especially for low-income countries (Prebisch, 1950; Singer, 1950). It is thus not surprising that open economy issues have been extensively introduced into heterodox theories of growth and distribution. We confine ourselves to three points to highlight some implications of these models.

First, open economy extensions change some implications of the models discussed earlier. Extensions of the KS model imply that the implications of a change in distribution have a more complicated effect in an open economy than in a closed one. If an increase in the wage share is due to an increase in the wage, a decline in external competitiveness is more likely to reduce aggregate demand and growth by reducing exports (Bhaduri and Margin, 1990), but if it is due to a reduction in the markup due to a reduction in industrial concentration, an increase in external competitiveness and expansion is more likely (Dutt, 1984). It is also likely that a change in external competitiveness is likely to change the markup, with a reduction in competitiveness exposing domestic producers to more foreign competition, and taking into consideration this feedback is more likely to imply that an increase in the real wage reduces aggregate demand (Blecker, 1989). These models also show how the real exchange rate influences the distribution of income (Blecker, 2011). Models of endogenous technical change due to learning by doing have been extended to examine the effects of export growth formalizing the ideas of Kaldor (1966) with (manufacturing) growth having a lagged effect of labor productivity due to learning by doing, which reduces the rate of change of domestic prices and increases the growth of exports and hence growth (Setterfield, 1997).

Second, open economy considerations introduce additional constraints on growth. Especially low-income countries can be constrained by the availability of foreign exchange in the presence of limited export opportunities, because of their need to import investment goods and intermediate goods; earlier two-gap models with saving and foreign exchange gaps have been extended to deal with additional growth determinants, including demand and fiscal constraints (see Taylor, 1991; Ros, 2001). Related to this is Thirlwall's (1979) analysis of balance of payments constrained growth that shows how, if a country has balanced trade (or limited access to foreign borrowing), and its terms of trade do not change, its growth rate is determined by the foreign the rate of growth and income elasticity of imports (positively), and the income elasticity of its own imports (negatively). A large theoretical and empirical literature on this model has emerged (Thirlwall, 2011), in which a multisector approach stresses the importance of sectoral changes for growth (Araujo and Lima, 2007).

Third, growth models of global trade and payments examine the implications of interactions between rich and poor countries using what have been called North–South models. Some show how trade according to short-run comparative advantage results in the exports of technologically sophisticated goods that have strong learning-by-doing effect from the North to the South and exports of simpler goods from the South to the North, results in uneven development even without any other differences between the two regions (see Krugman, 1981; Dutt, 1990a). Others introduce structural asymmetries between rich and poor countries, for instance, making rich counties monopolize the production of investment goods and assume their growth to be determined by aggregate demand along KS lines, while low-income countries are foreign exchange constrained and have a CM structure (Taylor, 1983). These models suggest that efforts to increase Southern growth by increased saving may be thwarted by terms of trade declines, and there may be North–South divergence in growth because high-income elasticity of Northern goods and low-income elasticity of Southern goods leads to Southern terms of trade declines, extending Thirlwall's approach (see Thirlwall, 2011). These models have also been extended to examine issues of international capital flows (Dutt, 1990a).

4.7 *The Environment*

On the relation between growth and the environment, some early models examined environmental issues in the form of land. Foley (2003) includes land that can be substituted for capital with a low elasticity in a CM model with Goodwin-type wage dynamics and labor productivity growth using the profitability approach. Assuming that land (representing the carrying capacity of the earth's atmosphere) is priced and yields a rent for capitalist owners, and firms take the cost of land into account in their technical choices, the economy ends up on a steady-state growth path, but if land is not priced, no steady state exists and the growth path collapses with a catastrophe due to an externality. Petith (2008), however, shows that if there is capital-augmenting technical change (unlike what Foley assumes), the rate of profit falls to zero even if there is land-augmenting technical change, implying that even when land is priced, steady-state growth is not possible. More recently, Fontana and Sawyer (2016) examine a PKK growth model along KS lines distinguishing between output growth driven by aggregate demand, labor supply growth, and the depletion rate of natural capital (which is depleted faster by higher output growth) to discuss mechanisms – market adjustments, government policy, and social norms (which they stress) – for making them consistent. Taylor *et al.* (2016) also develop a model in the PKK tradition to examine the accumulation of greenhouse gases and study the dynamics of capital and greenhouse gas emissions taking into account, among other things, the effects of the accumulation of the latter on output and employment, although offset by mitigation, fossil fuel consumption, and income distribution. The model shows that full abatement may be possible, but also examines the implications of high levels of fossil fuel use. While some useful contributions have been made, there could be more attention given to the adverse differential distributional consequences of current and future environmental damage, which are stronger for low-income people and countries.

5. Conclusion

The main conclusions that can be drawn from this survey of the vibrant, large, and rapidly growing literature on heterodox theories of growth and distribution are as follows:

1. There are many different heterodox theories embodying different visions of the growth process, some of which may be valid for certain times and places, but all of which can shape our intuitions about, and help our understanding of, growth and distributional processes.
2. Despite their diversity, they share some common features that distinguish them from most orthodox NC models. They stress the importance of uncertainty, power, markets, and institutions and how they make distribution and economic growth interact. They stress the normative importance of distributional equality without neglecting the importance of overall growth. In a negative sense, they do not insist on basing analysis on individual

optimizing behavior, which can lead to assuming away important features of real-world economies to make models tractable, although they – and the relations they embody – are not necessarily inconsistent with it. Instead, they focus on structural relations between what are considered important to growth and distribution processes in a systemic manner, something that can be formalized using general frameworks and treating alternative models are providing different ways of "closing" the framework.

3. They deal with many of the issues that are also covered by NC theories of economic growth, such as money, inflation, technical change, multisector issues, and open economy considerations, but in doing so often stress different issues, such as the roles of conflict, unemployment, structural change, and balance of payments constraints. They also explore issues usually neglected in NC theories or relegated to the discussion of the short or medium run, such as the role of aggregate demand, the problem of unemployment, and financial instability.

4. They do not necessarily imply full employment growth or growth equal to some exogenously given labor supply growth. Full employment is, in Keynes's (1936) sense, a special case. Even Solow (2005) has been critical of orthodox theories' neglect of aggregate demand and medium-run issues. In fact, the short and medium runs may not be very different from the long run that, as Kalecki argued, may be an average of the short runs. As a consequence, these models have implications that are at odds with many NC models, including the possible adverse consequences of technical change, the role of class conflict and power relations in affecting growth, and the possible problems resulting from financialization.

5. The models may be interpreted as being a part of a broader "system," involving additional political economy factors, which examine the coconstitution and interaction of aspects of societies that are often arbitrarily divided into the economic, the political, and the social. This system needs to take into account how different groups of people – such as classes – influence institutions (including laws, organizations, and social norms) while engaging in power struggles in markets, the state, and other spheres. This can be done in terms of parametric changes, such as those influencing wage and profit shares, interest rates, and tax rates, government expenditures, and other autonomous components of aggregate demand. However, these "parameters" may need to be endogenized, sometimes, in explicit mathematical forms using law-like relations when appropriate, but perhaps more often – especially for longer run changes – by considering different possibilities qualitatively.

Acknowledgment

I am grateful to two anonymous referees and to Luca Zamparelli for their useful comments on an earlier draft, which helped to considerably improve the content and organization of the paper.

Notes

1. Despite domination by the neoclassical approach, growth theory was largely seen as including contributions from other approaches (Stiglitz and Uzawa, 1969; Sen, 1970; Wan, 1971).

2. An earlier work by Frankel (1962) contains many of the central ideas of this approach but did not catch on.

3. Recent textbooks, including Barro and Sala-i-Martin (1995), Aghion and Howitt (1998), and Acemoglu (2009), completely ignore heterodox theories and the Harrod model has been transformed into a Solow model with fixed coefficients (Barro and Sala-i-Martin, 1995; Acemoglu, 2009)! It is ironic that Solow (2005, p. 5) writes in his introductory chapter to the *Handbook of Economic Growth*, which is devoted entirely to old and new neoclassical growth theory, that "Neoclassical growth theory is about the evolution of potential output. In other words, the model takes it for granted that aggregate output is limited on the supply side, not by shortages (or excesses) of effective demand." He continues that "some sort of endogenous knitting-together of the fluctuations and growth contexts is needed, and not only for the sake of neatness: the short run and its uncertainties affect the long run through the volume of investment and research expenditure, for instance …"

4. See the titles of books such as Harris (1978), Marglin (1984), Dutt (1990a), Foley and Michl (1999), and Hein (2014).

5. These different organizing principles need not be mutually exclusive.

6. Since, in general, no list of explicit assumptions completely determines the conclusion (there always being implicit assumptions), theories sometimes specify both.

7. Even for these, I should apologize for what may seem to be my immodesty in referring to my own writings. My defense: I am more familiar with them, and they liberally draw on the contributions of others.

8. The paper does not discuss Schumpeter and evolutionary approaches at any length, and ignores the neo-Austrian and institutionalist approaches. For the first, some heterodox contributions are briefly mentioned below, while neoclassical versions are discussed in Aghion and Howitt (1998). For the neo-Austrians, views on the subjectivity of knowledge or the complexity of social phenomena have stood in the way of formal modeling, and those models that do exist seem to modify neoclassical models in minor ways by jettisoning neoclassical production functions and adopting a discrete number of techniques using combinations of processes that reflect different degrees of the roundaboutness of production (Proops and Speck, 1996). Institutionalist theories in the heterodox tradition also tend not to be formal, and to the extent they are, are close to theories represented here.

9. The fixed input–output ratios can be interpreted as Leontief technology with fixed coefficients and constant returns to scale, but are usually interpreted more broadly to incorporate social norms and power relations that determine, for instance, the speed of work and the number of work shifts.

10. They use the accounting identities about income and production mentioned earlier and add assumptions (which can be relaxed, as shown in Section 4.1) about fixed labor–output and minimum capital–output ratios.

11. This approach, starting with a general framework and "closing" it in different ways to examine growth and distribution, follows Marglin (1984) and Dutt (1990a).

12. Some of these models do not assume given saving rates but take the overall saving rate to depend positively on the profit share. They do not explicitly examine who saves and how much, an issue which we will examine later. Some other presentations of the CM model endogenize the saving rate of capitalists; for instance, Foley and Michl (1999) do so by assuming that while workers spend all their income, capitalists save by maximizing their utility intertemporally in an infinite horizon framework, and derive their saving behavior in terms of this optimizing framework. This illustrates that assumptions made in heterodox models that take some parameter as given do not necessarily imply that they cannot be justified on the basis of some optimization exercise.

13. See Lavoie (1992, 2014) and especially Hein (2014) for a review of PKK growth theory, with the latter also covering related empirical work.

14. Harrod's (1939) early Keynesian model that does not fit our framework will be discussed in the next section.

15. Robinson's (1962) presentation assumes that a minimum profit rate is required for positive investment so that the g^I becomes steep at low levels of r in Figure 2 and meets the horizontal axis at a positive level of r. In this case, the g^I curve intersects the g^S line twice, with the higher equilibrium being stable and the lower one unstable.

16. A similar model was published earlier in Italian by de Monte (1975); see Lavoie (2014).

17. This follows the name given in Dutt (1990a). It has been given various other names, including the Kaleckian, neo-Kaleckian, or the canonical post-Keynesian models of growth and distribution (see Lavoie, 1992, 2014, and Hein, 2014).

18. The simplest variant takes g to be given, implying that growth is determined by autonomous investment. The variants discussed here all assume that the relevant investment function shows what determines the investment–capital ratio, I/K. Some other presentations assume a function form for the determinants of I/Y. Since $I/K = (I/Y)u$, it is straightforward to translate one form into the other.

19. These terms actually refer to the effect of changes in distribution for goods market equilibrium. When distribution is endogenized, the terms become more ambiguous (see Assous and Dutt, 2013).

20. See Skott (2012) and Hein et al. (2012) for recent discussions, reprsenting the critics and the defenders, respectively.

21. If c_c is taken to be exogenously given, the model behaves qualitatively in a manner similar to the earlier models. One change that this modification does introduce, however, is that when there is a rise in animal spirits and the growth rate increases in the KS model, the I/Y ratio rises rather than stays constant, as it does in the model in which equation (6) holds, in which in equilibrium, $I/Y = S/Y = s_c\pi$. If there is a positive relation between the growth rate and the investment–income and saving–income ratio for economies, as cross-country data seem to suggest, this modification can explain this relation in terms of the KS model.

22. The exogenously given growth rates of other components s of aggregate demand can be used. For instance, Allain (2015) takes the growth rate of government expenditure to be a constant.

23. See Taylor (1983). This approach is closely related to the structuralist approach in the social sciences in general. It can be clarified that neoclassical theories also involve a "general framework" and a specific "structure," but do not adopt this systemic approach as an organizing principle, building instead on the optimizing agent and (usually) market relations between them, deemphasizing the specificity of their structure, implicitly overlooking others that may also be plausible.

24. This is a simplified analysis. Since capacity utilization can change in the model, the rate of growth of sales and output is not equal to g. If firms make investment plans based on expected and actual output growth, the analysis needs to take into account that fact that $\hat{Y} = \hat{u} + g$.

25. Domar's (1946) related model mentioned earlier, although often bracketed with Harrod's, asks how much investment is needed to maintain full employment growth rather than examining the implications of actual investment behavior.

26. Heterodox models, unlike neoclassical models, often abstract from factor substitution for a given technology (though they have been modified to do so), and thus do not distinguish between technical choice and technological change; thus, we refer to changes in these coefficients as technical change.

27. More recent neoclassical macro models assume that interest rates are fixed in the short run and adjusted according to a monetary policy rule over time. Recent neoclassical growth models (see Acemoglu, 2009, for instance) typically neglect inflation and money. The orthodox theory of inflation still emphasizes monetary policy mistakes such as those caused by the politicization of central bank policy.

28. Monetary policy rules endogenizing the interest rate are examined by Rochon and Setterfield (2012).

References

Acemoglu, D. (2009) *Introduction to Modern Economic Growth*. Princeton, NJ: Princeton University Press.

Aghion, P. and Howitt, P. (1998) *Endogenous Growth Theory*. Cambridge, MA: MIT Press.

Allain, O. (2015) Tackling the instability of growth: A Kaleckian-Harrodian model with an autonomous expenditure component. *Cambridge Journal of Economics* 39(5): 1351–1371.

Amadeo, E.J. (1986) Notes on capacity utilization, accumulation and distribution. *Contributions to Political Economy* 5: 83–94.

Araujo, R. and Lima, G. (2007) A structural economic dynamics approach to balance-of-payments-constrained growth. *Cambridge Journal of Economics* 31(5): 755–774.

Arrow, K.J. (1962) The economic implications of learning by doing. *Review of Economic Studies* 29: 155–173.

Assous, M. and Dutt, A.K. (2013) Growth and income distribution with the dynamics of power in labor and goods markets. *Cambridge Journal of Economics* 37(6): 1407–1430.

Auerbach, P. and Skott, P. (1988) Concentration, competition and distribution—A critique of theories of monopoly capital. *International Review of Applied Economics* 2(1): 44–61.

Barbosa-Filho, N. and Taylor, L. (2006) Distributive and demand cycles in the US economy: A structuralist Goodwin model. *Metroeconomica* 57(3): 389–411.

Barro, R.J. and Sala-i-Martin, X. (1995) *Economic Growth*. New York: McGraw-Hill.

Baumol, W.J. (1967) Macroeconomics of unbalanced growth: The anatomy of urban crisis. *American Economic Review* 57: 185–196.

Bhaduri, A. (2006) Endogenous economic growth: A new approach. *Cambridge Journal of Economics* 30(1): 69–83.

Bhaduri, A. and Marglin, S.A. (1990) Unemployment and the real wage: The economic basis of contesting political ideologies. *Cambridge Journal of Economics* 14(4): 375–393.

Bleaney, M. (1976) *Underconsumption Theories: A History and Critical Analysis*. London: Lawrence and Wishart.

Blecker, R. (1989) International competition, income distribution, and economic growth. *Cambridge Journal of Economics* 13(3): 395–412.

Blecker, R. (2011) Open economy models of distribution and growth. In E. Hein and E. Stockhammer (eds.), *A modern Guide to Keynesian Macroeconomics and Economic Policies* (pp. 215–239). Cheltenham, UK: Edward Elgar.

Braunstein, E, van Staveren, I. and Tavani, D. (2011) Embedding care and unpaid work in macroeconomic modeling: A structuralist approach. *Feminist Economics* 17(4): 5–31.

Brewer, A. (2002) *Marxist Theories of Imperialism: A Critical Survey*. London: Routledge.

Caverzasi, E. and Godin, A. (2015) Post-Keynesian stock-flow-consistent modelling: A survey. *Cambridge Journal of Economics* 39(1): 157–187.

Committeri, M. (1986) Some comments on recent contributions on capital accumulation, income distribution and capacity utilization. *Political Economy* 2(2): 161–186.

Darity, W.A., Jr. (1981) The simple analytics of neo-Ricardian growth. *American Economic Review* 71(6): 978–993.

Desai, M. (1973) Growth cycles and inflation in a model of the class struggle. *Journal of Economic Theory* 6: 527–545.

Del Monte, A. (1975) Grado di monopolio e sviluppo economic. *Rivista Internazionale di Scienze Sociali* 83(3): 261–283.

Domar, E.D. (1946) Capital expansion, rate of growth, and employment. *Econometrica* 137–147.

Dos Santos, P.L. (2015) Not 'wage-led' versus 'profit-led', but investment-led versus consumption-led growth. *Journal of Post Keynesian Economics* 37(2): 661–686.

Duménil, G. and Lévy, D. (1999) Being Keynesian in the short term and classical in the long term: The traverse to classical long-term equilibrium. *Manchester School* 67(6): 684–716

Duménil, G. and Lévy, D. (2003) Technology and distribution. Historical trajectories à la Marx. *Journal of Economic Behavior and Organization* 52: 201–233.

Dutt, A.K. (1984) Stagnation, income distribution and monopoly power. *Cambridge Journal of Economics* 8(1): 25–40.

Dutt, A.K. (1989) Accumulation, distribution and inflation in a Marxian-Post Keynesian model with a rentier class. *Review of Radical Political Economics* 21(3): 18–26.

Dutt, A.K. (1990a) *Growth, Distribution and Uneven Development*. Cambridge, UK: Cambridge University Press.

Dutt, A.K. (1990b) Sectoral balance in development: A Survey. *World Development* 18(6): 915–930.

Dutt, A.K. (1990c) Growth, distribution and capital ownership: Kalecki and Pasinetti Revisited. In B. Dutta, S. Gangopadhyay, D. Mookherjee and D. Ray (eds.), *Economic Theory and Policy* (pp. 130–45). Delhi: Oxford University Press.

Dutt, A.K. (1992a) Unproductive sectors and economic growth: A theoretical analysis. *Review of Political Economy* 4(2): 178–202.

Dutt, A.K. (1992b) Conflict inflation, distribution, cyclical accumulation and crises. *European Journal of Political Economy* 8(4): 579–597.

Dutt, A.K. (1995) Internal finance and monopoly power in capitalist economies: A reformulation of Steindl's growth model. *Metroeconomica* 46(1): 16–34.

Dutt, A.K. (2006a) Maturity, stagnation and consumer debt: A Steindlian approach. *Metroeconomica* 57(3): 339–364.

Dutt, A.K. (2006b) Aggregate demand, aggregate supply and economic growth. *International Review of Applied Economics* 20(3): 319–336.

Dutt, A.K. (2013) Endogenous technological change in classical-Marxian models of growth and distribution. In T. Michl, A. Rezai and L. Taylor (eds.), *Social Fairness and Economics. Economic Essays in the Spirit of Duncan Foley* (pp. 264–285). Abingdon, UK: Routledge.

Dutt, A.K. (2016) Growth and distribution in heterodox models with managers and financiers. *Metroeconomica* 67(2): 364–396.

Dutt, A.K. (2017) Horizontal inequality, intersectionality, growth and distribution: General considerations and the case of class and race. Unpublished, University of Notre Dame.

Dutt, A.K., Charles, S. and Lang, D. (2015) Employment flexibility, dual labor markets, growth and distribution. *Metroeconomica* 66(4): 771–807.

Dutt, A.K. and Veneziani, R. (2011–12) Education, growth and distribution: Classical-Marxian economic thought and a simple model. *Cahiers d'économie politique* 61: 157–185.

Easterlin, R. (2001) Income and happiness: Towards a unified theory. *Economic Journal* 111: 465–484.

Flaschel, P., Franke, R. and Semmler, W. (1999) *Dynamic Macroeconomics: Instability, Fluctuations and Growth in Monetary Economies*. Cambridge, MA: MIT Press.

Foley, D.K. (1982) Realization and accumulation in a marxian model of the circuit of capital. *Journal of Economic Theory* 28(2): 300–319.

Foley, D.K. (2003) Endogenous technological change with externalities in a classical growth model. *Journal of Economic Behavior and Organization* 52: 167–189.

Foley, D.K. and Michl, T.R. (1999) *Growth and Distribution*. Cambridge, MA: Harvard University Press.

Fontana, G. and Sawyer, M. (2016) Towards post-Keynesian ecological macroeconomics. *Ecological Economics* 121: 186–195.

Frankel, M. (1962) The production function in allocation and growth: A synthesis. *American Economic Review* 52: 995–1022.

Friedman, B. (2005) *Moral Consequences of Growth*. New York: Knopf.

Freitas, F. and F. Serrano (2015) Growth rate and level effects, the stability of the adjustment of capacity to demand and the Sraffian supermultiplier. *Review of Political Economy* 27(3): 258–281.

Godley, W. and Lavoie, M. (2007) *Monetary Economics: An Integrated Approach to Credit, Money, Income, Production and Wealth*. Houndmills: Palgrave Macmillan.

Goodwin, R.M. (1967) A growth cycle. In C.H. Feinstein (ed.), *Socialism, Capitalism and Growth* (pp. 54–58). Cambridge: Cambridge University Press.

Harcourt, G.C. (1972) *Some Cambridge Controversies in the Theory of Capital*. Cambridge: Cambridge University Press.

Harris, D.J. (1978) *Capital Accumulation and Income Distribution*. Stanford: Stanford University Press.

Harrod, R. (1939) An essay in dynamic theory. *Economic Journal* 49(193): 14–33.

Hein, E. (2008) *Money, Distribution Conflict and Capital Accumulation. Contributions to 'Monetary Analysis'*. Basingstoke: Palgrave Macmillan.

Hein, E. (2014) *Distribution and Growth after Keynes*. Cheltenham, UK: Edward Elgar.

Hein, E., Lavoie, M. and Van Treeck, T. (2012) Harrodian instability and the 'normal rate'of capacity utilization in Kaleckian models of distribution and growth—A survey. *Metroeconomica* 63(1): 139–169.

Hein, E and van Treeck, T. (2010) 'Financialisation' in post-Keynesian models of distribution and growth. In M. Setterfield (ed.), *Handbook of Alternative Theories of Growth* (pp. 277–292). Cheltenham: Edward Elgar.

Kahn, R.F. (1959) Exercises in the analysis of growth. *Oxford Economic Papers* 11: 143–156.

Kaldor, N. (1940) A model of the trade cycle. *Economic Journal* 50(197): 78–92.

Kaldor, N. (1955–56) Alternative theories of distribution. *Review of Economic Studies* 23(2): 83–100.

Kaldor, N. (1957) A model of economic growth. *Economic Journal* 67: 591–624.

Kaldor, N. (1961) Capital accumulation and economic growth. In F.A. Lutz and D.C. Hague (eds.), *The Theory of Capital Accumulation* (pp. 177–222). London: Macmillan.

Kaldor, N. (1966) *Causes of the Slow Rate of Economic Growth in UK*. Cambridge, UK: Cambridge University Press.

Kaldor, N. (1979) Equilibrium theory and growth theory. In M.J. Boskin (ed.), *Economics and Human Welfare* (pp. 273–291). New York: Academic Press.

Kalecki, M. (1971) *Selected Essays on the Dynamics of the Capitalist Economy*. Cambridge, UK: Cambridge University Press.

Keynes, J.M. (1936) *The General Theory of Employment, Interest and Money*. London: Macmillan.

Krugman, P. (1981) Trade, accumulation, and uneven development. *Journal of Development Economics* 8: 149–161.

Kurz, H. (1990) Technical change, growth and distribution: A steady-state approach to 'unsteady' growth. In H. Kurz (ed.), *Capital, Distribution and Effective Demand* (pp. 20–39). Cambridge: Polity Press.

Lavoie, M. (1992) *Foundations of Post-Keynesian Economic Analysis*. Aldershot, UK: Edward Elgar.

Lavoie, M. (1995a) The Kaleckian model of growth and distribution and its neo-Ricardian and neo-Marxian critiques. *Cambridge Journal of Economics* 19(6): 789–818.

Lavoie, M. (1995b) Interest rates in post-Keynesian models of growth and distribution. *Metroeconomica* 46: 146–177.

Lavoie, M. (2014) *Post-Keynesian Economics: New Foundations*. Cheltenham, UK: Edward Elgar.

Lavoie, M. (2016) Convergence towards the normal rate of capacity utilization in neo Kaleckian models: The role of non-capacity creating autonomous expenditures. *Metroeconomica* 67(1): 170–201.

Lavoie, M. and W. Godley (2001–02) Kaleckian models of growth in a coherent stock–flow monetary framework: A Kaldorian view. *Journal of Post Keynesian Economics* 22: 277–311.

Lima, G.T. (2000) Market concentration and technological innovation in a dynamic model of growth and distribution. *Banca Nazionale del Lavoro Quarterly Review* 215: 447–475.

Lucas, R.E. (1988) On the mechanics of economic development. *Journal of Monetary Economics* 22: 3–42.

Marglin, S.A. (1984) *Growth, Distribution and Prices*. Cambridge, MA: Harvard University Press.

Metcalfe, J.S. and Foster, J. (2010) Evolutionary growth theory. In M. Setterfield (ed.), *Handbook of Alternative Theories of Growth* (pp. 64–94). Cheltenham: Edward Elgar.

Michl, T.R. (2009) *Capitalists, Workers, and Fiscal Policy: A Classical Model of Growth And Distribution*. Cambridge, MA: Harvard University Press.

Minsky, H. (1986) *Stabilizing an Unstable Economy*. New Haven, CT: Yale University Press.

Palley, T. (2008) Financialization: What it is and why it matters. In E. Hein, T. Niechoj, P. Spahn and A. Truger (eds.), *Finance-Led Capitalism? Macroeconomic Effects of Changes in the Financial Sector* (pp. 29–60). Marburg: Metropolis.

Palley, T. (2013) A neo-Kaleckian–Goodwin model of capitalist economic growth: Monopoly power, managerial pay and labour market conflict'. *Cambridge Journal of Economics* 38(6): 1355–1372.

Palley, T. (2015) The middle class in macroeconomics and growth theory: A three class neo-Kaleckian–Goodwin model. *Cambridge Journal of Economics* 39(1): 221–243.

Pasinetti, L. (1960) A mathematical formulation of the Ricardian system. *Review ofEconomic Studies* 27(2): 267–279.

Pasinetti, L. (1962) The rate of profit and income distribution in relation to the rate of economic growth. *Review of Economic Studies* 29(4): 267–279.

Pasinetti, L. (1983a) Conditions of existence of a two-class economy in the Kaldor and more general models of growth and income distribution. *Kyklos* 36(1): 91–102.

Pasinetti, L. (1983b) *Structural Change and Economic Growth: A Theoretical Essay on the Dynamics of the Wealth of Nations*. Cambridge, UK: Cambridge University Press.

Petith, H. (2008) Land, technical progress and the falling rate of profit. *Journal of Economic Behavior and Organization* 66: 687–702.

Prebisch, R. (1950) *The Economic Development of Latin America and Its Principal Problems*. Lake Success, NY: United Nations.

Proops, J.L.R. and Speck, S. (1996) Comparison of neoclassical and neo-Austrian growth models. *Structural Change and Economic Dynamics* 7: 173–192.

Rada, C. (2007) Stagnation or transformation of a dual economy through endogenous productivity growth. *Cambridge Journal of Economics* 31(5): 711–740.

Ramsey, F.P. (1928) A mathematical theory of saving. *Economic Journal* 38(152): 543–559.

Robinson, J.V. (1956) *The Accumulation of Capital*. London: Macmillan.

Robinson, J.V. (1962) *Essays in the Theory of Economic Growth*. London: Macmillan.

Rochon, L.-P. and Setterfield, M. (2012) A Kaleckian model of growth and distribution with conflict-inflation and Post Keynesian nominal interest rate rules. *Journal of Post Keynesian Economics* 34(3): 497–520.

Romer, P.M. (1986) Increasing returns and long-run growth. *Journal of Political Economy* 94: 1102–1137.

Ros, J. (2001) *Development Theory and the Economics of Growth*. Ann Arbor, MI: University of Michigan Press.

Rowthorn, R.E. (1977) Conflict, inflation and money. *Cambridge Journal of Economics* 1(3): 215–239.

Rowthorn, R.E. (1982) Demand, real wages and growth. *Studi Economici* 18: 3–54.

Ryoo, S. (2010) Long waves and short cycles in a model of endogenous financial fragility. *Journal of Economic Behavior & Organization* 74(3): 163–186.

Schumpeter, J.A. (1934) *The Theory of Economic Development*. Oxford: Oxford University Press.

Sen, A.K. (1970) Introduction. In A.K. Sen (ed.), *Growth Economics* (pp. 9–40). Harmondsworth, UK: Penguin.

Serrano, F. (1995) Long period effective demand and the Sraffian supermultiplier. *Contributions to Political Economy* 14: 67–90.

Setterfield, M. (1997) *Rapid Growth and Relative Decline: Modelling Macroeconomic Dynamics with Hysteresis*. London: Palgrave.

Shaikh, A. (2009) Economic policy in a growth context: A classical synthesis of Keynes and Harrod. *Metroeconomica* 60(3): 455–494.

Shaikh, A. (2016) *Capitalism: Competition, Conflict, Crises*. Oxford and New York: Oxford University Press.

Singer, H. (1950) The distribution of gains between investing and borrowing countries. *American Economic Review* 40(2): 473–485.

Skott, P. (1988) Finance, saving and accumulation. *Cambridge Journal of Economics* 12(3): 339–354.

Skott, P. (1989) *Conflict and Effective Demand in Economic Growth*. Cambridge: Cambridge University Press.

Skott, P. (2012) Theoretical and empirical shortcomings of the Kaleckian investment function. *Metroeconomica* 63(1): 109–138.

Skott, P. and Ryoo S. (2008) Macroeconomic effects of financialiation. *Cambridge Journal of Economics* 32: 827–862.

Solow, R.M. (1956) A contribution to the theory of economic growth. *Quarterly Journal of Economics* 70: 65–94.

Solow, R.M. (2005) Reflections on growth theory. In P. Aghion and S. Durlauf (eds.), *Handbook of Economic Growth*, Vol. 1 (pp. 3–10). Amsterdam: North Holland-Elsevier.

Sraffa, P. (1960) *Production of Commodities by Means of Commodities*. Cambridge: Cambridge University Press.

Steindl, J. (1952) *Maturity and Stagnation in American Capitalism*. Oxford: Basil Blackwell.

Stiglitz, J.E. and Uzawa, H. (eds.) (1969) *Readings in the Modern Theory of Economic Growth*. Cambridge, MA: MIT Press.

Stockhammer, E. (2004) Financialisation and the slowdown of accumulation. *Cambridge Journal of Economics* 28: 719–741

Swan, T.W. (1956) Economic growth and capital accumulation. *Economic Record* 32(2): 334–361.

Tavani, D. and Vasudevan, R. (2014) Capitalists, workers and managers: Wage inequality and effective demand. *Structural Change and Economic Dynamics* 30: 120–31.

Tavani, D. and Zamparelli, L. (2016) Public capital, redistribution and growth in a two-class economy. *Metroeconomica* 67(2): 458–476.

Taylor, L. (1983) *Structuralist Macroeconomics*. New York: Basic Books.

Taylor, L. (1991) *Income Distribution, Inflation and Growth*. Cambridge, MA: MIT Press.

Taylor, L. (2004) *Reconstructing Macroeconomics*. Cambridge, MA: Harvard University Press.

Taylor, L. (2012) Growth cycles, asset prices and finance. *Metroeconomica* 63(1): 40–63.

Taylor, L. and Bacha, E.L. (1976) The unequalizing spiral: A first growth model for Belindia. *Quarterly Journal of Economics* 90: 197–218.

Taylor, L., Rezai, A. and Foley, D. (2016) An integrated approach to climate change, income distribution, employment, and economic growth. *Ecological Economics* 121: 196–205.

Thirlwall, A.P. (1979) The balance of payments constraint as an explanation of international growth rate differences. *Banca Nazionale del Lavoro Quarterly Review* 128: 45–53.

Thirlwall, A.P. (1986) A Kaldorian Model of growth and development. *Oxford Economic Papers* 38(2): 199–219.

Thirlwall, A.P. (2011) Balance of payments constrained growth models: history and overview. *PSL Quarterly Review* 64(259): 307–351.

van Treeck, T. (2009) A synthetic, stock-flow consistent macroeconomic model of financialisation. *Cambridge Journal of Economics* 33(3): 467–493.

Vasudevan, R. (2016) Financial, distribution and accumulation: a circuit of capital model with a managerial class. *Metroeconomica* 67(2): 397–428.

Veneziani, R. and Mohun, S. (2006) Structural stability and Goodwin's growth cycle. *Structural Change and Economic Dynamics* 17: 437–451.

Wan, H. (1971) *Economic Growth*. New York: Harcourt Brace Jovanovich.

Wolff, E.N. (1987) *Growth, Accumulation, and Unproductive Activity*. Cambridge: Cambridge University Press.

You, J.-I. (1994) Endogenous technical change, accumulation, and distribution. In A. Dutt (ed.), *New Directions in Analytical Political Economy* (pp. 121–147). Aldershot: Edward Elgar.

You, J.-I. and Dutt, A.K. (1996) Government debt, income distribution and growth. *Cambridge Journal of Economics* 20(3): 335–351.

6

ENDOGENOUS TECHNICAL CHANGE IN ALTERNATIVE THEORIES OF GROWTH AND DISTRIBUTION

Daniele Tavani

Department of Economics
Colorado State University

Luca Zamparelli

Department of Social and Economic Sciences
Sapienza University of Rome

1. Introduction

The analysis of the role of technological change in the growth process is of central importance in classical political economy. In his *Wealth of Nations,* Adam Smith (1776[1981]) famously emphasized increasing returns and specialization as the main driver of economic progress, while in the third volume of *Capital*, Marx focused on the profit-driven motive to innovation in capitalist economies, and the corresponding conflictual nature of labor productivity growth (Marx, 1867). With the marginalist revolution and its main concern with the allocation of scarce resources over competing needs, technical progress fell out of fashion and was either assumed away or to take place exogenously, as it is the case in the (augmented) Solow (1956) model. Only in the early 1990s, a revived interest in the endogenous determinants of technical change enabled the introduction of insights by Schumpeter (1942) into dynamic neoclassical general equilibrium growth models (Romer, 1990; Grossman and Helpman, 1991; Aghion and Howitt, 1992). These theories have defined endogenous technical change as: (i) explained within the model rather than assumed to occur; (ii) costly to generate so that the problem of allocating resources to R&D becomes of crucial importance; (iii) dependent on preferences, in particular as it pertains to the allocation between current and future consumption, and on policy action.

Before the advent of endogenous growth, the neoclassical scene was dominated by the Solow growth model and its optimal growth counterpart (Ramsey, 1928; Cass, 1965;

Koopmans, 1965). As pointed out by Jones and Romer (2010), one reason for the success of the neoclassical growth model was its ability to match the Kaldor facts of long-run growth (Kaldor, 1961). Among those, here, we are mostly concerned with: (a) the constancy of factor shares in the long run; (b) a purely labor-augmenting profile of technical change; (c) an increasing capital intensity, and (d) the constancy of the output/capital ratio. In order to be consistent with the Kaldor facts, the neoclassical theory hinges crucially on the use of a smooth aggregate production function, and the resulting choice of the technique of production that equates the factor marginal products to factor prices.

The Cambridge capital controversy of the 1960s has warned in a definitive way about the logical shortcomings of neoclassical aggregate capital theory. While the neoclassical prescriptions about factor substitution and the distribution of income hold true in a one-good economy, it is not possible to deduct an aggregate production function with decreasing real marginal product of capital from an economy with heterogeneous capital goods (Samuelson, 1966; Garegnani, 1970). Thus, the Cambridge critique had disruptive implications for the neoclassical theory of growth and distribution. Not surprisingly, at the time when the capital debate was occurring, non-neoclassical economists began to look again at the process of technical change, as opposed to capital/labor substitution, in order to provide an alternative view of distribution compatible with the Kaldor facts, but at the same time immune from the pitfalls of the marginalist theory. Key examples of these efforts are the induced innovation hypothesis by Charles Kennedy (Kennedy, 1964), and Nicholas Kaldor's technical progress function (Kaldor, 1957).

Although neither Kaldor's nor Kennedy's view of technical change ever became mainstream, they laid the foundations for more recent work by economists working in alternative traditions toward modeling the interplay between the factor distribution of income and the evolution of labor productivity over time. This survey is meant to summarize the last two and a half decades of alternative literature on balanced growth models that reject the notion of an aggregate production function with well-defined marginal products, but whose long-run equilibria are consistent with the Kaldor facts. We will distinguish between classical-Marxian and post-Keynesian models, and analyze the implications that different model closures have for income distribution and productivity growth. Using these alternative models, we will look at three viewpoints on the evolution of technology: (i) a Kaldorian technical progress function, in which labor productivity grows in line with capital accumulation; (ii) a classical-Marxian technical progress function, where labor productivity growth depends on factor shares; and (iii) a technical progress function that relates labor productivity growth with tightness in the labor market. In addition, we provide an account of recent non-mainstream research on costly innovation—both private and public—and of an unbalanced growth model featuring a declining output/capital ratio with a strong Marxian flavor.

These broadly categorized alternative theories are compared with neoclassical exogenous and endogenous growth: despite a number of strong differences, there are striking similarities between the approaches. Broadly, the differences pertain with the basic question about what drives the pace of technical progress, as well as the assumptions regarding factor substitution and full employment (or the lack thereof). Neoclassical theories emphasize the role of intertemporal saving preferences and deviations from competitive markets, while alternative theories are concerned with income distribution, the state of the labor market, and investors' behavior and expectations as the main drivers of growth. On the other hand, the main common element is that endogenous technical change requires the natural rate of growth to be sensitive to investment decisions; but similarities can also be found in the very formal aspects of the long-run solutions to the various models. By highlighting both similarities and differences, this survey serves the purpose of focusing the debate between competing theories on their relative merits and shortcomings, thus offering an even playing field toward greater engagement between the different traditions (Setterfield, 2014).

The paper is organized as follows. Section 2 reviews exogenous and endogenous mainstream growth theories in order to provide a benchmark for comparison. Section 3 looks at three different specifications of endogenous technical change used in the alternative literature, while Sections 4 and 5 study their implications for different model closures: classical supply side closures with either exogenous distribution or labor supply, vis à vis two post-Keynesian accumulation closures (Kaleckian and Kaldorian, respectively). Section 6 reviews recent contributions that introduce mainstream endogenous growth insights in classical and post-Keynesian models. Section 7 concludes.

2. Neoclassical Growth Theory

2.1 Common Elements

The neoclassical (or marginalist) theory determines output and income distribution taking technology, consumer preferences, and endowments of productive factors as exogenous variables. This structure produces a few foundational elements common to both exogenous and endogenous growth. First, all models presuppose Say's law thus omitting any considerations about the role of aggregate demand in the growth process: growth is determined by supply factors alone. The existence of a continuum of techniques of production ensures that it is possible to substitute one factor with another until their endowments are fully employed: excess supply of one input would produce a reduction in its price, thus favoring the adoption of a technique of production that employs the factor more intensively. Second, income distribution is determined by the relative scarcity of the productive factors. The interaction between technology and factor endowments determines the equilibrium marginal product of each factor, which equals its rate of remuneration via profit-maximization by firms. Due to decreasing marginal products, relative factor prices decrease in the relative factors supply. Third, the society's preferences with regard to consumption and savings affect the endowment of the accumulable factors of production, and therefore output growth and income distribution. Fourth, the economic environment is typically (although not universally) modeled with the aid of a representative agent, who earns a salary as worker and receives interest income as the owner of capital assets. Thus, there is no class distinction in the economy: incomes are differentiated according to their source, not by the social class to which they accrue.

2.2 Exogenous Growth

Both the Solow (1956) growth model and its Ramsey–Cass–Koopmans counterpart featuring an endogenous saving rate (Ramsey, 1928; Cass, 1965; Koopmans, 1965) see technical change as purely exogenous. In fact, under the assumption of perfectly competitive goods and factors markets as well as marginal productivity pricing of capital and labor, neoclassical growth *requires* technical change to be generated outside the model because there are no resources left to innovate if both factors of production are paid their marginal product. This follows from Euler's theorem: if, for a given level of technology $\bar{A}$, output Y is produced according to a constant returns to scale and twice continuously differentiable function of capital and labor $F(K, L, \bar{A})$, Euler's theorem implies that $F_K K + F_L L = Y$, where F_i is the marginal product of factor i. Hence, remunerating capital and labor takes up the entire national product, and no resources are left to finance the production of technology-improving innovations. Accordingly, the growth rate of technology $\dot{A}/A \equiv g_A$ is necessarily exogenous. Focusing on balanced growth and assuming that technical progress is labor augmenting (Uzawa, 1961), we can rewrite the production function as $F(K, AL)$, where AL is a measure of labor in efficiency units, or effective workers. Let $k \equiv K/(AL)$. Then, output per effective worker is $y \equiv Y/(AL) = f(k)$. Population grows at the constant rate $n > 0$ and, as we will assume throughout the whole paper, capital does not depreciate. The steady state of the Solow model solves

$$\frac{f(k_{ss})}{k_{ss}} = \frac{n + g_A}{s}. \tag{1}$$

The left-hand side of equation (1) features the constant long-run output/capital ratio, which increases in the growth rate of the effective labor force $n + g_A$ and decreases in the saving rate.

While growth is exogenous, income distribution is endogenous: the long-run capital intensity (in efficiency units) k_{ss} regulates both factor prices and factor shares. Under marginal productivity pricing, the interest rate r equals the marginal product of capital, and in the long run $r = f'(k_{ss})$. Factor shares, on the other hand, coincide with the respective output elasticities: letting ω be the wage share in national income, its long-run value is $\omega_{ss} = 1 - f'(k_{ss})k_{ss}/f(k_{ss})$, where $f'(k_{ss})k_{ss}/f(k_{ss})$ is the elasticity of output with respect to capital (that is, the share of profits). Therefore, all relevant measures of income distribution are endogenous as they depend on the capital/labor ratio, save for the special (though admittedly popular) Cobb–Douglas case where output elasticities, and therefore income shares, are parametrically constant throughout the entire growth path. The saving rate and the exogenous growth rate of technology influence the long-run distribution of income by affecting the steady-state capital intensity in opposite ways. The direction of such influence is regulated by the elasticity of substitution between factors of production σ, defined as the percentage increase in the capital/labor ratio due to a percentage increase in the ratio of marginal products (in turn, equal to the wage/interest rate ratio). When $\sigma < 1$ (>1), an increase in the wage/interest rate ratio produces a less (more) than proportional boost in the capital/output ratio, so that the wage share increases (decreases). The long-run capital intensity increases in the saving rate: therefore, an increase in s raises (lowers) the long-run wage share if $\sigma < 1$ (>1). The opposite is true for the growth rate of technology, which is inversely related with the steady-state capital/labor ratio. Finally, when $\sigma = 1$, we are in the Cobb–Douglas case.

2.3 Endogenous Growth

Starting in the early 1990s, mainstream economists have investigated the role of ideas in generating increasing returns that allow for sustained economic growth in the long run. The endogenous growth models that followed, either based on increasing product variety (Romer, 1990) or increasing product quality (Grossman and Helpman, 1991; Aghion and Howitt, 1992), produce endogenous technical change that is fully explained within the model, and is affected by saving behavior and policy action. The enterprise was made possible by abandoning perfect competition in favor of monopolistic competition. By discovering new ideas, innovators are granted a patent and make the monopolistic profits necessary to cover the cost of R&D investment.

A version of the Romer (1990) model that allows an appreciation of the endogenous nature of technical change is the following. Consider a three-sector economy (final sector, intermediate goods sector, and R&D sector) with a constant, fully employed labor force. The final (manufacturing) good is produced competitively according to

$$Y = L_Y^{1-\alpha} \int_0^A x_i^\alpha di, \tag{2}$$

where L_Y is the number of manufacturing workers, x_i denotes the intermediate durable input i rented in the production of the final good, A is a measure of product variety or the number of existing intermediate input in the economy, and $\alpha \in (0, 1)$ is an elasticity parameter. One unit of raw capital can be transformed in one unit of any intermediate input, and therefore the total amount of intermediate inputs is equal to the economy's capital stock: $\int_0^A x_i di = K$. As it will be clear just below, the symmetric structure of the model ensures that all intermediate inputs are demanded in the same amount; therefore, $x_i = x$, $K = Ax$, and $Y = AL_Y^{1-\alpha}x^\alpha$. This last way of writing the production function shows that output is linear in A, the number of intermediate inputs. Alternatively, one can see that the number of varieties plays the role of labor-augmenting technology in the aggregate production function. In fact, given $x = K/A$, we have $Y = (AL_Y)^{1-\alpha}K^\alpha$. Since the marginal product of each intermediate input is independent of all the others, diminishing returns to capital can be overcome if accumulation results in an increase in the number of intermediate inputs rather than in the amount of each input produced.

Firms in the intermediate goods sector acquire from the R&D sector an infinitely-lived patent on the new variety of input they produce. Therefore, they operate under monopolistic conditions. Each firm chooses the profit-maximizing supply of its intermediate good, given a downward sloping inverse demand curve for its product $p(x)$, the one-to-one production technology, and the cost of capital r. The demand curve equals the marginal product of intermediate goods: $p(x) = \partial Y / \partial x = \alpha L_Y^{1-\alpha}x^{\alpha-1}$, and profits to be maximized are $\pi = p(x)x - rx$. The solution is $x = L_Y(\alpha^2/r)^{\frac{1}{1-\alpha}}$, and monopolists earn strictly positive profits, equal across all sectors:

$$\pi = \left(\frac{1-\alpha}{\alpha}\right)\alpha^{2/(1-\alpha)}r^{\alpha/(\alpha-1)}L_Y = \left(\frac{1-\alpha}{\alpha}\right)rx.$$

Technological advancements, on the other hand, are developed in the competitive R&D sector. Here, L_A workers are employed to produce new ideas according to

$$\dot{A} = \beta A L_A, \tag{3}$$

which means that the productivity of each R&D worker, βA, is linear in the stock of the existing ideas.[1] Labor moves freely between R&D and final production, and all workers are paid the same wage, equal to the marginal product of labor in the final sector: $w = (1 - \alpha)Y/L_Y$. If the allocation of workers between the two sectors is constant, and $\rho \in (0, 1)$ is the fraction of workers in R&D, to be determined within the model, the growth rate of technology is:

$$g_A = \beta\rho L, \tag{4}$$

which makes it clear that economic policy aimed at increasing the number of scientists has permanent growth effects. In fact, the allocation of workers between R&D and manufacturing represents the economy's choice between current consumption versus long-run growth, and it may be affected by means of taxes and subsidies to either sector.

If the research sector is competitive with free entry, the flow of profits in R&D must be zero. The value of an innovation is given by π/r, the discounted value of profit flow at the market interest rate r. Since one worker produces βA ideas in the unit time, an R&D firm employing L_A workers is faced with the following zero-profit condition:

$$\frac{\pi}{r}\beta A L_A - w L_A = 0, \quad \text{or } r = \frac{\beta A \pi}{w}. \tag{5}$$

We can now solve for the rate of return as a simple function of the elasticity of demand faced by the monopolist α, the R&D productivity parameter β, and the number of workers in the final good sector $(1 - \rho)L$ as follows:

$$r = \alpha\beta L_Y = \alpha\beta(1 - \rho)L.$$

To see the effect of the saving rate on long-run growth observe that, with a constant saving rate $s \in (0, 1)$ for simplicity, the growth rate of capital is

$$g_K = s\frac{Y}{K} = s\left(\frac{L_Y}{x}\right)^{1-\alpha} = s\frac{r}{\alpha^2} = \frac{s\beta(1 - \rho)L}{\alpha}.$$

Next, the balanced growth condition $g_K = g_A$ yields the share of workers in the R&D sector as

$$\rho(s) = \frac{s}{s + \alpha}. \tag{6}$$

A higher saving rate shifts the allocation of workers in favor of the R&D sector, because society prefers to improve future technology over current consumption. Since the growth rate of technology is linear in the number of researchers, a higher saving rate determines a permanent increase in the growth rate of the economy in contrast with the Solow model.

Consider also the implications of this class of models for income distribution. The labor share in output is endogenous as it depends on the fraction of workers in the R&D sector. In fact, using the wage equation above together with the labor market clearing condition, we have:

$$\omega = \frac{wL}{Y} = \frac{1 - \alpha}{1 - \rho(s)} = (1 - \alpha)\frac{s + \alpha}{\alpha}. \tag{7}$$

Equation (7) shows that the wage share increases in the saving rate. The wage rate is determined in the final good sector as the marginal product of labor, which, in turn, decreases in the share of workers in that sector: a higher saving rate shifts the composition of the labor force toward R&D, thus making final good-producing workers more productive and increasing wages. Finally, notice that the output/capital ratio is inversely related to the saving rate, just like in the neoclassical exogenous growth model. In fact, $Y/K = \lambda L/(s + \alpha)$, decreasing in the saving rate.

Kurz and Salvadori (1998) insightfully noted that income distribution in early neoclassical endogenous growth models depends on technology and profit-maximization only, and it is therefore exogenous. Our account is not inconsistent with their conclusion, once a fundamental difference in the assumptions of the models under consideration is singled out. In our analysis, the factor of production responsible for sustained growth (ideas) requires labor, a scarce input, in order to be produced. In the models considered by Kurz and Salvadori (1998), on the other hand, no original input is involved in the accumulation of the factors responsible for endogenous growth, whether these be physical capital, human capital, or ideas. The difference is thus reconciled here by simply assuming that innovations are produced using foregone consumption (in terms of final output) rather than labor; the latter is fully employed in producing the final good. Equations (2) and (3) become $Y = L^{1-\alpha} \int_0^A x_i^\alpha di$ and $\dot{A} = \beta\rho'Y$, where ρ' is the share of income invested in R&D effort (Aghion and Howitt, 2010). The marginal product of labor is now $F_L = w = (1 - \alpha)Y/L$, so that the wage share $\omega = 1 - \alpha$ is independent of the saving rate.

A crucial implication of the growth equation (4) is that the growth rate increases with the size of the labor force. This feature is known as the *scale effect* property of first-generation endogenous growth models and with population growing at a rate $n > 0$ implies an explosive growth rate. The scale effect property was questioned on empirical grounds by Jones (1995): he proposed a specification for the growth rate of varieties featuring a less-than proportional spillover from past discoveries. With

$$\dot{A} = \beta A^\vartheta \rho L, \vartheta \in (0, 1), \tag{8}$$

the growth rate of ideas is:

$$g_A = \beta A^{\vartheta - 1} \rho L. \tag{9}$$

Balanced growth requires a constant growth rate. Differentiating (9) with respect to time and imposing $\dot{g}_A = 0$ yields

$$g_A = \frac{n}{1 - \vartheta}. \tag{10}$$

Economic growth is therefore explained within the model, but is independent of savings and policy. For this reason, this class of models is commonly referred to as *semi-endogenous*. On the one hand, technical change is the outcome of profit-maximizing behavior, but, on the other hand, its long-run determinants are purely exogenous (technology and population growth) just like in the Solow model.[2] Regarding income distribution, the semi-endogenous model delivers an endogenous labor share increasing in the saving rate.

As a final observation, the comparison of endogenous vs. semi-endogenous growth models highlights the importance of the spillover generated by past discoveries in the production of new ideas, or alternatively the lack of robustness of the assumptions required to generate endogenous growth (Solow, 1994, 2007). With constant returns to ideas (the reproducible factor), growth is endogenous: thriftier consumers or innovation subsidies that increase the share of scientists in the overall labor force will have permanent growth effects. With diminishing returns, neither savings nor innovation subsidies have permanent effects on growth. In the language of dynamical system theory, endogenous growth models are *structurally unstable*: their conclusions are not robust to slight modifications in the elasticity parameter of the innovation technology.

3. Alternative Theories of Growth and Distribution

3.1 *Common Elements*

Even though different contributions have emphasized different aspects of the interplay between growth and distribution in the long run, there are a few common elements that span almost universally throughout the non-mainstream literature. A first feature is the use of a Leontief aggregate production function combining fixed proportions of capital and labor in producing output:

$$Y = \min[uBK, AL], \tag{11}$$

where B denotes the ratio of potential output (Y^p) to capital, A is labor productivity, and $u \equiv Y/Y^p$ is a measure of capacity utilization. Such production technology is not always explicitly assumed but it is functional as a critical tool toward mainstream economics, in that: (a) it implies a rejection of marginal productivity theory as marginal products are not defined, and (b) it allows for less than full employment of both capital and labor. In fact, because factor demands are inelastic to factor prices, there is no market-based equilibrating mechanism toward full utilization of all factors of productions. Thus, even when there is full utilization of capital—that is, when $u = 1$—the production technology allows for structural unemployment of labor. When effective demand is not strong enough to ensure full capacity utilization, that is, when $u < 1$, both capital and labor are unemployed.

A second, distinctive element of non-conventional theories is their focus on class as a defining feature of capitalist economies. The distinction between workers, on the one hand, and owners of the capital goods (capitalists), on the other hand, brings the functional income distribution front and center in the analysis. Given the production technology, the inverse relationship between wages and profits is represented by the distributive curve:

$$r = uB(1 - \omega). \tag{12}$$

where $\omega \equiv wL/Y = w/A$. The class distinction pertains also to different saving behavior: workers and capitalists have different propensities to save so that $s_w < s_\pi \equiv s$. Throughout the analysis, we will use a simplified version of differential savings by assuming $s_w = 0.$[3]

A third common feature is that technical change is (with some exceptions discussed in Section 6) *costless*. In the neoclassical endogenous growth literature, producing new technologies requires to allocate scarce resources to R&D investment, and is therefore costly. On the contrary, the problem of resource allocation toward the financing of innovation technology is seldom addressed in alternative treatments of economic growth, and technical change is basically explained within the model as an externality, whether it occurs through learning-by-doing or responds to either income distribution or employment, as it will be clear just below.

3.2 Approaches to Technical Change

In general, technological change can be represented by changes in the productivity of both labor and capital. However, balanced growth with constant returns to scale in production requires $g_B \equiv \dot{B}/B = 0$: capital productivity must remain constant in the long run, as shown by Uzawa (1961), and recently re-emphasized by Schlicht (2006); Jones and Scrimgeour (2008); Irmen (2016). For this reason, most models (with the exceptions discussed in Sections 4.3 and 4.4) simply assume a constant potential output/capital ratio, and only focus on labor productivity growth g_A.

We will then investigate three possible routes to model improvements in labor productivity. The first one is known as Kaldor-Verdoorn law, and it states that technical change is directly related either to capital accumulation or to output growth. Verdoorn (1949) explored empirically the relation between productivity growth and output growth; while Kaldor (1957) formulated the technical progress function, where labor productivity growth depends on the growth of capital stock per worker. The basic idea, however, has been a mainstay in the understanding of economic development since the inception of political economy, when Adam Smith linked productivity growth to the division of labor in turn limited by the size of the market (Smith, 1776[1981]). Later, Marshall (1920), Young (1928) and Arrow (1962) all related labor productivity to the economy's scale of production and capital stock through the concepts of external economies of scale, macroeconomic increasing returns, and learning by doing. Here, we will adopt two linear versions of the law: productivity growth depends either on the growth rate of aggregate capital stock or on the growth rate of capital per worker. Since alternative theories assume the fixed coefficient production function in (11) and that technical change (except in

Sections 4.3 and 4.4) leaves capital productivity constant over time, we can use capital growth (g_K) instead of output growth (g_Y) to state the Verdoorn law:

$$g_A = \phi_0 + \phi_1 g_K. \tag{13}$$

Denoting the growth rate of labor demand by g_L, the technical progress function in terms of capital per worker can be written as

$$g_A = \varphi_0 + \varphi_1(g_K - g_L), \tag{14}$$

with $\varphi_1 \in (0, 1)$.[4] As noted by several commentators (see, for example, Black, 1962) right after Kaldor proposed the technical progress function, (14) can be obtained from a Cobb–Douglas per-capita production function with exogenous technical change: $A = Y/L = A_0(K/L)^{\varphi_1}$ with φ_0 denoting the growth rate of the scale parameter A_0. Our analysis will show, however, that equation (14) has implications on growth and distribution that are quite non-neoclassical, once it is coupled with alternative closures.

A second option consists in postulating that labor-saving technical change depends on the labor share. This relation fits well with the notion of cost-minimization, and is founded in the classical-Marxian analysis of the choice of technique. New techniques of production are adopted only if they do not decrease the profit rate at the given real wage (Okishio, 1961); when the wage share (i.e., a firm's unit labor cost) rises, an increase in labor productivity is necessary if the firm wants to prevent a reduction in its rate of profit. Thus, labor-saving innovation is a way to re-establish profitability in the face of rising labor costs. Some of the contributions belonging to this tradition allow for variable capital productivity, and we will analyze them separately in Sections 4.3 and 4.4. For now, it is enough to focus on a constant output/capital ratio while assuming a direct relationship running from the wage share to the growth rate of labor productivity:

$$g_A = f(\omega), \ f' > 0, \tag{15}$$

as in Taylor (1991) and Dutt (2013a).

A third strand of recent literature (Dutt, 2006; Flaschel and Skott, 2006; Sasaki, 2010; Palley, 2012; Setterfield, 2013a) has looked at labor market tightness—as measured by the employment rate—as a driver of technical change. Shortages of labor would push firms to adopt innovations that save on labor requirements. This approach is conceptually similar to the one just discussed, because it builds on the implicit assumption that a tight labor market reduces firms' profit margins. However, we will see in Sections 5.1 and 5.2 that the focus on the labor market as opposed to distribution is favored within the Keynesian demand-led growth framework, as it is instrumental in reconciling actual and potential growth rates. Given the exogenous labor supply N, denote the employment rate by $e \equiv L/N$. We can therefore represent this approach to technical change as[5]

$$g_A = h(e), \ h' > 0. \tag{16}$$

Observe that equations (13)–(16) all arise from a general specification of the kind $\dot{A} = H(\cdot)A$, which exhibits the linear spillover of existing technologies that we discussed regarding the neoclassical endogenous growth case.

Finally, we will discuss two cases in which capital productivity is not always constant. The output/capital ratio might vary along the transitional dynamics toward the balanced growth path, as the model evolves toward a constant long-run output/capital ratio: such would be the case with induced technical change we will study in Section 4.3.1. Alternatively, the rejection of balanced growth has led authors to focus on the case of capital-using technical change involving negative capital productivity growth. Combined with a classical closure, a falling output/capital ratio determines a falling rate of profit: for this reason, such a pattern is typically referred to as Marx-biased technical change (MBTC) (Foley and Michl, 1999, chapter 7): we analyze it in Section 4.4. Both cases establish a direct causal relation between the labor share and labor productivity growth, and therefore belong to the tradition summarized by equation (15).

3.3 Balanced Growth with Endogenous Technical Change

Roy Harrod's essay on dynamic economics (Harrod, 1939) is conventionally seen as the beginning of modern growth theory. A stylized account of his contribution would define three different growth rates: the actual growth rate g^i_K, or the ratio of investment to capital stock; the "warranted" rate g^s_K, which is the ratio of savings to capital stock; and the "natural" rate g^p, equal to the sum of population growth and exogenous labor productivity growth. The Harrodian analysis devises two problems. First, full employment is the exception rather than the norm: the economy needs to expand at its natural rate to keep a steady employment rate, but nothing ensures this will happen because the determinants of the warranted and natural rate are unrelated. Second, there are no self-correcting mechanisms capable of dampening deviations of the actual rate from the warranted rate: this is known as the Harrodian instability problem. To some extent, the development of the theory of economic growth can be seen as an attempt to address these two issues. Our focus here is to investigate how the introduction of endogenous technical change affects the solution that different economic traditions have given to the first Harrodian problem.

Given the analytical framework described in Section 3.1, the warranted growth rate is

$$g^s_K = S/K = sr = suB(1 - \omega),$$

(17)

while the natural rate of growth is

$$g^p = n + g_A.$$

Notice that g^p also represents a rate of growth of potential output, since it is a measure of the overall growth in factors supply. The actual rate of growth of capital stock is theory-specific: below, we distinguish between the classical tradition, on the one hand, and post-Keynesian traditions on the other, in turn, drawing a difference between Kaleckian models and Kaldorian models.

The classical tradition is founded on the acceptance of Say's law, the notion that supply creates its own demand at the aggregate level. This principle is satisfied when all savings are automatically invested in capital accumulation, and it is equivalent to impose full utilization of capital stock: $u = 1$. In fact, there is no independent investment function, and we can directly assume

$$g^i_K \equiv g^s_K.$$

(18)

A crucial element of post-Keynesian economics, instead, is an investment demand function that is independent of saving behavior. In the (neo-) Kaleckian tradition, investment depends on utilization as a proxy for aggregate demand (an accelerator effect), and a measure of profitability. The latter determinant is justified either through the fact that a firm's current profits provide a source of internal funds that finance capital accumulation without resorting to credit markets, or can be used as an indication of future profitability. While early authors have used a specification involving the profit rate as the main determinant of investment demand (Taylor,

1985, 1991), after Bhaduri and Marglin (1990), neo-Kaleckian economists have focused on the profit share. Accordingly, the investment function can be written as follows:

$$g_K^i = \gamma + \eta_0 u + \eta_1(1 - \omega). \tag{19}$$

Finally, the Kaldorian tradition emphasizes the role of exports as the ultimate source of autonomous aggregate demand. Since labor productivity growth improves an economy's competitiveness, thus providing access to a larger share of global demand, we can assume that investment rises with labor productivity growth:

$$g_K^i = \gamma + \lambda g_A. \tag{20}$$

In fact, (20) can be seen as a reduced-form investment demand function in an open economy, where the coefficient λ captures trade-related factors such as the foreign trade multiplier and the price-elasticity of exports (see Setterfield, 2013b, for a derivation). We keep the intercept term γ to facilitate the comparison with the Kaleckian framework. In both (19) and (20), γ can be interpreted as the autonomous growth rate of investment demand—Keynes' animal spirits.

The equality $g_K^i = g_K^s$ defines the short-run equilibrium growth rate g^*. On the other hand, balanced growth requires that $g^* = g^p$, or we would face the first Harrodian problem with cumulative disequilibrium in the labor market. Below, we explore the implications for growth and distribution of different specification of g_A for classical and post-Keynesian economics.

4. Classical Closures

As already mentioned, all the contributions falling within the classical tradition presuppose Say's law, thus imposing full utilization of installed capacity in the general framework. The main differences pertain to models featuring a distributive closure and endogenous growth, as opposed to models featuring an exogenous labor supply closure and endogenous income distribution.

4.1 Distributive Closure

The classical-Marxian tradition has emphasized the role of the reserve army of labor in keeping the labor share in check. The most notable example in development economics is that of a dual economy with a large rural sector providing a basically unlimited pool of labor from which a small but growing manufacturing sector can draw (Lewis, 1954). A dual economy is not labor-constrained: rather, it is capital stock to be the limiting factor for growth. Accordingly, the classical closure consists in assuming a perfectly elastic labor supply at the going wage share. Income distribution is exogenous, and the wage share is fixed at its *conventional* value (Foley and Michl, 1999):

$$\omega = \bar{\omega}. \tag{21}$$

On the other hand, capital stock is assumed to be utilized at its normal rate: $u = 1$. This model delivers endogenous growth even without technical change. In fact, the growth rate is simply

$$g^* = sB(1 - \bar{\omega}). \tag{22}$$

Because there is no constraint arising from the size of the labor force, the rate at which the economy grows is governed by capital accumulation only. Labor supply is endogenous and it accommodates labor demand: $\dot{N}/N = g_L$. Notice the similarity of the steady state of this model with the Romer model using foregone consumption as an input to R&D: both models deliver an endogenous growth rate that increases in the saving rate, coupled with an exogenous distribution.

In this context, endogenous technical change adds very little to the analysis, as shown in Dutt (2011) and Dutt (2013a); in fact, the role of technical change is simply to determine the growth of employment through the long-run condition $g^* = g^p = g_L + g_A$. Assume, for example, that technology evolves according to (14): labor productivity growth is $g_A = \varphi_0/(1 - \varphi_1)$, and is therefore semi-endogenous; while employment growth satisfies $g_L = sB(1 - \bar{\omega}) - \varphi_0/(1 - \varphi_1)$. Similarly, if we model g_A through the Marxian motive described in (15), we find $g_L = sB(1 - \bar{\omega}) - f(\bar{\omega})$. In both cases, a higher saving rate as well as a higher profit share increase the growth rate of employment, while improvements in the innovation technology have the opposite effect. The third route to technical change (16) is incompatible with this framework: with unlimited labor supply, the employment rate is undefined.

4.2 Labor Supply Closure

The classical model has also been investigated under the assumption of exogenous labor supply (Pasinetti, 1974; Foley and Michl, 1999, chapter 6). The important question that this framework is called to answer is how adjustments in income distribution can maintain a constant employment rate in the absence of capital/labor substitution. When technical change is exogenous, the long-run equilibrium condition $g^* = g^p$ yields the Goodwin (1967) steady-state income distribution $1 - \omega_{ss} = (n + g_A)/sB$, which would be same in the Pasinetti (1962) model if technical change were introduced. The saving rate and labor productivity growth have opposite effects on the wage share. An increase in the saving propensity s lowers the profit share and the profit rate. The reason is that higher savings translate into higher long-run investment and employment growth. Given the exogenous growth rate of labor supply, a faster pace of accumulation puts pressure on wages relative to labor productivity, so that the wage share increases. Higher labor productivity growth, on the contrary, lowers the economy's labor requirements and the wage share falls as a consequence.

Let us now investigate the implications of endogenous technical change. When g_A follows (14), balanced growth yields

$$sB(1 - \omega_{ss}) = n + \frac{\varphi_0}{(1 - \varphi_1)}, \tag{23}$$

with $g_A = \varphi_0/(1 - \varphi_1)$. Not much changes in terms of income distribution: the labor share increases in the saving rate, and the only difference is that the role of exogenous labor productivity growth is played by the technological parameters of the technical progress function. Long-run technical change, on the other hand, is of the semi-endogenous variety: it is explained within the model, but it is independent of economic parameters (see Taylor, 2004, chapter 5). Strikingly, this model delivers implications about long-run growth and distribution that are virtually identical to those found in the Jones (1995) model. In fact, as we will discuss in Section 5.2, this is also the same steady state of a closed-economy Kaldor growth model with endogenous technical change.

When labor productivity follows the Marxian motive as in (15), income distribution still needs to adjust to satisfy the long-run balance $g^* = g^p$. Accordingly, ω_{ss} solves

$$sB(1 - \omega_{ss}) = n + f(\omega_{ss}). \tag{24}$$

The effect of the saving preferences on income distribution is the same as before: total differentiation of (24) shows $d\omega_{ss}/ds > 0$. A higher saving rate increases capital accumulation; maintaining the balance in the labor market requires either a reduction in the profit share or an increase in labor productivity, which is also achieved through a higher wage share. On the other hand, technical change and growth are fully endogenous as $g_A = f[\omega_{ss}(s)]$: the higher wage share that follows the increase in the saving rate has a positive effect on labor productivity growth. A comparison with the exogenous distribution model is instructive. With a conventionally determined wage share, capital accumulation is never constrained by labor supply. Conversely, the labor supply poses a binding constraint to capital accumulation in this model, but the constraint is loosened by the fact that investment can increase the growth rate of labor productivity through the distributive channel. We are not aware of contributions that investigated this result, which reaffirms the classical vision according to which effective labor is *de facto* endogenously produced by the capitalist system;[6] Dutt (2013a) studied this specification in the classical model of growth, but only under the conventional wage share assumption.

Finally, we can explore the implications of imposing (16), even though this specification of technical change has not been implemented in the literature. The balanced growth condition becomes

$$sB(1 - \omega_{ss}) = n + h(e_{ss}), \tag{25}$$

and it provides an equilibrium locus in the space of income distribution and the employment rate. In order to pin down equilibrium values, we can borrow from Goodwin (1967) and assume that real wages grow with the employment rate, say $g_w = m(e), m' > 0$, as a tighter labor market strengthens the bargaining power of workers. A constant wage share in the long run requires wages and labor productivity to grow at the same rate: thus, the condition $m(e_{ss}) = h(e_{ss})$ fixes the equilibrium employment rate and productivity growth, while the equilibrium wage share follows from (25). Employment and productivity are independent of the saving rate that, however, has a positive effect on the wage share similarly to the exogenous productivity growth case.

Although this model has not been studied in the literature, we can take the analysis one step further and introduce an explicit policy variable. Assume that real wage growth is also a function of labor market institutions z, for example, the degree of employment protection. If $g_w = m(e, z)$, labor market institutions affect the growth rate of labor productivity, as well as income distribution, through their effect on the equilibrium employment rate. Define z such that $m_z > 0$.[7] Then, the effect of a change in z on equilibrium employment and distribution depends on the sign of the partial derivative $m_e(e_{ss}, z) - h'(e_{ss})$. If the sign is positive, that is, if wages are more responsive than productivity to the employment rate, an increase in labor market protection lowers employment and productivity growth while raising the wage share. Vice versa, if the sign is negative, an increase in z has a positive effect on equilibrium employment but an adverse effect on the labor share. Either way, workers face a trade-off between employment and productivity on the one end, and the wage share on the other hand. Such trade-off is in contrast with the steady-state implications of the Goodwin (1967) model, where an increase in employment protection would reduce employment but would have no impact on income distribution.

4.3 *The Induced Innovation Hypothesis*

The pitfalls of the aggregate production function, as well as the dissatisfaction with the exogeneity of technical change in the neoclassical growth model, led some scholars to consider the microeconomic choice of factor-augmenting technologies made by profit-maximizing firms. In particular, while it became clear very soon that balanced growth requires technical change to take the pure labor-augmenting form, the economic rationale for such a biased pattern of technology was not as well understood.

Taking up an old insight by Hicks (1932), who argued that the quest for profit maximization would lead firms to augment the productivity of the factor of production whose share in total costs increases, Kennedy (1964) postulated the existence of an *innovation possibility frontier* (IPF). The IPF inversely relates the attainable growth rate of labor productivity to the growth rate of capital productivity: $g_B = \epsilon(g_A), \epsilon' < 0, \epsilon'' < 0$. The strict concavity of the IPF captures a notion of increasing complexity in the trade-off between labor-augmenting and capital-augmenting blueprints. The *induced innovation hypothesis* is Kennedy's idea that firms choose, myopically, a profile of technical change (g_A, g_B) so as to maximize the rate of change in unit cost reduction $\omega g_A + (1 - \omega)g_B$ under the constraint given by the IPF. The result of this program is that the growth rate of labor (capital) productivity becomes an increasing function of the wage (profit) share: $g_A = f(\omega), f' > 0$. This expression is formally identical to equation (15), but it does not assume constant capital productivity. The microeconomic appeal of the induced innovation hypothesis has led to a renewed interest to this theory in recent years (Foley, 2003; Julius, 2005; Rada, 2012; Tavani, 2012, 2013; Zamparelli, 2015).

Once the induced innovation hypothesis is adopted, the relation between productivity growth and income distribution in the classical growth model with exogenous labor supply changes dramatically. In its simplest form, the steady state of such classical model consists of the following equations:

$$g_B = \epsilon(g_A) = \epsilon[f(\omega_{ss})] = 0 \tag{26}$$

$$g_B + sB_{ss}(1 - \omega_{ss}) = n + f(\omega_{ss}). \tag{27}$$

In balanced growth, the output/capital ratio B has to remain constant: therefore, $g_B = \epsilon[f(\omega_{ss})] = 0$, which solves for a unique long-run value of the labor share: $\omega_{ss} = f^{-1}[\epsilon^{-1}(0)]$. The corresponding growth rate of labor productivity is then determined through the IPF: $g_A = \epsilon^{-1}(0)$. Finally, once the wage share is found, the balanced growth condition yields the long-run output/capital ratio as

$$B_{ss} = \frac{n + f(\omega_{ss})}{s(1 - \omega_{ss})}. \tag{28}$$

Important features of the induced innovation model are that: (a) factor shares *adjust* over time in order to ensure a labor-augmenting profile of technical change in the long run, and (b) income distribution depends only on the shape of the IPF. These results are substantially different from the classical model with constant capital productivity, and from the Solow growth model. We have shown how the saving rate in the classical model with endogenous labor productivity growth is a crucial determinant of income distribution, and even of per capita growth under the specification (15) of technical change. We have also discussed in Section 2 the influence of the saving rate on income distribution in neoclassical theory. Under the induced innovation hypothesis, on the contrary, the saving rate has no influence on income distribution and growth; however, similarly to the neoclassical case, it does affect the long-run level of capital productivity. Consider, in fact, an increase in the saving rate in equation (27), which puts pressure on the accumulation in the left-hand side. However, the position and shape of the IPF have not changed: the labor share is fixed, and so is the labor force growth rate. Therefore, the

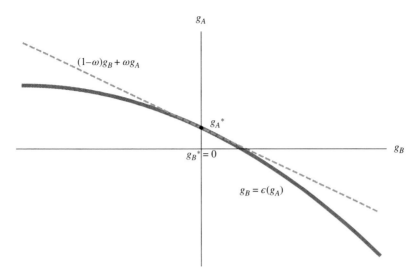

Figure 1. The Induced Innovation Hypothesis.

increase in savings must be counteracted by a decrease in the output/capital ratio, as it is clear from equation (28). Notice finally that the independence of income distribution from savings makes this model similar to the neoclassical endogenous growth model with foregone output as an R&D input.[8] Figure 1 displays Kennedy's IPF and the long-run profile of technical change in this model.

In a recent paper, Schlicht (2016) emphasizes the connections between the IPF and Kaldor's technical progress function; in fact, Kennedy (1964, p. 547n) already did notice that "if the technical progress function is known, the innovation possibility function can be derived from it." However, while the two theories are isomorphic in terms of their representation of technology, they have different steady-state implications regarding income distribution, as a comparison of (23) and (26) shows.

The induced innovation hypothesis has also been implemented in the neoclassical framework beginning with Drandakis and Phelps (1965), Nordhaus (1967), Samuelson (1965), and von Weizsacker (1966) and more recently by Funk (2002). Even with a neoclassical production function, income shares in the long run depend on the IPF alone and not on the production technology and the saving rate, provided that the elasticity of substitution be less than 1 (Drandakis and Phelps, 1965). Strengths and weaknesses of these models are illustrated in Brugger and Geherke (2017).

4.3.1 *Dynamics of Employment and the Output/Capital Ratio*

Incorporating the induced innovation hypothesis in the classical Goodwin (1967) growth cycle model highlights the adjustment process toward a constant output/capital ratio, as well as constant income shares and employment rate, in the long run. The most important implication of this model is the disappearance of the perpetual Goodwin cycles as the economy actually reaches the steady state, instead of fluctuating permanently around it (Shah and Desai, 1981). However, the direction of adjustment is not monotonic: Goodwin cycles typically persist in the short-to-medium run under standard parameterizations. The model adds the employment rate

$e = BK/(AN)$ as a dynamic variable, and makes use as before of a real-wage Phillips curve so that an increase in employment feeds into higher real wage growth: $g_w = m(e)$ in its simplest form. The aggregate economy is described by three differential equations (Foley, 2003; Julius, 2005):

$$g_B = \epsilon[f(\omega)] \tag{29}$$

$$g_\omega = m(e) - f(\omega) \tag{30}$$

$$g_e = \epsilon[f(\omega)] + sB(1 - \omega) - f(\omega) - n. \tag{31}$$

In steady state, setting as above $g_B = 0$ solves for the long-run labor share ω_{ss}, once again determined by the IPF only.[9] The long-run employment rate solves accordingly for $e_{ss} = m^{-1}[f(\omega_{ss})]$. Finally, because in steady state $\epsilon[f(\omega_{ss})] = 0$, the long-run output/capital ratio is obtained as the solution to equation (28) above, which also follows by setting $g_e = 0$ in (31). Importantly, the presence of induced innovation generates a negative feedback from the labor share to itself in equation (30): such feedback changes the dynamics of the growth cycle, turning the Goodwin steady state from a center into a stable spiral.

4.3.2 Assessment

The theory of induced technical change presented above is not immune to criticism: a first problem is that its logic involves a high level of abstraction, and it is not clear how to imagine an empirical counterpart to a strictly concave invention possibility frontier. Duménil and Levy (1995; 2010) have used a stochastic setting that better conforms with intuition, and delivers very similar implications for the choice of factor-augmenting technologies. A second, more important criticism is that the relationship between income distribution and factor productivities arises from the choice of a point along the IPF. But the position of the IPF is fully exogenous: the vertical intercept of the technical progress function in Figure 1—which determines the long-run growth rate of labor productivity—is a given of the theory. As such, the theory only explains the *direction* of technical change, that is, how changes in income distribution determine variations in labor productivity growth, as opposed to capital productivity growth: the theory is silent on the economic forces that give rise to a certain long-run growth rate, that is, the innovation *intensity*. In other words, labor-augmenting technical progress is basically available without costs to the economy, and the determination of income distribution is, in fact, driven by an exogenously given trade-off between factor-augmenting technologies (this point has been raised by Tobin, 1967, among others).

4.4 Unbalanced Growth: Marx-Biased Technical Change

Despite the balanced growth requirement that $g_B = 0$, actual historical patterns have shown that the output-capital ratio may decrease for long periods of time. As an empirical illustration, Figure 2 plots Penn World Table series for the labor share, capital productivity, and the profit rate in United States, China, United Kingdom, and Japan over country-specific extended periods characterized by falling capital productivity (with trend lines for the US and the UK). The three variables are related through the basic long-run distributive curve (12), evaluated at full utilization:

$$r = B(1 - \omega). \tag{32}$$

Figure 2. Marx-Biased Technical Change for Selected Countries. Source: Penn World Tables 9.0 (Feenstra *et al.*, 2015).

With a roughly trend-less labor share, decreasing capital productivity translates into a falling rate of profit of Marxian flavor. An almost constant labor share requires wages to grow in line with labor productivity: thus, the patterns displayed in Figure 2 are characterized by technical progress that is at the same time labor-augmenting ($g_A > 0$) and capital-using ($g_B < 0$) or, in the terminology by Foley and Michl (1999, chapter 7), Marx-biased technical change (MBTC). The analysis by Dumenil and Levy (2010) also refers to this pattern of technical change.

One question that arises when confronting falling profitability is why would firms adopt new production techniques that lower the profit rate: a basic criterion for the choice of technique (Okishio, 1961), in turn, similar to the quest for unit cost reduction that drives induced innovation, is to switch to a new technique if it does not decrease the profit rate at the current real wage. For simplicity, consider discrete time and two techniques characterized by productivity parameters (A, B) and $((1 + g_A)A, (1 + g_B)B)$, respectively. For a given real wage, the prospective profit rate associated with the new technique is

$$r' = B(1 + g_B)\left(1 - \frac{w}{A(1+g_A)}\right)$$
$$= B(1 + g_B)\left(\frac{1-\omega+g_A}{1+g_A}\right).$$

For the technique to be adopted, the prospective profit rate must be no less than the current profit rate. The required inequality can therefore be solved in order to identify a threshold value for the profit share $1 - \tilde{\omega}$ such that if the actual share of profits does not exceed this value, the technique will be adopted. Such *viability* criterion is:

$$1 - \omega \leq 1 - \tilde{\omega} \equiv \frac{g_A(1 + g_B)}{g_A - g_B}. \tag{33}$$

Under MBTC, $1 - \tilde{\omega}$ is always positive: thus, new techniques that increase labor productivity at the expenses of the output/capital ratio are viable. Notice that the higher the labor share, the easier it is to satisfy the viability condition. Therefore, a rising wage share makes the introduction of labor saving innovation more likely, which shows the resemblance of MBTC to theories of endogenous technical change captured in equation (15). What firms do not foresee when switching to the new technique, however, is that if real wages increase with labor productivity so as to maintain a constant wage share the profit rate falls following the decline in the output/capital ratio. Foley and Michl (1999, chapter 7) thus explain MBTC as analogous to a coordination failure: individually rational decision-making by firms results in a collectively self-defeating aggregate outcome. The historical patterns highlighted in Figure 2 leave little doubt about the relevance of MBTC.[10] Notice also that MBTC is compatible with transitional dynamics in the NW quadrant of Figure 1.

An important implication of MBTC is that subsequent labor-augmenting/capital-using innovations produce capital deepening that is "observationally equivalent" to the smooth capital-labor substitution in the Solow model. However, this process is driven by technical change, and not by factor substitution, as pointed out by Michl (1999): capital deepening leaves a trace that appears like a production function, but it is, in fact, just the *fossil* record of past technology. This observation has an obvious appeal for alternative economists: MBTC is immune from the logical flaws of the neoclassical aggregate production function highlighted by the Cambridge capital controversy of the 1960s, and therefore it provides a lens through which the process of capital deepening over time can be consistently accounted for.[11]

5. Post-Keynesian Closures

The rejection of Say's law is a cornerstone of Keynesian economics, and implies that output is demand-determined rather than constrained by supply factors. Post-Keynesian economists have incorporated Keynes' ideas into class-based models in order to emphasize the distributive implications of demand-driven growth. Here, we distinguish between a Kaleckian closure, where the rate of capacity utilization adjusts to ensure the equilibrium between the supply of savings and the demand for investment, and a Kaldorian closure, where the equilibrium in the goods market occurs through changes in income distribution. This sharp distinction is helpful from an expositional point of view, even though several contributions feature both adjustment mechanisms simultaneously (Palley, 1996; Cassetti, 2003; Sasaki, 2010; Taylor *et al.*, 2016).

5.1 Kaleckian Closure

As seen above, a distinctive element of Kaleckian economics is the dependence of investment demand on income distribution. While the classical tradition only considers the supply of savings and therefore sees economic growth as ultimately profit-driven, the Kaleckian investment function opens up the possibility of a paradox of costs to arise, so that aggregate demand and growth can be *wage-led*, in the now standard terminology.

We will analyze the role of investment demand and its relation with income distribution in the context of endogenous technical change. The original Kaleckian model (Kalecki, 1971) adds effective demand to a classical-Marxian framework. If firms charge a constant markup μ over real unit labor costs, the labor share is anchored to the value of the markup and fully determined by the equation

$$\omega = \frac{1}{1+\mu} = \bar{\omega},$$

which is formally equivalent to the classical closure (21). On the other hand, the short-run equilibrium between savings and investment is achieved through instantaneous adjustments in the utilization rate, which is a measure of aggregate demand. Using equations (17) and (19), and assuming in standard fashion that savings are more responsive than investment to changes in utilization, we can solve for the short-run equilibrium rate of capacity utilization and growth rate:

$$u^*(\bar{\omega}, \gamma, s) = \frac{\gamma + \eta_1(1-\bar{\omega})}{sB(1-\bar{\omega}) - \eta_0} \tag{34}$$

$$g^*(\bar{\omega}, \gamma, s) = sB(1-\bar{\omega})u^*(\bar{\omega}, \gamma, s).$$

Since output is demand-determined, an increase in the saving rate lowers aggregate consumption and the level of economic activity: this effect is known as the paradox of thrift. Further, because $u^*_\omega > 0$, the paradox of costs holds: an increase in the labor share pushes up consumption while it depresses investment. However, the former effect offsets the latter, and aggregate demand is wage-led. This mechanism highlights the fact that the paradox of costs is intimately connected to the paradox of saving: a redistribution that favors the class with the higher marginal propensity to consume has a boosting effect on aggregate demand.[12] Finally, both utilization and growth respond positively to autonomous investment: more bullish sentiments by investors result in a higher level of economic activity and a higher growth rate in the short run. This is a version of the Keynesian metaphor of the "widow's cruse."

In this model, growth can either be wage-led or profit-led. The simplest way to showcase the possibility of profit-led growth is to consider that if $\eta_0 = 0$—that is, if there is no accelerator effect and investment only responds to profitability—then $g_\omega^* = -\eta_1 < 0$, so that growth is profit-led. Through a continuity argument, it can be shown that profit-led growth will prevail when the accelerator effect on investment demand is small (or negative, which would mean that there are self-stabilizing forces at work on aggregate demand, as opposed to self-reinforcing mechanisms), but the sensitivity of investment to profitability is strong. On the other hand, autonomous investment always has a positive effect on growth. Finally, the paradox of thrift holds for economic growth, too. In fact, differentiating with respect to the saving rate and recalling that $s \in (0, 1)$, we find:

$$g_s = \left[(1 - \bar\omega)Bu^* \left(\frac{s - 1}{s}\right)\right] < 0.$$

5.1.1 Constant Markup and Endogenous Labor Supply

Let us now introduce technological change using the two specifications of labor productivity growth (14) and (15), in turn, in the context of the distributive closure. With the Kaldor–Verdoorn law (14), $g_A = \varphi_0 + \varphi_1[g(\bar\omega, \gamma, s) - g_L]$. In the short run, labor productivity growth is endogenous and reacts positively to demand shocks. Moreover, it maintains the wage-led or profit-led character of the short-run accumulation rate. When the economy approaches balanced growth in the long run, the endogenous labor supply and productivity growth both accommodate capital accumulation. In steady state, the equality $g^P = g(\bar\omega, \gamma, s)$ yields $g_A = \varphi_0/(1 - \varphi_1)$ and $g_L = g(\bar\omega, \gamma, s) - \varphi_0/(1 - \varphi_1)$. While the accumulation rate is endogenous, labor productivity growth is semi-endogenous: the unlimited labor supply is the key adjusting variable that enables accumulation to progress unconstrained by supply factors. Hein and Tarassow (2010) provide a similar analysis, but with fully endogenous labor productivity growth.

Alternatively, we can study the Kaleckian model where technical progress follows the classical-Marxian motive as in (15). Because distribution is exogenous, labor productivity growth is of the semi-endogenous variety, and does not add much to the analysis: $g_A = f(\bar\omega)$. With unlimited labor supply, the growth rate of labor demand will again be the variable that adjusts in order to ensure balanced growth: it solves $g_L = g(\bar\omega, \gamma, s) - f(\bar\omega)$. Such an adjustment process emphasizes capital accumulation as the main driver of growth, similarly to the classical framework. However, differently from the classical case, a higher saving rate reduces growth: the paradox of thrift holds just like in the short run. Finally, autonomous investment is unconstrained in driving accumulation.

5.1.2 Exogenous Labor Supply and Endogenous Markup

We turn now to endogenous technical progress in the Kaleckian model in the context of exogenous labor supply growth. First notice that if we impose the Kaldor–Verdoorn law in per-worker terms, the balanced growth condition delivers a semi-endogenous growth rate:

$$g(\omega, \gamma, s) = n + \frac{\varphi_0}{1 - \varphi_1}. \tag{35}$$

Such a case is surprisingly similar to the corresponding classical model as per equation (23). For (35) to hold, however, we cannot assume that both the markup and investment are exogenous: if we retain the Keynesian assumption of autonomous investment, we need the labor share to adjust. Regarding the comparative statics, total differentiation of (35) shows

$d\omega_{ss}/d\gamma = -g_\gamma/g_\omega$: an increase in autonomous investment will raise (lower) the wage share when growth is profit (wage)-led.

Second, we can let technical progress follow the classical-Marxian motive (15). In this case, the balanced growth condition is

$$g(\omega, \gamma, s) = n + f(\omega). \tag{36}$$

With endogenous distribution, both accumulation and labor productivity growth are fully endogenous, and increase in the labor share. A shift in autonomous investment surely increases the share of labor when short-run growth is profit-led, since $d\omega/d\gamma = g_\gamma/(f_\omega - g_\omega) > 0$. Under wage-led growth, instead, animal spirits and the wage share move together if the response of labor productivity growth to income distribution is stronger than the response of short-run accumulation, while they move in opposite directions if the converse is true. Exactly the opposite holds with regard to the effect of an increase in the saving rate on the wage share, given the paradox of thrift. In fact, $d\omega/ds = g_s/(f_\omega - g_\omega)$ is negative if growth is profit-led, and positive if $g_\omega > f_\omega$, that is, if accumulation is strongly wage-led. Thus, we see here a potential counterexample to the general case analyzed in this survey, namely, that savings and the share of labor always move together: the result is determined by the relative strength of the paradox of costs (g_ω) as opposed to the paradox of thrift (g_s) on accumulation. Because labor productivity is endogenous, under profit-led growth, the paradox of thrift holds in the long run as $dg_A/ds = f_\omega g_s/(f_\omega - g_\omega) < 0$; but the paradox of costs is not enough to offset it, and $d\omega/ds < 0$. If, on the other hand, the economy is strongly wage-led, the negative effect of the paradox of thrift on accumulation will be offset by the strength of the paradox of costs, and therefore the wage share will rise with the saving rate. Lima (2004) has generalized this case by assuming that f is a nonmonotonic function.

5.1.3 The Employment Rate as a Determinant of Technical Progress

As mentioned before, the dependence of labor productivity growth on employment as in (16) has been used extensively in the literature because it provides a solution to the first Harrodian problem with a Kaleckian closure and exogenous labor supply (Palley, 2012). The employment rate, in this case, adjusts to ensure that

$$g(\bar{\omega}, \gamma, s) = n + h(e_{ss}). \tag{37}$$

Since $h(e)$ is increasing, the steady-state employment rate retains the wage-led or profit-led character of the equilibrium growth rate, as well as the direct relationship with autonomous investment. Thus, even though utilization is always wage-led under the investment function (19), employment can be either wage-led or profit-led. Further, the "widow's cruse" argument also applies to the employment rate, as $de_{ss}/d\gamma > 0$. Third, the paradox of thrift holds, since $de_{ss}/ds < 0$. In this regard, notice the stark difference with the classical models, where employment and savings always go hand in hand. Finally, long-run productivity growth is fully endogenous, as it rises with the employment rate. Similar analyses can be found in Bhaduri (2006), Flaschel and Skott (2006), Lavoie (2006), and Sasaki (2010).

A related solution is the one proposed by Dutt (2006), with the important difference that distributive considerations are absent in his model. He postulates the specific functional form $g_A = h(e) = e^\theta$, which implies $g'_A/g_A = \theta(g_L - n)$. By construction, labor productivity growth in the long run reconciles actual and potential growth since $g_L - n = g - g_A - n = 0$. Dutt (2006) takes the argument one step further, and imposes slow adjustments in autonomous investment in response to the same forces (though working in the opposite direction). This generates indeterminacy and path dependence in the model. For instance, if a tighter labor market discourages investment growth, we can assume $\dot{\gamma}/\gamma = -\psi(g_L - n)$. The two equations that make up the corresponding dynamical system are linearly dependent on one another: the $\dot{\gamma} = 0$ and the $g_A = 0$ nullclines coincide, so that every point is an equilibrium point. Accordingly, the selection of equilibrium productivity and output growth depends on initial conditions and history. An extension of the model (Dutt, 2010) posits that changes in both labor productivity growth and autonomous investment respond positively to the difference between the employment rate (as opposed to its growth rate) and its "natural" level: $\dot{g}_A/g_A = \theta(e - \bar{e}); \dot{\gamma}/\gamma = -\psi(e - \bar{e})$. Contrary to the previous case, the steady-state level of employment is fixed at some exogenous equilibrium level, but indeterminacy still affects the growth rate of output and productivity growth due to the long-run endogenous rate of capacity utilization.

5.2 *Kaldorian Closure*

As is well known, Kaldor (1972) rejected the notion of equilibrium analysis as irrelevant. In line with the Smithian tradition, but with a stronger emphasis on the demand side of the economy, he argued that the growth process is characterized by dynamic increasing returns, path dependence and cumulative causation between the size of the economy and technological progress. Macroeconomic theory therefore should be history-specific and hardly representable by equilibrium analysis. Still, beginning with Dixon and Thirlwall (1975), modern Kaldorian growth theory has produced equilibrium frameworks that convey analytically Kaldor's main insights on growth. It has been developed along three different, although intertwined, research agendas: balanced-of-payments-constrained growth, North-South growth, and export-led cumulative causation growth. Here, we focus on the last one as it features the most prominent role for technical change. Discussions and comparative surveys of the three approaches can be found in McCombie and Thirlwall (1994), King (2010), and Blecker (2013).

A standard representation of Kaldorian cumulative causation would follow Cornwall and Setterfield (2002) in combining a demand regime, such as the one captured by the investment function (20), with a productivity regime given by the Kaldor–Verdoorn law (see also Naastepad, 2006). We model productivity growth according to the Kaldor–Verdoorn law in absolute terms (13). Equating (20) and (13) gives

$$g^* = \frac{\gamma + \lambda\phi_0}{1 - \lambda\phi_1}, \quad g_A = \frac{\gamma\phi_1 + \phi_0}{1 - \lambda\phi_1}, \tag{38}$$

whereas with endogenous labor supply, employment growth can be found residually as $g_L = g^* - g_A = \frac{\gamma(1-\varphi_1)+\varphi_0(1-\lambda)}{(1-\lambda\varphi_1)}$. Both the equilibrium capital and labor productivity growth are increasing in autonomous investment. Quoting from Taylor *et al.* (2016), "demand drives growth all the way" and creates the necessary supply conditions. A similar point was raised earlier by Cornwall (1972): a "Say's law in reverse" is at work in the Kaldorian process of growth, in that aggregate demand creates its own supply and not vice versa.

Kaldor (1956, p. 94) also suggested that the Keynesian principle of the multiplier can be alternatively used to provide either a theory of the level of economic activity or of income distribution. Using (17) and (38), we have $suB(1 - \omega) = \frac{\gamma + \lambda\phi_0}{1 - \lambda\phi_1}$, which shows that in the short-run investment generates the necessary savings either through changes in utilization or the wage share. We already explored the Keynesian framework with adjustments in capacity utilization:

here, we fix $u = 1$ and let income distribution be the accommodating variable. The long-run wage share can be found as solution to

$$sB(1 - \omega_{ss}) = \frac{\gamma + \lambda\phi_0}{(1 - \lambda\phi_1)}. \tag{39}$$

The adjustment of income distribution to changes in investment, the saving rate, or technology is based on the "forced saving" mechanism. If prices are more responsive than wages to excess demand, an increase in investment shifts the distribution of income in favor of the class with the higher propensity to save thus creating the additional savings necessary to accommodate higher growth. Conversely, the saving rate has an opposite effect on distribution: since higher savings reduce demand, if prices fall more rapidly than wages, the labor share rises and provides the increase in spending required to keep the macroeconomic balance. Finally, improvements in technology or trade conditions (ϕ_0, ϕ_1, λ) that increase equilibrium growth lower the wage share because, similarly to autonomous investment, they contribute to higher accumulation.

5.2.1 *Exogenous Labor Supply and Long-Run Growth*

The picture above changes drastically if we impose an exogenous growth rate of labor supply. The balanced growth condition becomes

$$\frac{\gamma + \lambda\phi_0}{1 - \lambda\phi_1} = n + \frac{\gamma\phi_1 + \phi_0}{1 - \lambda\phi_1}. \tag{40}$$

There is only one value of γ compatible with balanced growth, and it is fully determined by the innovation technology and the structural conditions affecting foreign trade. Investment loses its autonomous nature and becomes endogenous; as a consequence, aggregate demand plays no role. Still, we are not quite back to semi-endogenous growth: if a country's propensity to import and, in turn, the foreign trade multiplier depend on trade policy, and policy makers can affect the value of λ. In this case, growth becomes fully endogenous. Notice that if we describe a closed economy by assuming $\lambda = 0$, the steady state in (40) becomes equivalent to the semi-endogenous case discussed in the classical model with exogenous labor supply, save for the different specification of the Kaldor–Verdoorn law. This explains why some authors working within the Kaldorian tradition (Skott, 1989, 2010; Ryoo, 2016) assume that growth in mature economies is constrained by the exogenous rate of population growth.

The irrelevance of aggregate demand in the long run clearly does not sit well with Kaldor's view of the growth process. One possibility to reestablish the demand-driven nature of Kaldorian growth is to assume that the structural parameters of the model react to disequilibrium in the labor market. Following Setterfield (2006; 2013a; 2013b), we can posit $\phi_1 = \phi_1(e), \phi_1' > 0$. If a positive demand shock pushes growth above its natural rate ($g^* > g^P$), the employment rate rises because, given $g_L = g^* - g_A$, labor demand grows faster than labor supply. If the slope of the technical progress function increases as a response, the natural growth rate g^P rises and the initial demand shock has permanent growth effects. Palley (1996) has proposed a similar adjustment mechanism. He assumed that the innovation technology reacts to changes in capacity utilization rather than in the employment rate: since the equilibrium utilization rate is endogenous, this contribution combines the Kaleckian and the Kaldorian traditions.

The model is also capable of producing path dependence by imposing restrictions on its structural parameters. Under the restriction $\lambda\phi_1 = 1$, the equilibrium growth rate is undefined as the demand schedule and productivity regime schedule have the same slope. If, in addition, we assume that the two curves coincide we find a continuum of equilibria, whose selection will be determined by initial conditions and will be sensitive to demand shocks: growth is fully path-dependent (Palley, 2003; Setterfield, 2013b).[13] This conclusion, however, relies on the knife-edge condition.

5.2.2 Other Specifications of Technical Change

The Kaldor–Verdoorn relation is a core building block of Kaldorian growth. Nevertheless, it is interesting to explore the implications of other forms of technical change in a post-Keynesian environment characterized by full capacity utilization and endogenous income distribution. Assume first that labor productivity growth follows equation (15). In the short run, or in balanced growth with endogenous labor supply, the equilibrium is given by $sB(1 - \omega) = \gamma + \lambda f(\omega)$, which implicitly solves for the equilibrium wage share $\omega^* = \omega(s, \gamma)$. Just like in (39), the wage share is inversely related to autonomous investment while it increases with the saving rate. The short-run equilibrium growth rate is $g^* = \gamma + \lambda f[\omega(s, \gamma)]$, which highlights the ambiguous effect of autonomous investment. On the one hand, it directly increases the growth rate; on the other hand, however, its adverse distributional effect lowers the growth rate of labor productivity. Moreover, there is no paradox of saving: through its positive effect on the wage share, a higher saving rate increases labor productivity and output growth. Moving to the long run, balanced growth with exogenous labor supply requires

$$\gamma = n + (1 - \lambda)f[\omega_{ss}(s, \gamma)].$$

Once again, demand is irrelevant in the long run. Investment is not autonomous anymore, and it must adjust to satisfy supply constraints. Despite the fact that growth is supply-driven, the model is of the fully endogenous variety as the saving rate affects the equilibrium level of investment, income shares, and labor productivity growth. If $\lambda \in (0, 1)$, that is if the foreign sector effect on investment is not too large, a higher saving rate determines an increase in investment as $d\gamma/ds = (1 - \lambda)f[\omega_{ss}(s, \gamma)]/[1 - (1 - \lambda)f_\omega\omega_\gamma] > 0$; the effect on income distribution and growth, however, is ambiguous as $d\omega_{ss}/ds = \partial\omega_{ss}/\partial s + (\partial\omega_{ss}/\partial\gamma)d\gamma/ds \gtrless 0$.

Finally, if we let labor productivity growth rise with the employment rate as assumed in (16), the short-run equilibrium condition is $sB(1 - \omega) = \gamma + \lambda h(e)$. With full capacity utilization, the employment rate becomes a state variable in the model. Labor productivity growth is given in the short run and it does not affect the usual relation between income distribution, investment, and the saving rate: growth is demand-led, as investment creates the required savings through changes in income distribution. More interesting is the long-run equilibrium: the balanced growth condition is

$$\gamma = n + (1 - \lambda)h(e_{ss}).$$

Under this specification of technical change, demand matters even in the long-run. Autonomous investment increases capital accumulation, which determines a rise in the employment rate and, in turn, a higher natural growth rate. We are back to the "widow's cruse" result found in (37), with both steady-state employment and labor productivity growth increasing in response to stronger business confidence. However, the rise in the warranted growth rate necessary to keep the saving-investment balance occurs through a reduction in the wage share, rather than an increase in capacity utilization.

6. Costly Innovation

Until recently, researchers working within alternative frameworks have not considered the costly nature of the innovation process. Even though, to the best of our knowledge, there is no critical literature to draw from, one can think about a several explanations for this choice. First, in post-Keynesian economics, output and growth are demand-determined, supply only needs to accommodate demand conditions, and the assumption of a Kaldor–Verdoorn law such as (13) already well-captures the response of labor productivity growth to investment demand. Second, no matter whether one takes a classical or post-Keynesian viewpoint, inventive activity is highly uncertain, and does not lend itself to easy formalization as the output of a production process. Third, considering the costs incurred by firms when innovating requires to dive into the microeconomic allocation problem of choosing how to split resources between capital accumulation and inventive activity, which typically involves a profit-maximization problem. This may generate skepticism if profit maximization is identified with neoclassical marginal cost pricing.

And yet, in a world without a well-behaved production function but instead with labor and capital as perfect complements, firms have the ability to save on unit labor costs and increase profits through investment in labor-augmenting innovation. Since there is no question that the development of new technologies used for private production involves at least some expenditure, it is precisely the conflictual nature of the innovation process that calls for the inclusion of costly R&D into alternative models of growth and distribution. Here, we will distinguish between a series of recent contributions that focus on private R&D expenditure on the one hand, and public infrastructure spending on the other.

6.1 Private R&D

In recent contributions, Tavani and Zamparelli (2015) and Zamparelli (2015) study the problem of resource allocation on costly R&D by capitalist firms in the classical model with exogenous labor supply. We can follow the neoclassical endogenous growth theory in assuming that the flow of new ideas $\dot{A}$ depends positively on R&D inputs on the one hand, and linearly on the existing level of technology itself on the other hand. As already noted, a linear spillover from past ideas is useful to generate sustained growth in the long run. Contrary to (4), however, it is forgone consumption rather than labor to be employed in the production process of new technology. Accordingly,

$$\dot{A} = (R/Y)^{\zeta} A, \tag{41}$$

where R is the amount of R&D spending, homogeneous with output and capital stock, and $\zeta \in (0, 1)$ is the constant elasticity of innovation to R&D per unit of output. The normalization of R&D spending is necessary to avoid explosive growth: the growth rate of labor productivity would trend upward unless R&D investment is modeled as a share of output.

Once inventive activity becomes costly, capitalists have two alternative uses available for their saved profits: capital accumulation and innovation. Both types of investment raise total profits, but in different ways: innovation reduces unit labor costs in production, while capital accumulation increases the size of a firm's business. If we let δ be the share of saved profits invested in R&D, the growth rate of labor productivity is

$$g_A = \dot{A}/A = [s\delta(1 - \omega)]^{\zeta},$$

while physical capital accumulation obeys:

$$g_K = \dot{K}/K = s(1 - \delta)B(1 - \omega).$$

The representative capitalist will choose δ to maximize some measure of profitability. The solution to the problem will be an allocation of investment as a (possibly implicit) function of all variables involved: saving preferences, technology, and unit labor cost $\delta^* = \delta(s, B, \zeta, \omega)$. Then, using the profit-maximizing allocation in the balanced growth condition, we can write:

$$s[1 - \delta(s, B, \zeta, \omega_{ss})]B(1 - \omega_{ss}) = n + [s\delta(s, B, \zeta, \omega_{ss})(1 - \omega_{ss})]^\zeta. \qquad (42)$$

In line with the standard results of the classical model with exogenous labor supply, equation (42) shows that steady-state income distribution is endogenous, although the effect of a change in the saving rate on the labor share cannot be established without further information on the shape of δ^*. In equilibrium, labor productivity growth depends on the saving rate both directly and indirectly through its effect on the allocation of investment and on income distribution: $g_A^* = [s\delta(s, \omega_{ss})(1 - \omega_{ss})]^\zeta$. Tavani and Zamparelli (2015) obtain the values of investment in both capital stock and R&D as the solution of intertemporal optimization by forward-looking capitalist households. The relation between saving preferences, income distribution, and growth is in principle ambiguous, but a numerical implementation of the model calibrated to match long-run US data shows that a higher saving rate increases labor productivity growth as well as the labor share.

Bridging the induced innovation hypothesis with endogenous growth considerations, Zamparelli (2015) assumes that the position of the innovation possibility frontier depends on the expenditure on R&D, so that firms choose capital accumulation as well as both the intensity and direction of technical change by solving a myopic profit maximization problem. In steady state, increases in the saving rate raise both long-run growth and the labor share.

In Section 4, we discussed the two possible outcomes of the classical growth framework: endogenous growth with exogenous distribution and endogenous distribution with exogenous (or semi-endogenous) growth. On the other hand, Section 4.3 has shown how the induced innovation hypothesis implies that both growth and income distribution are basically exogenous and determined solely by Kennedy's innovation possibility frontier. The introduction of costly innovation has therefore substantial implications for the classical model, in that it delivers the simultaneous endogeneity of growth and income distribution with or without the induced innovation hypothesis. Moreover, in contrast with the Romer (1990) contribution, this model delivers both a fully endogenous growth rate and labor share even with foregone consumption and not labor providing resources to the R&D process. The main element driving this result is that both the total amount of saving and its allocation between capital accumulation and R&D investment depend on income distribution, unlike in the Romer model.

6.2 Public Investment

The importance of the costly nature of technical change does not imply that subsequent increases in productivity are carried out and paid for by the private sector only. Public infrastructure spending that directly affects the production possibilities of an economy also has implications for long-run growth. In fact, taxes levied on private agents will divert resources from private capital accumulation; but tax receipts can be used toward accumulation of public capital. Hence, the introduction of public infrastructure and its financing into the picture has features that are very similar to the trade-offs that are at the heart of the costly innovation literature. Following the seminal paper by Barro (1990), neoclassical endogenous growth theory has extensively analyzed the importance of public investment in long-run growth (see Irmen and Kuehnel, 2009, for a survey). Non-neoclassical economists have recently picked up the topic: examples can be found in Dutt (2013b) and Tavani and Zamparelli (2016, 2017). Our exposition here presents slightly modified versions of these contributions that better fit the overall framework of this survey.

Assume that both public capital G and private capital K are essential in production, and that potential output is given by

$$Y^p = G^\nu K^{1-\nu} = \chi^\nu K,$$

where $\nu \in (0, 1)$ is the elasticity of potential output to public capital, and $\chi \equiv X/K$ is the composition of aggregate capital stock. The interesting feature of this production function is that the productivity of private capital $B = \chi^\nu$ depends on how scarce public capital is relative to private capital, thus emphasizing the fundamental role of public infrastructure in the functioning of a market economy.

The government levies proportional taxes on profits at a rate $\tau \in (0, 1)$ in order to fund its infrastructure spending. Hence, $\dot{G} = \tau(1 - \omega)Y = \tau(1 - \omega)u\chi^\nu K$, and $g_G = \tau(1 - \omega)u/\chi^{1-\nu}$. The accumulation of private capital is affected by taxation, and obeys $g_K = s(1 - \tau)$ $(1 - \omega)u\chi^\nu$. The law of motion of the composition of aggregate capital stock is thus:

$$\frac{\dot{\chi}}{\chi} = g_G - g_K = (1 - \omega)u\chi^\nu \left[\tau/\chi - s(1 - \tau)\right]. \tag{43}$$

Focusing on a balanced growth path where private and public capitals grow at the same rate yields the long-run value of capital composition as:

$$\chi_{ss} = \frac{\tau}{s(1 - \tau)}, \tag{44}$$

which highlights the role of taxation in determining the long-run productivity of private capital.

This result can be combined with both the classical and the post-Keynesian closures in order to analyze the impact of public investment on growth and technical change. Let us start with the classical framework with exogenous distribution discussed in Section 4.1 where $u = 1$ and $\omega = \bar{\omega}$. Using (44), the growth rate of the economy can be found as $g_K(\tau) = [s(1 - \tau)]^{1-\nu}\tau^\nu(1 - \bar{\omega})$. It is endogenous and can be maximized by setting the tax rate equal to the output-elasticity of public capital: $\tau^* = \nu$. If in addition we assume that productivity growth follows the Kaldor–Verdoorn law as in (13), its long-run growth rate is $g_A = \phi_0 + \phi_1 g_K(\tau)$: technical change is fully endogenous, and can be maximized by levying a tax rate equal to τ^*. Endogenous adjustments in labor supply will ensure that the long-run condition $g_K(\tau) = \phi_0 + \phi_1 g_K(\tau) + g_L$ will be satisfied.

Consider instead the classical model with exogenous labor supply and endogenous distribution presented in Section 4.2, where $u = 1$ and $g_L = n$. In the long run, we find $[s(1 - \tau)]^{1-\nu}\tau^\nu(1 - \omega) = g_A + n$. If labor productivity growth is exogenous, fiscal policy affects income distribution only, and τ^* maximizes the labor share. If, conversely, we let productivity growth follow the Marxian motive (15), the balanced growth condition becomes $[s(1 - \tau)]^{1-\nu}\tau^\nu(1 - \omega) = f(\omega) + n$: both income distribution and productivity growth are endogenous and simultaneously maximized by levying a tax rate equal to τ^*.

To study this model under the post-Keynesian closure, we need to introduce a role for investment demand. Tavani and Zamparelli (2017) adopt the early Kaleckian investment function $g_K^i = \gamma + \eta r = \gamma + \eta(1 - \bar{\omega})u\chi^\nu$; the corresponding equilibrium capacity utilization rate is

$$u^* = \frac{\gamma}{(1 - \bar{\omega})\chi^\nu[s(1 - \tau) - \eta]},$$

while the short-run growth rate is

$$g_K(\tau, \gamma) = \left[\frac{s(1 - \tau)}{s(1 - \tau) - \eta}\right]\gamma.$$

If labor supply is endogenous and accommodates capital accumulation, the growth rate of the economy is fully endogenous in the long run and it increases in the tax rate (which constrains government spending) and autonomous investment. If, in addition, productivity growth follows the Kaldor–Verdoorn law, the endogeneity of the growth rate carries over to technical change: $g_A = \phi_0 + \phi_1 g_K(\tau, \gamma)$. Under the exogenous labor supply closure, on the contrary, the Kaldor–Verdoorn assumption produces semi-endogenous results: from the balanced growth condition $g_K(\tau, \gamma) = g_A + n$, we find

$$g_K(\tau, \gamma) = \frac{\varphi_0 + n}{1 - \varphi_1}; \quad g_A = \frac{\varphi_0 + \varphi_1 n}{1 - \varphi_1}.$$

Growth and labor productivity growth are fixed by innovation technology and population growth. Fiscal policy only determines the composition of aggregate capital. In fact, when labor supply is exogenous, achieving a fully endogenous growth rate requires public investment to directly affect productivity growth. For example, Tavani and Zamparelli (2017) assume

$$g_A = v(\chi_{ss}) = v\left(\frac{\tau}{s(1 - \tau)}\right), v' > 0,$$

with the underlying rationale that abundance of public capital produces more efficient infrastructures, which put private firms in a better position to innovate. An alternative route to full endogeneity of productivity growth can be found in Dutt (2013b). Elaborating on the framework developed in Dutt (2006) where productivity growth depends on the employment rate, he suggests that public investment may affect the elasticity of technical change to employment, that is:

$$g_A = h(e, \tau) = e^{\mu(\tau)}, \mu' > 0.$$

Higher public investment raises the responsiveness of productivity growth to employment. In an economy characterized by indeterminacy such as the one at the end of Section 5.1, this assumption delivers higher output growth and productivity growth in the long run.

7. Conclusion

In this paper, we surveyed the non-neoclassical literature on endogenous technical change of the last 25 years. We identified three main views on the determinants of technical change one can find in the literature: (i) a Kaldorian hypothesis that sees labor productivity growth as a byproduct of capital accumulation, (ii) a classical-Marxian hypothesis that links factors productivity growth to income distribution, and (iii) a hypothesis made in recent post-Keynesian literature according to which the growth rate of labor productivity is related to labor market tightness as measured by the employment rate. These alternative viewpoints can be embedded into growth models classified by their different closures. We first investigated a supply-side classical-Marxian closure based on Say's law, and we distinguished between a labor-abundant and a labor-constrained version of the model. We then explored two post-Keynesian closures with independent investment functions: a Kaleckian closure in which quantity adjustments in the rate of capacity utilization achieve the equilibrium between savings and investment; and a Kaldorian closure where the equilibrium in the goods market is brought about by changes in income distribution. We studied these Keynesian cases both with and without labor constraints.

One element of novelty in our account of these contributions is the comparison with neo-classical exogenous and endogenous—as well as semi-endogenous—growth theories. We find the comparison illuminating along several dimensions, and we summarize here the main implications of classical supply-side models and demand-driven models, in turn, focusing on their respective steady states.

First, we showed that there are strong similarities between a classical-Marxian model with endogenous labor supply (Foley and Michl, 1999, chapter 6) and a version of the product-variety endogenous growth model where R&D is financed by foregone consumption, an example of which can be found in Aghion and Howitt (2010, chapter 3). In both frameworks, the labor share is exogenously given, but the growth rate is endogenous and increases in the saving rate: it can potentially be affected by policy action.

Second, we highlighted the analogy between a classical model with exogenous labor supply together with a Kaldorian technical progress function (Taylor, 2004, chapter 5) and the semi-endogenous neoclassical growth model by Jones (1995). In both cases, the long-run rate of growth of labor productivity is determined endogenously, but is independent of saving preferences and it is therefore policy-invariant. However, income distribution is fully endogenous, in that the labor share is an increasing function of the saving rate. The endogeneity of income distribution occurs even in the Solow model, where, however, labor productivity growth is unexplained.

Third, the classical model with induced technical change resembles the neoclassical exogenous growth model as it features an adjusting long-run output-capital ratio inversely related to the saving rate; however, contrary to the neoclassical model, income distribution is independent of saving preferences and fully determined by the shape of Kennedy's innovation possibility frontier.

Fourth, the Romer (1990) model with labor as R&D input determines both growth and the labor share endogenously as increasing functions of the saving rate, similarly to classical models with costly R&D (Tavani and Zamparelli, 2015; Zamparelli, 2015). The latter contributions, however, achieve the endogeneity of factor shares even with forgone output as an input to the R&D process: key to this result is that both capital accumulation and R&D investment depend on income distribution.

Fifth, in the sole-unbalanced growth case we described, there is a striking parallel to be drawn between the capital deepening arising from the capital-labor substitution that drives the transitional dynamics of the Solow model and a Marx-biased pattern of technical change.

Despite these remarkable similarities, the differences between classical and neoclassical models are profound. To begin with, none of the classical models presupposes full employment of labor, which is a crucial element of all their neoclassical counterparts. Second, the neoclassical models hinge mostly on a representative household, while the classical models are class-based. Third, the classical models are immune from the Cambridge critique of the neoclassical production function. Fourth, the classical models are in principle compatible with growth-distribution cycles around the steady state, while the convergence to the steady state is monotonic in both the Solow model and the Romer model (Arnold, 2000).[14]

Demand-driven models in the post-Keynesian tradition add the rejection of Say's law to the features that put classical models in contrast with neoclassical growth. Since saving and investment decisions do not coincide, it is autonomous investment that provides the key behavioral variable to investigate the relation between capital accumulation, technical change, and income distribution.

First, in the short run or if labor supply is endogenous, both Kaleckian and Kaldorian models feature a fully endogenous growth rate increasing in autonomous investment: the difference lays in what is the adjusting variable in the two models. Under the Kaldorian closure, it is income distribution to adjust, similarly to the classical model with exogenous population growth or the semi-endogenous neoclassical model: the labor share rises with the saving rate. In Kaleckian models, on the other hand, the saving-investment equilibrium is realized through quantity adjustments in capacity utilization. From this point of view, there is a similarity with the classical model with exogenous distribution where, following an increase in the saving rate, higher employment growth accommodates the increase in the growth rate.

Second, if labor supply is exogenous and productivity growth follows the Kaldor–Verdoorn law, Keynesian models lose their demand-led flavor in the long run: the balanced growth condition requires investment to adjust given population growth, the innovation technology, and (in the Kaldorian case) trade conditions. We thus explored multiple ways to achieve demand-determined endogenous growth with exogenous labor supply: (i) postulating that labor productivity growth depends on the level of endogenous variables such as the labor share or the employment rate; (ii) assuming that innovation technology reacts to differences between actual and potential output, and (iii) generating path-dependence by letting capital accumulation and labor productivity growth be defined by the same equation.

Overall, our account has shown that changes in capital accumulation, be they supply- or demand-driven, tend to have distributional rather than growth effects when the labor force grows at an exogenous rate. The analytical accomplishment of both neoclassical and alternative endogenous growth theories has consisted in devising specifications of technological change that make the natural growth rate sensitive to investment decisions, so that supply constraints do not prevent accumulation from affecting growth in the long run. In so doing, they all rely on knife-edge conditions: as noted by Solow (2007), endogenous growth requires a linear differential equation in the level of technology. However, a key difference is the emphasis on different factors that may be responsible for long-run growth. Neoclassical growth theorists have emphasized the role of intertemporal saving preferences and deviations from competitive markets; alternative theorists have focused on income distribution, the state of the labor market, and investors' behavior as key determinants of the pace of technical progress.

Acknowledgments

We thank Roberto Veneziani for his encouragement, Peter Skott, Heckhard Hein and Rajiv Sethi for helpful conversations about this topic, and two anonymous referees for their constructive comments. The usual disclaimer applies.

Notes

1. Unless otherwise stated, we will use constants to denote positive numbers throughout the survey.
2. The notion of semi-endogenous growth that we just defined is essentially neoclassical, in that it states that growth is independent of the saving rate. As we will show in Section 4,

it fits well classical-Marxian models where the saving rate is the key economic variable representing economic decision making. More generally, semi-endogenous growth can be defined as an outcome where, despite assuming endogenous technical change, long-run growth does not depend on any *economic* variable. We refer to this notion when we discuss post-Keynesian models in Sections 5 and 6.

3. In his seminal paper, Pasinetti (1962) has shown that under $s_\pi > s_w > 0$, only the capitalists' saving rate matters for long-run income distribution, a result known as the "Pasinetti theorem." Michl (2009) has proven a contemporary version of the model with savings arising from optimizing behavior.

4. The relation between the technical progress function and the Verdoorn law has widely been discussed in the literature, see McCombie and Thirlwall (1994) and more recently McCombie and Spreafico (2016).

5. Skott (1989) has been the first to emphasize the relevance of the labor market in Keynesian growth models. Through the concept of an "output expansion function," he suggested that output growth is an inverse function of labor market tightness. As a consequence, high levels of employment produce a reduction in labor demand similarly to equation (16).

6. We thank an anonymous referee for suggesting to emphasize this point.

7. From now on, when no possible confusion arises, we will use the notation y_x to denote the partial derivative of y w.r.t. x. The context should make it clear when g_x indicates the growth rate of x as opposed to the derivative of the growth rate w.r.t. x.

8. The latter, however, is concerned with the intensity and not the direction of technical change. See the discussion concluding Section 4.3.1.

9. Tavani (2012; 2013) uses a Nash bargaining mechanism between workers and capitalists in order to endogenize wage-setting in this model. As a result, there is no independent dynamic equation for the labor share, and the shape of the IPF determines the long-run employment rate. However, these papers identify key institutional and policy variables (workers' bargaining power, job destruction rate, unemployment benefits) that affect the steady state of the model.

10. At the same time, an open modeling question is whether the coordination failure is a byproduct of the myopic nature of the firm's choice problem, and whether its extent could be reduced if firms adopted a longer horizon in their decision-making.

11. Although beyond the scope of this paper, the viability criterion provided by (33) has also been used to test the empirical relevance of competing theories of income distribution, namely the classical as opposed to the neoclassical theory. Michl (1999, 2002) devised early tests that appear to strongly reject the neoclassical theory for OECD countries. Basu (2010) has extended the logic of the test to a stochastic setting through the use of cross-country regressions: his finding confirms the rejection of the marginal theory of distribution.

12. Post-Keynesian authors (the literature is vast: here, it is enough to mention Bhaduri and Marglin, 1990; Taylor, 2004, chapter 8) have considered the possibility of aggregate demand being profit-led, so that $\partial u^*/\partial \omega < 0$. Especially with endogenous markups, this gives rise to a number of possible configurations of the interactions between demand and distribution. The focus of our paper is on the growth rate rather than the level of economic activity: the investment function we use is enough to generate profit-led growth.

13. This scenario is not exactly consistent with our simplified framework since it would require $\gamma = -\phi_0/\phi_1 < 0$. In the general version of the model, however, the intercept of the investment function can be negative and still remain economically meaningful.

14. Cycles in labor productivity growth and a measure of the real wage can occur in the Aghion and Howitt (1992) model.

References

Aghion, P. and Howitt, P. (1992) A model of growth through creative destruction. *Econometrica* 60: 323–351.

Aghion, P. and Howitt, P. (2010) *The Economics of Growth*. Cambridge, MA: MIT Press.

Arnold, L. (2000) Stability of the market equilibrium in Romer's model of endogenous technical change: A complete characterization. *Journal of Macroeconomics* 22(1): 69–84.

Arrow, K.J. (1962) The economic implications of learning-by-doing. *Review of Economic Studies* 29: 55–173.

Barro, R.J. (1990) Government spending in a simple model of endogenous growth. *Quarterly Journal of Economics* 98(5): S103–S125.

Basu, D. (2010) Marx-biased technical change and the neoclassical view of income distribution. *Metroeconomica* 61(4): 593–620.

Bhaduri, A. (2006) Endogenous economic growth: A new approach. *Cambridge Journal of Economics* 30(1): 69–83.

Bhaduri, A. and Marglin, S. (1990) Unemployment and the real wage: The economic basis for contesting political ideologies. *Cambridge Journal of Economics* 14: 375–393.

Black, J. (1962) The technical progress function and the production function. *Economica* 29(114): 166–170.

Blecker, R. (2013) Long-run growth in open economies: Export-led cumulative causation or a balance-of-payments constraint? In G.C. Harcourt and P. Kriesler (eds.), *The Oxford Handbook of Post-Keynesian Economics*, Vol. I (pp. 390–414) Theory and Origins. Oxford, UK: Oxford University Press.

Brugger, F. and Gehrke, C. (2017) The neoclassical approach to induced technical change: From Hicks to Acemoglu. *Metroeconomica* 68(4): 730–776.

Cass, D. (1965) Optimum growth in an aggregative model of capital accumulation. *Review of Economic Studies* 32(3): 233–240.

Cassetti, M. (2003) Bargaining power, effective demand and technical progress: A Kaleckian model of growth. *Cambridge Journal of Economics* 27(3): 449–464.

Cornwall, J. (1972) *Growth and Stability in a Mature Economy*. London, UK: Martin Robertson.

Cornwall, J. and Setterfield, M. (2002) A neo-Kaldorian perspective on the rise and decline of the golden age. In M. Setterfield (ed.), *The Economics of Demand-Led Growth: Challenging the Supply Side Vision of the Long Run* (pp. 67–86). Cheltenham, UK: Edward Elgar.

Dixon, R. and Thirlwall, A.P. (1975) A model of regional growth-rate differences on Kaldorian lines. *Oxford Economic Papers* 27(2): 201–214.

Drandakis, E.M. and Phelps, E.S. (1965) A model of induced invention, growth and distribution. *Economic Journal* 76(304): 823–840.

Duménil, G. and Lévy, D. (1995) A stochastic model of technical change: An application to the US economy, 1869–1989. *Metroeconomica* 46: 213–245.

Duménil, G. and Lévy, D. (2010) The classical-Marxian evolutionary model of technical change: Applications to historical tendencies. In M. Setterfield (ed.), *Handbook of Alternative Theories of Economic Growth* (pp. 243–273). Cheltenham, UK: Edward Elgar.

Dutt, A.K. (2006) Aggregate demand, aggregate supply and economic growth. *International Review of Applied Economics* 20(3): 319–336.

Dutt, A.K. (2010) Reconciling the growth of aggregate demand and aggregate supply. In M. Setterfield (ed.), *Handbook of Alternative Theories of Economic Growth* (pp. 220–240). London: Edward Elgar.

Dutt, A.K. (2011) Alternative models of growth and distribution with a simple formulation of endogenous technical change. In C. Gehrke and N. Salvadori (eds.), *Keynes, Sraffa, and the Criticism of Neoclassical Theory: Essays in Honor of Heinz Kurz* (pp. 67–83). Routledge.

Dutt, A.K. (2013a) Endogenous technological change in classical–Marxian models of growth and distribution. In T. Michl and A. Rezai (eds.), *Social Fairness and Economics: Essays in the Spirit of Duncan Foley* (pp. 264–285). New York, NY: Routledge.

Dutt, A.K. (2013b) Government spending, aggregate demand, and economic growth. *Review of Keynesian Economics* 1(1): 105–119.

Feenstra, R.C., Inklaar, R. and Timmer, M.P. (2015) The next generation of the Penn World Table. *American Economic Review* 105(10): 3150–3182. Available for download at https://doi.org/www .ggdc.net/pwt.

Flaschel, P. and Skott, P. (2006) Steindlian models of growth and stagnation. *Metroeconomica* 57(3): 303–338.

Foley, D.K. (2003) Endogenous technical change with externalities in a classical growth model. *Journal of Economic Behavior and Organization* 52(2): 167–189.

Foley, D.K. and Michl, T.R. (1999) *Growth and Distribution*. Cambridge, MA: Harvard University Press.

Funk, P. (2002) Induced innovation revisited. *Economica* 69: 155–171.

Garegnani, P. (1970) Heterogeneous capital, the production function and the theory of distribution. *Review of Economic Studies* 37(3): 407–436.

Goodwin, R. (1967) A growth cycle. In: C. Feinstein (ed.), *Socialism, Capitalism, and Economic Growth* (pp. 54–58). Cambridge, UK: Cambridge University Press.

Grossman, M. and Helpman, E. (1991) Quality ladders in the theory of growth. *Review of Economic Studies* 58(1): 43–61.

Harrod, R.F. (1939) An essay in dynamic theory. *Economic Journal* 49: 14–33.

Hein, E. and Tarassow, A. (2010) Distribution, aggregate demand and productivity growth: Theory and empirical results for six OECD countries based on a post-Kaleckian model. *Cambridge Journal of Economics* 34(4): 727–754.

Hicks, J.R. (1932[1960]) *The Theory of Wages*. London: Macmillan.

Irmen, A. (2016) A generalized steady-state growth theorem. *Macroeconomic Dynamics* 1–26. First View, Published online: 27 June 2016.

Irmen, A. and Kuehnel, J. (2009) Productive government expenditure and economic growth. *Journal of Economic Surveys* 23(4): 692–733.

Jones, C. (1995) R&D-based models of economic growth. *Journal of Political Economy* 103(4): 759–784.

Jones, C. and Romer, P. (2010) The new Kaldor facts: Ideas institutions, population, and human capital. *American Economic Journal: Macroeconomics* 2(1): 224–245.

Jones, C. and Scrimgeour, D. (2008) A new proof of Uzawa's steady-state growth theorem. *Review of Economics and Statistics* 90(1): 180–182.

Julius, A.J. (2005) Steady state growth and distribution with an endogenous direction of technical change. *Metroeconomica* 56(1): 101–125.

Kaldor, N. (1956) Alternative theories of distribution. *The Review of Economic Studies* 23(2): 83–100.

Kaldor, N. (1957) A model of economic growth. *Economic Journal* 67(268): 591–624.

Kaldor, N. (1961) Capital accumulation and economic growth. In F.A. Lutz and D.C. Hague (eds.), *The Theory of Capital* (pp. 177–222). New York, NY: St. Martins Press.

Kaldor, N. (1972) The irrelevance of equilibrium economics. *The Economic Journal* 82(328): 1237–1255.

King, J.E. (2010) Kaldor and the Kaldorians. In M. Setterfield (ed.), *Handbook of Alternative Theories of Economic Growth* (pp. 157–186). Cheltenham, UK: Edward Elgar.

Kalecki, M. (1971) *Selected Essays on the Dynamics of the Capitalist Economy*. Cambridge, UK: Cambridge University Press.

Kennedy, C. (1964) Induced bias in innovation and the theory of distribution. *Economic Journal* 74(295): 541–547.

Koopmans, T. (1965) On the concept of optimal economic growth. In J. Johansen (ed.), *The Econometric Approach to Development Planning* (pp. 225–287). Amsterdam: North-Holland.

Kurz, H. and Salvadori, N. (1998) The 'new' growth theory: Old wine in new goatskins. In F. Coricelli, M. di Matteo and F. Hahn (eds.), *New Theories in Growth and Development* (pp. 63–94). Berlin: Springer.

Lavoie, M. (2006) A post-Keynesian amendment to the new consensus on monetary policy. *Metroeconomica* 57(2): 165–192.

Lewis, W.A. (1954) Economic development with unlimited supplies of labor. *Manchester School of Economics and Social Studies* 22: 139–191.

Lima, G.T. (2004) Endogenous technological innovation, capital accumulation and distributional dynamics. *Metroeconomica* 55(4): 386–408.

Marshall, A. (1920[1960]) *Principles of Economics*. C.W. Guillebaud (ed.), 9th edn. London: Macmillan.

Marx, K. (1867 [1977]). *Capital: A Critique of Political Economy*, Vol. III. New York, NY: New York Books.

McCombie, J. and Spreafico, M. (2016) Kaldor' s 'technical progress function' and Verdoorn' s law revisited. *Cambridge Journal of Economics* 40(4): 1117–1136

McCombie, J. and Thirlwall, A.P. (1994) *Economic Growth and the Balance-of-Payments Constraint*. London, UK: Macmillan.

Michl, T.R. (1999) Biased technical change and the aggregate production function. *International Review of Applied Economics* 13(2): 193–206.

Michl, T.R. (2002) The fossil production function in a vintage model. *Australian Economic Papers* 41(1): 53–68.

Michl, T.R. (2009) *Capitalists, Workers, and Fiscal Policy*. Cambridge, MA: Harvard University Press.

Naastepad, C.W.M. (2006) Technology, demand and distribution: A cumulative growth model with an application to the Dutch productivity growth slowdown. *Cambridge Journal of Economics* 30: 403–434.

Nordhaus, W. (1967) The optimal rate and direction of technical change. In K. Shell (ed.), *Essays on the Theory of Optimal Economic Growth* (pp. 53–66). Cambridge, MA: MIT Press.

Okishio, N. (1961) Technical changes and the rate of profit. *Kobe University Economic Review* 7: 86–99.

Palley, T.I. (1996) Growth theory in a Keynesian model. *Journal of Post Keynesian Economics* 19(1): 113–135.

Palley, T.I. (2003) Pitfalls in the theory of growth: An application to the balance of payments-constrained growth model. *Review of Political Economy* 15(1): 75–84.

Palley, T.I. (2012) Growth, unemployment and endogenous technical progress: A Hicksian resolution of Harrod's knife-edge. *Metroeconomica* 63(3): 512–541.

Pasinetti, L.L. (1962) Rate of profit and income distribution in relation to the rate of economic growth. *Review of Economics Studies* 29(4): 267–279.

Pasinetti, L.L. (1974) *Growth and Income Distribution: Essays in Economic Theory*. Cambridge, UK: Cambridge University Press.

Rada, C. (2012) Social security tax and endogenous technical change in an economy with an aging population. *Metroeconomica* 63(4): 727–756.

Ramsey, F.P. (1928) A mathematical theory of saving. *Economic Journal* 38(152): 543–559.

Romer, P. (1990) Endogenous technological change. *Journal of Political Economy* 98(5): S71–S102.

Ryoo, S. (2016) Demand-driven inequality, endogenous saving rate and macroeconomic instability. *Cambridge Journal of Economics* 40: 201–225.

Samuelson, P.A. (1965) A theory of induced innovation along Kennedy-Weizsacker lines. *The Review of Economics and Statistics* 47(4): 343–356.

Samuelson, P.A. (1966) A summing up. *Quarterly Journal of Economics* 80(4): 568–583.

Sasaki, H. (2010) Endogenous technical change, income distribution and unemployment with inter-class conflict. *Structural Change and Economic Dynamics* 21: 123–134.

Schlicht, E. (2006) A variant of Uzawa's theorem. *Economics Bulletin* 5(6): 1–5.

Schlicht, E. (2016) Directed technical change and capital deepening: A reconsideration of Kaldor's technical progress function. *Metroeconomica* 67(1): 119–151.

Schumpeter, J.A. (1942) *Capitalism, Socialism, and Democracy*. New York: Harper and Brothers.

Setterfield, M. (2006) Thirlwall's law and Palley's pitfalls: A reconsideration. In P. Arestis, J. McCombie and R. Vickerman (eds.), *Growth and Economic Development: Essays in Honour of A.P. Thirlwall* (pp. 47–59). Cheltenham, UK: Edward Elgar.

Setterfield, M. (2013a) Exploring the supply side of Kaldorian growth models. *Review of Keynesian Economics* 1(1): 22–36.

Setterfield, M. (2013b) Endogenous growth: A Kaldorian approach. In G.C. Harcourt and P. Kriesler (eds.), *The Oxford Handbook of Post-Keynesian Economics*, vol. 1: Theory and Origins (pp. 231–256). Oxford, UK: Oxford University Press.

Setterfield, M. (2014) Neoclassical growth theory and heterodox growth theory: Opportunities for (and obstacles to) greater engagement. *Eastern Economic Journal* 40(3): 365–386.

Shah, A. and Desai, M. (1981) Growth cycles with induced technical change. *The Economic Journal* 91(364): 1006–1010.

Skott, P. (1989) *Conflict and Effective Demand in Economic Growth*. Cambridge, UK: Cambridge University Press.

Skott, P. (2010) Growth, instability and cycles: Harrodian and Kaleckian models of accumulation and income distribution. In M. Setterfield (ed.), *Handbook of Alternative Theories of Economic Growth* (pp. 108–131). Cheltenham, UK: Edward Elgar.

Smith, A. (1776 [1981]) *An Inquiry into the Nature and Causes of the Wealth of Nations*, R.H. Campbell and A.S. Skinner (eds.). Indianapolis, IN: Liberty Fund.

Solow, R. (1956) A contribution to the theory of economic growth. *Quarterly Journal of Economics* 70: 65–94.

Solow, R. (1994) Perspectives on growth theory. *Journal of Economic Perspectives* 8(1): 45–54.

Solow, R. (2007) The last 50 years in growth theory and the next 10. *Oxford Review of Economic and Policy* 23(1): 3–14.

Tavani, D. (2012) Wage bargaining and induced technical change in a linear economy: Theory and application to the US (1963-2003). *Structural Change and Economic Dynamics* 23: 117–126.

Tavani, D. (2013) Bargaining over productivity and wages when technical change is induced: Implications for growth, distribution, and employment. *Journal of Economics* 109: 207–244.

Tavani, D. and Zamparelli, L. (2015) Endogenous technical change, employment and distribution in the Goodwin model of the growth cycle. *Studies in Nonlinear Dynamics and Econometrics* 19(2): 209–226.

Tavani, D. and Zamparelli, L. (2016) Public capital, redistribution and growth in a two-class economy. *Metroeconomica* 67(2): 458–476.

Tavani, D. and Zamparelli, L. (2017) Government spending composition, aggregate demand, growth, and distribution. *Review of Keynesian Economics* 5(2): 239–258.

Taylor, L. (1985) A stagnationist model of economic growth. *Cambridge Journal of Economics* 9: 383–403.

Taylor, L. (1991) *Income Distribution, Inflation, and Growth*. Cambridge, MA: MIT Press.

Taylor, L. (2004) *Reconstructing Macroeconomics*. Cambridge, MA: Harvard University Press.

Taylor, L., Foley, D.K., Rezai, A., Pires, L., Omer, O. and Scharfenaker, S. (2016) Demand drives growth all the way. Schwartz Center for Economic Policy Analysis and Department of Economics, The New School for Social Research, Working Paper Series 2016-4.

Tobin, J. (1967) Comment to 'Some recent developments in the theory of production' by R.M. Solow. In M.B. Brown (ed.) *The Theory and Empirical Analysis of Production* (pp. 50–53). New York, NY: Columbia University Press.

Uzawa, H. (1961) Neutral inventions and the stability of growth equilibrium. *Review of Economic Studies* 28: 117–124.

Verdoorn, P.J. (1949) Fattori che regolano lo sviluppo della produttività del lavoro. *L'Industria* 1: 3–10.

Young, A.A. (1928) Increasing returns and economic progress. *Economic Journal* 38: 527–542.

von Weizsacker, C.C. (1966) Tentative notes on a two sector model with induced technical progress. *Review of Economic Studies* 33(3): 245–251.

Zamparelli, L. (2015) Induced innovation, endogenous technical change and income distribution in a labor-constrained model of classical growth. *Metroeconomica* 66(2): 243–262.

7

MINSKY MODELS: A STRUCTURED SURVEY

Maria Nikolaidi

University of Greenwich

Engelbert Stockhammer

Kingston University

1. Introduction

Since the global financial crisis, there has been a surge in interest in the work of Hyman Minsky and his financial instability hypothesis (FIH). Even the financial press (Financial Times Alphaville 20/8/2007),[1] the key economic policy institutions (White, 2009; IMF, 2012) and the mainstream economics literature (e.g. Eggertsson and Krugman, 2012 and Bhattacharya *et al.*, 2015) refer to Minsky respectfully. However, there is a literature on modeling Minsky's FIH within the field of heterodox economics that has been largely ignored by this interest in Minsky. The aim of this paper is to offer a survey of this literature.

Minsky's financial theory of economic crises explains how periods of tranquil growth lead to more financially fragile structures and speculative booms that can result in deep recessions and instability (Minsky, 1975, 1982, 1986 [2008]). In Minsky's theoretical framework, financial fragility increases due to endogenous forces that are linked with institutional transformations and the willingness of firms and banks to adopt riskier financial practices because of lower perceived uncertainty. Financial markets play also an important role in the generation of booms and busts since asset prices affect investment and debt relationships. There are at least four key features in Minsky's theory that have been extensively used in the Minskyan models so far. First, the debt ratio of firms tends to increase during the economic boom. Minsky expressed this over-indebtedness via his categorization of firms into hedge, speculative and Ponzi ones. His FIH suggests that during periods of tranquility, firms gradually shift from hedge to speculative or Ponzi regimes and the financial fragility becomes higher. Second, stock market prices, which tend to increase during economic expansions, have a positive impact on economic activity via his 'two price' theory of investment. Third, the accumulation of debt has generally a negative impact of economic activity. However, this negative impact might take

Analytical Political Economy, First Edition. Edited by Roberto Veneziani and Luca Zamparelli.

Chapters © 2018 The Authors. Book compilation © 2018 John Wiley & Sons Ltd. Published 2018 by John Wiley & Sons Ltd.

time to materialize because the rise in indebtedness is accompanied by (i) asset price inflation that boosts investment and (ii) a decline in the desired margins of safety of banks and firms that increases credit expansion. Fourth, one of the reasons why economic booms come to an end is the rise in the interest rate that comes from commercial banks' response to the rising indebtedness of borrowers or from central bank's policy that leads to an increase in interest rates during economic booms.

Minsky's writings are rich and innovative, but lack analytical clarity. Since the mid-1980s, there have been a growing number of papers that have tried to give a formal representation of Minsky's arguments. While all Minskyan models share that the financial variables play an important role in generating business cycles or instability, a closer examination reveals substantial differences in the mechanisms involved in the models as well as their dynamic properties. The aim of this paper is to survey the literature and identify differences and similarities in the mechanisms that give rise to business cycles or instability. We suggest a structure to classify Minsky-inspired models. We will use the term Minsky model for macroeconomic models that analyse the dynamic interaction between real and financial variables, build on Minsky and model some of the mechanisms he highlighted. We will distinguish between models that focus on debt or interest dynamics and models in which asset price dynamics play a key role. In the first type of models, the source of the dynamics is in the interaction of the goods market with the financial market and the key variable is the debt ratio or the interest rate. Within this category of models, we make a classification between (i) the Kalecki–Minsky models that assume a stable goods market, (ii) the Kaldor–Minsky models that postulate instability in the goods market, (iii) the Goodwin–Minsky models that incorporate debt dynamics into the traditional Goodwin interactions between the wage share and employment rate, (iv) the credit rationing Minsky models that consider explicitly credit rationing and the role that banks' financial position play in the provision of loans, (v) the endogenous target debt ratio Minsky models in which the accumulation of debt is driven by the stock-flow norms of the private sector that change endogenously during the economic cycle and (vi) the Minsky–Veblen models that combine consumer debt with the Veblenian ideas of emulation motives. Within the asset price dynamics models, we distinguish between (i) the equity price Minsky models that analyse the cycles and the instability that arise from the dynamics of equity prices and (ii) the real estate price Minsky models that study the dynamic interaction between mortgages and housing prices.

The paper is structured as follows. Section 2 provides an overview of the Minsky models and describes our suggested classification. Section 3 analyses the details of the Minsky models that concentrate on the debt or interest dynamics. Section 4 scrutinizes the Minsky models in which asset prices play a key role. Section 5 discusses mainstream models that have incorporated Minskyan ideas. Section 6 summarizes the key differences between the families of Minsky models, outlines their key limitations and briefly identifies directions for future research.

2. Overview and Structure of Minsky Models

There are several dimensions along which there are differences in the Minskyan models. Key differences include: Is the aim of the model to demonstrate the instability of the system or the emergence of endogenous cycles? Is the main source of instability in the interaction of the goods market and financial markets or is the source of the instability the financial sector itself? Is the key financial variable debt, the interest rate or asset prices? Does the interest rate change because of a change in portfolio decision, the behavior of commercial banks or the policy of the central bank? What is the residual source of finance? Do banks ration credit?

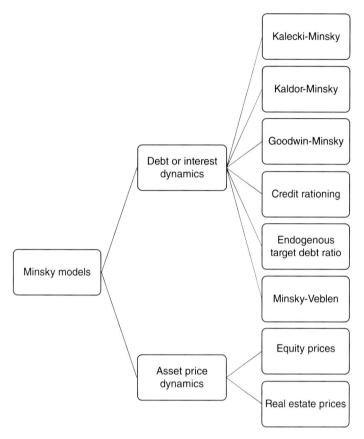

Figure 1. Families of Minsky Models.

We will refer to Minsky model when authors positively refer to Minsky and offer a formal macroeconomic model in which there are causally related cycles in financial markets and real markets or unstable interactions between the two. Figure 1 summarizes our suggested structure of Minsky models. Our broad distinction relies on whether the source of cyclical dynamics and instability is in the interaction between the goods markets and the financial market, with debt or interest rate dynamics being central, or whether it is primarily in the financial markets itself, with asset prices playing the key role. The relevant financial market in the traditional Minsky models is the equity market. However, there are also some Minsky models that pay particular attention to the interaction between housing price and mortgages despite the fact that housing prices are not considered an integral part of Minsky's analysis.

The Kalecki–Minsky models constitute the first group of debt or interest dynamics models. Here, the output is demand determined, the standard Keynesian stability condition on the goods market holds (marginal propensity to save is larger than the marginal propensity to invest), while asset prices and household debt are assumed away. In these models, the debt-to-capital ratio is used as an indicator of financial fragility. Also, many of these models (e.g. Lima and Meirelles, 2007; Nishi, 2012; Sasaki and Fujita, 2012) measure the financial fragility of firms by using Minsky's classification of hedge, speculative and Ponzi finance regimes based on the relationship between investment expenditures, profits and interest payments.[2] In the majority of the Kalecki–Minsky models, the interest rate is endogenous. The interest rates are set by commercial banks and increase in response to the rising debt-to-capital ratios of their costumers (e.g. Charles, 2008) or because of increasing economic activity (e.g. Lima and Meirelles, 2007). The labor market is not explicitly analysed in the Kalecki–Minsky models (an exception is Fazzari *et al.*, 2008).

The second group within the debt or interest dynamics models are the Kaldor–Minsky models. Kaldor (1940) proposed a model where the goods market is overshooting because of strong accelerator effects.[3] While in Kaldor and other related literature investment levels out at some point because of real constraints (e.g. supply side bottle necks), the Kaldor–Minsky model 'is made unstable by a strong investment accelerator, but the instability is contained by financial forces' (Foley, 1987, p. 364). In most Kaldor–Minsky models, the interest rate is endogenous (e.g. Foley, 1987). However, there are also models in which the interest rate is exogenous (e.g. Skott, 1994).

The third group is the Goodwin–Minsky models. Goodwin (1967) examined the cycles that can be generated by the interaction of wage share and employment rate. In his framework, the Say's law holds and output is determined by capital stock. In the Goodwin–Minsky models, debt is introduced via an investment function and interest payments squeeze profits and investment in the same way that wages do in the Goodwin model. A key difference of the Goodwin–Minsky models from the Kalecki–Minsky and the Kaldor–Minsky models is that labor market plays a central role via the Marxian idea of the reserve army of labor.

The fourth group is the credit rationing Minsky models. In contrast to the previous models, banks in these models apply credit rationing explicitly and this credit rationing is affected by banks' financial position. Credit rationing refers either to the volume of credit that is supplied by banks (Ryoo, 2013b; Nikolaidi, 2014) or to the interest rate that is charged by banks which, in turn, affects the amount of credit (Delli Gatti *et al.*, 2005, 2010). In these models, the interaction between the financial position of firms and the financial position of banks plays a central role in the emergence of cycles and instability.

The fifth group is the endogenous target debt ratio Minsky models (Dafermos, 2017; Jump *et al.*, 2017). In these models, the expenditures of the private sector and the dynamics of debt are affected by stock-flow norms (target debt ratios). These stock-flow norms change endogenously based on the Minskyan argument that the perception of risk alters during the economic cycle: in a period of tranquil or high growth, firms, or the private sector, in general, increase their target of debt; the opposite is true during period of low or volatile growth. This endogeneity of the target debt ratios is conducive to cycles and instability.

The sixth group is the Minsky–Veblen models. Applying Veblen's (1899 [1970]) ideas about the impact of social conventions on consumption, the Minsky–Veblen models assume that low-income households take on consumer debt in order to increase their consumption expenditures and emulate the high-income households (Kapeller and Schütz, 2014; Ryoo and Kim, 2014; Kapeller *et al.*, 2016). In these models, the credit provision is affected by households' balance sheet, which implies that there is credit rationing. The interest rate can be either endogenous or exogenous. Cycles arise because banks are willing to provide credit to low-income households when their indebtedness is low, but reduce credit availability once households' interest payments have become sufficiently high.

Within the group of asset price dynamics models, the first type is the equity price Minsky models. In these models, households invest in different financial assets, including equities, and their portfolio choice affects the equity price dynamics. The expected rate of return on equity plays a key role in generating instability or endogenous cycles (see, e.g. Taylor and O'Connell, 1985; Ryoo 2010, 2013a; Chiarella and Di Guilmi, 2011). When the expected rate of return increases, the price of equities goes up and this affects positively economic activity via investment and/or consumption. The second type of asset price models are the real estate price Minsky models. These models have been motivated by the global financial crisis and focus on the role of housing prices in the emergence of instability and cycles (Ryoo, 2016). House prices affect the provision of mortgages (since houses are used as collateral in the debt contracts). As mortgages increase, the demand for houses increases leading to further increases in the price of houses. As in the Minsky–Veblen models, the boom stops because of the rise in household indebtedness.

Table 1 gives an overview of the various features of the models covered in this survey. These features include (i) the overshooting, or not, of the goods market with respect to demand shocks, (ii) the existence of a Keynesian or a non-Keynesian goods market, (iii) the incorporation of household debt or corporate debt, (iv) the inclusion, or not, of equity or real estate prices, (v) the explicit incorporation, or not, of credit rationing, (vi) the inclusion, or not, of the effects of firms' or households' bankruptcy, (vii) the examination, or not, of the effects of the labor market, (viii) the inclusion, or not, of the distinction between hedge, speculative and Ponzi finance regimes, (ix) the inclusion of an endogenous or exogenous interest rate, (x) the incorporation, or not, of endogenous stock-flow norms and (xi) the formalization, or not, of the stability effects of financial regulation and fiscal policy.

Table 1 shows that the models also differ in the type of analytical framework that they use and the dynamic analysis that they conduct. Most Minsky models are small structural models with two or three dynamic variables, such as the leverage of firms, the investment rate and the interest rate. Some of them pay explicit attention to stock-flow consistency, while others do not. There are also some large stock-flow consistent (SFC) models that include complex financial structures and some Minskyan agent-based models (ABMs). The latter analyse financial fragility via the interaction between individual firms and banks, placing emphasis on network effects, or allow heterogeneous firms to have different strategies or balance sheet structures. While some Minsky models concentrate more on the conditions under which local instability can arise, other models pay their attention to the emergence of cycles which in many cases arise when the equilibrium points are locally unstable but global stability exists because of bounded functions.

3. Debt or Interest Dynamics

3.1 Kalecki–Minsky Models

In the Kalecki–Minsky models, the investment decisions of firms are captured by a Kaleckian investment function in which the rate of profit plays a key role. If the retained profits are not sufficient to cover the investment expenditures, firms demand bank loans which are always supplied (i.e. there is no explicit credit rationing). The debt ratio has negative effects on investment because it increases the interest payments of firms. Output is demand-determined and the marginal propensity to save is higher than the marginal propensity to invest, ensuring goods market equilibrium. Typically, there are two types of households: rentiers who save a proportion of their income and workers who consume all their income. There is no equity market and therefore asset prices are assumed away.

Table 1. Key Differences and Similarities between the Families of Minsky Models

Family		Stable goods market	Unstable goods market	Non-Keynesian goods market	Corporate debt	Household debt	Equity prices	Real estate prices	Credit rationing	Bankruptcy	Labor market	Endogenous interest rate	Hedge, speculative and Ponzi finance regimes	Endogenous stock-flow norms	Effects of fiscal policy	Effects of financial regulation	Small structural model	Stock-flow consistent model	Agent-based model	Cycles	Instability
Kalecki-Minsky	Charles (2008)	✓			✓							✓					✓				✓
	Fazzari et al. (2008)	✓			✓												✓			✓	✓
	Lima and Meirelles (2007)	✓			✓							✓	✓				✓				✓
	Nishi (2012)	✓			✓								✓				✓				✓
Kaldor-Minsky	Asada (2001)		✓		✓							✓					✓				✓
	Foley (1987)		✓		✓							✓					✓			✓	✓
	Jarsulic (1989)		✓		✓							✓					✓			✓	✓
	Semmler (1987)		✓		✓							✓					✓			✓	
	Skott (1994)		✓		✓												✓			✓	✓
Goodwin-Minsky	Keen (1995)			✓	✓						✓				✓		✓			✓	✓
Credit rationing	Delli Gatti et al. (2005, 2010)	✓		✓	✓				✓	✓									✓	✓	✓
	Nikolaidi (2014)				✓				✓					✓	✓			✓		✓	✓
	Ryoo (2013b)		✓		✓				✓		✓				✓		✓			✓	✓
Endogenous target debt ratio	Dafermos (2017)	✓			✓								✓	✓	✓			✓		✓	✓
	Jump et al. (2017)		✓		✓				✓					✓				✓	✓	✓	✓
Minsky-Veblen	Kapeller and Schütz (2014)					✓			✓	✓		✓	✓					✓		✓	✓
	Kapeller et al. (2016)					✓			✓	✓		✓	✓			✓		✓		✓	✓
	Ryoo and Kim (2014)					✓			✓			✓			✓			✓		✓	✓
Equity prices	Chiarella and Di Guilmi (2011)	✓			✓		✓			✓		✓	✓						✓	✓	✓
	Delli Gatti and Gallegati (1990)	✓			✓		✓					✓								✓	✓
	Delli Gatti et al. (1994)	✓			✓		✓					✓					✓			✓	
	Franke and Semmler (1989)	✓			✓		✓					✓					✓			✓	
	Ryoo (2010, 2013a)		✓		✓		✓				✓							✓		✓	✓
	Taylor and O'Connell (1985)	✓			✓		✓					✓					✓			✓	✓
Real estate prices	Ryoo (2016)	✓				✓		✓			✓							✓		✓	✓

Lima and Meirelles (2007), Charles (2008), Fazzari *et al.* (2008) and Nishi (2012) have developed the most prominent recent Kalecki–Minsky models. These models draw to a great extent on the models developed by Jarsulic (1990), Dutt (1995) and Lavoie (1995) which were the first models that incorporated debt and finance into the Kaleckian framework. In our review, we focus on the most recent models that pay more explicit attention to Minskyan dynamics. It is important to note that, with the exception of Fazzari *et al.* (2008), these models do not analyse cycles: they only focus on the conditions under which stability or instability arises. In addition, in many of these models, the categorization into hedge, speculative and Ponzi units is used and it is shown that instability is mostly associated with the speculative and Ponzi finance structures. Lastly, all the Kalecki–Minsky models are small structural models.

Our analysis will start with the models that consider that the interest rate changes in an endogenous way either because of commercial bank decisions (Lima and Meirelles, 2007; Charles, 2008), or because of changes in inflation that are passed on to the nominal interest rate (Fazzari *et al.*, 2008). Then we will analyse Nishi's (2012) model where the interest rate is considered exogenous.

Charles (2008) develops a Minsky model that is composed of firms, households and banks. Firms produce a single good that is used for consumption and investment purposes. Investment is financed via bank loans and retained profits. Equities are assumed away. There are two types of households: rentiers who save a proportion of their income and wealth and workers who consume all their income. Banks provide loans to firms on demand. Output is demand-determined. Commercial banks change the interest rates according to the indebtedness of firms.

Firms' desired investment rate (g^d) depends on animal spirits (α), the gross rate of profit (r) and the interest payments on accumulated debt. In particular, we have:

$$g^d = \alpha + \beta\,(r - id) \tag{1}$$

where i is the interest rate and d is the ratio of firms' debt (D) to capital (K). β is a positive parameter that captures the sensitivity of the investment rate to the net profit rate (which is equal to the gross rate of profit minus the interest payments to capital ratio).

The net borrowing of firms ($\dot{D}$) is derived from firms' budget constraint. Thus, it is equal to investment (I) minus net retained profits:

$$\dot{D} = I - s_f\,(R - iD) \tag{2}$$

where s_f is the retention rate and R are the gross profits. Dividing through by capital stock, we get:

$$\frac{\dot{D}}{K} = g - s_f\,(r - id) \tag{3}$$

where g is the effective investment rate.

Rentiers receive the distributed profits of firms and interest income on deposits. The total saving of the economy is equal to the saving of firms plus the saving of rentiers. Hence, the ratio of saving to capital stock (g^s) is given by:

$$g^s = s_f\,(r - id) + s_c((1 - s_f)(r - id) + id) \tag{4}$$

where s_c is capitalists' propensity to save out of their dividend income and interest on deposits.

Charles (2008) makes a distinction between the desired and the effective investment rate and assumes that the effective investment rate adjusts towards the desired one via the following formula:

$$\dot{g} = \upsilon(g^d - g) \tag{5}$$

where $\upsilon > 0$ is the adjustment speed.

Differentiating the debt-to-capital ratio, we get the law of motion of d:

$$\dot{d} = \frac{\dot{D}}{K} - gd \tag{6}$$

The interest rate is an increasing function of debt-to-capital ratio:

$$i = \bar{i} + \phi d \tag{7}$$

where $\bar{i}$ and ϕ are positive parameters. The assumption is that a higher debt-to-capital ratio increases perceived risk, inducing banks to increase the interest rate in order to compensate for this risk.

An increase in the debt-to-capital ratio has both positive and negative effects on effective investment rate. On the one hand, a higher debt-to-capital ratio tends to increase consumption (and thus capacity utilization and profit rate) since the rise in the interest payments over-compensates the decline in distributed profits, leading to higher rentier consumption. On the other hand, a higher debt-to-capital ratio tends to reduce the profit rate since firms have to pay higher interest. In Charles (2008), the adverse effects on investment over-compensate the positive ones and thus investment is debt-burdened.

The two-dimensional (2D) system of the model consists of the debt-to-capital ratio and the investment rate. Combining the debt-to-capital ratio with equation (7), we get an isocline that is quadratic in d. In a $g - d$ diagram, the isocline is U-shaped. Hence, we get two equilibrium points. The first equilibrium point is stable and is characterized by high investment rate and low debt-to-capital ratio. The second equilibrium point is a saddle point and exhibits a low investment rate and a high debt-to-capital ratio. Charles (2008) tries to connect the equilibrium points with the finance regimes of Minsky: the stable point resembles a hedge finance structure, while the saddle point is closer to the speculative or Ponzi finance structure.

Lima and Meirelles (2007) construct a macro-dynamic model which is similar to the model of Charles (2008). There are two crucial differences. The first one is that the authors formalize the hedge, speculative and Ponzi regime and use it in their dynamic analysis.[4] The second difference is that the authors assume an endogenous interest rate that depends on economic activity and not on the leverage ratio.[5] In particular, in their model, the law of motion of the interest rate is a function of the banking markup, which, in turn, depends on economic activity. The change in the interest is given by:

$$i = i_b \theta (u - \bar{u}) \tag{8}$$

where i_b is the base interest rate set by the central bank, θ is the responsiveness of the banking markup to capacity utilization, u is the capacity utilization and $\bar{u}$ is a threshold value for the capacity utilization. Lima and Meirelles (2007) consider both the case in which interest rate is pro-cyclical ($\theta > 0$) and the case in which it is counter-cyclical ($\theta < 0$). The commercial banks change the interest rate if economic activity is higher (lower) than the threshold value of the capacity utilization.

The 2D system of the model consists of the debt-to-capital ratio and the interest rate captured by equations (6) and (8). The authors identify the hedge, speculative and Ponzi finance regime areas in the $i - g$ diagram. The system has one equilibrium point and its stability properties depend on the finance regime in which it is located. If it is located in the hedge finance area, the equilibrium point is stable when the banking markup is pro-cyclical and the growth rate is higher than the interest rate. When the banking markup is counter-cyclical, the equilibrium is unstable irrespective of the other conditions. If the equilibrium point is located in the speculative finance area, it is unstable when the propensity to save of capitalists is sufficiently low. When this propensity is high enough, stability will arise only if the banking markup is pro-cyclical and the growth rate is higher than the interest rate. Finally, within a Ponzi regime, the equilibrium point is always unstable.

Fazzari *et al.* (2008) present a richer model that combines an investment function, which incorporates debt payments effects and an accelerator effect, with a non-linear Phillips curve. One key difference of their model with the other Kalecki–Minsky models is that the nominal interest rate increases when inflation goes up (the implicit assumption seems to be that the central bank has a real interest rate target which is fixed). Since inflation is a negative function of unemployment rate, it turns out that the nominal interest rate depends positively on economic activity.

Investment depends on output, via an accelerator mechanism, as well as the expected real cash flow of firms. It is assumed that there are two types of consumers: the forward-looking and backward-looking ones. The forward-looking consumers base their consumption on the expected income, while the backward-looking ones consume based on the income of the previous period. Overall, an increase in economic activity increases the disposable income of households, leading to higher consumption. Firms take on debt in order to finance the difference between investment and cash flow. It is implicitly assumed that the saving rate of firms is equal to 1. The net borrowing of firms is determined in a similar way as in equation (2). The authors use a sophisticated version of the Phillips curve that assumes that wage inflation depends on the productivity growth and the level as well as the change in unemployment, allowing thereby for unemployment hysteresis. Prices are determined via a markup over the unit labor costs and thus wage inflation directly affects price inflation.

The model has a complex and non-linear dynamic structure and the authors thus resort to simulations based on empirically motivated parameters in order to investigate its properties. They show that in their benchmark simulations, the system produces cycles after a positive demand shock. Initially, investment increases and gradually the debt ratio starts becoming higher. Simultaneously, higher economic activity leads to lower unemployment. This causes a rise in inflation (via the Phillips curve) which, in turn, leads to a rise in the nominal interest rate. The resulting increase in the debt service is the reason why the boom terminates at some point in time. The decline in economic activity ultimately leads to a reduction in the interest rate that makes the debt service lower, allowing the economy to recover. Fazzari *et al.* (2008) point out that, although the produced cycles eventually die out, they persist for a long period of time. They also illustrate that the responsiveness of the investment rate to the cash flow is one of the key parameters that affects the dynamic properties of their model. When this responsiveness increases, the amplitude of the cycles becomes higher; also, when the responsiveness becomes sufficiently high, the system produces asymptotic instability.

We now turn to the model of Nishi (2012) who assumes that the interest rate is exogenous. The structure of his model is very similar to the structure of Charles' (2008) model. A key difference is that in Nishi's investment function, the desired investment rate depends on the gross rate of profit and the interest payments separately, making it possible to get either a debt-burdened or a debt-led investment regime.

Nishi (2012) uses his model to examine how the various Minskyan finance regimes (hedge, speculative and Ponzi) can arise under different investment regimes.[6] His discussion has a more long-term focus and effectively uses the finance regimes to discuss different levels of the (fixed) interest rate. He shows that when the interest rate is low, we may have a hedge and speculative regime. When these non-Ponzi regimes are combined with a debt-burdened growth regime, the equilibrium point is stable. However, if the non-Ponzi regimes are combined with a debt-led growth regime, we may have an unstable equilibrium point. When the interest rate is sufficiently high, there is the possibility of a Ponzi regime. If the Ponzi regime is combined with a debt-led growth regime, we always have instability.

It is worth pointing out here that in the Kalecki–Minsky models presented above, the leverage ratio turns out to be pro-cyclical in most cases. However, Lavoie and Seccareccia (2001) have argued that the Kaleckian framework does not, in general, generate a pro-cyclical leverage ratio, because investment creates profits. Thus, while in the boom, individual firms might want to take on more debt, the boom conditions make profits high and firms can finance investment internally. This is referred to as the paradox of debt.[7] Charles (2016) has shown that in a Kalecki–Minsky model, the counter-cyclicality of the leverage ratio is less likely when the retention rate of firms is low and/or the propensity to invest out of profits is high.

To sum up, in the Kalecki–Minsky models, debt is accumulated as firms demand bank loans in order to finance their desired investment expenditures. In most of these models, the accumulation of debt has negative feedback effects on investment either directly (debt-burdened regime) or because of the fact that a higher debt ratio increases the interest rate (Charles, 2008). In some Kalecki–Minsky models, the interest rate can also increase when there is higher economic activity that induces commercial banks to increase their banking markup (Lima and Meirelles, 2007) or when central banks increase the base interest rate due to higher inflation (Fazzari et al., 2008).

3.2 Kaldor–Minsky Models

In Kaldor–Minsky models, firms' investment expenditures are positively affected by economic activity (either through the rate of profit or through the capacity utilization) and are negatively or positively affected by the accumulation of debt. Similar to the Kalecki–Minsky models, output is demand determined, loans are provided on demand (i.e. there is no explicit credit rationing) and there is no equity market. The hallmark of the Kaldor–Minsky model is that investment is overshooting. In contrast to the Kalecki–Minsky models, there is an unstable goods market: the marginal propensity to save is lower than the marginal propensity to invest (close to the equilibrium). This is a characteristic of the Kaldor models (see, e.g. Chiarella et al., 2000) that draw on Kaldor's (1940) trade cycle model in which the marginal propensity to save is lower than the marginal propensity to invest at intermediate levels of output.

Asada (2001) develops a highly stylized Kaldor–Minsky model where Minsky cycles can be produced. The author gives more emphasis to the assumptions that are needed to produce cycles, while less attention is paid to the economic intuition of the macroeconomic model. The structure of Asada's model is similar to the structure of Kalecki–Minsky models. His investment function can be written as follows:

$$g^d = \Phi(r, d, i, s_f) \tag{9}$$

where $\Phi_r = \partial\Phi/\partial r > 0$, $\Phi_d = \partial\Phi/\partial d < 0$, $\Phi_i = \partial\Phi/\partial i < 0$ and $\Phi_{sf} = \partial\Phi/\partial s_f > 0$.

The saving rate is given by:

$$g^s = s_f(r - id) + s_c((1 - s_f)(r - id) + id + \varepsilon d) \tag{10}$$

This saving function is similar to the saving function of Charles (2008). The main difference is that Asada includes a positive impact of a safe asset on saving. This safe asset is assumed to be a linear function of the debt-to-capital ratio, that is, it is equal to εd, where ε is positive parameter. Therefore, equation (10) implies that an increase in the debt-to-capital ratio has both positive and negative effects on the saving rate. A higher ε reinforces the positive effect of the debt ratio on the saving rate.

The interest rate is a positive function of the debt-to-capital ratio as in Charles (2008). The output-to-capital ratio increases when the sum of consumption-to-capital ratio and desired investment rate is higher than the current output-to-capital ratio:

$$\dot{y} = \sigma(c + g^d - y) \tag{11}$$

where $y = Y/K$ is the output-to-capital ratio, $c = C/K$ is the consumption-to-capital ratio and σ is a positive adjustment parameter.

The debt-to-capital ratio and the output-to-capital ratio constitute the 2D system of the model, captured by equations (6) and (11), respectively. Asada (2001) assumes, without much explanation, that the goods market is de-stabilizing, the output is debt-burdened, the leverage ratio is pro-cyclical and the debt ratio is self-stabilizing.

The author uses the Hopf bifurcation theorem in order to show the conditions under which a limit cycle arises. How does the cycle behave in this model? Suppose that the economy is initially characterized by a low output-to-capital ratio and a low debt-to-capital ratio. Since the debt-to-capital ratio is sufficiently low, the investment rate gradually becomes higher. When investment and output have become sufficiently high, the debt-to-capital ratio starts increasing. At some point, this increasing debt-to-capital ratio causes a decline in the investment rate and thus in output-to-capital ratio. Once the investment rate has become sufficiently low, the debt-to-capital ratio decreases and the economy enters into a new expansionary period.

Semmler (1987) has developed another model with Kaldor–Minsky features. He introduces financial variables into a profit-investment dynamic system where the saving function is S-shaped as in Kaldor. The system without the financial variables produces a limit cycle. In the system with the financial variables, the interest rate and the debt payment commitments have a negative impact on investment (i.e. investment is debt-burdened) and the debt-to-capital ratio rises during the expansions (i.e. leverage is pro-cyclical). The introduction of the financial variables can reduce the amplitude of the limit cycle (i.e. expansions become shorter and contractions become less severe) or can increase the possibility of instability.

Two other Kaldor–Minsky models are those developed by Foley (1987) and Jarsulic (1989) in which the interest rate plays a key role in the emergence of the cycles. In Foley's model, a decline in the interest rate increases borrowing which, in turn, increases investment and profitability. However, higher demand for credit produces a rise in the interest rate (via a loanable funds market) which has a negative impact on borrowing. Foley (1987) uses the Hopf bifurcation theorem in order to show the emergence of cycles. Jarsulic's (1989) model generates some similar dynamics. He postulates an investment function where the investment rate depends negatively on the interest rate and he also assumes that a higher investment rate increases the interest rate. His investment function is non-linear: he assumes that the investment rate starts declining when it is already high. As a result, his 2D system is bounded which allows him to use the Poincaré–Bendixson theorem to show the emergence of a limit cycle. According to this theorem, a 2D system that is bounded and has a unique locally unstable stationary point produces a limit cycle.

Skott (1994) develops a Kaldorian model in which some abstract financial variables are introduced in the investment function. In particular, he uses a financial fragility variable (F) and a tranquility variable (T). The financial fragility variable captures the sensitivity of the financial system to small disturbances that might affect the ability of economic units to fulfil their financial obligations. As a proxy of financial fragility, Skott (1994) uses the ratio of interest payments to the normal rate of profit ($F = id/\bar{r}$). As he points out, '... fragility and tranquillity evolve endogenously and, in accordance with Minsky's behavioural assumptions, it is assumed that changes in fragility depend on the degree of tranquillity: in the absence of financial difficulties agents adopt schemes of increasing optimism' (Skott, 1994, p. 53). Therefore, the change in the financial fragility ratio is given by:

$$\dot{F} = T \tag{12}$$

The tranquility variable is associated with the appearance or not of crises. When a system experiences a crisis, tranquility is at its minimum value since default and bankruptcy rates are high. Tranquility is at its maximum value when the financial system functions without disruptions and economic activity is high. As Skott (1994, p. 53) explains, '[f]inancial difficulties develop as a result of an incongruence between the optimism which motivated financial arrangements and the actual outcome. If the source of potential instability is located primarily in the business sector (...) then T should depend on financial fragility (inversely) and on realized profit rates (positively)'. Hence, he assumes that T is a negative function of F and a positive function of output-to-capital ratio:

$$T = Ay - BF \tag{13}$$

The investment function is written as:

$$g^d = \Lambda(y) + \varsigma F + \gamma T \tag{14}$$

where $\Lambda(y)$ is a function where $\Lambda_y = \partial\Lambda(y)/\partial y > 0$. Similarly to the Kalecki–Minsky models, an increase in economic activity increases investment. However, following Kaldor, it is assumed that investment is an S-shaped function, which implies that the investment rate is bounded (it stops increasing as output-to-capital ratio becomes too high). In addition, investment is positively or negatively affected by financial fragility (i.e. ς can be positive or negative) and is positively affected by the tranquility indicator ($\gamma > 0$). Since $F = id/\bar{r}$ and $T = Ay - BF$, equation (14) can be rewritten as follows:

$$g^d = \Lambda(y) + \gamma Ay + (\varsigma - \gamma B)\frac{id}{\bar{r}} \tag{15}$$

where $\bar{r}$ is the normal profit rate, while A and B are positive parameters. Equation (15) implies that an increase in economic activity positively affects the investment rate, while the interest payments on debt may have a positive or a negative effect on the investment rate. Saving is a function of output and output adjusts to the difference between investment and saving via an equation which is similar to equation (11) used by Asada (2001).

The fragility ratio and the output-to-capital ratio constitute the 2D system. Skott (1994) analyses the stability conditions for this 2D system by considering two cases. In the first case, the impact of financial fragility on investment is positive. It is shown that in this case, the model can be stable or unstable and does not produce cycles. In the second case, the impact of financial fragility on investment is negative. This makes it possible to generate cycles which are similar to the cycles generated by the model of Asada (2001). Since Skott's system is bounded due to the S-shaped investment function, he uses the Poincaré–Bendixson theorem to illustrate the conditions under which a limit cycle emerges.

To summarize, most Kaldor–Minsky models have a similar structure with the Kalecki–Minsky models. However, in the Kaldor–Minsky models, the main source of instability is the accelerator mechanism that is included in the investment function and renders the goods market unstable. Compared to the Kalecki–Minsky models, the analysis of the Kaldor–Minsky models pays more attention to the conditions under which cycles emerge. In some Kaldor–Minsky models, the interest rate is exogenous (e.g. Skott, 1994), while in other models, the endogenous change in the interest rate is a key part of the cyclical behavior (e.g. Foley, 1987; Jarsulic, 1989).

3.3 Goodwin–Minsky Models

Keen (1995) develops a Goodwin model with some Minskyan features that operate through the wage share equation: a higher debt ratio dampens investment and employment, which affects the wage share, which, in turn, affects the debt ratio. The use of the Goodwin framework implies that the Goodwin–Minsky models treat the labor market explicitly. This is a distinct feature compared to most other Minsky models in which labor market dynamics are absent.

Keen (1995) assumes full capital utilization and, as a result, output is determined by capital stock, which is driven by the past investment decisions of capitalists. This comes in contrast to the Kalecki–Minsky and Kaldor–Minsky models where output is demand-determined. Keen (1995) extends the Goodwin model to include banks, whose rising income share can squeeze industrial profits similar to how a rising wage share squeezes profits. Unlike the Goodwin model, where all profits are reinvested, Keen (1995) uses a non-linear (convex) investment function, which creates a pro-cyclical debt ratio. The interest rate is a positive function of the debt ratio. The theoretical problem of this model is that it does not offer a mechanism that equilibrates investment and saving.[8]

The gross investment rate (i.e. net investment rate plus depreciation rate) depends on the net profit rate of firms:

$$g = P(r - id) \qquad (16)$$

where P is a non-linear function of the net profit rate. We have that $r - id = \pi/v$ where v is the capital–output ratio, $\pi = 1 - \omega - b$ is the profit share, ω is the wage share and $b = iD/Y$ is the bankers' income share. This means that the gross investment rate ends up being a positive function of the profit share. The convexity of the investment function implies that the profit share has a gradually higher effect on the investment rate. In particular, for relatively low values of the profit share, investment is equal to profits but for relatively high values of the profit share, investment becomes higher than profits, which means that the accumulation of debt accelerates.

As in Goodwin's model, the wage share changes in an endogenous way. Since $\omega = w/x$, the change in the wage share is:

$$\dot{\omega} = (\Theta(l) - \chi)\omega \qquad (17)$$

where Θ is a non-linear positive function of the employment rate (l), χ is the growth rate of labor productivity, w is the wage rate and x is labor productivity. When the employment rate becomes higher, the wage share increases.

Since the employment rate is $l = Y/xN$, the law of motion of l is:

$$\dot{l} = (g - \chi - \tau)l \tag{18}$$

where τ is the growth rate of labor force and N is the labor force.

The net borrowing of firms depends on the difference between the investment rate and net profits. Keen (1995) normalizes debt by dividing it by output and assumes that firm retains all their profits. In similar lines with Charles (2008), the interest rate is an increasing function of the indebtedness of firms (Keen uses the debt-to-output ratio instead of the debt-to-capital ratio).

The three-dimensional (3D) system consists of the wage share and the employment rate, as in the Goodwin model, as well as the debt-to-capital ratio. Keen (1995) does not offer an analytical solution of the model, but moves swiftly to simulation.[9] Thus, the paper is more effective in illustrating the instabilities that can arise rather than clarifying the properties of the model. In his simulations, Keen (1995) shows that both stability and instability can arise in his dynamic system. Instability arises when the base interest rate is high and/or when the interest rate is low and the sensitivity of the interest rate to the debt-to-capital is high. The system breaks down because the rate of profit becomes negative primarily because of increasing firms' interest payments. Keen (1995) shows that a breakdown is prevented when counter-cyclical fiscal policy is introduced. However, in his simulations, fiscal policy does not eliminate cycles. Keen (2013) extends the model described above by including an explicit banking sector, endogenous money creation and a more explicit financial structure based on the SFC approach.

Sordi and Vercelli (2014) argue that Keen (1995) does not take into account that the goods market may be in a disequilibrium and they use an output adjustment mechanism. They propose a model based on Goodwin (1951) flexible accelerator. Therefore, in contrast to Keen (1995), output is demand-determined and investment is demand-driven (without direct effect of profitability or debt). In our classification, it is thus closer to the Kaldor–Minsky model. They derive a four–dimensional (4D) system with the wage share, the employment rate, the debt-to-capital ratio and the capital-to-output ratio as state variables and use the Hopf bifurcation theorem to prove the possibility of cycles. Instability in their model is more likely when investment responds strongly to expected output.

Stockhammer and Michell (2017) demonstrate that pseudo-Goodwin cycles can arise from a Minsky model that is paired with a reserve-army distribution function. Unlike the Goodwin–Minsky model, in their model, output is demand-determined and demand is debt-burdened and wage-led. The cycles are Minskyan debt cycles and income distribution fluctuates as it is dragged along by the business cycles. The economy thus exhibits pseudo-Goodwin cycles.

3.4 Credit Rationing Minsky Models

A key feature of the Minskyan models presented above is that banks play a relatively passive role. Although in some of these models, banks increase the interest rate when the debt ratio of firms increases (e.g. Charles, 2008) or banks are in some cases implicitly considered to co-determine the accumulation of debt, there is no explicit credit rationing based on the financial position of banks. This is at odds with Minsky who has argued that banks are active players in the emergence of financial fragility and credit expansion relies on their financial structure (e.g. Minsky, 1986 [2008], p. 265). The models of Ryoo (2013b), Nikolaidi (2014) and Delli Gatti et al. (2005, 2010) belong to the credit rationing Minsky models.[10]

Ryoo (2013b) develops an SFC model that consists of firms, households and banks. Firms take on debt and issue equities in order to externally finance their investment. Equity is the residual source of finance[11] and the equity-to-deposits ratio in the household portfolio choice is assumed to be constant. This implies that the price of equities needs to adjust in order to keep the ratio constant. Banks provide loans taking into account the profit-to-interest payment ratio and the profitability of banks. The bank capital ratio positively depends on the profitability of firms.

Ryoo (2013b) distinguishes between short cycles and long waves. Based on Skott (1989), the short cycles result from the interaction between destabilizing goods market dynamics à la Kaldor and stabilizing labor market dynamics. Investment depends on capacity utilization and there is an explicit function for economic growth whereby growth is affected positively by the profit share and negatively by the employment rate. The profit share is increasing in capacity utilization. As capacity utilization increases, growth rate responds strongly. The increase in growth rate increases employment. When employment becomes sufficiently high, it exerts a negative impact on economic growth, allowing the emergence of cycles.

The long wave of the model is captured by a 2D system which has the leverage ratios of firms and banks as state variables. It is shown that instability is more likely as the responsiveness of credit availability to bank profits increases. Using the Poincaré–Bendixson theorem, it is shown that cycles arise when the system becomes locally unstable. The rationale of the cycle is as follows. When the leverage ratio of firms and banks is low, the debt-to-capital ratio starts increasing because firms are considered to be creditworthy, and hence, more loans are provided by banks. As loans expand, the leverage of banks, which goes hand in hand with bank profitability, goes up. This enhances credit supply. However, when the leverage of firms becomes sufficiently high, firms start being considered less creditworthy. This causes a reduction in credit supply, which, in turn, leads to a decline in bank leverage and bank profitability which reinforces the decline in credit. The reduction in credit leads to a lower firm leverage. When the leverage ratios of both firms and banks have become sufficiently low, credit starts increasing again and a new cycle begins.

Ryoo (2013b) suggests that instability in his model can be reduced if a financial regulation rule is adopted according to which banks adjust their retention rate in order to achieve a specific leverage ratio. This rule relies on Minsky's writings about the ways through which banking instability can be tamed (see Minsky, 1986 [2008], ch. 13).

Nikolaidi (2014) develops an SFC model with firms, households, banks, government and a central bank. Both firms and banks have a target leverage ratio which captures their desired margins of safety that are deemed to change in an endogenous way: when economic activity is high (low), the target leverage ratios increase (decrease). The target leverage ratio of firms affects their desired investment. The higher the target leverage ratio of firms compared to the actual ratio, the higher their investment, ceteris paribus. Banks provide only a proportion of the loans demanded. They are more willing to reduce credit rationing when their leverage ratio is lower than the target one. Firms take on debt to finance their desired investment which is negatively affected by the leverage ratio of firms. Since there is credit rationing, the effective investment is lower than the desired investment. Banks' credit rationing is affected by their leverage ratio and the leverage ratio of firms.[12] Therefore, in boom periods, both the desired investment and the provision of loans become gradually higher, which might lead to instability. The opposite holds in bust periods. Instability is more likely when the target leverage ratios respond strongly to changes in economic activity.

The model can produce cycles (this is shown using the Hopf bifurcation theorem). The cycles can be described as follows. When investment activity is sufficiently high, the target leverage ratios of both firms and banks increase, leading to higher desired investment and lower credit rationing. This increases debt accumulation and the actual leverage ratios. However, once the leverage ratios have become sufficiently high, both firms and banks become less willing to participate in new debt contracts and economic activity starts slowing down. The decline in economic activity makes the leverage ratios lower and, at the same time, reduces the target leverage ratios of firms and banks reinforcing the contractionary forces. A new boom starts when the leverage ratios have declined sufficiently. Nikolaidi (2014) also examines the role of fiscal policy. It is shown that counter-cyclical fiscal policy can reduce the instability that stems from the behavior of firms and banks.

While most of the literature on Minsky uses small-scale or large-scale macro-models, there is also a family that emphasizes heterogeneity among firms and uses agent-based modeling techniques. Delli Gatti *et al.* (2005, 2010) have developed such models with heterogeneous firms and/or heterogeneous banks. Theoretically, these models draw on the financial accelerator argument that the availability of credit for firms depends on their net worth (Bernanke and Gertler, 1990; Greenwald and Stiglitz, 1993). However, in line with the credit rationing models discussed above, the credit conditions are also affected by the net worth of banks. In particular, the interest rate depends on the financial position of both firms and banks. Bankruptcy is explicitly introduced (which is an innovation compared to most Minsky models). When a firm goes bankrupt, this affects adversely the net worth of banks, leading to a higher interest rate. This, in turn, reduces the net worth of firms. Following stylized facts, firm size obeys a power law. This highly skewed distribution implies that idiosyncratic shocks can turn into macro shocks (if they affect one of the few very large firms). This is compounded by network effects that can cause bankruptcy cascades. It is worth mentioning that there is no aggregate demand function comparable to those of most previously discussed models, but output is determined by the optimizing behavior of net worth constrained firms. Unlike many of the models discussed in this survey, the main aim is not to analyse endogenous cycles but the conditions under which random shocks can turn into systemic crises. In some ways, the models are closer to the New Keynesian financial accelerator approach, but they also highlight Minskyan features.

To sum up, in credit rationing Minsky models, cycles and instability are affected by the behavior and the financial position of banks. In some models, the interest rate is exogenous and banks affect the volume of credit directly (Ryoo, 2013b; Nikolaidi, 2014), while in other models, the interest rate is a function of the financial position of firms and banks (Delli Gatti *et al.*, 2005, 2010). Banks contribute to the increase in financial fragility during the boom periods by increasing credit availability and/or providing credit at favorable terms. They can reinforce the destabilizing forces in the bust period since their financial soundness is affected by macroeconomic performance and this has feedback effects on credit conditions.

3.5 *Endogenous Target Debt Ratio Minsky Models*

In the endogenous target debt ratio Minsky models, firms, banks or the private sector, in general, have targets about their leverage ratios. These targets are also called stock-flow norms (based on Godley) or desired margins of safety (based on Minsky). The target debt ratios tend to increase when economic and financial performance is good and they tend to decline when economic and financial environment is perceived to be unfavorable and unstable. Higher target debt ratios increase desired investment or desired consumption and tend to reduce credit rationing. In the endogenous target debt ratio models, output is demand determined, the interest rate is exogenous and there is no consideration of the labor market.

The model of Nikolaidi (2014), described in the previous section, was the first model that used explicitly an endogenous target debt ratio. Dafermos (2017) incorporated this idea of an endogenous target debt ratio into a Godleyan analytical framework. Following Godley's projection analysis (e.g. Godley, 1999), his model consists of three sectors: the private sector (which is consolidated), the government sector and the foreign sector. The balances and the debt of these sectors are explicitly interrelated via Godley's financial balances approach. The private sector has a stock-flow norm (the target net debt-to-income ratio) which is allowed to change endogenously based on the Minskyan idea that the perception of risk and, hence, the desired margins of safety change during the economic cycle.

In his dynamic analysis, he first examines a system with the propensity to spend of the private sector and the private debt-to-income ratio as state variables. In this system, the propensity to spend of the private sector increases (decreases) when the target debt-to-income ratio is higher (lower) than the actual one. Using the Poincaré–Bendixson theorem, Dafermos (2017) shows that this system can produce cycles. Instability and cycles are more likely when the responsiveness of the propensity to spend to the target debt ratio is high. He also shows that when the target debt ratio is endogenized via a Minsky mechanism, an otherwise stable system can become unstable.

This model is also used to examine the implications of two fiscal rules: (i) a Maastricht-type fiscal rule in which government expenditures decline (increases) when government indebtedness is high (low) and (ii) a Godley–Minsky fiscal rule that is close to the idea of counter-cyclical fiscal policy. The simulation analysis in the paper shows that the Maastricht type fiscal rule is conducive to instability while the Godley–Minsky fiscal rule tends to stabilize the macro-economy.

Jump *et al.* (2017) develop a model with heterogeneous firms in which the aggregate target debt ratio is determined by firms' decisions via a switching mechanism. Firms choose between a hedge strategy with a low target debt ratio or a speculative strategy with a high target. The probability that firms select the speculative strategy increases as the interest payments relative to profits decreases and the volatility of output goes down. This implies that good and stable economic and financial performance induces more firms to select the speculative strategy, resulting in a higher aggregate target debt ratio. In the model, a higher target debt ratio affects investment positively (but actual debt negatively). The 3D system of the model consists of output, debt and the proportion of the firms that choose the hedge strategy. This system can produce limit cycles: in a stable growth period, firms switch to higher debt targets. The initial equilibrium becomes unstable and leads to a boom. Once volatility increases firms switch back to a hedge strategy. The model can also give rise to chaotic dynamics if firms are allowed to accumulate financial assets.

3.6 *Minsky–Veblen Models*

Despite the fact that household debt was not at the core of Minsky's analysis, there are some early Minsky models that have formalized consumer debt using Minskyan ideas (Palley, 1994, 1997). More recently, the Veblenian analysis of emulation motives has been used in some Minsky models to analyse the dynamics of consumer debt and the implications for financial fragility (Kapeller and Schütz, 2014; Ryoo and Kim, 2014; Kapeller *et al.*, 2016). In these models, low-income households take on debt in order to emulate the consumption of richer households.[13]

Ryoo and Kim (2014) develop a Kaldorian SFC model with households, firms and banks. Firms make investment expenditures by using equity and undistributed profits (they do not take out loans). There are two types of households: workers and rentiers. Workers demand consumer credit in order to increase their consumption and emulate the consumption of rentiers. Banks provide loans to workers taking into account their net income. Rentiers consume part of their income and wealth and do not take on debt. The 2D system of the model comprises the debt-to-capital ratio and the emulation motive. With this system, cycles may emerge (the authors use the Poincaré–Bendixson theorem to show that). When the indebtedness of workers is sufficiently low, workers are more willing to take on debt in order to emulate the rentiers and, simultaneously, banks are more willing to provide these loans. This increases the debt-to-capital ratio which has feedback effects into the emulation: workers have to pay a higher interest that reduces their income and increases the income of rentiers. This reinforces the consumption differential between workers and rentiers producing a further rise in the debt-to-capital ratio. Once the debt ratio has reached a sufficiently high level, workers become less willing to take on more debt and banks become less accommodative. Note that instability and cycles are more likely when banks' decision to provide loans is more accommodating and workers' decision to emulate the rentiers is sufficiently strong.

Kapeller and Schütz (2014) develop a large-scale SFC model that consists of firms, households and banks. There are three main differences between the model of Kapeller and Schütz (2014) and Ryoo and Kim (2014). First, Kapeller and Schütz (2014) incorporate three types of households instead of two: (i) type 1 worker households whose income share is constant, (ii) type 2 worker households whose income share is declining and (iii) rentiers. Emulation refers only to the intra-worker consumption: it is assumed that type 2 workers try to emulate the consumption of type 1 workers and the consumption of rentiers does not affect the consumption of workers. Second, in similar lines with Charles (2008), Kapeller and Schütz (2014) assume an endogenous interest rate which is a positive function of debt. Third, bankruptcy is introduced. Workers become bankrupt when they cannot cover their subsistence-level consumption. When this happens, banks' expectations are adversely affected and credit supply goes down.

In their simulations, Kapeller and Schütz (2014) produce cycles. Initially, the decline in the income of type 2 worker households relative to the income of type 1 worker households leads to an increase in their indebtedness which also leads to an increase in the interest rate. However, at some point in time, the rise in indebtedness causes bankruptcies that stop credit expansion leading to a decline in economic activity. After some periods, the economy recovers because bankruptcies reduce the debt of type 2 worker households, increasing their income.

Kapeller *et al.* (2016) extend the model developed by Kapeller and Schütz (2014) by introducing the role of fiscal policy and a more active banking sector. In their simulations, they investigate the effects of various government interventions (such as fiscal stimulus and bank bailouts) and financial regulation on the financial cycles. They show that the government interventions mitigate the impact of financial crises but they shorten the time between the crises since they are conducive to higher credit expansion. The financial crises become much less severe when a stricter financial regulation (captured by a higher responsiveness of credit availability to the leverage of banks) is implemented.

Overall, in the Minsky–Veblen models, consumer debt is the driver of financial fragility. Credit expansion depends positively on inequality and the financial soundness of households.

Financial booms come to an end when the interest payments of households have become sufficiently high. The endogeneity of the interest rate is not necessary in order to get financial cycles.

4. Asset Price Dynamics

The models described in the previous sections do not allow a role for asset price dynamics. This is at odds with Minsky's analysis according to which asset inflation positively affects investment and economic activity (see, for example, his 'two price' theory of investment). Actually, most Minskyan models that were developed in late 1980s and early 1990s paid particular attention to the role of asset prices. This changed after mid-1990s when most authors started developing Minskyan models using the Kaleckian framework where asset prices do not play a key role.[14] However, since 2010, there has been a resurgence of interest in Minsky models with asset prices. It is also interesting that the asset price Minsky models have traditionally confined their attention to equity prices—real estate prices have only very recently been incorporated into Minskyan frameworks.

4.1 Equity Price Minsky Models

The equity price Minsky models place particular attention on the equity price dynamics and their interactions with the real economy. In these models, there is an equity market and households take portfolio decisions that affect the demand for equity and thus the equity price, which, in turn, affects economic activity through consumption or investment. Equity market is the principal source of instability and both cycles and instability are investigated.

Taylor and O'Connell (1985) developed the first model that formalized Minsky's arguments and put equity prices at the core of the analysis. Their model economy consists of firms, households and a government. Banks are not explicitly considered. Firms issue equity in order to finance their investment expenditures. There are two types of households: workers who consume all of their income and rentiers who invest in three different assets: equity, money and government bonds. Money is exogenous and the interest rate changes endogenously.

Firms' desired investment rate depends on the actual rate of profit (r), a confidence variable that captures the difference between the expected and the actual rate of profit (ρ) and the interest rate (i):

$$g^d = \alpha + \zeta (r + \rho - i) \tag{19}$$

where ζ is the responsiveness of firms' investment to the expected difference between profit and interest costs. The variable ρ plays a key role in the model since it captures the role of expectations. When expectations improve, ρ increases, having a positive impact on the investment rate. Its law of motion is given by

$$\dot{\rho} = -\xi(i - \bar{i}) \tag{20}$$

According to equation (20), expectations improve when the interest rate is lower than a normal interest rate, $\bar{i}$. The dynamics of the model rely on the interaction between ρ and money. Suppose that there is an exogenous increase in the confidence of firms. Higher confidence has two countervailing effects on the interest rate. On the one hand, improved expectations increase investment and economic activity causing a rise in the interest rate via the traditional IS-LM mechanism. On the other hand, a higher expected rate of profit shifts wealth from money into equity. This reduction in the demand for money tends to reduce the interest rate. If the first effect dominates, the system converges towards its fixed point after some damped oscillations. This is because the model assumes a negative effect of the interest rate on expected profitability. If the second effect dominates, the system becomes unstable. This is more likely when there is high asset substitution.

Franke and Semmler (1989) extended the model of Taylor and O'Connell (1985) by including firm loans. Net borrowing increases when ρ becomes higher and the debt-to-capital ratio becomes lower. The underlying assumption is that banks take into account both the expected gross profitability and the indebtedness of firms when they decide about the provision of loans. There are no government bonds and households choose only between two assets: equities and deposits. The debt-to-capital ratio takes values between zero and one. When the debt ratio is equal to one, the risk of bankruptcy is at its maximum level and hence no further lending and borrowing can take place. This introduces a boundedness in the system. The change in ρ is a positive function of the difference between the rate of profit and the interest rate and a negative function of the debt-to-capital ratio. Overall, their model produces a dynamic interaction between ρ and the debt-to-capital ratio. This dynamic interaction can give rise to stability or cycles depending on the responsiveness of the law of motion of the debt-to-capital ratio to itself and ρ.

Delli Gatti and Gallegati (1990) develop a model which has many similarities with the model of Taylor and O'Connell (1985) but differ primarily in the way that the investment function and the portfolio choice are formalized. Firms invest taking into account their retained profits and the difference between asset prices and the price of investment goods. By using such an investment specification, the authors formalize Minsky's 'two price' theory of investment. Interestingly, it is assumed that the sensitivity of investment to profits increases during the upward phase of the business cycle (however, they do not include an explicit equation for that). The rationale for this pro-cyclical sensitivity is that during expansion, firms' profits increase and as a result both firms and banks consider that the projects are less risky and thereby investment relative to profits becomes higher. Households consume part of their income. Their demand for money depends on the transactions motive, the speculative motive and the finance motive. The demand for finance is equal to the financing gap: the difference between investment and retained profits. There is implicitly a portfolio choice between equity and money. The authors use the leverage ratio as an indicator of financial fragility. The leverage ratio is defined as the ratio of the financing gap to retained profits.

The 2D system of the model consists of the profits of firms and the price of equity. The change in profits is determined by the difference between investment and saving (the IS curve), while the law of motion of equity prices is obtained by the difference between the supply and the demand for money (the LM curve). The model can produce various dynamics depending on the relative strength of the different effects. The authors pay particular attention to the case in which profits, leverage and equity prices move hand in hand during the ascending phase of the business cycle.

Delli Gatti *et al.* (1994) extended the model of Delli Gatti and Gallegati (1990). They made two key changes. First, they included an explicit portfolio choice between equity and money. The demand for each asset depends on the expected rates of return. Second, they incorporated an equation in which the propensity to invest out of profits is a positive function of output. The model can produce cycles that behave as follows. During the ascending phase of the business cycle, the propensity to invest out of profits increases. As a result, investment and output become higher, increasing external finance and debt. At the same time, since economic activity increases dividends, investors decide to increase their holdings in equity and the price equity gradually improves. This equity price inflation boosts investment. However, at some point, internal funds do not increase sufficiently compared to debt commitments. At this point, we have a recession in which investment, output and the price of equity become lower. As a result, the propensity to invest with respect to profits gradually becomes lower. This produces a larger drop in investment and economic activity exacerbating the recession. Economic activity starts increasing again when debt commitments have been reduced sufficiently compared to profits.

More recently, Ryoo (2010, 2013a) developed an equity price Minsky model that builds on the above-mentioned models. There are five key differences: (i) asset prices affect economic activity not only via investment but also via consumption; (ii) money is assumed to be determined endogenously and the interest rate is exogenous; (iii) the interaction between the portfolio choice and debt dynamics is modeled more explicitly and the role of capital gains is taken into account; (iv) the model pays particular attention to stock-flow consistency and (v) a distinction is made between short cycles and long waves.

Ryoo's (2010, 2013a) model consists of households, firms and banks. Contrary to Ryoo (2013b), the equity-to-deposits ratio is not constant: the demand for equities increases when the return on equity becomes higher than the interest rate on deposits. Investment expenditures are financed via retained profits, banks loans and equities. Loans are assumed to increase when the profitability of firms improves; contrary to Ryoo (2013b), the availability of credit does not depend on the financial position of banks. As in Ryoo (2013b), equity issue acts as the residual source of finance for firms.

Ryoo (2013a) has developed a Kaleckian and a Kaldorian version of his model. In the Kaleckian version, the goods market is stable as in the Kalecki–Minsky models and capacity utilization is allowed to fluctuate. Investment is debt-led. This comes from the fact that (i) loans are equal to deposits and, as a result, a rise in loans leads to a rise in the wealth and the interest income of households, boosting consumption and (ii) investment depends only on capacity utilization and not on the rate of profit, which means that the interest payments of firms have no effect on investment. Ryoo shows that in such a Kaleckian model, the portfolio decisions of households can produce a cyclical behavior.

Let us now focus on the Kaldorian version of the model. As in Ryoo (2013b), the Kaldorian version distinguishes between short cycles and long waves. The short cycles are Kaldorian real cycles, while the long waves refer to financial cycles. The system that produces the long waves consists of three state variables: the equity-to-deposits ratio, the expected rate of return on equity and the debt-to-capital ratio.

In the long run, the actual capacity utilization is equal to the exogenously given desired one. The household wealth-to-capital ratio is given by $(p_e e + M)/K$, where p_e is the price of equities, e is the number of equities and M denotes deposits. Since in the model $D = M$ (i.e. loans are equal to deposits), we have that the household wealth-to-capital ratio is equivalent to the Tobin's q. Tobin's q can be written as a function of the equity-to-deposits ratio ($a = p_e e/D$) and debt-to-capital ratio:

$$q = \frac{p_e e + D}{K} = (1 + a)\, d \tag{21}$$

Tobin's q could be incorporated in the Kaleckian investment function in order to get a direct link between asset prices and investment. However, this would not change the essence of the dynamic analysis (Ryoo, 2013a, p. 49).

Households' consumption depends on disposable income and wealth. Using a linear specification, we have:

$$\frac{C}{K} = c_1 y_d + c_2 q \tag{22}$$

where y_d is the disposable income of households (equal to wages, dividends and interest on deposits) and c_1 and c_2 are positive parameters.

The ratio of equity-to-deposits (a) and the expected rate of return on equity (λ^e) change according to the following equations:

$$\dot{a} = \kappa(\eta(\lambda^e - i) - a) \tag{23}$$

$$\dot{\lambda}^e = \psi(\lambda - \lambda^e) \tag{24}$$

where λ is the (actual) rate of return on equity, κ and ψ are positive parameters and η is a positive non-linear function of the expected rate of return on equity (i.e. $\partial\eta/\partial\lambda^e > 0$). Equation (23) shows that households' desired equity-to-deposits ratio, $\eta(\lambda^e - i)$, is higher, the higher is the expected rate of return on equity compared to the interest rate on deposits (the latter is assumed to be equal to the interest rate on loans). The equity-to-deposits ratio increases when the desired one is higher than the actual one. Equation (24) implies that the expected rate of return on equity changes via an adaptive expectations mechanism whereby the expected rate of return on equity increases when the actual rate of return is higher than the expected one. From equations (23) and (24), we can derive the evolution of the price of equities. Ryoo (2013a) mentions that these equations can be viewed as a reduced form of the interactions between fundamentalists and chartists that are analysed in the behavioral finance literature but gives otherwise little explanation for these key equations that drive the cycle. Equations (23) and (24) can be derived from a momentum trader model where momentum traders (or chartists) and fundamentalists co-exist (Beja and Goldman, 1980). Fundamentalists expect the price to return to its fundamental value (thus the negative effect of a on $\dot{a}$), whereas the momentum traders expect a further increase in prices when asset price growth exceeds expected capital gains (equation (24)).

The debt-to-capital ratio increases as the profit-interest ratio becomes higher. According to Ryoo (2013a), the profit-interest ratio captures the fundamental margins of safety. Therefore, when this ratio becomes higher, firms are more willing to take on more debt and banks are more willing to expand credit. Thus, debt also changes endogenously over the cycle, it plays a role in transmitting the cycle to the real sector and interacts with asset prices; however, it is not essential for the cycle itself.

Ryoo (2013a) shows that closed orbits or explosive oscillations will occur if the impact of momentum traders ($\partial\eta/\partial\lambda^e$) is sufficiently large. The cycles in the model can be explained as follows. Suppose that initially, the expected rate of return is sufficiently high. As a result, households increase their demand for equity. The higher the demand for equity, the higher their price. This higher price increases the capital gains on equity and consequently the actual rate of return on equity. Since households have adaptive expectations about the expected rate of return on equity, the higher the actual rate of return the higher the expected rate of return on equity, and hence, the higher their demand for equity (i.e. the chartists dominate price formation). The equity-to-deposits ratio cannot increase continuously since there is imperfect asset substitution (households always wish to keep some deposits in their portfolio) and since households take into account the 'fundamentals'. As a result, the increase in the equity-to-deposits ratio becomes small as the expected rate of return in equity is too high. Hence, the demand for equities and the return on equity gradually start declining. This asset price deflation process does not continue forever again because of the reference to the 'fundamentals' and imperfect asset substitution. The new cycle begins when the expected rate of return starts increasing and becomes sufficiently high so as to induce a new rise in the equity-to-deposits ratio. These dynamics of the model resemble the dynamics of Taylor and O'Connell (1985) in the case where there is high asset substitution and as a result the system becomes unstable.

Chiarella and Di Guilmi (2011) propose a heterogeneous agents model that builds on and extends Taylor and O'Connell (1985) in several ways. On the financial side, they allow investors to hold equity, debt and money as financial assets. They distinguish between two groups of firms, those with debt (called speculative firms) and those without debt (referred to as hedge firms). Firms invest depending on their equity price, which, in turn, depends on the expectations of future returns (demand or debt obligations have no impact on investment). These returns are determined by the composition of financial market actors. Chiarella and Di Guilmi (2011) distinguish between chartists and fundamentalists, whose relative shares are determined stochastically. Their use of the terms chartists and fundamentalists differs somewhat from the literature. Chartists value speculative firms highly (but do not base evaluation on past experience) and fundamentalists value debt-free firms highly (but this valuation is not based on a fundamental value as conventionally defined). A high share of chartists drives up the prices of speculative firm equity; a high share of fundamentalists drives up the price of hedge firm equity. Equity prices, which drive investment, are the result of idiosyncratic shocks and the share of chartists. Firms produce with fixed coefficient production function (and infinitely elastic labor) and sell their output with a fixed markup. If profits fall below debt obligations, the firm goes bankrupt. New firms enter as a positive function of output growth. The model is discussed analytically using the mean–field approach and is simulated numerically. Chiarella and Di Guilmi (2011) report that the model matches firm stylized facts in terms of firm distributions and it exhibits cycles in output, equity prices, debt and bankruptcies.

To sum up, in the equity price Minsky models, the portfolio decision of households is introduced in order to analyse the destabilizing role of the equity market. This portfolio decision does not exist in most debt or interest dynamics models. Households allocate their wealth between different assets, for example, between equity and deposits (Franke and Semmler, 1989; Ryoo, 2010, 2013a), between equity and money (Delli Gatti and Gallegati, 1990) or between equity, money and government bonds (Taylor and O'Connell, 1985), taking into account the relative rate of return of each asset. Instability and cycles typically emerge when households invest more in the equity market and as a result the rate of return on equity improves, inducing a further rise in the demand for equities. Ryoo (2010, 2013a) and Chiarella and Di Guilmi (2011) introduce speculative dynamics by (explicitly or implicitly) distinguishing between fundamentalists and noise traders. This has feedback effects on economic activity since the resulting higher equity prices affect positively investment (via Tobin's q or expectations) or consumption (via the wealth effect). There are some equity price Minsky models that have equity as residual source of finance (e.g. Ryoo, 2010, 2013a) and others where debt act as a residual (e.g. Chiarella and Di Guilmi, 2011).

4.2 *Real Estate Price Minsky Models*

The real estate price Minsky models analyse housing debt, paying particular attention to the interaction between housing prices and collateral. The key real estate price Minsky model has been developed by Ryoo (2016).[15] Housing prices in this model play a similar role as the stock prices in the equity price Minsky models. Firms finance their investment expenditures by issuing equity and by using their internal funds. They do not take out corporate debt. There are two types of households: workers and rentiers. Workers take on mortgages and invest in the housing market, while rentier households invest in equities and deposits as in Ryoo (2013a). Banks provide mortgages to worker households taking into account their collateral.

Following Ryoo (2010, 2013a, 2013b), Ryoo (2016) makes again a distinction between Kaldorian short cycles and financial long waves. The long waves are captured by a 3D system in which the state variables are workers' housing wealth-to-capital ratio, the expected rate of return on houses and household debt-to-capital ratio. The housing wealth-to-capital ratio of workers (h^w) and the expected rate of return on houses (μ^e) change according to the following equations:

$$\dot{h}^w = \kappa(\eta(\mu^e - i)c^w - h^w) \tag{25}$$

$$\dot{\mu}^e = \psi(\mu - \mu^e) \tag{26}$$

where c^w is workers' household consumption-to-capital ratio, μ is the (actual) rate of return on housing and η is a positive non-linear function of the expected rate of return on housing (i.e. $\partial\eta/\partial\mu^e > 0$). Equation (25) shows that workers' desired housing wealth-to-consumption ratio, $\eta(\mu^e - i)$, is higher, the higher is the expected rate of return on housing, μ^e, compared to the interest rate on deposits (which is constant). The housing wealth-to-capital ratio increases when the desired housing wealth-to-capital ratio is higher than the actual wealth-to-capital ratio. Equation (26) shows that the expected rate of return on housing changes via an adaptive expectations mechanism. The third state variable of the 3D system, the debt-to-capital ratio, is positively affected by workers' household net income and their net worth.

In this system, instability is more likely when credit supply is highly responsive to the value of collateral, the sensitivity of housing supply to prices is low and the demand for houses is highly sensitive to expected capital gains. The cycles produced are similar to the cycles in the equity price Minsky models. Note that even with a constant debt-to-capital ratio, it is possible to get cycles in the h^w and μ^e space. In this case, the cycles can be described as follows. An increase in the expected housing price inflation produces a higher demand for houses. This gives a boost to housing prices and increases the actual rate of return on houses. Similarly to the equity price Minsky models, worker households have adaptive expectations about the expected rate of return on houses. As a result, the higher the actual rate of return on houses, the higher the respective expected rate of return. This brings about a boost to the demand for houses. At some point, workers' housing wealth-to-capital ratio stops increasing since households do not want to have a housing wealth-to-consumption rate above a specific upper limit. At this point, workers' desired housing wealth-to-capital ratio and the expected rate of return on houses start decreasing. This does not continue forever since households always want to invest a proportion of their net wealth in houses. When h^w and μ^e become sufficiently low, a new cycle begins where the expected rate of return on houses and workers' housing wealth-to-capital ratio start increasing again.

In the case in which the debt-to-capital ratio changes in an endogenous way, the increase in housing prices gives a boost to the value of the collateral. The higher the value of the collateral, the higher the credit provision by banks. At some point, the debt payment commitments become sufficiently high, decreasing loan expansion and consequently the debt-to-capital ratio.

5. Mainstream Minsky Models

Recently, there have been several attempts to incorporate Minskyan ideas into mainstream economic frameworks. By mainstream, we mean models that insist on explicit microfoundations and, in the area of macroeconomics, use dynamic stochastic general equilibrium (DSGE) models as the key reference point. Bhattacharya *et al.* (2015) present a model of financial markets where investors can choose between a risky and a safe asset. The payout from these assets depends on whether the economy is in a good or a bad state. Investors and bankers update their forecasts based on past experience. In a bad state, investors may default on their loans, which results in some deadweight loss. Bankers extend loans and charge interest on it based on the expected default rates and costs. Bhattacharya *et al.* (2015) demonstrate that competitive market outcomes are suboptimal as investors do not take into account the externalities of their default, that is, the deadweight loss and the risk premium effects of their defaults, because they are price takers on credit markets. The paper has explicit reference to Minsky and its novelty is in the explicit modeling of defaults. It neither demonstrates the existence of endogenous cycles, nor is it concerned with the macroeconomic effects of financial dynamics.

Farmer (2013) incorporates some Minskyan features into a rational expectations model with search of unemployment. His model is a multiple equilibrium model, where a belief function (also referred to as 'animal spirits') allows rational actors to choose between a continuum of possible equilibria. The belief function effectively determines the labor supply of the model and changes in animal spirits are thus transmitted (in proper New Classical fashion) via labor supply shocks. The main strength of the model is that animal spirits shocks have permanent labor market effects. Debt and financial fragility do not play a role in Farmer's model, nor is investment a key variable.

Eggertsson and Krugman (2012) build a model with two types of agents, which differ by their rate of time preference. The impatient agents will thus borrow from the patient ones. The model imposes an upper limit to borrowing and the main part of the paper discusses how in the case of an exogenous shock to the borrowing limit, the model exhibits Keynesian features like large multipliers and debt deflation problems. In a large deleveraging shock, the AD curve can become upwards sloping and more flexible labor market will mean a larger output reduction. The paper demonstrates that in a deleveraging economy, the Keynesian features will be strong; it has a prominent role for debt, but it does not discuss endogenous cycles. The main actors are households, not businesses. Overall, these models are attempts to incorporate some of Minsky's arguments in an optimization framework, but they do not fulfil Minsky's ambition to analyse endogenous real-financial dynamics.

6. Conclusion

This paper has suggested a categorization of Minsky-inspired models. While Minsky had been an obscure economist for much of his life, since the mid-1980s there has been a growing literature on the formalization of his arguments. This paper has surveyed the existing Minsky models highlighting their key differences and similarities. Our categorization makes a broad distinction between the models that focus on the dynamics of debt or interest, with no or a secondary role for asset prices, and the models in which asset prices play a key role in the dynamic behavior of the economy. Within the debt or interest dynamics models, debt typically behaves pro-cyclically and exerts a negative effect on demand. We made a distinction between the Kalecki–Minsky models that assume a stable goods market, the Kaldor–Minsky models which postulate instability in the goods market and the Goodwin–Minsky models that incorporate debt dynamics into the traditional Goodwin interactions between the wage share and employment rate. We also analysed the credit rationing Minsky models, in which credit provision depends on banks' financial position, and the endogenous target debt ratio Minsky models, which are driven by the stock-flow norms of the private sector that change endogenously during the economic cycle. The Minsky–Veblen models combine consumer debt with the Veblenian ideas of emulation motives. Unlike the previous models, this last group is about household debt rather than corporate debt. Within the asset price models, we distinguished between (i) the equity price Minsky models that analyse the cycles and the instability that arise from the dynamics of equity prices and (ii) the real estate price Minsky models that study the dynamic interaction between mortgages and housing prices.

Our survey has focused on theoretical models, but it is the case that the Minsky literature so far has concentrated on theoretical modeling and there is only a handful of rigorous empirical papers (e.g. Schroeder, 2009; Mulligan, 2013; Nishi, 2016; Davis *et al.*, 2017) which often focus on specific mechanisms (such as the pro-cyclical debt ratio) rather than testing the models discussed in this survey. There are four sets of questions that follow from this survey: What are the main points of differences between the Minsky models? Are they complementary or competing? What has been missing in the literature and what are its limitations? What are the implications for future research?

Different authors develop Minsky's arguments in a variety of different ways, both in terms of the key mechanisms involved and in terms of what is to be explained. In particular, some authors are eager to demonstrate that local instability can emerge without paying attention to the global properties of the models, while others want to demonstrate the emergence of endogenous cycles. Both the debt or interest dynamics models and the asset price dynamics models analyse the interaction between the real sector and the financial sector, but one important difference is that the asset price dynamics models can generate pure financial cycles. Moreover, the models covered differ in their investment functions, in the source of residual finance, in the key financial variables that matter and in the sector that is vulnerable to financial fragility. As regards the investment function, the distinction between Kaleckian and Kaldorian models refers to whether investment is overshooting with respect to demand; many of the models discussed have interest payments (or retained earnings) impacting on investment, whereas in the endogenous target debt ratio, models investment is affected by the target ratios which capture perceived uncertainty; in asset price dynamics models, equity prices have a direct impact on investment. Models also differ on whether debt or equity issue is regarded as the main source of residual finance. Debt dynamics models lend themselves more to credit as the residual source of finance while asset price dynamics may lend themselves to equity as residual source of finance; however, there is no one-to-one pairing. As regards the household debt models, the Minsky–Veblen models and the real estate price models differ on whether consumption emulation or wealth effects are the main drivers of debt accumulation.

What are the limitations of the Minskyan models analysed in this review? A first limitation is that there is no common framework of analysis. Some authors assume away asset prices, and others pay scant attention to debt. We do note that the debt or interest dynamics literature has so far not incorporated asset prices explicitly, whereas several of the asset price dynamics models do explicitly model debt. An increasing number of authors does use SFC models and thus are explicit on the links between financial stocks and flows. As of now there are few heterogeneous agents models and those that exist have only weakly developed demand sides. However, for the most part, the different arguments are not necessarily mutually exclusive. While the Kaleckian and the Kaldorian investment functions are mutually exclusive, debt cycles and asset prices cycles are not exclusive, nor are endogenous debt norms and asset price speculation. However, attempts to synthesize the arguments will soon hit the limits of tractability. Thus, to make progress and keep models manageable, it will be important to identify which mechanisms matter most in practice or clarify the conditions under which certain models are applicable.

A second limitation is that the link between the empirical literature and the theoretical models is loose. The vast majority of the authors make no attempt to estimate econometrically the key equations of their models or to calibrate the models in order to produce the patterns observed in the real data. Also, among the models discussed, only Ryoo (2010, 2013a, 2013b, 2016) asks how real cycles and Minsky cycles interact (Ryoo regards the financial cycles as long waves, but argues that business cycles are due to real factors).

Overall, Minskyans have made substantial progress in developing and formalizing Minsky's rich ideas. Future research should make a concerted effort to confront Minsky models with empirical data—both in the sense of testing the different mechanisms and evaluating their relative importance, but also in terms of calibrating the models and clarifying what the periodicity and the amplitude of the cycles is.

Acknowledgements

We thank two anonymous referees for their constructive comments and suggestions. The paper has also benefited from comments by Sébastian Charles, Yannis Dafermos, Giorgos Gouzoulis, Rob Jump, Ewa Karwowski, Yun Kim, Karsten Köhler, Hiroshi Nishi, Soon Ryoo and Bazil Sansom. An earlier version of the paper was presented at Kingston University and has benefited from discussion there. All mistakes are the authors'.

Notes

1. https://ftalphaville.ft.com/2007/08/20/6687/economist-idol-minskys-new-found-fame/
2. Foley (2003) was the first one who incorporated the hedge, speculative and Ponzi finance regime classification into an open economy macro model. This classification has also been incorporated into agent-based models (see, e.g. Delli Gatti *et al.*, 2003; Chiarella and Di Guilmi, 2011).
3. The choice of labels for our families is somewhat arbitrary. In particular, Kaldor (1940, p. 78) notes that his model is very similar to an earlier paper by Kalecki (1937). We think that our labels are reasonably accurate as most Kaleckian models assume or imply stable goods markets (see, e.g. Lavoie, 2014).
4. The distinction between hedge and speculative units relies on the comparison between the gross profits and the sum of investment expenditures and interest payments. When the former is higher than the latter, we have a hedge regime while, when the opposite holds, we have a speculative regime. In the extreme case where the gross profits are lower than the interest payments, we have a Ponzi regime.
5. There are some additional minor differences. In Lima and Meirelles' setup, the desired investment rate of firms depends on the interest rate and not on the interest payments on debt, a separate sensitivity to gross profits and interest rate is assumed, rentiers' propensities to save out of interest and dividends are different and investment is debt-led (although in the dynamic analysis, the investment rate is allowed to be debt-neutral by equalizing the propensities to save out of interest and dividends).

6. Nishi's (2012) distinction between hedge and speculative regimes relies on the comparison of gross profits with net borrowing and interest payments. This allows hedge units to borrow, which is not the case in Lima and Meirelles (2007) where hedge units do not borrow. The Ponzi regime is defined as in Lima and Meirelles (2007).

7. Lavoie (2014, p. 448) argues that when debt-led demand is combined with a counter-cyclical debt ratio, which he refers to as a 'Steindl regime', cycles can arise that work in the opposite direction of Minsky cycles.

8. The Keynesian mechanism of equilibrating investment and saving is blocked because Say's law is assumed to hold; the classical mechanism is blocked because the interest rate does not clear the market for loanable funds but is determined by the leverage ratio.

9. Such an analytical solution is provided by Grasselli and Costa Lima (2012).

10. The impact of banks' financial position on credit rationing is taken into account in the recent model of Kapeller *et al.* (2016). However, their model analyses household debt, while our credit rationing Minsky models refer exclusively to corporate debt.

11. Ryoo (2010) supports this assumption by presenting some evidence that the ratio of issues of equity to investment is very volatile and argues that this volatility is better captured when equity emission is modeled as a buffer.

12. The formulation of credit rationing draws on the SFC model of Le Heron and Mouakil (2008) who, in line with Minsky, assume that credit rationing depends both on borrower's and lender's risk.

13. Charpe *et al.* (2009) develop a Minskyan model with a Goodwin-type labor market in which workers take on debt in order to increase their consumption expenditures. The model is similar to the Minsky–Veblen models in that consumption expenditures are driving the financial dynamics and household debt is key. However, loans are solely determined by the fact that workers have an exogenous marginal propensity to consume which is larger than one and there is no explicit mechanism through which they emulate the consumption norms of richer households.

14. There are many SFC models that were developed in the 2000s and analysed the interactions between asset prices, the leverage of firms and the real economy (e.g. Lavoie and Godley, 2001-2; van Treeck, 2009). However, most of these models do not examine explicitly Minskyan dynamics.

15. Zezza (2008) develops an SFC model with housing prices. However, he does not take explicitly into account Minskyan dynamics.

References

Asada, T. (2001) Nonlinear dynamics of debt and capital: a post-Keynesian analysis. In Y. Aruka (ed.), *Evolutionary Controversies in Economics* (pp. 73–87). Tokyo: Springer-Verlag.

Beja, A. and Goldman, M.B. (1980) On the dynamic behavior of prices in disequilibrium. *The Journal of Finance* 35(2): 235–248.

Bernanke, B. and Gertler, M. (1990) Financial fragility and economic performance. *The Quarterly Journal of Economics* 105(1): 87–114.

Bhattacharya, S., Goodhart, C.A.E., Tsomocos, D.P. and Vardoulakis, A.P. (2015) A reconsideration of Minsky's financial instability hypothesis. *Journal of Money, Credit and Banking* 47(5): 931–973.

Charles, S. (2008) Teaching Minsky's financial instability hypothesis: a manageable suggestion. *Journal of Post Keynesian Economics* 31(1): 125–138.

Charles, S. (2016) Is Minsky's financial instability hypothesis valid? *Cambridge Journal of Economics* 40(2): 427–436.

Charpe, M., Flaschel, P., Proaño, C. and Semmler, W. (2009) Overconsumption, credit rationing and bailout monetary policy: a Minskyan perspective. *European Journal of Economics and Economic Policies: Intervention* 6(2): 247–270.

Chiarella, C. and Di Guilmi, C. (2011) The financial instability hypothesis: a stochastic microfoundation framework. *Journal of Economic Dynamics and Control* 35(8): 1151–1171.

Chiarella, C., Flaschel, P., Groh, G. and Semmler, W. (2000) *Disequilibrium, Growth and Labor Market Dynamics: Macro Perspectives*. Berlin and Heidelberg: Springer-Verlag.

Dafermos, Y. (2017) Debt cycles, instability and fiscal rules: a Godley-Minsky synthesis. *Cambridge Journal of Economics*, forthcoming.

Davis, L.E., de Souza J.P.A. and Hernandez, G. (2017) An empirical analysis of Minsky regimes in the US economy. Working Paper 2017–08, UMass Amherst.

Delli Gatti, D. and Gallegati, M. (1990) Financial instability, income distribution, and the stock market. *Journal of Post Keynesian Economics* 12(3): 356–374.

Delli Gatti, D., Di Guilmi, C., Gaffeo, E., Giulioni, G., Gallegati, M. and Palestrini, A. (2005) A new approach to business fluctuations: heterogeneous interacting agents, scaling laws and financial fragility. *Journal of Economic Behavior and Organization* 56(4): 489–512.

Delli Gatti, D., Gallegati, M. and Gardini, L. (1994) Complex dynamics in a simple macroeconomic model with financing constraints. In G. Dymski and R. Pollin (eds.), *New Perspectives in Monetary Macroeconomics* (pp. 51–76). Ann Arbor, US: University of Michigan Press.

Delli Gatti, D., Gallegati, M., Giulioni, G. and Palestrini, A. (2003) Financial fragility, patterns of firms' entry and exit and aggregate dynamics. *Journal of Economic Behavior and Organization* 51(1): 79–97.

Delli Gatti, D., Gallegati, M., Greenwald, B., Russo, A. and Stiglitz, J.E. (2010) The financial accelerator in an evolving credit network. *Journal of Economic Dynamics and Control* 34(9): 1627–1650.

Dutt, A.K. (1995) Internal finance and monopoly power in capitalist economies: a reformulation of Steindl's growth model. *Metroeconomica* 46(1): 16–34.

Eggertsson, G. and Krugman, P. (2012) Debt deleveraging, and the liquidity trap: a Fisher-Minsky-Koo approach. *The Quarterly Journal of Economics* 127(3): 1469–1513.

Farmer, R.E.A. (2013) Animal spirits, financial crises and persistent unemployment. *Economic Journal* 123(568): 317–340.

Fazzari, S., Ferri, P. and Greenberg, E. (2008) Cash flow, investment, and Keynes-Minsky cycles. *Journal of Economic Behavior and Organization* 65(3–4): 555–572.

Foley, D.K. (1987) Liquidity-profit rate cycles in a capitalist economy. *Journal of Economic Behavior and Organization* 8(3): 363–376.

Foley, D.K. (2003) Financial fragility in developing economies. In A.K. Dutt and J. Ros (eds.), *Development Economics and Structuralist Macroeconomics: Essays in Honor of Lance Taylor* (pp. 157–168). Cheltenham, UK and Northampton, US: Edward Elgar.

Franke, R. and Semmler, W. (1989) Debt financing of firms, stability, and cycles in a dynamical macroeconomic growth cycle. In W. Semmler (ed.), *Financial Dynamics and Business Cycles: New Perspectives* (pp. 38–64). New York and London: M.E Sharpe.

Godley, W. (1999) Seven unsustainable processes: medium-term prospects and policies for the United States and the world. Special Report, Levy Economics Institute of Bard College.

Goodwin, R.M. (1951) The non linear accelerator and the persistence of business cycles. *Econometrica* 19(1): 1–17.

Goodwin, R.M. (1967) A growth cycle. In C.H. Feinstein (ed.), *Socialism, Capitalism and Economic Growth: Essays Presented to Maurice Dobb* (pp. 54–58). Cambridge, UK: Cambridge University Press.

Grasselli, M.R. and Costa Lima, B. (2012) An analysis of the Keen model for credit expansion, asset price bubbles and financial fragility. *Mathematical Financial Economics* 6(3): 191–210.

Greenwald, B.C. and Stiglitz, J.E. (1993) Financial market imperfections and business cycles. *The Quarterly Journal of Economics* 108(1): 77–114.

IMF. (2012) *World Economic Outlook April 2012: Growth Resuming, Dangers Remain*. Washington, DC: IMF.

Jarsulic, M. (1989) Endogenous credit and endogenous business cycles. *Journal of Post Keynesian Economics* 12(1): 35–48.

Jarsulic, M. (1990) Debt and macro stability. *Eastern Economic Journal* 16(2): 91–100.

Jump, R.C., Michell, J. and Stockhammer, E. (2017) A strategy switching approach to Minskyan business cycles. Manuscript.

Kaldor, N. (1940) A model of the trade cycle. *Economic Journal* 50(197): 78–92.

Kalecki, M. (1937) The principle of increasing risk. *Economica* 4(16): 440–447.

Kapeller, J. and Schütz, B. (2014) Debt, boom, bust: a theory of Minsky–Veblen cycles. *Journal of Post Keynesian Economics* 36(4): 781–814.

Kapeller, J., Landesmann, M., Mohr, F.X. and Schütz, B. (2016) Government policies and financial crises: mitigation, postponement or prevention? The Vienna Institute for International Economic Studies Working Paper 126.

Keen, S. (1995) Finance and economic breakdown modelling Minsky's 'financial instability hypothesis'. *Journal of Post Keynesian Economics* 17(4): 607–635.

Keen, S. (2013) A monetary Minsky model of the Great Moderation and the Great Recession. *Journal of Economic Behavior and Organization* 86: 221–235.

Lavoie, M. (1995) Interest rates in post-Keynesian models of growth and distribution. *Metroeconomica* 46(2): 146–177.

Lavoie, M. (2014) *Post-Keynesian Economics: New Foundations*. Cheltenham, UK and Northampton, US: Edward Elgar.

Lavoie, M. and Godley, W. (2001–2) Kaleckian models of growth in a coherent stock-flow monetary framework: a Kaldorian view. *Journal of Post Keynesian Economics* 24(2): 277–311.

Lavoie, M. and Seccareccia, M. (2001) Minsky's financial fragility hypothesis: a missing macroeconomic link? In P. Ferri and R. Bellofiore (eds.), *Financial Fragility and Investment in the Capitalist Economy: The Economic Legacy of Hyman Minsky* Vol. 2 (pp. 76–96). Cheltenham, UK and Northampton, US: Edward Elgar.

Le Heron, E. and Mouakil, T. (2008) A post-Keynesian stock-flow consistent model for dynamic analysis of monetary policy shock on banking behaviour. *Metroeconomica* 59(3): 405–440.

Lima, G.T. and Meirelles, A.J.A. (2007) Macrodynamics of debt regimes, financial instability and growth. *Cambridge Journal of Economics* 31(4): 563–580.

Minsky, H.P. (1975) *John Maynard Keynes*. New York: Columbia University Press.

Minsky, H.P. (1982) *Inflation, Recession and Economic Policy*. New York: M.E. Sharpe.

Minsky, H.P. (2008) [1986] *Stabilizing an Unstable Economy*. New York: McGraw-Hill.

Mulligan, R. (2013) A sectoral analysis of the financial instability hypothesis. *The Quarterly Review of Economics and Finance* 53(4): 450–459.

Nikolaidi, M. (2014) Margins of safety and instability in a macrodynamic model with Minskyan insights. *Structural Change and Economic Dynamics* 31: 1–16.

Nishi, H. (2012) A dynamic analysis of debt-led and debt-burdened growth regimes with Minskian financial structure. *Metroeconomica* 63(4): 634–660.

Nishi, H. (2016) An empirical contribution to Minsky's financial fragility: evidence from non-financial sectors in Japan. Kyoto University, Graduate School of Economics Discussion Paper Series E-16-007.

Palley, T.I. (1994) Debt, aggregate demand, and the business cycle: an analysis in the spirit of Kaldor and Minsky. *Journal of Post Keynesian Economics* 16(3): 371–390.

Palley, T.I. (1997) Endogenous money and the business cycle. *Journal of Economics* 65(2): 133–149.

Ryoo, S. (2010) Long waves and short cycles in a model of endogenous financial fragility. *Journal of Economic Behavior and Organization* 74(3): 163–186.

Ryoo, S. (2013a) Minsky cycles in Keynesian models of growth and distribution. *Review of Keynesian Economics* 1(1): 37–60.

Ryoo, S. (2013b) Bank profitability, leverage and financial instability: a Minsky-Harrod model. *Cambridge Journal of Economics* 37(5): 1127–1160.

Ryoo, S. (2016) Household debt and housing bubble: a Minskian approach to boom-bust cycles. *Journal of Evolutionary Economics* 26(5): 971–1006.

Ryoo, S. and Kim, Y.K. (2014) Income distribution, consumer debt and keeping up with the Joneses. *Metroeconomica* 65(4): 585–618.

Sasaki, H. and Fujita, S. (2012) The importance of the retention ratio in a Kaleckian model with debt accumulation. *Metroeconomica* 63(3): 417–428.

Schroeder, S. (2009) Defining and detecting financial fragility: New Zealand's experience. *International Journal of Social Economics* 36(3): 287–307.

Semmler, W. (1987) A macroeconomic limit cycle with financial perturbations. *Journal of Economic Behavior and Organisation* 8(3): 469–495.

Skott, P. (1989) *Conflict and Effective Demand in Economic Growth*. Cambridge: Cambridge University Press.

Skott, P. (1994) On the modeling of systemic financial fragility. In A.K. Dutt (ed.), *New Directions in Analytical Political Economy* (pp. 49–76). Aldershot, UK and Brookfield, US: Edward Elgar.

Sordi, S. and Vercelli, A. (2014) Unemployment, income distribution and debt-financed investment in a growth cycle model. *Journal of Economic Dynamics and Control* 48: 325–348.

Stockhammer, E. and Michell, J. (2017) Pseudo-Goodwin cycles in a Minsky Model. *Cambridge Journal of Economics* 41(1): 105–125.

Taylor, L. and O'Connell, S.A. (1985) A Minsky crisis. *Quarterly Journal of Economics* 100(Supplement): 871–885.

Van Treeck, T. (2009) A synthetic, stock-flow consistent macroeconomic model of 'financialization'. *Cambridge Journal of Economics* 33(3): 467–493.

Veblen, T. (1970) [1899] *The Theory of the Leisure Class*. London: Allen and Unwin.

White, W. (2009) Modern macroeconomics is on the wrong track. *Finance and Development* 46(4): 15–18.

Zezza, G. (2008) U.S. growth, the housing market, and the distribution of income. *Journal of Post Keynesian Economics* 30(3): 375–401.

8

FINANCIALIZATION AND INVESTMENT: A SURVEY OF THE EMPIRICAL LITERATURE

Leila E. Davis

Middlebury College
Economics

1. Introduction

The 2008 financial crisis, beginning in the USA and spreading globally, drew the financial systems of advanced economies to the forefront of public awareness, and led to a surge of research on the size and role of the financial sectors of advanced economies. Importantly, however, this surge of attention comes on the coattails of a secular expansion in finance – across countries and by a range of measures – since the 1970s. In the USA, for which the most detailed data are available, financial sector growth is evident as a share of GDP, employment, total profits or outstanding financial assets (Krippner, 2005; Greenwood and Scharfstein, 2013; Montecino *et al.*, 2016). Similar trends occurred outside the USA as well: Philippon and Reshef (2013) document growth in the income share of finance across a set of developed economies (the UK, the Netherlands, the USA, Japan and Canada), and Jordà *et al.* (2016) measure an international expansion in private credit relative to income in the second half of the twentieth century.

This growth in the size and scope of modern finance is increasingly summarized as financialization. Broadly, financialization is perhaps most commonly defined as the 'increasing role of financial motives, financial markets, financial actors and financial institutions in the operation of domestic and international economies' (Epstein, 2005, p. 3).[1] Importantly, this expansion of finance is reflected not only in the size and scope of the financial sector, but also in the behaviour of nonfinancial actors and in nonfinancial outcomes (see Krippner (2005) for an early elaboration of this point). Thus, while precise definitions vary across analyses, the shared premise underlying accounts of financialization is that this expansion of finance is a critical feature of the post-1980 USA economy, with substantive implications for foundational economic relationships (Palley, 2007; Sawyer, 2013; Fine and Saad-Filho, 2014; Epstein, 2015).

A substantial branch of the literature on financialization analyses, in particular, the relationship between financialization and fixed investment. Striking shifts in the balance sheet structure

Analytical Political Economy, First Edition. Edited by Roberto Veneziani and Luca Zamparelli.

of nonfinancial corporations (NFCs) point to the financialization of traditionally nonfinancial firms, and suggest links between various aspects of financialization and investment. These trends are most fully documented for the USA (see Davis, 2016), where a shift in portfolio composition towards financial assets (Crotty, 2005) is, for instance, often used to suggest that financial investments increasingly replace – or 'crowd out' – fixed investment. Concurrently, firm balance sheets reflect changes in the structure of external finance, including growth in both indebtedness and own-stock repurchases, particularly among large firms (Davis, 2016). There is, correspondingly, an expansion in financial profits earned by nonfinancial firms (Krippner, 2005), and also in payments by NFCs to financial markets (Orhangazi, 2008a).

An increasingly complex relationship between NFCs and the financial sector is, also, evident in that some large NFCs, arguably, increasingly resemble financial firms (Froud *et al.*, 2006), and also in a growing 'portfolio conception' of the firm, wherein NFCs are viewed as bundles of assets rather than capital-accumulating enterprises (Crotty, 2005). These changes in firm behaviour have come with a slowdown in capital accumulation, despite rising profitability, pointing to an 'investment-profit puzzle' in which a declining share of profits is reinvested in physical capital (Stockhammer, 2005; van Treeck, 2008, 2009a; Gutiérrez and Philippon, 2016). As is discussed below, this puzzle may reflect, for instance, growing shareholder orientation, wherein NFCs increasingly focus on financial indicators of performance over firm growth and fixed investment (Stockhammer, 2004; Davis, 2017).

Building on these stylized facts, a growing literature finds that features of financialization are systematically related to investment. However, there remains lack of consensus on the primary channels through which this relationship occurs, and even on the direction of the relationship. An influential first wave of empirical research suggests a decisively negative effect of financialization on investment (Stockhammer, 2004; Demir, 2007, 2009a,b; Orhangazi, 2008a,b; van Treeck, 2008); this relationship is, similarly, reflected in a body of theoretical literature (Stockhammer, 2004, 2005; van Treeck, 2008, 2009a; Dallery, 2009). Conversely, however, Boyer (2000) considers conditions for 'finance-led' growth, and Aglietta and Breton (2001) emphasize the role of asset price inflations in capital accumulation. Skott and Ryoo (2008), furthermore, highlight sensitivity to the theoretical specification of the investment function (Harrodian or Kaleckian). Davis (2017) points to varied relationships between different features of financialization and firm investment rates in the USA, including a positive correlation between financial assets and investment, but a negative effect of shareholder orientation. Kliman and Williams (2014) contend, in contrast, that falling accumulation rates in the USA are wholly unrelated to financialization.

This paper surveys this literature on financialization and investment to take stock of where we are and what remains to be done. To understand the range of conclusions reached in this literature it is, first, important to recognize that the definition of financialization remains nebulous and often varies substantially across papers. This variance in definition has both advantages and disadvantages. On the one hand, financialization summarizes a broad, wide-reaching process of structural change, and there is no a priori reason to expect all aspects of this phenomenon affect investment analogously. A range of empirical indicators, thus, has the advantage of capturing different aspects of financialization. On the other hand, the term 'financialization' is often applied differentially across analyses despite an often-implicit pretense that the same phenomenon is analysed. As such, it is increasingly unclear what is meant when one concludes that 'financialization' does or does not depress investment.[2] More specifically, within countries different empirical measures are used to draw different conclusions about financialization and investment, without clear reference to distinctions between the indicators used. Across countries, conclusions from one country – for example, regarding shareholder ideology in the USA – are sometimes also applied to other countries despite vastly different institutional settings. One contribution of this survey is, thus, a delineation of distinctions between studies that claim to otherwise study the same thing: 'financialization' and investment.

To understand the conclusions reached in this literature it is instructive to divide the literature into two parts. The first emphasizes financial flow-based indicators of financialization and changes in the relative stocks of fixed and financial assets, debt and equity on firm balance sheets. In the USA, for example, Orhangazi (2008a) finds that both increased financial payments *made by* NFCs and increased financial profits *earned by* NFCs are negatively associated with fixed investment, particularly among large firms. This analysis captures systematic negative relationships between fixed investment and growing income flows between NFCs and the financial sector. Notably, these results have been widely interpreted to imply that financial asset acquisitions 'crowd out' physical investment. In presenting this part of the literature, I emphasize, in particular, this possibility of crowding out. Importantly, more recent analyses do not find conclusive evidence of crowding out (Kliman and Williams, 2014; Davis, 2017) and, more generally, the literature emphasizing financial flows is characterized by variability in conclusions. This variability reflects, in part, differences in sample definitions and/or scope of analysis, but also points to a more general limitation of this branch of the literature.

In particular, while these financial flow-based indicators of financialization capture important changes in where profits accrue in the post-1980 USA economy they also raise further questions. These flows stem from firm decisions to acquire financial assets, or to borrow, repurchase stock or pay dividends. Thus, this expansion of financial flows, as well as changes in the structure of firm balance sheets from which these flows derive, raises the question of what has changed in NFC decision making – for example, in managerial objectives – such that a break in firm behaviour occurs specifically in the post-1980 period. Put differently, why has firm financial behaviour changed after 1980 such that investment rates have slowed? These determinants have important implications for understanding the relationship between financialization and investment. For example, the implication of higher leverage (with, correspondingly, higher interest payments) for fixed investment differs if firms borrow to exploit profitable fixed investment opportunities, to repurchase shares or to fund banking divisions (Davis, 2017). As the literature on financialization and investment expands, significant scope remains for identifying specific behavioural mechanisms underlying the stylized facts that summarize financialization, and for delineating differences in these behavioural stories across countries.

The second branch of the literature analyses shareholder orientation, which is the most fully developed behavioural explanation linking financialization to investment to date. Since the 1980s, the 'maximization of shareholder value' has become an increasingly dominant corporate governance ideology, particularly among USA firms (Lazonick and O'Sullivan, 2000; Fligstein, 1990; Davis, 2009). Shareholder ideology is, in particular, linked to changes in corporate strategy from one aiming to 'retain and reinvest' to one aiming to 'downsize and distribute' (Lazonick and O'Sullivan, 2000). Arising from agency theory, shareholder value ideology contends that closer alignment of managerial interests with those of shareholders – for instance, via stock-based managerial compensation – improves corporate performance (Jensen, 1986; Jensen and Murphy, 1990). The literature on financialization and investment, however, establishes evidence that shareholder orientation has adverse implications for firm investment, emphasizing both increased managerial attention to financial performance indicators like earnings per share (Stockhammer, 2004; Davis, 2017) and corporate myopia (Stout, 2012).

This paper, accordingly, surveys the literature on financialization and investment by introducing these two branches of the literature. The paper is organized as follows: Section 2 introduces definitions of financialization in the literature on financialization and investment. Sections 3 and 4 introduce the two main strands of the literature: increased flows between NFCs and finance, and shareholder orientation. Section 3, also, suggests limitations of analysing financialization and investment exclusively on the basis of financial flows and points to the importance of a behavioural understanding of financialization and investment. Section 5 concludes and suggests avenues for future research. Finally, a point about scope. The empirical literature on financialization and investment has, to date, focused disproportionately on the USA, reflecting in part the size and international dominance of USA finance and also that key mechanisms, like those related to shareholder orientation, are closely linked to country-specific institutions defining the degree of shareholder power. This survey follows this emphasis in the existing literature, but also introduces the literature exploring the relationship between financialization and investment in developing countries, which has focused largely on financial flows (Section 3).

2. Defining Financialization

All analyses of financialization that emphasize NFCs and investment underscore either an increasingly complex relationship between NFCs and financial markets, or stronger NFC orientation to financial performance targets. Orhangazi (2008a), for example, uses the concept quite broadly to 'designate the changes that have taken place in the relationship between the nonfinancial corporate sector and financial markets' (p. 3). Somewhat more narrowly, Lazonick (2013) emphasizes the financialization of corporate resource allocation, wherein companies are increasingly evaluated by measures like earnings per share, rather than by the goods and services produced.

However, specific definitions, and their empirical operationalizations, differ substantially. This variance in definitions – and also, more generally, the fact that financialization is an ambiguously defined term – has been widely noted (for example, Stockhammer, 2004, p. 721; Orhangazi, 2008a, p. 863; Skott and Ryoo, 2008, p. 827; Fine, 2013; Fiebiger, 2016). Nonetheless, there is little attention on the extent to which these conceptualizations of financialization do/do not overlap, or the degree to which different definitions explain different results in the literature. Accordingly, an important starting point for surveying the literature on financialization and investment is recognition and discussion of the definitions of financialization across the existing literature.

To highlight the main approaches to financialization in the literature on investment, Table 1 summarizes empirical definitions of financialization across this literature, focusing on empirical papers that analyse the financialization of the nonfinancial corporate sector and/or investment. In addition to econometric analyses of investment, Table 1 includes papers that do not explicitly investigate investment behaviour, but establish empirical evidence of financialization linked to the nonfinancial corporate sector (for example, Krippner (2005), which measures the financial incomes of nonfinancial firms). The summary in Table 1 calls attention to a heterogeneous set of changes in firm financial behaviour, including increased shareholder payouts and/or dividend payments, the rate of return gap between fixed and financial assets, and financially derived incomes. This range of definitions captures, on the one hand, that – as financialization reflects a broad process of structural change – it is inherently multi-dimensional. Different analyses *should*, therefore, emphasize different features of this broad process and,

Table 1. Empirical Definitions of Financialization (Analyses of Financialization of Nonfinancial Corporations and/or Investment)

	Empirical Indicator of Financialization	Location and Time Frame of Analysis	Level of Analysis
A. The asset side of the balance sheet & financial sources of income			
Stockhammer (2004)	Interest and dividend income of the nonfinancial business sector (rentiers' income), relative to sectoral value added.	Germany (1963–1990) France (1979–1997); UK (1971–1996); USA (1963–1997)	Aggregate
Krippner (2005, 2011)	Interest, dividends and realized capital gains on investments (portfolio income), relative to corporate cash flow.	USA (1950–2001)	Aggregate
Orhangazi (2008a)[a]	Financial profits (interest income and equity in net earnings), relative to the capital stock.	USA (1973–2003)	Firm
Demir (2009b)	Rate of return on fixed assets less the rate of return on financial assets (i.e. the gap between returns on fixed and financial assets)[b]	Argentina (1992:2–2001:2) Mexico (1990:2–2003:2) Turkey (1993:1–2003:2)	Firm
Kliman and Williams (2014)	Financial assets ('portfolio investment')[c]	USA (1947–2007)	Aggregate
Seo et al. (2016)	Financial assets	Korea (1990–2010)	Aggregate
Davis (2017)	Total financial assets (relative to total assets), and the financial profit rate (interest and dividend income, relative to financial assets).	USA (1971–2014)	Firm
B. The liability side of the balance sheet & financial payments			
Orhangazi (2008a)[a]	Financial payments (interest payments, dividend payments, and stock buybacks) relative to the capital stock.	USA (1973–2003)	Firm
van Treeck (2008)	Interest payments and dividend payments, both relative to the capital stock.	USA (1965–2004)	Aggregate
Onaran et al. (2011)	Net dividends, net interest and miscellaneous payments (rentiers' income), relative to GDP.	USA (1962:q2–2007:q4)	Aggregate

(Continued)

Table 1. Continued

	Empirical Indicator of Financialization	Location and Time Frame of Analysis	Level of Analysis
Kliman and Williams (2014)	Dividend payments[a]	USA (1947–2007)	Aggregate
De Souza and Epstein (2014)	Net lending of nonfinancial corporate sector (or reduction in net use of external finance)	USA (1947–2011); UK (1991–2010); France (1971–2011); Netherlands (1980–2011); Germany (1995–2011); Switzerland (1995–2011)	Aggregate
Seo *et al.* (2016)	Dividend payments	Korea (1990–2010)	Aggregate
C. Shareholder value orientation			
Stockhammer (2004)	Interest and dividend income of the nonfinancial business sector (rentiers' income), relative to sectoral value added.	Germany (1963–1990) France (1979–1997); UK (1971–1996); USA (1963–1997)	Aggregate
van Treeck (2008)	Dividend payments	USA (1965–2004)	Aggregate
Orhangazi (2008a)[a]	Financial profits (interest income, dividend income) and financial payments (interest payments, dividend payments and stock buybacks), each relative to the capital stock.	USA (1973–2003)	Firm
Mason (2015)	Corporate borrowing and shareholder payouts (dividend payments and stock repurchases)	USA (1971–2012)	Aggregate
Davis (2017)	Average yearly industry-level stock repurchases (relative to equity).	USA (1971–2014)	Firm

[a]Orhangazi (2008b) defines similar indicators on the basis of aggregate data.
[b]The empirical definition of financial profits varies by country. For Argentina, financial profits are measured as interest income; for Mexico, financial profits are defined by net foreign exchange losses (gains), financial income (loss, and income (loss) from other financial operations; for Turkey, financial profits are defined as interest income and other income from other operations (p. 323). See also Demir (2007).
[c]The text of Kliman and Williams (2014) also reiterates a range of other possible indicators of financialization. The main text, however, most often refers to financialization in the context of 'rising dividend payments and the growth of corporations' portfolio investment' (p. 67).

similarly, different features of financialization may affect investment behaviour differently. However, ambiguity in the definition of financialization also obfuscates distinctions underlying analyses of financialization and investment. In particular, varied empirical operationalizations of financialization imply that, as the literature on financialization and investment grows, it is increasingly unclear what is meant when one concludes that '*financialization*' does/does not depress physical investment.

In addition to this heterogeneity, however, Table 1 also identifies three main approaches to measuring 'financialization'. These approaches correspond to the main outline of this survey: the first two feature increased financial flows between NFCs and finance (Section 3), and the third emphasizes shareholder orientation (Section 4). In particular, one set of analyses emphasizes growth in the financial incomes of traditionally *non*-financial firms (Stockhammer, 2004; Krippner, 2005; Demir, 2007, 2009b; Orhangazi 2008a,b; Davis, 2017). Growth in holdings of financial assets (i.e. the stock of assets from which these financial profits derive) is, also, included in this category (see also Döğüs, 2016). A second set of papers highlights increased payments made to finance by nonfinancial businesses, including interest, dividends and/or stock repurchases (Orhangazi 2008a; van Treeck, 2008; Onaran *et al.*, 2011; de Souza and Epstein, 2014; Kliman and Williams, 2014). Finally, a third set of studies aims to operationalize shareholder value orientation (Stockhammer, 2004; van Treeck, 2008; Orhangazi, 2008a; Mason, 2015; Davis, 2017); in some cases, these papers, also, *equate* financialization with shareholder value ideology. Note that Table 1 lists papers fitting into more than one of these three categories multiple times: for instance, Orhangazi (2008a) emphasizes aspects of financialization linked both to financial incomes and payments to finance.

At least two additional points fall out of this categorization. First, even within each subset of the literature there are meaningful differences in measures of financialization. For example, higher financial payments have been captured empirically by payments to creditors and shareholders (Orhangazi, 2008a); by dividend payments to shareholders (van Treeck, 2008); and by all shareholder payouts, including both dividends and repurchases (Mason, 2015). In the post-1980 USA these measures are qualitatively different: shareholder orientation is associated with a growing prioritization of shareholder payouts, and own-stock repurchases are consistent with the increasing prioritization of capital gains over long-term dividend growth (see Section 4). Second, the delineation between empirical indicators employed and the *mechanisms* that are emphasized is sometimes unclear. For instance, Stockhammer (2004), Demir (2007, 2009b) and Orhangazi (2008a,b) exploit, at least in part, similar indicators (an increase in financial profits/rentiers' income). Across these papers, however, the interpretation of the relationship between this measure of financialization and investment differs in important ways: Demir suggests financial profits crowd out fixed investment; Stockhammer uses the indicator to explain changes in firm behaviour associated with shareholder value; and Orhangazi's interpretation incorporates elements of both.

In addition to the categories outlined in Table 1, two additional branches of the literature on financialization and NFCs can be identified. One emphasizes links between the international reorganization of production, global value chains and the financialization of USA firms (Milberg, 2008; Milberg and Winkler, 2010, 2013). Milberg (2008), for example, analyses an 'offshoring-financialization' linkage, wherein offshoring fails to generate dynamic gains in investment by USA firms because these firms increasingly purchase financial assets and repurchase stock, rather than (domestically) reinvesting higher profits. Fiebiger (2016), also, links financialization and 'de-nationalization' in production, pointing to a range of measurement issues arising in the context of expanded USA production abroad after the mid-1990s. Outside of these contributions, however, this branch of the literature remains relatively sparse, in part due to data limitations and, in particular, explicit links to investment remain to be drawn.

A final theme emphasizes volatility and uncertainty, most often in the context of financial liberalization in developing and/or emerging market economies (Demir, 2009a,c; Akkemik and Özen, 2014; Seo *et al.*, 2016). Building on evidence that financial liberalization both increases macroeconomic uncertainty and increases firms' opportunities to invest in financial assets, uncertainty and/or risk become key parameters mediating firms' portfolio allocation decisions between illiquid capital investments and liquid financial investments (Demir, 2009b). Rising firm-level volatility also characterizes the USA experience over this period (Comin and Philippon, 2005); linking volatility and growth in firm financial asset holdings in the post-1970 USA, Davis (2017) introduces firm volatility into the investment function and captures a negative link between volatility and investment. The role of uncertainty and risk in mediating the relationship between financialization and investment remains, however, relatively under-explored. Existing evidence raises further questions about how firms' portfolio decisions may be differentially impacted by idiosyncratic risk and macro-level uncertainty, as well as about differences in the responsiveness of portfolio allocation decisions to risk in developed and developing economies.

3. Firm Financial Behaviour and Investment

The first branch of the literature on financialization and investment analyses the consequences of secular shifts in the balance sheet structure of NFCs, and the financial flows derived from these balance sheet stocks, for fixed investment. This literature draws primarily on Keynesian and Minskian approaches, which emphasize the importance of financial factors in investment (Eichner and Kregel, 1975; Minsky, 1975; Skott, 1989; Crotty, 1990, 1992; Lavoie, 2014). The role of financial factors in investment is, however, also widely accepted outside of the post-Keynesian literature (see, for example, Fazzari *et al.*, 1988).

This section follows the first two panels of Table 1 to introduce the main results in this segment of the existing literature. In each case, I first introduce the trends in the asset and liability sides of firms' balance sheets, respectively, that motivate analyses of financialization and investment. This literature highlights systematic relationships between changes in firm financial behaviour and investment, but also raises questions for further analysis, not least because the existing empirical literature points to sometimes-contradictory conclusions. In some cases, different results undoubtedly stem at least in part from different sample definitions and empirical methods; instances of these differences are pointed to in the discussion below. In other cases, different conclusions reflect different empirical approaches to defining financialization. Finally, and most importantly from a conceptual perspective, these differences motivate a behavioural approach to financialization and investment in future research that, in particular, emphasizes *determinants* underlying changes in firm financial behaviour.

3.1 *Financial Profitability and Financial Asset Holdings*

3.1.1 *Post-1970 Trends in Portfolio Composition and Profitability*

A first striking feature of the post-1970 period in the USA economy is secular growth in the financial asset holdings of the nonfinancial corporate sector. This portfolio shift is highlighted in Figure 1, which plots financial assets and fixed capital, each relative to sales between 1950 and 2014, in the median across USA NFCs. While both series are largely stable through the

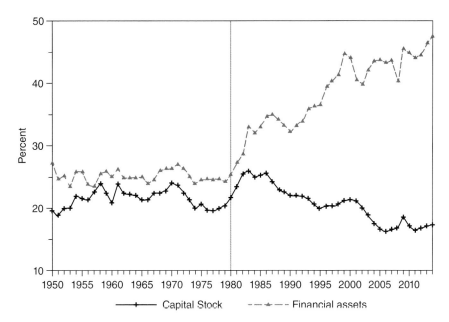

Figure 1. Fixed Capital and Financial Assets Relative to Sales (Yearly Median Across Nonfinancial Corporations).
Source: Compustat, author's calculations (reproduced from Davis, 2016).
Notes: The two series plot the across-firm yearly median of financial assets and fixed capital, each relative to firm-level sales between 1950 and 2014. Ratios are winsorized to account for outliers. Financial assets are defined as the sum of cash and short-term investments, current receivables, other current assets (less inventories) and 'other' investments and advances (Compustat items 1, 2, 68, 31, 32 and 69). The capital stock is defined as property, plant and equipment (Compustat item 141). Sales are drawn from Compustat item 12. The vertical line denotes 1980 to highlight the beginning of the period emphasized in the discussion.

1950s and 1960s, they diverge in the early 1980s; the ratio of financial assets to sales, in particular, climbs from approximately 25% in 1980 to 47.4% of sales in 2014. The firm-level decomposition in Davis (2016) indicates that this portfolio shift holds across firm size and industry, as well as when financial assets are normalized by other measures of firm size.

Together with this expansion in financial asset holdings comes growth in NFC incomes from financial sources. Krippner (2005, 2011) documents growth in portfolio income (interest, dividends and realized capital gains) relative to corporate cash flow earned by the nonfinancial corporate sector beginning in the 1970s and accelerating during the 1980s; this ratio signals a growing 'extent to which non-financial firms derive revenues from financial investments as opposed to productive activities' (2005, p. 182). Orhangazi (2008a,b), similarly, highlights growth in NFCs' financial incomes, documenting an increase in two specific sources of financial income – interest and dividend income – relative to internal funds after the early 1970s. Dumenil and Levy (2004a) document growth in French nonfinancial firms' holdings of other firms' stock, as well as corresponding growth in dividend income, thereby also accentuating 'strong increases in financial revenues in relation to revenues linked to the main activity of firms' (p. 118). Furthermore, while rentiers' income most commonly refers to economy-wide private-sector financial profits (clearly a broader concept than the financial profits of nonfinancial firms), growth in rentiers' income corroborates these trends, and also extends the evidence to a set of Organization of Economic Cooperation and Development (OECD) economies (Epstein and Power, 2003; Epstein and Jayadev, 2005; Dünhaupt, 2012). Rising financial incomes are also identified as a key manifestation of financialization in developing and emerging market economies, where financial liberalization has been followed by pressure to maintain high interest rates to sustain capital inflows (Demir, 2009a,b; Bonizzi, 2013).

These financial cash flows should, furthermore, be distinguished from financial profit rates. As such, growth in financial asset holdings and financial incomes, also, raises the question of the *rate* of return earned on financial assets. Dumenil and Levy (2004b) find that financial incomes – net interest, dividends, holding gains on assets and profits due to the devaluation of liabilities by inflation – increase overall profit rates in the USA between the early 1950s and 1982. After 1982, however, the gap between measures of the profit rate that do/do not incorporate financial factors largely disappears. Accordingly, financial relations most significantly improve USA firms' profitability at the beginning of firms' portfolio reallocation towards financial assets. This point is corroborated by the firm-level financial profit rates in Davis (2016), defined as firm-level interest and dividend earnings relative to financial assets (p. 135). This financial profit rate is positive for the full post-1970 period, but does not trend upwards with the exception of a small increase in large firms' financial profitability in the early 2000s (a period Dumenil and Levy's data does not include). Notably, the absence of a significant trend in financial profit *rates* is consistent with the fact that a large share of financial asset growth among USA firms is in highly liquid assets, yielding interest but not necessarily high returns (Davis, 2016).

It is, finally, important to note data limitations involved in measuring the total financial profits of nonfinancial firms. Total financial profits of NFCs include total interest income, dividend income (both from subsidiaries and affiliates, and other dividends) and capital gains (Krippner, 2005). Capital gains, in particular, include cash flows from net foreign exchange gains/losses, gains/losses from marketable securities and other short-term investments and gains/losses from sales of shares in other companies (Demir, 2009b). However, reporting requirements make it difficult to uniquely identify each of these income streams, such that total financial profits are difficult to document.

Thus, while Orhangazi (2008a), for example, documents a clear upward trend in two well-defined categories of financial income (interest and dividend income) at the sector level, this trend underestimates total financial profits both because it excludes other sources of financial income like capital gains (see Orhangazi, 2008a, p. 877), and because the Flow of Funds nets out within-USA within-sector holdings, such that dividends earned from stock of other USA NFCs are not included in dividends received (see Dumenil and Levy, 2004b, p. 102). Measurement issues arise in the firm-level data for the USA as well, in which it is neither possible to obtain a measure of capital gains nor to clearly identify all sources of financially derived income (see again Orhangazi, 2008a, p. 877; Davis, 2017). Notably, to measure capital gains at the sector level, Krippner (2005, 2011) uses (non-publicly available) Internal Revenue Service (IRS) data.[3] It is, accordingly, important to take note of differences in the definitions of financial profits across analyses.

3.1.2 *Do Financial Assets 'Crowd Out' Capital Investment?*

An influential set of empirical papers emphasize this expansion in financial assets and incomes, and consider whether the portfolio shift towards financial assets has come at the *expense* of physical investment. This channel has come to be known as the 'crowding out' thesis (for this usage see, as examples, Teixeira and Rotta, 2012, p. 454; van der Zwan, 2014, p. 14). This possibility is first analysed by Demir (2007, 2009a) and Orhangazi (2008a,b) who hypothesize that an increase in financial profits generates a portfolio reallocation towards financial investments that, in turn, reduces investment rates. Following Tobin (1965), if the yields of two categories of assets differ, these assets are held in proportions depending on their relative yields (p. 768); imperfections in financial markets and risk-diversification strategies ensure that nonzero quantities of both assets are held. Therefore, when internal funds are limited, there is 'substitutability of real and financial assets in portfolio balances' (Demir, 2009a, p. 314), such that 'increased financial investments could have a negative effect [on real investment] by crowding out real investment' (Orhangazi, 2008a, p. 865).[4]

This hypothesis is consistent with a growing 'portfolio view of investment' (Demir, 2009b, p. 316), wherein nonfinancial firms with increased access to financial markets exploit the availability of relatively quick and high financial returns. All else equal, an increase in the rate of return on financial assets effectively increases the 'hurdle' rate NFCs must expect to earn on fixed capital in order to allocate funds towards fixed assets, thereby reducing fixed investment rates as firms allocate (limited) funds towards financial investments (Demir, 2009b). While Demir emphasizes emerging markets, Crotty (2005), similarly, argues in the USA case that a key dimension of financialization is a 'shift in the beliefs and behavior of financial agents .... to a "financial" conception [of the nonfinancial firm] in which the NFC is seen as a "portfolio" of liquid subunits' (p. 88; see, similarly, Fligstein, 1990). Uncertainty, furthermore, implies firms may prefer investment in liquid, reversible financial assets over irreversible fixed capital when financial assets offer higher or even *comparable* rates of return (Crotty, 1990; Tornell, 1990; Demir, 2009a). This point is important: an *excess* of financial over real rates of return is not necessary for financial profitability to reduce investment rates; instead, a *decline in the gap* between real and financial profitability or an increase in uncertainty may be sufficient to depress investment.

This hypothesis is most often tested empirically by introducing financial cash flows or financial profit rates into estimations of the investment function.[5] The inclusion of financial profits into investment specifications is common across the literature on financialization and investment, whether directly via total financial earnings (Stockhammer, 2004; Orhangazi, 2008a,b; Demir, 2009c; Onaran et al., 2011; Seo et al., 2016; Tori and Onaran, 2017), the differential between rates of return on real and financial assets (Demir, 2007, 2009b) or the financial profit rate (Davis, 2017). Note that while Stockhammer's (2004) theoretical model concerns shareholder orientation (discussed in Section 4), the main empirical proxy for financialization – the interest and dividend income of the nonfinancial business sector – is closely tied to this section of the literature.

The empirical results in each of these papers point to a negative relationship between financial income and investment rates *in some specifications or subsamples*. This relationship is, perhaps, the strongest in Demir's (2009b) estimates for Argentina, Mexico and Turkey, which test whether an increase in the gap between real and financial profit rates *decreases* fixed investment. Demir finds a positive and statistically significant effect of this gap on investment, robust across specifications (p. 320). Orhangazi (2008a), similarly, finds a strongly statistically significant negative relationship between financial profits (normalized by the capital stock) and investment, although only among *large* firms. In fact, the relationship between financial incomes of the full sample of USA NFCs and investment is *positive*, albeit statistically insignificant. At the aggregate level, Stockhammer (2004) finds statistically significant evidence of a negative relationship between financial profits and capital investment in the USA and, in some specifications, also in the UK, but little evidence of a negative relationship in France or Germany. Notably, the statistical significance of this relationship disappears for the USA as well when also controlling for financial *payments* (Stockhammer, 2004, p. 735); these estimations that include both financial incomes and payments align with the statistically insignificant full-sample result in Orhangazi (2008a) and also the aggregate estimations in Orhangazi (2008b).[6]

Thus, while these papers point to a negative relationship between NFCs' financial incomes and investment in some specifications, the results are sufficiently mixed to suggest that evidence of 'crowding out' is not clearly robust across contexts and specifications. As such, this literature raises questions about the necessary conditions for 'crowding out' to hold. Perhaps most importantly, the theoretical robustness of the predicted negative relationship hinges on the assumption that *internal funds are limited*. This assumption of limited internal funds excludes, however, two relevant cases: first, a case in which *financial earnings* augment a firm's available funds such that (some proportion of) these total funds may be allocated towards physical investment and, second, a case in which firms *borrow to augment internal funds*.

The first possibility is that financial earnings augment firms' pools of internal funds, which can then be allocated in some proportion towards fixed or financial assets. Importantly, there is no a priori reason to expect these funds will be allocated entirely towards financial acquisitions, much less cause a further *reduction* in the acquisition of fixed assets. Demir (2009c), for example, finds that cash flows from financial investments have a positive effect on fixed investment in Turkey, although this positive effect is substantially smaller in magnitude than the (positive) effect of cash flow from operating profits. This result suggests that, in some circumstances, financial profits act as a dynamic 'hedging mechanism' that offer NFCs additional cash flow in subsequent periods, particularly in times of high uncertainty (p. 959). In other words, cash flows from financial investments may have a long-run positive effect on fixed capital investment. Notably, this analysis emphasizes financial *cash flows*; in contrast, Demir's (2009b) findings emphasize financial *rates of return* (i.e. financial profits per unit of financial assets), wherein a relative improvement in financial profitability relative to real profitability leads to a portfolio reallocation towards financial assets that depresses fixed investment.

In some contexts, however, financial profit rates may also *complement* 'real' earnings. Davis (2017), for example, presents evidence consistent with the negative predicted relationship between financial profit rates and investment above across all USA NFCs; however, firm size sub-samples point to a *positive* short-run relationship between financial profitability and investment for the largest quartile of firms.[7] This result suggests possible complementarities between financial profits and the nonfinancial aspects of firms' businesses that are only captured by the largest firms in the USA economy (Davis, 2017, p. 18). For instance, this result may corroborate examples of (large) NFCs' expansion into the provision of financial services, including NFC provision of car loans and store-issued credit cards (Froud *et al.*, 2006). These cases of captive finance not only generate financial profits, but also capture demand for a firm's nonfinancial output, thereby supporting fixed investment. This discussion, furthermore, suggests that – for firms able to capture these types of complementarities – a large differential between returns to lending and borrowing may not be necessary to generate NFC movement into financing activities.

Second, access to external finance (new borrowing) that augments a firm's pool of internal funds also implies that the acquisition of financial assets need not come at a trade-off with fixed investment.[8] Because firms make investment and financing decisions subject to a finance constraint, decisions regarding uses of funds are interdependent with decisions regarding external finance. Notably, in the USA context, the post-1980 expansion of financial incomes and financial investments is concurrent with an expansion in gross debt on NFC balance sheets (see Section 3.2), suggesting that – at least at the sector-level – firms are not constrained in new borrowing. In this context, 'crowding out' – or what Kliman and Williams (2014) term 'diversion' of the share of profits invested in production towards financial uses – need not have taken place.

Kliman and Williams (2014), instead, contend that USA NFCs' financial asset acquisitions were 'almost wholly funded by means of newly borrowed funds throughout the entire post-World War II period' (p. 77). While this conclusion is based on aggregate data showing the relative magnitudes of changes in financial asset holdings and liabilities, such that it is not possible to disambiguate what funds are used for what (only that, at the sector level, there are 'enough' funds to cover new financial assets out of new borrowing), this conclusion is also supported by the firm-level estimations in Davis (2017). Investment specifications that include NFCs' outstanding stock of financial assets, in addition to the flows of income earned off these assets, point to a positive and strongly robust relationship between firm-level financial asset holdings and fixed investment (in the short-term, over time and across firm-size specifications). Thus, holding expected returns constant, 'firms acquire financial assets – which ameliorate inherent risks of long-term and irreversible capital investments – concurrently with fixed capital' (p. 20), similarly, suggesting that financial assets have *not* directly crowded out fixed capital investment among USA firms. Seo *et al.* (2016), similarly, find no evidence of a crowding out relationship between financial asset acquisitions and fixed investment in Korea.

Among firms facing constraints in access to external finance, however, the acquisition of financial assets may come at a trade-off with fixed capital investment. Thus, the fact that Demir (2009b) finds robust evidence of crowding out in emerging market economies is consistent with the expectation that credit rationing constrains a more significant set of firms in an emerging market context. Demir, furthermore, draws on these results to point to the persistence of capital market imperfections in Argentina, Mexico and Turkey, arguing that – despite predictions that financial liberalization should deepen capital markets and reduce agency costs, in turn, increasing capital market efficiency – there is no robust evidence of a reduction in credit rationing for these real-sector firms. In addition to highlighting the role of credit constraints, this discussion speaks to a broader point: namely, that the key mechanisms through which financialization is linked to changing investment behaviour are likely to vary across countries, in line with historical and institutional differences (see Lapavitsas and Powell, 2013; Seo *et al.*, 2016; Karwowski and Stockhammer, 2017), as well as – within countries – both over time and by 'types' of firm (for example, those that are credit constrained versus those that are not).

3.2 Debt and Investment

A dramatic rise in NFC (gross) leverage is, also, a key stylized feature of the post-1980 period in the USA economy that has been emphasized extensively in the financialization literature. This expansion of debt is evident both at the sector level (Palley, 2007), and also at the firm level among large corporations (Davis, 2016). Figure 2 plots the firm-level yearly means of total outstanding debt relative to total capital between 1950 and 2014 for the full USA non-financial corporate sector, capturing a dramatic expansion in debt over the post-1980 period. As indicated by the discussion in Section 3.1.2, new borrowing is closely linked to accounts of financialization and investment, particularly in the post-1980 USA economy. As *a source*

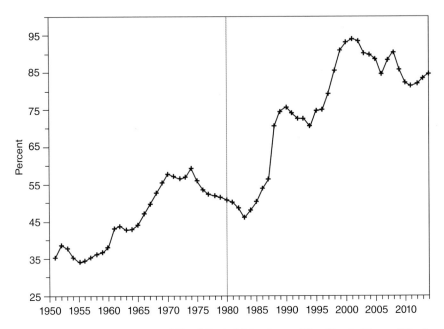

Figure 2. Gross Debt as a Percentage of Fixed Capital (The Across-Firm Yearly Mean of Nonfinancial Corporations).

Source: Compustat, author's calculations (series reproduced from Davis, 2016).

Notes: The series plots the across-firm yearly mean of total outstanding debt relative to the firm-level capital stock between 1950 and 2014. The ratio is winsorized to account for outliers. Debt is defined as the sum of current and long-term debt (Compustat items 34 and 142) Sales are drawn from Compustat item 12. The vertical line denotes 1980 to highlight the beginning of the period emphasized in the discussion.

of funds, new borrowing can be channelled towards three types of *uses of funds*: investment in fixed capital, investment in financial assets (or, analogously, saving) or 'swapping' debt for equity.

Importantly, the financialization literature suggests a 'de-linking' between borrowing and physical investment in the post-1980 USA economy. Kliman and Williams (2014) contend, for instance, that borrowed funds are an 'increasingly large source of the funds that drive the financialization process' (p. 76), where 'financialization' refers to dividend payments and financial asset acquisitions. Using firm-level data, Mason (2015) points to a declining correlation between new borrowing and physical investment after the early 1980s. Similarly, the USA nonfinancial corporate sector's dependence on external borrowing for investment falls after the early 1980s, such that a declining share of sector-level capital investment is financed with external funds (de Souza and Epstein, 2014). De Souza and Epstein (2014), also, document similar trends for five European countries with major financial centres (the UK, Germany, the Netherlands, Switzerland and France). Notably, in Germany, the UK and Switzerland, this trend is sufficiently dramatic that the nonfinancial corporate sectors become net *lenders* of funds to the rest of the economy, reversing traditional patterns of inter-sectoral lending.

Given this 'de-linking', the literature on financialization suggests at least two possible reasons why firms (increasingly) borrow, without channelling these borrowed funds into traditional investment. First, a large – and growing – subset of the financialization litera-ture suggests that growth in debt and shareholder payouts in the USA economy are linked (Dumenil and Levy, 2011; Kliman and Williams, 2014; Mason, 2015; Fiebiger, 2016). Of particular importance is the possibility that 'financing for stock repurchases has been mainly from borrowing rather than from profits' (Fiebiger, 2016, p. 355), such that debt increasingly replaces equity on NFC balance sheets. However, complete consideration of this channel also requires a discussion of shareholder value orientation, and is postponed to Section 4.

It is, second, plausible that (at least some part of) the expansion in borrowing is used to fund financial asset acquisitions. As discussed above in the context of crowding out, if fi-nancial asset acquisitions draw from borrowed funds, they need not come at a trade-off with fixed investment. Importantly, this point raises the question of *why* firms may borrow simply in order to hold more financial assets. Perhaps most notably, borrowing to fund financial as-set acquisitions is consistent with the possibility that large NFCs are increasingly engaged in the provision of financial services. The clearest evidence of this possibility comes from case studies of large firms – like General Electric, General Motors and Ford – that have expanded their scope into banking activities (Froud *et al.*, 2006). In the case that nonfinancial firms in-creasingly act like *financial* firms, their balance sheets structures should also more closely resemble those of financial firms (and, accordingly, be characterized by larger gross holdings of both debt and financial assets). More generally, however, this example indicates the impor-tance of tying changes in NFC financial structure to behavioural changes, so as to disentangle, for example, the possibility that financial investments 'crowd out' capital investments, from the possibility that firms borrow to fund financial investments.

3.3 *Behavioural Explanations of the Financialization of NFCs*

As emphasized by this discussion, changes in firm financial portfolio and financing structure – as well as the financial flows that derive from these balance sheet stocks – are common across the existing empirical literature on financialization and investment. However, this discussion also highlights that the *reasons* why firm portfolio and financing behaviour have changed are important for disentangling the effects on investment. These financial flows stem from firm decisions to acquire financial assets, or to borrow, repurchase stock or pay dividends, and – accordingly – raise the question of *why* NFCs have changed their portfolio and financing be-haviour over the post-1980 period such that these indicators rose in a dramatic and sustained way. Because firms make investment decisions subject to a finance constraint, the decision to invest is inherently interdependent with the decision of how to finance that investment, as well as with the decision not to allocate that finance towards another use – for example, to acquire financial assets or to finance (discretionary) shareholder payouts. As such, financial profits and NFC payments to the financial sector are both endogenous to the investment decision, and – as an explanation of the financialization of NFCs – cannot isolate what has changed in the post-1980 economy such that firms have changed their financial behaviour in a sustained way. Put differently, the interpretation of estimated coefficients drawn from reduced form re-lationships between flows of financial income and firm-level investment behaviour hinges on the theoretical basis of the investment function. Lack of clarity in the theoretical basis of the investment function, in turn, generates ambiguity regarding the behavioural and theoretical basis of estimated relationships.

As such, the implications of the same measure of financialization – for example, financial asset acquisitions – for investment differ if a firm acquires financial assets because they offer higher and faster rates of return than fixed assets, as compared to if a firm holds financial assets as part of a financial services division (wherein traditionally *non*financial firms engage in borrowing and lending for profit). Similarly, an increase in NFC payments to finance due to higher interest payments (deriving from increased leverage) draws, on the one hand, on a firm's pool of available funds. On the other hand, however, higher leverage – and the corresponding increase in interest payments – is the result of a firm's decision to borrow in pursuit of some objective: for example, profits, targeting a stock price increase by financing repurchases, or covering rising interest obligations (Davis, 2017). Importantly, the implications for fixed investment likely vary with this objective. Borrowing to invest in an attractive capital investment project, for example, differs from borrowing to repurchase stock.

Similarly, while improved demand conditions may traditionally be expected to drive a portfolio reallocation towards physical capital, thereby reducing NFC holdings of financial assets, this expectation in fact hinges on the nature of a firm's activities. If, for example, a significant proportion of an otherwise 'non'-financial firm's activities are financial (derived from the provision of financial services), and if the firm generates substantial complementarities between the financial and nonfinancial aspects of its business, the relationship between financial asset holdings and investment may instead be positive, as improved demand conditions could induce a firm's management to also expand the firm's financial services division. These examples speak to a broader point: continued research on financialization and investment requires development of a more complete behavioural narrative of *why* NFCs have 'financialized' – including changes in firm activities and managerial objectives that accompany this financialization process – to more fully elaborate the consequences for investment.

4. Shareholder Value Orientation

The primary behavioural channel analysed extensively in the existing literature, which links firms' financial outcomes to changes in firm behaviour, emphasizes a shift in corporate governance norms associated with the growing entrenchment of shareholder value ideology (Lazonick and O'Sullivan, 2000; Davis, 2009). Arising out of the application of agency theory to firms, shareholder value ideology contends that agency problems between shareholders (owners) and managers lead to inferior corporate performance. The agency problem is argued to derive from moral hazard: managers may apply 'insufficient effort', undertake 'extravagant investments', pursue 'entrenchment strategies' to make themselves indispensable, or exploit expensive perks like private jets or box tickets to ball games (Tirole, 2006, p. 17). To mitigate this moral hazard, agency theory suggests specific mechanisms to better-align managerial and shareholder interests including a hostile market for corporate control (Jensen, 1986, p. 324) and stock-based executive compensation (Jensen and Murphy, 1990). While these mechanisms are designed to improve firm performance, the literature on financialization has linked changes in firm behaviour associated with growing shareholder orientation – and, in particular, increased managerial attention to financial measures of firm performance defined on a short-term basis – to declining fixed investment rates.

4.1 *The Entrenchment of Shareholder Orientation in the USA Economy*

The development of institutions supporting the maximization of shareholder value is particularly dramatic in the USA economy. Because these changes depend significantly on country-specific institutions defining the degree of shareholder power, it is, therefore, useful to specifically introduce the USA case. In the USA, these changes are summarized by a shift from the Chandlerian managerial firm of the initial post-WWII period – in which professional managers ran corporations with little shareholder oversight (Chandler, 1977) – to a 'financialized' or 'rentier-dominated' firm following the shareholder revolution (Stockhammer, 2004; Crotty, 2005; Mason, 2015). This 'financialized' or 'rentier-dominated' firm is characterized by a shift in managerial priorities towards an emphasis on shareholder interests and, in particular, the interests of *short-term* shareholders (Stout, 2012).

A wide-reaching set of institutional and regulatory changes over the post-1980 period – including growth in institutional investors, an expansion in stock-based executive pay, and regulatory changes encouraging stock buybacks – have supported this shift in corporate governance norms, encouraging attention to shareholder payouts and the 'maximization of shareholder value'. First, the post-1980 period is characterized by significant changes in the structure of stock ownership, wherein institutional and activist investors increasingly dominate shareholding. Growth in the share of USA equities managed by institutional investors rises from 33% of total stock market capitalization in 1980 to 67% of by 2010 (Blume and Keim, 2012). Institutional ownership is, also, importantly, characterized by a shorter duration of stock ownership. Accordingly, stock market turnover has risen substantially over this period. Figure 3 highlights this increase in stock market turnover in the USA between 1980 and 2014; in this figure, the stock market turnover ratio is defined as the total annual value of shares traded relative to average market capitalization. Together with the expansion in institutional investors,

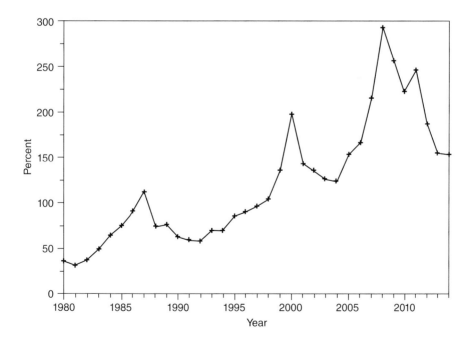

Figure 3. Stock Market Turnover, USA Stock Market (1980–2014).
Source: World Bank, Stock Market Turnover Ratio (Value Traded/Capitalization) for United States, retrieved from FRED, Federal Reserve Bank of St. Louis.
Notes: This figure shows the total value of shares traded each year divided by the average market capitalization for this period.

increased turnover reflects a marked departure from the pre-1980 period – dominated by long-term household-level stockholding – towards increasingly 'impatient' stock market finance (Crotty, 2005).

The expansion of institutional investors, together with changes in Securities and Exchange Commission (SEC) rules increasing the ease of communication between shareholders, has manifested in 'shareholder activism, with large outsider investors publicly pushing management to increase payouts and adopt "value-enhancing" policies, pushing for seats on the board, sponsoring resolutions, and threatening to sell their shares en masse' (Mason, 2015, p. 12). Crotty (2005) argues that this 'impatient finance' has contributed to growing emphasis on capital gains over long-term measures of firm performance and growth. Stout (2012), similarly, frames the expansion of institutional stock ownership in terms of the increasing power of *short-term shareholders* relative to *long-term shareholders*, generating 'corporate myopia' (p. 65). Short-term stockholding comes with a different set of incentives and, in particular, generates preferences for quick capital gains over long-term dividend growth. The rise of institutional and activist investors has, thus, arguably changed the constraints subject to which NFC managers operate, requiring greater managerial attention to stock-based indicators of performance.

Second, an expansion in stock-based executive pay directly affects managerial preferences by linking executives' individual payoffs to the firm's stock performance (Lazonick and O'Sullivan, 2000). Frydman and Jenter (2010) document an upswing in stock option compensation in the early 1980s and emphasize, 'The purpose of option compensation is to tie remuneration directly to share prices and thus *give executives an incentive to increase shareholder value*' (p. 5; emphasis added; see also Lazonick, 2013). The expansion of stock-based executive pay has, notably, also been supported by tax code changes, including a 1993 amendment to the tax code (Code 152(m)) stipulating a $1 million cap on nonperformance-based pay, but no cap on 'performance'-based pay. 'Performance' has, in turn, become increasingly synonymous with stock-price performance (Stout, 2012). Institutional investors have also been involved in the push for stock-based managerial pay (Lazonick 2009; Krippner, 2011). Hartzell and Starks (2003), for example, document that institutional ownership is tied to pay-for-performance sensitivity in executive compensation, where 'performance' again reflects stock price performance. A related change lies in a growing 'market for managers': whereas the initial post-WWII period was characterized largely by promotion within firms, an expanding 'market for management' has meant top management is increasingly likely to be brought in from outside the firm (Crotty, 2005; Kaplan and Minton, 2011; Mason, 2015).

These institutional changes are, third, supported by regulatory changes supporting own-stock repurchases. Of particular note is SEC Rule 10b-18, which first opened scope for (legal) large-scale repurchases by protecting managers from the threat of insider trading charges for targeting the firm's stock price (Grullon and Michaely, 2002; Lazonick, 2013; Davis, 2016). Further rule updates in 1991 and 2003 expand these safe harbour provisions, and shorten the waiting period between exercising and selling stock options (Lazonick, 2013; Davis, 2016). The dramatic post-1980 expansion in stock repurchases among USA corporations is closely correlated with these regulatory changes (Lazonick and O'Sullivan, 2000; Crotty, 2005; Davis, 2016). This secular expansion in repurchases is shown in Figure 4, which plots average industry-level repurchases across USA NFCs between 1970 and 2014; Figure 4 also indicates that this trend begins in 1983 (following SEC Rule 10b-18). Repurchase growth is accompanied by (more gradual) dividend growth; thus, total shareholder payouts exhibit secular growth after 1980, and dividends comprise a declining share of these total payouts over time (Grullon and Michaely, 2002). Importantly, own-stock repurchases clearly capture NFC

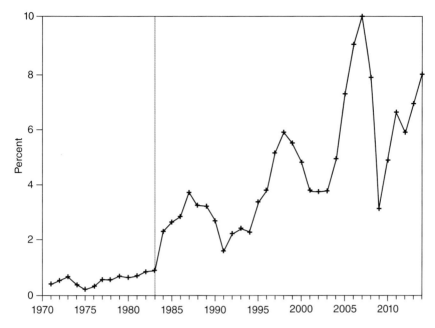

Figure 4. Gross Stock Repurchases Relative to Total Outstanding Equity (The Across-Firm Yearly Mean of Nonfinancial Corporations).
Source: Compustat, author's calculations.
Notes: The series plots the across-firm yearly mean of gross stock repurchases relative to the outstanding equity between 1971 and 2014. The ratio is winsorized to account for outliers. Gross repurchases are drawn from Compustat item 115. Total outstanding equity is drawn from Compustat item 144. The vertical line denotes 1983 to define the period after the implementation of SEC Rule 10b-18.

emphasis on shareholder value. By repurchasing shares, managers increase stock-based performance measures (like return on equity, or earnings per share), for otherwise given profits. Thus, repurchases both appease institutional investors, and directly affect the part of executive pay comprised of stock-based instruments.

4.2 *Shareholder Value and the Post-Keynesian Theory of the Firm*

Growth in NFC own-stock repurchases, importantly, draws a clear link between shareholder orientation and changes in NFC financial behaviour associated with the financialization of non-financial firms (namely, increased shareholder payouts). In turn, shareholder value orientation has been linked to investment via changes in managerial objectives and/or the constraints subject to which managers make portfolio and financing decisions. The increasing entrenchment of shareholder value ideology has, first, been linked to firm investment behaviour via changing managerial objectives (Stockhammer, 2004; Davis, 2017). The rationale for analysing the impact of shareholder orientation on firm behaviour via changes in managerial *objectives* is perhaps most clearly reflected in the growing share of stock-based executive pay, which directly aligns managerial and shareholder interests. As such, managers are increasingly oriented towards short-term profitability – and, more specifically, stock-based performance indicators – such that managerial willingness to tie up funds in long-term irreversible fixed capital declines.

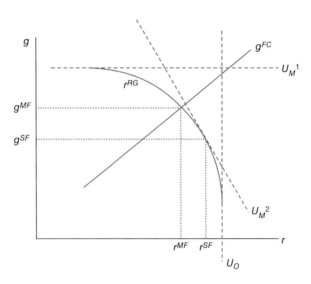

Figure 5. The Investment Decision in Stockhammer (2004).
Source: Adapted from Stockhammer (2004); r is the profit rate and g is the investment (growth) rate,
g^{FC} is the finance constraint; r^{RG} is the growth-profit trade-off; U_o is the utility function of owners
(defined as $U_o = u(r)$), and U_M is the utility function of managers. With the shift from managerial
capitalism to shareholder value orientation, managerial utility functions shift from $U_M^{\,1} = u(g)$ to
$U_M^{\,2} = u(g,r)$. Investment declines from g^{MF} (growth in the managerial firm) to g^{SF} (growth in the
shareholder-oriented firm), and profit rates rise from r^{MF} to r^{SF}. See Stockhammer (2004) and Lavoie
(2014) for additional details regarding the theoretical framework.

Building on the post-Keynesian theory of the firm in Lavoie (2014), Stockhammer (2004)
develops a theoretical framework analysing the impact of changes in managerial preferences
on investment, via a shift from 'growth-maximizing' to 'profit-maximizing' objectives. The
investment decision, pictured in Figure 5, is determined by managerial objectives, the firms'
finance constraint (g^{FC}), and the firms' output expansion function (r^{RG}) (Stockhammer, 2004;
for additional elaborations of this framework see also Dallery, 2009; Hein and van Treeck,
2010; Lavoie, 2014). The finance constraint defines the maximum level of growth that can be
financed by a given rate of profit. The output expansion frontier, in turn, defines the profit rate
that can be achieved for a given investment rate (growth strategy). The firm is assumed to operate on the concave portion of the output-expansion function, such that additional investment
harms profits – that is, there is a 'growth-profit trade-off'.[9]

The theoretical specification emphasizes the separation between ownership and control to
introduce the possibility of divergence between managerial and shareholder preferences. Prior
to the entrenchment of shareholder ideology, managers maximize firm growth (the investment
rate), despite shareholders' preferences for profit maximization. As such, managerial preferences are defined by U_M^1 in Figure 5 (where $U_M^1 = u(g)$), whereas owners' preferences (U_O)
are a function of profits (r). As shareholder value orientation becomes increasingly entrenched,
managerial preferences become increasingly 'profit-maximizing' (shown by the rotation
to $U_M^2 = u(g,r)$). As Figure 5 indicates, this increasingly 'profit-maximizing' managerial
orientation, accordingly, drives a decline in the firm's investment rate (from the investment
rate of the 'managerial firm', g^{MF}, to the lower investment rate of the 'shareholder-dominated
firm', g^{SF}).[10]

Changes in firm financial behaviour associated with shareholder value – including, most notably, increased financial payout ratios – may, furthermore, change the position of the firm's finance constraint (Hein and van Treeck, 2008; Hein and van Treeck, 2010). In particular, the finance frontier rotates so as to further constrain the investment rate available to firms. Hein and van Treeck, (2010) contend that shareholder value orientation is, accordingly, associated not only with a change in managerial objectives, but also with a change in the firm's *constraints* as shareholders 'compel firms to distribute a larger portion of profits' (p. 210). Note, however, that an increase in distributed profits can also be understood as endogenous to the change in managerial preferences: namely, shareholder payouts increase and affect the position of the finance constraint *because* of the change in managerial objectives. As such, any changes in the position of the finance frontier are, in fact, also a consequence of changing managerial *objectives*. Furthermore, if shareholder payouts are financed, at least in part, through increased borrowing, this expansion in borrowing (reflecting additional finance available to the firm) can offset the shift in the firms' finance constraint. Finally, Fiebiger (2016) contends that a concurrent shift in production from the domestic to the international sphere mitigates the extent to which the utility function describing managerial preferences rotates in the context of shareholder orientation; in particular, international fixed investment may, to some extent, have replaced domestic fixed investment.

4.3 *Empirical Evidence on Shareholder Value and Investment*

An empirical literature, also, provides econometric support for the hypothesis that growing shareholder orientation among NFC managers is associated with declining firm investment rates. This literature includes distinct approaches to operationalizing shareholder value orientation, which reiterate the bifurcation in empirical approaches to measuring financialization empirically shown in Table 1. In particular, some contributions rely primarily on NFCs' financial *payouts* (Orhangazi, 2008a,b); others emphasize, more specifically, *shareholder* payouts (van Treeck, 2008; Mason, 2015); and still others equate shareholder orientation with increasing financial *incomes* (Stockhammer, 2004).

Stockhammer (2004) provides an early empirical analysis of shareholder orientation that extends the theoretical approach to the firm described in Section 4.2 to an empirical estimation of the investment function using aggregate data. The key empirical indicator of financialization is the rentiers' income of nonfinancial business (interest and dividend income earned by nonfinancial business, at the sector level). This indicator is designed to capture the extent of managerial orientation towards financial profits. For the USA, Stockhammer finds a negative relationship between rentiers' income and capital accumulation in most specifications, and concludes that these results provide preliminary evidence that financialization depresses capital accumulation (although it is important to note that the mechanism is shareholder value orientation and, thus, is one specific manifestation of financialization). Orhangazi (2008a), also, points to the possibility that the relationship between financial incomes and investment may be indicative – in part – of shareholder orientation, as higher financial profits can reflect 'impatient finance' (Crotty, 2005) and increased short termism (Orhangazi, 2008a, p. 868).

It is, however, important to note that there is not a direct mapping between the firm-level framework in Section 4.2 and the empirical analysis of this framework in Stockhammer (2004). First, by applying the firm-level framework to aggregate data, the empirical model excludes possible interactions between micro-level and macro-level outcomes. Skott and Ryoo (2008) note that, if each individual firm moves along its output-expansion frontier to a lower investment rate, aggregate demand falls. Thus, 'an individual firm may face a perceived trade-off but this perceived trade-off does not extend to the macroeconomic level: changes in accumulation and financial behaviour affect aggregate demand and thereby the position of the frontier' (Skott and Ryoo, 2008, p. 834). While this aggregation issue may not be vital for specifying the behaviour of an individual firm, it is important in the empirical extension of the firm-level model to the aggregate setting. Second, the theoretical framework emphasizes a distinction between profit-maximizing and growth-maximizing objectives; however, the empirical framework emphasizes a different distinction, between *total* profits and *financially derived* profits.

Furthermore, given the importance of increased payouts to shareholders in accounts of shareholder value orientation, the relationship between financial *payouts* and investment offers a more direct test of the effect of shareholder ideology on investment. Orhangazi (2008a) finds, first, a negative and statistically significant relationship between total NFC payments to financial markets (interest payments, dividend payments and repurchases), concentrated among large firms. As an explicit test of the relationship between shareholder orientation and investment, however, this approach is limited, given that total financial payments include payments to both creditors and to shareholders. In particular, shareholder orientation is plausibly identified with an increasing prioritization of shareholder over creditor interests, such that it is important to distinguish payouts to shareholders versus creditors. Notably, Davis (2017) finds an insignificant relationship (and a very small point estimate) between a firm's cost of borrowing and investment; the difference between the results in Davis (2017) and Orhangazi (2008a) suggest that the strength of Orhangazi's result captures payouts to shareholders rather than to creditors. Similarly, at the aggregate level, van Treeck (2008) includes interest and dividend payments separately in the empirical specification, finding a statistically significant negative effect of each variable on investment, but that the magnitude of the coefficient on dividend payments exceeds that on interest payments. Finally, given that buybacks are an increasingly important method of returning cash to shareholders, Mason (2015) points to the importance of combining repurchases with dividends to measure total shareholder payouts.

Departing from both financial-flow based indicators, Davis (2017) proxies shareholder value orientation by average industry-level repurchases, to capture the effect of increasingly entrenched norms encouraging managerial attention to stock-based performance indicators on investment. Both rentiers' income and shareholder payouts are endogenous to the investment decision (and, as noted above, to the position of an individual firm's finance constraint), whereas average industry repurchases are plausibly exogenous to an individual firm. These results point to a negative relationship between average industry-level repurchases and fixed investment across all USA NFCs; furthermore, the magnitude of the estimate increases when focusing on the largest quartile of firms. Thus, holding all else equal in terms of expected profits, debt, and other financial variables, a 'value' maximizing firm invests less in fixed capital than a firm with traditional growth or profit-maximizing objectives. Furthermore, as is discussed above, a range of changes in financial behaviour are expected to accompany the increasing entrenchment of shareholder orientation including, notably, changes in debt and corporate borrowing. Mason (2015), for instance points to a declining correlation between borrowing and new physical investment, suggesting that – with a shift towards shareholder value maximizing objectives – firms increasingly take on external debt to repurchase outstanding stock, rather than to invest in new physical capital.

It is important to note that these mechanisms are highly institutionally contingent and depend substantially on institutions defining the degree of shareholder power in a particular economy. The analysis of shareholder orientation, therefore, offers a clear caution against applying institutionally specific features of financialization in cross-country contexts. If, for instance, one argues that rentiers' income is indicative of growing managerial orientation to shareholder orientation, and this change in managerial preferences crowds out fixed investment, it is unlikely that this relationship between financial incomes and investment will also apply in economies where the degree of shareholder power is lower. Stockhammer's (2004) analysis speaks to this point: evidence of the effect of shareholder orientation on investment holds only in the USA and in some specifications in the UK, whereas France and Germany – both countries where the degree of shareholder power is lower – exhibit no such relationship. Analysing the salience of a link between shareholder orientation and investment in Korea, Seo *et al.* (2016), similarly, fail to find evidence of such a relationship.

5. Conclusions

This paper has surveyed the strand of the financialization literature that emphasizes fixed investment and capital accumulation. In this literature, there is growing consensus that certain features of financialization – in the USA context, most notably shareholder orientation and corporate short-termism – depress physical investment. Given the key role of fixed investment in economic growth, this literature raises important questions about the long-term macroeconomic effects of increased attention to short-term financial market-based indicators of firm performance in the USA economy. Notably, the possibility of economically meaningful negative links between financialization and capital accumulation is also echoed in a more recent mainstream literature that finds that, beyond a certain threshold, financial sector growth negatively effects GDP growth (Cecchetti and Kharoubi, 2012; Law and Singh, 2014; Arcand *et al.*, 2015). Together, these results increasingly call into question a long-held tenet in mainstream macroeconomics: that more finance leads to more growth (Levine, 1997). Thus, as a largely heterodox literature on financialization has raised the question of 'how big is too big?' with respect to the size of the financial system (Epstein and Crotty, 2013), in the mainstream literature as well there is 'an emerging notion: that there can be "too much finance"' (Jordà *et al.*, 2016, p. 32).

This survey also indicates directions for future research. As discussed above, for example, the key role of risk and uncertainty in mediating firms' demand for liquid versus illiquid assets suggests that linkages between financialization, risk, uncertainty and investment behaviour should be further analysed in future research. The existing literature, furthermore, focuses on corporations – both due to data availability (given corporations' public reporting requirements) and because key themes in the literature on financialization (like shareholder orientation) are closely tied to the stock market. However, selection into the corporate form is nonrandom (Demir, 2009a); additionally, the role of the corporate sector in total business investment varies over time and place. Systematic differences in the characteristics of listed and nonlisted firms – for instance, in access to debt and equity finance – raise the possibility of distinct relationships between financialization and the investment behaviour of public and private firms. More broadly, considerable scope remains to isolate key characteristics of the relationship between financialization and investment for different types of firms: public and private, foreign and domestic, those in developed and developing economies. Finally, while most research to date has utilized annual data, higher-frequency data have the potential to offer new insight into determinants of firm portfolio choice. While annual data are well-suited to describing longer-term trends, the end-of-year values on annual income and balance sheet statements cannot capture short-term portfolio adjustments (specifically of liquid financial assets) throughout the year (see Demir (2009b) for an analysis that, instead, uses semi-annual data).

These directions for future research can all contribute to further development of a behavioural narrative explaining links between post-1980 changes in firm financial behaviour and investment. Shareholder orientation, particularly in the USA context, is an increasingly well-developed behavioural channel tying changes in firm behaviour to financial outcomes. Nonetheless, it is important to recognize that trends like an expansion in NFC financial asset holdings and/or financial profits can have different implications for fixed investment in different contexts. For instance, financial earnings may crowd out investment if driven by expanded opportunities to earn high returns on liquid assets in the context of uncertainty and the presence of credit constraints. However, the same 'crowding out' may not hold if financial asset holdings reflect an expansion in the scope of NFC *activities* towards involvement in banking services. Thus, space remains to build on this existing literature, to draw links between observed changes in firm financial structure and the specific changes in firm objectives, constraints, or activities that generate these outcomes. Doing so – particularly given that the term 'financialization' denotes a broad and wide-reaching process of structural change – opens scope for the possibility that different channels associated with financialization affect investment in different ways.

Notes

1. A full review of the research on financialization lies outside the scope of this survey. By way of brief introduction, however, this literature explores the relationship between financialization and a range of both financial and nonfinancial outcomes, including household debt (Scott and Pressman, 2009; Kim, 2013); macroeconomic dynamics (Boyer, 2000; Aglietta and Breton, 2001; Skott and Ryoo, 2008; van Treeck, 2009b); inequality in both the personal and functional distributions of income (Onaran *et al.*, 2011; Lin and Tomaskovic-Devey, 2013; Dünhaupt, 2014; Hein, 2015; Kohler *et al.*, 2015; Stockhammer, 2017); and commodities markets and food prices (Gosh, 2009; Isakson, 2014; Pradhananga, 2016).

2. In describing the expanding body of work on financialization more broadly, Michell and Toporowski (2013), similarly, write that the term 'financialization' has come to 'have different meanings according to the context and the individual using the term. With different meanings, the term loses its efficacy as a device for communicating ideas: Users of the term believe that they are communicating effectively because other people are using the term, whereas they may be communicating about different ideas…' (p. 68). See also Lapavitsas (2011) and Fiebiger (2016) for similar points.

3. Similar issues arise in defining total financial assets (the necessary denominator for a financial profit rate) reflecting, in particular, the identification of 'other' financial assets at both the firm level and the aggregate level (Crotty, 2005; Davis, 2016). Similarly, real profit rates should – whenever possible – be measured relative to a measure of the capital stock excluding land (Demir, 2009b).

4. See also Taylor and O'Connell (1985) for a model of Minsky crises that emphasizes the impact of changing profit expectations on portfolio decisions between liquid assets (money) and illiquid assets.

5. Because financing decisions and investment decisions are interdependent, the inclusion of financial earnings in investment estimations raises questions about endogeneity and

bias. These questions are, of course, common to the broader investment literature. The most common approach to these endogeneity problems, particularly in firm-level analyses, is the Arellano-Bond Generalized Method of Moments, which allows for the simultaneous inclusion of firm fixed effects and a lagged dependent variable (to capture well-documented persistence in investment rates), and can also be used to instrument variables endogenous to the firms' investment decision, like financial profits and financial asset holdings, with their own lags.

6. Stockhammer (2004) suggests a high degree of collinearity between financial payments and financial incomes at the sector level is responsible for the decline in the precision of these estimates.

7. At least two differences are useful to note between the USA-based firm-level analyses in Orhangazi (2008a) and Davis (2017). First, whereas Orhangazi (2008a) measures financial incomes relative to outstanding capital, Davis (2017) utilizes a financial profit *rate* (i.e. financial incomes normalized by financial assets). Perhaps more importantly, it is useful to note a difference in the sample of USA NFCs in these two analyses. Orhangazi, in particular, excludes firms with negative (real) profit rates, which excludes a significant share of the full sample given the (increasing) incidence of negative profitability in Compustat data over this period. In effect, this restriction biases Orhangazi's sample towards relatively larger firms. It is, however, difficult to identify the effect of these sample differences on the estimation results in the two papers.

8. This general point, of course, extends to all other uses of funds, including payments to shareholders (dividends payments/stock repurchases), discussed below.

9. The specification of the finance constraint reflects that internal and external funding differ for the firm, such that managers are only willing to accept a given leverage rate (borrowers' risk), and banks provide credit to firms that are already profitable, taking the current profit rate as a proxy for a firm's 'reliability' (lenders' risk); thus, investment, which depends on available finance, depends on the profit rate. The concave portion of the growth-profit trade-off reflects growing managerial inefficiency associated with excessively fast growth of the firm, the 'Penrose effect' (see Stockhammer, 2004, pp. 724–726).

10. Note, however, that maximizing shareholder returns need not be equivalent with profit maximization. As shareholder payouts have increasingly taken the form of supporting stock price increases (or stock-price related performance metrics, like earnings per share), 'value' maximization may diverge from profit maximization. If the stock price is considered a key indicator of firm 'value' (by these financial performance-based metrics), then two identical firms earning the same profits could generate different 'shareholder returns' depending on their financial policy and payout behavior: if one firm repurchases stock, then by decreasing the total stock of outstanding equity, the per-share price increases (Davis, 2016) – at least in the short-term. Then, despite equivalent profitability, the manager of the firm that has repurchased stock appears to have more successfully improved stock market performance and shareholder value.

References

Aglietta, M. and Breton, R. (2001) Financial systems, corporate control and capital accumulation. *Economy and Society* 30(4): 433–466.

Akkemik, K. and Özen, S. (2014) Macroeconomic and institutional determinants of financialization of non-financial firms: case study of Turkey. *Socio-Economic Review* 12(1): 71–98.

Arcand, J., Berkes, L. and Panizza, U. (2015) Too much finance? *Journal of Economic Growth* 20(2): 105–148.

Blume, M. and Keim, D. (2012) Institutional investors and stock market liquidity: trends and relationships. Available at https://papers.ssrn.com/sol3/papers.cfm?abstract_id=2147757, accessed on Jan 14, 2017.

Bonizzi, B. (2013) Financialization in developing and emerging countries. *International Journal of Political Economy*: 42(4): 83–107.

Boyer, R. (2000) Is a finance-led growth regime a viable alternative to Fordism? A preliminary analysis. *Economy and Society* 29(1): 111–145.

Cecchetti, S. and Kharoubi, E. (2012) Reassessing the impact of finance on growth. Bank for International Settlements Working Paper # 381.

Chandler, A. (1977) *The Visible Hand: The Managerial Revolution in American Business*. Cambridge, MA: Harvard University Press.

Comin, D. and Philippon, T. (2005) The rise in firm-level volatility: causes and consequences. *NBER Macroeconomics Annual 2005* 22: 166–228.

Crotty, J. (1990) Owner-manager conflict and financial theories of investment instability: a critical assessment of Keynes, Tobin and Minsky. *Journal of Post Keynesian Economics* 12(4): 519–542.

Crotty, J. (1992) Neoclassical and Keynesian approaches to the theory of investment. *Journal of Post Keynesian Economics* 14(4): 483–496.

Crotty, J. (2005) The neoliberal paradox: the impact of destructive product market competition and 'modern' financial markets on nonfinancial corporation performance in the neoliberal era. In G. Epstein (ed.), *Financialization and the World Economy* (pp.77–110). Northampton, MA: Edward Elgar.

Dallery, T. (2009) Post-Keynesian theories of the firm under financialization. *Review of Radical Political Economics* 41(4): 492–515.

Davis, G. (2009) *Managed by the Markets*. Oxford: Oxford University Press.

Davis, L. (2016) Identifying the 'financialization' of the nonfinancial corporation in the US economy: a decomposition of firm-level balance sheets. *Journal of Post Keynesian Economics* 39(1): 115–141.

Davis, L. (2017) Financialization and the nonfinancial corporation: an investigation of firm-level investment behavior in the U.S. *Metroeconomica* 00: 1–38. https://doi.org/10.1111/meca.12179

Demir, F. (2007) The rise of rentier capitalism and the financialization of real sectors in developing countries. *Review of Radical Political Economics* 39(3): 351–359.

Demir, F. (2009a) Capital market imperfections and financialization of real sectors in emerging markets: private investment and cash flow relationship revisited. *World Development* 37(5): 953–964.

Demir, F. (2009b) Financial liberalization, private investment and portfolio choice: financialization of real sectors in emerging markets. *Journal of Development Economics* 88(2): 314–324.

Demir, F. (2009c) Financialization and manufacturing firm profitability under uncertainty and macroeconomic volatility: evidence from an emerging market. *Review of Development Economics* 13(4): 592–609.

de Souza, J. and Epstein, G. (2014) Sectoral net lending in six financial centers. Political Economy Research Institute Working Paper Series # 346.

Dögüs, I. (2016) A Minskian criticism on the shareholder pressure approach of financialisation. Zentrum fuer Oekonomische und Soziologische Studien, #1868-4947/53.

Dumenil, G. and Levy, D. (2004a) *Capital Resurgent*. Cambridge, MA: Harvard University Press.

Dumenil, G. and Levy, D. (2004b) The real and financial components of profitability. *Review of Radical Political Economics* 36(1): 82–110.

Dumenil, G. and Levy, D. (2011) *The Crisis of Neoliberalism*. Cambridge, MA: Harvard University Press.

Dünhaupt, P. (2014) An empirical assessment of the contribution of financialization and corporate governance to the rise in income inequality. Berlin School of Economics and Law, Institute for International Political Economy Working Paper No. 41/2014.

Dünhaupt, P. (2012) Financialization and the rentier income share – evidence from the USA and from Germany. *International Review of Applied Economics* 26(4): 465–487.

Eichner, A. and Kregel, J. (1975) An essay on post-Keynesian theory: a new paradigm in economics. *Journal of Economic Literature* 13(4): 1293–1314.

Epstein, G. (2005) Introduction: financialization and the world economy. In G. Epstein (ed.), *Financialization and the World Economy* (pp. 1–16). Northampton, MA: Edward Elgar.

Epstein, G. (2015) Financialization: there's something happening here. Political Economy Research Institute Working Paper #394.

Epstein, G. and Crotty, J. (2013) How big is too big? On the social efficiency of the financial sector in the United States. Political Economy Research Institute Working Paper #313.

Epstein, G. and Jayadev, A. (2005) The rise of rentier incomes in OECD countries: financialization, central bank policy and labor solidarity. In G. Epstein (ed.), *Financialization and the World Economy* (pp. 46–74). Northampton, MA: Edward Elgar.

Epstein, G. and Power, D. (2003) Rentier incomes and financial crises: an empirical examination of trends and cycles in some OECD countries. *Canadian Journal of Development Studies* 24(2): 229–248.

Fazzari, S., Hubbard, R. and Peterson, B. (1988) Financing constraints and corporate investment. *Brookings Papers on Economic Activity* 1: 141–206.

Fiebiger, B. (2016) Rethinking the financialisation of non-financial corporations: a reappraisal of US empirical data. *Review of Political Economy* 28(3): 354–379.

Fine, B. (2013) Financialization from a Marxist perspective. *International Journal of Political Economy* 42(4): 47–66.

Fine, B. and Saad-Filho, A. (2014) Politics of neo-liberal development: Washington Consensus and Post-Washington Consensus. In H. Weber (ed.), *The Politics of Development: A Survey* (pp. 154–166). Abingdon: Routledge.

Fligstein, N. (1990) *The Transformation of Corporate Control*. Cambridge, MA: Harvard University Press.

Froud, J., Johal, S., Leaver, A. and Williams, K. (2006) *Financialization and Strategy: Narrative and Numbers*. New York, NY: Routledge.

Frydman, C. and Jenter, D. (2010) CEO compensation. NBER Working Paper No. 16585.

Gosh, J. (2009) The unnatural coupling: food and global finance. *Journal of Agrarian Change* 10(1): 72–86.

Greenwood, R. and Scharfstein, D. (2013) The growth of finance. *The Journal of Economic Perspectives* 27(2): 3–28.

Grullon, G. and Michaely, R. (2002) Dividends, share repurchases, and the substitution hypothesis. *Journal of Finance* 57(4): 1649–1684.

Gutiérrez, G. and Philippon, T. (2016) Investment-less growth: an empirical investigation. *NBER Working Paper* 22897.

Hartzell, J. and Starks, L. (2003) Institutional investors and executive compensation. *The Journal of Finance* 58(6): 2351–2374.

Hein, E. (2015) Finance-dominated capitalism and re-distribution of income: a Kaleckian perspective. *Cambridge Journal of Economics* 39(3): 907–934.

Hein, E. and van Treeck, T. (2008) 'Financialisation' in post-Keynesian models of distribution and growth – a systematic review. IMK Working Paper #10/2008.

Hein, E. and van Treeck, T. (2010) Financialisation and rising shareholder power in Kaleckian/Post-Kaleckian models of distribution and growth. *Review of Political Economy* 22(2): 205–233.

Isakson, R. (2014) Food and finance: the financial transformation of agro-food supply chains. *The Journal of Peasant Studies* 41(5): 749–775.

Jensen, M. (1986) Agency cost of free cash flow, corporate finance and takeovers. *American Economic Review* 76(2): 323–329.

Jensen, M. and Murphy, K. (1990) Performance pay and top management incentives. *Journal of Political Economy* 98(2): 225–264.

Jordà, Ò., Schularick, M. and Taylor, A. (2016) Macrofinancial history and the new business cycle facts. *NBER Macroeconomics Annual* 2016, 31.

Kaplan, S. and Minton, B. (2011) How has CEO turnover changed? *International Review of Finance* 12(1): 57–87.

Karwowski, E. and Stockhammer E. (2017) Financialisation in emerging economies: a systematic overview and comparison with Anglo-Saxon economies. *Economic and Political Studies*, 5(1): 60–86.

Kim, Y. (2013) Household debt, financialization and macroeconomic performance in the US, 1951–2009. *Journal of Post Keynesian Economics* 35(4): 675–694.

Kliman, A. and Williams, S. (2014) Why 'financialisation' hasn't depressed US productive investment. *Cambridge Journal of Economics* 39(1): 67–92.

Kohler, K., Guschanski, A. and Stockhammer, E. (2015) How does financialisation affect functional income distribution? A theoretical classification and empirical assessment. Kingston University London Economics Discussion Papers 2015-5.

Krippner, G. (2005) The financialization of the American economy. *Socio-Economic Review* 3(2): 173–208.

Krippner, G. (2011) *Capitalizing on Crisis: The Political Origins of the Rise of Finance*. Cambridge, MA: Harvard University Press.

Lapavitsas, C. (2011) Theorizing financialization. *Work, Employment and Society* 25(4): 611–626.

Lapavitsas, C. and Powell, J. (2013) Financialisation varied: a comparative analysis of advanced economies. *Cambridge Journal of Regions, Economy and Society* 6(3): 359–379.

Lavoie, M. (2014) *Post-Keynesian Economics: New Foundations*. Northampton, MA: Edward Elgar.

Law, S. and Singh, N. (2014) Does too much finance harm economic growth? *Journal of Banking & Finance* 41: 36–44.

Lazonick, W. (2009) The explosion of executive pay and the erosion of American prosperity. *Enterprises et Histoire* 57(4): 141–164.

Lazonick, W. (2013) From innovation to financialization: how shareholder value ideology is destroying the US economy. In M. Wolfson and G. Epstein (eds.), *The Handbook of Political Economy of Financial Crises* (pp. 491–511). New York, NY: Oxford University Press.

Lazonick, W. and O'Sullivan, M. (2000) Maximizing shareholder value: a new ideology for corporate governance. *Economy and Society* 29(1): 13–35.

Levine, R. (1997) Financial development and economic growth: views and agenda. *Journal of Economic Literature* 35(2): 688–726.

Lin, K. and Tomaskovic-Devey, D. (2013) Financialization and US income inequality: 1970–2008. *American Journal of Sociology* 118(5): 1284–1329.

Mason, J.W. (2015) Disgorge the cash: the disconnect between corporate borrowing and investment. Available at http://rooseveltinstitute.org/disgorge-cash-disconnect-between-corporate-borrowing-and-investment-1/, accessed on January 13, 2017.

Michell, J. and Toporowski, J. (2013) Critical observations on financialization and the financial process. *International Journal of Political Economy* 42(4): 67–82.

Milberg, W. (2008) Shifting sources and uses of profits: sustaining US financialization with global value chains. *Economy and Society* 37(3): 420–451.

Milberg, W. and Winkler, D. (2013) *Outsourcing Economics: Global Value Chains in Capitalist Development*. Cambridge: Cambridge University Press.

Milberg, W. and Winkler, D. (2010) Financialisation and the dynamics of offshoring in the USA. *Cambridge Journal of Economics* 34(2): 275–293.

Minsky, H. (1975) *John Maynard Keynes*. New York: McGraw-Hill Professional.

Montecino, J., Epstein, G. and Levina, I. (2016) Long-term trends in intra-financial lending in the US (1950–2012). *Eastern Economic Journal* 42(4): 611–629.

Onaran, O., Stockhammer, E. and Grafl, L. (2011) Financialisation, income distribution and aggregate demand in the USA. *Cambridge Journal of Economics* 35(4): 637–661.

Orhangazi, O. (2008a) Financialisation and capital accumulation in the non-financial corporate sector. *Cambridge Journal of Economics* 32(6): 863–886.

Orhangazi, O. (2008b) *Financialization and the US economy*. Cheltenham: Edward Elgar.

Palley, T. (2007) Financialization: what it is and why it matters. Political Economy Research Institute Working Paper #153.

Philippon, T. and Reshef, A. (2013) An international look at the growth of modern finance. *The Journal of Economic Perspectives* 27(2): 73–96.

Pradhananga, M. (2016) Financialization and the rise in co-movement of commodity prices. *International Review of Applied Economics* 30(5): 547–566.

Sawyer, M. (2013) What is financialization? *International Journal of Political Economy* 42(4): 5–18.

Scott, R. and Pressman, S. (2009) Consumer debt and the measurement of inequality in the US. *Review of Social Economy* 67(2): 127–146.

Seo, H., Kim, H. and Kim, J. (2016) Does shareholder value orientation or financial market liberalization slow down Korean real investment? *Review of Radical Political Economics* 48(4): 633–660.

Skott, P. (1989) *Conflict and Effective Demand in Economic Growth*. Cambridge: Cambridge University Press.

Skott, P. and Ryoo, R. (2008) Macroeconomic implications of financialisation. *Cambridge Journal of Economics* 32(6): 827–862.

Stockhammer, E. (2004) Financialisation and the slowdown of accumulation. *Cambridge Journal of Economics* 28(3): 371–404.

Stockhammer, E. (2005) Shareholder value orientation and the investment-profit puzzle. *Journal of Post Keynesian Economics* 28(2): 193–215.

Stockhammer, E. (2017) Determinants of the wage: a panel data analysis of advanced and developing economies. *British Journal of Industrial Relations* 55(1): 3–33.

Stout, L. (2012) *The Shareholder Value Myth: How Putting Shareholders First Harms Investors, Corporations, and the Public*. San Francisco: Berett-Koehler Publishers, Inc.

Taylor, L. and O' Connell, S. (1985) A Minsky Crisis. *Quarterly Journal of Economics* 100: 871–885.

Teixeira, R. and Rotta, T. (2012) Valueless knowledge-commodities and financialization: productive and financial dimensions of capital autonomization. *Review of Radical Political Economics* 44(4): 448–467.

Tirole, J. (2006) *The Theory of Corporate Finance*. Princeton: Princeton University Press.

Tobin, J. (1965) Money and economic growth. *Econometrica* 33(4): 671–684.

Tornell, A. (1990) Real vs. financial investment: can Tobin taxes eliminate the irreversibility distortion? *Journal of Development Economics* 32(2): 419–444.

Tori, D and Onaran, O. (2017) The effects of financialisation and financial development on investment: evidence from firm-level data in Europe. Greenwich Papers in Political Economy No. 44.

Van der Zwan, N (2014) Making sense of financialization. *Socio-Economic Review* 12(1): 99–129.

Van Treeck T. (2008) Reconsidering the investment-profit nexus in finance-led economies: an ARDL-based approach. *Metroeconomica* 59(3): 371–404.

Van Treeck T. (2009a) A synthetic, stock-flow consistent macroeconomic model of 'financialisation'. *Cambridge Journal of Economics* 33(3): 467–493.

Van Treeck T. (2009b) The political economy debate on 'financialization' – a macroeconomic perspective. *Review of International Political Economy* 16(5): 907–944.

9

QUANTITATIVE EMPIRICAL RESEARCH IN MARXIST POLITICAL ECONOMY: A SELECTIVE REVIEW

Deepankar Basu

University of Massachusetts Amherst

1. Introduction

Marxist political economy has a long and distinguished tradition of quantitative empirical analysis, going all the way back to Marx himself. Using tax returns data to infer patterns of top income distribution and nutrition data to understand conditions of the working class population in Volume I of *Capital*, Marx anticipated Thomas Piketty by more than 150 years and the discipline of development economics by about 100. Lenin's monumental work, *The Development of Capitalism in Russia*, had used extensive quantitative data on distribution of landholdings, small peasant industries and factory industries in Russia and Europe to argue against the Narodnik claim that capitalism could not develop in a backward country like Russia.

This robust tradition has been kept alive by the painstaking research of numerous Marxist scholars, who have used, over the years, improved statistical techniques and better measurement for quantitative empirical work. In this chapter, I review some of this literature, focusing specifically on quantitative empirical research in the following areas: (a) construction of Marxist national accounts, (b) analysis of classical theories of relative prices, (c) probabilistic political economy, (d) profitability analyses and (e) analysis of classical-Marxian growth, distribution and biased technical change. The choice of these topics derives from my own research interests and expertise. Naturally, then, many other interesting and important lines of empirical research in Marxian political economy will not be surveyed in this chapter. That is why this is a *selective* survey, as the title of the chapter makes clear and so, I make no claims about comprehensiveness.

The rest of the chapter is organized as follows. In Section 2, I provide a quick review of theoretical debates in the labour theory of value that started with the so-called transformation problem in Volume III of Capital. I argue that the Sraffa-based critique of the 1970s was the culmination of a long tradition that had criticized Marx on his handling of the transformation problem, and, more importantly, that this episode was extremely productive for Marxist

Analytical Political Economy, First Edition. Edited by Roberto Veneziani and Luca Zamparelli.

political economy. It challenged Marxist scholarship and elicited creative responses. I briefly outline five different Marxist responses to the Sraffa-based critique, and then spend more time, in subsequent sections, discussing two of these responses that have generated impressive quantitative empirical work. But before taking that up, I review research work, in Section 3, on a topic that has widespread acceptance among Marxist scholars, both as to its usefulness and to its broad methodology: construction of national accounts on the basis of Marxist principles.

In Section 4, I return to the value controversy and survey quantitative empirical research associated with the Standard Interpretation, where the primary issue under investigation is the deviation of prices from values. In Section 5, I continue discussion of the value controversy and review work that derives from a probabilistic approach to political economy. In the following two sections, I survey work on topics that have generated impressive research output but do not directly connect to the value controversy. Section 6 discusses the literature on profitability analysis, and Section 7 surveys empirical work related to the classical-Marxian theories of growth, distribution and technical change. In the concluding section, I summarize the main lines of the review and also highlight two interesting puzzles. Mathematical proofs and definitions are collected in an Online Appendix that is available from this book's website and/or from the author upon request.

2. The Value Controversy

The relationship between the 'value' and 'price' of commodities has been an important issue of investigation in the classical-Marxian tradition for more than two centuries. In the context of such discussions, 'value' is defined as the total socially necessary abstract labour time directly and indirectly needed to produce (and therefore embodied in) a commodity with current technology and average intensity of work effort. Thus, values of commodities are measured in units of time, for example, hours. On the other hand, the category of 'price' refers to the set of prices that would arise in the long run when rates of profit are equalized across all industries (these long-run equilibrium prices are referred to in the literature as *prices of production*, or *production prices*, or *natural prices*). The price of production, like any other price, of a commodity is measured in units of money, for example, U.S. dollars. Both Ricardo and Marx were aware of the fact that *relative* prices (of production) and *relative* values were related to each other in complicated ways and need not necessarily coincide. But they had different ways of understanding this relationship. That is where I start the story.

2.1 *Ricardo, Marx and Bortkiewicz*

Ricardo thought that the two ratios—relative prices and relative values—were approximately equal for individual commodities. After examining ample textual evidence, Stigler (1958) summarized this contention with the famous quip that Ricardo had a 93% labour theory of value, with the 93% figure capturing the approximation involved. On the other hand, Marx understood that profit rate equalization and different compositions of capital across industries would necessarily lead to a deviation of relative prices (of production) from relative values of individual commodities. Hence, he conceptualized the equivalence between values and prices at the aggregate level (Marx, 1991). For him, the process of equalization of the rate of profit was driven by the movement of capital across industries from lower (than average) to higher (than average) rates of profit. This process tended to push the economy, in the long run, towards a state where all industries earned a uniform rate of profit and commodities exchanged at prices of production. Since industries differed in their composition of capital, this meant that individual prices and values necessarily diverged from each other.

For Marx, emergence of a uniform rate of profit (and prices of production) was primarily a way of conceptualizing the redistribution of surplus value across industries enforced by competitive pressures. He thought that *both* surplus value and total value would be preserved in this process of 'transformation' of values into prices (of production). That is why he proposed the aggregate value–price equivalence as the cornerstone of his labour theory of value in Volume III of Capital: total value = total price, and total surplus value = total profits.

At this point, the reader might wonder as to how Marx could have claimed the equivalence between total value and total price (or total surplus value and total profits) when the quantities in the two sides of this equality are measured in different units. After all, as I have noted above, values are measured in units of (labour) hours and prices are measured in units of a currency (dollars, say). The answer lies in the fact that Marx implicitly used, all through the three volumes of Capital, what Duncan Foley (1982) has called a monetary expression of value (MEV) or what later theorists have called a monetary expression of labour time (MELT).[1] The MELT is the quantity of money (i.e. units of the currency) that is equivalent to 1 hour of social labour. Thus, a value magnitude could be multiplied with the MELT to generate its price (monetary) equivalent. Using the MELT, Marx could freely move between values and prices so that when he discusses price–value deviations, both terms (of the equality or inequality) are expressed in terms of the same units.

With this small but necessary detour on units of measurement, let us return to the main narrative. Immediately upon the publication of Volume III of Capital in 1894, critics (like the Austrian economist Eugen von Böhm-Bawerk) discovered two problems in Marx's transformation procedure: prices of inputs had not been transformed (even as prices of outputs had been), and the rate of profit had been calculated in value terms (whereas a consistent procedure would need to calculate it in price terms). While the two errors in Marx's procedure could be easily corrected, as shown by the German statistician-economist Ladislaus von Bortkiewicz in 1907, it was no longer possible, using the correct procedure, to derive both aggregate value–price equalities that Marx had asserted. In a sense, this was the first step away from Marx's analysis: *only one* of the aggregate value–price equalities could hold (von Bortkiewicz, 1949).

2.2 The Standard Interpretation and the Sraffa-Based Critique

Revival of interest in Marxian economics in the 1960s and 1970s saw further development and elaboration of the Bortkiewicz argument in the works of, among others, Francis Seton, Nobuo Okishio and Michio Morishima. The Seton–Okishio–Morishima contribution recast the question in the Leontief-Sraffa input–output framework, thereby making explicit the use-value basis and sectoral interdependence of capitalist production. At the same time, it generalized the analysis of Marx (five industries) and Bortkiewicz (three departments) to an *n*-commodity world. The Seton–Okishio–Morishima contribution demonstrated that in a general circulating capital model, *relative* prices and a uniform rate of profit could be derived rigorously from data on technology and the real wage (commodity) bundle. But, an additional 'normalization condition' was needed to derive absolute prices, and either of Marx's aggregate value–price equalities could be used for the purpose (Seton, 1957; Okishio, 1963; Morishima and Catephores, 1978). This was the second step away from Marx's analysis: *none* of the aggregate value–price equalities could be derived; instead, one of them had to be *assumed* as a normalization condition.

The Seton–Okishio–Morishima framework of the labour theory of value, sometimes known as the Standard Interpretation, was subjected to a serious Sraffa-based critique in the 1970s, most prominently by Ian Steedman (1977). The main thrust of the critique was an argument of redundancy. Given data on technology and the real wage bundle, one could calculate the uniform rate of profit and prices of production. Hence, there was no need for value categories. Value was conceptually redundant. Even though this critique was not new—the same point had been made previously by Paul Samuelson (1971) and seven decades earlier by the Russian economist Dmitriev (1974/1902)—it was forceful and provocative. Paradoxically, the Sraffa-based critique was also extremely productive for Marxist political economy. In responding to the Sraffa-based critique, Marxist political economy renewed itself. By the early 1980s, one could discern several strands of Marxist political economy that had emerged as a response to the Sraffa-based critique. Many of these strands opened up new, or continued older, lines of scholarly work and research. Without claiming to be comprehensive, I would direct the attention of readers to five strands.

2.3 *Marxist Responses to the Sraffa-Based Critique*

The first response that developed in the 1970s through the work of scholars like Ben Fine, Laurence Harris, Simon Mohun and others emphasized the difference between the Ricardian understanding of value as 'embodied labour' and the Marxian understanding as 'abstract labour'. While this strand opened up interesting theoretical questions, to the best of my knowledge, it did not materialize into a progressive research program with quantitative empirical work (for a recent exposition of this strand, see Fine *et al.*, 2004).

The second response came from within the Seton–Okishio–Morishima framework in the form of the Fundamental Marxian Theorem (FMT). The FMT demonstrated that positive profits can arise if and only if there is positive surplus value. Since it is a 'if and only if' claim, the FMT is a weak response to the Sraffa-based critique. It shows that surplus value is necessary for profits, but equally well that profits are necessary for surplus value. Moreover, the FMT did not lead to any empirical work.

The third response emerged in the work of Anwar Shaikh (1977, 1984), who continued to use a Standard Interpretation of the labour theory of value. His main claim was similar to Ricardo's: value and price magnitudes are *approximately* equal at the level of individual commodities. In his 1984 paper, Shaikh developed a theoretical argument demonstrating that the deviation of prices from values would be 'small' and then used data from the Italian and U.S. economies to show that his claim is empirically valid. Anwar Shaikh's work on this question has given rise to a large literature that I will review below in the section on 'classical theories of relative prices'.

The fourth response came from the work of two mathematicians, Emmanuel Farjoun and Moshé Machover, who brought a probabilistic approach to political economy. Farjoun and Machover (1983) argued that most economic variables—like price, rate of profit and wage—are non-degenerate random variables, each with their own probability distribution functions. This means that equilibrium in a capitalist economy should be characterized by a *distribution* of the rate of profit, instead of a single, uniform rate of profit. Looked at from within a probabilistic perspective, the Sraffa-based critique is based on the erroneous postulate of *a* uniform rate of profit as characterizing long-run equilibrium; hence, its conclusions are invalid. In addition to offering a rebuttal of the Sraffa-based critique, Farjoun and Machover (1983) also developed a positive theory of the distribution of the rate of profit and value–price deviations.

This approach, which I will call Probabilistic Political Economy, has seen some recent interesting work that significantly extends the original work of Farjoun and Machover (1983). I review some of this literature below in the section on 'probabilistic political economy'.

The final response to the Sraffa-based critique came through the New Interpretation (NI) of Marxian economics, developed independently by Duncan Foley and Gérard Duménil in the late 1970s. The NI emphasized Marx's insistence that the value–price equivalence be conceptualized at the aggregate level *only*. But instead of trying to derive such equivalence from more primitive principles, the NI *defined* the labour theory of value to be that equivalence. The twin conceptual innovations of 'value of money' and 'value of labour power' anchored the aggregate equivalence, and created a theoretically informed and consistent accounting framework (for details, see Section B of the Online Appendix). While this aggregate accounting framework does not rule it out, the NI has not generated any work that directly addresses the value–price relationship at lower levels of aggregation. Instead, researchers who adhere to the NI have used the consistent accounting framework as a springboard for interesting empirical work in other areas like profitability analysis, analysis of biased technical change, etc.

Before I review the empirical work related to the classical theory of prices, the probabilistic interpretation of value theory, profitability analysis and biased technical change, I would like to acquaint readers with an important body of empirical work in the Marxist tradition: construction of National Accounts using a consistent classical Marxist framework.

3. Marxian National Accounts

The aim of Marxian national accounts is to generate estimates of the total value produced in an economy over a period of time, as also its component parts—constant capital, variable capital and surplus value. There is a long tradition that has attempted this task, including Mage (1963), Wolff (1977), Moseley (1982), Shaikh and Tonak (1994), Mohun (2005), Olsen (2011) and Paitaridis and Tsoulfidis (2012). In this paper, I will focus my comments on the groundbreaking work of Shaikh and Tonak (1994), which is, in a sense, a culmination of the previous literature on this issue and also the most comprehensive work to date.[2] Traditional national accounts provide the basic data source for constructing Marxian national accounts. But to use the data from traditional national accounts for estimating Marxian value categories, two important distinctions have to be conceptualized and empirically operationalized: (a) the distinction between production and nonproduction activities; and (b) the distinction between productive and unproductive labour.

3.1 *Theoretical Considerations*

To understand the first distinction, we can divide the basic activities of social reproduction into two mutually exclusive and exhaustive groups: production and non-production. The difference between the two is crucial: while production results in the creation of new use values (wealth) on a net basis, non-production uses up wealth without creating new wealth. Non-production activities can, in turn, be divided into three mutually exclusive and exhaustive groups: distribution, social maintenance and personal consumption. Distribution involves activities that transfer use values, titles to use values or sums of money from one set of economic agents to another. Social maintenance refers to all activities that are geared towards the maintenance and reproduction of the social order. Personal consumption includes all activities involved in the maintenance and reproduction of individuals within the social order.

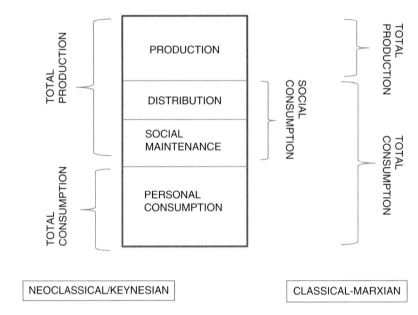

Figure 1. Alternative Classifications of the Four Basic Activities of Social Reproduction in the Neoclassical/Keynesian and Classical-Marxian traditions.

All schools of economic thought distinguish between production and consumption. Moreover, they agree that production creates wealth and consumption uses up wealth. The difference between the neoclassical and classical-Marxian traditions arises from the characterization of the activities of distribution and social maintenance. For the neoclassical (and Keynesian) tradition, these activities are understood as production as long they are marketable and some entity is willing to pay for the activity or the product arising therefrom. The classical-Marxian tradition differs sharply by arguing that distribution and social maintenance should *not* be understood as production; rather, they should be understood as social consumption. This is because they *use up* rather than creating new use values.

These alternative classifications of the basic activities of social reproduction by the neoclassical/Keynesian and classical-Marxian traditions can be summarized in Figure 1. For the neoclassical/Keynesian tradition, personal consumption is coterminous with total consumption and total production is the sum of distribution, social maintenance and production. In sharp contrast, for the classical-Marxian tradition, distribution and social maintenance together make up social consumption, and the sum of social and personal consumption gives total consumption. Total production, on the other hand, is just production proper.

To grasp the second distinction, that is, the distinction between productive and unproductive labour, we can begin by noting that production, distribution and social maintenance can each involve three different types of labour—labour that creates use values for direct use, labour that creates use values for sale for income and labour that creates use values for sale for profit. The classical-Marxian framework argues that the first type of labour creates use values, the second type creates use values and value and the third type creates use values, value and surplus value. With this understanding, the classical-Marxian tradition defines productive labour as all labour that produces surplus value. All other labour is defined to be unproductive because it does not produce surplus value (and capital).[3]

3.2 Empirical Operationalization

The empirical operationalization of Marxian national accounts for the U.S. economy relies on three data sources: (a) input–output (IO) tables for benchmark years, (b) national income and product accounts (NIPA) for non-benchmark years and (c) Bureau of Labour Statistics (BLS) data for all years.

Traditional IO tables contain comprehensive information about two types of interindustry flows in an economy over a period of time (usually a year). First, for each industry they provide information about the inputs used up and the value added created, the sum of the two being the gross output (revenue). Second, they provide information about the precise manner in which the gross product of any industry is used, that is, either as an intermediate input in some industry or for a final use (personal consumption, investment, government purchases or net export).

Therefore, the first step in the construction of Marxian national accounts is to start with data from the published IO tables, re-classify industries to operationalize the distinction between production and nonproduction activities and add the gross output for all industries in the former category to arrive at an estimate of total value produced. To do so, a researcher needs to answer the following question: which industries should be included in the production sector? To answer this question, we need to keep a peculiarity of IO tables in mind. They record transactions in terms of producers' prices, instead of purchasers' prices. Hence, the value of a commodity gets realized in two steps. In the first step, the producer sells the commodity to a wholesaler or retailer, and in the second step, the wholesaler or retailer sells it to the final user. Thus, *the sum of the gross output of production and trade activities provide an estimate of the total value produced in the economy.*[4]

To be more precise, the production sector includes three types of industries: all industries that produce *goods* like agriculture, mining, manufacturing, etc.; all *productive services* industries like transportation, entertainment, lodging, cooking, healthcare, education, utilities, etc.; and all government enterprises. On the other hand, the trade sector includes the wholesale and retail trade industries, including government trading enterprises, and a part of the real estate sector—the part that deals with building, equipment and car rentals (because rental sale is akin to selling the commodity piecemeal over its lifetime).

Following Shaikh and Tonak (1994), we can call the production and trade sector together as the 'primary flows' sector and note that the gross output of this sector is the total value produced in the economy. While industries in the primary flows sector derive their revenues from the production and sale of the commodity product, revenues of all other industries—which take the form of ground rent, finance charges and fees, interest charges, royalties of various types, insurance charges and taxes—are derivatives of primary flows in the following sense: they are either a recirculation of money flows generated by primary flows, or are a circulation of socially validated claims upon parts of primary flows, or both. Hence, we can club together all other industries into the 'secondary flows' sector and note that their 'output' cannot be counted as creating new value.

With an estimate of the total value (TV^*) as the sum of the gross output of the industries in the primary flows sector (production, GO_p, and trade, GO_t)

$$TV^* = GO_p + GO_t \qquad (1)$$

we move to the next step and estimate the constant capital (C^*) as the sum of material inputs (M'_p) and depreciation (D_p) of the production sector

$$C^* = M'_p + D_p \qquad (2)$$

It is worth pointing out that while we have included the gross output of the trade sector in the computation of total value, we have excluded the material inputs (M'_t) and depreciation (D_t) of the trade sector from the calculation of constant capital. To understand the reason for this let us compare two scenarios.

In the first scenario, producers directly sell commodities to final users; in the second scenario, producers sell commodities to wholesaler/retailers at the 'producers' price', and the latter then sell the commodities to final users at the 'purchasers' price'. Note that there is no difference between the two scenarios as far as the process of production is concerned. Since a classical-Marxian perspective assumes that value can only be produced in the sphere of production, the total value and its components—constant capital, variable capital and surplus value—are going to be the same in the two scenarios. The only difference between the two scenarios arises with regard to the *distribution* of surplus value. In the first scenario, the total surplus value is realized as the profit of the producer. In the second scenario, the total surplus value is realized as the profit of the producer *and* the total trade margin, that is, the total revenue of the trade sector. Total trade margin, in turn, is the sum of intermediate inputs, wages and profits of the trade sector. Hence, when we calculate total value, we need to add the gross output of production and trade, but when we compute constant (and variable) capital, we need to exclude the trade sector (because the value of intermediate inputs in the trade sector is part of surplus value and not constant capital).

With estimates of total value and constant capital, we can compute Marxian value added (MVA^*) as

$$MVA^* = TV^* - C^* \tag{3}$$

So far, we have not yet had to use the distinction between productive and unproductive labour, but in the next step, when we compute variable capital, it will become salient. Variable capital (V^*) is defined as the total wage bill of the productive workers in the production sector. Thus, the first task in computing variable capital is to separate out the productive and unproductive workers in the production sector.

The primary source of information on employment for the U.S. economy is the NIPA, which provides data on persons engaged in production (PEP) for all industries. PEP is the sum of full-time equivalent employees (FEE) and self-employed persons (SEP). The NIPA data do not contain any information to distinguish productive and unproductive labour. Hence, we turn to employment data provided by the BLS, which distinguishes between supervisory workers and production/non-supervisory workers. Using the ratio of the latter to total employment is a good estimate of the share of productive workers in any industry. Hence, if j indexes industries in the production sector, then an estimate of productive workers in industry j is given by

$$L^p_j = \rho_j \times PEP_j \tag{4}$$

where ρ_j is the ratio of productive workers to total employment in industry j (from BLS), and PEP_j is the total employment in industry j (from NIPA). Then, the sum total of all productive workers in production is given by

$$L^p = \sum_j L^p_j \tag{5}$$

where the index j runs over all industries in the production sector.

With an estimate of total productive workers in production in place, the next task is to compute their wage bill (or employee compensation). To do so, we need to draw on data from both the NIPA and BLS. Unit wage of productive (production and non-supervisory) workers is available from the BLS. But BLS wage data do not include wage supplements like employer contributions to social security and pension funds. Since the cost of labour power should include total wage and wage equivalents, we turn to data on employee compensation from the NIPA that includes supplements to wages. We can use both sets of information to define employee compensation for productive workers in industry j as

$$e\,c_j = \left(w'_p\right) \times \left(\frac{EC}{WS}\right)_j \qquad (6)$$

where w'_p is the unit wage of production and non-supervisory workers (from BLS), EC is the employee compensation (from NIPA), and WS is wage and salary accruals (from NIPA). The product of employee compensation and productive labour summed over all industries in the production sector provides an estimate of variable capital

$$V^* = \sum_j V_j = \sum_j \left(ec_j \times L_j^p\right) \qquad (7)$$

where the index j runs over all industries in the production sector, and L_j^p is the productive labour in industry j.[5]

The final step is to calculate the surplus value as

$$S^* = MVA^* - V^* \qquad (8)$$

which allows us to compute the rate of surplus value as

$$s\,v^* = \frac{S^*}{V^*} \qquad (9)$$

and the rate of profit as

$$r^* = \frac{S^*}{K} \qquad (10)$$

where K is the total stock of fixed non-residential gross private capital valued at replacement cost.

Using the methodology outlined above, Shaikh and Tonak (1994) report several interesting findings about the U.S. economy over the period from 1948 to 1989. First, they find that there is a dramatic increase in the share of non-production workers in the total pool of workers. This reflects the corresponding increase in the share of non-production activities in the aggregate economy. Shaikh and Tonak (1994) offer the increase of non-production activities as a possible explanation of the productivity slowdown in the U.S. economy from the early 1970s.[6] Second, they find that the rate profit has a pronounced tendency to fall over the period of analysis. This, according to them, supports Marx's hypothesis about the tendency for the rate of profit to fall over time (I will have more to say on this important topic in Section 6.2). The third striking finding from Marxian national accounts is that the 'social wage' of production workers have been negative for most of the post-war period. This means that production workers, as a group, have paid more taxes to the State than they have received back in benefits.[7] The final interesting finding is that values are 'close to' prices, a finding that I will examine in greater detail in Section 4.

The usefulness of the classical-Marxian idea of distinguishing between production and non-production activities, and between productive and unproductive labour is also highlighted in recent work on the employment-output linkage. Basu and Foley (2013) note that one of the ways in which received wisdom on economics was taken by surprise in and after the financial and economic crisis of 2008–2009 was with regard to predicting the depth of the downturn and the weakness of the recovery. While there was some discussion of jobless recoveries, the mainstream literature has not been able to appreciate the significant weakening of the *linkage* between output growth, as measured by the growth rate of real GDP, and changes in the un-employment rate over the whole business cycle. Thus, not only does unemployment fall by much less during recoveries than would be predicted by the past (jobless recoveries), it also increases by much more during recessions than would be predicted by past trends (severe job loss downturns).

Basu and Foley (2013) demonstrate that this weakening of the linkage between measured aggregate output and employment has been gathering pace since the early 1980s. One way to understand this weakening is to realize that the standard national accounts overestimate value added (real GDP) because they fail to exclude sectors that do not produce value—like finance, insurance and real estate—from the ambit of calculation. Basu and Foley (2013) use a simple classical-Marxian methodology to re-calculate value added by excluding the finance, insurance and real estate from the standard measures of aggregate real GDP. They call this the 'measurable value added' and show that it tracks movements in the unemployment rate much better than the standard measures of aggregate output. While this partly accounts for the weakening of the linkage between measured aggregate output and employment (driven by the growth to dominance of the financial sector in the post-war U.S. economy), Basu and Foley (2013) also discuss other issues, like globalization of production and flexibilization of employment, as possible contributing factors.

4. Classical Theory of Relative Prices

The basic framework for empirical analysis of the value–price relationship in the Standard Interpretation literature derives from a theoretical relationship between relative prices and rel-ative values mediated by ratios of integrated capital–labour ratios. I will give a very brief sketch of the argument here; for details see Section A of the Online Appendix and Shaikh (1984).

Let $p_{ij} = \frac{p_i}{p_j}$ and $\lambda_{ij} = \frac{\lambda_i}{\lambda_j}$ be the relative price and relative value of commodity i and j, re-spectively; then

$$p_{ij} = \lambda_{ij} \times \left\{ \frac{1 + \frac{r}{w} k_i^T}{1 + \frac{r}{w} k_j^T} \right\} \tag{11}$$

where r and w refer to the uniform rate of profit and wage rate, respectively, and

$$k_i^T \equiv \frac{K_i^T}{L_i^T} = \frac{K_i + K_i^{(1)} + K_i^{(2)} + K_i^{(3)} + \cdots}{L_i + L_i^{(1)} + L_i^{(2)} + L_i^{(3)} + \cdots} \tag{12}$$

is the (vertically) integrated capital–labour ratio, that is, the ratio of integrated capital stock, K_i^T, and integrated labour, L_i^T (Pasinetti, 1973). The integrated labour, L_i^T, is the sum of the direct labour required to produce commodity i, and the sum of the labour required to produce the means of production required in the production of commodity i, and the labour required to produce the means of production of the means of production required in the production of commodity i, and so on (integrated capital, K_i^T, is defined in an analogous manner).

The theoretical results contained in equations (11) and (12) have two important implica-tions. First, the result was derived without imposing *any* aggregate normalization condition. In particular, it avoids imposing either of the aggregate equalities that Marx thought would hold: total prices = total value, and total surplus value = total profits. This increases the generality and applicability of the result, and also distinguishes it from the NI, where an aggregate value–price equality *is* the labour theory of value.

Second, it offers a *partial rebuttal* of the claim that price and values must diverge from each other because sectoral organic compositions are very different from each other. It is *partial* because it accepts that prices and values will diverge, and it is a *rebuttal* because it shows that the divergence will be small. To see the latter claim, note that the integrated capital–labour ratio is a *weighted average* of actual capital–labour ratios for all stages of production going back indefinitely. Hence, its variation across sectors is bound to be much smaller than variation in actual capital labour ratios. To be more precise, this argument suggests that even when actual capital–labour ratios k_i and k_j are very different from each other, we can have $k_i^T \cong k_j^T$ as long as the economy is sufficiently interdependent. This means that the term multiplying relative values on the Right hand side (RHS) of equation (11) is 'close' to unity. Hence, this opens up the possibility that relative prices and relative values might be 'close' to each other even when there is large variation in capital–labour ratios across sectors.

The model in equations (11) and (12) is also the basis of empirical analysis of the claim that values and prices are approximately equal. There are two methods of analysis that have been used in the literature, a regression-based method and a non-regression-based method.

4.1 Regression-Based Methodology

Taking logarithms of equation (11) gives the bivariate regression model that has been widely used for empirical analysis

$$\ln\left(p_{ij}\right) = \alpha + \beta \times \ln\left(\lambda_{ij}\right) + u_{ij} \tag{13}$$

where a comparison with equation (11) suggests that

$$\alpha + u_{ij} = \ln\left(\frac{1 + \frac{r}{w}k_i^T}{1 + \frac{r}{w}k_j^T}\right)$$

A high value of R^2 (the coefficient of determination) from the estimation of equation (13)—most researchers using this method have found values of the R^2 in excess of 0.9—is interpreted as evidence in support of the Standard Interpretation (or Ricardian) hypothesis that relative values and relative prices are approximately equal (Shaikh, 1984; Cockshott and Cottrell, 1997; Tsoulfidis and Maniatis, 2002).

There seems to be a methodological problem in this approach because the magnitude of the R^2 is not the correct way to test the underlying theory. To see this, note that the theory in equations (11) and (12) does not have *any* implications for the R^2 in the bivariate regression model (13) estimated by OLS. Instead, the theory suggests that $k_i^T \cong k_j^T$ so that the researcher needs to test whether

$$\frac{1 + \frac{r}{w}k_i^T}{1 + \frac{r}{w}k_j^T} = 1 \tag{14}$$

which is equivalent to testing if

$$\ln\left(\frac{1 + \frac{r}{w}k_i^T}{1 + \frac{r}{w}k_j^T}\right) = 0 \tag{15}$$

Hence, because the expected value of the error term in equation (13) is zero by construction, the theory in equation (11) would lead to the test of the following joint null hypothesis

$$H_0 : \alpha = 0 \ \& \ \beta = 1 \tag{16}$$

with respect to the parameters in equation (13) and can be conducted as a F-test. Moreover, the test of the null hypothesis in equation (16) has a straightforward graphical interpretation: in a bivariate regression of log relative prices on log relative values, as represented by equation (13), the regression line passes through the origin and has a slope of unity.[8] None of the papers that have used this methodology have tested the null hypothesis in equation (16), including Shaikh (1984), Petrovic (1987), Cockshott and Cottrell (1997) and Tsoulfidis and Maniatis (2002). This lacuna could be addressed in future research.

4.2 Non-Regression-Based Methodologies

Non-regression-based methodologies have proceeded by constructing various measures of 'distance' between the vector of prices and the vector of values. To operationalize this methodology let us define the following n-vector (assuming that there are n sectors in the economy):

$$x = \left[\frac{p_1}{\lambda_1} \ \frac{p_2}{\lambda_2} \ \frac{p_3}{\lambda_3} \ \cdots \ \frac{p_n}{\lambda_n} \right] \tag{17}$$

Each element of the n-vector is the ratio of the price—price of production, or market price or some other price—and the value of the product in that sector in the economy.[9] If the vector x was the unit vector i (which is an n-vector of ones), then for all the n sectors, values and prices would be identically equal. Hence, the basic method of analysis in this approach is to define a measure of 'distance' between x and the unit vector i (which represents the benchmark case where the equality of value and price holds completely) and see whether it is relatively small.

Petrovic (1987) uses a measure of distance called root-mean-square-per-cent-error (RMS%E), which is the (positive) square root of the (arithmetic) mean squared (per cent) deviation between x and i:

$$RMS\%E = \sqrt{\frac{1}{n} \sum_j \left(\frac{p_j}{\lambda_j} - 1 \right)^2} \tag{18}$$

Ochoa (1989) uses a similar measure of distance called mean absolute deviation (MAD), which is the (arithmetic) mean of the absolute deviation between elements of x and i

$$MAD = \frac{1}{n} \sum_i \left| \frac{p_j}{\lambda_j} - 1 \right| \tag{19}$$

and Shaikh (1998) uses a related measure called mean absolute-weighted deviation (MAWD), which is an weighted average of the absolute deviation between elements of x and i

$$MAWD = \sum_j \left| \frac{p_j}{\lambda_j} - 1 \right| \mu_j$$

where $\mu_j = \lambda_j z_j / \sum \lambda_j z_j$ is the weight applied to the jth term, and z denotes the integrated profit–wage ratio (for an exact definition of z, see A.11 and A.12 in Section A of the Online Appendix).

All these measures suffer from the problem that their value depends on the choice of the *numeraire*. To deal with this problem, Steedman and Tomkins (1998) propose an alternative measure of distance:

$$d = \sqrt{2(1 - \cos\alpha)} \tag{20}$$

where α is the angle between the vectors x and i. Motivated by the discussion in Steedman and Tomkins (1998), Fröhlich (2013) uses the tangent of the angle between the vectors x and i as his preferred measure of (angular) distance: $\tan\alpha = \frac{\sigma_x}{\mu_x}$, where σ_x and μ_x are the standard deviation and mean, respectively, of the elements of the vector x. In line with this literature, Shaikh (2016) proposes another unit-independent and scale-free measure, which he calls the *classical distance measure*, as

$$\delta_c \sum_j \left|\frac{p_j}{\text{d}_j} - 1\right| \omega_j \tag{21}$$

where $\text{d}_j = \mu \text{w}_j \lambda_j$ and μ denotes the monetary equivalent of total labour time (ratio of aggregate value added measured in monetary units and total labour time), w_j denotes the jth sector's relative wage (ratio of wage in sector j to the total wage in the whole economy), λ_j denotes, as before, the value of commodity j and $\omega_j = p_j X_j / \sum_j p_j X_j$.

The general finding in this literature is that the distance measure attains 'small' values for a whole range of capitalist economies for which these distance measures have been computed. For instance, the smallest value of RMS%E in table 1 in Petrovic (1987) is 4.45% (for the Yugoslav economy in 1978); similarly, the smallest value of α in table A1 in Fröhlich (2013) is 3.16 degrees (for the German economy). In a similar vein, Shaikh (2016) finds that the classical distance measure evaluated with prices of production and values (what he calls direct prices) for the U.S. economy over the period 1947–1998 attains a value of about 13% (table 9.16, Shaikh, 2016). These are interesting findings and seem to support Ricardo's claim that values and prices of production are approximately equal.

5. Probabilistic Political Economy

Classical economists have conceptualized competition in capitalist economies as a complex and turbulent process. Their distinct and powerful conception of capitalist competition was formulated through the theory of capital mobility. They argued that in capitalist economies, individual capitals, that is, individual capitalist firms, are constantly under pressure to move from industries with lower than (economy-wide) average rate of profits towards industries with above average rates of profit. While the entry of capital into high profit industries would increase industry-level output and put downward pressure on prices and profit rates, the exit of capital from low profit industries would reduce industry-level output and push up prices and the rate of profit. Hence, the process of capital mobility would manifest itself as a pervasive *tendency* for the rate of profit to equalize across industries.

It is possible to interpret the tendency for profit rate equalization across industries as a description of the long-run behaviour of capitalist economies, as Marx did in Volume III of Capital. Understanding the long run as an ideal state of rest—the state towards which the economy is driven over very long periods of time—one can compute the set of prices that prevail in the long run as 'prices of production' using a single profit rate for all industries. Later theorists like Piero Sraffa used this procedure, and a large literature has followed him in studying classical questions about prices (of production), technology and profitability in this framework (see, for instance, Kurz and Salvadori, 1995; Shaikh, 2016).[10]

An alternative way to approach the mobility of capital is to interpret the tendency of profit rate equalization in a probabilistic framework. As the economy is buffeted by demand and supply shocks and as the flow of information is always less than perfect, the incessant movement of individual capitals in search of higher profit rates never settles down. Hence, the manifestation of capitalist competition should be visualized not as the emergence of a uniform rate of profit across all industries but as the generation of a stable *probability distribution* of industry-level profit rates.

5.1 *Probabilistic Political Economy, Mark I*

Farjoun and Machover (1983) proposed such a probabilistic interpretation of capital mobility in capitalist economies and developed arguments to derive the equilibrium distribution of two key variables of interest to Marxist political economy, the rate of profit and what they call the 'specific price' (which is defined as the price per unit of embodied labour). The empirical work that follows from this framework relates to testing whether actually observed profit rates and specific prices have the distribution that is posited by the theoretical arguments.

What is the distribution of the rate of profit in capitalist economies? Based on an analogy from statistical mechanics, Farjoun and Machover (1983) hypothesize that the rate of profit has a *gamma distribution* (details of the two-parameter gamma distribution can be found in Section C1 of the Online Appendix).

> In seeking theoretical expression for the distribution of R [rate of profit], a useful heuristic guide is provided by statistical mechanics. In a gas at equilibrium, the total kinetic energy of all the molecules is a given quantity. It can be shown that the 'most chaotic' partition of this total kinetic energy among the molecules results in a gamma distribution. Now, if we consider that in any given short period, there is a more-or-less fixed amount of social surplus ... and that capitalist competition is a very disorderly mechanism for partitioning this surplus among capitalists in the form of profit, then the analogy of statistical mechanics suggests that R may also have a gamma distribution. (Farjoun and Machover, 1983, p. 68)

Their next task was to derive the distribution of the specific price

$$\Psi(i) = \frac{p(i)}{\Lambda(i)} \tag{22}$$

where i indexes transactions taking place in some period T, $p(i)$ is the price paid in transaction i and $\Lambda(i)$ is the total amount of human labour embodied in the commodities that participated in transaction i. Thus, the specific price, $\Psi(i)$, is the price paid per unit of labour content in transaction i. An argument that relies on decomposing total price of any commodity into the sum of non-labour inputs, labour input and profit, and iterating back through the various stages of production of the non-material inputs can be used to show that the numerator in equation (22) is the sum of two terms

$$p(i) = w(i) + \pi(i) \tag{23}$$

where $w(i)$ is the sum of total wages paid to all workers who participated directly and indirectly in the production of commodities involved in transaction i, and $\pi(i)$ is the sum of total profits earned by all firms directly and indirectly involved in the production of commodities involved in transaction i.[11] If there are m firms in the economy, then the sum in equation (23) can be broken into value-added contributions (because value added is the sum of wages and profits) coming from each of these firms (some of which may be zero). Moreover, since this logic holds for each transaction, we can dispense with the index i. Thus,

$$\Psi = \sum_{j=1}^{m} \frac{w_j + \pi_j}{\Lambda} \tag{24}$$

where the sum in equation (24) runs over the total number of firms in the economy. Since any capitalist economy will have a large number of firms, some version of the central limit theorem can be invoked on equation (24) to suggest that the specific price is distributed as a normal random variable. Farjoun and Machover (1983) also derive the mean and variance of Ψ as $\mathbb{E}(\Psi) = 2$, and $\mathbb{V}(\Psi) = 1/3$, and thus propose that

$$\Psi \sim \mathbb{N}(2,\ 1/3) \tag{25}$$

What does the distribution of the observed rate of profit look like? Farjoun and Machover (1983, Ch. 8) present data on profit rates in the British non-oil manufacturing Industry in 1972 and 1981. After plotting the empirical distribution (figures 5 and 7), they impose a gamma distribution with shape and scale parameters 4.72 and 32, respectively, on top. The empirical distribution seems to visually match the imposed gamma distribution. This can be interpreted as suggestive evidence in support of the claim that the rate of profit is distributed as a gamma random variable.

In a recent study of the German economy for 2000 and 2004, Fröhlich (2013) has strengthened the visual results in Farjoun and Machover (1983) with more rigorous statistical tests. He finds that the empirical distribution of the rate of profit in Germany is well approximated by a gamma distribution with shape and scale parameters of 2.78 and 20.29 in 2004, and 2.03 and 15.65 in 2000. Moreover, a two-sample Kolmogorov–Smirnov test is not able to reject the null hypothesis that rate of profit data in 2000 and 2004 were drawn from the same continuous distribution (p-value $= 0.74$).[12] Fröhlich (2013) also tests the proposition that the 'specific price' (price per unit of labour content) is distributed as $\mathbb{N}(2,\ 1/3)$. He finds that the mean of specific price is close to 2 in both 2000 and 2004. But the distribution is better approximated as lognormal instead of normal. His results suggest that the logarithm of specific price is distributed as $\mathbb{N}(0.66,\ 0.21)$.

5.2 Probabilistic Political Economy, Mark II

The key shortcoming of Farjoun and Machover's (1983) analysis was that it used *ad hoc* arguments to derive the equilibrium distribution of the rate of profit; thus, it was not clear why the profit rate should have a gamma distribution. An alternative, but related, tradition in probabilistic political economy has built on the innovative ideas of statistical equilibrium developed in Foley (1994) to address this problem. This relatively recent literature has replaced the *ad hoc* arguments of Farjoun and Machover (1983) with a rigorous derivation of the equilibrium distribution (see Alfarano et al., 2012; Scharfenaker and Semieniuk, 2016).

The key idea used to derive the equilibrium distribution is the principle of maximum entropy (PME), which Foley (1994) had taken from the work of the physicist E. T. Jaynes (1957, 1978), and which was implicitly present in the informal arguments of Farjoun and Machover (1983). For a continuous random variable, X, with a probability density function, $f(x)$, defined over the whole real line, *entropy* is defined as $-\int_{-\infty}^{\infty} f(x) \log(f(x))dx$. This is understood as the degree of uncertainty associated with the possible realizations of the random variable, X. Interpreted as a principle of statistical inference, PME states that the random variable should be assigned a probability distribution that maximizes entropy subject to relevant constraints. Intuitively, maximizing entropy is akin to maximizing the uncertainty about the realizations of the random variable, and equivalently minimizing the informational bias of the inference procedure.

> Information theory provides a constructive criterion for setting up probability distributions on the basis of partial knowledge, and leads to a type of statistical inference which is called the maximum-entropy estimate. It is the least biased estimate possible on the given information; i.e., it is maximally noncommittal with regard to missing information. (Jaynes, 1957)

The probability distribution that emerges as the solution to the maximum entropy program, which we can call the *maximum entropy distribution*, is the best prediction we can make about the distribution of the random variable in question given our informational limitations (captured by the constraints). The constraint that the probabilities sum to unity, $\int_{-\infty}^{\infty} f(x)dx = 1$, will always be applicable, and with this as the only constraint the uniform distribution will be the maximum entropy distribution. Specific problems might furnish additional constraints, which will then give rise to other maximum entropy distributions.

Alfarano *et al.* (2012) use data from *Thomson Datastream* on 623 long-lived publicly traded non-bank U.S. firms, that is, those firms which were present in every year in the dataset over their period of study, 1980–2006, to plot empirical densities of the annual rate of profit (ratio of operating income and total assets). Yearly plots of the empirical densities show a tent-shaped distribution on a semi-log scale for most years, indicating that the Laplace distribution might be a good benchmark for the profit rate of long-lived firms (figure 3, Alfarano *et al.*, 2012). Various goodness-of-fit tests on the empirical distribution functions suggest that the hypothesis of a Laplace distribution cannot be rejected in most cases (appendix A, Alfarano *et al.*, 2012). In a follow-up exercise, Alfarano *et al.* (2012) expand their sample to all firms and plot empirical densities conditional on survival spans of firms for at least T years. They find that for small T, the distributions are asymmetric and much more leptokurtic to the left of the mode (figure 6, Alfarano *et al.*, 2012). In a similar contribution, Scharfenaker and Semieniuk (2016) use data for U.S. firms from the Compustat/CRSP Annual Northern American Fundamentals database for the period between 1962 and 2014, to show that firm-level profit rate distributions are approximated well with a Laplace distribution before 1980 and with an asymmetric Laplace distribution in the period since then. What could explain the increasing asymmetry of the Laplace distribution since 1980? An interesting hypothesis would be to use information from the conditional density plots from Alfarano *et al.* (2012), which suggests that in Scharfenaker and Semieniuk's (2016) sample, the proportion of short-lived firms might have increased since the early 1980s. Thus, neoliberalism might have had a negative impact on the average lifespan of firms.

To derive the empirically observed probability distributions of the rate of profit, Scharfenaker and Semieniuk (2016) and Alfarano *et al.* (2012) adopt different strategies. Scharfenaker and Semieniuk (2016) derive equilibrium distributions of the profit rate as the solution to maximum entropy programs with suitable constraints. The Laplace distribution (which is relevant for the period 1962–1980) arises as a maximum entropy distribution when there are two constraints: the probabilities sum to unity, $\int_{-\infty}^{\infty} f(x)dx = 1$; and the mean of the absolute deviation of the profit rate from an exogenous measure of central tendency is a constant, $\int_{-\infty}^{\infty} |x - \mu| f(x) dx = c$,

$$\max_{\{f(x) \geq 0 | x \in \mathbb{R}\}} \int_{-\infty}^{\infty} f(x) \log (f(x)) \, dx \tag{26}$$

subject to

$$\int_{-\infty}^{\infty} f(x) \, dx = 1 \tag{26.1}$$

and

$$\text{and} \int_{-\infty}^{\infty} |x - \mu| f(x) \, dx = c \tag{26.2}$$

The asymmetric Laplace distribution (which is relevant for the period 1980–2014) emerges as the maximum entropy distribution when there are three constraints, instead of two: the probabilities sum to unity, $\int_{-\infty}^{\infty} f(x) dx = 1$; and, the infra-modal observations have a different mean constraint from the supra-modal observations, that is, $\int_{-\infty}^{\mu} (\mu - x) f(x) dx = c_1$ and $\int_{\mu}^{\infty} (x - \mu) f(x) dx = c_2$, which provides another two constraints.

In these maximum entropy programs, argue Scharfenaker and Semieniuk (2016), the constraints are supposed to summarize our understanding about the process of capitalist competition. While these constraints can be seen as necessary to generate the maximum entropy distributions that the researcher is looking for (in this case the Laplace distributions), they are not fine grained enough to capture any intuitions about the process of competition. For instance, why should the mean constraint be specified in absolute deviation form and not in squared deviation form? Our understanding of competition does not allow us to choose between, for instance, these two specifications.

One way to proceed is to derive the maximum entropy distributions from a more primitive process that captures our intuitions about capitalist competition a little better. Alfarano et al. (2012) take this more ambitious route and derive the equilibrium distribution as a diffusion process. This is a continuous time stochastic process, X_t, which emerges as a solution to the following stochastic differential equation:

$$d X_t = -\frac{D}{2\sigma} \text{sign} (X_t - m) \left| \frac{X_t - m}{\sigma} \right|^{\alpha - 1} dt + \sqrt{D} dW_t \tag{27}$$

where D is a constant diffusion parameter, $\alpha, \sigma > 0$, $m \in \mathbb{R}$ and W_t is a Brownian motion (for a very brief introduction to diffusion processes, see Section C2 of the Online Appendix). The advantage of deriving the equilibrium distribution as a diffusion process is that this formulation allows the competitive process to be decomposed into a drift function and a diffusion function, with the drift function capturing the tendency for equalization of profit rates that operate on all firms and the diffusion function capturing idiosyncratic, firm-level forces.

I would like to end this brief review of probabilistic political economy with two critical comments. First, the classical view of competition as the mobility of capitals across industries and sectors seem to have implications about the distribution of the industry-level rate of profit, not the firm-level rate of profit. The tendency of the rate of profit to equalize operates at the level of industries and sectors and not firms. Thus, it might be useful to complement the existing analysis of the distribution of firm-level profit rates with an analysis of the distribution of industry-level profit rates. Second, the probabilistic approach to capitalist competition seems to boil down to the following: (a) identifying the theoretical distribution function that best describes the empirical distribution of the rate of profit; (b) identifying the constraint(s) that can be imposed on a maximum entropy program to get the theoretical distribution that was identified in the previous step as the maximand distribution; or, identifying a stochastic differential equation that can give the theoretical distribution identified in the previous step as its solution; and (c) using economic theory to motivate or justify the specific constraint(s) that was used in maximum entropy program or the specific stochastic differential equation that was used in the previous step. Thus, the burden of economic reasoning now falls squarely on some moment constraints in a maximum entropy program or a specific form of the drift and diffusion function defining a diffusion process. On this score, much work needs to be done to convince researchers that some new insight is gained from this approach about the real capitalist economy.

6. Profitability Analysis

Marxian political economy understands capitalism as a system driven by the logic of capital accumulation. Since the rate of profit is a key determinant of capital accumulation, a large Marxist literature has developed around the analysis of profitability, with at least two sub-strands. The first strand focuses on what we may call decomposition analysis, where short- or medium-run temporal movements in the rate of profit are, on the one hand, used to explain key developments in capitalist economies, and on the other, explained by movements of its components, suitably defined. One of the key substantive issues motivating this strand of profitability analysis has been the possible link between the rate of profit and structural crises of capitalism. A second, more recent, strand analyses long-run movements in the rate of profit and has used econometric analysis to empirically address Marx's law of the tendential fall in the rate of profit (understood as a long-run phenomenon).

6.1 Decomposition Analysis

Decomposition analysis comes in two varieties, determined by the time span of analysis, a medium-run analysis and a short-run analysis.

6.1.1 Medium-Run Decomposition Analysis

When a medium-run perspective is adopted, fluctuations of aggregate demand are abstracted from. Hence, to study the drivers of profitability over a medium-run time scale, a decomposition of the rate of profit into the share of profit and the output–capital ratio is typically used, that is,

$$r \equiv \frac{\Pi}{K} = \left(\frac{\Pi}{Y}\right) \times \left(\frac{Y}{K}\right) \tag{28}$$

where r is the rate of profit, Π is total profits, K is the stock of fixed capital and Y is value added. In the decomposition in equation (28), the profit share, Π/Y represents income distribution between capitalists and workers, and technology is represented by the output–capital ratio Y/K. Changes in the two factors are used to explain the observed movements of the rate of profit. This is followed by a detailed analysis of the evolution of both these components by further decomposing them into sub-components. To do so, the profit share is decomposed as follows:

$$\frac{\Pi}{Y} = \frac{Y - W}{Y} = 1 - \frac{W}{Y} = 1 - \frac{w}{y} \tag{29}$$

where W is the total wage bill, $w = W/(L * P_y)$ is the real product wage, $y = Y/(L * P_y)$ is the real labour productivity and P_y is some index of the price of value added (e.g. GDP deflator); and the output–capital ratio is decomposed as

$$\frac{Y}{K} = \left(\frac{Y_r}{K_r}\right) \times \left(\frac{P_y}{P_k}\right) = \left(\frac{Y_r/L}{K_r/L}\right) \times \left(\frac{P_y}{P_k}\right) \tag{30}$$

where Y_r is real value added, K_r is real capital stock, P_y is an index of the price of value added and P_k is an index of the price of capital stock. Dividing real value added and the real capital stock by the total labour input (measured in hours of number of workers) in the expression for the output–capital ratio in equation (30), we see that it is the product of a real ratio and a price ratio. The real ratio has real labour productivity in the numerator and a measure of the 'composition of capital' in the denominator. The price ratio has an index of the price of output in the numerator, and a price of capital stock in the denominator. Hence, changes in the real ratio can be conceptualized in terms of the effect of changes in the composition of capital on labour productivity, an approach that Marx often adopted.

Change in, or the growth rate of, each of the components in these decompositions is studied and then related to changes in broader political economic factors like the contours of class struggle, evolution of state policies, cross-border mobility of capital and other relevant factors. This approach has been used to study medium-run capitalist evolution, as also episodes of crises under capitalism (Duménil et al., 1984, 1985; Michl, 1988; Duménil and Lévy, 1993; Foley and Michl, 1999; Duménil and Lévy, 2004; Marquetti et al., 2010; Duménil and Lévy, 2011; Basu and Vasudevan, 2013; Mohun, 2013).

6.1.2 Short-Run Decomposition Analysis

When a short-run profitability analysis is of interest, the profit rate decomposition includes three terms. In addition to technology and distribution, capacity utilization rate is used as a variable to capture the effect of fluctuations in aggregate demand. Letting Z refer to capacity output, the three-part decomposition can be written as

$$r \equiv \frac{\Pi}{K} = \left(\frac{\Pi}{Y}\right) \times \left(\frac{Y}{Z}\right) \times \left(\frac{Z}{K}\right) \tag{31}$$

where the first term on the right Π/Y is the profit share, the second term Y/Z is the capacity utilization rate and the last term Z/K is the capacity–capital ratio. Just like in the medium-run analysis, each of the three terms in the decomposition is further decomposed into its real and nominal components for further, and detailed, study. Following the pioneering work of Weisskopf (1979), many scholars have used and extended this strand of the literature (e.g. Henley, 1987; Bakir and Campbell, 2009; Kotz, 2009; Izquierdo, 2013; Basu and Das, 2015).

6.2 Econometric Analysis of the LTFRP

Marx's claim in Volume III of Capital that the rate of profit has a tendency to fall with capitalist development, which he called the law of the tendential fall in the rate of profit (LTFRP), has generated an enormous literature over the past decades. While the theoretical literature has developed sophisticated arguments, the empirical literature on this issue, till very recently, was relatively less developed. Many researchers merely used exploratory data analysis, like visual inspection of time series plots or fitting trend lines to the profit rate series, to test the validity of the LTFRP.

Basu and Manolakos (2013) pointed out that there were two important shortcomings of this empirical literature. First, it did not take account of the time series properties of the rate of profit. This was important because whether the profit rate series was stationary or non-stationary would have important implications on empirical analyses of its long-run behaviour, including the validity of the LTFRP. Second, Marx's account of the LTFRP accorded an important role to counteracting factors but none of the existing studies took this into account.[13] Basu and Manolakos (2013) argued that failure to account for the effect of the counteracting factors on the observed time series of the rate of profit would invalidate any tests of the LTFRP.

The second point is important and bears some discussion. In Volume III, Marx offered a simple and powerful argument for the LTFRP. Capitalist competition and the struggle between capital and labour push capitalist firms to adopt labour-saving technical changes. The pronounced bias of technical change under capitalism expresses itself as the inexorable mechanization of the production process. This results in the continuous growth of the organic composition of capital, which pushes down the rate of profit. After outlining this argument for the LTFRP, Marx immediately notes the presence of powerful 'counteracting factors' in capitalist economies that would halt or even reverse the LTFRP: (1) the increasing intensity of exploitation of labour, which could increase the rate of surplus value; (2) the relative cheapening of the elements of constant capital; (3) the deviation of the wage rate from the value of labour power; (4) the existence and increase of a relative surplus population; and (5) the cheapening of consumption and capital goods through imports. Marx also mentioned an increase in share capital as a sixth counteracting influence. Yet the relationship between share capital and the rate of profit is not clear and therefore we can abstract from this variable, following Foley (1986).

The important point is that in periods when the counteracting factors were weak, the rate of profit would fall; when the counteracting factors were strong, the rate of profit would stop falling and might even rise. The result is that the observed profit rate series would not display a secularly declining trend. Hence, neither visual inspection of time series plots nor fitting trend lines to the profit rate series were the correct ways to test the validity of the LTFRP. To test the LTFRP, a researcher would first need to remove the effect of the counteracting factors from the profit rate series and only then investigate for the presence of a downward long-run trend. This is precisely what a regression analysis could do. Hence, Basu and Manolakos (2013) developed an econometric model to test the LTFRP where they regressed the logarithm of the rate of profit on a constant and a linear time trend, and controlled for the effect of the counteracting factors by including them in the model as additional covariates. After dealing with the possibility of a spurious regression and using data for the U.S. economy for the period, 1948–2007, they find evidence in support of the LTFRP: the rate of profit declined by 0.2% per annum over the period of analysis after counteracting factors had been controlled for.

7. Classical-Marxian Theories of Growth, Distribution and Technical Change

Over the past few decades, an impressive body of research has developed a classical-Marxian framework for studying growth, distribution and patterns of technical change in capitalist economies (see, for instance, Duménil and Lévy, 1995; Foley and Marquetti, 1997; Foley and Michl, 1999, 2004; Michl, 1999, 2002, 2009; Duménil and Lévy, 2003; Foley and Taylor, 2006). A key feature of this literature is that, having taken the Cambridge capital controversy seriously, it eschews the use of a smooth production function. This is an important contribution to the development of a framework for the analysis of growth of capitalist economies that is an alternative to the neoclassical framework.

This alternative framework recognizes the importance of biased technical change in capitalist economies. It has been observed that technical change is biased in capitalist economies, in the sense that labour and capital productivity does not grow symmetrically through time. In fact for a large group of capitalist countries and over long periods of time, labour productivity has been observed to have increased even as the output–capital ratio (capital productivity) has declined (or stagnated). In the language of macroeconomics, such a pattern of technical change would be characterized as labour-saving and capital-using. Interestingly, it also matches the depiction of the process of technical change under capitalism developed by Marx. Hence, Foley and Michl (1999) call this Marx-biased technical change (MBTC) and Duménil and Lévy (2003) describe it as trajectories à la Marx.

There are two reasons why such patterns of biased technical change might be interesting from a Marxist perspective. First, since the share of profits in national income has been relatively stable over long periods of time, especially before the 1980s, periods of rising labour productivity and declining output–capital ratio—the pattern seen with MBTC—puts downward pressure on the rate of profit and could precipitate a period of crisis. Hence, MBTC can become an important component of explanations of crisis tendencies in capitalist economies. Second, MBTC gives rise to an important proposition relating to the viability of technical change, that is, whether a new technique of production will be adopted by profit-maximizing capitalist firms, that can be used to derive competing testable implications about income distribution corresponding to a neoclassical and a classical-Marxian viewpoint. Hence, MBTC can be used to devise a test between the neoclassical and classical-Marxian theories of growth and distribution.

To get a handle on the second point, let us recall some definitions. A technique of production is the pair (x, ρ), where x is labour productivity and ρ is the output–capital ratio. The set of all currently existing techniques of production represents 'technology', and technological progress is addition of new techniques to technology. In a capitalist society, the distribution of income between the two fundamental classes—the wage rate w and the rate of profit v—can be represented by

$$w = x - kv \tag{32}$$

where w is the wage rate and $k = x/\rho$ is the capital intensity of a technique of production.[14] Represented in $v - w$ space, the relationship in equation (32) is a downward sloping straight line with an intercept x and slope $-k$, as depicted in Figure 2. We can call it the distribution schedule because it represents the class struggle over the distribution of income in capitalism.

To pose the question about the choice of technique, suppose the current best-practice technique of production is given by (x, ρ) and a new technique (x', ρ') becomes available with $x' = x(1 + \gamma)$, and $\rho' = \rho(1 = \chi)$. Note that each technique of production corresponds to a different distribution schedule in Figure 2. Now, suppose the current (real) wage rate is w and further that capitalist firms expected it to grow at some positive rate $\eta > 0$, so that $w' = w(1 + \eta)$, and let π denote the current profit share, that is, $\pi = (1 - w/x)$. Is the new technique of production 'viable', that is, would a profit-maximizing capitalist firm choose the new technique of production?

Let v_n^e denote the expected rate of profit that would arise if the new technique of production were to be adopted. Then,

$$v_n^e = \left(1 - \frac{w'}{x'}\right) \rho' \tag{33}$$

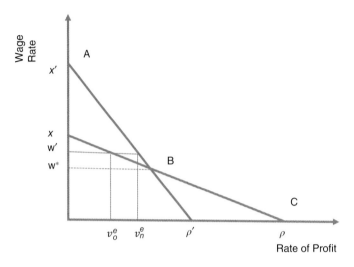

Figure 2. Marx-Biased Technical Change and the Choice of Technique.

If, on the other hand, the current technique of production continues to be used but the wage rate increases to w', the profit rate would be

$$v_o^e = \left(1 - \frac{w'}{x}\right)\rho \tag{34}$$

If the expected wage rate w' is bigger than the 'switch point' wage rate (the wage rate given by the intersection of the two distribution schedules)

$$w' > w^* \tag{35}$$

then the corresponding relationship among the profit rates is given by

$$v_n^e > v_o^e \tag{36}$$

That is, the expected profit rate when using the new technique of production is higher than the expected profit rate with the old technique. Hence, profit-maximizing capitalist firms will adopt the new technique of production, that is, the new technique of production will be viable. A little algebra shows that equation (36) will be satisfied if the following holds:

$$\pi < 1 + \frac{\chi(1+\gamma)}{(1+\eta)(\gamma-\chi)} = \pi^* \tag{37}$$

In the above analysis, the switch point wage rate (w^*) plays an important role. If the expected wage rate is higher than w^* then the firm will switch from the old to the new technique of production; if the expected wage rate is lower than or equal to w^*, then the firm will continue using the old technique. It is in this sense that the intersection of the two distribution schedules is a *switch* point.

But how does this relate to the neoclassical model? Recall that in a neoclassical framework, technology is represented by a smooth production function, for example, a Cobb–Douglas production function. In such a set-up, even a small change in the wage rate leads to a new technique of production being chosen. This is because in a neoclassical set-up the curve that represents the north–east frontier of the intersection of the two distribution schedules—the curve ABC—would be a smooth convex (to the origin) curve. Hence, every point on such a curve would be a switch point. Thus, in terms of the classical-Marxian model, the neoclassical position is represented by the condition that $w' = w^*$ or $\pi = \pi^*$, whereas the Marxian position is that $w' > w^*$ or $\pi < \pi^*$.

Basu (2010) considers two variants of the model in equations (35)–(37). The first variant has zero expected growth in the real wage rate, that is, $\eta = 0$; and the second has the expected real wage rate growing in tandem with labour productivity, that is, $\gamma = \eta$. The second variant is more realistic because it accords well with historical data suggesting roughly equal growth rate of productivity and wages before the 1980s. Hence, Basu (2010) uses the second variant to conduct empirical analysis in a cross-country regression framework with the following model

$$\pi_i^* = \alpha + \beta \pi_i + \text{controls} + u_i \tag{38}$$

To test the neoclassical versus the classical-Marxian models, he tests the joint null hypothesis

$$H_0 : \alpha = 0 \,\&\, \beta = 1 \tag{39}$$

with an F-test. Since the neoclassical model suggests that the viability parameter and the actual profit share are equal, rejection of the null hypothesis in equation (39) can be interpreted as evidence against the neoclassical model.

Using data from the Extended Penn World tables 2.1, Basu (2010) conducts the test for the period 1963–2000 for two sets of countries: (a) 25 OECD countries; and (b) 117 developed and developing countries (which include the 25 OECD countries). He reports high values of the F-statistic (which are significant at standard levels) for both sets of countries and concludes that there is strong evidence against the neoclassical viewpoint. Using data from the period 1963–1998, Michl (2009) also finds strong evidence—from cross-sectional, time series and pooled regressions—against the neoclassical model.

An alternative approach to test for the existence of MBTC is explored in Marquetti (2004) and by de Souza (2016). The basic idea used in these papers is the following. The incentive for labour-saving technical change increases under high wage pressure. Hence, there should be a causal relationship running from real wages to labour productivity. Since both real wages and labour productivity are unit root non-stationary variables, an eminently plausible hypothesis is that they are co-integrated, implying that there is a long-run relationship between the two variables. Moreover, it is this long-run relationship that, driven by MBTC, gives rise to non-trending profit and wage shares. Marquetti (2004) uses this methodology with time series data on the U.S. economy for the period 1869–1999 and finds evidence in favour of MBTC. de Souza (2016) extends the analysis to a panel data setting for manufacturing industries. Using the EU-Klems dataset covering 11 industries in 19 developed countries, and the UNIDO dataset covering 22 industries in 30 developing countries, he finds evidence of MBTC.

8. Conclusion

In this chapter I have reviewed some recent strands of quantitative empirical research in Marxist political economy. I started out by providing a quick overview of the debate surrounding the value controversy. Value is a foundational concept in Marxian political economy, and its interpretation and relationship to observable variables denominated in prices has been a source of lively debate and, often, bitter controversy. Starting almost immediately with the publication of Volume III of Capital in 1894, critics have argued that Marx's work in the three volumes of Capital does not provide an internally consistent labour theory of value. Repeating points made earlier by critics like Dmitriev and Samuleson, Ian Steedman (1977) elaborated this critique—what he called a Sraffa-based critique—in a forceful manner in the 1970s. The main claim in the critique was that value categories are redundant to the analysis of capitalism because prices of production and a uniform rate of profit can be computed directly from data on technology and distribution (the real wage bundle).

One can discern at least five different responses to the Sraffa-based critique that I have briefly indicated in Section 2.3. In this chapter, I have focused on the three Marxist strands that have not only responded to the redundancy critique but also opened up progressive research programs with nontrivial empirical components: the Standard Interpretation as developed by Anwar Shaikh; the Probabilistic Interpretation developed by Farjoun and Machover; and the New Interpretation developed by Duncan Foley and Gerard Dumenil. Each of these responses accepts the fact that prices of production and a uniform rate of profit can be computed from data on technology and distribution. But, each argue in their own way, that this does not make value categories redundant.

Before reviewing this literature, I took a detour by reviewing a literature that has wide acceptance—both as to its necessity and basic methodology—in the Marxist tradition, viz., construction of national accounts that is consistent with Marxist political economy. Starting with traditional input–output (and national accounts) data, the operationalization of two key conceptual features can take us to Marxist national accounts: the distinction between production and nonproduction activities, and the distinction between productive and non-productive labour.

There is a long and distinguished literature that has worked on this issue, including Mage (1963), Wolff (1977) and Moseley (1982), and has culminated in Shaikh and Tonak (1994). There is an urgent need to carry this work forward by applying Shaikh and Tonak's (1994) methodology, with certain modifications that may be necessary (e.g. Mohun, 2005), to construct and disseminate Marxist national accounts for as many countries as data limitations make possible. This is an area that can fruitfully engage future Marxist scholars and it is encouraging to see that work on these issues is being continued (e.g. Paitaridis and Tsoulfidis, 2012; Rotta, 2014).

Returning to the value controversy, I first discussed the response to the Sraffa-based critique developed in and through the work of Anwar Shaikh in the late 1970s. The argument contained in Shaikh (1984) provides, to my mind, a partial rebuttal of the Sraffa-based critique by converting the question into an empirical one. According to this 'standard interpretation' response, the interesting question is not that values and prices diverge, which is uncontroversial, but by how much? In essence, this strand advances Ricardo's neglected claim that values and prices are approximately equal. In Shaikh (1984), a theoretical argument is constructed to show that even in the face of wide divergence of organic composition of capital across sectors, relative prices can be 'close' to relative values because they depend on vertically integrated capital labour ratios and not actual capital–labour ratios. Using data from several capitalist economies, this strand then demonstrates that relative values and relative prices are strongly correlated, or that a suitable measure of distance between the vector of prices and values is small.

The second response to the Sraffa-based critique that I discuss emerged from the work of Farjoun and Machover (1983), who argued for a probabilistic approach to Marxist political economy. Farjoun and Machover's rebuttal of the Sraffa-based critique rested on asking a simple question: is there any justification for the assumption of a single, uniform rate of profit? The answer is: no. Empirical evidence shows that in any economy at any point in time, there is a distribution of the rate of profit, rather than a single value of the rate of profit. Thus, long-run equilibrium of capitalist economies is characterized by equilibrium distributions of the rate of profit, and not a single uniform rate of profit. Once the assumption of a uniform rate of profit is abandoned, the whole Sraffa-based critique collapses.

In addition to the rebuttal of the Sraffa-based critique, Farjoun and Machover (1983) also develop a positive program of probabilistic political economy. They argue that the rate of profit follows a gamma distribution, and develop an elaborate argument to show that the specific price (price per unit of labour embodied) follows a normal distribution. While the distribution of the rate of profit is derived on the basis of an analogy from statistical mechanics, the distribution of the specific price is derived by taking recourse to some central limit theorem. Evidence presented by Fröhlich (2013) for the German economy shows that the rate of profit does indeed follow a gamma distribution but that the specific price follows a log-normal distribution (instead of a normal distribution). This strand of the literature has been significantly extended in recent work by Alfarano *et al.* (2012) and Scharfenaker and Semieniuk (2016), both of which open up interesting avenues for future research.

The third response to the Sraffa-based critique that I discuss emerged as the 'new interpretation' of Marx's value theory, developed independently by Foley (1982) and Duménil (1983/1984). The new interpretation's rebuttal of the Sraffa-based critique relies on developing a theoretically informed, internally consistent *ex post* accounting framework. Two definitions anchor this accounting framework. First, the value of money is defined as the ratio of the total labour embodied in the net output (measured in labour time units) and the money value added (measured in prices). Second, the value of labour power is defined as the product of the nominal money wage and the value of money. These two definitions imply that profits are proportion to unpaid labour time, and value added is proportional to total labour time (the latter by definition). This is the way in which the redundancy argument is addressed in the NI: since value and price is equal at the aggregate level, the question of redundancy itself becomes redundant.

Even though the deviation of individual values and prices could be investigated in the NI framework, researchers adhering to this interpretation have studied other questions. One issue that has been studied extensively is the evolution of the rate of profit rate in relation to developments in the economy, followed by a decomposition analysis to study factors that drive medium- and/or short-run dynamics. Another issue has been to study the validity of Marx's law of the tendential fall in the rate of profit using modern econometric methods. A third issue that has been investigated relates to patterns of growth, distribution and technical change in capitalist economies.

This brief review of recent quantitative empirical research in Marxist political economy has highlighted some of the interesting issues that are currently being investigated in this tradition. When we look at all the existing approaches at once, some puzzles and conundrums do emerge. I would like to end this review by highlighting two of these intriguing issues. My hope is that these real and challenging puzzles will pique the interest of new generations of researchers and help in the effort to move Marxian political economy beyond *mere* discussions of what Marx 'really' meant.

The first puzzling issue comes to the fore when we think of the conclusions of Section 3 (Marxian national accounts) and Section 4 (classical theory of price–value deviation) together. The literature reviewed in Section 4 suggests that prices of production and values are approximately equal. When we juxtapose this with the work reported in Section 3, it seems that national monetary aggregates do reflect national labour values, at both aggregate and disaggregated levels (to the extent allowed by IO tables). If this is correct, then what are the implications of this for unequal exchange through the balance of payments? Is this just a matter of differences in national vertically integrated labour–capital ratios? Or, are the principles governing the flows recorded in the balance of payments outside the equilibrating logic underlying the prices of production? What is the implication of this for theories of imperialism that hinge on the notion of unequal exchange between countries (or blocs of countries)?

The second puzzle emerges from a juxtaposition of the discussion in Section 4 (classical theory of price–value deviation) and the NI (which I have briefly outlined in Section 2.3 and in Section B of the Online Appendix). Unequal exchange at the micro-level is central to the vision of the NI. It underlies the metaphor—first developed by Baumol (1974)—that all capitals contribute to a world pool of surplus value according to the labour they exploit, and draw from it according to their competitive edge. The key mechanism that effects this redistribution of surplus value is the price mechanism, that is, the deviation of market prices from values. For the net value added, these deviations must sum to zero, as the NI emphasizes. If sectoral price–value deviations are also small, as the literature on classical price–value deviations reviewed in Section 4 claims, then this raises a puzzle. How do we explain the incomes of commercial capital and financial capital in terms of the process of circulation?

Acknowledgements

I have benefitted from comments from two anonymous referees of this journal. I would also like to thank, without implicating in any way for the content of this paper, Duncan Foley, Tom Michl, Simon Mohun and Anwar Shaikh for comments on an earlier version.

Notes

1. 'If 1 hour of work is embodied in 6 pence, and the value of a day's labour-power is 5 shillings …' (Marx, 1990, p. 430). 'Let the value of labour-power be 3 shillings, and let the necessary labour-time amount to 6 hours' (Marx, 1990, p. 659). 'If we suppose that the value produced by one worker in an average social working day is expressed in a sum of money to the value of 6 shillings …' (Marx, 1991, p. 119).
2. See chapter 6 in Shaikh and Tonak (1994) for a critical review of the literature that precedes their work.
3. Note that the difference between productive and unproductive labour has nothing to do with necessity, usefulness or rationality. It is a narrow and precise distinction based on whether that labour creates surplus value.
4. All magnitudes in this section are measured in monetary units.
5. Mohun (2005) provides better estimates of productive labour and the wage bill of productive labour by doing away with some approximations that Shaikh and Tonak (1994) were forced to make due to unavailability of data.
6. While there is broad agreement in the Marxist tradition on the need to distinguish productive and unproductive labour, there are alternative interpretations of the effect of unproductive labour on the macroeconomy. For alternative interpretations, see Paitaridis and Tsoulfidis (2012) and Mohun (2014). From a class perspective, Mohun's (2014) distinction between what he calls the 'unproductive working class' and supervisors is important. His empirical work has emphasized the constancy of the share of the unproductive working class, and the rise in the share of supervisors, since the early 1960s. This observation has important insights to offer on the growing income and wealth inequality under neoliberal capitalism.

7. Note that computation of the 'social wage' is based on many distributional assumptions. For instance, to compute the net taxes paid by production workers, the researcher needs to decide what proportion of total social welfare expenditures on health, education, roads, parks, etc., accrues to the working class (and what proportion accrues to the capitalist class).

8. Using this methodology would also avoid the problem that results of the analysis are impacted by units of measurement, an issue that has been discussed a lot in the literature (see, for instance, Shaikh, 2016, pp. 387–390). Changes in the unit of measurement will not have an impact on the results of the F-test.

9. The denominator in each element of the vector in equation (17) is multiplied by 'the monetary equivalent of total labor time' (Shaikh, 2016, p. 392), which is the ratio of total price and total value of the gross output. This ensures that the numerator and denominator in each element in equation (17) have the same units. But it also raises an interesting question. Should value–price conversions use the 'MELT' of the NI, where net output is used? Or, should value–price conversions use the 'monetary equivalent of total labour time' (METLT) of the Standard Interpretation, where gross output is used? Since the total labour involved in production in a period only adds new value, even as it preserves the value in constant capital and transfers it, to the commodity, the use of net output seems more appropriate. Hence, the MELT seems to be a better conversion factor to use than the METLT.

10. In the 1980s, there was an important debate on the classical view of competition, the mobility of capital and distribution of industry rates of profit. An empirical strand of this literature that I have been unable to discuss in this paper is available in, among others, Semmler (1982), Glick (1985) and Duménil and Lévy (1987).

11. This is the same vertical integration argument that was developed by Pasinetti (1973) and was also used in part by Shaikh (1984). See Section A of the Online Appendix for details, especially the derivation of equations (A.4), (A.5) and (A.6).

12. A two-sample Kolmogorov–Smirnov test is used to test the null hypothesis that two empirical distributions are drawn from the same theoretical distribution. Operationalizing the test involves calculating the 'distance' between the two empirical distribution functions and testing whether it is 'small'. Standard statistical packages like R and STATA have built-in functions to conduct the test.

13. The only exceptions were Feldstein and Summers (1977) and Michl (1988). While these studies tried to account for some of the counteracting factors, they did not take account of the unit root properties of the rate of profit (or of some of the counteracting factors).

14. Note that $w = \dfrac{W}{L} = \dfrac{X-\Pi}{L} = \dfrac{X}{L} - \dfrac{\Pi}{K}\dfrac{K}{L} = x - kv$.

References

Alfarano, S., Milaković, M., Irle, A. and Kauschke, J. (2012) A statistical equilibrium model of competitive firms. *Journal of Economic Dynamics and Control* 36(1): 136–149.

Bakir, E. and Campbell, A. (2009) The effect of neoliberalism on the fall in the rate of profit in business cycles. *Review of Radical Political Economics* 38(3): 365–373.

Basu, D. (2010) Marx-biased technical change and the neoclassical view of income distribution. *Metroeconomica* 61(4): 593–620.

Basu, D. and Das, D. (2015) Profitability in India's organized manufacturing sector: the role of technology, distribution and demand. *Working Paper 380, Political Economy Research Institute, University of Massachusetts Amherst.*

Basu, D. and Foley, D.K. (2013) Dynamics of output and employment in the US economy. *Cambridge Journal of Economics* 37(5): 1077–1106.

Basu, D. and Manolakos, P.T. (2013) Is there a tendency for the rate of profit to fall? Econometric evidence from the US economy, 1948–2007. *Review of Radical Political Economics* 45(1): 75–94.

Basu, D. and Vasudevan, R. (2013) Technology, distribution and the rate of profit: understanding the current crisis. *Cambridge Journal of Economics* 37(1): 57–89.

Baumol, W.J. (1974) The transformation of values: what Marx "Really" meant (an interpretation). *Journal of Economic Literature* 12(1): 51–62.

Cockshott, W.P. and Cottrell, A.F. (1997) Labour time versus alternative value bases: a research note. *Cambridge Journal of Economics* 21(4): 545–549.

de Souza, J.P.A. (2016) Real wages and labour-saving technical change: evidence from a panel of manufacturing industries in mature and labour surplus economies. *International Review of Applied Economics.* Published online 25 August. https://doi.org/10.1080/02692171.2016.1225017

Dmitriev, V.K. (1974 [1902]) *Economic Essays on Value, Competition and Utility.* Edited with an Introduction by D.M. Nuti. Translated by D. Fry. Cambridge, UK: Cambridge University Press.

Duménil, G. (1983/1984) Beyond the transformation riddle: a labour theory of value. *Science & Society* 47(4): 427–450.

Duménil, G. and Lévy, D. (1987) The dynamics of competition: a restoration of the classical analysis. *Cambridge Journal of Economics* 11(2): 133–164.

Duménil, G. and Lévy, D. (1993) *The Economics of the Profit Rate: Competition, Crises, and Historical Tendencies in Capitalism.* Aldershot, UK: Edgar Elgar.

Duménil, G. and Lévy, D. (1995) A stochastic model of technical change: an application to the US economy (1869–1989). *Metroeconomica* 46(3): 213–245.

Duménil, G. and Lévy, D. (2003) Technology and distribution: historical trajectories à la Marx. *Journal of Economic Behavior and Organization* 52(2): 201–233.

Duménil, G. and Lévy, D. (2004) *Capital Resurgent: Roots of the Neoliberal Revolution.* Translated by D. Jeffers. Cambridge, MA: Harvard University Press.

Duménil, G. and Lévy, D. (2011) *The Crisis of Neoliberalism.* Cambridge, MA: Harvard University Press.

Duménil, G., Glick, M. and Rangel, J. (1984) The tendency of the rate of profit to fall in the United States, part 1. *Contemporary Marxism* 9: 148–164.

Duménil, G., Glick, M. and Rangel, J. (1985) The tendency of the rate of profit to fall in the United States, part 2. *Contemporary Marxism* 11: 138–52.

Farjoun, E. and Machover, M. (1983) *Laws of Chaos: A Probabilistic Approach to Political Economy.* London, UK: Verso.

Feldstein, M. and Summers, L. (1977) Is the rate of profit falling? *Brookings Papers on Economic Activity* 1: 211–228.

Fine, B., Lapavitsas, C. and Saad-Filho, A. (2004) Transforming the transformation problem: why the "new interpretation" is a wrong turning. *Review of Radical Political Economics* 36(3): 3–19.

Foley, D.K. (1982) The value of money, the value of labour power and the Marxian transformation problem. *Review of Radical Political Economics* 14(2): 37–47.

Foley, D.K. (1986) Understanding Capital: Marx's Economic Theory. Cambridge, MA: Harvard University Press.

Foley, D.K. (1994) A statistical equilibrium theory of markets. *Journal of Economic Theory* 62(2): 321–345.

Foley, D.K. and Marquetti, A. (1997) Economic growth from a classical perspective. In J. Texeira (ed.), *Proceeding: International Colloquium on Money, Growth, Distribution and Structural Change: Contemporaneous Analysis.* Department of Economics, University of Brasilia, Brazil.

Foley, D.K. and Michl, T.R. (1999) *Growth and Distribution*. Cambridge, MA: Harvard University Press.

Foley, D.K. and Michl, T.R. (2004) A classical alternative to the neoclassical growth model. In G. Argyros, M. Forstater and G. Mongiovi (eds.), *Growth, Distribution and Effective Demand: Alternatives to Economic Orthodoxy. Essays in Honor of Edward J. Nell*. Armonk, NY: M. E. Sharpe.

Foley, D.K. and Taylor, L. (2006) A heterodox growth and distribution model. In N. Salvadori (ed.), *Economic Growth and Distribution: On the Nature and Causes of the Wealth of Nations*. Cheltenham, UK: Edward Elgar.

Fröhlich, N. (2013) Labour values, prices of production and the missing equalization tendency on profit rates: evidence from the German economy. *Cambridge Journal of Economics* 37(5): 1107–1126.

Glick, M. (1985) Competition versus monopoly: profit rate dispersion in US manufacturing industries. Ph.D. Dissertation, New School for Social Research, New York.

Henley, A. (1987) Labour's share and profitability crisis in the US: recent experience and post-war trends. *Cambridge Journal of Economics* 11(4): 315–330.

Izquierdo, S.C. (2013) The cyclical decline of the profit rate as the cause of crises in the United States (1947–2011). *Review of Radical Political Economics* 45(4): 463–471.

Jaynes, E.T. (1957) Information theory and statistical mechanics. *The Physical Review* 106(4): 620–630.

Jaynes, E.T. (1978) Where do we stand on maximum entropy? In: R.D. Rosenkrantz and E.T. Jaynes (eds.), *Papers on Probability, Statistics and Statistical Physics*. Dordrecht, Netherlands: Kluwer Academic Publishers.

Kotz, D. (2009) Economic crises and institutional structures: a comparison of regulated and neoliberal capitalism in the US. In J. Goldstein and M. Hillard (eds.), *Heterodox Macroeconomics: Keynes, Marx, and Globalization* (pp. 176–188). London and New York: Routledge.

Kurz, H.D. and Salvadori, N. (1995) *Theory of Production: A Long Period Analysis*. Cambridge: Cambridge University Press.

Mage, S.H. (1963) The law of the falling tendency of the rate of profit: it's place in the Marxian theoretical system and relevance to the United States. Ph.D. Dissertation, Department of Economics, Columbia University.

Marquetti, A. (2004) Do rising real wages increase the rate of labour-saving technical change?: Some econometric evidence. *Metroeconomica* 55(4): 432–441.

Marquetti, A., Filho, E.M. and Lautert, V. (2010) The profit rate in Brazil, 1953–2003. *Review of Radical Political Economics* 42(4): 485–504.

Marx, K. 1990 [1867] *Capital: A Critique of Political Economy*. Volume I. Translated by B. Fowkes. London, UK: Penguin Books.

Marx, K. 1991 [1894] *Capital: A Critique of Political Economy*. Volume III. Translated by D. Fernbach. London, UK: Penguin Books.

Michl, T.R. (1988) The two-stage decline in US nonfinancial corporate profitability, 1948–86. *Review of Radical Political Economics* 20(4): 1–22.

Michl, T.R. (1999) Biased technical change and the aggregate production function. *International Review of Applied Economics* 13(2): 193–206.

Michl, T.R. (2002) The fossil production function in a vintage model. *Australian Economic Papers* 41: 53–68.

Michl, T.R. (2009) *Capitalists, Workers and Fiscal Policy: A Classical Model of Growth and Distribution*. Cambridge, MA: Harvard University Press.

Mohun, S. (2005) On measuring the wealth of nations: the US economy, 1964–2001. *Cambridge Journal of Economics* 29(5): 799–815.

Mohun, S. (2013) Rate of profit and crisis in the US economy: a class perspective. In L. Taylor, A. Rezai and T.R. Michl (eds.), *Social Fairness and Economics: Economic Essays in the Spirit of Duncan Foley* (pp. 171–198). London and New York: Routledge.

Mohun, S. (2014) Unproductive labour in the US economy, 1964–2010. *Review of Radical Political Economics* 46(3): 355–379.

Morishima, M. and Catephores, G. (1978) *Value, Exploitation, Growth: Marx in the Light of Modern Economic Theory*. London, UK: McGraw-Hill Book Co.

Moseley, F.B. (1982) The rate of surplus-value in the United States: 1947–77. Ph.D. Dissertation, Department of Economics, University of Massachusetts, Amherst.

Moseley, F.B. (2000) The "new solution" to the transformation problem: a sympathetic critique. *Review of Radical Political Economics* 32(2): 282–316.

Ochoa, E.M. (1989) Values, prices, and wage-profit curves in the US economy. *Cambridge Journal of Economics* 13(3): 413–430.

Okishio, N. (1963) A mathematical note on Marxian theorems. *Weltwirtschaftliches Archiv* 91: 289–299.

Olsen, E.K. (2011) Modeling the economic surplus in a SAM framework. *American Journal of Economics and Sociology* 70(5): 1175–1207.

Paitaridis, D. and Tsoulfidis, L. (2012) The growth of unproductive activities, the rate of profit, and the phase-change of the U.S. economy. *Review of Radical Political Economics* 44(2): 213–233.

Pasinetti, L. (1973) The notion of vertical integration in economic analysis. *Metroeconomica* 25: 1–29.

Petrovic, P. (1987) The deviation of production prices from labour values: some methodology and empirical evidence. *Cambridge Journal of Economics* 11(3): 197–210.

Rotta, T.N. (2014) Productive stagnation and unproductive accumulation in the United States, 1947–2011. Ph.D. Dissertation, Department of Economics, University of Massachusetts, Amherst.

Samuelson, P.A. (1971) Understanding the Marxian notion of exploitation: a summary of the so-called transformation problem between Marxian values and competitive prices. *Journal of Economic Literature*, 9(2): 399–431.

Scharfenaker, E., and Semieniuk, G. (2016) A Statistical Equilibrium Approach to the Distribution of Profit Rates. Metroeconomica. https://doi.org/10.1111/meca.12134

Semmler, W. (1982) Competition, monopoly and differentials of profit rates: theoretical considerations and empirical evidence. *Review of Radical Political Economics* 15(2): 125–133.

Seton, F. (1957) The "transformation problem". *The Review of Economic Studies* 24(3): 149–160.

Shaikh, A. (1977) Marx's theory of value and the transformation problem. In J. Schwartz (ed.), *The Subtle Anatomy of Capitalism*. Santa Monica, CA: Goodyear Publishing Co.

Shaikh, A. (1984) The transformation from Marx to Sraffa. In E. Mandel and A. Freeman (eds.), *Ricardo, Marx, Sraffa*. London, UK: Verso.

Shaikh, A. (1998) The empirical strength of the labour theory of value. In R. Bellofiore (ed.), *Marxian Economics: A Reappraisal. Essays on Volume III of Capital. Volume 2: Profits, Prices and Dynamics*. New York, NY: St. Martin's Press.

Shaikh, A. (2016) *Capitalism: Competition, Conflict, Crises*. Cambridge, UK: Cambridge University Press.

Shaikh, A. and Tonak, E.A. (1994) *Measuring the Wealth of Nations: The Political Economy of National Accounts*. Cambridge, UK: Cambridge University Press.

Steedman, I. (1977) *Marx after Sraffa*. London, UK: New Left Books.

Steedman, I. and Tomkins, J. (1998) On measuring the deviations of prices from values. *Cambridge Journal of Economics* 22(3): 379–385.

Stigler, G.J. (1958) Ricardo and the 93% labour theory of value. *American Economic Review* 48: 357–367.

Tsoulfidis, L. and Maniatis, T. (2002) Values, prices of production and market prices: some more evidence from the Greek economy. *Cambridge Journal of Economics* 26(3): 359–369.

von Bortkiewicz, L. (1949 [1907]) On the correction of Marx's fundamental theoretical construction in the Third Volume of Capital. In P.M. Sweezy (ed.), *Karl Marx and the Close of his System by Eugen von Böhm-Bawerk & Böhm-Bawerk's Criticism of Marx by Rudolf Hilferding*. New York: Augustus M. Kelley. 199–221.

Weisskopf, T.E. (1979) Marxian crisis theory and the rate of profit in the post-war US economy. *Cambridge Journal of Economics* 3(4): 341–378.

Wolff, E.N. (1977) Unproductive labour and the rate of surplus value in the United States, 1947–67. In P. Zarembka (ed.), *Research in Political Economy* (Vol. 1). Greenwich, CT: JAI Press.

Wolff, R.D., Roberts, B. and Callari, A. (1982) Marx's (not Ricardo's) 'transformation problem': a radical reconceptualization. *History of Political Economy* 14(4): 564–582.

Supporting Information

Additional Supporting information may be found in the online version of this article at the publisher's website:

Online Appendix

10

VALUE, PRICE, AND EXPLOITATION: THE LOGIC OF THE TRANSFORMATION PROBLEM

Simon Mohun

School of Business and Management
Queen Mary University of London

Roberto Veneziani

School of Economics and Finance
Queen Mary University of London

1. Introduction

When economic activity is organized through markets, the notion of price is central. In the neoclassical individualist tradition, price and value are synonyms; prices emerge in competitive markets from the interaction of optimizing individual households and firms with given endowments, preferences, and technology, and in that sense, the theory of value is subjective. In the Marxian tradition, value is distinct from price and only labor creates value. Such a labor theory of value is objective, and prices are long-run centers of gravity around which market prices fluctuate. The relation between labor value and long-run price is the content of what has become known as the "transformation problem."

The outcome of the last wave of major debates in the 1960s and 1970s has led to the view that the classical-Marxian labor theory of value is logically inconsistent and so irremediably flawed. And even if some of the insights of Marx's theory of value can be salvaged, they are irrelevant for any meaningful positive or normative purposes: as Paul Samuelson (1971) famously put it in his "blackboard theorem," price magnitudes and value magnitudes are independent of each other, with a relation of mutual irrelevance. A similar negative judgment

We are grateful to Antonio Callari, Emmanuel Farjoun, Duncan Foley, Moshe Machover, Gary Mongiovi, Fred Moseley, Erik Olsen, Bruce Roberts, Bertram Schefold, Julian Wells, Rick Wolff, Naoki Yoshihara, the participants in the Tenth Analytical Political Economy Workshop (London, May 2016), and two anonymous referees for helpful and sometimes detailed comments. The usual disclaimer applies.

was also shared by commentators who were less hostile to Marxist theory in general. Joan Robinson famously argued, for example, that value theory "provides a typical example of the way metaphysical ideas operate. Logically it is a mere rigmarole of words, but for Marx it was a flood of illumination and for latter-day Marxists, a source of inspiration" (Robinson, 1964, p. 39). Given the central role of value theory in Marxian economics, these conclusions have led many commentators to consider the whole of Marx's theory as dead.

This paper argues that such judgments are based on a particular interpretation of Marx's notion of value and of its role in the understanding of capitalist economies. But rather than provide another "solution" to the transformation problem, our aim is to outline a unified theoretical framework that can clarify its logic and in so doing emphasize the wide variety of possible interpretations of value theory for which the transformation problem has no implications. To do this, we employ an axiomatic approach.

Following (Thomson, 2001, p. 332), an axiomatic study has

> the following components: 1. It begins with the specification of a domain of problems, and the formulation of a list of desirable properties of solutions for the domain. 2. It ends with … descriptions of the families of solutions satisfying various combinations of the properties.

From this perspective, it is possible to conceive of any approach to value theory as (implicitly) defining a set of problems (including definitions of the main variables: prices, values, technology, competition, and so on); formulating a list of desirable properties (axioms) of the labor theory of value, including the specification of the role of value analysis; and then exploring the set of "solutions" to those problems. The axiomatic method then provides a new perspective on some old issues. In particular, the standard approach to the transformation problem—analyzed in Section 5 below—can be seen as identifying an impossibility result: under a certain interpretation of value theory, and on the basis of some axioms concerning value and price magnitudes, the set of solutions is empty. But the axiomatic method also provides a general formal and conceptual framework for analyzing different views on Marxian value theory.

One striking aspect of the debates on Marxian value and price theory is the lack of agreement on virtually anything, including on what the actual issue of contention is. Part of the reason is that the discussion is ideologically loaded. But a large part of the controversy stems from different views concerning the key concepts, the basic methodology, and the actual role of value theory. Different approaches do not simply provide alternative solutions to a given problem, for there is no single way of posing that problem. In terms of Thomson's description above, different approaches often identify a completely different set of problems the solutions to which will have different properties. The advantage of an axiomatic framework is to provide a unified framework to clarify these differences.[1]

There is an enormous literature on the relation between value and price dating back to the publication of *Capital III* in 1894 (Marx, 1981). So, three clarifications concerning the scope of our analysis are in order. First, there are several reviews of earlier debates, including Hunt and Glick (1987), Desai (1988), and Howard and King (1992). This paper focuses only on recent approaches (from around 1980), most of which start from the acknowledgement that, as originally posed, the transformation problem has no solution.[2] Second, we do not provide a survey of all of the (recent) interpretations of Marxian value theory but restrict ourselves to those that have a clear and explicit quantitative dimension. Qualitative interpretations, for example, occasioned by the rediscovery of Rubin (1972), fall outside of our survey. Third, as a logical inquiry into the structure of value theory, we provide no exegetical evidence. All of the approaches we survey can be presented and supported by careful analysis of Marxian texts.

2. What Is Value Theory For?

One of the main arguments of this paper is that disputes on the transformation problem derive from different views about the aim and scope of value theory (in Marx and beyond). And the popular view that Marx's theory is fundamentally flawed derives from the erroneous extrapolation of the logical problems of *one* of the interpretations of value theory to all possible approaches. In this section, we provide a classification and discussion of the main views.

2.1 *Description, Prediction, and Evaluation*

What is the labor theory of value for? The received view is that its main aim is predictive: labor values are meant to explain (relative, equilibrium) prices. Yet, even within a predictive interpretation, labor magnitudes may be relevant to explain other phenomena of capitalist economies. For example, one may argue that the labor theory of value establishes a relation between profits and exploitative relations, thus allowing one to explain investment and growth More generally, however, it is not clear that Marxian value theory can only be interpreted as a predictive exercise. For "there are at least three distinct non-metaphysical interpretations of the labour theory of value, viz. (i) descriptive, (ii) predictive and (iii) normative" (Sen, 1978, p. 175).

As for (i), Sen (1978, p. 176) notes that "Any description relies on factual statements. But it also involves a selection from the set of factual statements that can be made pertaining to the phenomenon in question: some facts are chosen and others ignored. The selection process is part of the exercise of description, and not a 'metaphysical' exercise." One descriptive interpretation of the labor theory of value is that of capturing the process of formation of equilibrium prices in capitalist economies, as in the standard view. But this is certainly not the only possibility. One may argue that in the labor theory of value, "it is the *activity* of production that is being described, and the selection criterion is focused on 'personal participation'" (Sen, 1978, p. 177). It focuses analysis on human effort and refuses "to give the same status to the ownership of [natural resources and capital] in describing participation in production as personal participation through labour" (Sen, 1978).[3] Thus, alternative formulations of the labor theory of value "have to be judged in terms of the motivation of the exercise of description in the particular case in question" (Sen, 1978, p. 178).

Regarding (iii), the labor theory of value can also be interpreted primarily as providing the foundations for a normative, evaluative exercise and an indictment of capitalist relations of production. For example, one may argue that it explains the origin of profits as accruing from the exploitation of workers and therefore shows the illegitimacy of capitalist earnings, and the source of significant inequalities of well-being. Or it may be taken as providing the foundations of a distributive approach based on contribution and effort.

Thus, even at the most abstract level, there is no single, natural interpretation of the labor theory of value. In addition to the standard predictive view, other interpretations that emphasize its descriptive or evaluative role are possible. These interpretations are not mutually inconsistent. For even within a descriptive approach, the specific interpretation chosen may depend on the actual motivation of the analysis, which can be predictive or evaluative. Recognition of this diversity of interpretation is important when seeking to identify the primary analytical focus of the various approaches: there are a great variety of interpretations of Marxian value theory. Moreover, even within each interpretation (descriptive, predictive, or evaluative), several alternative formulations of the labor theory of value are possible. In the rest of this section, we try to identify some of them.

2.2 *The Equilibrium Price View*

This is the standard approach, and historically the oldest. It contends that Marx's value theory provides an explanation of the equilibrium prices of a competitive market economy. Marx's approach is seen as falling within the classical economists' long-period approach in which profits are interpreted as a surplus. It will be convenient to distinguish two variants, a strong one and a weak one.

Definition 1. According to the *strong equilibrium price view*, relative equilibrium prices are equal to relative values.

Definition 2. According to the *weak equilibrium price view*, relative equilibrium prices are determined by relative values.

The notion of "determination" in Definition 2 can be defined in different ways. Thus, relative equilibrium prices might be determined by relative values in the sense that there exists a clear deterministic functional relation linking the two sets of magnitudes (see, for example, Section 5 below). Alternatively, relative equilibrium prices might be equal to relative values up to a predefined margin of error. We leave the concept of determination undefined in order to accommodate a range of possible views.

2.3 *The Profit & Exploitation View*

In this approach, the basic idea is that the purpose of the labor theory of value is to reveal the origin of profits, the key variable in capitalist economies. At its most basic, capitalist society is a class society of workers and capitalists; these classes exist in antagonistic relation to each other, and that antagonism is based on the extraction of surplus labor from one class (the working class) by the other (the capitalist class). Extraction of surplus labor is called "exploitation," and it characterizes all types of class society. But while exploitation is obvious in, for example, slave societies (slaves are compelled to produce more than they consume) and feudal societies (serfs are compelled to work on the lord's land for part of the week), it is not obvious in capitalist societies where market transactions are voluntary. The purpose of the labor theory of value is then to show how voluntary participation in markets nonetheless generates exploitation. In sum, value theory provides the foundations for the Marxian theory of exploitation, showing that profits result from the exploitation of labor.

Definition 3. According to the *profit & exploitation view*, profits are determined by the exploitation of labor.

2.4 *The Appropriate Level of Analysis*

A further important distinction concerns the appropriate level of value analysis. The standard approach to the labor theory of value is microeconomic and conceives of Marxian value theory as an alternative to Walrasian general equilibrium for the explanation of equilibrium prices.

More generally, one can identify a general approach—that can be called, to simplify, the microeconomic view—according to which, value analysis focuses primarily on disaggregated variables, such as prices, or an agent's individual exploitation status, or the labor values of individual commodities.

Definition 4. According to the *microeconomic view*, the labor theory of value applies to disaggregated magnitudes.

Many recent approaches have rejected this microeconomic view, and have interpreted Marxian value theory as explaining primarily macroeconomic features of capitalist economies, such as the aggregate production of surplus value, or the aggregate exploitation rate.

Definition 5. According to the *macroeconomic view*, the labor theory of value is primarily a theory of aggregates.

The different views identified above are not mutually exclusive. An emphasis on aggregate macroeconomic relations as the primary unit of analysis does not mean that microeconomic variables are ignored, or irrelevant. If the equilibrium price view focuses on the relation between labor values and prices, it nevertheless has to incorporate a notion of exploitation for labor values to make sense. So, a value theory that provides an explanation of equilibrium relative prices in capitalist economies must also provide an explanation of equilibrium profits as the product of exploitation. Similarly, if the profit & exploitation view is based on showing how exploitation results from market participation, then some specification of prices is required. Hence, an explanation of profits in terms of exploitation must also provide an account of the prices in which these profits are measured. So, categorizing approaches in the literature to each view is more a matter of determining their emphasis than their exclusive concentration.

Neither are these views exhaustive. But they do encompass the main approaches that are expressed in mathematical language. And given the latter, we emphasize the particular assumptions that drive their different emphases.

3. The Basic Marxian Framework

Marx's vision of production was an advance of capital by a capitalist in order to make profit, an extra sum of money over and above that which the capitalist had to advance to purchase nonlabor means of production, and to purchase the use of labor. These inputs were combined in a production process to produce an output which when sold generated revenues that both replaced the capital advanced and produced more money as profit. The challenge was to find a general explanation for this profit.

For clarity, we set aside the complications related to unproductive labor, fixed capital, international trade, the public sector, joint production, and so on, and consider the simplest production structure, a closed, private economy in which each sector i produces only one type of commodity.[4] There are n such commodities produced in a given production period, using physical inputs in the form of circulating capital and one type of homogeneous labor. Production takes time. Suppose that production processes have a uniform duration and let t denote a generic production period. Let the total value of the output of any sector i during period t, Λ_{it}, be the labor time required to produce the gross output of that sector, Q_{it}. (Unless the context requires it, we will henceforth drop the subscript t.)

Marx argued that what made commodities exchangeable in the market for sums of money, and hence commensurable, was that they were all products of labor. He spent some time refining what he meant by this labor (abstract rather than concrete, simple rather than compound, social rather than private, and necessary rather than wasted), and he measured it in units of socially necessary labor time.[5] Then, the value of a commodity is the sum of the (indirect) labor time embodied in the nonlabor inputs (means of production) and the (direct) labor time expended by workers when using these means of production. Indirect labor time is transferred from the nonlabor means of production to the product of the production process and reappears as part of the value of output. While its location changes, its amount remains the same. For this reason, Marx called the capital advanced to purchase nonlabor means of production "constant capital." When the output is sold, the capitalist recovers the capital he advanced to purchase nonlabor means of production. But he also recovers the capital he advanced to purchase labor inputs, *and* he appropriates a profit. Both of these Marx attributed to the value-creating capacity of human labor: laboring activity uniquely has the ability to produce more than it costs. For this reason, Marx called the capital advanced to purchase labor inputs "variable capital."[6] The extra, over, and above the sum of constant capital and variable capital, Marx called "surplus value." Formally, in labor value terms,

$$\Lambda_i = C_i + V_i + S_i \tag{1}$$

where C_i is total constant capital employed, V_i is total variable capital employed, S_i is total surplus value appropriated by capitalists in sector i, and all magnitudes are measured in units of labor time.

Thus far, these are just definitions. Two steps are required to turn them into a labor *theory* of value. Let the unit value of sector i be given by $\lambda_i = \frac{\Lambda_i}{Q_i}$. While value is measured in units of labor time, that measure is definitional, and it has to be combined with value being measured as a sum of money when the commodity that embodies it is sold. It is this combination that turns a labor *definition* of value into a labor *theory* of value. So, the first step is to assert that if prices were determined by labor values, then at unit level, and for all i,

$$p_i = \frac{\lambda_i}{\lambda_m} \tag{2}$$

where p_i denotes the unit price of commodity i, denominated in units of money; since λ_i is denominated in units of time, the value of money, λ_m, must be denominated in units of time per unit of money.[7]

The second step is to provide some specification of the value of money. For Marx, reflecting the monetary arrangements and institutions of his time, money was a commodity (generally gold); its value was determined, like all commodities, by the labor time required for its production, and its price was unity.[8] Hence, for any value of money, the price of commodity i is determined by its value. Equation (2) specifies the labor theory of value as Marx inherited it from Ricardo (but with more sophisticated notions of labor and labor time).

Three further points concerning equation (2) should be emphasized. First, given the value of money, equation (2) is a statement of "equal" or "equivalent" exchange. Prices exactly reflect values, so that for each and every commodity, its purchaser pays and its seller receives its full value in money terms. That is, for each and every commodity, *its value is exactly conserved in any market transaction*. It will be convenient henceforth to call the prices at which this is true "simple prices."

Second, equation (2) applies to each and every commodity, including labor power (the value-creating capacity of human labor). Applying it to labor power, and denoting its price as w_i, the wage rate per unit of labor time in sector i, and the value of labor-power per unit of labor purchased in sector i as vlp_i, then

$$w_i = \frac{vlp_i}{\lambda_m} \tag{3}$$

As soon as labor mobility is presumed, in long-period equilibrium, the wage rate will be uniform across all sectors, with $w_i = w$, all i, and so, by equation (3), $vlp_i = vlp$, for all sectors i.

Third, suppose that workers do not save and spend their wages on consumer goods (means of subsistence).[9] Let L be the total number of hours worked in the economy. Letting $\mathbf{b} = (b_1, \ldots, b_n)'$ denote the vector indicating the amount of each good i consumed, and denoting whatever the ruling prices are by $\mathbf{p} = (p_1, \ldots, p_n)$, for the economy as a whole $wL = \mathbf{pb}$, so that

$$w = \mathbf{p}\frac{\mathbf{b}}{L} \tag{4}$$

Let $\lambda = (\lambda_1, \ldots, \lambda_n)$. Combining equations (3) and (4), and assuming equal exchange (equation (2)),

$$vlp = \frac{\lambda \mathbf{b}}{L} \tag{5}$$

or the value of labor power per hour of labor hired is the value of the bundle consumed per hour.[10]

Dividing equation (1) through by Q_i and using equation (2):

$$p_i = \frac{\lambda_i}{\lambda_m} = \left(\frac{C_i}{Q_i} + \frac{V_i}{Q_i} + \frac{S_i}{Q_i}\right)\frac{1}{\lambda_m} = \frac{c_i}{\lambda_m} + \frac{v_i}{\lambda_m} + \frac{s_i}{\lambda_m} \tag{6}$$

By definition, variable capital in sector i is advanced to purchase labor-power in sector i, and in value terms, this must be equal to vlp per hour of labor hired, multiplied by the number of hours purchased l_i. So, $v_i = vlp \cdot l_i$, and since $v_i + s_i = l_i$, then $s_i = (1 - vlp)l_i$. Define the rate of surplus value in sector i as $e_i = s_i/v_i$. Then, $e_i = e_j = e$ for all i and j: because labor mobility implies a uniform wage rate and hence a uniform value of labor power, the rate of surplus value must be uniform across sectors,

$$e = \frac{1 - vlp}{vlp} \tag{7}$$

Thus far, the basic structure of Marx's labor theory of value is the same as Ricardo's: prices are determined by values. And hence, for the same reason as Ricardo discovered (see Sraffa's *Introduction* to Ricardo, 1951), the labor theory of value cannot be true if it is combined with competition. Let the rate of profit earned by capitalists in sector i be given by

$$r_i = \frac{\dfrac{s_i}{\lambda_m}}{\dfrac{c_i}{\lambda_m} + \dfrac{v_i}{\lambda_m}} = \frac{s_i}{c_i + v_i} \tag{8}$$

Marx defined the general rate of profit r^M as

$$r^M = \frac{\dfrac{s\mathbf{Q}}{\lambda_m}}{\left(\dfrac{\mathbf{c}}{\lambda_m} + \dfrac{\mathbf{v}}{\lambda_m}\right)\mathbf{Q}} = \frac{s\mathbf{Q}}{(\mathbf{c} + \mathbf{v})\mathbf{Q}} \tag{9}$$

where $\mathbf{Q}$ is the $n \times 1$ vector of gross output and the (row) value vectors $\mathbf{c}$, $\mathbf{v}$, and $\mathbf{s}$ are defined in similar manner to the vector λ. In long-period equilibrium, as long as there is capital mobility, competition must equalize the rate of profit across all activities, so that $r_i = r$ for all i. Yet, given equation (7), two competing capitalists who advance identical total quantities of capital, but in different constant and variable amounts, to produce an identical output cannot earn the same rate of profit; more surplus value and hence a higher rate of profit must accrue to the capitalist who advances more variable capital. This is incompatible with capitalist competition, so that, if the rate of profit is to be equalized, value must be transferred from the capitalist who advances more variable capital to the capitalist who advances less.

To be exact, whereas the prices in equations (2) and (6) are simple prices, the prices $\mathbf{p}^M = (p_1^M, \ldots, p_n^M)$ that support an equalized rate of profit are "prices of production," where

$$p_i^M = (1 + r^M)\left(\frac{c_i}{\lambda_m} + \frac{v_i}{\lambda_m}\right) \tag{10}$$

Then, for a given value of money, the capitalist who advances more (less) variable capital must sell his commodity at a price of production less (more) than its simple price. In this manner, competition redistributes value. Hence, as long as proportions of constant and variable capital differ across different production processes, the labor theory of value understood as equation (2) cannot hold, because it is incompatible with capitalist competition.

Differing time structures of embodied labor had bedevilled the Ricardian labor theory of value. Marx translated this into a difference between price of production and simple price on the one hand, and the proportions in which capital was advanced as constant or variable on the other hand. So, define the composition of capital in sector i as k_i where $k_i = \frac{c_i}{v_i}$. Then, combining equations (6) and (7) and rearranging,

$$\lambda_m p_i = (k_i + 1 + e)v_i$$

Similarly, define the whole economy composition of capital k as $k = \frac{c\mathbf{Q}}{v\mathbf{Q}}$. Then, using equation (9), equation (10) can be rewritten as

$$\lambda_m p_i^M = \frac{k + 1 + e}{k + 1}(k_i + 1)v_i$$

On division, and simplifying,

$$\frac{p_i}{p_i^M} = \left(\frac{k+1}{k_i+1}\right) \Big/ \left(\frac{k+1+e}{k_i+1+e}\right)$$

so that

$$k_i \gtreqless k \Leftrightarrow p_i \lesseqgtr p_i^M$$

Marx's prices of production are greater (less) than their corresponding simple prices in those sectors where the sectoral organic composition of capital is higher (lower) than the economy-wide organic composition of capital. But all sectoral transfers of value will cancel out in the aggregate because it is easily checked that $\mathbf{p}^M\mathbf{Q} = \frac{\lambda\mathbf{Q}}{\lambda_m} = \mathbf{p}\mathbf{Q}$. Furthermore, it is definitionally true that aggregate profits, $\Pi = r^M(\frac{\mathbf{c}}{\lambda_m} + \frac{\mathbf{v}}{\lambda_m})\mathbf{Q}$, are equal to aggregate surplus value at simple prices $\frac{s\mathbf{Q}}{\lambda_m}$.

In sum, Marx developed Ricardo's labor theory of value not only by refining the concept of labor time but also by transferring the focus away from simple prices. Equation (2) does not, in general, hold, and price-of-production-simple-price deviations are the norm. That is, unequal exchange, or nonequivalent exchange, is the norm. For Marx, what anchored the system to labor values were the two aggregate equalities; first, aggregate gross value is invariant to whether it is measured in simple prices or prices of production, and second, aggregate surplus value measured in simple prices is identical to aggregate profits measured in prices of production. Thus, the proportionality of price and value magnitudes holds only at the aggregate level, and only at that level is there equal or equivalent exchange.

But there are two difficulties with this account. First, if prices of production systematically differ from their corresponding simple prices in a long-period equilibrium, then the right-hand side of equation (10) appears to be wrongly specified. In a long-period equilibrium, inputs must be evaluated at prices of production, not simple prices. Hence Marx's procedure seems incomplete. Second, by the same token, the average rate of profit in equation (9) appears to be wrong, since it too should be defined in price of production terms. This is arguably more serious, because if the rate of profit is wrongly defined, its use to define prices of production will generate inconsistency. The transformation problem is therefore concerned with the following questions: under what circumstances, if any, should Marx's procedure be corrected? And if Marx's procedure is suitably corrected, under what circumstances, if any, can Marx's account of a capitalist economy in terms of a labor theory of value be maintained?

4. Classical Long-Period Equilibrium

Because many inputs have to be combined to produce output, if inputs are to be evaluated at prices of production, the input–output structure of the economy has to be specified in more detail. Let A_{ij} and L_j denote, respectively, the amounts of physical input i and labor used in the production of the total amount of good j. The corresponding amounts per unit of output are denoted as $a_{ij} = A_{ij}/Q_j$ and $l_j = L_j/Q_j$, and we shall denote the $n \times n$ input–output matrix and the $1 \times n$ vector of labor inputs, respectively, as $\mathbf{A} = [a_{ij}]$ and $\mathbf{l} = (l_1, \ldots, l_n)$. The ith column of $\mathbf{A}$ is denoted by $\mathbf{A}_{\cdot i}$.[11] The vector of aggregate net output is $\mathbf{y} = (\mathbf{I} - \mathbf{A})\mathbf{Q}$, where $\mathbf{I}$ is the $n \times n$ identity matrix.[12]

Correcting Marx for incompleteness and inconsistency involves correcting equations (9) and (10). Let $\mathbf{p}^e$, w^e, and r^e denote the vector of production prices, and the corresponding (uniform) wage rate and profit rate, which are in principle distinguished from the market prices of the same variables, and may be interpreted as equilibrium values.

Axiom 1 (Long Period). *Long-period equilibrium prices ("prices of production" or "production prices") are the prices that support an equalized rate of profit:*

$$\mathbf{p}^e = (1 + r^e)(\mathbf{p}^e \mathbf{A} + w^e \mathbf{l}) \tag{11}$$

Equation (11) is a system of n equations in $n + 2$ unknowns. The system can be closed by specifying the value of either of the distributive variables, (r^e, w^e), and by choosing a numéraire, which determine equilibrium prices and the other distributive variable.[13] In this paper, we follow the literature and suppose that equation (11) is solved by specifying the wage rate. This can be done in a number of ways. One possibility is to take the money wage as given, which we explore in Section 6, so that it is the same whether prices are simple prices or prices of production. This implies that across the transformation, the real wage rate will change. Another possibility, which we consider in Section 5, is to specify the wage as a real wage, in terms of the commodities $\mathbf{b}$ the wage purchases, whether at simple prices or prices of production. This implies that across the transformation, the money wage rate will change.

However the wage is specified, aggregate equilibrium profits are total revenues less total costs, denoted as $\Pi^e = \mathbf{p}^e\mathbf{Q} - (\mathbf{p}^e\mathbf{AQ} + w^e L)$, and the rate of profit can be written as

$$r^e = \frac{\Pi^e}{\mathbf{p}^e\mathbf{AQ} + w^e L} \tag{12}$$

For most of the approaches we consider (but not all, as we shall see), there is no disagreement over Axiom 1. The issue that separates different approaches is rather how to specify a value theory that is compatible with Axiom 1.

5. The Transformation Problem as an Impossibility Result: The Dualist Approach

Equation (2) is explicit about the value of money, labor values, and prices, and thereby avoids dimensional confusion between units of money and units of labor time. However, if equation (2) holds for all i, then for any i and j, it must be the case that

$$\frac{p_i}{p_j} = \frac{\lambda_i}{\lambda_j} \tag{13}$$

Of course, letting commodity j be the money-commodity restores equation (2), and further assuming the value of money to be unity normalizes all labor values. But the dominant approach in the literature up to the 1970s treats this as a secondary consideration of choice of numéraire, and instead sees the statement of the labor theory of value directly as equation (13). The labor theory of value was taken as specifying that relative prices are determined by relative labor values. Notably, money is absent from this interpretation of Marx (notwithstanding Marx's own emphasis on money in the first three chapters of Marx, 1976). With money reduced to an arbitrary choice of normalization, there was no conceptual linkage between labor values and monetary prices. Instead, there was an underlying (intrinsic, invisible, and essential) system of labor values and associated exploitation, and a phenomenal (extrinsic, visible, and superficial) system of prices and profit rate. The question then was how the visible system could be derived from the invisible system. If Marx's method was wrong, both incomplete and inconsistent, then how should/could prices be derived from values? For around 80 years from the mid-1890s, the issue was posed and analyzed in this manner. With separate price and value systems, this tradition has become known as the "dualist" approach.

Since the value of a commodity is the sum of the value embodied in the means of production and the labor that works with those means of production, we can write the value equations as $\lambda = \lambda\mathbf{A} + \mathbf{l}$, so that labor values are uniquely determined by $\lambda = \mathbf{l}(\mathbf{I} - \mathbf{A})^{-1}$. Hence, immediately, $\lambda\mathbf{y} = L = \mathbf{lQ}$, or the value of net output is the total hours worked. The value of the labor embodied in the means of production is just the value of constant capital, so that $c_i = \lambda\mathbf{A}_{.i}$; and, as before, $v_i + s_i = l_i$.

Within the dualist tradition, a common approach has been to assume that workers do not save but spend all of their income, and to follow Marx (1976, chapter 6, pp. 274–275) in specifying the value of labor power as the value of the commodities purchased with the wage. Then the value of labor power (per hour of labor hired) is the value of the real wage (per hour), as in equation (5). Notice that this specification requires *equivalent exchange in all individual exchanges*, as in equation (2). It immediately follows that the rate of surplus value in equation (7) can be rewritten as

$$e = \frac{L - \lambda\mathbf{b}}{\lambda\mathbf{b}} = \frac{1 - (\lambda\mathbf{b}/L)}{\lambda\mathbf{b}/L} \tag{14}$$

which is nonnegative as long as $L - \lambda \mathbf{b} \geq 0$. Hence, the value equations could be written more fully as

$$\lambda = \lambda \mathbf{A} + (1 + e)\lambda \frac{\mathbf{b}}{L}\mathbf{l} \tag{15}$$

In this manner, the value equations are completely specified by the input–output structure of the economy, the labor coefficients, and the real wage. Hence, they are quite separate from anything to do with prices.

Axiom 2 (Dualism). *Value magnitudes are determined independently from price magnitudes. More specifically, for all i, (i) the value of constant capital is $c_i = \lambda \mathbf{A}_{\cdot i}$; (ii) the value of variable capital (value of labor power) is $v_i = (\lambda \mathbf{b}/L)l_i$; and (iii) the total new value produced is equal to total direct labor employed, $v_i + s_i = l_i$.*

With the wage rate specified as whatever is necessary to purchase $\mathbf{b}/L$, the classical equation for prices of production, equation (11), becomes

$$\mathbf{p}^e = (1 + r^e)\left(\mathbf{p}^e\mathbf{A} + \mathbf{p}^e\frac{\mathbf{b}}{L}\mathbf{l}\right) = (1 + r^e)\mathbf{p}^e\mathbf{M} \tag{16}$$

where $\mathbf{M} = \mathbf{A} + \frac{\mathbf{b}}{L}\mathbf{l}$ is the augmented input coefficient matrix. The system of equations (16) is linear and homogeneous, and a necessary condition for a solution is that the determinant $|\mathbf{I} - (1 + r^e)\mathbf{M}|$ is zero. If $\mathbf{M}$ is indecomposable, then it has a unique positive eigenvalue $1/(1 + r^e)$ to which it can be associated a corresponding unique (up to a positive scalar) positive eigenvector $\mathbf{p}^e$.[14] Choosing a numéraire to close the system then completes the solution.

How then does this result bear on the derivation of the price system from the value system? The short answer is that it does not. Since the augmented input coefficient matrices for the value system $\mathbf{M} + e\frac{\mathbf{b}}{L}\mathbf{l}$ and for the price system $\mathbf{M}$ are different, then the solutions to equations (15) and (16) will be different, and so prices cannot be proportional to labor values. The point is that in the two systems, the nonwage net product is distributed differently. In the "value system," it is distributed in proportion to variable capital advanced (defined in Axiom 2), whereas in the "production price system," it is distributed in proportion to total capital advanced. The same physical quantity of nonwage net product (albeit differently evaluated in labor values and production prices) is distributed over different amounts of capital. So the price and value systems are different. This is summarized in the following theorem.

Theorem 1 (The Transformation Problem). Under **Dualism** and **Long Period**, it is generally impossible that relative prices are equal to relative values. In other words, the *strong equilibrium price view* is logically untenable.

Within the dual, long-period framework, a first reaction to Theorem 1 has been to abandon the *strong equilibrium price view* in favor of the *weak equilibrium price view* and maintain that although relative values are not necessarily equal to relative prices, they still determine them in some sense. While under Axioms 1 and 2, it has long been known that it is possible to derive a precise relation between prices of production and labor values (Pasinetti, 1977, Appendix to chapter 5; Roemer, 1981, section 8.2), this relation is far from the simple one that Marx proposed. For all sectors i, price-value differences depend on how the composition of capital in the production of i differs from that in the production of the commodity used as numéraire, both compositions being evaluated at prices of production. But they also depend upon the "the intricate network of relations between rate of profit and prices in the whole economic system"

(Pasinetti, 1977, p. 136). Vector–matrix multiplication and matrix inversion might show a one-to-one correspondence between labor values and prices of production, but that correspondence is very much more complicated than the relatively simple relations which Marx adduced (see also Mohun, 2004).

Further, the weak equilibrium price view provides at best a partial answer to the problems raised by Theorem 1. For consider the aggregate proportionalities that for Marx anchored prices to labor values: whatever the complexities at the individual level, at the aggregate level, the relationship is simple. Let TV and S denote, respectively, the total amount of value and the aggregate surplus value produced in the economy. Similarly, let TR and Π denote, respectively, aggregate revenues and aggregate profits: these may be equilibrium amounts, or just observed market magnitudes.[15] Dimensionally, if price and value magnitudes are denominated, respectively, in money units and in labor time, then any relation between these value and price aggregates must be mediated by the value of money, and the aggregate relation between them can be stated as:

Axiom 3 (Aggregate Proportionalities). *Total revenue is proportional to total value and total profits are proportional to total surplus value. Formally, (i)* $\lambda_m TR = TV$ *and (ii)* $\lambda_m \Pi = S$.

Further, were it the case that either $\lambda_m = 1$, or labor values were defined in terms of money, or prices of production were defined in terms of labor hours, the dimensional distinction between monetary magnitudes and quantities denominated in labor time would be eliminated, and then we could write:

Axiom 4 (Aggregate Equalities). *Total revenue is equal to total value and total profits are equal to total surplus value. Formally, (i)* $TR = TV$ *and (ii)* $\Pi = S$.

While the issue of dimensionality is theoretically important, we do not discuss it at this point: we list both Axioms 3 and 4 and leave their variables undefined, allowing different approaches to adopt different notions of price and value magnitudes.

It may be objected that the relation between labor and monetary aggregates should not be considered as an axiomatic property. Rather, the existence of such a relation should be, and indeed usually is, proved as a *result* in a given economic environment, under certain conditions. Yet, its central relevance in value theory is such that "its epistemological status in our understanding is as a postulate. We seek a model which will make our postulated belief true" (Roemer, 1982, p. 152). For an axiomatic study involves the specification of a domain of problems, and the formulation of a list of desirable properties of solutions for the domain. Axioms 3 and 4 formalize one of the key properties of Marxian value theory.

This distinction between Axioms 3 and 4 makes little difference to our results here. For, in general, there is no scalar λ_m such that $\lambda_m \mathbf{p}^e \mathbf{Q} = \lambda \mathbf{Q}$ and $\lambda_m \Pi^e = S = \lambda(\mathbf{Q} - \mathbf{AQ} - \mathbf{b})$: by Theorem 1, production prices are not proportional to labor values, and because there are n equations in equation (16) but $n + 1$ variables, one further equation can be specified; this allows either (i) or (ii) in Axiom 3 but not both. Thus, a fortiori, Axiom 4 cannot hold either.

Specifying a numéraire amounts to choosing some commodity or composite commodity whose "value" is invariant to evaluation at simple prices and prices of production (which is why Seton, 1957, called the choice of a numéraire an "invariance postulate"). Since only one such numéraire can be chosen, this is clearly a serious embarrassment for the interpretation that prices of production are derived from labor values. For if the choice of numéraire is that total revenue is proportional to total value, then total profit will not be proportional to total surplus value, in which case the explanation of profit as originating in surplus value fails.

Conversely, if the choice of numéraire maintains proportionality between total surplus value and total profits, then the macroeconomic labor theory of value fails.

The stronger version of the transformation problem can then be stated as follows.

Theorem 2 (The Strong Transformation Problem). Dualism, Long Period, and **Aggregate Proportionalities** are inconsistent. In other words, the *weak equilibrium price view* is logically untenable if either **Aggregate Proportionalities** or **Aggregate Equalities** is imposed.

Within the standard dualist approach to value theory, two main ways out of the impossibility highlighted by Theorems 1 and 2 have been suggested.[16] The standard solution has been to drop **Aggregate Proportionalities** (or **Aggregate Equalities**) and to deflate the relevance of the *weak equilibrium price view* to emphasize the *profit & exploitation view*. This is the literature on the so-called *Fundamental Marxian Theorem* (Okishio, 1963; Morishima, 1973, 1974; Roemer, 1981). For note that although Axiom 3 does not hold, comparison of the characteristic equations of the two systems shows immediately that, regardless of choice of numéraire: (i) $r^e > 0$ if and only if $e > 0$, (ii) $r^e < e$ (unless $\mathbf{A} = \mathbf{0}$), and (iii) each of r^e and e is a monotonically increasing function of the other.

The second solution originally proposed by Okishio (1963) and later developed by Morishima (1973, 1974) consists of a significant weakening of **Aggregate Proportionalities** (or **Aggregate Equalities**), requiring it to hold only at "the long-run equilibrium balanced-growth output vector (or the von Neumann equilibrium output vector)" (Morishima, 1974, p. 623). In fact, it is not difficult to show that if the aggregate output vector coincides with the column eigenvector associated with the largest positive eigenvalue of $\mathbf{M}$, then total revenues equal total value and total surplus value equals total profits.[17] Furthermore, Morishima has shown that, under standard assumptions, there exists a dynamic process—an iteration procedure—whereby the economy reaches the state of long-run equilibrium balanced growth (or the von Neumann equilibrium), and the price and output vectors converge to the von Neumann equilibrium vectors.

Shaikh (1977) has also proposed an iterative approach, arguing that it resolves the incompleteness issue of Marx's own approach. He interprets the Marxian prices of production in equation (10) as the first stage of a recursive procedure that can be written as

$$\mathbf{p}_{k+1}^{M} = \left(1 + r_k^{M}\right) \mathbf{p}_k^{M} \mathbf{M}, \quad \text{for } k = 0, 1, \ldots \tag{17}$$

with $1 + r_k^{M} = \dfrac{\mathbf{p}_k^{M} \mathbf{Q}}{\mathbf{p}_k^{M} \mathbf{M} \mathbf{Q}}$ for all $k = 0, 1, \ldots$ and initializing the iteration by setting $\mathbf{p}_0^{M} = \lambda$. He then shows that in the limit, $\mathbf{p}_k^{M}$ and r_k^{M} converge to the dualist solutions $\mathbf{p}^e$ and r^e of equation (16). Further, equation (17) and the definition of r_k^{M} imply that $\mathbf{p}_{k+1}^{M} \mathbf{Q} = \mathbf{p}_k^{M} \mathbf{Q}$ is true at all stages k of the iteration and therefore part (i) of Axiom 3 (**Aggregate Proportionalities**) holds.

These iterative solutions do not really address the issues raised by the transformation problem because they do not provide a way out of the impossibility highlighted by Theorem 2. Morishima's solution based on the iterative procedure restricts the validity of value theory to a rather special case, namely, the von Neumann equilibrium, which is reached by a very specific dynamic process. While Shaikh's iterative approach is not restricted to a specific equilibrium path, this generality comes at a cost. First, while equation (17) shows how Marx's own "transformation procedure," once extended, can lead from simple prices to production prices, Theorem 2 remains valid and therefore part (ii) of Axiom 3 does not hold.[18] Second, as Shaikh (1977) acknowledges, it is well known that a characteristic equation such as equation (16) can be solved iteratively for $\mathbf{p}^e$ and r^e beginning from some arbitrary initial p_0 and r_0. But then, it is quite unclear that his result identifies a specific, unique relation between values expressed as simple prices and prices of production.

More generally, both the fundamental Marxian theorem and the iterative solutions state how in general the value and price systems are related, but that is all. There are no causative relations between the two systems, which are different from each other and independent of each other. It remains true that all that is necessary to determine production prices is knowledge of the physical structure of the economy: the input–output coefficients, the labor coefficients, and the real wage. Value magnitudes play no role. Further, the same information that is needed to solve the value equations (15) is all that is needed to solve equation (16). The value equations are therefore redundant.

This was the position reached by the end of the 1970s. And yet, there are several oddities in this received view. For one example, money is a casual afterthought in the dualist approach, emerging out of a possible normalization. This seems to miss an empirically and theoretically essential aspect of capitalist economies. For another, the value of labor power is taken to be the value of the real wage (Axiom 2(ii)) and the same real wage is used to augment the input coefficient matrix. Hence, the real wage is held invariant to transformation, which implies that the money wage in the "price world" is different from the implicit money wage in the "value world." But no economic rationale is given for this latter. For reasons such as these, more recent approaches question the coherence of this dualistic separation of the "value world" from the "price world," and generically, they have come to be known as *"single-system"* approaches. Because they question this separation in different ways, they each have a different set of axioms from those of the dualist approach and from each other.

6. The New Interpretation

The *new interpretation* (henceforth, NI) has been proposed, independently, by Duménil (1980, 1984) and Foley (1982, 1986).[19] For them, the fundamental question is not how to derive prices of production from values that are prior in some sense, but rather how the theory of exploitation, based on the value difference between labor power and labor, is compatible with the theory of capitalist competition. But while the theory of exploitation is essential to the understanding of capitalism, the theory of competition embraces more than the characterization of a long-run price equilibrium. So, combining the theory of capitalist exploitation with the theory of capitalist competition must show the compatibility of class exploitation with each and every price system (of which a long-run equilibrium price system is but one example). Consequently, the NI adopts both a descriptive interpretation of value theory as providing a broad theoretical framework for "understanding the dynamics of accumulation and distribution in capitalist-commodity producing economies" (Foley, 2014, p. 17), and a *profit & exploitation view*.

The NI formulation proceeds in two steps. First is an interpretation of the labor theory of value. For the individual commodity, the labor theory of value is specified by equation (2) for some definition of the value of money. This is how it appeared in Smith's precapitalist "early and rude state," as a "commodity law of exchange;" Ricardo extended this to a capitalist economy with produced means of production and found that, in general, such a commodity law of exchange did not hold. It was rather superseded by the "capitalist law of exchange," specified as the determination of prices that supported an equalized rate of profit.[20] Marx then tried to show that the capitalist law of exchange merely modified the commodity law of exchange in the sense that it took value from where it was produced and redistributed it according to total capital advanced. In Marx's particular procedure, the deviations generated by this redistribution summed to zero, and the NI argues that, in a certain (ontological) sense, they could not meaningfully do anything else. It is this insight that motivates the NI, and it is specified accordingly as a fundamental *conservation principle*.

Axiom 5 (Conservation Principle). *For any specification of prices, the total value created by labor in all value-creating production processes is conserved in exchange. Formally,*

$$\mathbf{p}\mathbf{y} = \frac{\lambda \mathbf{y}}{\lambda_m} = \frac{L}{\lambda_m} \tag{18}$$

Two features of Axiom 5 should be emphasized. First, it says that when the commodity law of exchange (equation (2)) does not in general apply for each individual commodity, it nevertheless *does* apply for the aggregate of commodities in net value added; their value in aggregate is conserved in exchange. Thus, at its core, the NI adopts a *macroeconomic view*.[21] Second, Axiom 5 *defines* the value of money in the NI:

$$\lambda_m = \frac{L}{\mathbf{p}\mathbf{y}} \tag{19}$$

The second step of the NI concerns the specification of the value of labor power. The reason that equation (2) does not in general apply to individual commodities is because of their different production conditions (their different compositions of capital). So, in general, individual commodities must exchange at prices different from their simple prices in order that value is redistributed through exchange. This must apply to each and every commodity purchased by the wage. Hence, if all the wage is spent,

$$\mathbf{p}\frac{\mathbf{b}}{L} \neq \frac{\lambda}{\lambda_m} \frac{\mathbf{b}}{L} \tag{20}$$

Yet labor power itself is not a produced commodity, there is no composition of capital involved, no rate of profit in its production that competition will tend to equalize, and hence no price of production of labor power. Consequently, in the sale of labor power for a wage, the law of commodity exchange continues to apply. That is,

Axiom 6 (Weak Single-System). *In the sale of labor power for a wage, the capitalist law of exchange has no effect, and the commodity law of exchange continues to apply so that*

$$w = \frac{v l p}{\lambda_m} \tag{21}$$

In sum, because of different compositions of capital, equation (2) cannot in general hold. But for the NI, equation (2) does continue to hold, first for the aggregate of commodities in value added (Axiom 5); and second, in the sale of labor power for a wage (Axiom 6). These are the key features of the NI, summarized in the following theorem.

Theorem 3 (New Interpretation). Under **Conservation Principle** and **Weak Single-System**, the *profit & exploitation view* is logically consistent. Furthermore, aggregate net output is proportional to total value added and aggregate profit is proportional to aggregate surplus value.

Observe that, since the left-hand sides of equations (20) and (21) are equal if all the wage is spent, then Axiom 2(ii) in the dualist approach cannot hold. Thus, in specifying the value of labor power as the value of the real wage rate, the dualist approach presumes equal exchanges in what the wage is spent on, and *that is precisely what cannot be the case*. The NI argues that the dualist approach is therefore incoherent in its treatment of the wage rate and the value of labor power. Rather than the real wage, the NI takes the money wage rate as given. By equation (21), the given money wage rate determines the value of labor power, and, using equation (19), the value of labor power can be written as

$$vlp = \frac{wL}{\mathbf{py}} \tag{22}$$

As for prices of production, the NI formulation is the same as equation (11) in Axiom 1, but without specifying w^e in terms of the workers' consumption bundle. There is no requirement in the NI either to specify the wage as what it is spent on, or indeed to presume that all of the wage is spent. Then, from equation (11), one can derive a one-to-one inverse relation between the wage rate and the profit rate that, by equation (22), can be specified in terms of the value of labor power. The higher the value of labor power, the lower the rate of profit. But once the value of labor power is fixed, then the rate of profit and the corresponding production prices can be derived.

In one sense, there is little substantive difference between the dualist prices of production and the NI prices of production in that both derive from equation (11) in Axiom 1, for appropriate specifications of the wage rate. But consider again equation (22). This says that the value of labor power is the wage share of value added *at any set of prices*. This result is central to the NI because it demonstrates the existence of class exploitation. Using Marx's metaphor, the value of labor power divides the total "working day" into a period of "necessary labor" in which the working class produces a value equivalent to its wages, and a further period of "surplus labor" in which it produces a value that is expropriated by the capitalist class as profit. At any moment in time, class struggle (for example, over the social norms for the reproduction of the working class) determines how this "working day" is divided. That is, class struggle determines how much of the net value added the working class produces is won back in the form of wages, and this class struggle determination of the wage share is no different whether prices are simple prices or production prices. As long as exploitation exists, the wage share must be less than one.

The NI thereby shows that *the existence of capitalist exploitation is independent of any account of price formation*. That is, in the NI, equation (22) always holds, whereas equation (11) might not. Hence, the NI is also a framework for empirical analysis, since the total number of hours worked, aggregate value added in price terms, and the average hourly wage rate are all measurable quantities.

One may object that, albeit formally correct, the previous argument does not clarify why one needs the labor theory of value to capture exploitative relations. For, in the NI, the existence of exploitation at the aggregate level reduces to the fact that the wage share is less than 1. This objection is not entirely convincing. The NI does not *define* exploitation as corresponding to a wage share smaller than 1: the equivalence, at the aggregate level, between exploitation and the existence of profits is *derived* from more primitive axioms concerning the nature and determinants of value and surplus value. Further, such equivalence does not imply that monetary phenomena are all that matters while the notion of exploitation, and labor accounts, are irrelevant. In recent work, for example, Veneziani and Yoshihara (2015, 2017) and Yoshihara (2010) have extended the NI in order to define exploitation at the level of individual agents and social classes. They have shown that even at the micro level, the existence of exploitation is synonymous with positive profits. The exploitation status of individuals and classes, and labor accounts more generally, provide important positive and normative insights on capitalist economies and their class structure, which are not reducible to the wage share being smaller than 1. Further, they have shown in Yoshihara and Veneziani (2013) that, contrary to a common view, the concept of exploitation is not just a complicated way of capturing the productivity of the economy. Under the NI, the existence of profits is *not* synonymous with the existence of a surplus denominated in any arbitrary commodity (as the *Commodity Exploitation Theorem* implies, for example, in Roemer, 1981). Rather, a wage share smaller than 1 is synonymous with the exploitation of *labor*.

As a theory, however, the NI is incomplete for two reasons. First, there is no theoretical determination of *vlp* other than in the general terms of class power and class struggle. And second, while it defines λ_m as equation (19), it has no theoretical account either of its formation or its movement over time. While equation (19) does imply that λ_m will fall through time because of both productivity increases and pure price inflation, there is no account of pure price inflation. While this incompleteness detracts neither from the generality of the NI as an account of exploitation, nor from its usefulness as a foundation for empirical analysis, it nonetheless requires further theoretical development. As such, it specifies a progressive research agenda.

7. An Althusserian Approach

A rather different interpretation to the NI has been proposed by Wolff *et al.* (1982, 1984a, 1984b) (henceforth, WCR) and further extended and generalized by Roberts (1997, 2009). WCR see themselves as "applying the perspectives and insights of the Althusserian tradition to the reinterpretation of Marx's theoretical and economic texts" (Wolff *et al.*, 1982, p. 565). Within this framework, the notion of causation implicit in the dualist approach is rejected as both reductive and essentialist, resting on some essence determining some consequent (such as in the standard reading of Marx, values determining prices). In its place is a focus on "overdetermination": mutual and reciprocal determination together with relations of constitutivity. Constitutivity is "the power of each aspect of society not merely to affect other aspects, but also to effect them, constitute them, participate in determining the nature of, as well as the changes in, every other aspect" (Wolff *et al.*, 1982, p.565). Because production and circulation are both overdetermined, the concepts of value and price, understood as the form that value takes in exchange, are interdependent, and constitute each other. They further change according to the degree of complexity of the economic processes that actualize class relations, so that discourses themselves are changed.

In particular, the concepts of *Capital III* are, taken together, a different discourse from those of *Capital I*; the new determinations of *Capital III* (such as interindustry competition) require new concepts (such as the average rate of profit), and the changing discourse requires corresponding changes in the meanings of value and the form it takes in exchange. Because *Capital I* constructs capitalist class relations to show how surplus value derives from unpaid labor time, and because *Capital III* shows how the form of surplus value, as profit, is also a relation between paid and unpaid labor time, then WCR are adopting a *profit & exploitation* view.[22]

Within this methodological approach, value is "the quantity of social labor-time 'attached to' the commodity in production, given the nature and functioning of the processes involved in commodity circulation. The form of value in exchange is … the quantity of social labor-time 'attached to' the commodity in circulation, given the particular processes of production" (Wolff *et al.*, 1984a, p. 123). Value and value-form are equal in *Capital I*, but only as a preliminary step. In general, and in actual capitalist economies, they differ quantitatively, both being jointly determined by production and circulation conditions. It follows that, while "value-form" is a price, it is a price denominated in labor time rather than in money. Given their focus on individual values and prices, WCR adopt a *microeconomic view*. More precisely, WCR adopt Axiom 1 (**Long Period**), but interpret it differently. For them, prices of production are the magnitudes of *labor time* that allow the reproduction of the capitals of each industry with a uniform profit rate. Hence, they can be called "labor prices of production" and denoted $\mathbf{p}^{wcr}$. Thus, in the discourse of *Capital III*, Axiom 1 becomes the basic statement of the value-form, with its production prices $\mathbf{p}^{wcr}$ measured in labor time.[23] Interpreted in this way,[24] Axiom 1 both constitutes and is constituted by the basic statement of value that is written as Axiom 7:

Axiom 7 (Strong Single-System). *The value of each commodity is the sum of the prices of production of its constant capital plus the living labor required. Formally,*

$$\lambda = \mathbf{p}^{wcr}\mathbf{A} + \mathbf{l} \tag{23}$$

Letting $\mathbf{p}^e = \mathbf{p}^{wcr}$, equations (11) and (23) provide a codetermination of value and value-form. Together they define a system of $2n$ equations in $2n + 1$ unknowns (λ, $\mathbf{p}^{wcr}$, and r), which can be solved in the same manner as dualism's equation (16). Then a unique normalization can be specified by defining the rate of profit as a ratio of labor amounts as follows.

Axiom 8 (Labor Prices of Production). *The rate of profit is the ratio of total unpaid labor to total capital advanced in labor time. Formally,*

$$r = \frac{L - \mathbf{p}^{wcr}\mathbf{b}}{\mathbf{p}^{wcr}\mathbf{A}\mathbf{Q} + \mathbf{p}^{wcr}\mathbf{b}} \tag{24}$$

Letting $\mathbf{p}^e = \mathbf{p}^{wcr}$, by equations (11) and (24), it follows that

$$\mathbf{p}^{wcr}\mathbf{Q} = \mathbf{p}^{wcr}\mathbf{A}\mathbf{Q} + L \tag{25}$$

which implies that

$$\mathbf{p}^{wcr}\mathbf{y} = L \tag{26}$$

Equation (26) expresses "a necessary equality between ... the direct labor-time expression of the net product ... and ... the expression in labor-time terms for the revenues which are realized by the two classes together when that net product is distributed between them through the circulation process" (Wolff *et al.*, 1982, p. 579).[25]

On the basis of the foregoing, and noting that $\mathbf{p}^{wcr}\mathbf{Q} = \lambda\mathbf{Q}$ follows immediately by post-multiplying equation (23) by $\mathbf{Q}$ and comparing with equation (25), the WCR Theorem can be stated as follows.

Theorem 4 (Single System). Let $\mathbf{p}^e = \mathbf{p}^{wcr}$. Under **Long Period, Strong Single-System**, and **Labor Prices of Production**, the *profit & exploitation view* is logically consistent. Furthermore, **Aggregate Equalities** is satisfied.

WCR conclude that the traditional interpretation that "a valid Marxian transformation must explain prices and the rate of profit as exclusively determined by physically embodied direct and indirect labor time ... is ... *not* the only basis on which to confront the price-value relation. Reading Marx's *Capital* as expressing a view of the role of labor-time categories which is quite thoroughly opposed to the Ricardian approach in all its variants has allowed us to resolve the traditional puzzles of the transformation problem by posing them in different fashion" (Wolff *et al.*, 1984b, pp. 435–436).

However, two features of the WCR system should be emphasized that raise doubts concerning this conclusion and more generally, the WCR approach to Marxian value theory. First, the role of equation (23) in the WCR system is unclear, because it simply adds n more variables and n more equations. It is therefore not completely obvious that equations (11) and (23) adequately fulfill the constitutive roles that WCR allocate for them. Conceptually, equation (23) can be interpreted as a part of a complete value accounting system in which constant capital, variable capital, and surplus value are all expressed in value magnitudes. Yet, formally, values are defined purely *ex post* and play no role either in the definition or in the determination of any other variable in the WCR system. WCR solve equations (11) and (24) for $\mathbf{p}^e = \mathbf{p}^{wcr}$ and r, and the value equations (23) are irrelevant to that solution.[26] Notice further that, directly from equation (24), total profit in labor units and total surplus value are the same. So the only relevance of the value equations (23) is in showing that Axiom 4(i) holds. If that is all that equation (23) is good for, its status as a fundamental constitutive relation seems somewhat artificial.

Second, money plays no role in Axioms 1 and 7–8. While prices of production are denominated in labor times, one of these prices (say, the kth) will be a labor-time price of gold; dividing all other labor-time prices by this labor-time price of gold translates labor-time prices into money prices, so that $P_j = \frac{p_j^{wcr}}{p_k^{wcr}}$, which is the WCR interpretation of Marx's equation (2) in an overdetermined *Capital III* world. Yet, as in the dualist interpretation—and unlike in other approaches—money plays no direct role in the WCR system, for its analysis of labor time accounting is independent of and prior to the introduction of money and the definition of its value.

8. A Macromonetary Approach

Moseley (2016) also offers an explicit methodological account of values and prices. He proposes that Marx's analysis be interpreted as focusing first on the production of surplus value, and then on its distribution, so that a sequential (rather than a simultaneous) account is necessary. This contrasts, for example, with WCR, who see both value and its form (price) as being simultaneously determined for a given level of abstraction. Moseley offers an interpretation that sees first a macrodetermination of total surplus value for the economy as a whole, and then a microdetermination of how this total is divided between different industries. Given the logical primacy of the macrorelations, we characterize Moseley as adopting a *macroeconomic view*.

8.1 The Macrodetermination of Surplus Value

Moseley stresses an interpretation of the circuit of capital that sees a given amount of money advanced as (constant and variable) capital that reproduces itself together with an increment called surplus value. Because it is this latter that has to be explained, the money advanced is taken as given. His approach implies that neither equation (2) nor its implication, equation (13), represents Marx's labor theory of value. Instead, the latter is solely concerned with the determination of aggregate surplus value in money terms on the basis of aggregate money capital advanced. While "aggregate" might be taken to imply that something is aggregated, Moseley denies this on methodological grounds. Obviously, the money advanced is spent on definite quantities of inputs, but what is purchased is a microeconomic issue that cannot be considered until aggregate surplus value is first determined. So while inputs are purchased at unit prices that are presumed to be prices of production, these latter are (methodologically) posited yet undetermined and so cannot be explicitly considered at this macroeconomic stage. Similarly, since these prices determine the quantities that are purchased, those quantities cannot be explicitly considered. All that can be considered is the total quantity of money laid out, and its division into what is spent on means of production, and what is spent on labor power.

Let $C^\$$ and $V^\$$ denote the total amounts of money advanced as constant and variable capital, respectively, and let $S^\$$ denote the money surplus value produced. By definition, money surplus value is just the difference between total revenue $M^\$$ and the capital advanced to produce it:

$$S^\$ = M^\$ - C^\$ - V^\$ \tag{27}$$

The new value created in the circuit of capital is L, the sum of necessary labor V^{hrs}, and surplus labor S^{hrs}. As in the NI, Moseley then imposes Axiom 5, the **Conservation Principle** ("the key assumption in Marx's labor theory of value" [Moseley, 2016, p. 31]), according to which aggregate new value produced is proportional to total labor L. In the notation of this section,

$$V^\$ + S^\$ = \frac{(V^{hrs} + S^{hrs})}{\lambda_m}$$

Consequently,

$$S^\$ = \left(\frac{V^{hrs}}{\lambda_m} - V^\$\right) + \frac{S^{hrs}}{\lambda_m}$$

Moseley then applies Marx's definition of necessary labor as a *macroeconomic* definition.

Axiom 9 (Necessary Labor). *Necessary labor in the aggregate is the labor that produces the monetary equivalent of the total capital advanced as wages, so that*

$$V^{hrs} = \lambda_m V^\$ \tag{28}$$

Combining Axiom 9 with Axiom 5 immediately yields Moseley's main result:

$$S^\$ = \frac{S^{hrs}}{\lambda_m} \tag{29}$$

Theorem 5 summarizes these results.

Theorem 5. Under the **Conservation Principle** and **Necessary Labor**, the *profit & exploitation view* is logically consistent. Furthermore, aggregate net output is proportional to total value added and aggregate profit is proportional to aggregate surplus value.

For Moseley, equation (29) is "Marx's 'surplus labour' theory of surplus-value ... the main conclusion of Volume I" (Moseley, 2016, p. 34) and hence the basic statement of Marx's labor theory of value.

Theorems 5 and 3 are remarkably similar. They both rely on the **Conservation Principle** (Axiom 5). Furthermore, the NI's Axiom 6 and Moseley's Axiom 9 can hardly be considered as radically different. Formally, Axiom 6 appears to be stronger than Axiom 9: whereas the NI applies equation (2) to the commodity labor power in Axiom 6, the NI's use of an hour as the basic unit is arbitrary, and multiplying equation (21) through by the total number of hours hired yields equation (28). The converse is also true however. Moseley's methodological emphasis that the various monetary aggregates are scalar magnitudes because prices are as yet unspecified is irrelevant in the treatment of $V^\$$. For with respect to variable capital in money terms, there are no undetermined prices. Moseley begins with the "per-worker-day" relation between variable capital as wages and variable capital as necessary labor, aggregates up across all "worker-days," and then treats the resultant aggregate relation as a given. But since the wage rate is known, one can also proceed in the opposite direction and so Moseley's Axiom 9 implies the NI's Axiom 6. Thus far then, the analytical difference between Moseley's interpretation and the NI is slight.

8.2 *The Distribution of Surplus Value*

Having determined total surplus value in money terms, $S^\$$, by equation (29), the general rate of profit r^{mos} is then defined as the ratio of $S^\$$ to the total money capital advanced:

$$r^{mos} = \frac{S^\$}{C^\$ + V^\$} \tag{30}$$

This, in turn, is used to define Moseley's prices of production:

$$P_i^{mos} = M_i^\$ = \left(C_i^\$ + V_i^\$\right)(1 + r^{mos}) \tag{31}$$

Notice that first, r^{mos} is determined prior to prices of production; second, the inputs for each industry are commodities purchased at already existing prices (of production), so that there is nothing to transform; and third, these prices of production are not unit prices but industry gross revenues. These latter are the money capital advanced in industry i plus a portion of total money value produced, that portion being determined by the ratio of money capital advanced in industry i to that advanced in the economy as a whole (because equation (31) can be written as $P_i^{mos} = M_i^\$ = \frac{(C_i^\$ + V_i^\$)}{(C^\$ + V^\$)}(C^\$ + V^\$ + S^\$)$).

Moseley's sequential approach here appears to diverge from the NI (compare equation (11) for a given money wage and equation (31)). His rate of profit is formed out of the aggregate money magnitudes of *Capital I*, and, for Moseley, these latter are aggregates of quantities priced at prices of production. Hence, equation (31) does not determine prices of production; it only serves to distribute aggregate money surplus value among the various individual capitals. Yet, converting equation (31) into unit levels, it is easy to see that it can only do that if equation (30) is, in fact, that equalized rate of profit that forms prices of production at unit level. For prices of production have been posited at the outset, and the mathematics only allows for one solution value of the rate of profit.

Moseley further argues that Marx's two aggregate proportionalities are always both satisfied, because in his framework, they are not equations but identities. By Theorem 5, part (ii) of Axiom 3 (**Aggregate Proportionalities**) is satisfied. And the total revenues of *Capital I* are identical to the total revenues of *Capital III* because everything is denominated (whether implicitly or explicitly) in prices of production. But that is neither part (i) of Axiom 3 nor part (i) of Axiom 4 (**Aggregate Equalities**), both of which concern the relation between total revenue at *Capital III* prices and total value measured in hours.

Since Moseley proposes that his interpretation is what Marx himself wrote/meant, he has to specify some relation between *Capital I* (or, identically, *Capital III*) total revenues and total value measured in hours. There is obviously no difficulty in showing this for value-added, for that is what equations (28) and (29) do. But no deduction is possible for total revenue and total value, since $C^\$$ is denominated in prices of production that are not proportional to labor values. Hence, he requires a further axiom.

Axiom 10 (Constant Capital Proportionality). *The labor value of constant capital is imputed as*

$$C^{mos,hrs} = \lambda_m C^\$ \tag{32}$$

Then, the combination of equations (18), (28), and (32) shows that part (i) of Axiom 3 is also satisfied, yielding the following theorem.

Theorem 6 (Moseley). Under the **Conservation Principle, Necessary Labor**, and **Constant Capital Proportionality**, the *profit & exploitation view* is logically consistent. Furthermore, **Aggregate Proportionalities** holds.

Theorem 6 is distinctive of Moseley's approach, and it shows that in his framework, both of Marx's aggregate proportionalities hold. Nonetheless, compared with Theorem 5, this comes at a significant cost, since it requires an arbitrary redefinition of the value of constant capital. While Axiom 10 provides a symmetry to Moseley's treatment of constant capital, variable capital, and surplus value, the interpretation of $C^{mos,hrs}$ is unclear, for this imputed value of constant capital is *neither* the hours historically necessary *nor* the hours currently necessary to produce the means of production (Moseley, 2016, pp. 259–260). It is rather a quantity of hours that is wholly determined by the prevailing value of money and the aggregate amount of money advanced as constant capital. Its interpretation is therefore obscure, and the argument appears contrived, suggesting that the only reason behind the redefinition of constant capital in Axiom 10 is to achieve a claim of Marxist textual fidelity via Theorem 6. Setting aside the theoretically questionable Axiom 10 and focusing on Theorem 5, Moseley's approach is not substantially different from the NI.

9. The Temporal Single-System Interpretation

An approach to Marxian value theory that has recently attracted both attention and controversy is the Temporal Single-System Interpretation (TSSI) (Freeman, 1996; Kliman and McGlone, 1988, 1999; Kliman, 2001, 2007). The TSSI adopts a *profit & exploitation view* and a *microeconomic view*, and supports a *weak price view*, arguing that values determine prices, although these are not equilibrium prices.

Consider the production period t. As production takes time, one can distinguish between the beginning of t, when inputs are bought, and the end of t/beginning of $t + 1$ when outputs emerge from production and are sold. So far, we have not made this distinction because all of the main approaches (and indeed almost all schools of economics) evaluate inputs at current or replacement cost rather than historical cost. One reason is that we are interested in firms as going concerns, and in a situation in which prices are changing, we want to know whether the firm is viable and can reproduce itself. With a labor theory of value, there is another reason: we want to be able to attribute the value of net output to the labor that produced it. The TSSI insists on a temporalism and historical cost pricing (Kliman and McGlone, 1999, p. 34) and we write the temporalist perspective as the following axiom.

Axiom 11 (Temporalism). *In every production period t, the values and prices of inputs are determined at the beginning of t, before the values and prices of outputs, which are determined at the end of t/beginning of $t + 1$, so that the former are determinants of the latter.*

Axiom 11 is supposed to capture the inherently dynamic nature of capitalist economies. In the rest of this section, the time subscript t refers to the beginning of production period t, whereas we use the time subscript $t + 1$ to denote the end of period t and beginning of $t + 1$.

The TSSI further rejects the view that labor values and monetary prices emerge from separate systems. This is instantiated in two different axioms. The first one states that money magnitudes enter the determination of values.

Axiom 12 (Value Single-System). *Price magnitudes enter the definition of values. More specifically, for all i and t, (i) the value of constant capital is $c_{it} = \lambda_{m,t}\mathbf{p}_t\mathbf{A}_{.it}$; and (ii) the value of variable capital is $v_{it} = \lambda_{m,t}w_t l_{it}$.*

Assuming that total new value produced in every sector is equal to total direct labor employed, $v_{it} + s_{it} = l_{it}$, Axiom 12 immediately implies that equation (6) becomes

$$\lambda_{t+1} = \lambda_{m,t}\mathbf{p}_t\mathbf{A}_t + \mathbf{l}_t \tag{33}$$

The second part of the TSSI rejection of dualism is a stronger claim on the relation between prices and values.

Axiom 13 (Price Single-System). *Values and prices differ because of random, sector-specific deviations. Formally, for all t, there exists a vector $\mathbf{g}_t = \lambda_{m,t+1}\mathbf{P}_{t+1} - \lambda_{t+1}$ such that $\mathbf{g}_t\mathbf{Q}_{t+1} = 0$.*

Combining Axioms 12 and 13, it immediately follows that

$$\lambda_{m,t+1}\mathbf{P}_{t+1} = \lambda_{m,t}\mathbf{p}_t\mathbf{A}_t + \mathbf{l}_t + \mathbf{g}_t \tag{34}$$

Thus, assuming workers to spend all their income, so that $w_t = \mathbf{p}_t\frac{\mathbf{b}_t}{L_t}$, aggregate nominal profits are $\Pi_{t+1}^N = (\mathbf{p}_{t+1} - \mathbf{p}_t\mathbf{A}_t - \mathbf{p}_t\frac{\mathbf{b}_t}{L_t}\mathbf{l}_t)\mathbf{Q}_{t+1}$. Let $i_{t+1} = \frac{\lambda_{m,t}}{\lambda_{m,t+1}} - 1$, where i_{t+1} is the TSSI inflation rate. Then, aggregate real profits, Π_t^R, and aggregate surplus value, $S_{t+1} = \mathbf{s}_t\mathbf{Q}_{t+1}$, are defined as follows:

$$\Pi_{t+1}^R = \left[\frac{\mathbf{p}_{t+1}}{1+i_{t+1}} - \mathbf{p}_t\mathbf{A}_t - \mathbf{p}_t\frac{\mathbf{b}_t}{L_t}\mathbf{l}_t\right]\mathbf{Q}_{t+1} \tag{35}$$

$$S_{t+1} = \mathbf{l}_t\mathbf{Q}_{t+1} - \lambda_{m,t}\mathbf{p}_t\mathbf{b}_t \tag{36}$$

That profits are defined in real terms is important in that the aggregate proportionality of profits and surplus value is interpreted in terms of real profits, not nominal profits (see Theorem 7 below).

Axioms 12 and 13 concern the relation between labor values and *market* prices. As concerns prices of production and the general profit rate, the TSSI makes two assumptions. First, it has a rather specific view concerning the determination of the general profit rate, which can be formally put as follows.

Axiom 14 (TSSI Profit Rate). *The general profit rate is given by the ratio between aggregate surplus value (converted into monetary units) and the historic, market cost of advanced inputs. Formally,*

$$r_t^{TSSI} = \frac{\mathbf{s}_t\mathbf{Q}_{t+1}}{\lambda_{m,t}\left(\mathbf{p}_t\mathbf{A}_t + \mathbf{p}_t\frac{\mathbf{b}_t}{L_t}\mathbf{l}_t\right)\mathbf{Q}_{t+1}}, \quad \text{for all } t. \tag{37}$$

The second assumption specifies prices of production not as those supporting a long-period equilibrium but as determined by a markup on historic market prices.

Axiom 15 (TSSI Production Prices). *Production prices are derived from applying the average profit rate to historic costs evaluated at past market prices. Formally,*

$$\mathbf{p}_{t+1}^{TSSI} = \left(1 + r_t^{TSSI}\right)\mathbf{p}_t\left(\mathbf{A}_t + \frac{\mathbf{b}_t}{L_t}\mathbf{l}_t\right), \quad \text{for all } t. \tag{38}$$

Based on this axiomatic system, TSSI proponents maintain that the literal truth of *all* of Marx's propositions can be shown:

Theorem 7 (TSSI). Assume that $\lambda_{m,t} > 0$ all t. Then, under **Temporalism, Value Single-System, Price Single-System, TSSI profit rate**, and **TSSI production prices**, "(a) all of Marx's aggregate value-price equalities hold; (b) values cannot be negative; (c) profit cannot be positive unless surplus value is positive; (d) value production is no longer irrelevant to price and profit determination; (e) the profit rate is invariant to the distribution of profit; (f) productivity in luxury industries affects the general rate of profit" (Kliman and McGlone, 1999, p. 55).

Claims (a) and (c) follow immediately from Axiom 13: postmultiplying equations (33) and (34) by $\mathbf{Q}_{t+1}$, using equations (35) and (36), and noting that $\mathbf{g}_t \mathbf{Q}_{t+1} = 0$ by assumption, it follows that $\lambda_{m,t+1} \mathbf{P}_{t+1} \mathbf{Q}_{t+1} = \lambda_{t+1} \mathbf{Q}_{t+1}$ and $\lambda_{m,t} \Pi_t^R = S_t$, for all t. Claim (b) follows from equation (33) by assuming $\mathbf{p}_t$ to be nonnegative at all t. Claims (e) and (f), and the part of claim (d) concerning the profit rate, immediately follow from Axiom 14.[27] It is also easy to show that in the TSSI, the key claims of price and value theory also hold if production prices are considered instead of market prices.[28]

In all frameworks considered so far, prices of production are the long-run prices that support an equalized rate of profit, and consequently they are equilibrium prices. But the TSSI axioms do not specify what is to be regarded as equilibrium in its temporal framework.[29] Indeed, the vector $\mathbf{p}_{t+1}^{TSSI}$ is determined on the basis of a uniform profit rate, a long-run condition which the TSSI regards as "a very particular case" (Kliman, 2001, p. 99), or a rather restrictive postulate (Freeman, 1996); yet this holds in the TSSI even outside a steady state by assuming that the profit rate is an average rate of profit. But "If market prices do not coincide with prices of production, there is no reason to think that the profit rate will be uniform across sectors. To assume a uniform profit rate in such circumstances amounts to imposing an arbitrary condition on the sectoral mark-ups" (Mongiovi, 2002, p. 408).

Kliman and McGlone deny that the TSSI "eliminates the inconsistency in Marx's value theory by supplying extra unknowns, in effect by modeling a perpetual disequilibrium in which 'anything goes'" (Kliman and McGlone, 1999, p. 50), because $\mathbf{p}_t$ and r_t^{TSSI} are determined prior to $\mathbf{p}_{t+1}^{TSSI}$, and thus in equation (38), there are n equations and n unknowns. Yet, despite the large number of assumptions, the formal structure of the TSSI is underdetermined. Consider the relation between TSSI values and market prices. At a steady state, equations (35) and (36) become

$$\lambda = \lambda_m \mathbf{pA} + \mathbf{l} \tag{39}$$

$$\lambda_m \mathbf{p} = \lambda_m \mathbf{pA} + \mathbf{l} + \mathbf{g} \tag{40}$$

But then there are $n + 1$ degrees of freedom, unless *first*, it is assumed that in a steady state $\mathbf{g} = \mathbf{0}$, or equivalently, that $\lambda = \lambda_m \mathbf{p}$, so that goods exchange at simple prices, and *second*, a formal definition of λ_m is provided. As regards the first point, since $\mathbf{g}_t$ is determined after market prices are realized, the alternative to value-price proportionality is to deny the steady state so that prices determine values "historically." But then, all variables are determined *ex post* by observed, unexplained market prices, with little explanatory power. As regards the second point, there is no definition of the value of money in the TSSI and so the model is undetermined. To assume $\lambda_{m,t} = 1$, all t, and state that this implies no loss of generality (e.g., Kliman and McGlone, 1999, p. 36) is unconvincing. In equations (39) and (40), *if* one assumes $\mathbf{g} = \mathbf{0}$ to avoid underdetermination, then the choice of λ_m is largely immaterial in that commodities are already assumed to exchange at their simple prices. But outside of a steady state, it is difficult to justify the assumption that $\lambda_{m,t} = 1$, all t.[30] The absence of a definition of $\lambda_{m,t}$ casts some doubt on Theorem 7, which crucially rests on the assumption that the undefined variable $\lambda_{m,t}$ is positive at all t.

That an explicit definition of $\lambda_{m,t}$ is unnecessary to prove Theorem 7 highlights some conceptual differences with competing approaches. In the NI, for example, prices and values are distinct and $\lambda_{m,t}$ is used "to move back and forth between money and labour accounts" (Foley, 2000, p. 7). Moreover, it is Axioms 5 and 6, and the specific definition of $\lambda_{m,t}$ that follows from them, that make it possible in the NI to retain "the central ideas of the labor theory of value, ... [although] they cannot and do not retain all of the results that hold when prices are proportional to labor values" (Foley, 1982, p. 42). In the TSSI, instead, there exist no distinct money and value accounts, and the single-system qualification reduces to the assumption that, apart from out-of-steady-state deviations, values are proportional to market prices. Thus, as shown by equations (39) and (40), $\lambda_{m,t}$ is just an undefined factor of proportionality between values and prices, which can be arbitrarily (and, from the TSSI standpoint, without loss of generality) assumed equal to unity.

Temporalism, "disequilibrium," and the extra unknowns, $\mathbf{g}_t$, are necessary to have some sort of "transformation problem" to solve. But as Duménil and Lévy comment on equation (33), "Sequential values are clearly consubstantial with prices, within a *labor-market price* theory of value" (Duménil and Lévy, 2000, p. 127). Equations (33) and (34) show the temporal and logical primacy of observed market prices: the sequence $\{\mathbf{p}_t\}_{t=0,...}$ unidirectionally determines the time paths of all other variables $\{\lambda_t, \mathbf{g}_t, \lambda_{m,t}, \mathbf{p}_t^{TSSI}\}_{t=0,...}$. This is some distance from the classical theory of value.

10. Stochastic Approaches

Despite many conceptual and formal differences, all of the interpretations considered thus far share a common feature: value theory and price theory are analyzed within a *deterministic* framework. In this section, we discuss two less known approaches that substantially deviate from this assumption. They rather conceptualize the main economic magnitudes (prices, values, technology, distribution, and so on) as generated by *stochastic* processes and the transformation problem as relating to *average* values of the relevant variables. In this sense, both approaches adopt what may be defined the *strong average equilibrium price view*. Moreover, the focus of both approaches is on the prices and values of individual commodities and the relation between the two sets of variables at a highly disaggregated level. Thus, they adopt a *microeconomic view*.

10.1 Stochastic Prices

From a descriptive perspective, Farjoun and Machover (1983) (henceforth, FM) argue that in general, "labour is, *par excellence*, the essential substance of an economy, and should therefore be taken ... as the fundamental yardstick. ... [Economics] *is about the social productive activity of human beings, social labour ... the study of the social processes and structures by means of which and through which social labour is organized and performed, and the output of this labour distributed and allocated to various uses*" (FM, p. 85). This supports a *predictive view* that labor magnitudes are interpreted probabilistically as the best predictors of actual market monetary magnitudes (prices and profit rates). The fundamental theoretical tenet of their approach is that "the labour theory of value was led into a theoretical crisis not because of the supposed incoherence of the concept of labour-value, nor because it assumed free competition, but because it attempted to reconcile value categories with the fallacious assumption of the uniformity of the rate of profit" (FM, p. 19).

In terms of our axiomatic approach, on the one hand, they take technology as part of the essential data of an economy, and define labor values as the standard input–output employment multipliers, accepting the dualist approach to value magnitudes, including constant and variable capital, and adopting Axiom 2 (**Dualism**). On the other hand, however, they reject Axiom 1 (**Long Period**) and in general any theory of prices based on the assumption of a uniform profit rate. They argue not only that such uniformity is never observed in practice, even as an approximation, but also that "the uniformity assumption is in principle incompatible with a theorization of the capitalist system as a system of free competition and private property in the means of production" (FM, p. 28). For competitive forces constantly tend to create new opportunities for profit and "in a capitalist economy the very forces of competition, *which are internal to the system*, are responsible not only for pulling an abnormally high or low rate of profit back towards normality, *but also for creating such 'abnormal' rates of profit in the first place*" (FM, p. 34). Such competitive forces include not only various pricing and marketing strategies but also technical innovations, which take place at an uneven and uncoordinated pace, and "technical revolutions" (FM, p. 138), which "tend to scramble any putative uniformity in the rate of profit" (FM, p. 35). The uniform profit rate assumption misses the essentially dynamic nature of capitalism.

This entails a different theorization of capitalist economies. First, FM argue that actual market variables should be analyzed adopting "a probabilistic model, in which price, the rate of profit (and other economic parameters, such as capital intensity) are treated from the very beginning not as determinate numerical quantities, but as random variables, each having its own probability distribution" (FM, p. 25). Formally, let K_f and Π_f^{mkt} be, respectively, the total amount of fixed capital (valued at current market prices) owned by firm f and its current profits. The rate of profit of firm f is $r_f = \frac{\Pi_f^{mkt}}{K_f}$. Let w_l be the gross wage paid for the lth worker-hour, and let p_j^{mkt} and λ_j be, respectively, the actual market price paid for a commodity (or a bundle of commodities) in the jth transaction and its labor content. Define $\psi_j = \frac{p_j^{mkt}}{\lambda_j}$: ψ_j is the price paid in the jth transaction per unit of labor content. The first tenet of FM's approach concerns the probabilistic nature of processes generating market outcomes.

Axiom 16 (Stochastic Prices). *Marxian value theory focuses on actual market phenomena and magnitudes. Observed profit rates r_f, wage rates w_l, and prices p_j^{mkt}, are all random variables with given empirical distributions.*

The second key departure from the standard approach concerns the definition of equilibrium. "If a competitive market economy has a state of equilibrium, it must be a state in which a whole range of profit rates coexist; it must be a *dynamic* state, in the sense that the rate of profit of each firm keeps changing all the time; it can only be a state of *equilibrium* in the sense that the *proportion* of capital (out of the total social capital) that yields any particular rate of profit remains approximately constant" (FM, p. 36). This is a statistical equilibrium notion that differs from both the standard Walrasian concept and the long-period approach.

Axiom 17 (Stochastic Equilibrium). *Under perfect competition, the system gravitates toward an equilibrium probability distribution of each random variable, whose general form (at least) is theoretically ascertainable and empirically verifiable.*

Axioms 2, 16, and 17 represent the theoretical core of FM's approach. In order to provide a solution to the transformation problem, however, they need to impose some auxiliary assumptions that allow them to use standard results in probability theory.[31]

First, they postulate that the cumulative density functions of all random variables "can be assumed, with negligible error, to be smooth" (FM, p. 69). Next, using a recursive argument, they show that the price p_j^{mkt} paid for a certain commodity (or bundle of commodities) χ can be represented as the sum of the total amount of wages, v_j', paid to all workers who participated directly or indirectly in the production of χ, plus the sum total of profits, s_j', made by all firms involved directly or indirectly in the production of χ ("each in respect of its workers' part in the production of this particular commodity" [FM, p. 113]).[32] Therefore, interpreting p_j^{mkt}, v_j', and s_j' as realizations of three random variables whose relation is captured by the identity $p_j^{mkt} = v_j' + s_j'$, one has

$$\psi_j = \frac{v_j'}{\lambda_j} + \frac{s_j'}{\lambda_j} \tag{41}$$

By equation (41), it follows that the average of ψ is $E\psi = E(\frac{v'}{\lambda}) + E(\frac{s'}{\lambda})$. Using labor values to weight the goods involved in each transaction, by definition, $E(\frac{v'}{\lambda}) = \sum_j \alpha_j \frac{v_j'}{\lambda_j}$ and $E(\frac{s'}{\lambda}) = \sum_j \alpha_j \frac{s_j'}{\lambda_j}$ where $\alpha_j = \frac{\lambda_j}{\sum_j \lambda_j}$. But then at a dynamic equilibrium, $E(\frac{v'}{\lambda}) = \frac{\sum_j v_j'}{\sum_j \lambda_j}$ is the sum total of wages divided by the total amount of labor performed in t, and so $E(\frac{v'}{\lambda}) = Ew$, and we can write $E(\frac{s'}{\lambda}) = e^* E(\frac{v'}{\lambda})$, where $e^* = \frac{\sum_j s_j'}{\sum_j v_j'}$ is "the ratio in which the total value-added embodied in the aggregate ... of all commodities sold during [t] is apportioned between profits and wages" (FM, p. 118). Therefore,

$$E\psi = (1 + e^*)Ew \tag{42}$$

This implies that the market prices of commodities are proportional to labor values on average. Furthermore, by the Law of Large Numbers, it follows that if χ is a large aggregate of commodities sold at total price $p^{mkt}(\chi)$ and embodying an amount of labor $\lambda(\chi)$, then with high probability and a good level of approximation $\frac{p^{mkt}(\chi)}{\lambda(\chi)} = E\psi$, and by equation (42)

$$\frac{p^{mkt}(\chi)}{\lambda(\chi)} = (1 + e^*)Ew \tag{43}$$

Equation (43) holds as an approximation for any large aggregate of commodities, including, for example, the consumption basket of the whole of the working class, **b**.

Next, note that, by definition, the aggregate rate of exploitation is

$$e^M = \frac{L - \lambda(\mathbf{b})}{\lambda(\mathbf{b})} \tag{44}$$

Under the assumption that workers spend all their income, $p^{mkt}(\mathbf{b}) = Ew \cdot L$ and therefore $e^M = \frac{p^{mkt}(\mathbf{b}) - \lambda(\mathbf{b})Ew}{\lambda(\mathbf{b})Ew}$ or, equivalently, by equation (43), with $\chi = \mathbf{b}$,

$$(1 + e^M)Ew = \frac{p^{mkt}(\mathbf{b})}{\lambda(\mathbf{b})} = E\psi$$

which implies that e^M must be equal, or very nearly equal, to e^*.

Finally, let W_f denote the total wage bill paid by firm f and let $z_f = \frac{W_f}{K_f}$ be its organic composition of capital. Define the variable $x_f = \frac{r_f}{z_f}$: x_f is "similar to what Marx calls the *rate of surplus-value*, except that here, too, we measure $[r_f]$ and $[z_f]$ in money terms, whereas he uses labor-values" (FM, p. 69). Let $e_0 = \frac{Er_f}{Ez_f}$: e_0 is the proportion in which the aggregate value added is divided between capital and labor in the economy.

The rates e^* and e_0 are not calculated on the same basis: e_0 "is defined with reference to the *firm space*; if we calculate $[e_0]$, for the period $[t]$, we obtain the ratio in which the *new* value-added *generated during this period* is being shared between capital and labor. On the other hand, $[e^*]$ is defined with reference to the *market space*; it measures the ratio in which the price, which is also the total value-added embodied in [a bundle of commodities χ] – some of which has been generated *before* the period $[t]$ – was shared between capital and labour" (FM, p. 118). Nonetheless, in equilibrium, "the two ratios must be extremely close to each other, because the ratio between total profits and total wages cannot change rapidly" (FM, p. 118). Therefore,

$$E\psi = (1 + e_0)Ew$$

It is now possible to see how these results provide a solution to the transformation problem. Consider Marx's "simple prices" p_j in equation (2). Unlike in FM's framework, they are ideal, rather than market, prices and they are deterministic magnitudes, rather than random variables. If equation (2) holds, then there exists some scalar ψ_0 such that $\frac{p_j}{\lambda_j} = \psi_0$ for all j, including labor power. In Section 3, $\psi_0 = \frac{1}{\lambda_m}$, but FM suggest to normalize prices taking the (ideal) unit wage as the price unit, so that $p_0 = w = 1$, $\psi_0 = \frac{1}{\lambda_0}$, and $\frac{p_j}{\lambda_j} = \frac{1}{\lambda_0}$ for all j. Then, noting that $\lambda(\mathbf{b}) = \lambda_0 L$, equation (44) can be written as

$$e^M = \frac{1 - \lambda_0}{\lambda_0} \tag{45}$$

which, in turn, implies $\frac{1}{\lambda_0} = 1 + e^M$ and therefore,

$$\frac{p_j}{\lambda_j} = 1 + e^M, \quad \text{for all } j \tag{46}$$

Noting that $Ew = w = 1$ by construction, it is possible to see the connection between equation (46), and therefore Marx's "simple prices," p_j, and equations (42) and (43) defining the relation between market prices, p_j^{mkt}, and values in FM's probabilistic approach. Because ψ_j is in general a nondegenerate random variable, equation (46) does not hold in general and individual commodities are unlikely to be exchanged in proportion to their labor values. Nonetheless, under the assumptions of FM's model, equation (43) shows that "when it comes to large and 'unbiased' aggregates of commodities, the specific price of such an aggregate (total price/total labour-content) can, with high probability, be taken as very nearly constant" (FM, p. 135) and the market prices of such aggregates are very close to "simple prices." Equation (42) shows that the same result holds also on average.

Similar conclusions can be reached about the profit rates obtained by capitalist firms on the market. At simple prices, the average rate of profit measured in labor time, r^{FM}, is equal to

$$r^{FM} = \frac{(1 - \lambda_0)L}{\lambda(\mathbf{K}_G)} = \frac{L - \lambda(\mathbf{b})}{\lambda(\mathbf{K}_G)} \tag{47}$$

where $\mathbf{K}_G$ is the vector of total capital stocks employed in the economy. Recall that $\mathbf{Q}$ is the gross output vector. Let $\mathbf{I}_G$ denote the vector of intermediate goods used in production: by definition $L = \lambda(\mathbf{Q}) - \lambda(\mathbf{I}_G)$. Then, substituting the latter expression into equation (47) and noting that since $\mathbf{Q}$, $\mathbf{I}_G$, and $\mathbf{K}_G$ are very large aggregates of commodities, equation (43) holds, we can write

$$r^{FM} = \frac{p^{mkt}(\mathbf{Q}) - p^{mkt}(\mathbf{I}_G) - p^{mkt}(\mathbf{b})}{p^{mkt}(\mathbf{K}_G)} \tag{48}$$

But the right-hand side of equation (43) is equal to the average rate of profit, and therefore,

$$r^{FM} = Er \tag{49}$$

In other words, the value rate of profit is equal to the average money rate of profit, proving the link between profits and surplus value.

We can summarize the previous results in the following theorem:

Theorem 8 (The Probabilistic Labor Theory of Value). Under **Dualism, Stochastic Prices**, and **Stochastic Equilibrium**, both the *strong average equilibrium price view* and the *average profit & exploitation view* are logically consistent. Furthermore, **Aggregate Proportionalities** is satisfied.

The approach proposed by FM is innovative and sophisticated. Methodologically, it can be considered as one precursor of the literature on econophysics (Wright, 2005; Cockshott *et al.*, 2009) and of statistical equilibrium theories (Foley, 1994). But it is important to stress that it solves the transformation problem in a very specific and limited sense. The distribution of the random variable $\frac{p_j}{\lambda_j}$ may be rather narrowly clustered around the mean, but it is by no means degenerate. Therefore, commodities do not exchange at labor values—even approximately—when taken individually. Marx's simple prices are a good approximation of market prices only on average (equation (42)), or when large aggregates of commodities are considered (equation (43)), and the probabilistic approach does not (and cannot) provide any explanation of price/value deviations. Nor does it provide any theory of observed market prices, based on labor values or otherwise.

Indeed, labor values play a central role in FM's theorization of the dynamics of capitalist economies, as they capture the deeper technological structure of capitalist production beneath the surface of market phenomena—the real "cost" of goods to society in terms of real human social effort in production. For example, they are arguably the most appropriate measures of labor productivity and can explain long-run effects of technological innovations, including the so-called *law of decreasing labor content* (FM, chapter 7). Yet, in a dynamic perspective, the causality runs from price magnitudes to labor values: actual and expected production costs and profitability determine capitalist innovation activities and choice of techniques, and therefore labor values (see also Flaschel *et al.*, 2013).

One may argue that this lack of theoretical power is compensated by a more realistic set of assumptions and a stronger empirical grounding. For if FM's arguments are correct, then for predictive purposes and from an empirical viewpoint, Marx's simple prices may be taken to be a good approximation of actual market prices. This result, however, is by no means unique to FM's approach. Indeed, a well-known puzzle in the empirical literature on the transformation problem is a very strong correlation between production prices and embodied labor values (see, for example, Shaikh, 2016, chapter 9, and Cockshott and Cottrell, 1997).[33]

10.2 *Stochastic Technology*

The stochastic approach recently proposed by Schefold (2016) shares some important features with FM. Most importantly, like FM, Schefold (2016) adopts the standard definition of values as expressed in Axiom 2 (**Dualism**). However, he differs from FM in two key respects. First, he adopts Axiom 1 (**Long Period**) thereby both endorsing a dualist approach to the definition of values, and defining equilibrium and prices of production in the standard Sraffian fashion. Second, consistent with the adoption of Axiom 1, Schefold rejects Axiom 16 and a focus on market variables. The stochastic nature of the economy emerges from the sphere of production, and not from market processes: it is the fundamental technical data of the economy that should be interpreted as generated by stochastic processes. Formally,[34]

Axiom 18 (Stochastic Technology). *Technology* $(\mathbf{A}, \mathbf{l})$ *is a random variable.*

Although Axioms 1, 2, and 18 represent the theoretical backbone of Schefold (2016)'s approach, the solution to the transformation problem, as with FM, requires some auxiliary assumptions that further specify the properties of the main random variables.

The first assumption concerns the production structure of the economy. Let $\mu = (\mu_1, \mu_2, \ldots, \mu_n)$ be the vector of eigenvalues of the matrix $\mathbf{A}$, where μ_1 is the (strictly positive) dominant eigenvalue.

Assumption 1. *All nondominant eigenvalues of* $\mathbf{A}$ *are (approximately) zero. Formally,* $\mu_i \approx 0$, *for all* $i \neq 1$.

It is well known that $\mu_i = 0$, for all $i \neq 1$ if and only if $\mathbf{A} = \mathbf{cf}$, for some two vectors $\mathbf{c} > \mathbf{0}$, $\mathbf{f} > \mathbf{0}$ where $\mathbf{c}$ is a column vector, $\mathbf{f}$ a row vector, and $\mathbf{A}$ has rank 1. If $\mathbf{A}$ is interpreted as a random matrix that is a perturbation of $\mathbf{A} = \mathbf{c1}$, with $\mathbf{1} \equiv (1, \ldots, 1)$, then the nondominant eigenvalues are only approximately equal to zero. To be precise, suppose the elements of a semipositive and indecomposable matrix $\mathbf{A}$ on each row (i) are distributed independently and identically around a mean specific for the row, and (ii) are random, with a variance that is so large that many single elements equal to zero are admitted. Suppose further that this matrix approximates the form $\mathbf{A} = \mathbf{c1}$, and its dimension is sufficiently large. Then, the nondominant eigenvalues tend to zero, even if the coefficients of $\mathbf{A}$ are perturbed considerably.[35]

In order to state the next assumptions, we need some additional notation. Let $\mathbf{u}_i$ and $\mathbf{i}_i$ denote, respectively, the right (column) and left (row) eigenvectors of $\mathbf{A}$, corresponding to the eigenvalue μ_i, where $\mathbf{u}_1$ and $\mathbf{i}_1$ pertain to the dominant eigenvalue. The components of $\mathbf{u}_1$ are "in the same proportions as Sraffa's standard commodity. This standard vector may also be interpreted as the average industry, introduced by Marx in the third volume of *Das Kapital*" (Schefold, 2016, p. 172). Accordingly, $\mathbf{u}_1$ is called the Sraffa-vector. As for $\mathbf{i}_1$, it is the vector "for which prices would be equal to labor values at all rates of profits, if it were the labour vector" (Schefold, 2016, p. 173), and hence is called the Marx-vector.

The gross output vector and the vector of labor inputs can be expressed as a linear combination, respectively, of the right-hand and the left-hand eigenvectors. Formally, $\mathbf{Q} = \sum_{i=1}^{n} \mathbf{u}_i$ and $\mathbf{l} = \sum_{i=1}^{n} \mathbf{i}_i$. The next assumption then imposes a constraint on the sectoral deviations of the gross output vectors and the labor vector from the Sraffa-vector and the Marx-vector: $\mathbf{d}^u = \mathbf{Q} - \mathbf{u}_1$ and $\mathbf{d}^i = \mathbf{l} - \mathbf{i}_1$.

Assumption 2. *The deviations of activities from the average industry and the deviations of the labor vector from the Marx-vector are not correlated. Formally,* $cov(\mathbf{d}^u, \mathbf{d}^i) = 0$.

The next assumption focuses on some properties of surplus products and the labor vector.

Assumption 3. *The deviations of the labor vector from the Marx-vector and the vector* **s** *of surplus products are not correlated. Formally,* $cov(\mathbf{s}, \mathbf{d^i}) = 0$.

If the input matrix is a perturbation of $\mathbf{A} = \mathbf{cf}$, for a generic $\mathbf{f} > 0$, then one more, crucial assumption is necessary, which concerns the average of the deviations of the labor vector from the Marx-vector. For every vector γ, let $\bar{\gamma}$ denote the average of the components of γ.

Assumption 4. *On average, the deviations of the labor vector from the Marx-vector disappear. Formally,* $\bar{d}^i = 0$.

According to Schefold (2016, p. 174), Assumption 4 "means that, because the individual deviations of the labour vector from the Marx-vector do not disappear but its average disappears, the labour theory of value does not hold for the single prices but on average, as it were." Formally, Assumptions 2 and 3 imply, respectively, that $\mathbf{d^i d^u} = n \bar{d}^i \bar{d}^u$ and $\mathbf{d^i s} = n \bar{d}^i \bar{s}$, and by Assumption 4, the latter vector products are both equal to zero. If, however, the input matrix is a perturbation of $\mathbf{A} = \mathbf{c1}$, then Assumption 4 follows as a *result* as proved in the theory of stochastic matrices. Either way, this is the key property to prove the following theorem.[36]

Theorem 9 (The Average Labor Theory of Value). Under **Assumptions 1–4, Dualism, Long Period**, and **Stochastic Technology**, both the *strong average equilibrium price view* and the *average profit & exploitation view* are logically consistent. Furthermore, **Aggregate Equalities** is satisfied.

According to Schefold (2016, p. 176), Theorem 9 is "a most surprising result, obtained after 120 years of discussions of the transformation problem." It establishes that "the Marxian transformation of values into prices is correct after all, despite many refutations, if the economic system under consideration is random" (Schefold, 2016, p. 165). Theorem 9 is indeed a remarkable result as it provides a solution to the transformation problem within the standard dualist framework, due to an innovative interpretation in terms of random matrices. Furthermore, Schefold (2016, section 3) relates some key aspects of the formalism to Marx's texts, providing an interesting interpretation of dialectics.

Nonetheless, two caveats should be made concerning the interpretation of the results. First, "Prices are here not derived from values, but without having recourse to values from the structure of production or of the values in use, represented by **A** and **l**, and from the distribution, represented by r. The formal redundancy of the theory of surplus value remains" (Schefold, 2016, p. 177).

Second, Schefold criticizes and rejects the NI because some of its results are "little more than a tautology" (Schefold, 2016, p. 170). Yet, from a logical perspective, Schefold's approach is very similar in that the key Marxian insights, and Theorem 9, follow straightforwardly by virtue of the axioms and definitions. This is not to suggest that this approach (or others) is trivial. Rather it emphasizes the fact that in *all* approaches, the results follow in some sense from the relevant definitions and from the axiomatic framework characterizing a given approach.

Indeed, our axiomatic treatment very clearly suggests that the strength of Theorem 9 lies entirely in the strength of the underlying axioms, and the axioms are not entirely convincing, or at least are insufficiently motivated. For example, concerning Assumption 2 Schefold (2016, p. 173) simply says: "Now there is in fact no reason why the deviations of activities from the average industry and the deviations of the labour vector from the Marx-vector should be correlated." Yet there is no reason why they should not be correlated (or at least no independent reason is provided). Even more puzzlingly, concerning Assumption 4, he simply says "that on average the deviations of the labour vector from the Marx-vector disappear. This is a new assumption" (Schefold, 2016, p. 174). To be sure, as mentioned earlier, Assumption 4 can be obtained as a result from more basic premises, namely, the assumption that $\mathbf{A}$ is a stochastic matrix that can be approximately seen as the perturbation of $\mathbf{A} = \mathbf{c1}$. Yet, it is unclear why— either theoretically or empirically—the matrix of material input requirements should be even approximately of rank 1, let alone have essentially identical columns. At a deeper level, one may even question the assumption that the technology matrix $\mathbf{A}$ can be meaningfully considered to be random in the statisticians' sense of the word, as it is the outcome of certain processes of innovation and choice of techniques.[37]

11. Conclusions

This paper provides a new interpretation of the literature on the transformation problem by using the language of modern axiomatic theory. This approach has significant advantages in terms of clarifying the exact nature and scope of the argument. On the one hand, it allows us to show that, on its own terms, the transformation problem is an impossibility result. At a purely logical level, there is nothing to discuss about it and there is no hope of "solving" it. On the other hand, however, it forcefully shows that the result depends both on a certain interpretation of Marxian value theory *and* on a specific set of assumptions and definitions—a specific axiomatic structure.

In the standard dualist approach that has dominated the debate from the publication of *Capital III* up until the 1970s, money plays no role and labor values and monetary magnitudes are assumed to form two conceptually separate systems. There is an underlying (intrinsic, invisible, and essential) system of labor values and associated exploitation, and a phenomenal (extrinsic, visible, and superficial) system of prices and profit rate. Marxian value theory is then interpreted as a predictive tool that bridges the gap between the two systems: relative labor values are meant to explain equilibrium relative prices. Because no robust relation between labor and monetary magnitudes can be proved in the dualist framework, the conclusion is that Marxian value theory is at best irrelevant, if not irremediably inconsistent.

The axiomatic approach adopted in this paper has the advantage of clarifying the key assumptions and the logical structure of the received approach, and it has allowed us to show that neither its general conception of value theory, nor the specific axioms adopted are logical truths. Both can be, and indeed have been, modified in various logically consistent and theoretically relevant directions. In closing this paper, it is worth summarizing what we believe are the key departures from the standard view of these recent approaches (albeit, as we have shown, with different emphases).

First, a strictly predictive interpretation of Marxian value theory is unnecessarily reductive. The labor theory of value can be meaningfully interpreted as a tool for describing and understanding the basic structure and dynamics of capitalist economies, and in particular the relation between profits and exploitation, even if embodied labor values are not good theoretical predictors of prices of production.

Second, dimensionality is important. The standard approach is dualist in that it interprets labor accounts and monetary magnitudes as unrelated and separate systems. Its focus on *relative* values and prices eliminates and therefore obscures the fact that these magnitudes are denominated in different units. Once that difference is kept explicit, then the translation between the two relates labor magnitudes and monetary magnitudes in a way that the dualist approach does not manage.

This leads immediately to the third feature: the labor theory of value is a monetary theory (because a capitalist economy is a monetary economy) and that must require a conversion rate to move back and forth from labor accounts to money accounts. So the value of money is a central concept. But more than that, money is not a veil, concealing a set of real transactions; it is rather how value appears when it is separated from the commodity. This further implies that the wage transaction is a monetary one: the sale of labor power is for a monetary wage, and the value of labor power is that wage multiplied by the value of money.

No survey is theoretically innocent. We began in Section 2 by noting a number of possible interpretations of the labor theory of value. At its most general and abstract level, the labor theory of value is a statement that as long as labor is mobile, a decentralized allocation of labor is organized via the natural prices of all activities when these are proportional to the human effort expended in such activities. This allocation of labor is modified by the distribution via class relations of the monetary form of the surplus product. The theoretical challenge is to understand how this modification works in a context of class exploitation. While this motivates the NI in particular, the various approaches we have surveyed all have something that underpins their different assumptions/axioms. This paper has surveyed the logic of the latter, but it should be clear that that logic can only take us so far.

Our survey then does not provide the final word on Marxian value theory. Among other things, we have developed our analysis at a purely theoretical level, and have neglected the important issue of its empirical relevance. We hope to have shown, however, that the central question is not whether the transformation problem can be solved, but rather whether modern approaches to value theory can provide a theoretically rigorous framework that can underpin the analysis of contemporary capitalist economies.

Notes

1. There is no single, unequivocal way of defining an approach axiomatically. It is largely a matter of emphasis whether certain features should be considered as part of the specification of the domain of problems, or rather of the desirable properties of solutions for the domain. Different axiomatic descriptions may be appropriate depending on the theoretical exercise. The axiomatic method is not "a substitute for intuition … but instead … a way of articulating [the intuitions that hold in specific situations] into operationally useful conditions pertaining to an entire class of cases" (Thomson, 2001, p. 356).

2. Although the discussion in Section 5 touches upon various issues that are central in the Sraffian literature, the latter falls beyond the scope of our paper. For Sraffians, the labor theory of value has no relevance, and the issues that were central to Ricardo and Marx can be analyzed with Sraffa's long-period framework. For a discussion, see Steedman (1977) and Mongiovi (2002).

3. This can be interpreted both as a descriptive and as a normative claim. As such, it offers one possible reason why we focus on a labor theory of value rather than, say, on a "steel theory of value" and the corresponding transformation from "steel values" at simple prices to prices of production.

4. These simplifying assumptions are made for expositional purposes, since the transformation problem arises, and has traditionally been discussed, within the simplified context analyzed here. It is worth stressing, however, that modern approaches to Marxian price and value theory provide solutions to the transformation problem that are independent of these simplifying assumptions. See, for example, Flaschel (1983, 2010) and Flaschel

et al. (2013) on joint production and fixed capital; Duménil *et al.* (2009) and Veneziani and Yoshihara (2015, 2017) on heterogeneous labor.

5. These refinements of labor and labor time are not the subject of this paper. Henceforth, the qualifier "socially necessary" will be dropped; but units of time in this paper are assumed to be always so qualified.

6. In this paper, we follow Marx and assume, without loss of generality, that wages are paid *ex ante*.

7. The inverse of λ_m is denominated in units of money per unit of time, and is accordingly called "the monetary equivalent of labor time." While some authors work with this directly, we use the value of money throughout.

8. In his numerical examples, Marx was generally explicit about this; for example, he wrote, "if 2 ounces of gold when coined are £2 ..." (Marx, 1976, p. 163), and "If then, twenty-four hours of labour, or two working days, are required to produce the quantity of gold represented by 12 shillings ..." (Marx, 1976, p. 294). For an analysis of Marx's concept of money, see Foley (1986). We do not pursue the philosophical and exegetical literature on money in this paper. A sample might include Nelson (1999) and Lapavitsas (2017).

9. The assumption that workers do not save is conceptually central to the dualist approach. For expositional clarity we maintain it throughout the paper to facilitate the comparison of alternative approaches. Yet none of the key arguments of the paper depends on ruling out workers' savings.

10. We assume throughout that hours of labor power hired are unproblematically translated into hours of labor worked.

11. We assume that $\mathbf{A}$ is nonnegative, productive, and indecomposable, and $\mathbf{l}$ is strictly positive.

12. These quantities are all determined *ex post*; they are givens of the analysis, and no assumption concerning constant returns to scale is made (nor is it necessary, Flaschel, 2010).

13. Given our assumptions on technology $(\mathbf{A}, \mathbf{l})$, it is well known that, due to a theorem of Frobenius, Perron, and Remak, for a range of values of the distributive variables, once either of (r^e, w^e) is specified, equation (11) has a unique, economically meaningful solution. See, for example, Roemer (1981) and Flaschel (2010).

14. By equation (16), the (equalized) rate of profit in equation (12) becomes $r^e = \frac{\Pi^e}{\mathbf{p}^e\mathbf{AQ}+\mathbf{p}^e\mathbf{b}}$.

15. We prefer "total revenue" to the terminologically imprecise "total price" that is typically used in the literature.

16. A third, more recent solution within the dualist approach is examined in Section 10.2 below.

17. Dimensionality issues are not relevant here since the price vector is the eigenvector of the augmented input coefficients matrix $\mathbf{M}$, and is determined up to a positive multiplicative constant, so that only relative prices matter.

18. According to Shaikh, (2016, chapter 6) and the references therein, the reason why part (ii) fails to hold is because of transfers between the "circuit of capital" and the "circuit of revenue."

19. See also Lipietz (1982), Mohun (1994, 2004), Duménil and Foley (2008), and Foley and Mohun (2016). It is worth noting that other authors had anticipated *some* of the key elements of the NI such as the definition of the value of labor power (Robinson, 1965; Schefold, 1973) or the existence of a conversion rate between money and labor accounts (Desai, 1979). However, Duménil and Foley were the first to put these elements together into a unified approach.

20. The terminology "commodity law of exchange" to describe equation (2), and "capitalist law of exchange" to describe the determination of prices that support an equalized rate of profit, is used by Foley and Mohun (2016).

21. As already noted, the adoption of the *macroeconomic view* does not imply that microeconomic variables are ignored, or irrelevant in the NI. Indeed, Duménil *et al.* (2009) have extended the NI at the meso-level by analyzing value creation at the sectoral level. Further, in a series of recent contributions, Veneziani and Yoshihara (2015), Veneziani and Yoshihara (2017), and Yoshihara (2010) have shown axiomatically that the NI can provide an appropriate criterion to analyze individual exploitation status.

22. Roberts (1997, 2009) defends a strong version of the *profit & exploitation view* that holds at the level of individual industries or processes.

23. Of course, only relative prices of production are thereby determined; the further normalization equation (26) is discussed below.

24. Furthermore, Axiom 1 so reinterpreted is not understood as describing the long-period position of the economy but as representing, for Marxism, the "condition for equivalent exchange" under the competitive capitalist conditions of *Capital III*, Part I. We are grateful to Bruce Roberts for this suggestion.

25. Alternatively, instead of Axiom 8, equation (26) could be given axiomatic status with equation (24) derived as a result. This choice makes no difference for our conclusions. We do think, however, that Axiom 8 reflects Wolff *et al.* (1982, 1984a, b)'s own presentation of the approach.

26. Roberts (1997, 2009) has developed the WCR approach by further analyzing the relation between prices and values, and by considering economies with joint production and heterogeneous labor. Yet, the fundamental axiomatic structure of the approach is the same and it remains true that prices are defined independently of values but the converse is not true.

27. The part of claim (d) concerning the role of values in the *determination* of prices is not entirely clear and we shall return to it later.

28. In Theorem 7, TSSI proponents also include: "(g) labor-saving technical change itself can cause the profit rate to fall" (Kliman and McGlone, 1999, p. 55). But claim (g) cannot be proved based only on Axioms 11–15. Indeed, the asserted TSSI relation between labor-saving innovations and movements in the rate of profit is controversial (for example, Veneziani, 2004). Different interpretations of (price and) value theory certainly have implications for the analysis of the dynamics of a capitalist economy, but space constraints preclude their exploration in this paper.

29. The following discussion draws heavily on Veneziani (2004).

30. Sometimes, TSSI proponents suggest that the definition of $\lambda_{m,t}$ can be derived by post-multiplying equation (34) by $\mathbf{Q}_{t+1}$, and rearranging to obtain

$$\frac{1}{\lambda_{m,t+1}} = \frac{\mathbf{p}_{t+1}\mathbf{Q}_{t+1}}{\lambda_{m,t}\mathbf{p}_t\mathbf{A}_t\mathbf{Q}_{t+1} + \mathbf{l}_t\mathbf{Q}_{t+1}}$$

Unfortunately, this equation does not provide a *definition* of $\lambda_{m,t+1}$: it describes its motion, provided that $\lambda_{m,0}$ is independently defined. And there is no such definition in the TSSI literature. For further discussion, see Mohun and Veneziani (2009).

31. See Fröhlich (2012) for an econometric analysis of the basic assumptions of FM.

32. Therefore, v'_j and s'_j are different from v_i and s_i used, for example, in equation (6): they are monetary (not value) magnitudes and capture the interconnectedness of the economic

system. Thus, v'_j measures the wages paid to the workers involved in the production of the goods in transaction j, plus the wages paid in the production of the intermediate goods necessary to produce such goods, and so on.

33. But note that the input–output methodology of these empirical studies implicitly assumes all labor to be productive, which raises some delicate issues in interpreting such correlations as having anything to do with values.

34. "Essentially, matrices are random, if the elements on each row (which represents the process) are i.i.d. with a distribution around a mean specific for the row" (Schefold, 2016, p. 166).

35. "Tend to zero" here means, as usual, that the modulus of any eigenvalue is smaller than any preassigned positive number. For a more thorough discussion of the relevant assumptions, see Schefold (2013).

36. Observe that Theorem 9 proves that **Aggregate Equalities** holds. This is because, in Schefold's framework, only relative prices matter. The proof of Theorem 9 is in the Addendum (in the Additional Supporting Information in the online version of this article).

37. We are grateful to Gary Mongiovi for this suggestion.

References

Cockshott, W.P. and Cottrell, A.F. (1997) Labour time versus alternative value bases: a research note. *Cambridge Journal of Economics* 21: 545–549.

Cockshott, W.P., Cottrell, A.F., Michaelson, G.J., Wright, I.P. and V.M. Yakovenko, (2009) *Classical Econophysics*. London: Routledge.

Desai, M. (1979) *Marxian Economics*. Oxford: Blackwell.

Desai, M. (1988) The transformation problem. *Journal of Economic Surveys* 2: 295–333.

Duménil, G. (1980) *De la Valeur aux Prix de Production*. Paris: Economica.

Duménil, G. (1984) The so-called 'transformation problem' revisited: a brief comment. *Journal of Economic Theory* 33: 340–348.

Duménil, G. and Foley, D.K. (2008) The Marxian transformation problem. In S. Durlauf and L.E. Blume (eds.), *The New Palgrave Dictionary of Economics* (2nd edn). London: Palgrave Macmillan. https://doi.org/10.1057/9780230226203.1052

Duménil, G., Foley, D.K. and Lévy, D. (2009) A note on the formal treatment of exploitation in a model with heterogenous labor. *Metroeconomica* 60: 560–567.

Duménil, G. and Lévy, D. (2000) The conservation of value: a rejoinder to Alan Freeman. *Review of Radical Political Economics* 32: 119–146.

Farjoun, E. and Machover, M. (1983) *Laws of Chaos*. London: Verso.

Flaschel, P. (1983) Actual labor values in a general model of production. *Econometrica* 51: 435–454.

Flaschel, P. (2010) *Topics in Classical Micro-and Macroeconomics*. New York: Springer.

Flaschel, P., Franke, R. and Veneziani, R. (2013) Labor productivity and the law of decreasing labor content. *Cambridge Journal of Economics* 37: 379–402.

Foley, D.K. (1982) The value of money, the value of labor power, and the Marxian transformation problem. *Review of Radical Political Economics* 14: 37–47.

Foley, D.K. (1986) *Understanding Capital*. Cambridge, MA: Harvard University Press.

Foley, D.K. (1994) A statistical equilibrium theory of markets. *Journal of Economic Theory* 62: 321–345.

Foley, D.K. (2000) Recent developments in the labor theory of value. *Review of Radical Political Economics* 32: 1–39.

Foley, D.K. (2014) What is the labor theory of value and what is it good for? Mimeo, The New School for Social Research.

Foley, D.K. and Mohun, S. (2016) Value and price. In G. Faccarello and H. Kurz (eds.), *Handbook of the History of Economic Thought, Volume 3: Developments in Major Fields of Economics* (pp. 589–610). London and Cheltenham: Edward Elgar.

Freeman, A. (1996) Price, value and profit. A continuous, general treatment. In A. Freeman and G. Carchedi (eds.), *Marx and Non-equilibrium Economics* (pp. 180–233). Aldershot: Elgar.

Fröhlich, N. (2012) Labour values, prices of production and the missing equalization tendency of profit rates: evidence from the German economy. *Cambridge Journal of Economics* 37: 1107–1126.

Howard, M.C. and King, J.E. (1992) *A History of Marxian Economics – Vol. 2, 1929-1990*. Princeton: Princeton University Press.

Hunt, E.K. and Glick, M. (1987) Transformation problem. In J. Eatwell, M. Milgate and P. Newman (eds.), *The New Palgrave Dictionary of Economics* (pp. 356–362). London, Macmillan.

Kliman, A. (2001) Simultaneous valuation vs. the exploitation theory of profit. *Capital and Class* 73: 97–112.

Kliman, A. (2007) *Reclaiming Marx's "Capital"*. Lanham: Lexington Books.

Kliman, A. and McGlone, T. (1988) The transformation non-problem and the non-transformation problem. *Capital and Class* 35: 56–83.

Kliman, A. and McGlone, T. (1999) A temporal single-system interpretation of Marx's value theory. *Review of Political Economy* 11: 33–59.

Lapavitsas, C. (2017) *Marxist Monetary Theory*. Leiden: Brill.

Lipietz, A. (1982) The so-called "Transformation Problem" revisited. *Journal of Economic Theory* 26: 59–88.

Marx, K. (1976 [1867]) *Capital Volume 1*. Harmondsworth: Penguin.

Marx, K. (1981 [1894]) *Capital Volume 3*. Harmondsworth: Penguin.

Mohun, S. (1994) A re(in)statement of the labour theory of value. *Cambridge Journal of Economics* 18: 391–412.

Mohun, S. (2004) The labour theory of value as foundation for empirical investigations. *Metroeconomica* 55: 65–95.

Mohun, S. and Veneziani, R. (2009) The Temporal Single-System Interpretation: underdetermination and inconsistency. *Marxism 21* 6: 277–299.

Mongiovi, G. (2002) Vulgar economy in Marxian garb: a critique of Temporal Single System Marxism. *Review of Radical Political Economics* 34: 393–416.

Morishima, M. (1973) *Marx's Economics*. Cambridge: Cambridge University Press.

Morishima, M. (1974) Marx in the light of modern economic theory. *Econometrica* 42: 611–632.

Moseley, F. (2016) *Money and Totality. A Macro-Monetary Interpretation of Marx's Logic in Capital and the End of the 'Transformation Problem'*. Leiden and Boston: Brill.

Nelson, A. (1999) *Marx's Concept of Money*. London: Routledge.

Okishio, N. (1963) A mathematical note on Marxian theorems. *Weltwirtschaftliches Archiv* 91: 287–299.

Pasinetti, L.L. (1977) *Lectures on the Theory of Production*. New York: Columbia University Press.

Ricardo, D. (1951 [1821]) *On the Principles of Political Economy and Taxation. Volume I of The Works and Correspondence of David Ricardo*, edited by Piero Sraffa with the collaboration of M. H. Dobb. Cambridge: Cambridge University Press.

Roberts, B. (1997) Embodied labour and competitive prices: a physical quantities approach. *Cambridge Journal of Economics* 21: 483–502.

Roberts, B. (2009) RICARDO: Standard Commodity :: MARX: - -?- -. *Review of Political Economy* 21: 589–619.

Robinson, J. (1964) *Economic Philosophy* (2nd edn). Harmondsworth: Penguin.

Robinson, J. (1965) A reconsideration of the labour theory of value. In J. Robinson (ed.), *Collected Economic Papers III* (pp. 173–181). Oxford: Blackwell.

Roemer, J.E. (1981) *Analytical Foundations of Marxian Economic Theory*. Cambridge, MA: Harvard University Press.

Roemer, J.E. (1982) *A General Theory of Exploitation and Class*. Cambridge, MA: Harvard University Press.

Rubin, I.I. (1972 [1928]) *Essays on Marx's Theory of Value*. Detroit: Black and Red Books.

Samuelson, P.A. (1971) Understanding the Marxian notion of exploitation: a summary of the so-called transformation problem between Marxian values and competitive prices. *Journal of Economic Literature* 9: 399–431.

Schefold, B. (1973) Wert und Preis in der marxistischen und neokeynesianischen Akkumulationstheorie. *Mehrwert, Beiträge zur Kritik der politischen Ökonomie* 2: 125–175.

Schefold, B. (2013) Approximate surrogate production functions. *Cambridge Journal of Economics* 37: 1161–1184.

Schefold, B. (2016) Profits equal surplus value on average and the significance of this result for the Marxian theory of accumulation. *Cambridge Journal of Economics* 40: 165–199.

Sen, A.K. (1978) On the labour theory of value: some methodological issues. *Cambridge Journal of Economics* 2: 175–190.

Seton, F. (1957) The transformation problem. *Review of Economic Studies* 24: 149–160.

Shaikh, A. (1977) Marx's theory of value and the 'Transformation Problem'. In J. Schwartz (ed.), *The Subtle Anatomy of Capitalism* (pp. 106–139). Los Angeles, Goodyear Publishing.

Shaikh, A. (2016) *Capitalism: Competition, Conflict, Crises*. New York: Oxford University Press.

Steedman, I. (1977) *Marx after Sraffa*. London: NLB.

Thomson, W. (2001) On the axiomatic method and its recent applications to game theory and resource allocation. *Social Choice and Welfare* 18: 327–386.

Veneziani, R. (2004) The Temporal Single-System Interpretation of Marx's economics: a critical evaluation. *Metroeconomica* 55: 96–114.

Veneziani, R. and Yoshihara, N. (2015) Exploitation in economies with heterogeneous preferences, skills and assets: an axiomatic approach. *Journal of Theoretical Politics* 27: 8–33.

Veneziani, R. and Yoshihara, N. (2017) One million miles to go: taking the axiomatic road to defining exploitation. *Cambridge Journal of Economics* 41: 1607–1626.

Yoshihara, N. (2010) Class and exploitation in general convex cone economies. *Journal of Economic Behavior & Organization* 75: 281–296.

Yoshihara, N. and Veneziani, R. (2013) Exploitation of labour and exploitation of commodities: a 'New Interpretation'. *Review of Radical Political Economics* 45: 517–524.

Wolff, R., Callari, A. and Roberts, B. (1984a) A Marxian alternative to the traditional transformation problem. *Review of Radical Political Economics* 16: 115–135.

Wolff, R., Roberts, B. and Callari, A. (1982) Marx's – not Ricardo's – 'Transformation Problem': a radical reconceptualization. *History of Political Economy* 14: 564–582.

Wolff, R., Roberts, B. and Callari, A. (1984b) Unsnarling the tangle. *History of Political Economy* 16: 431–436.

Wright, I. (2005) The social architecture of capitalism. *Physica A* 346: 589–620.

Supporting Information

Additional Supporting information may be found in the online version of this article at the publisher's website:

Data S1.

11

A PROGRESS REPORT ON MARXIAN ECONOMIC THEORY: ON THE CONTROVERSIES IN EXPLOITATION THEORY SINCE OKISHIO (1963)

Naoki Yoshihara

University of Massachusetts Amherst
Kochi University of Technology, and Hitotsubashi University

1. Introduction

Given the recent and common trends of growing disparity in income and wealth and the increase in poverty among advanced countries, the issue of the long-run distributional feature of wealth and income in the capitalist economy should be at the heart of economic analysis, as Piketty (2014) emphasizes. Piketty (2014) also suggests that divergence in the distribution of wealth and income is explained by the significant inequality between the earnings rate of financial assets and the growth rate, since the former represents the increase in rewards for capital holders while the latter does the increase of the real wage rate. Although controversial, his argument reminds us of Marx's view of the capitalist economy as a conflicting distributional relationship between capitalists and workers.

Marx recognized the conflicting distributional relationship as *exploitative*, and argued that an exploitative relation between capitalists and workers is generic and persistent in the capitalist economy. Since then, the notion of exploitation has been one of the prominent concepts relevant to capitalist economic systems, particularly in a number of debates and analyses of labor relations, especially focusing on the weakest segments of the labor force (see, e.g., ILO, 2005a, 2005b).

However, the nature of exploitation in the capitalist economy is unclear, while it is a matter of observation that feudal lords exploit serfs in the feudal system in that the serf spends part of his/her time working for him/herself and another part on uncompensated work for the lord. Marx argued that a wage worker is also forced to give up part of his/her life to the capitalist. That is, while the serf must work for the lord according to feudal law and usage, the relationship

Analytical Political Economy, First Edition. Edited by Roberto Veneziani and Luca Zamparelli.

between capitalists and workers is mediated by a market contract that the worker is formally free not to enter. Nonetheless, the worker cannot but spend part of his/her time working for a given capitalist by entering into a contract, since otherwise he/she could not procure his/her necessities because of a lack of access to means of production.

Given these background arguments, the *unequal exchange of labor* (UE) may well be considered as a *descriptive feature* of exploitation in the capitalist economy, in that exploitative relations involve systematic differences between the amount of labor that individuals contribute to the economy *in some relevant sense* and the amount of labor they receive *in some relevant sense* through their income. Exploitation as UE (hereafter, UE exploitation) may also have some *normative features* relevant to a diagnosis of the capitalist economy. For instance, it captures certain inequalities in the distribution of material well-being and free hours[1] that are – at least *prima facie* – of normative relevance. Indeed, they are relevant for the *inequalities of well-being freedom* as discussed by Rawls (1971) and Sen (1985) because material well-being and free hours are two key determinants of individual well-being freedom.[2] Second, an UE exploitation-free allocation coincides with the so-called *proportional solution*, a well-known fair allocation rule whereby every agent's income is proportional to his/her contribution to the economy (Roemer and Silvestre, 1993).

Although the notion of UE exploitation seems to be intuitive, the application of this notion to the capitalist economy involves a fundamental difficulty: unlike the case of feudal exploitation, the division of a worker's labor into working for him/herself and working for a capitalist is not a matter of observation since the market contract between buyers and sellers of labor power is simply observed as an equal exchange of labor. Therefore, the existence of UE due to the exploitative relationship in the capitalist economy should be measured through economic analysis. To promote such an analysis, one of the central issues in exploitation theory is to stipulate a suitable operational method to measure the difference between the labor expended and the labor received by an individual via his/her income, without which we cannot credibly diagnose the capitalist economy as an exploitative economic system.

As such a measure, Okishio (1963) provides a formal definition of exploitation to diagnose the capitalist economy as an exploitative economic system under the so-called *Fundamental Marxian Theorem* (FMT). Although Okishio's (1963) definition of exploitation is essentially faithful to the classical labor theory of value and theory of surplus value, it intrinsically relies on the assumption of two-class economies with simple Leontief production technology, homogeneous labor, and homogeneous preferences for consumption and leisure. Indeed, outside of these simple economies, the appropriate definition of the labor "contributed to" and "received by" agents is no longer obvious; moreover, the core diagnoses of the capitalist economy such as the FMT no longer hold under Okishio's (1963) definition of UE exploitation, which has led to several proposals for alternative definitions.

This report examines the development of exploitation theory since the contribution of Okishio (1963) by reviewing the main controversies regarding the proper formal definition of UE exploitation.[3] In the first place, assuming homogeneous labor and homogeneous preferences for consumption and leisure, we review Okishio's definition of exploitation and its generalized versions such as Morishima (1974) and Roemer (1982) through a debate on the FMT in economies with more general production technology. Given that the FMT holds with Okishio's (1963) definition in economies with simple Leontief production technology, if the FMT with any generalization of this definition is not preserved under more general production technology, this would suggest the *incoherence* of such a definition rather than the limitation of the basic Marxian perception of capitalist economies as exploitative. Indeed, it seems to be plausible to think that a purely technological matter such as the complexity of production technology should not be essential to determine the position of each agent in the exploitative relation. Similarly, we also discuss the validity of alternative generalizations of Okishio's (1963) definition from the viewpoint of the so-called *Class-Exploitation Correspondence Principle* (CECP), which was first shown by Roemer (1982) by using Okishio's (1963) definition in economies with simple Leontief production technology. We summarize these arguments and suggest the limitation and noneligibility of these classical definitions.

Second, we review the *property relation definition of exploitation* (PR exploitation), proposed by Roemer (1982, 1994) as an alternative to UE exploitation. Again assuming homogeneous labor and identical preferences for consumption and leisure, the definition of PR exploitation is a mathematical extension of Okishio's definition. Moreover, it is generally true that under this definition, the capitalist economy can be conceived of as exploitative. However, the PR theory of exploitation denies the relevance of exploitation as a primary normative concern: Roemer (1994) argues that the primary normative concern should be the injustice of the unequal distribution of productive assets rather than UE exploitation *per se*. Given this criticism of the notion of UE exploitation, we also review some arguments in political philosophy and sociology such as those proposed by Cohen (1995), Wright (2000), and Vrousalis (2013), which criticize the PR theory of exploitation and encourage the revival of the UE theory of exploitation. Based on their arguments, Roemer's claim that the theory of exploitation is reduced to a theory of distributive injustice can be invalidated.

Third, allowing heterogeneous labor skills, heterogeneous preferences for consumption and leisure, and general production technology, we review the recent development of an axiomatic theory of exploitation. Among the works of this approach, this report focuses on the *Profit-Exploitation Correspondence Principle* (PECP) (Veneziani and Yoshihara, 2015a). Then, an extension of the exploitation form *à la* the New Interpretation (NI) originally introduced by Duménil (1980) and Foley (1982) is shown to be uniquely eligible among the main definitions provided in the literature.

The remainder of this paper is organized as follows. Section 2 discusses the robustness and economic implications of the debates on the FMT initiated by Okishio (1963) and developed mainly in the 1970s and 1980s, followed by a discussion of the CECP. Section 3 introduces the criticism of UE exploitation from the standpoint of PR exploitation, and Section 4 provides the counterarguments to PR exploitation by Cohen (1995), Wright (2000), and Vrousalis (2013). Section 5 provides an overview of recent axiomatic studies of exploitation. Finally, Section 6 concludes the report and provides a perspective on the remaining subjects of exploitation theory.

2. The Main Developments in Mathematical Marxian Economics from the 1970s until the 1990s

In this section, we provide an overview of the main arguments regarding a proper definition of exploitation in mathematical Marxian economics developed until the 1990s. We begin with the significant contribution by Nobuo Okishio, known for the FMT, and then discuss the successive developments and relevant debates on this theorem, mainly initiated by Michio Morishima and John Roemer during the 1970s and 1980s.

2.1 The Formulation of Labor Exploitation (LE) by Okishio and the FMT

An economy comprises a set of agents, $\mathcal{N} = \{1, .., N\}$, with generic element $v \in \mathcal{N}$.[4] Denote the cardinal number of this set by N. Similarly, the cardinal number for any subset, $S \subseteq \mathcal{N}$, is denoted by S. There are n types of (purely private) commodities that are transferable in markets.

Production technology, commonly accessible by any agent, is represented by a production possibility set $P \subseteq \mathbb{R}_- \times \mathbb{R}_-^n \times \mathbb{R}_+^n$ with generic element $\alpha \equiv (-\alpha_l, -\underline{\alpha}, \overline{\alpha})$, where $\alpha_l \in \mathbb{R}_+$ is the *effective* labor input; $\underline{\alpha} \in \mathbb{R}_+^n$ are the inputs of the produced goods; and $\overline{\alpha} \in \mathbb{R}_+^n$ are the outputs of the n goods. The net output vector arising from α is denoted as $\hat{\alpha} \equiv \overline{\alpha} - \underline{\alpha}$. P is assumed to be closed and convex-cone such that (i) $\mathbf{0} \in P$; (ii) for any $\alpha \in P$ with $\overline{\alpha} \geq \mathbf{0}$, $\alpha_l > 0$ holds; and (iii) for any $c \in \mathbb{R}_+^n$, there exists $\alpha \in P$ such that $\hat{\alpha} \geq c$. Property (ii) implies that labor is indispensable for the production of a positive amount of a commodity, while property (iii) implies that any nonnegative vector of commodities can be produced as a net output. A specific type of production technology P is of a *Leontief type* if there exists a pair (A, L), where A is an $n \times n$ nonnegative square matrix of material input coefficients and L is a $1 \times n$ positive vector of labor input coefficients, such that P is represented by the following form:

$$P_{(A,L)} \equiv \left\{ \alpha \equiv (-\alpha_l, -\underline{\alpha}, \overline{\alpha}) \in \mathbb{R}_- \times \mathbb{R}_-^n \times \mathbb{R}_+^n \mid \exists x \in \mathbb{R}_+^n : \alpha \leqq (-Lx, -Ax, x) \right\}.$$

Here, A is assumed to be productive and indecomposable. Another specific type of production technology P is of a *von Neumann type* if there exists a profile (A, B, L) such that P is represented by the following form:

$$P_{(A,B,L)} \equiv \left\{ \alpha \equiv (-\alpha_l, -\underline{\alpha}, \overline{\alpha}) \in \mathbb{R}_- \times \mathbb{R}_-^n \times \mathbb{R}_+^n \mid \exists x \in \mathbb{R}_+^m : \alpha \leqq (-Lx, -Ax, Bx) \right\}$$

where A is an $n \times m$ matrix, the generic component of which, $a_{ij} \geqq 0$, represents the amount of commodity i used as an input to operate one unit of the jth production process; B is an $n \times m$ matrix, the generic component of which, $b_{ij} \geq 0$, represents the amount of commodity i produced as an output by operating one unit of the jth production process; and L is a $1 \times m$ positive row vector of direct labor input coefficients. In the following discussion, we sometimes use the notation A_i (respectively, B_i) to refer to the ith row vector of A (respectively, B).

In this section and in the next sections, assume that for each production period, the maximal amount of labor supply by every agent is equal to unity and there is no difference in labor skills (human capital) among agents. Let $b \in \mathbb{R}_+^n$ be the basic consumption bundle, which is the minimum consumption necessary for every agent when supplying one unit of labor. Let $\omega \in \mathbb{R}_+^n \setminus \{\mathbf{0}\}$ be the social endowments of commodities.

Assuming a private ownership economy, let ω^v be the initial endowment of commodities owned by agent $v \in \mathcal{N}$. In the following discussion, let $\mathcal{W} \equiv \{v \in \mathcal{N} \mid \omega^v = \mathbf{0}\}$ be the set of propertyless agents. Typically, $\mathcal{W}$ would represent the set of workers who own no material means of production. In summary, one *capitalist economy* is described by a profile $\langle \mathcal{N}; P; (\omega^v)_{v \in \mathcal{N}} \rangle$.

Given a capitalist economy $\langle \mathcal{N}; P_{(A,L)}; (\omega^v)_{v \in \mathcal{N}} \rangle$, let v represent a vector of each commodity's labor value. Note that, according to classical economics and Marx, the labor value of commodity i, v_i, is defined as the sum of the amount of labor directly and/or indirectly input to produce one unit of this commodity. Therefore, this value is mathematically formulated by the solution of the system of equations, $v = vA + L$. Here, since matrix A is productive and vector L is positive, $v \in \mathbb{R}_{++}^n$ is the unique solution of the system of equations. Then, the labor value of any commodity vector $c \in \mathbb{R}_+^n$ is given by $vc \geqq 0$.

Let $w \in \mathbb{R}_+$ represent a wage rate. Assume that any agent, $v \in \mathcal{W}$, can purchase the consumption vector, b, with wage revenue, w, per working day. Moreover, let $p \in \mathbb{R}_+^n \setminus \{0\}$ represent a vector of market prices for n types of commodities. Then:

Definition 1. *A balanced-growth equilibrium (BGE) for a capitalist economy* $\langle \mathcal{N}; P_{(A,L)}; (\omega^v)_{v \in \mathcal{N}} \rangle$ *is a profile* $(p, w) \in \mathbb{R}_+^{n+1} \setminus \{0\}$ *that satisfies the following:*

$$p = (1 + \pi)[pA + wL] \quad \& \quad w = pb$$

where the scalar $\pi \geq 0$ represents the equal profit rate.[5]

Definition 2. (Okishio, 1963): *In a capitalist economy* $\langle \mathcal{N}; P_{(A,L)}; (\omega^v)_{v \in \mathcal{N}} \rangle$, *labor exploitation (hereafter, LE) exists if and only if* $vb < 1$.

That is, within one working day, normalized to unity, vb corresponds to the necessary labor hours for each $v \in \mathcal{W}$, so that $1 - vb$ represents the surplus labor hours. Therefore, the existence of LE is none other than the existence of positive surplus labor.

Under Definition 2, Okishio proves the validity of the basic Marxian view, which conceives the capitalist economy as exploitative, as the following theorem shows:

Fundamental Marxian Theorem (FMT). (Okishio, 1963): Let (p, w) be a BGE associated with an equal profit rate π for capitalist economy $\langle \mathcal{N}; P_{(A,L)}; (\omega^v)_{v \in \mathcal{N}} \rangle$. Then,

$$\pi > 0 \Leftrightarrow vb < 1.$$

Since Okishio (1963), numerous studies have examined the robustness of the FMT. Of these, we review the works of Morishima (1974) and Roemer (1980), which discuss the generalization of the FMT to a model of the von Neumann type, in order to show the robustness of the FMT in economies with fixed capital, joint production, and the possibility of technical choices.[6]

Let $x_j \geq 0$ represent an activity level of the jth production process, so that a profile of social production activities is represented by a nonnegative $m \times 1$ column vector, $x \equiv (x_j)_{j=1,\dots,m}$. For a von Neumann capitalist economy, $\langle \mathcal{N}; P_{(A,B,L)}; (\omega^v)_{v \in \mathcal{N}} \rangle$, we can, respectively, define the notions of BGEs, labor values, and LE as follows:

Definition 3. *A BGE for a capitalist economy* $\langle \mathcal{N}; P_{(A,B,L)}; (\omega^v)_{v \in \mathcal{N}} \rangle$ *is a profile of nonnegative and nonzero vectors,* $((p, w), x) \in \mathbb{R}_+^{n+1} \times \mathbb{R}_+^m$, *that satisfy the following:*

$$pB \leq (1 + \pi)[pA + wL]; Bx \geq (1 + \pi)[A + bL]x; pBx > 0; \&w = pb.$$

Definition 4. (Morishima, 1974): *Given a capitalist economy,* $\langle \mathcal{N}; P_{(A,B,L)}; (\omega^v)_{v \in \mathcal{N}} \rangle$, *the labor value of a consumption bundle,* $c \in \mathbb{R}_+^n$, *is the solution,* Lx^c, *of the following constrained optimization program:*

$$\min_{x \geq 0} Lx \quad s.t. \quad [B - A]x \geq c.$$

Then, *LE* is said to exist if and only if $Lx^b < 1$.

Definition 4 extends Definition 2 into von Neumann capitalist economies.

Morishima (1974) shows that, under the BGE, the equivalence between the existence of LE and a positive equal profit rate is preserved, even in a von Neumann capitalist economy:

Generalized Fundamental Marxian Theorem (GFMT). (Morishima, 1974): Let $((p, w), x)$ be a BGE associated with the equal profit rate, π, for capitalist economy $\langle \mathcal{N}; P_{(A,B,L)}; (\omega^v)_{v \in \mathcal{N}} \rangle$. Then,

$$\pi > 0 \Leftrightarrow Lx^b < 1.$$

By contrast, Roemer (1980) defines an alternative equilibrium notion, called a *reproducible solution* (RS), which is to preserve its coherency with the profit-maximizing behavior of every capital owner, $v \in \mathcal{N} \setminus \mathcal{W}$. He then examines the robustness of the FMT under this equilibrium. That is,

Definition 5. (Roemer, 1980): An *RS* for a capitalist economy $\langle \mathcal{N}; P_{(A,B,L)}; (\omega^v)_{v \in \mathcal{N}} \rangle$ is a profile of nonnegative and nonzero vectors, $((p^*, w^*), x^*) \in \mathbb{R}_+^{n+1} \times \mathbb{R}_+^m$, that satisfies the following:[7]

(a) $x^{v*} \in \arg\max_{x^v \geq 0} p^* B x^v + (p^* \omega^v - [p^* A + w^* L] x^v)$,   such   that $[p^* A + w^* L] x^v \leq p^* \omega^v$ ($\forall v \in \mathcal{N} \setminus \mathcal{W}$), where $x^* \equiv \sum_{v \in \mathcal{N} \setminus \mathcal{W}} x^{v*}$;

(b) $(B - [A + bL]) x^* + \omega \geq \omega$;

(c) $w^* = p^* b$;

(d) $[A + bL] x^* \leq \omega$.

In this definition, (a) requires that every capital owner maximizes the monetary value of her capital for the next period, given the equilibrium price vector; (b) requires the *reproducibility* of the economy itself, in that the aggregate capital stock at the beginning of the next period, $(B - [A + bL]) x^* + \omega$, is at least as much as that at the beginning of the present period, ω;[8] (c) stipulates the labor market equilibrium; (d) is the feasibility condition of social production. An RS is a Walrasian equilibrium with an additional condition of the reproducibility.

Roemer's Fundamental Marxian Theorem (RFMT). (Roemer, 1980): For any capitalist economy, $\langle \mathcal{N}; P_{(A,B,L)}; (\omega^v)_{v \in \mathcal{N}} \rangle$, and any *RS*, $((p^*, w^*), x^*)$, the following two statements are equivalent:

(1) $p^* [B - A] x^* - w^* L x^* > 0 \Leftrightarrow Lx^b < 1$;

(2) $\forall x, x' \geq 0, \ Lx = Lx', [\exists i \in \{1, \ldots, n\} : (B_i - A_i) x > (B_i - A_i) x'] \Rightarrow \exists x'' \geq 0 : \ Lx'' = Lx', (B_i - A_i) x'' = (B_i - A_i) x', \& \exists i' \in \{1, \ldots, n\} : (B_{i'} - A_{i'}) x'' > (B_{i'} - A_{i'}) x.$

In the above theorem, statement (1) implies the equivalence between the positivity of total profit, $p^* [B - A] x^* - w^* L x^*$, at the RS and the existence of LE in terms of Definition 4. By contrast, statement (2) characterizes the necessary and sufficient condition for statement (1) to hold. Suppose two production activities, say x and x', have the same corresponding labor inputs. Then, according to statement (2), if the net output of some commodity, say i, via activity x is strictly greater than that via activity x', then there is another commodity, say i', such that the net output of i' via some suitable production activity x'', which may be identical to or different from x', is strictly greater than that via x. This statement is named the *independence of production* by Roemer (1980). If it fails, there is a commodity that can be produced only as a joint product in fixed proportions with another commodity. Thus, the RFMT implies that, in any capitalist economy, the equivalence relationship between positive profits and the existence of LE holds for any RS if and only if no commodity is produced only as a joint product of another good (in terms of condition (2)) in this economy.

To see the difference between the GFMT and RFMT, consider the following example.

Example 1. Consider a von Neumann economy, $\langle \mathcal{N}; P_{(A,B,L)}; (\omega^v)_{v \in \mathcal{N}} \rangle$, such that

$$A = \begin{bmatrix} 1 & 1 \\ 1 & 0 \end{bmatrix}, B = \begin{bmatrix} 2 & 3 \\ 2 & 1 \end{bmatrix}, L = (1,1), b = \begin{bmatrix} 1 \\ 1 \end{bmatrix}, \text{ and } \omega = \begin{bmatrix} 2 \\ 1 \end{bmatrix}.$$

In this economy, condition (2) of the RFMT is violated, because $B - A = \begin{bmatrix} 1 & 2 \\ 1 & 1 \end{bmatrix}$ and $L = (1,1)$, which implies that while the second production process is superior to the first production process in the production of commodity 1, no production process is superior to the second production process in the production of commodity 2.

Note that in this economy, the set of BGEs is characterized by

$$\{((p,w),x) \in \{((0,1),1)\} \times \mathbb{R}^2_+ \mid x \neq \mathbf{0}\}$$

where all BGEs are associated with $\pi = 0$. By contrast, the set of RSs is characterized by

$$\left\{ ((p^*,w^*),x^*) \in \mathbb{R}^2_+ \times \{1\} \times \left\{ \begin{bmatrix} 0 \\ 1 \end{bmatrix} \right\} \mid p_1^* + p_2^* = 1 \right\}$$

where, if $p_1^* > 0$, then $\pi^* = \frac{p_1^*}{2p_1^* + p_2^*} > 0$; while, if $p_1^* = 0$, then $\pi^* = 0$.

Next, in this economy, the labor value of the commodity bundle b is $Lx^b = 1$, where x^b is any nonnegative vector satisfying $x_1^b + x_2^b = 1$. Thus, according to Definition 5, there is no exploitation in this economy.

Therefore, the GFMT holds in this economy, since in any BGE, the corresponding profit rate is $\pi = 0$, while there is no exploitation. However, we can find an RS $((p^*,w^*),x^*)$, with $p_1^* > 0$, whose corresponding profit rate is $\pi^* > 0$. Thus, if the economy arrives at this equilibrium, then positive profits are generated in conjunction with no exploitation, which violates condition (1) of the RFMT. This contrast between the GFMT and RFMT can be observed when the economy does not satisfy condition (2) of the RFMT. □

Okishio–Morishima's proposal for the formulation of LE given in Definitions 2 and 4 is consistent with the basic perception of the labor theory of value, since it is formulated completely independently of price information. Given this formulation, however, Example 1 suggests that the equivalence between positive profits and the existence of exploitation no longer holds for RSs in a general economic environment with the possibility of fixed capital, joint production, and technical choices. First, the extension of the equilibrium notion from the BGE to the RS seems to be reasonable whenever we view a capitalist economy as a resource allocation mechanism working via the capitalists' profit-seeking motivation under market competition. Second, there is no reason to eliminate such an economy as in Example 1 from the subject of our analysis. However, this negative result may suggest that Okishio–Morishima's definition of LE is inappropriate rather than that the basic Marxian perception of the capitalist economy as exploitative is not confirmed, since it seems strange that such a purely technological condition as the existence of a *nonindependently produced commodity* makes the capitalist economy nonexploitative.

There is another, even more serious criticism of Okishio–Morishima's definition, given by Bowles and Gintis (1981), Roemer (1982), and Samuelson (1982). To see this, we return to a Leontief capitalist economy, $\langle \mathcal{N}; P_{(A,L)}; (\omega^v)_{v \in \mathcal{N}} \rangle$. Then, take any commodity, k, and let $v_i^{(k)}$, for each commodity i, be the aggregate amount of commodity k directly and/or indirectly input to produce one unit of the commodity i. Let $v^{(k)} \equiv (v_i^{(k)})_{i \in \{1,\dots,n\}}$ be a vector of *commodity k-values.* Analogical to the case of the vector of labor values, $v^{(k)}$ can be defined as the solution of the following system of equations:

$$v^{(k)} = v^{(k)}[A + bL] + \left(1 - v_k^{(k)}\right)\left[A_k + b_k L\right]$$

where A_k is the kth row vector of matrix A. Then,

Definition 6. In a capitalist economy, $\left\langle \mathcal{N}; P_{(A,L)}; (\omega^v)_{v \in \mathcal{N}} \right\rangle$, the *exploitation of commodity k* exists if and only if $v_k^{(k)} < 1$.

Generalized Commodity Exploitation Theorem (GCET). (Bowles and Gintis, 1981; Roemer, 1982; Samuelson, 1982): Let (p, w) be a BGE associated with the equal profit rate, π, for capitalist economy $\left\langle \mathcal{N}; P_{(A,L)}; (\omega^v)_{v \in \mathcal{N}} \right\rangle$. Then,

$$\pi > 0 \Leftrightarrow vb < 1 \Leftrightarrow v_k^{(k)} < 1.$$

Establishing the GCET leads us to see Okishio–Morishima's definition of LE as representing the productiveness of an overall economic system. This is because the existence of commodity k's exploitation is the exact numerical representation of the productiveness of an overall economic system if we select commodity k as the numéraire, in that the overall economic system is productive enough to guarantee the possibility of surplus products via the efficient use of commodity k as a factor of production. Analogically, we can interpret the existence of LE in terms of Definition 2 as the numerical representation of the productiveness of an overall economic system by selecting labor as the numéraire. Therefore, the equivalence between the FMT and GCET indicates that the necessary and sufficient condition for positive profits is that the whole economic system is sufficiently productive to guarantee the possibility of surplus products, which is a trivial proposition. This view prompted criticism of Okishio's original motivation and interpretation of the FMT, in that it may simply affirm the productiveness of the capitalist economy, rather than the Marxian perception of the capitalist economy as an exploitative system.[9] However, the criticism should be directed to the suitability of Okishio–Morishima's formulation, since such a definition fails to present the intrinsic feature of UE exploitation, which should not be reduced to the productiveness of an overall economic system.

2.2 CECP

Although the FMT has been criticized as mentioned above, there is another well-known analysis to validate the Marxian perception of the capitalist economy as an exploitative system: that is, the CECP proposed by Roemer (1982).

2.2.1 A General Model

We first set up a more general economic model than that presented in Section 2.1 and its corresponding equilibrium notion. These settings are also used in Section 5.

Given $\mathcal{N}$ and P defined in Section 2.1, agents can be heterogeneous in terms of their capital endowments $(\omega_t^v)_{v \in \mathcal{N}}$ in each period t. Moreover, for each $v \in \mathcal{N}$, $s^v > 0$ represents his/her skill level. Let $C \subseteq \mathbb{R}_+^n \times [0, 1]$ be the consumption space common to all agents, and for each $v \in \mathcal{N}$, let $u^v : C \to \mathbb{R}_+$ be his/her welfare function. All available welfare functions are assumed to be strongly increasing in consumption bundles and decreasing in the supply of labor hours. Thus, one capitalist economy is defined by the list $\mathcal{E} \equiv \left\langle \mathcal{N}; P; (u^v, s^v, \omega_0^v)_{v \in \mathcal{N}} \right\rangle$.

As in Roemer (1980, 1982), the time structure of production is explicitly considered and production activities are financed with current wealth. Agent v's wealth, at the beginning of period t, is given by $p_{t-1}\omega_t^v$: this is fixed at the end of period $t-1$ given market prices p_{t-1}. Thus, given a price system $\langle\{p_{t-1},p_t\},w_t\rangle$ in period t, each agent $v \in \mathcal{N}$ engages in an optimal choice of production plan $\alpha_t^v \in P$. Here, each agent (i) purchases a bundle of capital goods $\underline{\alpha}_t^v$ at price p_{t-1} under his/her wealth constraint, $p_{t-1}\omega_t^v$, and employs labor power, α_{lt}^v, at the beginning of this period; (ii) purchases an optimal amount of commodity bundle δ_t^v at price p_{t-1} under budget constraint $p_{t-1}(\omega_t^v - \underline{\alpha}_t^v)$ for speculative purposes, to be sold at the end of the period with an expected price p_t; and (iii) chooses an optimal labor supply and consumption plan, $(c_t^v, l_t^v) \in C$, where c_t^v will be purchased at the end of this period with an expected price (p_t, w_t) under the budget constraint of his/her revenue from both production and speculation. This choice behavior is determined as a solution to the optimization problem (MP_t^v), as follows:

$$MP_t^v : \max_{(c_t^v,l_t^v)\in C;\delta_t^v\in\mathbb{R}_+^n;\alpha_t^v\in P} u^v\left(c_t^v,l_t^v\right)$$

$$\text{s.t. } \left[p_t\overline{\alpha}_t^v - w_t\alpha_{lt}^v\right] + w_t\Lambda_t^v + p_t\delta_t^v \geq p_t c_t^v + p_t\omega_{t+1}^v, \text{ where } \Lambda_t^v \equiv s^v l_t^v;$$

$$p_{t-1}\delta_t^v + p_{t-1}\underline{\alpha}_t^v \leq p_{t-1}\omega_t^v;$$

$$p_t\omega_{t+1}^v \geq p_{t-1}\omega_t^v.$$

Then, denote the set of solutions to the problem (MP_t^v) by $O_t^v(\{p_{t-1},p_t\},w_t)$.

We focus on the stationary equilibrium price vector, $p^* = p_{t-1} = p_t$ ($\forall t$). Moreover, we focus on the nontrivial equilibrium satisfying $\pi \equiv \max_{\alpha'\in P}\frac{p^*\overline{\alpha}'-p^*\underline{\alpha}'-w_t\alpha_l'}{p^*\underline{\alpha}'} \geq 0$. In this case, according to the monotone increasing characteristic of u^v at c_t^v, there always exists an optimal solution having $\delta_t^v = 0$. By focusing on this optimal solution, we can remove the description of δ_t^v without loss of generality. Therefore, we consider the following equilibrium notion:

Definition 7. For a capitalist economy, $\mathcal{E}$, an RS is a profile $((p^*, w_t^*); ((c_t^{*v}, l_t^{*v}); \alpha_t^{*v})_{v\in\mathcal{N}})$ of a price system and economic activities in each period, t, satisfying the following conditions:

(i) $((c_t^{*v}, l_t^{*v}); \alpha_t^{*v}) \in O_t^v(p^*, w_t^*)$ ($\forall t$) (each agent's optimization);

(ii) $\sum_{v\in\mathcal{N}} \widehat{\alpha}_t^{*v} \geq \sum_{v\in\mathcal{N}} c_t^{*v}$ ($\forall t$) (demand–supply matching at the end of each period);

(iii) $\sum_{v\in\mathcal{N}} \alpha_{lt}^{*v} = \sum_{v\in\mathcal{N}} \Lambda_t^{*v}$ ($\forall t$) (labor market equilibrium);

(iv) $\sum_{v\in\mathcal{N}} \underline{\alpha}_t^{*v} \leq \sum_{v\in\mathcal{N}} \omega_t^v$ ($\forall t$) (social feasibility of production at the beginning of each period).

Henceforth, we assume the stationary state on economic activities of agents and delete the time description, t.

2.2.2 Class and Exploitation

Although the above definitions of MP_t^v and the RS are the most general, let us focus on a specific case of such a general form of capitalist economies within this subsection. First, we assume that all agents have the same level of skill, so that $s^v = 1$ for each $v \in \mathcal{N}$, without loss of generality. Therefore, $\Lambda_t^v = l_t^v$ holds for each $v \in \mathcal{N}$. Second, we focus on the following case: for each $v \in \mathcal{N}$, $u^v(c,l) \equiv \psi^v(c)$. That is, all agents are indifferent to the increase in leisure. In this case, for any economy $\mathcal{E} = \langle\mathcal{N};P;(\psi^v, 1, \omega^v)_{v\in\mathcal{N}}\rangle$ and any RS $((p, w); ((c^v, l^v); \alpha^v)_{v\in\mathcal{N}})$,

$l^v = 1$ and $pc^v = \pi p\omega^v + w$ hold for any $v \in \mathcal{N}$. Let $\Pi^v(p, w) \equiv \pi p\omega^v + w$ be the net revenue of $v \in \mathcal{N}$ at RS-prices (p, w).

Based on Roemer (1982), we define the class structure of the capitalist economy as follows:

Definition 8.   For a capitalist economy, $\mathcal{E} = \langle \mathcal{N}; P; (\psi^v, 1, \omega^v)_{v \in \mathcal{N}} \rangle$, let $((p, w); ((c^v, 1); \alpha^v)_{v \in \mathcal{N}})$ be an RS. Then, for each $v \in \mathcal{N}$:

   (i) v is a member of the *capitalist class*, $C^1(\subseteq \mathcal{N})$ if and only if $\alpha_l^v > 1$;
   (ii) v is a member of the *petit bourgeois class*, $C^2(\subseteq \mathcal{N})$ if and only if $\alpha_l^v = 1$;
   (iii) v is a member of the *quasi-proletariat class*, $C^3(\subseteq \mathcal{N})$ if and only if $\alpha_l^v < 1$; and
   (iv) v is a member of the *pure proletariat class*, $C^4(\subseteq \mathcal{N})$ if and only if $\alpha_l^v = 0$.

Under this definition, $\alpha_l^v > 1$ implies that agent v should employ others' labor in the equilibrium, meaning that such an agent is an employer; $\alpha_l^v = 1$ implies that agent v should be self-employed in the equilibrium; and $\alpha_l^v < 1$ implies that agent v could spend a part of his/her labor in his/her own shop but must sell his/her remaining labor to others. Finally, $\alpha_l^v = 0$ implies that this agent can optimize only by selling all of his/her labor to others.

Based on Okishio–Morishima's definition of exploitation, Roemer (1982) provides a more comprehensive definition of exploitative relations as follows. First, for any bundle $c \in \mathbb{R}_+^n$, let us denote the production possibility set to produce c as a net output by $\phi(c) \equiv \{\alpha \in P \mid \hat{\alpha} \geqq c\}$. Then:

Definition 9.   For a capitalist economy, $\mathcal{E} = \langle \mathcal{N}; P; (\psi^v, 1, \omega^v)_{v \in \mathcal{N}} \rangle$, let $((p, w); ((c^v, 1); \alpha^v)_{v \in \mathcal{N}})$ be an RS. Then, for each $v \in \mathcal{N}$:

   (i) v is *exploited* if and only if $1 > \max_{f^v \in \mathbb{R}_+^n : pf^v = \Pi^v(p,w)} \min_{\alpha \in \phi(f^v)} \alpha_l$;
   (ii) v is *an exploiter* if and only if $1 < \min_{f^v \in \mathbb{R}_+^n : pf^v = \Pi^v(p,w)} \min_{\alpha \in \phi(f^v)} \alpha_l$.

Note that when $P = P_{(A,B,L)}$, then $\alpha^v = (-Lx^v, -Ax^v, Bx^v)$ and so $\min_{\alpha \in \phi(f^v)} \alpha_l = Lx^{f^v}$, where Lx^{f^v} is given by Definition 4. Likewise, when $P = P_{(A,L)}$, then $\alpha^v = (-Lx^v, -Ax^v, x^v)$ and so $\min_{\alpha \in \phi(f^v)} \alpha_l = vf^v$.

Given these formulations of class structure and exploitation, Roemer (1982) shows the following:

Theorem of the Class-Exploitation Correspondence Principle (CECP): For any $\mathcal{E} = \langle \mathcal{N}; P_{(A,L)}; (\psi^v, 1, \omega^v)_{v \in \mathcal{N}} \rangle$ and any RS $((p, w); ((c^v, 1); \alpha^v)_{v \in \mathcal{N}})$ with $\pi > 0$,

   (i) every agent $v \in C^1$ is an exploiter;
   (ii) every agent $v \in C^3 \cup C^4$ is exploited; and
   (iii) for any $k = 1, 2, 3$ and any $v \in C^k$ and any $\mu \in C^{k+1}$, $p\omega^v > p\omega^\mu$ holds.

Given Okishio–Morishima's definition of exploitation, the CECP establishes that for any capitalist economy with Leontief production technology and any RS with a positive maximal profit rate, every member of the capitalist class C^1 is an exploiter while every member of the working class $C^3 \cup C^4$ is exploited. Moreover, every member of the capitalist class is richer than every member of the working class. This states that in the equilibrium class membership and exploitation status emerge endogenously: the wealthy can rationally choose to belong to the capitalist class among other available options and become an exploiter, while the poor have no other option than being in the working class and are exploited. Thus, it provides a more comprehensive analysis of the capitalist economy as an exploitative system than the

FMT, since the latter is only concerned with the (average rate) of exploitation for propertyless agents in $\mathcal{W}$.

Unfortunately, as in the case of the FMT, the robustness of the CECP is also problematic if a more general production technology is considered: given Definition 9, the CECP does not hold in an economy with $P_{(A,B,L)}$. This finding can be confirmed by checking the economy presented in Example 1.[10] From Definition 8(iv), any agent in $\mathcal{W}$ belongs to C^4. Therefore, to verify the CECP, such an agent must be exploited in terms of Definition 9(i). However, in Example 1, at an RS (p^*, w^*) with $p_1^* > 0$ and $w^* > 0$, $p^*b = \Pi^v(p^*, w^*)$ holds for any $v \in \mathcal{W}$, and $Lx^b = 1$. Therefore, since $\max_{f^v \in \mathbb{R}_+^n : p^*f^v = \Pi^v(p^*,w^*)} Lx^{f^v} \geq Lx^b = 1$ for any $v \in \mathcal{W}$, no agent in C^4 is exploited. This means the violation of the CECP.

Given this negative result, Roemer (1982, chapter 5) rightly argues that this is the most serious criticism of Okishio–Morishima's definition of exploitation, rather than the failure of the basic Marxian perception of the capitalist economy as an exploitative system. This is because, taking the CECP as a guiding postulate even though it is a theorem, "we learn something about what the formal model must look like" (Roemer, 1982, p. 152).

Roemer (1982, chapter 5) also provides an alternative to Okishio–Morishima's definition. For any price system $(p, w) \in \mathbb{R}_+^{n+1}$ and any $c \in \mathbb{R}_+^n$, let $\phi(c; p, w) \equiv \{\alpha \in \arg\max_{\alpha' \in P} \frac{p\overline{\alpha'} - w\underline{\alpha'_l}}{p\underline{\alpha'}} \mid \hat{\alpha} \geq c\}$. Then,

Definition 10. For a capitalist economy, $\mathcal{E} = \langle \mathcal{N}; P; (\psi^v, 1, \omega^v)_{v \in \mathcal{N}} \rangle$, let $((p, w); ((c^v, 1); \alpha^v)_{v \in \mathcal{N}})$ be an RS. Then, for each $v \in \mathcal{N}$:

(i) v is *exploited* if and only if $1 > \max_{f^v \in \mathbb{R}_+^n : pf^v = \Pi^v(p,w)} \min_{\alpha \in \phi(f^v;p,w)} \alpha_l$;

(ii) v is an *exploiter* if and only if $1 < \min_{f^v \in \mathbb{R}_+^n : pf^v = \Pi^v(p,w)} \min_{\alpha \in \phi(f^v;p,w)} \alpha_l$.

Unlike Definitions 2, 4, and 9, Definition 10 formulates the labor value of a commodity vector as a function of equilibrium prices. Therefore, it is not faithful to the labor theory of value. Roemer (1982, chapter 5) claims that given Definition 10, the CECP holds in the general economy, and relying on this claim, he also criticizes the labor theory of value, by arguing that to preserve the CECP, labor values must be properly defined as "logically posterior" to equilibrium prices.

Unfortunately, his claim is wrong in that, given Definition 10, the CECP still fails in an economy with $P_{(A,B,L)}$. This point again can be verified by the economy in Example 1.[11] At an RS (p^*, w^*) with $p_1^* > 0$ and $w^* > 0$, it is verified that

$$\phi(b; p^*, w^*) = \{\lambda\alpha^* \mid \lambda \geq 1\} \text{ for } \alpha^* \equiv (-Le_2, -Ae_2, Be_2) \text{ where } e_2 \equiv \begin{bmatrix} 0 \\ 1 \end{bmatrix}.$$

Therefore, $\min_{\alpha \in \phi(b;p^*,w^*)} \alpha_l = 1 \leq \max_{f^v \in \mathbb{R}_+^n : p^*f^v = w^*} \min_{\alpha \in \phi(f^v;p^*,w^*)} \alpha_l$, which implies that no agent in C^4 is exploited in terms of Definition 10. Thus, although Roemer's (1982) view about the epistemological role of the CECP is correct, his proposal about the proper definition of UE exploitation cannot be validated.

3. The PR Exploitation by Roemer (1982)

Roemer (1994) argues that UE exploitation should be replaced with exploitation as the distributional consequences of an unjust inequality in the distribution of productive assets and resources. What constitutes unjust inequality in capitalist societies? Roemer (1994) argues that this is the unequal distribution of alienable assets.[12]

Based on this view, Roemer (1994) proposes the *PR exploitation*. Namely, *a group or individual (capitalistically) exploits another group or individual* if and only if the following three conditions hold: (i) were the latter to withdraw from society, endowed with his/her per capita share of social alienable goods and own labor skill, then his/her welfare would improve compared with under the present allocation; (ii) were the former to withdraw under the same conditions, then his/her welfare would worsen compared with under the present allocation; and (iii) were the latter to withdraw from society, endowed with his/her own endowments, then the former would be worse off than at present.

Such a definition can be formulated within the framework of cooperative game theory. Let $(V^1, \ldots, V^N) \in \mathbb{R}_+^N$ be a profile of each agent's welfare level in society. Let $P(\mathcal{N})$ be the power set of $\mathcal{N}$ and let $K : P(\mathcal{N}) \to \mathbb{R}_+$ be a *characteristic function* of society, which assigns to every coalition $S \subseteq \mathcal{N}$, with S agents, an aggregate payoff, $K(S)$, if it withdraws from the economy.

The types of features that characteristic function K would have to include as a welfare allocation rule of the alternative society depends on the nature of the alternative society. For instance, in a capitalist society, function K would be defined in terms of the welfare allocation implementable from the equal distribution of alienable assets. Consider an economy $\mathcal{E} = \langle \mathcal{N}; P_{(A,L)}; (u, 1, \omega^v)_{v \in \mathcal{N}} \rangle$, where u is the common welfare function of all agents. Define a feasible allocation for this economy as a profile $((c^v, l^v)_{v \in \mathcal{N}}, x) \in C^N \times \mathbb{R}_+^n$ satisfying (i) $Ax \leqq \omega$; (ii) $Lx = \sum_{v \in \mathcal{N}} l^v$; and (iii) $(I - A)x \geqq \sum_{v \in \mathcal{N}} c^v$. If a feasible allocation $((c^{*v}, l^{*v})_{v \in \mathcal{N}}, x^*)$ is implemented as an RS for the capitalist economy $\mathcal{E}$, then its corresponding welfare allocation is denoted by $(V^{*1}, \ldots, V^{*N})$, where $V^{*v} \equiv u(c^{*v}, l^{*v})$ for each $v \in \mathcal{N}$.

Denote the welfare allocation rule of an alternative society by $K^{CE} : P(\mathcal{N}) \to \mathbb{R}_+$. For each coalition, $S \subseteq \mathcal{N}$, then consider the following optimization program (CE):

$$\max_{((c^v, l^v)_{v \in S}, x)} \sum_{v \in S} u(c^v, l^v)$$

$$\text{s.t. } (I - A)x \geqq \sum_{v \in S} c^v; \quad Lx = \sum_{v \in S} l^v \leqq S; \ \& \ Ax \leqq \frac{S}{N}\omega. \qquad (CE)$$

Denote the solution of program (CE) by $((c^{**v}, l^{**v})_{v \in S}, x^S)$. Then, the characteristic function, K^{CE}, is defined by $K^{CE}(S) \equiv \sum_{v \in S} u(c^{**v}, l^{**v})$ for each $S \subseteq \mathcal{N}$.

The program (CE) presumes a counterfactual situation in which group S withdraws from the capitalist society to form a *commune* comprising the members of this group, and then investigates the expected sum of the welfare levels achievable in that alternative society. That is, the program maximizes the aggregate of the welfare levels attainable by group S endowed with its accessible aggregate capital stock, $\frac{S}{N}\omega$. Here, $\frac{S}{N}\omega$ is the sum of the capital stocks of all members in S derived from the counterfactual equal distribution of the overall material means of production, ω. The solution to this program constitutes the value $K^{CE}(S)$ as the total payoff attainable by group S if it forms a communal society by withdrawing from the present society. Following Roemer (1982), the *property-relation exploitation of a capitalist society (capitalist PR exploitation)* is defined by means of this K^{CE}, as follows:

Definition 11. (Roemer, 1982): At a welfare allocation $(V^{*1}, \ldots, V^{*N})$ of a capitalist economy, $\langle \mathcal{N}; P_{(A,L)}; (u, 1, \omega^v)_{v \in \mathcal{N}} \rangle$, *coalition $S \subseteq \mathcal{N}$ is capitalistically exploited (respectively,* *capitalistically exploiting)* if and only if the complement $\mathcal{T} \equiv \mathcal{N} \backslash S$ is in a relation of dominance to S, and the following two conditions hold:

(i) $\sum_{v \in S} V^{*v} < K^{CE}(S)$ (respectively, $\sum_{v \in S} V^{*v} > K^{CE}(S)$);

(ii) $\sum_{v \in \mathcal{T}} V^{*v} >$ $K^{CE}(\mathcal{T})$ (respectively, $\sum_{v \in \mathcal{T}} V^{*v} < K^{CE}(\mathcal{T})$).

That is, condition (i) of Definition 11 states that a capitalistically exploited coalition is worse off in terms of its attainable payoff in the capitalist society than in the communal society endowed with an equal distribution of material means of production. Moreover, condition (ii) of Definition 11 states that the complement of the capitalistically exploited coalition would be better off in terms of its attainable payoff in the capitalist society than in the communal society of this complement. It would be expected that a capitalistically exploiting coalition would exist within this complement. In addition to the definition given in Roemer (1982), Roemer (1994) introduces a third condition: (iii) the aggregate welfare of group $\mathcal{T}$ would be worse off if group S withdraws, taking $\omega^S \equiv \sum_{v \in S} \omega^v$ with it from the capitalist society.[13] This condition would naturally follow whenever the welfare allocation $(V^{*1}, \dots, V^{*N})$ is derived from the RS in our setting of the Leontief capitalist economy.

A nonexploitative society in terms of Definition 11 can be formulated as a society without an unequal distribution of material capital goods, as confirmed by the following definition.

Definition 12.   (Roemer, 1982): For any Leontief production economy, $\langle \mathcal{N}; P_{(A,L)};$ $(u, 1, \omega^v)_{v \in \mathcal{N}} \rangle$, a *welfare allocation* $(V^{*1}, \dots, V^{*N})$ *lies in a communal core* if and only if any coalition $S \subseteq \mathcal{N}$ is not capitalistically exploited by the allocation.

Definition 12 implies that the core property of a communal society is equivalent to the nonexistence of capitalist exploitation in terms of Definition 11.

What types of feasible allocations can a communal core contain? The welfare allocation lies in the communal core if (i) it is generated from the situation in which all individuals in $\mathcal{N}$ constitute a communal society, (ii) all individuals engage in a cooperative production activity using the overall set of material capital goods, ω, and (iii) all individuals share the reward of the activity equally. Such an allocation is a nonexploitative allocation in terms of Definition 11.[14]

Unlike the traditional Marxian theory of exploitation, the capitalist PR exploitation formulated in Definition 11 never refers to UE. Rather, it straightforwardly refers to the unequal distribution of material means of production as the basic feature of exploitation in the capitalist economy. However, Definition 11 extends Okishio–Morishima's definition of UE exploitation, as pointed out by Roemer (1982). Indeed, given the RS $((p^*, w^*), x^*)$ in the capitalist economy $\langle \mathcal{N}; P_{(A,L)}; (u, 1, \omega^v)_{v \in \mathcal{N}} \rangle$, if any worker, $v \in \mathcal{W}$, is identified as an exploited agent by Okishio–Morishima's definition of exploitation, then he/she would be a member of an exploited coalition in terms of Definition 11. Furthermore, Definition 11 allows us to identify all exploited agents beyond the members of $\mathcal{W}$ as well as all members of the exploiters. Henceforth, the PR theory of exploitation provides a finer definition of exploitation than do UE theories. In summary, whenever we are interested in exploitation as a feature of social relations, Roemer (1994) concludes that we should discuss it based on the PR definition rather than the UE definition of exploitation.

Given this alternative definition, Roemer (1994) questions whether the issue of exploitation is an intrinsic normative problem worth discussing in the context of contemporary societies. He argues that exploitation *per se* is at best a morally secondary phenomenon. Instead, he believes that the normatively primary concern that we should be addressing is the injustice of property relations. For instance, according to Definition 11, capitalist PR exploitation exists in the RS $((p^*, w^*), x^*)$ of the economy $\langle \mathcal{N}; P_{(A,L)}; (u, 1, \omega^v)_{v \in \mathcal{N}} \rangle$, whenever alienable capital goods are unequally distributed.[15] However, although inequality in the distribution of alienable resources could be conceived of as unjust when all agents are homogeneous in their welfare functions and skills, the issue is less straightforward when these functions and skills are heterogeneous and diverse. Given that the heterogeneity and diversity of agents are generic features of contemporary societies, it seems to be necessary for us to develop a more comprehensive theory of distributive justice, which should be the normatively primary concern in contemporary societies, rather than the development of exploitation theory.

Therefore, what types of theories of distributive justice should be addressed? As a solution, Roemer (1994, 1998) develops a *theory of equality of opportunity*, based on the debates on equality by Dworkin (2000), Arneson (1989), and Cohen (1989). His theory can be summarized by the following axiom:

Principle of voluntary disadvantage: The distribution of alienable resources between any agents, $v \in \mathcal{N}$ and $v' \in \mathcal{N}$, is *just* if and only if any difference in v's and v''s enjoyment of the resources reflects a difference in their choices, desserts, or faults.

Any inequality violating this principle implies *involuntary disadvantage*, which should be deemed to be distributive injustice.

Note that involuntary disadvantage implies disadvantages due to circumstantial factors for which individuals should not be deemed to be responsible, such as those due to household environments, native talents, disaster, and so on. It is reasonable to regard an agent's disadvantage in the private ownership of material capital goods as involuntary, at least in his/her initial stage of economic activities. For instance, in the above-mentioned capitalist economy $\langle \mathcal{N}; P_{(A,L)}; (u, 1, \omega^v)_{v \in \mathcal{N}} \rangle$, there is supposedly no difference in agents' native talents, and the possibility of disaster is not considered. Therefore, the inequality in the private ownership of material capital goods is the sole source of involuntary disadvantages in this economy. In this respect, an equilibrium allocation in the economy $\langle \mathcal{N}; P_{(A,L)}; (u, 1, \omega^v)_{v \in \mathcal{N}} \rangle$ implies involuntary disadvantages if and only if it entails capitalist PR exploitation in terms of Definition 11.

In summary, given the above arguments, the existence of exploitation *à la* Roemer's theory of PR exploitation is equivalent to distributive injustice *à la* Roemer's theory of equality of opportunity, at least in any Leontief capitalist economy with no heterogeneity or diversity of agents. Hence, in such homogeneous societies, it is sufficient to argue distributive injustice in terms of the theory of equality of opportunity. Moreover, the theory of equality of opportunity can diagnose allocations of alienable resources as unjust, even in societies with heterogeneity and/or diversity among agents. Therefore, the issue of exploitation can be replaced with, or be reduced to, the issue of distributive injustice because of the theory of equality of opportunity. It is sufficient that we diagnose societies using the theory of equal opportunity, which is the main message derived from Roemer's PR theory of exploitation in conjunction with the theory of equality of opportunity.

4. Recent Trends of Exploitation Theory in Political Philosophy and Sociology

Roemer's PR theory of exploitation was so influential that, while the Marxian theory of exploitation was almost dismissed in economics, given the absence of substantial studies in this field since Roemer (1994), many counterarguments were developed, particularly in political philosophy and sociology. Among these, this section reviews Cohen's (1995) criticism of PR exploitation and the recent works of Vrousalis (2013) and Wright (2000) on reviving UE exploitation theory.

4.1 Cohen's (1995) Criticism of PR Exploitation

Cohen (1995) criticizes Roemer's (1994) claim that normatively fundamental injustice is the maldistribution of assets rather than their unreciprocated flow (i.e., the UE transfer of products). Let us consider agents v and μ, who are equal in talent and external assets but who have different preferences for income and leisure in that v is an idler and μ is a workaholic. Then, v let μ work on v's means of production after μ has finished working on his own. As a consequence, a part of μ's product derived from her working on v's means of production goes to v. In this case, there is nothing unjust since there is no unjust extraction.

Based on this argument, Roemer concludes that the UE transfer *per se* is not unjust and that unequal asset distribution is normatively fundamental injustice. By contrast, according to Cohen, the injustice of such a distribution is *normatively derivative*. Indeed, Cohen (1995) argues that an unreciprocal transfer of products is unjust if and only if it occurs for the wrong reason. The transfer is unjust when it is caused not by *different preferences* but by an *unequal asset endowment*. Moreover, an unequal asset endowment is unjust because of its tendency to induce an unjust product flow. Therefore, although it is causally primary in the explanation of the possibility and occurrence of unjust transfers, it remains normatively secondary unjust. Based on this argument, the UE transfer in the above example is simply not unjustly exploitative.[16]

Note that Cohen (1995) also thinks that taking the UE transfer itself as coherently unjust and exploitative causes difficulties. The position to regard the UE transfer as such implicitly affirms at least a strongly qualified version of the self-ownership principle.[17] Such a position cannot criticize *cleanly generated capitalism*,[18] since such a brand of capitalism was generated without violating the self-ownership principle.

By contrast, based on Cohen's (1995) argument, cleanly generated capitalism can be criticized: even in such a capitalist economy, the worker μ is exploited by the capitalist v, since v gets some of what μ produces (for no return) by virtue of the differential ownership of means of production. Furthermore, since such asset inequality causes v to get some of what μ produces, it is unjust that v would get it. Moreover, the unequal distribution of means of production is unjust because it tends to cause such an unjustly unreciprocal transfer.

4.2 A Conceptual Definition of Vrousalis (2013) in Political Philosophy

Vrousalis (2013) offers the following argument for the conceptual definition of exploitation in capitalist economies:

Definition 13. (Vrousalis, 2013): Agent v *economically exploits* agent μ if and only if v and μ are embedded in a systematic relationship in which, (a) v *instrumentalizes μ's economic vulnerability to v* in order to (b) *appropriate (the fruits of) μ's labor*.

To clarify this definition, we examine each concept in Definition 13 individually.[19]

First, the *instrumentalization* of a subject implies that the subject is being used as a means to an end. Note that, according to Vrousalis (2013), neither unfairness nor the intentionality of instrumentalization is necessary for the definition of exploitation. As we will see, Vrousalis (2013) provides examples of the "nonunfair" utilization of others' attributes, which is still deemed to be exploitative. Vrousalis (2013) also discusses that one can unintentionally or unknowingly instrumentalize another's vulnerability and thereby exploit that person.

Second, before discussing the notion of *economic vulnerability*, let us mention that Vrousalis (2013) describes two types of vulnerability: absolute and relational. An agent suffers *absolute vulnerability* when he/she is at substantial risk of a significant loss in the relevant metric (welfare, resources, capabilities, etc.). The absence of absolute vulnerability is guaranteed by security, which implies such losses will not occur. However, absolute vulnerability does not refer to an agent's power over another person. By contrast, the notion of *relational vulnerability* is defined as follows: μ *is relationally vulnerable to* v if v has some sort of power over μ in that (i) μ lacks something that he/she wants/needs, F, that is a requirement for μ to flourish; (ii) μ can only obtain F from v; and (iii) v has it within his/her discretion to withhold F from μ.[20]

Now, the notion of *economic vulnerability* is defined as follows: μ *is economically vulnerable to* v if and only if μ is relationally vulnerable to v by virtue of μ's position relative to v in the relations of production. Here, it refers to the systematic relations of effective ownership in that v's ownership of a means of production and μ's lack thereof (or, μ's ownership is substantially less than v's), as a result of which v has *economic power over* μ in the sense that v has the relevant ability and opportunity to get μ to do something by virtue of his/her control over a greater share of resources than μ.

In summary, if v instrumentalizes μ's economic vulnerability to v, then in doing so, v takes advantage of his/her economic power over μ. Under capitalism, if μ has no means of production but v does, or μ owns substantially less than v, then μ is economically vulnerable to v. In other words, v is given economic power over μ and can get μ to supply his/her labor power to v. For instance, assuming an equal distribution of internal resources,[21] the wealth owned by capitalists (or agent v) systematically gives them a decisive bargaining advantage over workers (or agent μ), which means capitalists take advantage of their economic power over workers, but never the other way around.[22,23]

Finally, condition (b) of Definition 13 needs clarification: v appropriates μ's labor when μ toils for H hours, and v appropriates a use value of $H - G$ hours of toil, where G can be any number satisfying $H > G \geq 0$.[24]

In Definition 13, UE, which is represented by condition (b), is simply a necessary condition for economic exploitation, since conditions (a) and (b) of Definition 13 together constitute economic exploitation. For instance, gift-giving implies UE, but no one thinks of (even systematic) gift-giving as exploitative. If one party freely decides to pass on a large part of whatever use value he/she creates (with his/her own labor power) to another party of society, the resulting inequality in the consumption of (surplus) labor need not be objectionable.

4.3 *A Conceptual Definition of Exploitation by Wright (2000) in Sociology*

Wright (2000) defines exploitation as follows:

Definition 14. (Wright, 2000): Exploitation exists if the following three criteria are satisfied:

(1) *The inverse interdependent welfare principle*: The material welfare of exploiters causally depends upon the reduction of the material welfare of the exploited;

(2) *The exclusion principle*: This inverse interdependence of the welfare of exploiters and the exploited depends upon the exclusion of the exploited from access to certain productive resources; and

(3) *The appropriation principle*: The exclusion generates a material advantage to exploiters because it enables them to appropriate the labor effort of the exploited.

In a market economy, both parties to an exchange gain relative to their condition before making the exchange: both workers and capitalists gain when an exchange of labor power for a wage occurs. While such mutual gains from trade can occur, the magnitude of the gain by one party may still be at the expense of another party.[25] Thus, criterion (1) should be satisfied and, according to Wright (2000), we should not assume that market exchanges do not satisfy (1) because of mutual gains from trade.

Wright (2000) argues that exploitation is the process through which certain inequalities in income are generated by inequalities in rights and powers over productive resources. Such inequalities in income occur by the ways in which exploiters, by virtue of their exclusionary rights and powers over productive resources, are able to appropriate the labor effort of the exploited.

Before closing this subsection, it is worth noting that Definition 14 is insufficient as a definition of exploitation, and nor is it as elaborate a conceptual configuration as Definition 13. Definition 14 simply lists the indispensable principles of exploitation as its essential features, although the three principles are intuitively appealing and well acknowledged. Moreover, it is easy to check that Definition 13 satisfies all three principles in Definition 14. Indeed, the appropriation principle is obviously satisfied, and the exclusion principle is satisfied by the definition of economic vulnerability. Finally, Definition 13 also satisfies the inverse interdependence welfare principle as long as the fruit of labor is defined as a use value contributing to human welfare.

4.4 Relations of Exploitation with Economic Oppression and Distributive Injustice

This subsection examines the logical relation of exploitation to similar notions of economic oppression and/or distributive injustice using the conceptual definition of exploitation developed by Vrousalis (2013) and Wright (2000).

4.4.1 Exploitation and Distributive Injustice

Based on the notion of economic exploitation in Definition 13, Roemer's claim that the issue of exploitation can be reduced to that of distributive injustice is not valid. To argue this point, Vrousalis (2013) applies the notion of cleanly generated capitalism defined in Section 4.1 and provides us with the following example:

Example of Grasshopper and Ant: Grasshopper spends the summer months singing, whereas Ant spends all her time working. When the winter comes, Grasshopper needs shelter, which he presently lacks. Ant has three options:

(i) She can do nothing to help Grasshopper, in which case, the corresponding payoff allocation, (V^{*An}, V^{*Gh}) is $(V^{*An}, V^{*Gh}) = (10, 1)$;

(ii) She can offer Grasshopper her own shelter on the condition that he signs a sweatshop contract to pay the rent, in which case, $(V^{*An}, V^{*Gh}) = (12, 2)$; and

(iii) She can offer Grasshopper her own shelter rent-free, where the cost of maintenance is equal to -1, then $(V^{*An}, V^{*Gh}) = (9, 3)$.

Now, it is plausible to think that Ant has an obligation to help Grasshopper. However, one need not have a view on this to believe that (ii) is morally worse than (iii), in part because the choice of (ii) constitutes exploitation. Indeed, according to the Roemerian principle of voluntary disadvantages discussed in the last section, (i), (ii), and (iii) are equally acceptable. This fact implies that even if it is agreed that option (ii) involves exploitation, it cannot be condemned as distributive injustice by means of Roemer's theory of equality of opportunity.

The above argument suggests that Roemer's claim that exploitation implies distributive injustice cannot be validated as long as Definition 13 is presumed. The reason why exploitation survives in the absence of distributive injustice is that, according to Definition 13, the notion of exploitation aims to diagnose the structure of an economic transaction involving an asymmetric power relation that systematically generates an UE. In other words, exploitation constitutes a procedural injury to status, which is not reducible to distributive injury.

4.4.2 *Exploitation and Nonexploitative Economic Oppression*

Exploitation is nothing but a category of *economic oppression*. Generally speaking, economic oppression could be conceived of as social relations satisfying the inverse interdependence welfare principle and the exclusion principle in Definition 14. According to Wright (2000), various forms of economic oppression can be categorized into the following two notions: exploitation and *nonexploitative economic oppression*.

In nonexploitative oppression, the advantaged group does not itself need the excluded group. Although the welfare of the advantaged does depend on the exclusion principle, there is no ongoing interdependence between their activities and those of the disadvantaged. However, in exploitation, exploiters depend upon the effort of the exploited for their own welfare. Hence, exploiters depend upon and need the exploited.

We can find a sharp contrast between these two notions by considering the difference in the treatment of indigenous people in North America (nonexploitative economic oppression) and South Africa (exploitation) by European settlers. First, in both cases, we can find a causal relationship between the material advantage to the settlers and the material disadvantage to the indigenous people. This fact implies that both cases satisfy the inverse interdependence welfare principle. Second, in both cases, this causal relation is rooted in processes by which indigenous people were excluded from a crucial productive resource, namely, land. Hence, both cases satisfy the exclusion principle.

However, in South Africa, the settlers appropriated the fruits of labor of the indigenous population, first as agricultural labor and later as mine workers. This finding implies that the relation between the settlers and indigenous people in South Africa was exploitative.

By contrast, in North America, the labor effort of the indigenous people was generally not appropriated. The indigenous people were simply excluded from the capitalistic economic activities developed by the settlers. This finding implies that the settlers in North America could adopt a strategy of genocide in response to the conflict generated by this exclusion, because they did not need the labor effort of Native Americans. Thus, the relation between the settlers and indigenous people in North America is an example of nonexploitative economic oppression.

5. Recent Developments of Exploitation Theory in Economics: An Axiomatic Approach

According to Cohen (1995), Vrousalis (2013), and Wright (2000), exploitation should be conceptualized as the systematic structure of economic transactions, in which some of the fruits of the labor of the exploited agents is appropriated by the exploiters under the institutional framework of asymmetric power relations resulting from private ownership. Thus, while the

UE theory of exploitation is conceptually sophisticated and well motivated by these works, the issue of proper formal definitions of UE exploitation has yet remained unresolved, as we saw in Section 2.

Note that if a definition of UE exploitation is appropriate, it should point out the existence of a transfer mechanism by which UE is mediated: UE occurs by a mechanism that transfers (a part of) the productive fruits of the exploited to the exploiter. In perfectly competitive markets, neglecting the issue of rent, net outputs are distributed into wage income and profit income. Moreover, every party receives an equal wage per unit of (effective) labor. Therefore, the appropriation of more of the productive fruits by exploiters must be explained as a source of income other than wages, that is, profits. In other words, a valid formal definition of UE exploitation should be able to verify the correspondence between UE and profits.

Summarizing the above argument leads to the following logical implication as our desideratum:

(a) The formal definition of UE exploitation is valid $\Rightarrow$ (b) in any economic equilibrium, the generation of positive profits must imply an UE transfer from each propertyless worker and vice versa, according to the presumed definition of exploitation.

Statement (b) is referred to as the *Profit-Exploitation Correspondence Principle* (**PECP**).

The PECP looks similar to the FMT, but they are both conceptually and formally different. Conceptually, the FMT, in general, refers to the (average) rate of exploitation (i.e., the rate of surplus value) for the working class as a whole.[26] By contrast, the PECP requires equivalence between the generation of positive profits and situation in which each propertyless worker is identified as exploited for any capitalist economy. Formally, the PECP and the FMT are logically independent, as discussed below.

Veneziani and Yoshihara (2015a) axiomatically characterize the definitions of UE exploitation that satisfy the PECP, shedding new light on the debate about the proper definition of UE exploitation. First, they propose a general model of capitalist economies that allows for heterogeneity in each agent's preferences for consumption goods and leisure, heterogeneity in their endowments of material and human capital, and a general closed-convex cone type of production set. Second, given such a general model, they axiomatically characterize the formal definitions of UE exploitation in which the PECP is preserved in any equilibrium. As a result, few definitions of exploitation proposed in the literature preserve the PECP, with only the definition à la the NI (Duménil, 1980; Foley, 1982) being an exception.

5.1 Alternative Definitions of Exploitation and the Domain Axiom of Admissible Definitions of Exploitation

Recall that the model of capitalist economies considered in Sections 2.1 and 2.2.2 assumes no difference in agents' labor skills or preferences for leisure. In this section, we assume a more general model of a capitalist economy, $\mathcal{E} = \langle \mathcal{N}; P_{(A,B,L)}; (u^{\nu}, s^{\nu}, \omega_0^{\nu})_{\nu \in \mathcal{N}} \rangle$, that includes the heterogeneity of labor skills and preferences for consumption bundles and leisure. Here, we discuss the axiom proposed by Veneziani and Yoshihara (2015a), which represents the minimal necessary condition for admissible definitions of UE exploitation. Then, we introduce alternative definitions of exploitation proposed in the literature on mathematical Marxian economics.

As a preliminary step, given any P, we define the set of production activities feasible with k units of labor inputs by $P(\alpha_l = k) \equiv \{(-\alpha'_l, -\underline{\alpha}', \overline{\alpha}') \in P \mid \alpha'_l = k\}$. Moreover, given $c \in \mathbb{R}^n_+$, we define the set of efficient production activities to produce c as a net output by $\partial\phi(c) \equiv \{\alpha \in \phi(c) \mid \forall\alpha' \in \phi(c), (-\alpha'_l > -\alpha_l \Rightarrow \exists i : -\underline{\alpha}'_i \leq -\underline{\alpha}_i < 0)\}$.[27]

Any definition of exploitation should be able to identify, associated with each equilibrium allocation, the set of exploiting agents, $\mathcal{N}^{ter} \subseteq \mathcal{N}$, and the set of exploited agents, $\mathcal{N}^{ted} \subseteq \mathcal{N}$, such that $\mathcal{N}^{ter} \cap \mathcal{N}^{ted} = \varnothing$ holds. Moreover, it should capture the feature of UE as the difference between the amount of labor supplied by each agent and the amount of labor "received" through each agent's income. In particular, the supplied labor amount should be greater than the received labor amount for each exploited agent. Such properties should be preserved as a core feature of exploitation regardless of the way in which UE exploitation is measured.

Note that for the capitalist economies considered herein, each agent's supply of labor is identified by Λ^v. By contrast, how to formulate the labor amount that each agent can "receive" through his/her earned income remains open to debate. Based on the forms of "received" labor, a number of possible definitions of exploitation exist.

Summarizing the above arguments, Veneziani and Yoshihara (2015a) propose an axiom that represents the minimal necessary condition for any definition of exploitation, whenever it is deemed to be admissible as the form of UE:

Labor Exploitation (LE). (Veneziani and Yoshihara, 2015a): Given any definition of exploitation, for any capitalist economy $\mathcal{E}$ and any RS $((p, w); ((c^v, l^v); \alpha^v)_{v \in \mathcal{N}})$, the set of exploited agents, $\mathcal{N}^{ted} \subseteq \mathcal{N}$, should have the following property: there exists a profile of commodity bundles, $(c_e^v)_{v \in \mathcal{W}} \in \mathbb{R}_+^{nW}$, such that, for any $v \in \mathcal{W}$, $pc_e^v = w\Lambda^v$ holds, and for some production point, $\alpha^{c_e^v} \in \partial\phi(c_e^v)$:

$$v \in \mathcal{N}^{ted} \Leftrightarrow \alpha_l^{c_e^v} < \Lambda^v.$$

That is, axiom **LE** requires that any admissible definition of UE exploitation must identify whether each propertyless agent is exploited for each RS under any economy. More specifically, the axiom stipulates that the set of propertyless exploited agents be identified as follows: according to each specific admissible definition, there should be a profile, $(c_e^v)_{v \in \mathcal{W}}$, for each propertyless agent's commodity bundle affordable by that agent's revenue, and its corresponding profile $(\alpha^{c_e^v})_{v \in \mathcal{W}}$ of production activities, where each $\alpha^{c_e^v}$ can produce the corresponding commodity bundle c_e^v as a net output in a technologically efficient way. Then, the exploitation status of each propertyless agent can be identified by comparing his/her amount of labor supply Λ^v with the amount of labor input $\alpha_l^{c_e^v}$ that he/she is able to "receive" through his/her income $w\Lambda^v$.

Axiom **LE** is a rather weak condition in that it only refers to the exploitation status of propertyless agents in each RS. This should be reasonable as a minimal necessary condition for the admissible domain. In other words, a definition of exploitation is not necessarily deemed to be proper, even if it satisfies **LE**. In fact, there may be infinitely many definitions of exploitation that satisfy **LE**, and all the main definitions proposed in the mathematical Marxian economics literature satisfy this axiom.[28]

To see the last point, let us consider three main definitions under general economies with possibly heterogeneous agents. First, the following two definitions are, respectively, natural extensions of Definitions 4 and 10 to economies with possibly heterogeneous agents:

Definition 15. (Morishima, 1974): For any capitalist economy, $\mathcal{E}$, and any $v \in \mathcal{W}$, who supplies Λ^v and purchases $c^v \in \mathbb{R}_+^n$, $v \in \mathcal{N}^{ted}$ if and only if $\Lambda^v > \min_{\alpha \in \phi(c^v)} \alpha_l$.

Definition 16. (Roemer, 1982, chapter 5): For any capitalist economy, $\mathcal{E}$, any RS, $((p, w); ((c^v, l^v); \alpha^v)_{v \in \mathcal{N}})$, and any $v \in \mathcal{W}$, who supplies Λ^v and purchases $c^v \in \mathbb{R}_+^n$, $v \in \mathcal{N}^{ted}$ if and only if $\Lambda^v > \min_{\alpha \in \phi(c^v; p, w)} \alpha_l$.

Finally, for any capitalist economy, $\mathcal{E}$, and any RS, $((p, w); ((c^v, l^v); \alpha^v)_{v \in \mathcal{N}})$, let $\alpha^{p,w} \equiv \sum_{v \in \mathcal{N}} \alpha^v$. Moreover, for any $c \in \mathbb{R}_+^n$, we define a nonnegative number, $\tau^c \in \mathbb{R}_+$, as satisfying $\tau^c p \widehat{\alpha}^{p,w} = pc$. Then:

Definition 17. (Veneziani and Yoshihara, 2015a): For any capitalist economy, $\mathcal{E}$, any RS, $((p, w); ((c^v, l^v); \alpha^v)_{v \in \mathcal{N}})$, and any $v \in \mathcal{W}$, who supplies Λ^v and can purchase $c^v \in \mathbb{R}_+^n$, $v \in \mathcal{N}^{ted}$ if and only if $\Lambda^v > \tau^{c^v} \alpha_l^{p,w}$.

In Definition 17, for each $v \in \mathcal{W}$, τ^{c^v} represents v's share of national income, and thus $\tau^{c^v} \alpha_l^{p,w}$ is the share of social labor that this agent receives through the wage income sufficient to purchase c^v. It is conceptually related to the NI definition of exploitation *à la* Duménil (1980) and Foley (1982), which was originally defined in Leontief economies with homogeneous agents. In the NI, *the value of money* is defined by the labor amount per unit of national income,[29] and the wage multiplied by the value of money is the value of labor power, as Foley (1986, p. 43) states: "the amount of average social labor workers receive a claim to in the wage for each hour they actually work – that is, as the average wage multiplied by the value of money." In Definition 17, for each $v \in \mathcal{W}$, $\tau^{c^v} \alpha_l^{p,w} = w \Lambda^v \frac{\alpha_l^{p,w}}{p \widehat{\alpha}^{p,w}}$ holds by $w \Lambda^v = pc^v$. Since $w \Lambda^v$ is v's wage income and $\frac{\alpha_l^{p,w}}{p \widehat{\alpha}^{p,w}}$ corresponds to the value of money in the NI, $\Lambda^v > \tau^{c^v} \alpha_l^{p,w}$ means that v is exploited as "a worker expends more labor hours than he or she receives an equivalent for in wages" (Foley 1986, p. 122).

5.2 PECP

Now, we are ready to formulate the axiom of PECP, given as follows:

Profit-Exploitation Correspondence Principle (PECP). [Veneziani and Yoshihara (2015a)]: For any capitalist economy, $\mathcal{E}$, and any RS, $((p, w); ((c^v, l^v); \alpha^v)_{v \in \mathcal{N}})$:

$$\left[p \widehat{\alpha}^{p,w} - w \alpha_l^{p,w} > 0 \Leftrightarrow \mathcal{N}^{ted} \supseteq \mathcal{W}_+ \right]$$

where $\mathcal{W}_+ \equiv \{ v \in \mathcal{W} \mid \Lambda^v > 0 \} \neq \varnothing$.

That is, whatever the definition of exploitation is, it must follow that for any capitalist economy and any RS, total profits are positive if and only if any propertyless employee is exploited in terms of this definition, assuming the definition of exploitation is deemed appropriate. This is required by **PECP**.

For the available class of capitalist economies considered here, there is no requirement of a restriction that excludes the existence of fixed capital goods, the possibility of joint production, or of technical changes. In addition, unlike in condition (2) of the RFMT discussed in Section 2, there is no restriction that excludes the existence of a dependently produced commodity. Moreover, heterogeneity in agents' preferences and/or skills is also permitted. The equilibrium notion presumed here is also sufficiently general that there is no requirement of a subsistence wage condition. Therefore, the correspondence between profits and exploitation is required for a large class of economies, as assumed by the standard general equilibrium theory.

However, **PECP** *per se* is not so strong. Indeed, it even allows for a situation in which some propertyless employees are exploited in an equilibrium with zero total profit.[30] This finding implies that, at least within the class of economies with homogeneous agents, **PECP** is logically weaker than the statement of the FMT, as within such economies, the latter implies that no propertyless employee is exploited in any equilibrium with zero profit. By contrast, while the FMT implies that the rate of exploitation for the whole working class is positive in any equilibrium with positive total profits, **PECP** requests that every propertyless worker is exploited, which is a stronger claim than that of the FMT.

As noted at the start of this section, if a definition of exploitation satisfying axiom **LE** is proper, it must satisfy **PECP**. Based on this perspective, Veneziani and Yoshihara (2015a) study the necessary and sufficient condition for **PECP**, as stated in the following theorem:[31]

Theorem 1. (Veneziani and Yoshihara, 2015a): For any definition of exploitation satisfying **LE**, the following two statements are equivalent for any capitalist economy, $\mathcal{E}$, and any *RS*, $((p,w);((c^v,l^v);\alpha^v)_{v \in \mathcal{N}})$:

(1) **PECP** holds under this definition of exploitation;
(2) If $p\hat{\alpha}^{p,w} - w\alpha_l^{p,w} > 0$, then for any $v \in \mathcal{W}_+$, there exists a production activity $\alpha_\pi^v \in$
$P(\alpha_l = \Lambda^v) \cap \partial P$ such that $\hat{\alpha}_\pi^v \in \mathbb{R}_+^n$, $p\hat{\alpha}_\pi^v > w\Lambda^v$, and $(\alpha_{\pi l}^v, \underline{\alpha}_{-\pi}^v, \overline{\alpha}_\pi^v) \geqq \eta^v(\alpha_l^{c^v}, \underline{\alpha}^{c^v}, \overline{\alpha}^{c^v})$
hold for some $\eta^v > 1$.

That is, condition (2) of Theorem 1 is the necessary and sufficient condition for any definition of exploitation satisfying **LE** to preserve **PECP**. Condition (2) states that if total profits are positive in the present equilibrium, then for each propertyless employee, $v \in \mathcal{W}_+$, there exists a suitable efficient production point, α_π^v, activated by the present amount of labor supply, Λ^v, which in conjunction with production activity, α^{c^v}, can verify that this agent is being exploited. Recall that, according to axiom **LE**, production activity α^{c^v} is identified by the presumed definition of exploitation, and the corresponding labor input $\alpha_l^{c^v}$ represents agent v's "received" labor. Production activity $\alpha_\pi^v \in P(\alpha_l = \Lambda^v) \cap \partial P$ is defined as the proportional expansion of production point α^{c^v} up to the point of his/her present labor supply, Λ^v, and that produces a nonnegative net output, $\hat{\alpha}_\pi^v \in \mathbb{R}_+^n$, that is nonaffordable by v at the present equilibrium because $p\hat{\alpha}_\pi^v > w\Lambda^v$. Therefore, since $\Lambda^v = \alpha_{\pi l}^v > \alpha_l^{c^v}$ holds for such a selection of α_π^v, we can confirm that agent $v \in \mathcal{W}_+$ is exploited at this RS, according to the given definition satisfying **LE**.

Theorem 1 does not provide a normative characterization of the presumed definition of exploitation, but rather a demarcation line (condition (2)) by which one can test which of infinitely many potential definitions preserves the essential relation of exploitation and profits in capitalist economies. Thus, if a definition of exploitation satisfying **LE** does not generally meet condition (2), then it will not satisfy **PECP**, which implies that it is not a proper definition of UE exploitation.

Some may criticize the methodological positions of **PECP** and Theorem 1, claiming that **PECP** should be proved as a theorem rather than treated as an axiom. In fact, as Okishio and Morishima did, the methodological standpoint of the FMT was, assuming a specific definition of exploitation, to verify that a capitalist economy can be conceived of as exploitative.

By contrast, Theorem 1 presumes a correspondence between positive profits and exploitation for every propertyless employee as an axiom and then tests the validity of each alternative definition of UE exploitation by checking whether it satisfies this axiom. Such a methodology has been implicitly adopted within debates on the FMT. Typically, whenever a counterexample has been raised against the FMT with a major definition of exploitation by generalizing the model of economies, this criticism has been resolved by proposing an alternative definition and proving that the FMT is held with this alternative form under the generalized economic model. This implicitly suggests that in the overall debate on the FMT, the validity of each form of exploitation has been tested by the robustness of the equivalence between exploitation and positive profits. However, even if such an interpretation is acceptable, the structure of the debate on the FMT could not function as such, because it may involve an infinite repetition of counterexample and alternate proposal. By contrast, by providing an axiomatic characterization such as Theorem 1, the validity of every form of UE exploitation is testable simply by checking condition (2).

Another argument justifies the treatment of **PECP** as an axiom. In any Leontief economy, regardless of whether agents are heterogeneous in preferences and/or skill levels, the equivalence of positive profits and exploitation of each propertyless employee and the equivalence of zero profit and no exploitation are preserved for any definition of exploitation, as long as it satisfies **LE**.

Theorem 2. (Veneziani and Yoshihara, 2015a): For any capitalist economy, $\langle \mathcal{N}; P_{(A,L)};$ $(u^\nu, s^\nu, \omega_0^\nu)_{\nu \in \mathcal{N}} \rangle$, and any RS, $((p, w); ((c^\nu, l^\nu); \alpha^\nu)_{\nu \in \mathcal{N}})$, **PECP** holds for any definition of exploitation satisfying **LE**.

Proof. Take any definition of exploitation that satisfies **LE**. Then, for any Leontief economy and any RS, (p, w), we can find a profile of reference commodity bundles, $(c_e^\nu)_{\nu \in \mathcal{W}} \in \mathbb{R}_+^{n\mathcal{W}}$. Then, regardless of the heterogeneity of welfare functions and skills, the corresponding profile of production activities, $(\alpha^{c_e^\nu})_{\nu \in \mathcal{W}}$, is uniquely given by

$$\alpha^{c_e^\nu} \equiv \left(-vc_e^\nu, -A(I-A)^{-1} c_e^\nu, \left[I + A(I-A)^{-1} \right] c_e^\nu \right) \text{ for each } \nu \in \mathcal{W}.$$

Thus, $\alpha_l^{c_e^\nu} = vc_e^\nu$. Let $p\widehat{\alpha}^{p,w} - w\alpha_l^{p,w} > 0$ for this RS. This finding implies that, under the Leontief economy

$$p = (1 + \pi) pA + wL \text{ for some } \pi > 0.$$

Then, as is well known, $\frac{p}{w} > v$. Thus, by $w\Lambda^\nu = pc_e^\nu$ from **LE**, we have $\Lambda^\nu = \frac{p}{w} c_e^\nu > vc_e^\nu$, for any $\nu \in \mathcal{W}_+$. Therefore, according to **LE**, any propertyless employee is exploited in terms of the presumed definition of exploitation. $\qquad\square$

However, once the production technology of economies is replaced by a more general type such as the von Neumann production technology, some definitions of exploitation violate **PECP**, even if they satisfy **LE**. Does this suggest that the validity of the basic Marxian perception of capitalist economies as exploitative crucially depends on the degree of the complexity of the production technology? Or, does it suggest that such counterexamples are generated because of the *incoherency* of these definitions in that they cannot properly identify the set of exploited agents whenever a more complex production technology is applied? Veneziani and Yoshihara (2015a) take the latter view. For the complexity of production technology such as the existence of fixed capital and of alternative techniques should not be essential for the exploitation status of each agent. Rather, these counterexamples should be viewed as representing the non-validity of the presumed definitions of exploitation.

Theorem 1 does not identify a unique definition that meets **PECP**, but rather a class of definitions that satisfy condition (2). Yet, Veneziani and Yoshihara (2015a, corollary 1) show that it has surprising implications concerning the main approaches in exploitation theory. There are economies in which, for all $v \in \mathcal{W}_+$, condition (2) is never satisfied if $\alpha^{c^v}_e$ is given by Definition 15 or 16, and thus **PECP** does not hold. By contrast, Definition 17 satisfies condition (2), and thus **PECP** holds *for all $\mathcal{E}$ and all* RS:

Corollary 1. (Veneziani and Yoshihara, 2015a): There exists a capitalist economy, $\mathcal{E}$, and an RS for this economy such that neither Definition 15 nor Definition 16 satisfies **PECP**.

The proof of Corollary 1 is given in Section 2.2.2 by using the economy in Example 1. In that economy, assume an RS $(p^*, 1)$ with $p^*_1 > 0$. Then, every agent, $v \in \mathcal{W}_+$, consumes $c^v = b$ and $\min_{\alpha \in \phi(c^v)} \alpha_l = \min_{\alpha \in \phi(c^v; p^*, 1)} \alpha_l = 1 = \Lambda^{*v}$, while $\pi^* > 0$. This finding implies that neither Definition 15 nor Definition 16 satisfies **PECP**.

Corollary 2. (Veneziani and Yoshihara, 2015a): For any capitalist economy, $\mathcal{E}$, and any RS, Definition 17 satisfies **PECP**.

These corollaries suggest that, at least among the main competing proposals of exploitation forms, Definition 17 is the sole appropriate form.

The above arguments are sufficient to show that among the main proposals in the literature, the NI one is the only definition of UE exploitation that can be used to measure UE coherently regardless of the complexity of production technology. However, other arguments also support the NI form of UE exploitation. First, following Roemer's (1982) view on the epistemological role of the CECP, Yoshihara (2010) formulates **Class-Exploitation Correspondence Principle (CECP)** as an axiom that any proper definition of exploitation should meet and then shows that the NI definition is the unique one satisfying this axiom among the main definitions. This is even more supportive for the NI definition since **CECP** may provide a more comprehensive view of capitalist exploitative relations than **PECP**. Second, Yoshihara and Veneziani (2009) introduce an axiom called **Relational Exploitation (RE)** that requests that an exploiter exists if and only if an exploited agent exists as a minimal condition to capture the social relational feature of exploitation. Then, they show that any definition satisfying **RE**, together with a small number of rather weak axioms, is uniquely the NI definition.

Another interesting argument supports the NI definition. Although Definition 17 formulates exploitation as the UE, it is also possible to formulate the unequal exchange of any commodity, k, in an analogical way. In this case, is an argument such as the GCET reestablished by using such a definition of unequal exchange? The answer is negative, according to Yoshihara and Veneziani (2013).

Let us define exploitative relations as an unequal exchange of commodity k, analogical to Definition 17:

Definition 18. (Yoshihara and Veneziani, 2013): For any capitalist economy, $\mathcal{E}$, and any RS, $((p, w); ((c^v, l^v); \alpha^v)_{v \in \mathcal{N}})$, any agent, $v \in \mathcal{N}$, supplies some amount of commodity k, $\omega^v_k \geq 0$, as a factor of production, and consumes $c^v \in \mathbb{R}^n_+$. Then, agent v is k-exploited if and only if $\omega^v_k > \tau^{c^v} \underline{\alpha}^{p,w}_k$.

Yoshihara and Veneziani (2013) prove that the equivalence between positive profits and existence of k-exploited agents in terms of Definition 18 does not hold. For instance, assuming an economy with a homogeneity of welfare functions and labor skills, consider an RS with zero profit. Then, it follows that, for any $v \in \mathcal{N}$, $\tau^{c^v} = \frac{1}{N}$. By contrast, whenever the initial endowment of capital good k is unequal, there generically exists an agent, v', endowed with $\omega^{v'}_k > \frac{1}{N}\omega_k$. Then, it is easy to construct an equilibrium with zero profit under which this agent is deemed to be k-exploited, which violates the equivalence of k-exploitation with positive profits in terms of Definition 18.

Summarizing these arguments, if we take the NI definition such as in Definition 17, it follows that the unequal exchange of any productive factor other than labor and UE are not logically equivalent. Therefore, there can be no room for criticism of this definition by means of an analogical argument of the GCET, unlike the criticism of Okishio–Morishima's definition.

6. Concluding Remarks

One of the most prominent contributions of Okishio (1963) is that he inspired the controversy about the proper definitions of exploitation. Although Okishio's definition of exploitation (Definition 2 in this paper) was essentially faithful to the labor theory of value and theory of surplus value, the sequence of later controversies suggests the limitation and noneligibility of such a classical definition. Instead, based on the axiomatic analysis reviewed in Section 5, the NI type (Definition 17 in this paper) is deemed to be appropriate as a coherent measure of UE exploitation applicable to a broader class of economies with complex structures of production and the heterogeneity of agents.

Moreover, Definition 17 also satisfies a property of *Minimal objectivism* (Veneziani and Yoshihara, 2011) in that, unlike Definitions 15 and 16, the exploitation status of agents is determined independent of possibly arbitrary consumption decisions. Furthermore, it has a clear empirical content by being firmly anchored to actual economic data: only actual production decisions and the social allocation of labor, income, and production activities matter.

Recent discussions such as Vrousalis (2013) and Wright (2000), through the debate over Roemer's (1982, 1994) PR exploitation theory, conceptualize UE exploitation as UE transfer under the systematic asymmetric power structure due to private ownership, by which UE exploitation is shown to be irreducible to the issue of distributive injustice. Indeed, the issue of UE exploitation refers to the asymmetric structure of production relations among *citizens with capacity*. The UE feature can be criticized from a viewpoint of distributive justice, but it is simply one aspect of injustice involved in exploitative production relations.

Contemporary theories of distributive justice typically refer primarily to the treatment of citizens who suffer disadvantages in access to suitable labor markets due to bad luck, incapacity, disability, or their social background. These citizens might be deemed to be economically oppressed but not exploited, according to Wright's (2000) terminology.

By contrast, the issue of *working poor*, which has even affected regular workers in advanced countries during recent decades, is more relevant to the issue of UE exploitation, since it is not simply a matter of the insufficiency of welfare compensation, but is more related to the power relations between capital and labor and the strength of labor unions. Note that this issue also suggests that addressing a special concern to propertyless employees is still important in UE exploitation theory, as, for instance, more than 30% of current households in Japan lack financial assets.

Overall, UE exploitation theory and theories of distributive justice play mutually complementary roles in diagnosing the present society; one does not dominate the other and nor are they mutually exclusive and substitutable. This finding suggests that in some contexts, the issues of redressing distributive injustice and of improving exploitative working conditions might be traded off, given the scarce budgets of the welfare state. In such a situation, it would be necessary to develop a theory of comprehensive social welfare functions to accommodate the criteria of distributive justice and of UE exploitation, in addition to the standard criterion of economic efficiency.

In this respect, UE exploitation theory has not thus far been sufficiently cultivated; it can only identify the proper measure to diagnose the *existence of UE exploitation*. The next step to develop UE exploitation theory would be to study the severity of UE exploitation in each society. Proceeding with this line of research would require a new subject to identify a *proper measure of the degree of UE exploitation*.

Definition 17 in this paper also suggests that nonexploitative resource allocations should serve as the *proportional solution*, as proposed by Roemer and Silvestre (1993). Although reducing concerns about exploitation to concerns about distributive injustice is not legitimate, it is still an intrinsically interesting problem to study the ethical properties of nonexploitative allocations. With regard to this point, Roemer (2010, 2015) recently shows that the proportional solution, that is, the allocation rule of nonexploitation, would be implementable in a moral state of society in which every citizen behaves in accordance with the Kantian categorical imperative. Such a moral state of society is formulated by Roemer (2010) as a social state of the Kantian equilibrium. This line of research would be interesting for Marxian economists to study further.

Last, this paper mainly discussed the generation of UE exploitation in a perfectly competitive economy. However, we have not addressed the persistency of exploitative relations[32] nor the generation of exploitative relations under capitalist economies with imperfect labor contracts.[33] The former problem would be relevant, in a broader sense, to the controversies over the Okishio Theorem (Okishio, 1961), another significant contribution by Nobuo Okishio. We leave this point to future research.

Acknowledgments

The author record his special thanks to the editor in charge and the three referees for their detailed comments that improved the paper substantially. The author is also thankful to Makoto Saito, So Kaneko, Kazuhiro Kurose, and Taiji Furusama for their comments on an earlier version of this draft. The main content of this paper is based on the two intensive lectures given by the author, "Lectures on Marxian Economic Theory" at the third Summer School of Analytical Political Economy held at Hitotsubashi University on August 31, 2013 and "A Progress Report on Marxian Economic Theory" at the first Young Seminar of the Japan Society for Political Economy held at Sensyu University on October 4, 2013. The author is grateful to Jota Ishikawa, Yoshi Sato, and Takashi Ohno for their work and cooperation in organizing these events. Finally, an earlier version of this paper was presented at the Workshop of Economic Theory and Political Economy at the University of Massachusetts, Amherst in November 2013. The author is grateful to all of the participants of the workshop, especially Peter Skott and Deepankar Basu for their useful discussions.

Notes

1. See Fleurbaey (2014) for this point.
2. The notion of well-being freedom emphasizes an individual's ability to pursue the life he/she values. According to Rawls–Sen theory, inequalities in the distribution of well-being freedom are formulated as *inequalities of capabilities*, whereas they are formulated as *inequalities of (comprehensive) resources* in Dworkin's (2000) theory.
3. Because of this limited purpose, we mainly refer to the literature relevant to the proper formal definition of UE exploitation in mathematical Marxian economics, although many

other influential works exist in that field such as the "macro-monetary" approach of Fred Moseley and the "temporal single-system" framework of Andrew Kliman and others.

4. Let $\mathbb{R}$ be the set of real numbers and $\mathbb{R}_+$ (*respectively,* $\mathbb{R}_-$) the set of nonnegative (*respectively,* nonpositive) real numbers. For all $x, y \in \mathbb{R}^n$, $x \geq y$ if and only if $x_i \geq y_i$ ($i = 1, \ldots, n$); $x \geq y$ if and only if $x \geq y$ and $x \neq y$; and $x > y$ if and only if $x_i > y_i$ ($i = 1, \ldots, n$). For any set, X and Y, $X \subseteq Y$ if and only if for any $x \in X$, $x \in Y$; $X = Y$ if and only if $X \subseteq Y$ and $Y \subseteq X$; and $X \subsetneq Y$ if and only if $X \subseteq Y$ and $X \neq Y$.

5. The condition of $w = pb$ means that the wage rate is so low that any propertyless agent cannot but expend all of the wage revenue for the basic consumption bundle, which corresponds to the case where the aggregate labor supply is excessive with respect to the aggregate labor demand in the equilibrium.

6. Note that generalizations of the FMT to a Leontief economy with *heterogeneous labor* have also been examined by Morishima (1973), Bowles and Gintis (1977, 1978), and Krause (1981). This line of research focuses on solving the reduction problem of heterogeneous labor into one common unit, and/or the dilemma of the heterogeneity of labor and the respective rates of exploitation. Thus far, the robustness of the FMT in this line of generalization has remained firm.

7. As Roemer (1980) explicitly shows, there is essentially no difference between the BGE (given in Definition 1) and the RS in capitalist economies with Leontief production technology. However, these two notions of equilibria differ whenever a more general model of capitalist economies is considered.

8. As Roemer (1980, p. 507) states, "What equilibrium or solution concept is adopted in Marxian-Sraffian analysis? The concern is with whether the economic system can reproduce itself: whether it can produce enough output to replenish the inputs used, and to reproduce the workers for another period of work."

9. For a more detailed discussion on the implications of the GCET, see Roemer (1982) and Yoshihara and Veneziani (2010a, 2010b). Studies such as Fujimoto and Fujita (2008) and Matsuo (2009) criticize the GCET, supporting Okishio–Morishima's definition of LE. Such critics emphasize that the coefficients L and b are not simply technologically determined but reflect the state of class struggle. This point is true, but it does not deny that Okishio–Morishima's definition is mainly used to represent the productiveness of an overall economic system.

10. Although the economy in Example 1 violates condition (2) of the RFMT, this is not essential for deriving a negative result. Indeed, as Yoshihara (2010, corollary 1) explicitly shows, we can develop essentially the same proof, even for an economy without an inferior process.

11. Again, the violation of condition (2) of the RFMT in the economy in Example 1 is not essential for this negative result. For this point, see Yoshihara (2010, corollary 2).

12. Alienable assets are typically financial assets and/or material capital goods. By contrast, inalienable assets are typically talents and/or skills immanent in individuals.

13. The condition that $\mathcal{T}$ is in a relation of dominance to $\mathcal{S}$ in Definition 11 is not formally specified by Roemer (1982). This condition is, first, to ensure the existence of economic interactions between $\mathcal{T}$ and $\mathcal{S}$. Second, it is to eliminate certain perverse cases such as an invalid supported with costly medication by the rest of society, who would be worse off and the rest of society better off after their respective withdrawal according to K^{CE}.

Indeed, because of this dominance condition, the relationship between the invalid and the rest of society is not exploitative even though Definition 11(i) and (ii) are satisfied: they are not in a relation of dominance (see Roemer, 1994, p. 21, footnote 4).

However, the condition of dominance *alone* may be insufficient to define exploitation. For instance, as discussed in Section 4.4.2, we may say that the European settlers and indigenous people in North America were in a relation of dominance, but they were not in an exploitative relation even if Definition 11(i) and (ii) were satisfied. In this respect, the third condition (iii) by Roemer (1994) requests that in order to identify capitalist PR exploitation, T depends on S in the situation for its fortune to flourish. By adding this condition, the relationship between the European settlers and indigenous people was not PR exploitative.

14. For a more detailed discussion, see Veneziani and Yoshihara (2015b, section 4.4).
15. The additional condition (iii) of capitalist PR exploitation is met under the RS, as mentioned above.
16. Consider also the case that v and μ have dissimilar external assets but the same preference for income and leisure. Because of these different endowments, suppose that v must get less product than μ for the same labor input if each of them, respectively, chooses to work autarchically. Thus, an inequality in income and leisure is derived from unequal asset endowments. Cohen (1995) acknowledges that this situation is not exploitative, although it does represent the injustice generated by unequal asset endowments.
17. That is, a person should be sovereign with respect to what he/she will do with his/her energies.
18. That is, a form of capitalism in which a capital-lacking worker is on one side and a capital-endowed capitalist is on the other, that does not arise from "primitive accumulation" through massacre, plunder, forced extraction, or, more generally, by transgressing some norm of distributive justice. Rather, it arises from "clean" social interactions: a laborer, starting from equality of external assets, manages to accumulate significant quantities of capital through toil and savings, thereby turning him/herself into a capitalist.
19. Here, we mainly summarize Vrousalis's own account without necessarily endorsing it, although some of his claims may need more careful discussion based on economic theory, as mentioned in footnote 23.
20. Vrousalis (2013) does not consider condition (iii) of relational vulnerability to be a necessary condition for exploitation, since there is nothing contradictory in the thought that v is forced to exploit μ and therefore lacks the said discretion.
21. Internal resources imply talents and/or skills inherent in individuals. By contrast, any other types of resources that are transferrable are often called external resources. For a more detailed argument on these concepts, see Cohen (1995).
22. Therefore, economic vulnerability in the definition of economic exploitation refers to the relations of production that must be *unilateral* in nature as Vrousalis (2013, p. 137) states: "there can be no 'reciprocal' economic power-over: if Bill Gates and Warren Buffett own approximately the same amount of wealth, then neither power-overs the other economically." Note that the general notion of relational vulnerability also allows the case of two parties that are *mutually* relationally vulnerable to each other in that one party's resources are a necessity of the other and vice versa.
23. To logically ensure this claim, we would need to develop a more detailed, step-by-step argument, based upon economic theory, which is beyond the scope of this paper.

24. Note that although the notion of economic exploitation only refers to the extraction of labor, any other form of extraction from the exploited can be argued in the general notion of exploitation, such as the case of sexual exploitation, which is also discussed by Vrousalis (2013).

25. For this point, Wright (2000, pp. 1566–1567) explains as follows: "Let us examine the three criteria for exploitation specified above in a capitalist economy with perfect competition in which there are only two categories of economic actors: capitalists who own the means of production – and thus have the effective power to exclude others from access to those assets – and workers who own only their labor power. .... Are the inverse interdependent welfare principle and the exclusion principle satisfied in this case? Is the material welfare of capitalists causally dependent upon the exclusion of workers from access to capital assets? The test here is whether or not it is the case that workers would be better off and capitalists worse off if property rights were redistributed so that workers would no longer be "excluded" from capital. It seems hard to argue that this is not the case: in the initial condition capitalists have a choice of either consuming their capital or investing it, as well as the choice of whether or not they will work for earnings. Workers only have the latter choice. To be sure, they can borrow capital (and in a world of perfect information they would not need collateral to do so since there would be no transaction costs, no monitoring costs, no possibility of opportunism), but still workers would be better off owning capital outright than having to borrow it."

26. As shown by Yoshihara and Veneziani (2012), in a von Neumann economy with the heterogeneity of propertyless workers' welfare functions, the positivity of the average rate of exploitation may coexist with the nonexploitation of some propertyless workers, simply because of their consumption choices. This fact implies that even if the FMT holds in such economies, it may be that some propertyless workers are not exploited.

27. By this definition, for the frontier of the production possibility set P, $\partial P \equiv \{\alpha \in P \mid \nexists \alpha' \in P : \alpha' > \alpha\}$, we have $\partial\phi(c) \subseteq \partial P \cap \{\alpha \in \phi(c) \mid \hat{\alpha} \not> c\}$.

28. Of course, this does not imply that the axiom **LE** is trivial. For instance, the definition proposed by Matsuo (2008) does not satisfy **LE**.

29. In other words, the ratio of aggregate direct labor time to aggregate money value added.

30. However, any definition of exploitation satisfying **LE** does not allow the existence of exploited propertyless employees in conjunction with zero profit.

31. Note that, though all of the following analyses herein presume economies with a homogeneous type of labor with heterogeneous levels of skills, the completely parallel results can be obtained even if we consider economies with heterogeneous types of labor, as shown in Veneziani and Yoshihara (2017).

32. For the current standpoint of this subject, refer to Veneziani (2007, 2013) and Veneziani and Yoshihara (2015b; section 4).

33. For more information on this line of research, refer to Yoshihara (1998) and Skillman (2014).

References

Arneson, R. (1989) Equality and equal opportunity for welfare. *Philosophical Studies* 56: 77–93.

Bowles, S. and Gintis, H. (1977) The Marxian theory of value and heterogeneous labour: a critique and reformulation. *Cambridge Journal of Economics* 1: 173–192.

Bowles, S. and Gintis, H. (1978) Professor Morishima on heterogeneous labour and Marxian value theory. *Cambridge Journal of Economics* 2: 311–314.

Bowles, S. and Gintis, H. (1981) Structure and practice in the labor theory of value. *Review of Radical Political Economics* 12: 1–26.

Cohen, G.A. (1989) On the currency of egalitarian justice. *Ethics* 99: 906–944.

Cohen, G.A. (1995) *Self-Ownership, Freedom and Equality*. Cambridge: Cambridge University Press.

Duménil, G. (1980) *De la Valeur aux Prix de Production*. Paris: Economica.

Dworkin, R. (2000) *Sovereign Virtue: The Theory and Practice of Equality*. Cambridge: Harvard University Press.

Fleurbaey, M. (2014) The facets of exploitation. *Journal of Theoretical Politics* 26: 653–676.

Foley, D.K. (1982) The value of money, the value of labor power, and the Marxian transformation problem. *Review of Radical Political Economics* 14: 37–47.

Foley, D.K. (1986) *Understanding Capital*. Cambridge, MA: Harvard University Press.

Fujimoto, T. and Fujita, Y. (2008) A refutation of commodity exploitation theorem. *Metroeconomica* 59: 530–540.

International Labour Office. (2005a) *Human Trafficking and Forced Labour Exploitation*. International Labour Office, Geneva.

International Labour Office. (2005b) *Forced Labour: Labour Exploitation and Human Trafficking in Europe*. International Labour Office, Geneva.

Krause, U. (1981) Heterogeneous labour and the fundamental Marxian theorem. *Review of Economic Studies* 48: 173–178.

Matsuo, T. (2008) Profit, surplus product, exploitation and less than maximized utility. *Metroeconomica* 59: 249–265.

Matsuo, T. (2009) Generalized commodity exploitation theorem and the net production concept. *Bulletin of Political Economy* 3: 1–11.

Morishima, M. (1973) *Marx's Economics*. Cambridge: Cambridge University Press.

Morishima, M. (1974) Marx in the light of modern economic theory. *Econometrica* 42: 611–632.

Okishio, N. (1961) Technical changes and the rate of profit. *Kobe University Economic Review* 7: 85–99.

Okishio, N. (1963) A mathematical note on Marxian theorems. *Weltwirtschaftliches Archiv* 91: 287–299.

Piketty, T. (2014) *Capital in the Twenty-First Century*. Cambridge, MA: Harvard University Press.

Rawls, J. (1971) *A Theory of Justice*. Cambridge, MA: Harvard University Press.

Roemer, J.E. (1980) A general equilibrium approach to Marxian economics. *Econometrica* 48: 505–530.

Roemer, J.E. (1982) *A General Theory of Exploitation and Class*. MA: Harvard University Press.

Roemer, J.E. (1994) *Egalitarian Perspectives: Essays in Philosophical Economics*. Cambridge: Cambridge University Press.

Roemer, J.E. (1998) *Equality of Opportunity*. MA: Harvard University Press.

Roemer, J.E. (2010) Kantian equilibrium. *Scandinavian Journal of Economics* 112: 1–24.

Roemer, J.E. (2015) On the problem of socialist economic design. *Journal of Theoretical Politics* 27: 34–42.

Roemer, J.E. and Silvestre, J.E. (1993) The proportional solution for economies with both private and public ownership. *Journal of Economic Theory* 59: 426–444.

Samuelson, P. (1982) The normative and positive inferiority of Marx's values paradigm. *Southern Economic Journal* 49: 11–18.

Sen, A.K. (1985) Well-being agency and freedom: the Dewey lectures. *Journal of Philosophy* 82: 169–224.

Skillman, G.L. (2014) Capitalist exploitation without capitalist production: the consequences of imperfect contracting. *Journal of Theoretical Politics* 26: 629–652.

Veneziani, R. (2007) Exploitation and time. *Journal of Economic Theory* 132: 189–207.

Veneziani, R. (2013) Exploitation, inequality and power. *Journal of Theoretical Politics* 25: 526–545.

Veneziani, R. and Yoshihara, N. (2011) Strong subjectivism in the theory of exploitation: a critique. *Metroeconomica* 62: 53–68.

Veneziani, R. and Yoshihara, N. (2017) One million miles to go: taking the axiomatic road to defining exploitation. *Cambridge Journal of Economics* 41: 1607–1626.

Veneziani, R. and Yoshihara, N. (2015a) Exploitation in economies with heterogeneous preferences, skills and assets: an axiomatic approach. *Journal of Theoretical Politics* 27: 8–33.

Veneziani, R. and Yoshihara, N. (2015b) Unequal exchange, assets, and power: recent development in exploitation theory. In Binder, C., Codognato, G., Teschl, M., Xu, Y. (Eds.), *Individual and Collective Choice and Social Welfare*, Studies in Choice and Welfare. Springer-Verlag Berlin Heidelberg.

Vrousalis, N. (2013) Exploitation, vulnerability, and social domination. *Philosophy and Public Affairs* 41: 131–157.

Wright, E.O. (2000) Class, exploitation, and economic rents: reflections on Sorensen's "Sounder Basis". *American Journal of Sociology* 105: 1559–1571.

Yoshihara, N. (1998) Wealth, exploitation, and labor discipline in the contemporary capitalist economy. *Metroeconomica* 49: 23–61.

Yoshihara, N. (2010) Class and exploitation in general convex cone economies. *Journal of Economic Behavior & Organization* 75: 281–296.

Yoshihara, N. and Veneziani, R. (2009) Exploitation as the unequal exchange of labour: an axiomatic approach. IER Discussion Paper Series A. No.524, The Institute of Economic Research, Hitotsubashi University.

Yoshihara, N. and Veneziani, R. (2010a) Commodity content in a general input-output: a comment. *Metroeconomica* 61: 740–748.

Yoshihara, N. and Veneziani, R. (2010b) Exploitation and productivity: the generalised commodity exploitation theorem once again. *Bulletin of Political Economy* 4: 45–58.

Yoshihara, N. and Veneziani, R. (2012) Profits and exploitation: a reappraisal. *Advances in Mathematical Economics* 16: 85–109.

Yoshihara, N. and Veneziani, R. (2013) Exploitation of labour and exploitation of commodities: a "new interpretation". *Review of Radical Political Economics* 45: 517–524.

12

SOUTH–SOUTH AND NORTH–SOUTH ECONOMIC EXCHANGES: DOES IT MATTER WHO IS EXCHANGING WHAT AND WITH WHOM?

Omar S. Dahi

Hampshire College

Firat Demir

University of Oklahoma

1. Introduction

The term "South–South economic relations" captures a host of economic exchanges within the global South including trade in goods and services, capital flows, technology transfer, labor migration, and remittances as well as preferential trade agreements (PTA) and investment agreements and voting blocs within multinational institutions. For the most part, "South–South trade" is used as shorthand to capture all those modes of interactions and South–South trade and South–South economic relations tend to be used interchangeably. In much of the postwar period through the 1980s, South–South economic relations were a flashpoint for debate between supporters and critics of universal free trade, state-led development, and import substitution industrialization (ISI). The relatively scarce literature tended to focus overwhelmingly on the benefits or drawbacks of trade integration among developing countries.

The supporters' rationale was the ostensible benefits for industrialization in the South. Prebisch (1959) had famously advocated the "enlargement of national markets through the gradual establishment of a common market" in Latin America to take advantage of specialization and economies of scale (p. 268). Myrdal (1956 p. 261) supported South–South integration to help the global South overcome the colonial legacy that biases them in favor of North–South trade.[1] Linder (1967) had argued that similarities in consumer preferences, resource base, technological development, as well as institutions are likely to make South–South integration and trade more beneficial to Southern industrialization than North–South trade.

Analytical Political Economy, First Edition. Edited by Roberto Veneziani and Luca Zamparelli.

Chapters © 2018 The Authors. Book compilation © 2018 John Wiley & Sons Ltd. Published 2018 by John Wiley & Sons Ltd.

The critics on the other hand saw in South-South integration all that was wrong about ISI. According to Havrylyshyn and Wolf (1987, p. 158) if a Southern country "does a great deal of trade with other developing countries, the implication is that it has distorted its domestic prices." South–South trade according to Deardorff (1987) and Havrylyshyn and Wolf (1987) was an attempt to recoup the losses from ISI. Given its inability to penetrate Northern markets due to the high cost and low quality of its consumer and capital goods, a large industrializer like Brazil would offload them to neighboring Paraguay due to preferential treatment. Amsden (1980, 1983, 1984, 1987, 1989), using her analysis of East Asian industrialization, countered these critics by arguing that much of South–South trade in capital goods was intra-industry and in intermediate products, most of which was not subject to preferential treatment. Moreover, she argued, South–South trade facilitated technology transfer and a "learning by exporting" in countries trying to climb the industrial ladder.

Research on South–South trade as an alternative remained relatively marginal throughout this period even when the structuralist literature on uneven development extensively critiqued North–South trade due to asymmetrical economic structures and patterns of specialization (Findlay, 1980; Darity, 1990; Dutt, 1992). As noted by Darity and Davis (2005, p. 154):

> The role of government policy is not at the forefront of most of these [uneven development] papers. If we believe these processes operate and perpetuate international inequality, precisely how do we reverse them? Via industrial policy, South-South trade, South-South finance, autarky? Rarely does the formal literature on North-South trade and growth answer the question of how the world should be changed.

There is good reason for this lack. Research on South–South relations remained minimal because South–South trade and capital flows themselves remained relatively negligible throughout most of the postwar period. It was not until the 1990s that South–South economic relations took off and eventually brought the academic literature along with them. However, the post-1990s boom was fundamentally different from earlier ones. While most earlier studies focused on South–South relations under the ISI and the "old regionalism," the rise in the past three decades has been under the neoliberal era and the "new regionalism" in which most countries of the globe have experienced significant trade and financial liberalization relative to the earlier period together with a simultaneous retrenchment of industrial policy.

Several themes emerge from this newly bourgeoning literature. First, South–South trade and finance is now a significant economic and political force for South countries as well as for the global economy. There is a near consensus therefore that South–South economic relations *do matter* and that they have the potential to have a significant developmental impact. Moreover, this impact may be positive or negative, that is, that it may help or hinder the long-term developmental goals of exchanging parties. Second, much of South–South manufactures trade is concentrated in high-technology-and-skill content, opening the door for potential long-run dynamic gains from trade. However, these gains are being increasingly concentrated within a small number of South countries. The global South is, in fact, splitting into two groups, which we refer to as the Emerging South and the Rest of South with very different outcomes. While there is evidence for gains through South–South trade, there is also evidence that the Emerging South is rising at the expense of the Rest of South. Finally, the South–South exchanges have expanded significantly to cover issues including financial flows and technology transfer, among other topics. The overall conclusion of this diverse literature is that while it does matter who is exchanging what and with whom, South–South trade is not a panacea for the development challenges in Southern countries. On the contrary, South–South exchange themselves may become a potential threat for development for some of the Southern countries.

The rest of the paper proceeds as follows. Section 2 provides a framework for situating the literature by reviewing the traditional targets of development as well as the benefits and drawbacks of integration into the global economy in both South–South and North–South directions. By establishing the general goals for development in the global South and the means to achieving those goals, we can better appreciate the debates in the academic literature on the relative merits of South–South and North–South trade. Section 3 provides a discussion on the definition of North and South and offers a statistical overview of South–South economic relations that also helps contextualize the debates within the literature. Section 4 introduces the theoretical and empirical literature on the relative costs and benefits as well as relative constraints and bottlenecks in South–South and North–South economic exchanges. Section 5 provides a discussion of the China in Africa debate that helps explain the complexities in South–South exchanges. Section 6 debates whether South–South is still a useful analytical category with the potential of uplifting developing countries as a whole. Section 7 concludes.

2. Economic Development and Global Integration within the Global South

In order to understand the evolution of the literature on South–South trade, it is necessary to anchor the discussion on the main question that the literature is responding to. The debate about South–South trade and its comparative merit relative to North–South trade is in essence a debate about economic development strategies within the global South. Linking South–South relations to trade was explicitly made by developing countries themselves starting with the Bandung Declaration of 1955 to the New International Economic Order of 1974 within UNCTAD to South–South coalitions such as the Like Minded Group within the World Trade Organization (WTO) (Dahi and Demir, 2016). Through those various initiatives, the majority of developing countries have declared the goals of development to be solving the problem of poverty, raising the living standards of their citizens, and achieving a level of economic independence to accompany political independence. This leads to two central questions: What kind of processes lead to achieving those goals, and how does integration into the world economy help or hinder those processes?

The answers to those questions have been at the core of debates within economic development and international economics fields over the past half-century. Though the debate itself is outside the scope of this paper, much of the literature reviewed here assumes that the engines of economic development and structural change within the global South emanates from increasing industrialization, technology-and-skills upgrading, as well as the development of effective institutions.[2] Economists have long argued that there exists a positive relationship between industrialization and income growth (Leontief, 1963; Kaldor, 1967; Chenery *et al.*, 1986; Murphy *et al.*, 1989) though this relationship has not gone without critiques (Easterly and Levine, 2001). Technological upgrading and entering into knowledge-based economies are also shown to be engines of growth (Romer, 1990; Landes, 1998; Rodrik, 2007). Overall, there appears to be a consensus in this literature suggesting that what you produce and export matters for long-run development and growth.

Accepting the goals of development and the general means to achieving those goals leads to the key questions facing developing countries. What kind of barriers or binding constraints, internal or external, does the average developing country face in achieving those goals, and what may be the benefits or drawbacks from integration into the global economy? Internally, most developing countries found themselves in vicious cycles of low savings and capital investments, dependence on primary product exports, underdeveloped institutions, low levels of financial depth and high levels of capital market imperfections, as well as a variety of information and coordination failures. These internal constraints also shape the developmental potential of South–South versus North–South exchanges through adaptive capabilities, suitability of new technologies, transferability of skills and technology, and differences in demand structures. This is not to mention that many countries with extended experience with colonialism often had domestic vested interests in agricultural or natural resource extraction rather than in industrial development. Externally, the significant gaps that existed at the industrial and technological level were coupled by power and knowledge asymmetries, particularly as the United States and the United Kingdom wrote the rules of the game in the post-WWII era through the Bretton Woods institutions.

What then are the purported benefits of integration into the world economy? The mainstream orthodoxy since the 1970s has argued that integration into the world economy is the best path for development and growth and that inward orientation hurts development (Little *et al.*, 1970; Krueger, 1977, 1997; Bhagwati, 1978; Michaely *et al.*, 1991; Dollar, 1992; Harrison, 1996; Dollar and Kraay, 2004). Integration has many potential benefits. Openness, particularly in trade, allows countries to access advanced technology that facilitates the process of growth and structural transformation and helps overcome domestic market constraints, enabling the industrial sector to achieve economies of scale, among other benefits (Grossman and Helpman, 1991). Likewise, financial liberalization is expected to drive down the cost of capital (Henry, 2000), increase investment and growth (Bekaert *et al.*, 2001, 2005), and lower financial constraints on growth (Rajan and Zingales, 1998).

In short, developing countries want to industrialize and upgrade their technological capacity, and integration into the world economy may provide them with the means to do so. Nevertheless, the question then becomes whether North–South or South–South economic relations particularly help or hinder achieving developing country goals. The rest of the paper traces the evolution of this debate.

3. Evolving Nature of South–South and North–South Exchanges

3.1 *Where Is the South?*

Defining the South and the North is not an easy task and the exact categorization of countries into one of these two groups partly depends on the research question at hand as well as the underlying assumptions for particular theoretical approaches. The countries of the South are usually defined as those developing (or underdeveloped/less developed/Third World/peripheral) countries in Latin America and the Caribbean, Africa, and most of Asia excluding Japan and Oceania, as well as transition economies. This makes the North defined as developed (First World/center/core/metropolis) countries including those in North America (except Mexico), Western Europe, Japan, Oceania, and Israel.

The critique that both the North and the South are composed of a wide range of countries with high levels of heterogeneity in their economic, social, and political structures as well as in their factor endowments, development policies, historical experiences, etc., is a valid one. Furthermore, these countries have a diverse set of interests and treating them as homogenous units may create a fallacy of composition.[3] The literature we review is mostly aware of these objections and the North and South classification does not assume that countries are homogenous within each group. Rather, it is based on the stylized facts showing that similarities are more than differences within each group and that there are some fundamental differences between countries across these groups. Another issue is that the list of Northern club membership is a dynamic one even though there is strong hysteresis. Last, how much of this country hetero-geneity needs to be emphasized depends on the research question. For example, differences in economic development trajectories of Southern countries for the last 30 years necessitate an additional distinction to separate Emerging South economies (i.e., Newly Industrialized Countries [NICs]/semiperiphery) from the Rest of South.

Notwithstanding these objections, we argue that the North versus South distinction is a useful one with some caveats, particularly regarding emerging market economies with fast-track industrialization and technology-and-skills upgrading. Using Occam's razor, we chose the definition with the least number of assumptions and have classified countries in three groups: the North (23 countries), the Emerging South (55 countries), and the Rest of South (157 countries).[4] "The North" refers to the industrialized high-income countries. "Emerging South" refers to the more advanced and, at a minimum, partially industrialized countries of the South, most of them from what the World Bank refers to as the middle-income group, and a few from the NICs group. The term "developing," in the true sense of the word, refers to these countries. "Rest of South" includes those Southern countries that are not included in the Emerging South category. Global South (or when we simply state, South–South), on the other hand, refers to all countries of Emerging South and Rest of South combined. We should note that while most countries of the global South are in this group, the majority of Southern population lives in Emerging South countries.

In our classification, we have taken into account countries' incomes, production and trade structures, factor endowments, and human and institutional development, and have kept the group of countries constant over time. Allowing country switching between groups would create inconsistency as we would have to exclude countries that move up the economic ladder, and to do so would introduce a selection bias. Furthermore, moving the new graduates from the global South class would prevent us from understanding how these now-rich countries have become rich. The rule of thumb in these decisions, especially in applied research, is the timing of a particular country's move up (or down) the development ladder. The obvious examples are Argentina's downgrading from North to South in early 20th century and the upgrading of South Korea in late 20th century.

3.2 *Stylized Facts on South–South and South–North Exchanges*

For most of post-WWII period, South–South trade remained marginal, fluctuating at around 10% of world trade in merchandise goods. Historically, an interesting feature of South–South trade is that it is concentrated in relatively sophisticated manufactures compared to South–North trade (Amsden 1989). Since early 1990s, South–South trade has grown substantially, reaching as high as 28% of world merchandises trade by 2013 (Figure 1).[5] North–South and South–North trade, however, remained relatively stable, with a slight increase for the latter. The importance of South–South exports in total Southern exports has also increased substantially, reaching from around 20% in the 1950s to 60% in 2013. And yet, a majority of this, around 70%, is from trade between Emerging South countries. Likewise, more than 85% of South–North trade originates from Emerging South countries as seen in Figure 2.

During this period, the production structures of some Southern countries have gone through a major metamorphosis, becoming more industrial rather than agricultural or natural

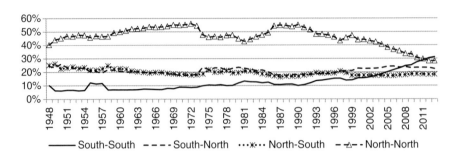

Figure 1. The Share of South and North in World Merchandise Goods Trade, 1948–2013.
Source: IMF Direction of Trade Statistics (2014) and authors' calculations.
Notes: South–South, South–North, North–South, and North–North refer to the share of each group of exporters in world merchandise exports.

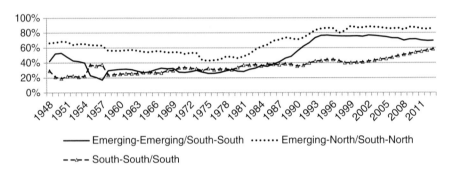

Figure 2. Share of Emerging South within South–South and South–North Merchandise Exports, 1948–2013.
Source: IMF Direction of Trade Statistics (2014) and authors' calculations.
Notes: Emerging–Emerging/South–South and Emerging North/South–North refers to the share of Emerging–Emerging country trade and Emerging North trade in total South–South and South–North trade, respectively. South–South/South refers to the share of South–South trade in global South exports to the rest of the world.

resource-dependent. In fact, as shown in Figure 3, the share of Emerging South countries in world manufactures exports steadily increased from 10% in 1962 to 45% in 2012, while the share of the Rest of South countries remained negligible, fluctuating at around 2%–3% of world trade since the 1980s. The situation with high-technology-and-skill-intensive manufactures is even worse such that the share of Rest of South stayed at or below 1% and has never been more than 2% of world trade. Meanwhile, the share of Emerging South in world exports of high-skill goods increased from 2% in 1962 to 55% in 2012, surpassing the share of the North (45%) (Figure 4).

We see a similar trend in South–South financial flows even though they have remained negligible up until very recently, and this is reflected in the relatively minimal literature we have on the subject. In fact, before the 1990s, most of the South was in a state of financial autarky with regard to equity and private debt flows. Besides Southern countries emerging as a source of debt, equity of aid coincides with the rise of few Emerging markets after the 2000s (UNDP, 2013). In 2013, FDI inflows to the South amounted to 61% of global inflows (including both

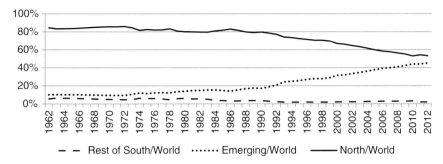

Figure 3. Share of South, Emerging South, and North in World Manufactures Exports, 1962–2012.
Source: MIT Media Lab (2015) and authors' calculations.
Notes: Rest of South/World, Emerging/World, and North/World refer to the share of Rest of South, Emerging South, and the North in world manufactures exports.

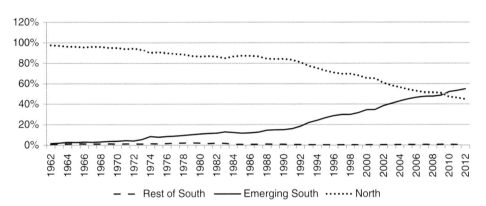

Figure 4. Share of South and North in World High-Skill Manufactures Exports, 1962–2012.
Source: IMF Direction of Trade Statistics (2014) and authors' calculations.
Notes: The definition of product classifications is provided in the appendix.

the North and the South), while FDI outflows from the South reached its highest level of 39% within global outflows. We discuss the financial aspect of South–South exchanges further in Section 4.4.

4. Theory and Empirics of South–South Trade and Finance

4.1 *Static Theories of Trade*

The traditional Ricardian and HOS (Heckscher–Ohlin–Samuelson) model approaches the issue of South–South trade with suspicion as it sees growing South–South trade coming at the expense of North–South trade. The static HOS model predicts that in countries with higher capital/labor ratios (i.e., the North), the relative cost of capital-intensive goods will be lower, while in countries with lower capital/labor ratios (i.e., the South), the relative costs will be lower for labor-intensive goods, reflecting the effect of factor endowments on each group of countries' comparative advantage in international trade. Through specialization, the capital-abundant countries will export more capital-intensive products to labor-abundant countries and receive more labor-intensive products in return. If we considered factor endowments as skilled and unskilled labor, we would get the same outcome. Countries with higher skilled/unskilled labor ratios will export more skill-intensive products and import relatively lower-skill-intensive products. We should note that the static nature of the HOS assumes that international division of labor and specialization should be based on current factor endowments.

The HOS model was extended to account for the rise of the NICs (i.e., the Emerging South), so that they appear as middle countries (Deardorff 1987). Unlike the older theories, which assume two countries with two goods and two factors of production, this formulation assumes a three-country and two-good model where factor endowments lie on a continuum, with relative labor abundance on one end, and relative capital abundance on the other. A middle country is somewhere in between and imports labor-intensive goods from a less-developed Southern country (i.e., Rest of South) and capital-intensive goods from a Northern country. At the same time, the Emerging South country exports capital-intensive goods to the low-income Southern country and labor-intensive goods to the Northern country (Krueger, 1977; Baldwin, 1979; Khanna, 1987; Deardorff, 1987). Therefore, the Rest of South competes with the Emerging South in labor-intensive but not in capital-intensive products, while the North competes with the Emerging South in capital-intensive but not in labor-intensive products.

Static neoclassical trade theory treats the South–South trade in capital or skill-intensive goods as a result of misguided ISI policies, which distorted relative prices and caused allocative inefficiencies and welfare losses. Accordingly, those Southern countries that had failed to develop high-quality and competitive capital-and-skill-intensive products dump their lower quality and overpriced industrial products on other Southern countries. Thus, Southern consumers end up being penalized by being forced to buy low-quality refrigerators, televisions, machinery, or cars from their Southern partners, driven by trade diversion from the North (Diaz-Alejandro, 1973; Havrylyshyn and Wolf, 1987; Bhagwati *et al.*, 1998; Panagariya, 2000). This critique of South–South trade is therefore also a critique of the ISI model in developing countries. The basic idea behind the ISI was antithetical to the static HOS model as it argued that industrial upgrading is not only possible but it is also desirable for less developed countries with low capital/labor and skill-intensity ratios.

4.2 *Dynamic Theories of Trade*

The development of neoclassical new trade theory starting with Krugman (1979) led to another wave of criticisms of South–South economic integration efforts. By then, it had become obvious that most world trade was between similarly endowed economies, that is, North–North rather than North–South, and it was intra-industry rather than interindustry, running against the predictions of the HOS theory. New trade theory introduced imperfect competition, including monopoly rights over new technology, increasing returns, differentiated products, and mobile capital, with special attention to intra-industry trade. Unlike the static neoclassical trade theory, the evolution of factor endowments, technology, skill intensities, and factor productivity has come to the center stage of trade analysis.

Compared to the neoclassical theory, heterodox trade and development theory had always focused on dynamic gains, or lack thereof, from international trade. Issues seemingly introduced by new trade theory, such as imperfect competition, increasing returns and endogenous technological change (together with surplus labor), were already a key feature of early classical development theory (Ros, 2001, 2008, 2013, ch. 2). While the heterodox macroeconomic literature on North–South and South–South trade is rich and diverse, the main debates on the subject mostly originated from the structuralist school.[6] Therefore, we will mostly compare neoclassical trade theory with the structuralist and related literature in this section. In what follows, we will summarize the main points from the neoclassical and structuralist schools on South–South versus North–South trade, emphasizing the binding constraints and developmental effects of economic interactions that favor one over the other. We should also note that the division between the neoclassical and structuralist literature has increasingly become blurred as it is possible to find arguments for and against South–South trade from both schools.

4.2.1 *Productivity Spillovers, Technology Frontier, and Adaptive Capabilities*

One strain of neoclassical new trade theory argues that North–South trade integration is mutually more beneficial as it allows for exploitation of economies of scale, and faster adoption of newer and better technologies and skills, leading to skills-and-technology upgrading and productivity gains, which would not be possible under South–South trade. Otsubo (1998), for example, argue that only after the South has liberalized trade with the North and begun producing according to their comparative advantage (i.e., labor-intensive goods), will there be a chance for the expansion of intra-industry South–South trade. Schiff (2003), Schiff *et al.* (2002), and Schiff and Wang (2006, 2008) also suggest that the highest impact on Southern total factor productivity (TFP) comes from the North through trade-induced technology diffusion. That is, the potential for technology transfer is higher when the technology gap between the trading partners is larger. As the South is positioned further away from the international technology frontier, North–South trade offers a higher chance of technology diffusion than South–South trade. North–South trade integration is also suggested to accelerate vertical specialization or value-chain fragmentation, allowing for faster catching up with the North (Krugman, 1995). Thus, with regard to technological acquisition, Southern countries are to have a wider range of choices in the Northern technology market and therefore can adopt the best technologies with the least cost and effort. In this literature, as will be discussed further later, capacity and capability of technology adoption are seen as one and the same thing.

On the other hand, for other strands of this literature, the existence of a vast technological gap between the North and the South limits gains from North–South trade and prohibits expansion of intra-industry trade. As the gap is smaller in South–South direction, there is arguably a bigger potential for learning by exporting in more sophisticated manufactures. This view challenges the orthodox view about technology transfer. What is suggested here is the opposite of the earlier view: the closer two countries are in technological development, the more likely they are to benefit mutually from trade since the technology is more appropriate for local conditions, including consumer preferences (more on this in Section 4.2.2), production structures, resource bases, and institutions (World Bank, 2006; Caglayan *et al.*, 2013; Dahi and Demir, 2013; Regolo, 2013; Bahar *et al.*, 2014; Cheong *et al.*, 2015; Demir, 2016; Demir and Hu, 2016).

On this issue, the new trade theory has converged to the older structuralist tradition, which made the exact same arguments in favor of South–South trade (Amsden, 1980, 1987; UNIDO, 2005). Particularly, because of its higher skill-and-technology intensity, South–South trade is argued to have dynamic long-run benefits (Amsden, 1980, 1983, 1984, 1987, 1989; Chang, 2002, 2000, 2001; Wade, 1990). Assuming that learning and other spillover effects are the highest in the production of higher skill manufactures, South–South trade therefore offers higher potential for long-term development as it stimulates greater industrial production and skill-and-technology upgrading. Besides, South–South trade offers more opportunities in

Table 1. Share of High- and Medium-Skill Exports in Total Exports in Each Direction of Trade

High-skill	South–South	South-Emerging	South–North	Emerging-South	Emerging–Emerging	Emerging-North
1962–1969	2%	2%	0%	1%	2%	1%
1970–1979	2%	1%	1%	2%	4%	4%
1980–1989	3%	1%	1%	4%	9%	8%
1990–1999	3%	2%	1%	7%	18%	17%
2000–2008	5%	2%	1%	8%	28%	22%
2009–2012	7%	1%	1%	10%	27%	21%

Medium-skill	South–South	South-Emerging	South–North	Emerging-South	Emerging–Emerging	Emerging-North
1962–1969	14%	13%	3%	6%	8%	2%
1970–1979	15%	6%	2%	13%	14%	5%
1980–1989	18%	10%	4%	20%	20%	10%
1990–1999	15%	10%	4%	29%	23%	16%
2000–2008	21%	8%	4%	29%	21%	20%
2009–2012	24%	9%	4%	30%	23%	22%

Source: MIT Media Lab (2015) and authors' calculations.
Notes: Skill-classification is based on Lall (2000). High-skill refers high-technology and skill-intensive manufactured goods. For product codes, see the Appendix. The values refer to the share of high and medium-skill goods in total exports within each direction of trade.

intra-industry trade in industrial products than the North–South trade, which is interindustry, with the South exporting relatively lower skill-and-technology-intensive products.[7] The importance of manufactured goods for industrial upgrading and growth was first raised by Kaldor (1967). While the classical development theory and the structuralist approaches have long argued that what you export matters for long-run development, which is seen as a dynamic process reinforced by sectors that enjoy increasing returns, neoclassical new trade theory, despite starting from different assumptions and often arriving at different policy conclusions, has increasingly recognized the importance of export structure and export diversification for skills upgrading and growth (Antweiler and Trefler, 2002; Imbs and Wacziarg, 2003; An and Iyigun, 2004; Hausmann *et al.*, 2007).

Table 1 shows that while the share of medium-skill manufactures in intra Rest of South trade has been around 14%–24%, on average, in each decade since 1960s, it was around 2%–4% in Rest of South–North trade. The same is true for high-skill goods. For intra-Emerging South trade in medium and high-skill goods, we again find a similar pattern. During the 1960s, 1970s, and 1980s, for example, the share of medium-skill goods in intra-Emerging South trade was more than twice higher than in Emerging South–North trade. Table 2 supports these findings by showing the destination market distribution of medium and high-skill exports of Southern countries. During the Great Recession period of 2009–2012, for example, 35% of Rest of South high-skill exports were to other similar countries and 42% were exported to Emerging South countries. In fact, for most of the years between 1962 and 2012, more than half of Rest of South exports of medium- and high-skill goods were to global South countries, be that Rest of South or Emerging South.

Table 2. Share of High- and Medium-Skill Goods in South–South Trade

High-skill	South–South	South-Emerging	Emerging-South	Emerging–Emerging
1962–1969	25%	30%	11%	27%
1970–1979	25%	16%	6%	19%
1980–1989	17%	14%	4%	21%
1990–1999	7%	30%	3%	34%
2000–2008	23%	42%	2%	42%
2009–2012	35%	42%	3%	51%
Medium-skill	South–South	South-Emerging	Emerging-South	Emerging–Emerging
1962–1969	24%	28%	17%	38%
1970–1979	35%	22%	17%	31%
1980–1989	23%	26%	12%	32%
1990–1999	9%	44%	9%	38%
2000–2008	22%	44%	9%	35%
2009–2012	24%	53%	9%	43%

Source: MIT Media Lab (2015) and authors' calculations.
Notes: Medium-skill and High-skill refer to medium- and high-skill manufactured goods. The values refer to the share of high and medium-skill goods in each direction of trade as a percentage of total exports of these goods to all directions. The differences from 100 percent gives the shares of exports to the North.

Furthermore, being the technological laggard, the South is argued to be in a dependent relationship regarding the direction of technological change. Particularly, being at the technological frontier, the North controls the direction of technological innovation, which is conditioned by Northern endowments and preferences, making it more capital-intensive (Stewart, 1982; 1992, p. 81; Kaplinsky, 1990; Acemoglu, 2015). Thus, products produced by the North are biased against Southern preferences and are inappropriate in terms of production techniques and product characteristics, which the South accepts because of lack of alternatives. Conversely, South–South exports, which embody older technologies, might be more appropriate for skill and technology adoption, matching Southern production and demand structures as well as factor endowments and market size than Northern exports with cutting-edge technologies (Stewart, 1982; Chudnovsky, 1983; Amsden, 1984, 1987; Bhalla, 1985; Kaplinsky, 1990; Nelson and Pack, 1999). Environmental appropriateness, including climate conditions or land use patterns and soil fertility of a chosen technology, adds another dimension to this debate as large-scale versus small-scale production processes have different implications for resource-poor or environmentally risky Southern countries that lack the resources to guarantee environmental safety and protections (Schumacher, 1973; Atta-Ankomah, 2014). Akamatsu's (1962) "flying geese" made similar arguments about the rise of Japanese industrialization. The size of the market and scale economies also affects the choice of technology available to Southern and Northern producers (Stewart, 1982; Kaplinsky, 1990; He *et al.*, 2012; Atta-Ankomah 2014). Therefore, technologies that are more suitable for Southern firms in smaller markets will not be necessarily available from Northern suppliers, whose capital goods are more suitable for large markets.

The assimilation argument of Stewart (1992) and Nelson and Pack (1999), among others, matches with what Lall (2000, 2001) refers to as the capabilities approach to technological change. Accordingly, developing country firms are constrained by imperfect knowledge of technological alternatives, and finding appropriate technologies is a difficult and costly process. Imported new technologies require creating new skills and know-how to master their tacit knowledge, which varies by the kind of technology in question. Learning costs and adaptive capabilities therefore create barriers for technology adoption and limit the ability of Southern firms to choose the best technology available from the North. Thus, national abilities, not comparative advantage in factor endowments, determine a country's ability to master and use effectively a given technology. The greater the gap in tacit technological knowledge required in the production processes, the smaller the possibility for technological acquisition and knowledge growth. Therefore, the adoption costs are an increasing function of the knowledge and technology gap between the importers and suppliers (Amsden, 1987, p. 133). It must be stressed that the relevant literature argues for targeted industrial policy in promoting technological development, whether through North–South or South–South exchanges as has been shown for the case of Costa Rica, Brazil, India, South Korea, and elsewhere (Salazar-Xirinachs et al., 2014).

More recent advances in neoclassical research also support these observations. Acemoglu (2001), 2002, p. 783, 2007, 2015) and Acemoglu and Zilibotti (2001), for example, argue that market size, the relative scarcity of factor endowments, including their elasticity of substitution, and skills scarcity bias the direction of technological change. The technologies developed in the North therefore will be inappropriate to the needs of the South as they will not correspond to lower capital and skill intensities in developing countries. Caselli and Coleman (2001) also show that the level of human capital development and industrial development level of importing countries influence technology adoption. In the industrial organization field, there is indeed a long literature exploring how the choice of technology is endogenous to firm, market, and consumer characteristics.[8]

Given the similarities in technological development, South–South trade therefore allows for easier technological innovation (Amsden, 1984, 1987; Lall et al., 1989; Lall, 2000, 2001). These production systems are also more likely to be labor-intensive, and thus, allow for a more efficient use of surplus labor in the South while lowering license costs (Pack and Saggi, 1997). Recent empirical work using case studies shows that developing country technologies might indeed fit better for local needs, demand structures, market size, factor endowments, and adaptive capabilities (He et al., 2012; Atta-Ankomah, 2014; Agyei-Holmes, 2016; Xu et al., 2016).

4.2.2 Preference, Demand, and Income Similarity

Another seeming convergence between the neoclassical and structuralist literature is the recent work on Linder's preference similarity theory on consumer demand, which provides support for South–South over North–South trade (Hallak, 2006, 2010; Fajgelbaum et al., 2015). Linder (1967) suggested that inventors, innovators, and entrepreneurs are stimulated by home demand as they develop products to fit home market tastes and preferences. Later, they export products to those countries with tastes and preferences similar to those at home. Thus, the reason why most Northern trade is with other Northern countries and why it is intra-industry is because of the demand structure: the incomes, tastes, and preferences of developed countries are similar, and therefore they buy differentiated but similar products from each other (Krugman, 1980). South–South trade may therefore fit the demand structure of Southern consumers better than North–South trade. Furthermore, because entry barriers are higher in South–South direction, be that because of higher trade barriers, transaction, and transportation costs, colonial-era distortions that favor Northern countries, language differences, or lack of trade financing and credit, Southern consumers buy inappropriate Northern goods that do not match their demand structures, reducing overall welfare.[9] The South also loses in North–South trade as it cannot export products that it is most efficient at producing (Linder, 1967, p. 37).

Accordingly, there are differences in consumer demand structures in the North and the South as certain products have "high," while others have "low"-income characteristics and preference structures (Copeland and Kotwal, 1996; Murphy and Schleifer, 1997; Hallak, 2006, 2010; Fajgelbaum et al., 2015). Lancaster's (1971) approach to consumer demand also argues that consumers desire certain characteristics of goods rather than the goods themselves. The perceived quality differences between Southern and Northern goods of the same type also create some friction between Northern and Southern consumer preferences. For example, while there is little evidence showing that Chinese leather bags or watches are of lower quality than Italian bags or Swiss watches, the price differences are significant, reflecting differences in consumer demand for Southern and Northern goods (Brucks et al., 2000; Fontagne et al., 2008). Loren and Eric (2016), for example, showed that despite a lack of quality differences, Chinese excavators are sold at a significant price discount to foreign competitors. Therefore, specialized products in South–South trade may be subject to smaller perceived quality biases than in North–South trade, allowing Southern producers a better chance of exporting.

Recent empirical work supports Linder's theses showing that the level of institutional and cultural similarity as well as closeness in incomes, endowments, technological, and preference structures between countries boost bilateral trade as well as the potential for economic convergence and spillovers through economic exchanges (Hallak, 2006, 2010; Demir and Dahi, 2011; Bergstrand and Egger, 2013; Dahi and Demir, 2013, 2016; Regolo, 2013; Bahar et al., 2014; Fajgelbaum et al., 2015; Cheong et al., 2015; Demir, 2016; Demir and Hu, 2016). Regolo (2013), for example, finds that endowment similarity between country pairs stimulates greater export diversification. Bergstrand and Egger (2013) also find that country pairs of similar economic sizes or capital and labor endowments are more likely to engage in bilateral PTA and investment agreements (BIAs) than others. Bahar et al. (2014) show that having neighbors with similar comparative advantage increases a country's export growth in similar products. Besides, they show that countries with more similar incomes, endowments, and population have more similar exports. Likewise, Hallak (2006, 2010) shows that income similarity increases bilateral trade flows between countries.

4.2.3 Economies of Scale and Market Size Asymmetries

Unlike the discussion in Sections 4.2.1 and 4.2.2, similarities in production and trade structures, consisting (arguably) of primary commodities, are claimed to make it harder to benefit from economies of scale in South–South trade. Faulty government interventions under the ISI through price distortions and errors in the choice of subsidized sectors as well as the geographical location of industrial plants are argued to lower the chances of economies of scale in South–South trade (Schiff, 2003). South–South trade integration is also suggested to have asymmetric effects on trading partners, conditional on their positioning in the industrialization ladder. More advanced Southern countries are more likely to reap larger benefits as they export their lower quality manufactured goods to other less-developed Southern countries. Therefore, weaker Southern countries are claimed to be better off in North–South than South–South trade. Because of economic power asymmetry, industries with the most dynamic development potential are also more likely to relocate to bigger and richer Southern countries, leading to their divergence from the Rest of South (Puga and Venables, 1997; Schiff, 2003; Venables, 2003).

4.2.4 *Quality Upgrading*

The quality of exported goods is shown to be endogenous to importer characteristics such as income levels or similarities in tastes and preferences. Through panel data on Mexican manu-facturing plants, Verhoogen (2008) shows that more productive plants produce higher quality goods to penetrate Northern (particularly United States) markets. This is a stylized fact that was previously highlighted by the structuralist literature as well. Amsden (1989), for exam-ple, suggests that South Korean exports to the North enabled product quality upgrades. Hallak (2006), Bastos and Silva (2010), Manova and Zhang (2012), and Dahi and Demir (2016) find that export unit values, signaling product quality, increase with the income levels of importing nations, reflecting increasing consumer demand for quality with income. In fact, Manova and Zhang (2012) show that even the very same firms charge higher prices, reflecting higher qual-ity, in richer country markets. One major implication of these findings is that North–South trade may provide additional benefits through productivity and quality improvements for Southern producers.

4.2.5 *Uneven Development, Path Dependency, and Trade*

While previously outside the scope of mainstream trade theory, there is now a bourgeoning neoclassical literature emphasizing the importance of initial conditions in explaining long-run differences in incomes and growth (Krugman, 1987, 1991; Lucas, 1988; Becker *et al.*, 1990; Matsuyama, 1991). As Feenstra (1996) pointed out, the assumption of perfect international diffusion of knowledge is a necessary condition for the neoclassical convergence story to ma-terialize. Without this assumption, the same models can lead to convergence clubs within but not between different groups of countries.

   Furthermore, Northern colonial rule and slave trade are shown to have had significantly neg-ative effects on bilateral trade, institutional development, democracy, income growth, human capital, trust, and income inequality within the South (Findlay, 1992; Acemoglu *et al.*, 2001; Angeles, 2007; Bagchi, 2008; Iyer, 2010; Wietzke, 2015). Interestingly, the empirical neoclas-sical trade literature has long been aware of the effect of colonial past on trade as shown by the positive and significant colonial past dummies in Gravity regressions. However, most of these studies do not assume any interdependency between the rise of the West with the fall of the Rest, treating skill-biased technological and structural change in Northern economies as exogenous of their involvement in the South. Furthermore, learning-by-doing and induced-technological change, which have been the corner stones of endogenous growth and new-trade theories, have not been applied to North–South exchanges. As Acemoglu (2015: 456) noted "the orthodoxy …, which ignores the biased and localised nature of technological change, is still widespread in much of macro-economics."

   On the other hand, the structuralist school from its beginnings has questioned the premise that North–South trade is beneficial to all trading parties. Initially developed by Raul Prebisch, the structuralist literature argues that the South exports primary products and/or simple manufactures, in return, for advanced industrial products from the North and there-fore remain in a constant state of underdevelopment.Unlike the arguments put forward in section 4.2.3, a rich literature from this tradition shows myriad ways in which North–South interactions create outcomes more favorable to the North, leaving the South in a dependent position to the North (Bacha, 1978; Findlay, 1980; Taylor, 1981; Dutt, 1986, 1987, 1989, 1990, 1992, 1996; Darity and Davis, 2005).

One strain of this literature argues that differences in income elasticities of demand for Southern and Northern goods generate uneven development given the international division of labor whereby the South produces primary products or low-end manufactures with low-income elasticities, while the North produces high-skill-and-technology-intensive goods with higher income elasticities (Prebisch, 1950; Singer, 1950, 1975). Endogenous technological change is also suggested to cause uneven development in North–South trade. The invention of synthetic substitutes for Southern primary goods, for example, is shown to turn the terms of trade against the South, thereby slowing its growth (Dutt, 1996).

The asymmetric nature of North–South trade is also analyzed through the engine of a global growth metaphor where increasing Northern growth moves the terms of trade in favor of the South, stimulating growth and capital accumulation in the South (Lewis, 1980; Taylor, 1981). However, given the structure of Southern and Northern exports, the North–South interaction is doomed to be uneven (Findlay, 1980, 1984; Taylor, 1981; Dutt, 1989, 1990; Darity and Davis, 2005; Ros, 2013, ch. 4). Furthermore, in this framework, Southern growth is always dependent on Northern growth and is not self-sustaining. For example, a positive technological shock in the South increases Southern productivity and growth, leading to an expansion of Southern supply of goods as well as Southern demand for Northern goods, both of which turns the terms of trade against the South. Falling terms of trade, in turn, lowers Southern foreign exchange earnings and profits, eventually slowing down its growth (Singer, 1950, 1975; Prebisch, 1950, 1959; Lewis, 1969; Dutt, 2012). Interestingly, WTO (2003) celebrated the increase in South–South trade in manufactures and financial flows, citing favorably Prebisch's hypothesis on declining terms of trade in the context of discussing the importance of manufactures for industrial growth. Furthermore, the World Bank (2008) pointed out that South–South trade can help reduce the South's growth dependence on Northern growth.

The earlier structuralist literature, however, did not suggest that South–South trade would reverse the asymmetric nature of North–South exchanges. In fact, there is nothing to stop the same dynamics from progressing within the South–South as long as there are the same type of asymmetries between Southern trading partners as is the case today between Emerging South and the Rest of South.

4.2.6 *Entry Barriers*

Finally, any assessment of the payoff matrix in trade by direction should hold that due to long-standing structural (colonial legacy and neocolonial ties) and policy factors (trade and nontrade barriers), South countries still do not have the same tendency or ease of trade by direction. South–South trade is subject to higher trade barriers, making it more difficult for firms to start exporting, survive and grow in Southern markets. Weak destination institutions, for example, increase entry costs and lower the entry, growth, and survival rates while discouraging firms from exporting to new markets (Anderson and Marcouiller, 2002; Belloc, 2006; Levchenko, 2007; Aeberhardt *et al.*, 2014; Söderlund and Tingvall, 2014; Fernandes *et al.*, 2016). Traditional trade barriers in the form of tariffs are also higher in South–South trade than North–South (Dahi and Demir, 2016). Therefore, North–South trade can offer more opportunities to Southern exporters than those in South–South trade.

4.3 *Preferential Trade and Investment Agreements and South–North Exchanges*

Asymmetries in bargaining power, knowledge, negotiating capacity, and retaliatory capabilities are argued to bias bilateral trade and investment agreements, favoring the Northern over Southern partners (Thrasher and Gallagher, 2008; Dahi and Demir, 2013, 2016). While these asymmetries are arguably also present in the South–South direction, the gap is smaller, allowing more policy space to developing countries to experiment with economic policies that are most suitable to their needs. An obvious reflection of such asymmetries is that four Northern actors, the United States, the European Union, Canada, and Japan, were responsible for 52% of all trade-related disputes filed at WTO between 1995 and 2015 (Dahi and Demir, 2016, p. 40). The share of low-income countries in total number of complaints was less than 7%, while the middle-income South countries accounted for 45% of the total during the same period (Dahi and Demir, 2016, p. 38). The case with investor-state disputes is no different. Dahi and Demir (2016, p. 47) report that between 1998 and 2014, global South countries were on the defending end 90% of the time, out of a total of 589 disputes filed though international investment agreements (IIAs). Of this number, more than 70% were brought by Northern investors against global South countries (with the remainder launched by other countries in the global South). The threat of a lawsuit works as a deterrent for the South not to employ policies that might be challenged by foreign investors, particularly in the face of exorbitant amounts of awards involved. That is why UNCTAD (2015: 125) argued that IIAs are not "harmless political declarations" and they, in fact, enable Northern investors to "challenge core domestic policy decisions … for instance in the area of environmental, energy and health policies."

On the issue of trade diversion caused by PTAs, South–South trade is unlikely to be trade diverting from South–North as trade barriers are significantly higher in South–South than in any other direction (Cernat 2001; Kowalski and Shepherd, 2006; Kee *et al.*, 2009; Medvedev, 2010; Dahi and Demir, 2016, ch. 4). Linder (1967) also suggested that the positive effects of South–South trade agreements are less ambiguous than those for the North, and even if they are trade diverting, they were still welfare enhancing as long as the diversion is from the North. Empirically speaking, the biggest trade enhancing effect of PTAs is found in South–South direction (Kowalski and Shepherd, 2006; Dahi and Demir, 2013; Behar and Cirera-i-Criville, 2013). Decreasing cost of intermediate goods imports from other Southern markets can also increase Southern export penetration in industrial goods in Northern markets (Fugazza and Robert-Nicoud, 2006).

As is consistently shown in the empirical trade literature, colonial-link variables almost always appear to be a significant predictor of bilateral trade flows. Therefore, Dahi and Demir (2013, 2016) suggest that PTAs may also be an indirect way of correcting for colonial linkages that distort international trade in favor of North–South direction.[10] Obviously, South–South trade suffers from smaller number of such colonial distortions. Dahi and Demir (2013) also see South–South PTAs as a developmentalist tool because of their larger positive effect on manufactured goods exports than North–South PTAs. The international political economy literature on South–South integration also suggested that PTAs and BITs help diversify the alliances of Southern countries and facilitate a more flexible policy space against the Northern dominance in global economy (Hveem, 1999; Hettne, 2005; Doctor, 2007; Thrasher and Gallagher, 2008).

The significant increase in the number of South–South PTAs and BITs suggests that policy makers in the South are aware of their positive effects. The average annual number of new

PTA pairs was 30 between 1958 and 1988, it increased to 267 between 1989 and 2013, and 75% of these agreements were in the South–South direction (Dahi and Demir, 2016). In 2013 alone, for example, 222 new country pairs signed PTAs, 66% of which were between Southern countries. Likewise, 88% of BITs were signed after 1990, reaching 3140 by 2015. Of those BITs signed since 1990, 56% were between Southern countries (Dahi and Demir, 2016, p. 47).

4.4 *South–South versus North–South Finance*

Unlike the extensive literature on trade linkages, theoretical and empirical work on South–South and North–South financial linkages is only very recent and is in much shorter supply. The main reason is the relatively more recent history of such exchanges, which started to grow mostly after the financial liberalization wave of the early 1990s. The data quality and availability issues are also more severe for financial flows than trade flows. Most existing work on the topic has focused on long-term capital flows as FDI differs significantly from other types of financial flows in its effects on productivity, capital formation, growth, and employment. Global FDI flows reached $1.8 trillion in 2015 up from $54 billion in 1980 and $205 billion in 1990 (UNCTAD, 2017a). Even more strikingly, an increasing percentage of these flows is now to and from the South, and increasingly within the South–South direction. While more than 80% (90%) of all inflows (outflows) were to (from) the North even back in 2000, almost 60% (40) of all were to (from) the South in 2014. Mainland China alone ranked number 3 in both FDI inflows and outflows in 2015. Furthermore, 8 of the top 20 host economies and 6 of the top 20 home economies were from the South in 2015. Within aggregate FDI flows to the South, South–South flows increased significantly, reaching around 63%–65% of all outflows from developing countries in 2010 (UNCTAD, 2011; World Bank, 2011). In the case of Africa, for example, 78% (44%) of all announced greenfield FDI inflows and 94% (88%) of outflows were in South–South direction in 2016 (2015). In Asia, 50% (52%) of all announced Greenfield FDI inflows and 82% (79%) of all outflows were in South–South direction in 2016 (2015) (UNCTAD, 2017b. pp. 45, 50).

Within the neoclassical framework, North–South capital movements, particularly FDI flows, facilitate technology transfer and productivity spillovers, allowing the South to catch up with the North. The predicted spillover effects include better technology, modern management techniques and managerial skills, R&D investment, and more experience in international markets as well as the possibility of learning by watching (Fosfuri *et al.*, 2001; Fabbri *et al.*, 2003; Navaretti *et al.* 2003; Almeida, 2007; Desai *et al.*, 2008; Huttunen, 2007; Arnold and Javorcik, 2009). As the productivity and knowledge gaps are larger in the North–South dimension, so are the expected spillovers effects.

And yet, as discussed in Sections 4.2.1 and 4.2.2, institutional and cultural similarities as well as closeness in technological and preference structures between countries can affect the potential for spillovers and convergence through economic exchanges (Bergstrand and Egger, 2013; Regolo, 2013; Bahar *et al.*, 2014; Cheong *et al.*, 2015). Recent work on Linder hypothesis suggests that South–South FDI may offer some additional benefits over North–South FDI. Fajgelbaum *et al.* (2015), for example, show that countries with similar incomes and development levels are more likely to receive FDI from each other, given their similarities in consumer tastes and preferences. And yet, Demir and Duan (2017) find no evidence of positive productivity growth or convergence effects from bilateral FDI flows in South–South, North–South, South–North, or North–North directions.

Financial development asymmetries between trading partners can also contribute to the uneven pattern of development in South–North trade. Kletzer and Bardhan (1987), Rajan and Zingales (1998), Demirguc-Kunt and Maksimovic (1998), Beck (2002), Svaleryd and Vlachos (2005), and Hur *et al.* (2006) argue that credit-market imperfections cause differential comparative costs even with identical technologies and endowments and therefore industries that are more dependent on external finance such as those in capital intensive sectors grow faster in countries with better developed financial systems. In an extension of this work, Demir and Dahi (2011) argue and provide empirical support to the hypothesis that the comparative disadvantage of the South against the North in financial development can be alleviated in South–South trade where such asymmetries are smaller. As a result, a financially underdeveloped Southern country can have a better chance of exporting higher skill-and-technology-intensive products that are more reliant on external finance to other Southern countries.

South–South trade is also argued to be less sensitive to exchange rate shocks than South–North trade. Caglayan *et al.* (2013) suggest that because of lack of financial development as well as the original sin problem in the South, exchange rate shocks affect Northern and Southern exporters differently. In an extension of this work, Caglayan and Demir (2016) explore the effects of exchange rate changes on trade flows after controlling for the skill-content and origin/destination of products. They report that higher skill exports are the least affected product category from exchange rate movements, thus affecting Southern and Northern economies differently. Furthermore, they find that while South–South and South–North exports are significantly affected by exchange rate shocks, North–South exports are not.

Regarding South–South capital flows, recent empirical work suggests that Southern investors have a comparative advantage in operating in institutionally less developed and higher risk countries (Cuervo-Cazurra and Genc, 2008; Darby *et al.*, 2010; Aleksynska and Havrylchyk, 2013; Demir and Hu, 2016). Therefore, this advantage can help Southern investors overcome their disadvantaged position in technology, operational and management capabilities, experience, internal and external financing sources, marketing, size, and colonial linkages (i.e., their lack of it), and enable them penetrate Southern markets (Dahi and Demir, 2016; Demir and Hu, 2016). Likewise, less developed Southern host countries can have less restricted access to foreign capital through Southern multinationals.

On the more critical side of the literature, increasing South–South financial flows is blamed for undermining Northern country efforts to improve Southern institutions as they have weaker institutions and conditionality requirements (Lyman, 2005; Economist, 2006; Graham-Harrison, 2009; Mbaye, 2011; Warmerdam, 2012; Strange *et al.*, 2013). In contrast, North–South FDI is expected to improve Southern institutions as the Northern investors are endowed with better institutions than Southern ones (Mauro, 1995; Hall and Jones, 1999; Kaufmann *et al.*, 1999; Acemoglu *et al.*, 2001, 2005; Alfaro *et al.*, 2008). Directly through conditionality requirements, such as anticorruption or better rule of law demands in PTAs and BITs, or indirectly through the demonstration channel, (i.e., the introduction of new methods of business practices), Northern investors can help improve institutional quality in the South (Kwok and Tadesse, 2006). Northern investors can also improve host country institutions through lobbying and exerting pressure on local policy makers (Dang, 2013; Long *et al.*, 2015). Yet, Demir (2016) finds no evidence of positive institutional effects of FDI flows at the bilateral level in North–South or any other direction but reports some negative effects at the aggregate level for South–South flows.

Table 3 provides a summary of the literature on South–South and South–North exchanges in trade and finance that we discussed in Section 4.

Table 3. Classification of South–South Theories (Mainstream and Heterodox)

1. In favor of North–South trade and finance

1.1 Static Theories

Diaz-Alejandro (1973), Krueger (1977), Baldwin (1979), Khanna (1987), Deardorff (1987), Havrylyshyn and Wolf (1987), Bhagwati *et al.* (1998), Panagariya (2000)	Allows for specialization, technology transfer, and comparative advantage.

1.2 Dynamic Theories

Otsubo (1998), Schiff (2003), Schiff *et al.* (2002), Schiff and Wang (2006, 2008)	Expansion of intra-industry trade. Increases TFP through faster and better technology diffusion. It also enables economies of scale.
Puga and Venables (1997), Venables (2003), Schiff (2003).	South–North is better for smaller/weaker Southern countries as they are disadvantaged in economic power and market size against larger Southern countries.
Krugman (1995)	Allows for vertical specialization/value-chain fragmentation
Hallak (2006), Bastos and Silva (2010), Manova and Zhang (2012), Dahi and Demir (2016)	Export unit values (product quality) increase in importer incomes, allowing for productivity and quality improvements.
Anderson and Marcouiller (2002), Belloc (2006), Levchenko (2007), Aeberhardt *et al.* (2014), Fernandes *et al.* (2016), Söderlund and Tingvall (2014)	Lower Northern entry barriers make it easier for firms to export, enter, diversify, survive, and grow.
Fabbri *et al.* (2003), Fosfuri *et al.* (2001), Almeida (2007), Desai *et al.* (2008), Arnold and Javorcik (2009), Navaretti *et al.* (2003), Almeida (2007), Huttunen (2007)	FDI spillovers through better technology, modern management techniques and managerial skills, R&D investment, more experience in the international markets, and higher possibility of learning by watching.
Lyman (2005), Kwok and Tadesse (2006), Graham-Harrison (2009), Warmerdam (2012), Dang (2013), Long *et al.* (2015), Mbaye (2011),	North–South FDI and financial flows improve Southern institutional quality through conditionality requirements, lobbying, and demonstration channel.South–South financial flows encourage rogue states and hurt institutional development efforts in the South.

2. In favor of South–South trade and finance

2.1 Dynamic Theories

Linder (1967), Hallak (2006, 2010), World Bank (2006), UNCTAD (2011, p. 42), Bergstrand and Egger (2013), Regolo (2013), Amighini and Sanfilippo (2014), Cheong *et al.* (2015), Bahar *et al.* (2014), Cheong *et al.* (2015), Fajgelbaum *et al.* (2015), Demir and Duan (2017)	Similarities in institutions, culture, endowments, production structures, preferences, incomes, and technological development increase bilateral trade and finance and boost facilitate economic convergence and spillovers. They also allow for easier technology adoption and enable Southern investors to address local consumer needs better.
Dutt (1989, 1990), Findlay (1980, 1984), Taylor (1981), Darity and Davis (2005), Lewis (1980), Taylor (1981), World Bank (2008), Ros (2013, ch. 4),	North–South trade causes dependent growth in the South. South–South exchanges allow for decoupling from Northern business cycles and increase global economic stability.

(Continued)

Table 3. *Continued*

Cuervo-Cazurra and Genc (2008), Darby *et al.* (2010), Aleksynska and Havrylchyk (2013)	South–South investment flows can benefit from the comparative advantage of Southern investors in operating in institutionally less developed and more risky countries.
Amighini and Sanfilippo (2014), Demir and Hu (2016)	
Prebisch (1959), Akamatsu (1962), Amsden (1980, 1983, 1984, 1987, 1989), Fugazza and Robert-Nicoud (2006), Amighini and Sanfilippo (2014), Dahi and Demir (2013), Demir and Dahi (2011)	Higher skill and technology-intensive content of South–South trade allows for better skills upgrading and endogenous technological change. Allows for more export diversification and higher skill content in exports.
Amsden (1980, 1987), UNIDO (2005), Caglayan *et al.* (2013), Regolo (2013), Dahi and Demir (2013), Stewart (1982, 1992, p. 81), Kaplinsky (1990), Bhalla (1985), Nelson and Pack (1999), Schumacher (1973), Atta-Ankomah (2014), Lall (2000, 2001), Pack and Saggi (1997), Lall *et al.* (1989), Copeland and Kotwal (1996), Murphy and Shleifer (1997), Agyei-Holmes (2016), Atta-Ankomah (2014), Xu *et al.* (2016), He *et al.* (2012), Demir and Duan (2017)	The North controls the direction of technological innovation, which is conditioned by Northern endowments and preferences, making it more capital-intensive. Southern technologies are better fit for production and demand structures, resource bases, institutions, factor endowments, and market size in the South. They are more cost-effective and easier to learn, adapt, and upgrade. They are also more fit to consumer preferences.
Hveem (1999), Hettne (2005), Doctor (2007), Thrasher and Gallagher (2008), Kaplinsky (2008), Gallagher *et al.* (2012), Dahi and Demir (2013, 2016), UNCTAD (2015)	Smaller gaps in bargaining power, negotiating capacity, and retaliatory capabilities allow for more balanced BITs and PTAs and create more flexible policy space
Myrdal (1956), Kowalski and Shepherd (2006), Demir and Dahi (2011), Dahi and Demir (2013, 2016), Behar and Cirera-i-Criville (2013)	Higher trade and skill-growth effects of South–South PTAs
Caglayan *et al.* (2013), Caglayan and Demir (2016)	South–South trade may be less sensitive to exchange rate shocks
Brautigan (2009)	Chinese lending lowers corruption risk in Southern countries.
3. Critical of North–South exchanges	
Singer (1950, 1975), Prebisch (1950, 1959), Bacha (1978), Taylor (1981), Dutt (1986, 1987, 1989, 1990, 1992, 1996, 2012), Findlay (1980), Darity and Davis (2005), Acemoglu and Zilibotti (2001), Acemoglu (2015)	Causes uneven development favoring the North through terms of trade changes, dependent growth, and skill-biased technological change. Hurts industrialization efforts by forcing South to specialize in primary and labor intensive goods.
Acemoglu *et al.* (2001, 2015), Iyer (2010), Wietzke (2015), Bagchi (2008)	Northern colonialism and slave trade had negative effects on institutional development, democracy, income growth, human capital, trust, and income inequality in the South.

(Continued)

Table 3. *Continued*

5. Critical of South–South exchanges	
Kaplinsky *et al.* (2007)), Jenkins (2009), Brautigan (2009), Gallagher and Porzecanski (2008, 2010), Giovanetti and Sanfilippo (2009), Adisu *et al.* (2010), Kaplinsky *et al.* (2010), Jenkins and Edwards (2006, 2014), Peters (2005), Jenkins and Peters (2009); Ros (2013), Cabral *et al.* (2016), Dahi and Demir (2016), Demir and Duan (2017), Shankland and Gonçalves (2016), Scoones *et al.* (2016)	South–South exchanges benefit Emerging South at the expense of Rest of South. Rise of China crowds out Southern exporters and cause primarization and deindustrialization.
Amanor and Chichava (2016), Cabral *et al.* (2016), Scoones *et al.* (2016), Demir and Duan (2017)	South–South technology transfer and adaptive capabilities are subject to same limitations as North–South exchanges.
Baah and Jauch (2009), Jauch (2011)	Chinese investments in Africa are neocolonial, focusing on resource extraction, and are antilabor and exploitative.
Mohan and Kale (2007), Mohan *et al.* (2014), Mohan and Lampert (2013), Demir (2016), Demir and Duan (2017)	The net effect of Southern investments in local economies depends on country characteristics.

5. China and the Emerging South in Africa

The increasing importance of South–South exchanges in trade and finance is most visible in the China in Africa literature, which brings together the complex intersection of trade, aid, FDI, migration, and geopolitics. We dedicate a separate section here for several reasons. First, compared to other debates on South–South exchanges, interactions between China and various African countries have received particular attention in North America and Europe. In addition, China and Africa tend to represent opposite ends of the development spectrum, that is, a rising industrial power versus a relatively agrarian and primary good exporting region. Furthermore, on many development accounts, Africa appears as a net loser from the neoliberal period, while China appears as a winner. This makes investigating the outcome of their increased interaction particularly compelling. Finally, China in Africa best illustrates how the academic literature has evolved to allow for greater complexity in analyzing South–South interactions.

The earlier literature on the topic tended to be simplistic. As Ado and Su's (2016) survey argue, "research publications on the Chinese in Africa are mostly oriented toward findings that highlight a win-lose paradigm" (p. 42), underscoring the ideological bias in some of this literature, as is also pointed out by Power *et al.* (2012). Following Kaplinsky (2013), we classify the China in Africa debate by the levels of complexity of "China" and "Africa" as analytical categories that highlight the dynamism and the heterogeneity of country experiences involved therein. Particularly, we suggest three analytical categories: (a) China and Africa as two homogeneous actors whose interactions would either benefit or harm the other or both; (b) recognizing Africa as too heterogeneous and diverse to expect a unitary impact of Chinese presence, and to (c) a most complex approach, which recognizes that both China and Africa are heterogeneous with multiple actors, processes, and impacts. The articles surveyed here are classified accordingly in Table 4. The main benefit of this classification is that it reveals not just the fact that China–Africa engagement is complex but *how* it is complex.

Table 4. Selective Survey of China–Africa Literature by Complexity

1. Both China and Africa as homogeneous	
Brautigan (2009)	Chinese aid and investment is largely beneficial.
Alden (2007)	China as competitor, partner, colonizer: elements of all three, but large positive potential.
Busse *et al.* (2016)	Positive terms of trade impact, crowding out of African firms and no impact of aid and FDI on African growth
2. Africa heterogeneous, China homogenous	
Kaplinsky *et al.* (2007)), Kaplinsky (2008), Adisu *et al.* (2010), Brenton and Walkenhorst (2010), Kaplinsky *et al.* (2010), Edwards and Jenkins (2014)	Channels of impact: trade, aid, FDI reflecting strategic, and political economy factors. China endangers manufacturing, governance, and institutional development, triggers resource-curse, crowds out domestic investment, and has limited local employment effects.
Jenkins and Edwards (2006)	Direct channels more important than indirect due to lack of export similarity between China and SSA
Aguilar and Goldstein (2009)	China in Angola increases Angolan engagement with international community and brings significant infrastructural investments.
Baah and Jauch (2009), Jauch (2011)	Chinese investments engage in neocolonial practices and labor exploitation.
Xu *et al.* (2016)	Positive effects of Chinese aid on technology transfer.
Atta-Ankomah (2014), Agyei-Holmes (2016)	More appropriate technology transfer through more labor-intensive, cost-effective, and profitable imported capital goods.
Cheru (2016)	Joint ventures of China in Ethiopia and the use of the country as launching pad for regional investments.
3. Both China and Africa as heterogeneous	
Kaplinsky (2013)	Multiple actors in both China and Africa, indirect effects just as important as direct ones, and interaction contains both equalizing and unequalizing tendencies.
Mohan and Lampert (2013)	Labor exploitation and migrant worker integration varies by Chinese firm, country, institutional, cultural, and other factors.
Strauss and Saavedra (2009)	Ethnographic studies showing how cultural norms, structures, practices, critical engagements, and other interactions over time shape the China–Africa relationship.
Cabral *et al.* (2016), Amanor and Chichava (2016), Shankland and Gonçalves (2016)	Chinese and other Southern investment in Africa are subject to the same types of constraints and bottlenecks present in North–South exchanges.

Source: Kaplinsky (2013) and authors.

As alluded to by Power *et al.* (2012), China's Africa presence is often interpreted by its Cold War era engagements, signified by the iconic Tanzania-Zambia Railway, built during 1970–1975, which contained several elements that were later erroneously considered as *new* in terms of China's current engagement in Africa. First, it was a massive investment, costing about $600 million dollars, more than the Aswan dam in Egypt had cost the Soviets. Second, it was efficiently and rapidly done. Despite containing 300 tunnels, 10 km of bridges, and covering a distance of 1860 km, it was completed in only five years and two years ahead of schedule. Third, it contained a large number of workers, many of whom were Chinese (of the 75,000 workers who worked on the project, 25,000 were Chinese, and the remaining were Tanzanian). These three elements: massive infrastructure project, efficiency in implementation, and the presence of Chinese laborers are common tropes covered by the later literature.

The first wave of the China in Africa literature was born in reaction to the overwhelmingly alarmist discussions in the West. Some, if not all, of this literature was excessively optimistic, highlighting the benefits more than potential risks (Alden, 2007; Mawdsley, 2008; Brautigan, 2009; Chan, 2013; Kachiga, 2013). Brautigan (2009) questions the "myths" on China in Africa by arguing that contrary to Western aid, Chinese aid and concessionary loans reduce the possibility of corruption and embezzlement in host countries as they are often contracted directly through Chinese companies. Likewise, Alden (2007) assesses China–Africa policy through three possibilities that are partner, competitor, and colonizer, and finds elements of each in this relationship. While he finds that Chinese presence provides significant infrastructural benefits, it may also undermine African local industrial development and hurt indigenous democratization efforts. Jenkins and Edwards (2006) examine the direct and indirect impact of both China and India on African development in both natural resource and textile sector and find only limited crowding out effect on African exports in third country markets.

Kachiga (2013) through case studies on Nigeria, Sudan, Angola, Zimbabwe, and South Africa illustrates both the unique aid and investment strategies of China and how they compare and differ from those of the West. Like Western aid, Chinese aid comes with conditionalities and expectations of strategic payoffs, including tying them to purchases of Chinese goods and services. Nevertheless, given China's principle of sovereignty and noninterference, Kachiga argues that China's aid more closely fulfills the meaning of the word than that from the West as African countries are freer to set their own priorities on spending aid money. Carmody (2013), focusing on the BRIC countries, also highlights the positive developmental effects of these countries' involvement in Africa.

Kaplinsky *et al.* (2007)), Kaplinsky (2008), and Kaplinsky *et al.* (2010) provide a more critical and balanced analysis of China effect in Africa. Kaplinsky (2008) is a cornerstone of the second level of complexity of China in Africa studies and finds that China may be undermining industrial development in sub-Saharan Africa (SSA) through two channels. First, increasing Chinese imports of natural resources turns the terms of trade against manufacturing.[11] Second China's manufacturing growth is outcompeting African manufacturing, which has direct as well as indirect effects through third countries. For example, China's trade with the United States may help or hinder SSA exports to the United States. In addition, high saving rates of China help lower global interest rates and stimulate investment in SSA. Finally, increasing Chinese participation in international financial institutions may help relax their conditionality requirements imposed on SSA in aid flows given that China has now become a major donor for aid to the South (Gallagher *et al.*, 2012; Strange *et al.*, 2013).

In a follow-up work, Kaplinsky *et al.* (2010) focus on three areas: trade, production/FDI, and aid. Regarding trade, unlike Jenkins and Edwards (2006), Kaplinsky *et al.* (2010)

suggest that the opening up of the United States to imports from China (particularly in textiles after January 2005) resulted in significant declines in SSA manufactures exports to the U.S. market, hurting unemployment and poverty reduction efforts. The decline in exports and industrial employment is not sufficiently countered by growth in resource-extractive industries as the latter is more capital-intensive and involves more concentrated forms of ownership. Similarly, Giovanetti and Sanfilippo (2009) show significant crowding out of African exporters by Chinese manufactures exports to the United States, EU, and other African countries. Furthermore, Adisu *et al.* (2010) find that while Chinese investments create only minimal employment effects, they significantly hurt local trade in host economies. Similarly, Brenton and Walkenhorst (2010) highlight the competition risk China poses on domestic industries in North Africa, while Edwards and Jenkins (2014) find a strong crowding out effect of China on South Africa's exports to SSA in medium and low technology manufactures. Busse *et al.* (2016), in their assessment of Chinese trade, aid and FDI effects on per capita growth rates among SSA countries find that while imports from China have a negative displacement effect on African growth, exports to China do not have any significantly positive effect.

Furthermore, Cheru (2016) examines the case of Ethiopia and points to the use of certain countries such as Ethiopia and Kenya by China and India as regional hubs and launching pads. Aguilar and Goldstein (2009), focusing on Angola, show that China's increasing interest in oil and metals resulted in significant investment and credit extension and helped build critical infrastructure. However, they also find minimal employment creation and, with credit being tied to imports from Chinese suppliers, little boost to domestic production. Contrary to perceptions about lack of accountability, they find persistent Chinese attention to the use of their credit and loans.

As discussed earlier, one of the biggest themes in the literature has been the potential payoffs from South–South technology transfer. Focusing on rice farms in Tanzania, Agyei-Holmes (2016) finds that imported power tillers from China and India are more suitable for local needs than those from Northern countries as they are more labor-intensive, cost-effective, and profitable. Likewise, focusing on furniture manufacturing industry in Kenya, Atta-Ankomah (2014) compares the effects of imported technologies from the North with those from China and with locally developed indigenous methods. He reports that local and Chinese technologies are more labor-intensive, allowing for higher employment creation and poverty reduction. They are also more cost-effective, allowing poor entrepreneurs to start up their businesses with a higher degree of automation than would be possible otherwise. The products produced with these technologies are also reported to be more pro-poor as they meet the needs of poor consumers better at lower prices. Xu *et al.* (2016) report similar positive effects of knowledge transfer potential of Chinese aid programs in Tanzania, Ethiopia, Zimbabwe, and Mozambique through the agricultural technology demonstration centers.

In contrast, Cabral *et al.* (2016) argue that Brazilian agricultural modernization initiatives in Ghana, Mozambique, and Zimbabwe are subject to similar constraints and distortions that are present in North–South exchanges. Amanor and Chichava (2016) also find similar constraints in trilateral exchanges in agricultural development policies among Brazil, Ghana, and Mozambique. Shankland and Gonçalves (2016) also question the better suitability of Southern technologies in other Southern countries by analyzing the debates around the pro-Savana project of Brazil and Japan in Mozambique that was expected to boost agricultural productivity and lower poverty rates while increasing employment. They conclude that just being South–South does not ensure that such exchanges will not be subject to the same types of limitations present in North–South dimension. Conflicting priorities, differing development narratives, and problems in the suitability of local technologies to other Southern countries' needs remain as problematic in South–South exchanges as in North–South. Regarding the effect of Brazilian and Chinese development cooperation in Africa, Scoones *et al.* (2016) also argue that the benevolent effects of South–South cooperation may be more in theory than in reality and that the existing evidence hints at a reproduction of North–South style uneven development within South–South relations.

Finally, a series of articles have begun examining issues of labor and migration. Baah and Jauch (2009) and Jauch (2011) argue that Chinese businesses in Africa are neocolonial, focusing on resource extraction, and are highly antilabor, and exploitative with minimal labor rights. These businesses also fail to develop local capabilities. Mohan and Kale (2007), Mohan *et al.* (2014), and Mohan and Lampert (2013), while not disputing the exploitative tendencies of Chinese businesses, argue for a more nuanced understanding of the spatially complex state-capital dynamics, the fractious capital, Chinese and African workers, and other structural factors that are contributing to shaping the outcome of Chinese engagements in Africa. Mohan and Lampert (2013) sees heterogeneous union activity and labor practices depending on country and even the Chinese company in question. Strauss and Saavedra (2009) also bring together a vast array of works, highlighting heterogeneous country experiences in their exchanges with China.

In summary, the literature on China in Africa has moved away from sweeping judgments and extreme pessimism and optimism and toward both a more detailed assessment of heterogeneous impact, not just across but also within countries and by sectors as well as a recognition of the multiplicity of actors on both sides.

6. Is South–South Still a Meaningful Category?

Moving forward, a big question for the South–South literature is existential: to what extent is "South–South" still a meaningful analytical category given the huge disparities within the South? Figures 1–4 show what might be another great divergence between and within Southern countries themselves (Dahi and Demir, 2016). What has been called the rise of the South is actually the rise of a *few* in the South albeit the largest and most populous countries. What is more alarming is that their rise is coming at the expense of the Rest of South. As Figures 1–3 show, more than 30% of world trade is now in South–South direction and 58% of total Southern exports were to other Southern countries in 2013. And yet, 70% of this global South–South trade was between Emerging South countries. In fact, 10 Emerging South countries accounted for more than 60% of South–South trade in 2013 and China alone was responsible for 21% of it (IMF, 2014).[12] Likewise, 86% of global South–North trade was from Emerging South to North and top 10 countries accounted for 60% of total South–North trade in 2013 (with China accounting for more than 25% of the total).[13]

The skill content of Southern exports is also highly skewed in favor of a few Emerging economies. Figure 2 shows that the share of Rest of South in world manufactures exports was almost nonexistent in 2012, less than 2%, while Emerging South countries accounted for 45% of the total. Figure 4 shows that the share of Rest of South in global high-skill manufactures exports was 0% in 2012, while that of Emerging South was 55%. In fact, fossil fuels alone accounted for 58% of all Rest of South exports in 2012 (MIT Media Lab, 2015).[14] We should note, however, that the Emerging South as a whole accounts for 75% of Southern population and 86% of Southern output. The top 10 South–South exporters host 47% of Southern population and are responsible for 52% Southern output. China and India are the heavyweights in these calculations, jointly accounting for 42% of Southern population and 33% of total Southern output in 2012.

This country heterogeneity is mostly neglected in the South–South literature. Particularly, the issue that Emerging South–Rest of South exchanges may well recreate the same type of dependency within the South as in North–South is not explored much. Over 74% percent of all Rest of South's exports were in primary commodities in 2012, compared to 64% in 1970, which hints at the return of the traditional center–periphery relationship but this time between Emerging South and Rest of South (MIT Media Lab, 2015). As argued by Ros (2013), the rise of China changed the terms of trade in favor of primary goods during the 2000s, benefiting primary good exporting Southern countries in an opposite pattern to that predicted by the Prebisch-Singer hypothesis. However, this is a double-edged growth spurt, encouraging deindustrialization in the long run.[15] China (mainland) accounted for more than a third of world consumption of all metals, 50% of global coal consumption, 15% percent of global crude oil demand, 73% of iron ore, 38% of copper ore, 60% of global soy beans demand, and 27% of world demand in natural rubber in 2014 (MIT Media lab, 2016). Thus, as discussed in the previous section on China in Africa, growing Chinese demand for primary commodities had two distinct effects on Southern countries. For primary good producers, it triggered a structural transformation, called primarization, so that increasing demand for primary products and favorable terms of trade pushed them to specialize in primary goods and to move away from manufactures. For primary good importing semi-industrialized economies, increasing competition from China in export markets and the rising cost of imported primary inputs have crowded them out of other Southern and Northern markets, decimating their manufacturing industries. Both groups of countries here face deindustrialization/primarization, as the shares of industry employment, output, and investment decrease and they experience a downgrading to less technology-and-skill-intensive, low-productivity activities, mostly in primary goods or low-skill service sectors (UNCTAD, 2003, 2006; Peters, 2005; Jenkins and Peters, 2009; Gallagher and Porzecanski, 2008, 2010; McMillan and Rodrik, 2011; Dahi and Demir, 2016; Rodrik 2016).

Tables 5 and 6 highlight the effect of China on world trade, and particularly that of Latin America. Since the 1990s, China emerged as a major exporter of high-, medium-, and

Table 5. Share of Chinese Exports and Imports in World Trade, 1990, 2003, and 2012

	Exports			Imports		
	1990	2003	2012	1990	2003	2012
Total	4.2%	9.4%	15.1%	3.9%	8.0%	12.3%
Primary	2.7%	2.6%	2.2%	2.4%	5.5%	10.6%
Nat-resource intensive	1.8%	4.0%	7.5%	3.1%	6.4%	14.6%
Low-skill	13.3%	24.2%	32.4%	6.4%	8.5%	7.3%
Medium-skill	2.6%	5.8%	11.3%	4.1%	7.1%	9.3%
High-skill	3.0%	13.4%	28.8%	4.1%	12.9%	20.1%

Source: Dahi and Demir (2016, table 5.3).
Notes: Based on Lall (2000), Total, Primary, and Nat-Resource Intensive refer to the export (import) shares of total merchandise goods, primary commodities, and natural-resource-intensive manufactured goods in world trade of these goods. Low-skill, Medium-skill and High-skill refer to low-, medium- and high-skill manufactured goods. China includes Hong Kong. Exports and imports are valued fob and cif, respectively.

Table 6. Structure of China-Latin America Trade, 1990, 2003, and 2012

	Exports to Latin America			Imports from Latin America		
	1990	2003	2012	1990	2003	2012
Primary	10.4%	1.9%	2.3%	31.8%	36.9%	45.5%
Nat-resource intensive	7.2%	8.5%	7.9%	31.4%	31.7%	41.6%
Low-skill	46.2%	29.8%	25.4%	19.0%	8.5%	1.6%
Medium-skill	28.0%	21.9%	28.4%	16.1%	11.2%	4.2%
High-skill	7.6%	37.0%	35.0%	1.4%	11.6%	6.5%

Source: Dahi and Demir (2016, table 5.6).
Notes: Latin America includes the Caribbean.

low-skill manufactures.[16] Between 1990 and 2012, China's shares in world exports of these goods increased from 13% to 32% for low-skill goods, from 2.6% to 11% for medium-skill goods, and from 3% to just below 29% for high-skill goods. Meanwhile, its import share of primary goods and natural-resource-intensive manufactures increased from less than 4% to 12%, and from 2% to 10%, respectively. Similarly, in 2012, more than 45% of Chinese imports from Latin America were primary commodities and 41.6% were natural-resource-intensive manufactures, jointly accounting for 87% of its imports from the entire region. In contrast, in that year, 35% of its exports to Latin America were high-skill and 28% were medium-skill manufactures, jointly accounting for more than 63% of Chinese exports to the region. This is exactly what the structuralist economists were afraid of: a vicious cycle of increasing deindustrialization and primarization process in the South. Looking at particular economies, in 2012, 74% of Argentine and 61% of Chilean exports to China were of primary commodities. Together with natural-resource-intensive manufactures, primary goods accounted for 92.6% of Argentine and 99.5% of Chilean exports to China in 2012. Even in the case of more successful industrializing countries such as Brazil, the future looks grim as 92% of Brazilian exports to China were of either primary commodities or natural resource intensive manufactures in 2012.

Table 7 shows the structure of South–China trade in 1990 compared to 2012. The trend here also suggests increasing primarization of exports from the Rest of South to China. In fact, 75% of Rest of South exports to China were of primary goods in 2012, compared to only 13% in 1990. The manufactures exports from the Rest of South fell radically across all skill levels, while the share of primary goods increased. While we observe similar changes in Emerging South–China trade, it is not as radical. Overall, the experience of Latin America and SSA show that export growth is not synonyms with export-led growth.

Despite this heterogeneity however, South–South is still a meaningful unit of analysis in two ways. First, even if some countries have now reached high-income levels, these countries are few (such as South Korea). On the other hand, most countries, including most of the Emerging South, are still at low- or middle-income levels. Therefore, it would be inappropriate to remove these countries from the global South. Our emphasis on heterogeneity is meant to illustrate that these interactions, particularly between Emerging South and Rest of South, may be unequalizing rather than mutually beneficial unless addressed through policy interventions or regional harmonization. Second, as illustrated by some of the literature reviewed, the term "South–South" carries with it a geopolitical and power dimension rather than simply a technical one. The gap in bargaining power and global influence is still significantly smaller

Table 7. Structure of South-China Trade

	Rest of South			
	Exports		Imports	
	1990	2012	1990	2012
Primary	13.0%	75.2%	14.1%	3.0%
Nat-resource intensive	18.4%	11.2%	9.1%	9.8%
Low-skill	16.3%	1.7%	48.2%	37.8%
Medium-skill	46.6%	8.7%	22.6%	34.1%
High-skill	5.4%	2.0%	5.5%	14.0%
	Emerging South			
	Exports		Imports	
	1990	2012	1990	2012
Primary	8.5%	15.6%	8.1%	3.3%
Nat-resource intensive	12.2%	12.9%	7.7%	6.7%
Low-skill	39.4%	9.0%	43.4%	21.8%
Medium-skill	27.5%	15.8%	27.1%	24.2%
High-skill	11.4%	42.8%	12.2%	40.4%

Source: Dahi and Demir (2016, table 5.9).

within much of the South than between South and North. Moreover, countries such as China self-identifying as "developing" or "South" may be an attempt to utilize the prestige of South–South relations to advance their interests. However, the evidence from negotiating blocs within the WTO showed that South–South cooperation was able to reap meaningful results for the global South as a whole (Dahi and Demir, 2016, chapter 2).

Muhr (2016) argued that social relations and social realities are influenced by discourse and the labels of solidarity, cooperation, and alternative economic models that emanate from within the global South are themselves important and capable of being transformative. Therefore, they should not be dismissed as mere exaggerations or smokescreens to mere exploitation. He points to the case of Latin America, showing how South–South mobilization has proven to be capable of building a progressive alternative, and that ultimately interests and solidarity are not mutually exclusive. And yet, as our review highlights, South–South exchanges involve a variety of perspectives, visions, and motivations, including diverse social, cultural, and political dynamics at home and host countries, and are inherently heterogeneous in nature. Consequently, increasing South–South trade and finance are likely to create diverse outcomes, some positive and, inevitably, some negative. What is needed therefore is recognition of this diversity in the theoretical and empirical analysis of South–South economic exchanges.

7. Conclusion

This paper has traced the evolution of the South–South versus North–South economic exchanges literature. The paucity of South–South trade and financial flows in the postwar period implied that the debate on South–South relations was less of an actual assessment of its implications and more a proxy debate over the (obviously erroneous) state-led versus market-led economic development paradigms in the global South. There was certainly much less at stake than today. Particularly with the industrial rise of large developing countries, South–South trade and finance now makes up significant shares of global as well as Southern country exchanges and much of these exchanges are in increasingly sophisticated products.

However, this dramatic increase in the intensity and scope of these exchanges has implied a greater willingness to embrace complexity in measuring the development positives and benefits. Simplistic assessments have given way to more sophisticated and pointed examinations of certain forms of interactions within the South. At the same time, the lion's share of the benefits of South–South exchanges is accruing to the larger, more populous and more industrialized South countries. For South–South exchanges to be mutually beneficial what is needed is to identify the necessary conditions that maximize spillovers and gains in the form of technology transfer, skills-upgrading, institutional development, policy space and global governance, labor and environment policy, etc. The fact that all developing countries, large or small, still face significant pressures from the North implies an opportunity for South–South arrangements that are mutually beneficial (Dahi and Demir, 2016). However, once left to mere market forces, the evidence points to an increasing uneven development within the global South. Therefore, whether or not South–South exchanges can still offer a developmental promise that might be missing in North–South exchanges depends on how it is appropriated and shaped by movements within the global South.

Acknowledgments

We thank Mustafa Caglayan, Amitava K. Dutt, Kevin Gallagher, Ilene Grabel, Arslan Razmi, Jaime Ros, Roberto Veneziani, and two anonymous reviewers for excellent comments on previous drafts. We also thank session participants at the URPE/ASSA meetings in 2014, 2015, and 2017, the EEA meetings in 2015 and 2017, the Analytical Political Economy Workshop at the University of Notre Dame in 2015, and the seminar participants at the faculty of economics at the University of Montenegro in 2016. Firat Demir thanks the Fulbright Commission and the Faculty of Economics at the University of Montenegro for his Fulbright visit during 2015–2016 when this project was started. Omar S. Dahi thanks the Dean of Faculty Office at Hampshire College and the School of Critical Social Inquiry at Hampshire College for financial support.

Notes

1. In this paper, we use the term "North–South" as a default term for relations between developed and developing countries unless we are specifically referring to Southern exports to the North, in which case we use "South–North." Our personal preference is to use "South–North" as a default term since it decenters the North and is in line with adopting a South-based perspective. However, since this is a survey paper, and the standard usage in the development and trade literature is North–South, we stick with that term.
2. We leave various critiques of modernization theory outside the scope of this review, including the critique that industrialization efforts in the South have confused ends (human development) with means (capital accumulation).
3. For example, what is good for one Southern country may not be necessarily good for other Southern countries (Razmi and Blecker, 2008).
4. The full list of countries in each category is included in the Appendix.
5. The trade data we use here and in the rest of the paper do not correct for triangular trade, reexports and processing trade, or intrafirm trade through global value chains, which risk

an upward bias in the implied net value added of South–South as well as North–South exchanges. Therefore, we should not equate trade values with net value added, which would require an input–output analysis.

6. Structuralism in economics emphasizes the interdependence of relations among various economic actors and how institutions and "distributional relationships across its [an economy's] productive sectors and social groups play essential roles in determining its macro behavior" (Taylor, 2004: 1). In the case of North–South exchanges, the Marxian literature on the causes of uneven development between the North and the South is also very rich and explores the role of uneven exchange, primitive accumulation, and imperialism in the rise of the West at the expense of the Rest (Lenin, 1917; Luxemburg, 1913; Baran, 1957; Furtado, 1964; Frank, 1966; Emmanuel *et al.*, 1972; Amin, 1976, 1990; Wallerstein, 1976; Brewer, 1990; Chase-Dunn, 1990; Trotsky, 2001).

7. Note that Dahi and Demir (2016) show that intra-industry trade is higher in Rest of South–North and Emerging South–North directions than in any other.

8. For an extensive review, see Atta-Ankomah (2014).

9. For a theoretical analysis of welfare effects, see Foellmi *et al.* (2007) and Fajgelbaum *et al.* (2011).

10. Myrdal (1956, p. 261) also argued that, because of the colonial legacy, "governments and businesses in underdeveloped countries are conditioned and trained to negotiate and cooperate with their opposite partners in advanced countries but not with the governments and businesses in other underdeveloped countries."

11. See Ros (2013) for a similar discussion. Busse et al. (2016) interpret this as a positive development since it benefits African natural resource and primary good exporters.

12. These 10 countries are China (20.8%), South Korea (7.4%), Hong Kong (6%), Taiwan (5.2%), Russia (4.6%), Singapore (4.2%), Saudi Arabia (4%), India (3.6%), UAE (3.3%), and Malaysia (2.9%).

13. These 10 countries are China (25.5%), Mexico (8.3%), Russia (6.4%), Korea (3.7%), Saudi Arabia (3.4%), Poland (3%), Czech Republic (2.6%), India (2.5%), Ireland (2.4%), and Taiwan (2.3%).

14. SITC codes: 3330, 3340, 3341, 3342, 3343, 3350, 3354.

15. Interestingly, these warnings are also raised by IMF (2013, Ch. 4).

16. We should note that there is a disagreement in the literature regarding the net value added of Chinese exports. Lemoine and Ünal-Kesenci (2004) and Feenstra and Wei (2010) suggest that including processing trade in export values causes an overestimation of Chinese export sophistication. For works that critically reestimate the real content of Chinese exports, see, for example, Koopman *et al.* (2008), Yao (2009), and Assche and Gangnes (2010).

References

Acemoglu, D. (2001) Factor prices and technical change: from induced innovations to recent debates. MIT Department of Economics Working Paper No. 01–39, Massachusetts Institute of Technology.

Acemoglu, D. (2002) Directed technical change. *Review of Economic Studies* 69(4): 781–809.

Acemoglu, D. (2007) Equilibrium bias of technology. *Econometrica* 75(5): 1371–1409.

Acemoglu, D. (2015) Localised and biased technologies: Atkinson and Stiglitz's new view, induced innovations, and directed technological change. *Economic Journal* (583): 443–463.

Acemoglu, D., Johnson, S. and Robinson, J.A. (2001) The colonial origins of comparative development: an empirical investigation. *American Economic Review* 91(5): 1369–1401.

Acemoglu, D., Johnson, S. and Robinson, J. (2005) Institutions as the fundamental cause of long-run growth. In P. Aghion and S. Durlauf (eds.), *Handbook of Economic Growth*, Vol. 1A (pp. 385–472). San Diego: Elsevier.

Acemoglu, D. and Zilibotti, F. (2001) Productivity Differences. *The Quarterly Journal of Economics* 116(2): 563–606.

Adisu, K., Sharkey, T. and Okoroafo, S.C. (2010) The Impact of Chinese investment in Africa. *International Journal of Business and Management* 5(9): 3–9.

Ado, A. and Su, Z. (2016) China in Africa: a critical literature review. *Critical Perspectives on International Business* 12(1): 40–60.

Aeberhardt, R., Buono, I. and Fadinger, H. (2014) Learning, incomplete contracts and export dynamics: theory and evidence from French firms. *European Economic Review* 68: 219–249.

Aguilar, R. and Goldstein, A. (2009) The Chinisation of Africa: the case of Angola, *World Economy* 32(11): 1543–1562.

Agyei-Holmes, A. (2016) Tilling the soil in Tanzania: what do emerging economies have to offer? *European Journal of Development Research* 28(3): 379–396.

Akamatsu, K. (1962) A historical pattern of economic growth in developing countries. *Journal of Developing Economies* 1(1): 3–25.

Alden, C. (2007) *China in Africa*. London: Zed Books.

Aleksynska, M. and Havrylchyk, O. (2013) FDI from the South: the role of institutional distance and natural resources. *European Journal of Political Economy* 29: 38–53.

Alfaro, L., Kalemli Ozcan, S. and Volosovych, V. (2008) Why doesn't capital flow from rich to poor countries? An empirical investigation. *The Review of Economics and Statistics* 90: 347–368.

Almeida, R. (2007) The labor market effects of foreign owned firms. *Journal of International Economics* 72: 75–96.

Amanor, K.S. and Chichava, S. (2016) South–South Cooperation, Agribusiness, and African Agricultural Development: Brazil and China in Ghana and Mozambique. *World Development* 81: 13–23.

Amighini, A. and Sanfilippo, M. (2014) Impact of South–South FDI and trade on the export upgrading of African economies. *World Development* 64: 1–17.

Amin, S. (1976) *Unequal Development: An Essay on the Social Formations of Peripheral Capitalism.* New York: Monthly Review Press.

Amin, S. (1990) *Delinking: Towards a Polycentric World*. London: Zed Books.

Amsden, A. (1980) The industry characteristics of intra-Third World trade in manufactures. *Economic Development and Cultural Change* 29(1): 1–19.

Amsden, A. (1983) De-skilling, skilled commodities, and the NIC's emerging competitive advantage. *American Economic Review; Papers and Proceedings* 73(2): 333–337.

Amsden, A. (1984) *The division of labor is limited by the rate of growth of the market: The Taiwanese machine tool industry revisited*. Mimeo, Harvard Business School.

Amsden, A. (1987) The directionality of trade: historical perspective and overview. In O. Havrylyshin (ed.), *Proceedings of World Bank Symposium: Exports of Developing Countries: How Direction Affects Performance* (pp. 123–138). Washington, DC: World Bank.

Amsden, A. (1989) *Asia's Next Giant: South Korea and Late Industrialization*. New York: Oxford University Press.

An, G. and Iyigun, M.F. (2004) The export skill content, learning by exporting and economic growth. *Economics Letters* 84: 29–34.

Anderson, J. and Marcouiller, D. (2002) Insecurity and the pattern of trade: an empirical investigation. *Review of Economics and Statistics* 84(2): 342–352.

Angeles, L. (2007) Income inequality and colonialism. *European Economic Review* 51(5): 1155–1176.

Antweiler, W. and Trefler, D. (2002) Increasing returns and all that: a view from trade. *American Economic Review* 92(1): 93–119.

Arnold, J.M. and Javorcik, B.S. (2009) Gifted kids or pushy parents? Foreign direct investment and plant productivity in Indonesia. *Journal of International Economics* 79: 42–53.

Assche, A.V. and Gangnes, B. (2010) Electronics production upgrading: is China exceptional? *Applied Economics Letters* 17(5): 477–482.

Atta-Ankomah, R. (2014) *China's presence in developing countries' technology basket: the case of furniture manufacturing in Kenya*. PhD thesis, The Open University, UK.

Baah, A.Y. and Jauch, H. (2009) Chinese Investments in Africa. In A.Y. Baah and H. Jauch (eds.), *Chinese Investments in Africa: A Labour Perspective* (pp. 35–76). Ghana: African Labor Research Network.

Bacha, E.L. (1978) An interpretation of unequal exchange from Prebisch-Singer to Emmanuel. *Journal of Development Economics* 5(4): 319–330.

Bagchi, A.K. (2008) Historical perspectives on development. In A. K. Dutt and J. Ros (eds.), *International Handbook of Development Economics*, Vol. 1 (pp. 16–31). Northampton, MA: Edward Elgar.

Bahar, D., Hausmann, R. and Hidalgo, C.A. (2014) Neighbors and the evolution of the comparative advantage of nations: evidence of international knowledge diffusion? *Journal of International Economics* 92(1): 111–123.

Baldwin, R.E. (1979) Determinants of trade and foreign investment: further evidence. *Review of Economics and Statistics* 61(1): 40–48.

Baran, B. (1957) *The Political Economy of Growth*. New York: Monthly Review Press.

Bastos, P. and Silva, J. (2010) The quality of a firm's exports: where you export to matters. *Journal of International Economics* 82(2): 99–111.

Beck, T. (2002) Financial development and international trade: Is there a link? *Journal of International Economics* 57: 107–131.

Becker, G.S., Murphy, K.M. and Tamura, R.F. (1990) Human capital fertility and economic development. *Journal of Political Economy* 98: 12–37.

Behar, A. and Cirera-i-Criville, L. (2013) Does it matter who you sign with? Comparing the impacts of North-South and South-South trade agreements on bilateral trade. *Review of International Economics* 21(4): 765–782.

Bekaert, G., Harvey, C.R. and Lundblad, C. (2001) Emerging equity markets and economic development. *Journal of Development Economics* 66: 465–504.

Bekaert, G., Harvey, C.R. and Lundblad, C. (2005) Does financial liberalization spur growth? *Journal of Financial Economics* 77(1): 3–55.

Belloc, M. (2006) Institutions and international trade: a reconsideration of comparative advantage. *Journal of Economic Surveys* 20(1): 3–26.

Bergstrand, J.H. and Egger, P. (2013) What determines BITs? *Journal of International Economics* 90(1): 107–122.

Bhagwati, J.N. (1978) *Foreign Trade Regimes and Economic Development: Anatomy and Consequences of Exchange Control Regimes*. Cambridge, MA: Ballinger Press.

Bhagwati, J.N., Panagariya, A. and Srinivasan, T.N. (1998) *Lectures on International Trade*. Cambridge, MA: MIT Press.

Bhalla, A.S. (1985) Concept and measurement of labour intensity. In A. S. Bhalla (ed.), *Technology and Employment in Industry: A Case Study Approach*, 3rd edn. (pp. 11–13). Geneva: International Labour Organization.

Brautigan, D. (2009) *The Dragon's Gift: The Real Story of China in Africa*. Oxford: Oxford University Press.

Brenton, P. and Walkenhorst, P. (2010) Impacts of the rise of China on developing country trade: evidence from North Africa. *African Development Review* 22(1): 577–586.

Brewer, A. (1990) *Marxist Theories of Imperialism. A Critical Survey* (2nd edn). London: Routledge and Kegan Paul.

Brucks, M., Zeithaml, V.A. and Naylor, G. (2000) Price and brand name as indicators of quality dimensions for consumer durables. *Journal of the Academy of Marketing Science* 28: 359–374.

Busse, M., Erdogan, C. and Mühlen, H. (2016) China's impact on Africa–the role of trade, FDI and aid. *Kyklos* 69(2): 228–262.

Cabral, L., Favareto, A., Mukwereza, L. and Amanor, K. (2016) Brazil's agricultural politics in Africa: more food international and the disputed meanings of "family farming". *World Development* 81: 47–60.

Caglayan, M., Dahi, O.S. and Demir, F. (2013) Trade flows, exchange rate uncertainty, and financial depth: evidence from 28 emerging countries. *Southern Economic Journal* 79(4): 905–927.

Caglayan, M. and Demir, F. (2016) Exchange rate movements, skill-content and direction of trade. Mimeo, University of Oklahoma.

Carmody, P.R. (2013) *The Rise of the BRICS in Africa: The Geopolitics of South-South Relations*. London: Zed Books Ltd.

Caselli, F. and Coleman, II, W. (2001) Cross-country technology diffusion: the case of computers. *American Economic Review* 91(2): 328–335.

Chan, S. (2013) *The Morality of China in Africa: The Middle Kingdom and the Dark Continent*. London: Zed Books.

Chang, H.-J. (2002) *Kicking Away the Ladder: Development Strategy in Historical Perspective*. London: Anthem Press.

Chang, H.-J. (2006) *The East Asian Development Experience: The Miracle, the Crisis and the Future*. London: Zed Books.

Chase-Dunn, C. (1990) Resistance to imperialism: semiperipheral actors. *Review* 13(1): 1–31.

Chenery, H.B., Robinson, S. and Syrquin, M. (1986) *Industrialization and Growth* (p. 45). Washington: World Bank.

Cheong, J., Kwak, D.W. and Tang, K.K. (2015) Heterogeneous effects of preferential trade agreements: how does partner similarity matter? *World Development* 66: 222–236.

Cheru, F. (2016) Emerging Southern powers and new forms of South-South cooperation: Ethiopia's strategic engagement with China and India. *Third World Quarterly* 37(4): 592–611.

Chudnovsky, D. (1983) The entry into the design and production of complex capital goods: the experiences of Brazil, India, and South Korea. In M. Fransman (ed.), *Machinery and Economic Development* (pp. 54–92). New York: St. Martin's Press.

Copeland, B. and Kotwal, A. (1996) Product quality and the theory of comparative advantage. *European Economic Review* 40: 1747–1760.

Cuervo-Cazurra, A. and Genc, M. (2008) Transforming disadvantages into advantages: developing-country MNEs in the least developed countries. *Journal of International Business Studies* 39(6): 957–979.

Dahi, O.S. and Demir, F. (2013) Preferential trade agreements and manufactured goods exports: does it matter whom you PTA with? *Applied Economics* 45(34): 4754–4772.

Dahi, O.S. and Demir, F. (2016) *South–South Trade and Finance in the Twenty-First Century*. New York: Anthem Press.

Dang, D.A. (2013) How foreign direct investment promote institutional quality: evidence from Vietnam. *Journal of Comparative Economics* 41: 1054–1072.

Darby, J. Desbordes, R. and Wooton, I. (2010) Does Public Governance always Matter? How Experience of Poor Institutional Quality Influences FDI to the South, No 3290, CESifo Working Paper Series, CESifo Group Munich.

Darity, W. Jr. (1992) A model of "Original Sin": rise of the West and lag of the rest. *American Economic Review Papers and Proceedings* 82(2): 162–167.

Darity, W. Jr. and Davis, L.S. (2005) Growth, trade and uneven development. *Cambridge Journal of Economics* 29: 141–170.

Deardorff, A.V. (1987) The directions of developing country trade: examples of pure theory. *Proceedings of World Bank Symposium: Exports of Developing Countries: How Direction Affects Performance* (9–22). Washington, DC: World Bank.

Demir, F. (2016) Effects of FDI flows on institutional development in the South: does it matter where the investors are from? *World Development*, 78, 341–359.

Demir, F. and Dahi, O.S. (2011) Asymmetric effects of financial development on South–South and South–North trade: panel data evidence from emerging markets. *Journal of Development Economics* 94: 139–149.

Demir, F. and Duan, Y. (2017) Bilateral FDI flows, productivity growth and convergence: the North vs. the South. *World Development*, Forthcoming.

Demir, F. and Hu, C. (2016) Institutional differences and direction of bilateral FDI flows: are South-South flows any different than the rest? *The World Economy* 39(12): 2000–2024.

Demirguc-Kunt, A. and Maksimovic, V. (1998) Law, finance and firm growth. *Journal of Finance* 53: 2107–2137.

Desai, M.A., Foley, C.F. and Forbes, K.J. (2008) Financial constraints and growth: multinational and local firm responses to currency depreciations. *Review of Financial Studies* 21(6): 2857–2888.

Diaz-Alejandro, C.F. 1973. Some characteristics of recent export expansion in Latin America. Economic Growth Center Discussion Paper no. 183, Yale University.

Doctor, M. (2007) Why bother with inter-regionalism? Negotiations for a European Union-Mercosur agreement. *Journal of Common Market Studies* 45(2): 281–314.

Dollar, D. (1992) Outward oriented developing economies really do grow more rapidly: evidence from 95 LDCs, 1976–85. *Economic Development and Cultural Change* 40(3): 523–544.

Dollar, D. and Kraay, A. (2004) Trade, growth, and poverty. *The Economic Journal* 114(493): F22–F49.

Dutt, A.K. (1986) Vertical trading and uneven development. *Journal of Development Economics* 20(2): 339–359.

Dutt, A.K. (1987) Keynes with a perfectly competitive goods market. *Australian Economic Papers* 26(49): 275–293.

Dutt, A.K. (1989) Uneven development in alternative models of North–South trade. *Eastern Economic Journal* 15(2): 91–106.

Dutt, A.K. (1990) *Growth, Distribution, and Uneven Development*. Cambridge, UK: Cambridge University Press.

Dutt, A.K. (1992) The NICs, global accumulation and uneven development: implications of a simple three-region model. *World Development* 20(8): 1159–1171.

Dutt, A.K. (1996) Southern primary exports, technological change and uneven development. *Cambridge Journal of Economics*, 20(1), 73–89.

Dutt, A.K. (2012) Distributional dynamics in post Keynesian growth models. *Journal of Post Keynesian Economics* 34(3): 431–452.

Easterly, W. and Levine, R. (2001) It´s not factor accumulation: stylized facts and growth models. *World Bank Economic Review* 15(2): 177–220.

Economist. (2006) Africa and China: African Heads of State Gather for a Summit in China. November 3. Retrieved from https://www.economist.com/node/8126261/print?story_id=8126261 (Accessed on May 1, 2015).

Edwards, L. and Jenkins, R. (2014) The margins of export competition: a new approach to evaluating the impact of China on South African exports to sub-Saharan Africa. *Journal of Policy Modeling* 36(1): S132–S150.

Emmanuel, A., Bettelheim, C. and Pearce, B. (1972) *Unequal Exchange: A Study of the Imperialism of Trade*. New York: Monthly Review Press.

Fabbri, F., Slaughter, M.J. and Haskel, J.E. (2003) Does nationality of ownership matter for labor demands? *Journal of the European Economic Association* 1(2–3): 698–707.

Fajgelbaum, P., Grossman, G.M. and Helpman, E. (2011) Income distribution, product quality, and international trade. *Journal of Political Economy* 119(4): 721–765.

Fajgelbaum, P., Grossman, G.M. and Helpman, E. (2015) A linder hypothesis for foreign direct investment. *The Review of Economic Studies* 82(1): 83–121.

Feenstra, R.C. (1996) Trade and uneven growth. *Journal of Development Economics* 49: 229–256.

Feenstra, R.C. and Wei, S.-J. (eds.) (2010) *China's Growing Role in World Trade*, National Bureau of Economic Research Conference Report. Chicago: University of Chicago Press.

Fernandes, A., Freund, C. and Pierola, C. (2016) Exporter behavior, country size and stage of development: evidence from the exporter dynamics database. *Journal of Development Economics* 119: 121–137.

Findlay, R. (1978) Relative backwardness, direct foreign investment, and the transfer of technology: a simple dynamic model. *Quarterly Journal of Economics* 92(1): 1–16.

Findlay, R. (1980) The terms of trade and equilibrium growth in the world economy. *American Economic Review* 70(3): 291–299.

Findlay, R. (1984) Growth and development in trade models. In R. Jones and P. Kenen (eds.), *Handbook of International Economics*, Vol. 1 (pp. 185–236). Amsterdam: Elsevier Science.

Findlay, R. (1992) The roots of divergence: Western economic history in comparative perspective. *American Economic Review Papers and Proceedings* 82(2): 158–161.

Fontagne, L., Gaulier, G. and Zignago, S. (2008) Specialization across varieties and North-South competition. *Economic Policy* 53: 53–91.

Foellmi, R., Hepenstrick, C. and Zweimuller, J. (2007) *Income effects in the theory of monopolistic competition and international trade*. Mimeo, University of Zurich.

Fosfuri, A., Motta, M. and Ronde, T. (2001) Foreign direct investment and spillovers through workers' mobility. *Journal of International Economics* 53(1): 205–222.

Frank, A.G. (1966) *The Development of Underdevelopment*.Boston: New England Free Press.

Fugazza, M. and Robert-Nicoud, F. (2006) Can South-South trade liberalization stimulate North-South trade? *Journal of Economic Integration* 21: 234–253.

Furtado, C. (1964) *Development and Underdevelopment*. Berkeley: University of California Press.

Gallagher, K.P., Irwin, A. and Koleski, K. (2012) The new banks in town: Chinese Finance in Latin America. Inter-American Development Bank Report.

Gallagher, K. and Porzecanski, R. (2008) China matters: China's economic impact in Latin America. *Latin American Research Review* 43(1): 185–200.

Gallagher, K.P. and Porzecanski, R. (2010) *The Dragon in the Room: China and the Future of Latin American Industrialization*. Palo Alto: Stanford University Press.

Graham-Harrison, E. (2009) China trade outweighs corruption fears for Africa. *Reuters*. Retrieved from https://www.reuters.com/article/2009/11/05/businesspro-us-china-africa-corruption-a-idUSTRE5 A44I220091105 (Accessed on May 02, 2016).

Grossman, G.M. and Helpman, E. (1991) Trade, knowledge spillovers, and growth. *European Economic Review* 35(2–3): 517–526.

Giovanetti, G. and Sanfilippo, M. (2009) Do Chinese exports crowd-out African goods? An econometric analysis by country and sector. *European Journal of Development Research* 21(4): 506–530.

Hall, R. and Jones, C. (1999) Why do some countries produce so much more output per worker than others? *Quarterly Journal of Economics* 114: 83–116.

Hallak, J. (2006) Product quality and the direction of trade. *Journal of International Economics* 68(1): 238–265.

Hallak, J.C. (2010) A product-quality view of the Linder hypothesis. *The Review of Economics and Statistics* 92(3): 453–466.

Hanauer, L. and Morris, L. (2014) Chinese engagement in Africa: drivers, reactions, and implications for U.S. policy. RAND Corporation Research Reports. Retrieved from https://www.rand.org/pubs/ research_reports/RR521.html (Accessed on May 02, 2016).

Harrison, A. (1996) Openness and growth: a time series, cross-country analysis for developing countries. *Journal of Development Economics* 48: 419–447.

Hausman, R., Hwang, J. and Rodrik, D. (2007) What you export matters. *Journal of Economic Growth* 12: 1–25.

Havrylyshyn, O. and Wolf, M. (1983) *Recent Trends Among Developing Countries*. Washington, DC: World Bank.

Havrylyshyn, O. and Wolf, M. (1987) What Have We Learned about South-South Trade. In O. Havrylyshin (ed.), *Proceedings of World Bank Symposium: Exports of Developing Countries: How Direction Affects Performance* (pp. 149–166). Washington, DC: World Bank.

He, P., Ding, H. and Hua, Z. (2012) Strategic choice of flexible production technology using game theory approach. *Robotics and Computer-Integrated Manufacturing* 28(3): 416–424.

Henry, P.B. (2000) Stock market liberalization, economic reform, and emerging market equity prices. *Journal of Finance* 55: 529–564.

Hettne, B. (2005) Beyond the "new regionalism." *New Political Economy* 10(4): 543–571.

Hur, J., Raj, M. and Riyanto, Y.E. (2006) Finance and trade: a cross-country empirical analysis on the impact of financial development and asset tangibility on international trade. *World Development* 34(10): 1728–1741.

Huttunen, K. (2007) The effect of foreign acquisition on employment and wages: evidence from Finnish establishments. *Review of Economics and Statistics* 89(3): 497–509.

Hveem, H. (1999) Political regionalism: master or servant of economic internationalization? In B. Hettne, A. Inotai and O. Sunkei (eds.), *Globalism and the New Regionalism* (pp. 85–115). New York: Palgrave Macmillan.

Imbs, J. and Wacziarg, R. (2003) Stages of diversification. *American Economic Review* 93(1): 63–86.

IMF (2013) *World Economic Outlook*. IMF, April.

IMF (2014) Direction of Trade Statistics Online Database. http://data.imf.org/?sk=9D6028D4-F14A-464C-A2F2-59B2CD424B85 (Accessed on December 1, 2014).

Iyer, L. (2010) Direct versus indirect colonial rule in India: long-term consequences. *Review of Economics and Statistics* 92(4): 693–713.

Jauch, H. (2011) Chinese investments in Africa: twenty-first century colonialism? *New Labor Forum* 20(2): 48–55. The Murphy Institute/City University of New York.

Jenkins, R. (2009) The Latin American case. In R. Jenkins and E.D. Peters (eds.), *China and Latin America: Economic Relations in the Twenty-First Century* (pp. 21–64). Bonn and Mexico City: German Development Institute.

Jenkins, R. and Edwards, C. (2006) The Economic impact of China and India on sub Saharan Africa: trends and prospects. *Journal of Asian Economics* 17(2): 207–225.

Jenkins, R. and Peters, E.D. (eds.) (2009) *China and Latin America: Economic Relations in the Twenty-First Century*. Bonn and Mexico City: German Development Institute.

Kachiga, J. (2013) *China in Africa: Articulating China's Africa Policy*. Trenton, N.J.: Africa World Press.

Kaldor, N. (1967) *Causes of the Slow Rate of Economic Growth of the United Kingdom: An Inaugural Lecture*. Cambridge: Cambridge University Press.

Kaplinsky, R. (1990) *The Economies of Small: Appropriate Technology in a Changing World*. London: Intermediate Technology Publications.

Kaplinsky, R. (2013) What contribution can China make to inclusive growth in SSA? *Development and Change* 44(6): 1295–1316.

Kaplinsky, R., McCormick, D. and Morris, M. (2007) The impact of China on sub-Saharan Africa. Institute of Development Studies working paper 291.

Kaplinsky, R., McCormick, D. and Morris, M. (2010) China and sub Saharan Africa: impacts and challenges of a growing relationship. In V. Padayachee (ed.), *The Political Economy of Africa* (pp. 389–409). London: Routledge.

Kaufmann, D., Kraay, A. and Zoido-Lobato´n, P. (1999) *Governance matters*. World Bank Research Paper No. 2196. Washington, DC: The World Bank.

Kee, H.L., Nicita, A. and Olarreaga, M. (2009) Estimating trade restrictiveness indices. *The Economic Journal* 119: 172–199.

Khanna, A. (1987) Market distortions, export performances, and export direction: India's exports of manufactures in the 1970s. *Proceedings of World Bank Symposium: Exports of Developing Countries: How Direction Affects Performance* (pp. 47–56). Washington, DC: World Bank.

Kletzer, K. and Bardhan, P. (1987) Credit markets and patterns of international trade. *Journal of Development Economics* 27(1–2): 57–70.

Koopman, R., Wang, Z. and Wei, S.-J. (2008) How much of chinese exports is really made in China? Assessing domestic value-added when processing trade is pervasive. Working Paper No. 14109, National Bureau of Economic Research.

Kowalski, P. and Shepherd, B. (2006) South–South trade in goods. *OECD Trade Policy*, Working Paper No. 40.

Krueger, A.O. (1977) *Growth, Distortions, and Patterns of Trade among Many Countries*. Princeton Studies in International Finance, no. 40. Princeton: Princeton University Press.

Krueger, A.O. (1997) Trade policy and economic development: how we learn. *American Economic Review* 87(1): 1–6.

Krugman, P.R. (1979) Increasing returns, monopolistic competition, and international trade. *Journal of International Economics* 9(4), 469–479.

Krugman, P. (1980) Scale economies, product differentiation, and the pattern of trade. *American Economic Review* 70(5): 950–959.

Krugman, P. (1987) The narrow moving band, the Dutch disease and the consequences of Mrs. Thatcher. *Journal of Development Economics* 27: 41–55.

Krugman, P. (1991) History versus expectations. *Quarterly Journal of Economics* 196(2): 651–667.

Krugman, P. (1995) Growing world trade: causes and consequences. *Brookings Papers on Economic Activity* 1: 327–377.

Kwok, C.C. and Tadesse, S. (2006) The MNC as an agent of change for host-country institutions: FDI and corruption. *Journal of International Business Studies* 37(6): 767–785.

Lall, S. (2000) The technological structure and performance of developing country manufactured exports, 1985–1998. *Oxford Development Studies* 28(3): 337–370.

Lall, S. (2001) *Competiveness, Technology and Skills*. Cheltenham: Edward Elgar.

Lall, S., Ray, A. and Ghosh, S. (1989) The determinants and promotion of South-South trade in manufactured products. In V. Ventura-Dias (ed.), *South-South Trade: Trends, Issues, and Obstacles to its Growth* (pp. 131–164). New York: Praeger Publishers.

Lancaster, K. (1971) *Consumer Demand: A New Approach*. New York: Columbia University Press.

Landes, D.S. (1998) Homo Faber, Homo Sapiens: knowledge, technology, growth, and development. In D. Neef (ed.), *The Knowledge Economy* (pp. 53–67). London: Butterworth–Heinemann.

Lemoine, F., Ünal-Kesenci, D. (2004) Assembly trade and technology transfer: the case of China. *World Dev.* 32: 829–850.

Lenin, V.I. (1917) Imperialism, the highest stage of capitalism. In *Selected Works*, Vol. 1. Moscow: Foreign Languages Publishing House.

Leontief, W. (1963) The structure of development. *Scientific American* 209(3): 148–166.

Levchenko, A. (2007) Institutional quality and international trade. *Review of Economic Studies* 74(3): 791–819.

Lewis, W.A. (1969) *Some Aspects of Economic Development*. Ghana: The Ghana Publishing Corporation.

Lewis, W.A. (1980) The slowing down of the engine of growth. *American Economic Review* 70(3): 555–564.

Linder, S. B. (1967) *Trade and Trade Policy for Development*. New York: Praeger Publishers.

Little, I., Scitovsky, T. and Scott, T.M. (1970) *Industry and Trade in Some Developing Countries: A Comparative Study*. London: Oxford University Press.

Loren, B. and Eric, T. (2016) Constructing a ladder for growth: policy, markets, and industrial upgrading in China. *World Development* 80: 78–95.

Lucas, R.E. (1988) On the mechanics of economic development. *Journal of Monetary Economics* 22(1): 3–42.

Luxemburg, R. (1913) *The Accumulation of Capital* (transl. from German, 1951). London: Routledge and Kegan Paul.

Lyman, P. (2005) China's rising role in Africa. Testimony on Council on Foreign Relations, July 21. Retrieved from https://www.cfr.org/china/chinas-rising-role-africa/p8436 (Accessed on May 9, 2014).

Manova, K.B. and Zhang, Z. (2012) Export prices across firms and destinations. *Quarterly Journal of Economics* 127: 379–436.

Matsuyama, K. (1991) Increasing returns, industrialization and indeterminacy of equilibrium. *Quarterly Journal of Economics* 106(2): 617–650.

Mauro, P. (1995) Corruption and growth. *Quarterly Journal of Economics* 110(3): 681–712.

Mawdsley, E. (2008) Fu Manchu versus Dr. Livingstone in the dark continent? Representing China, Africa, and the West in British Broadsheet Newspapers. *Political Geography* 27(5): 509–529.

Mbaye, S. (2011) *Africa Will Not Put Up with a Colonialist China*. The Guardian. https://www.theguardian.com/commentisfree/2011/feb/07/china-exploitation-africa-industry (Accessed on May 2, 2016).

McMillan, M. and Rodrik, D. (2011) *Globalization, structural change, and productivity growth*. NBER Working Paper 17143. Cambridge, MA: NBER.

Medvedev, D. (2010) Preferential trade agreements and their role in world trade. *Review of World Economies* 146: 199–222.

Michaely, M., Papageorgious, D. and Choksi, A. (1991) *Liberalizing Foreign Trade: Lessons of Experience in the Developing World*. Cambridge, MA: Blackwell.

MIT Media Lab. (2015) *The Atlas of Economic Complexity*. Center for International Development at Harvard University. Retrieved from https://atlas.media.mit.edu/en/resources/data/ (Accessed on March 1, 2015).

Mohan, G. and Kale, D. (2007) *The Invisible Hand of South-South Globalization: Chinese Migrants in Africa. A Report for the Rockefeller Foundation prepared by The Development Policy and Practice Department*. UK: The Open University.

Mohan, G. and Lampert, B. (2013) Negotiating China: reinserting African agency into China–Africa relations. *African Affairs* 112(446): 92–110.

Mohan, G., Lampert, B., Tan-Mullins, M. and Chang, D. (2014) Chinese Migrants and Africa's Development: New Imperialists or Agents of Change? London: Zed Books.

Muhr, T. (2016) "Beyond 'BRICS': ten theses on South-South cooperation in the twenty-first century. *Third World Quarterly* 37(4): 630–649.

Murphy, K.M. and Shleifer, A. (1997) Quality and trade. *Journal of Development Economics* 53: 1–15.

Murphy, K.M., Shleifer, A. and Vishny, R.W. (1989) Industrialization and the big push. *Journal of Political Economy* 97(5): 1003–1026.

Myrdal, G. (1956) *An International Economy*. London: Routledge and Kegan Paul.

Navaretti, G.B., Turrini, A. and Checchi, D. (2003) Adjusting labor demand: multinational versus national firms: a cross-European analysis. *Journal of European Economic Association* 1: 708–719.

Nelson, R. and Pack, H. (1999) The Asian miracle and modern growth theory. *Economic Journal* 109(457): 416–436.

Otsubo, S. 1998. New regionalism and South-South trade: could it be an entry point for the South toward global integration? APEC Discussion Paper, No. 18.

Pack, H. and Saggi, K. (1997) Inflows of foreign technology and indigenous technological development. *Review of Development Economics* 1(1): 81–98.

Panagariya, A. (2000) Preferential trade liberalization: the traditional theory and new developments. *Journal of Economic Literature* 38(2): 287–331.

Peters, E.D. (2005) *Economic Opportunities and Challenges Posed by China for Mexico and Central America*. Bonn: Dt. Inst. Fur Entwicklungspolitik.

Power, M., Mohan, G. and Tan-Mullins, M. (2012) China's Resource Diplomacy in Africa: Powering Development? New York: Palgrave Macmillan.

Prebisch, P. (1950) *The Economic Development of Latin America and Its Principal Problems*. New York: United Nations Department of Economic Affairs.

Prebisch, P. (1959) Commercial policy in the underdeveloped countries. *American Economic Review Papers and Proceedings* 49(2): 251–273.

Puga, D. and Venables, A.J. (1997) Preferential trading arrangements and industrial location. *Journal of International Economics* 43: 347–368.

Rajan, R.G. and Zingales, L. (1998) Financial dependence and growth. *American Economic Review* 88: 559–586.

Razmi, A. and Blecker, R.A. (2008) Developing country exports of manufactures: moving up the ladder to escape the fallacy of composition? *The Journal of Development Studies* 44(1): 21–48.

Regolo, J. (2013) Export diversification: how much does the choice of the trading partner matter? *Journal of International Economics* 91: 329–342.

Rodrik, D. (2007) Industrial development: some stylized facts and policy directions. In UN-DESA (ed.), *Industrial Development for the 21st Century: Sustainable Development Perspectives* (pp. 7–28). New York: United Nations department of Economic and Social Affairs.

Rodrik, D. (2016) Premature deindustrialization. *Journal of Economic Growth* 21(1): 1–33.

Romer, P.M. (1990) Endogenous technological change. *Journal of Political Economy* 98(5): S71–S102.

Ros, J. (2001) *Development Theory and Economic of Growth*. Ann Arbor: University of Michigan Press.

Ros, J. (2008) Classical development theory. In A. K. Dutt and J. Ros (eds.), *International Handbook of Development Economics*, Vol. 1 (pp. 111–124). Northampton, MA: Edward Elgar.

Ros, J. (2013) Latin America's trade and growth patterns, the China Factor, and Prebisch's Nightmare. *Journal of Globalization and Development* 3(2): 1–16.

Salazar-Xirinachs, J.M., Nübler, I. and Kozul-Wright, R. (2014) Transforming economies. Making industrial policy work for growth, jobs and development. *ILO/UNCT, AD*. Geneva: International Labor Organization.

Schiff, M. (2003) The unilateral/ bilateral/ regional/ multilateral approaches to trade liberalization. Background paper for Trade for Development UN Millennium Project, New York.

Schiff, M. and Wang, Y. (2006) North-South and South-South trade-related technology diffusion: an industry-level analysis of direct and indirect effects. *Canadian Journal of Economics* 39(3): 831–844.

Schiff, M. and Wang, Y. (2008) North-South and South-South trade-related technology diffusion: how important are they in improving TFP growth? *Journal of Development Studies* 44(1): 49–59.

Schiff, M., Wang, Y. and Ollareaga, M. (2002) *Trade-related technology diffusion and the dynamics of North-South and South-South integration*. The World Bank Policy Research, Working Paper, No. 2861.

Schumacher, F. (1973) *Small is Beautiful: A Study of Economics as If People Mattered*. London: Blond and Briggs.

Scoones, I., Amanor, K., Favareto, A. and Qi, G. (2016) A new politics of development cooperation? Chinese and Brazilian engagements in African agriculture. *World Development* 81: 1–12,

Shankland, A. and Gonçalves, E. (2016) Imagining agricultural development in South–South cooperation: the contestation and transformation of ProSAVANA, *World Development* 81: 35–46

Singer, H.W. (1950) The distribution of gains between investing and borrowing countries. *American Economic Review Papers and Proceedings* 40(2): 473–485.

Singer, H.W. (1975) *The Strategy of International Development: Essays in the Economics of Backwardness*. A. Cairncross and M. Puri (eds.). London: Macmillan.

Söderlund, B. and Tingvall, P. (2014) Dynamic effects of institutions on firm-level exports. *Review of World Economy* 150(2): 277–308.

Stewart, F. (1982) *Technology and Underdevelopment* (2nd edn). London: Macmillan.

Stewart, F. (1992) *North-South and South-South: Essays on International Economics*. Hong Kong: St. Martin's Press.

Strange, A., Parks, B., Tierney, M.J., Fuchs, A., Dreher, A. and Ramachandran, V. (2013) *China's development finance to Africa: a media-based approach to data collection*. Center for Global Development Working paper 323.

Strauss, J. and Saavedra, M. (2009) Introduction: China, Africa and Internationalization. *The China Quarterly* 199: 551–562.

Svaleryd, H. and Vlachos, J. (2005) Financial markets, the pattern of industrial specialization and comparative advantage: evidence from OECD countries. *European Economic Review* 49: 113–144.

Taylor, L. (1981) South-North trade and Southern growth: bleak prospects from a structuralist point of view. *Journal of International Economics* 11(4): 589–602.

Taylor, L. (2004) *Reconstructing Macroeconomics*. Cambridge, MA: Harvard University Press.

Trotsky, L. (2001) *History of the Russian Revolution*. New York: Pathfinder Press.

Thrasher, R. D. and Gallagher, K. (2008) *21st century trade agreements: Implications for long-run development policy*. The Pardee Papers, No. 2. Boston: Boston University.

UNDP (United Nations Development Programme). (2013) *Human Development Report 2013. The Rise of the South: Human Progress in a Diverse World*. New York: United Nations.

UNIDO. (2005) *Industrial Development, Trade and Poverty Alleviation through South-South Cooperation*. New York: United Nations.

United Nations Conference on Trade and Development (UNCTAD). (2003) *Trade and Development Report*. Geneva: United Nations.

United Nations Conference on Trade and Development (UNCTAD). (2006) *Trade and Development Report*. Geneva: United Nations.

United Nations Conference on Trade and Development (UNCTAD). (2011) *World Investment Report 2011*. New York and Geneva: United Nations.

United Nations Conference on Trade and Development (UNCTAD). (2015) *World Investment Report 2015*. Geneva: United Nations.

United Nations Conference on Trade and Development (UNCTAD). (2017a) *UNCTADSTAT*. Geneva: United Nations. http://unctadstat.unctad.org/EN/ (Accessed on 5/10/2017).

United Nations Conference on Trade and Development (UNCTAD). (2017b) *World Investment Report 2016*. Geneva: United Nations.

Venables, A. (2003) Winners and losers from regional integration agreements. *The Economic Journal* 113: 747–761.

Verhoogen, E. (2008) Trade, quality upgrading, and wage inequality in the mexican manufacturing sector. *The Quarterly Journal of Economics* 123(2): 489–530.

Wade, R. (1990) *Governing the Market: Economic Theory and the Role of Government in East Asian Industrialization*. Princeton: Princeton University Press.

Wallerstein, I. (1976) Semi-peripheral countries and the contemporary world crisis. *Theory and Society* 3(4): 461–483.

Warmerdam, W. (2012) Is China a liberaliInternationalist? *The Chinese Journal of International Politics* 5: 201–243.

Wietzke, F.-B. (2015) Long-term consequences of colonial institutions and human capital investments: sub-national evidence from Madagascar. *World Development* 66: 293–307.

World Bank. (2008) *Global Development Finance*. Washington, DC: World Bank.

World Bank. (2011) *Global Development Horizons 2011, Multipolarity: The New Global Economy*. Washington, DC: World Bank.

World Trade Organization (WTO). (2003) *World Trade Report 2003*. Geneva: WTO Publications.

Xu, X., Li, X., Qi, G., Tang, L. and Mukwereza, L. (2016) Science, technology, and the politics of knowledge: the case of China's Agricultural Technology Demonstration Centers in Africa. *World Development* 81: 82–91.

Yao, S. (2009) Why are Chinese exports not so special? *China & World Economy* 17(1): 47–65.

Appendix

A.1 *Country Classification: North, Emerging South, and Rest of South*

The North refers to the following countries: Austria, Australia, Belgium, Canada, Denmark, Germany, Finland, France, Greece, Iceland, Israel, Italy, Japan, Luxembourg, Netherlands, New Zealand, Norway, Portugal, Spain, Sweden, Switzerland, the United Kingdom, and the United States.

The Emerging South includes: Algeria, Argentina, Angola, Armenia, Azerbaijan, Bosnia and Herzegovina, Bulgaria, Bolivia, Brazil, Chile, China, Colombia, Costa Rica, Croatia, Cyprus, Czech Republic, Dominican Republic, Ecuador, Egypt, Estonia, Guatemala, Hong Kong, Hungary, India, Indonesia, Ireland, Jordan, Kazakhstan, Korea, Lithuania, Latvia, Malaysia, Mexico, Morocco, Oman, Pakistan, Paraguay, Peru, Philippines, Poland, Romania, Russian Federation, South Africa, Singapore, Slovenia, Slovakia, Syria, Thailand, Tunisia, Turkey, Taiwan, Ukraine, Uruguay, Venezuela, and Vietnam.

All other countries are classified as the Rest of South.

A.2 *Product Classification*

The product classifications are from Lall (2000) and are based on the following three-digit product codes using SITC Rev2.

High-skill-manufactures: 716, 718, 751, 752, 759, 761, 764, 771, 774, 776, 778, 524, 541, 712, 792, 871, 874, 881.

Medium-skill-manufactures: 781, 782, 783, 784, 785, 266, 267, 512, 513, 533, 553, 554, 562, 572, 582, 583, 584, 585, 591, 598, 653, 671, 672, 678, 786, 791, 882, 711, 713, 714, 721, 722, 723, 724, 725, 726, 727, 728, 736, 737, 741, 742, 743, 744, 745, 749, 762, 763, 772, 773, 775, 793, 812, 872, 873, 884, 885, 951.

Low-skill manufactures: 611, 612, 613, 651, 652, 654, 655, 656, 657, 658, 659, 831, 842, 843, 844, 845, 846, 847, 848, 851, 642, 665, 666, 673, 674, 675, 676, 677, 679, 691, 692, 693, 694, 695, 696, 697, 699, 821, 893, 894, 895, 897, 898, 899.

Resource-intensive-manufactures: 012, 014, 023, 024, 035, 037, 046, 047, 048, 056, 058, 061, 062, 073, 098, 111, 112, 122, 233, 247, 248, 251, 264, 265, 269, 423, 424, 431, 621, 625, 628, 633, 634, 635, 641, 281, 282, 286, 287, 288, 289, 323, 334, 335, 411, 511, 514, 515, 516, 522, 523, 531, 532, 551, 592, 661, 662, 663, 664, 667, 688, 689.

Primary products: 001, 011, 022, 025, 034, 036, 041, 042, 043, 044, 045, 054, 057, 071, 072, 074, 075, 081, 091, 121, 211, 212, 222, 223, 232, 244, 245, 246, 261, 263, 268, 271, 273, 274, 277, 278, 291, 292, 322, 333, 341, 681, 682, 683, 684, 685, 686, 687.

Unclassified goods: All remaining products not included in any of above groups.

INDEX

Page numbers in **bold** refer to Tables; page numbers in *italics* refer to Figures.

Analytical Political Economy, First Edition. Edited by Roberto Veneziani and Luca Zamparelli.
Chapters © 2018 The Authors. Book compilation © 2018 John Wiley & Sons Ltd. Published 2018 by John Wiley & Sons Ltd.